etisalat

YELLOW PAGES

Maï Café & Splash! Pool

Lounge around at our ultimate chill-out spot on the 5th floor rooftop, surrounding the amazing infinity Splash pool. Expect oversized beach chairs and lounge pods, complimented by our eclectic mix of laid-back tunes and sunny grooves. Don't forget to bring your flip-flops!

Exciting international flavors await at Maï Café, featuring Arabic delights, fresh healthy bites and all-time classics. Maï Café is your perfect spot for a leisurely lunch, relaxing dinner or a quick snack at anytime of the day.

Thursday Evening Brunch
6.30-10.30 pm

Kick start your weekend at Maï Café, with our BBQ Evening Brunch for just AED 135 net including soft drinks or AED 199 net including free flowing house beverages. Shisha also available.

Maï Café
Aloft Abu Dhabi Hotel @ ADNEC
For reservations call 02 654 5111

ريادة جهود
المحافظة على الحبارى وتعزيزها

LEADING AND PROMOTING
HOUBARA CONSERVATION

INTERNATIONAL FUND FOR
HOUBARA CONSERVATION

www.houbarafund.org

Your marketplace in the Arab world!

24 - 29 April 2013

Follow us for daily updates

ADBookFair   @ADIBF

Register now!

www.adbookfair.com

 معــرض أبـوظبي الدولي للكتـاب
Abu Dhabi International Book Fair

A project by
 هيئة أبوظبي للسياحة والثقافة
ABU DHABI TOURISM & CULTURE AUTHORITY

Organised by
 كتاب Kitab

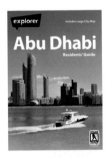

Abu Dhabi Explorer 2012/10th Edition
First Published 1999
2nd Edition 2002
3rd Edition 2003
4th Edition 2004
5th Edition 2006
6th Edition 2007
7th Edition 2009
8th Edition 2010
9th Edition 2010
10th Edition 2012   ISBN 978-9948-450-97-9

Copyright © Explorer Group Ltd, 1999, 2002, 2003, 2004, 2006, 2007, 2009, 2010, 2011, 2012.
All rights reserved.

Front Cover Photograph – Abu Dhabi Corniche – Pete Maloney

Printed and bound by Emirates Printing Press, Dubai, United Arab Emirates.

Explorer Publishing & Distribution
PO Box 34275, Dubai
United Arab Emirates
Phone   +971 (0)4 340 8805
Fax   +971 (0)4 340 8806
Email   info@askexplorer.com
Web   askexplorer.com

Welcome...

...to the 10th anniversary edition of the **Abu Dhabi Residents' Guide**, the ultimate insider's guide to living in and loving this fascinating emirate.

From red-tape procedures to hotels and restaurants, we've got everything covered to help you make the most of your time in Abu Dhabi. Whether you're still at home thinking about the move or have been living here for years, this guide will help you make the most out of life.

Abu Dhabi is a modern, thriving metropolis – one that is constantly growing and changing. We can only fit so much exhaustive information onto these pages, so whether you want to find a school, a hospital or the nearest bakery; you're looking for the latest shops to open in your community; or you're after reviews for the newest bars, clubs and restaurants, make askexplorer.com your companion to life in Abu Dhabi.

Finally, don't forget that Explorer publishes hundreds of maps and activity guides that help to make the good life in the UAE even better. Discover more at askexplorer.com/shop.

In your hands, in the glovebox, in your rucksack; on your laptop, tablet or smartphone. Wherever you're going and whatever you're doing, be sure to take us with you.

There's more to life...
The Explorer Team

   ask**explorer**.com

Contents

UAE:
A Country
Profile

UNITED ARAB EMIRATES

Located in the heart of the Middle East, the United Arab Emirates (UAE) is home to over 150 nationalities. While proud and protective of its Islamic culture, it is also one of the most progressive, cosmopolitan and open-minded countries in the region. From the desert wilderness of Abu Dhabi's Empty Quarter to the brash metropolis of Dubai and across to the rugged coastline of the country's east, its many landscapes lie waiting to be explored. Whether you're new to this remarkable land or have been living here for years, there's always something new to discover.

Location

Located on the eastern side of the Arabian Peninsula, the UAE borders Saudi Arabia and the Sultanate of Oman, with coastlines on both the Arabian Gulf and the Gulf of Oman. The country comprises seven emirates: Abu Dhabi, Ajman, Dubai, Fujairah, Ras Al Khaimah, Sharjah and Umm Al Quwain. Abu Dhabi is by far the largest emirate, occupying over 80% of the country; the emirate of Dubai is second largest, although Abu Dhabi and Dubai share similar population sizes (p.9).

The country is perhaps best known for the modern, rapidly expanding metropolises of Abu Dhabi and

Dubai, but visitors may be surprised by the variety of landscapes when they venture beyond the cities. The coast is littered with coral reefs and more than 200 islands, most of which are uninhabited. The interior of the country is characterised by sabkha (salt flats), stretches of gravel plain, and vast areas of sand desert. To the east rise the Hajar Mountains ('hajar' is Arabic for 'rock') which, lying close to the Gulf of Oman, form a backbone through the country, from the Musandam Peninsula in the north, through the eastern UAE and into Oman.

UAE Fact Box

Coordinates: 24°00' North 54°00' East
Total land area: approx. 83,600 sq km
Total coastline: 1,318km
Highest point: 1,527m
Abu Dhabi total land area: 67,340 sq km

The highest named point is Jebel Yibir at 1,527 metres. The Rub Al Khali, or Empty Quarter, occupies a large part of the south of the country. Stretching into Saudi Arabia, Oman and Yemen, it's the largest sand desert in the world, covering an area roughly the same size as France, Belgium and the Netherlands. This stark desert is interrupted only by salt flats and occasional oases, and its spectacular sand dunes rise to more than 300 metres.

Climate

The UAE has a subtropical and arid climate. Sunny blue skies and high temperatures can be expected for most of the year. Rain falls on an average of only 25 days per year, mainly in winter (December to March). In the UAE, it rarely rains very heavily or for long periods. However, in the Hajar Mountains, the amount of rainfall can be much higher and flash floods in the wadis are not unheard of. Although infrequent, when it comes, heavy rainfall can really take its toll on the city of Abu Dhabi within a relatively short period. Not all roads have adequate drainage and even those that do are not designed for massive downpours, so drains get blocked by sand. In addition, many of Abu Dhabi's drivers are not accustomed to wet conditions and tend to respond by putting their hazard lights on, which can be confusing for other drivers. Heavy rain, although infrequent, can quickly lead to flooding and disruption to business; schools and companies have had to close due to impassable roads in the past.

During winter, there are occasional sandstorms when the sand is whipped up off the desert. This is not to be confused with a shamal, a north-westerly wind that comes off the Arabian Gulf and can cool temperatures down. Sandstorms cover anything left outside in gardens or on balconies and can even blow inside, so make sure your doors and windows are shut.

Abu Dhabi Theatre

Temperatures range from a low of around 10°C (50°F) in winter to a high of 48°C (118°F) in summer. The mean daily maximum is 24°C (75°F) in January, rising to 41°C (106°F) in August. Humidity is usually between 50% and 65%. However, when combined with the high summer temperatures, even 60% humidity can produce extremely uncomfortable conditions. The most pleasant time to visit the UAE is in the cooler winter months, when temperatures are perfect for comfortable days on the beach and long, lingering evenings outside. For up-to-date weather reports, log on to weather.adac.ae or ncms.ae, or call the Abu Dhabi International Airport Meteorological Department forecaster on 02 575 7326.

HISTORY

Abu Dhabi's early existence is closely linked to the arrival and development of Islam in the greater Middle East region. Islam developed in modern-day Saudi Arabia at the beginning of the seventh century AD with the revelations of the Quran being received by the Prophet Muhammad. Military conquests of the Middle East and North Africa enabled the Arab empire to spread the teachings of Islam from Mecca and Medina to the local Bedouin tribes inhabiting the surrounding areas. This unifying foundation enabled the Arab empire to expand further into the Middle East and North Africa.

Emirs Or Sheikhs?

While the term emirate comes from the ruling title of 'emir', the rulers of the UAE are called 'sheikhs'.

Periods of dominance from other empires followed over the centuries, with the Turks, Mongols and Ottomans all exerting their influence over the region. In the early 19th century, the British and Portuguese

UAE TIMELINE

Stone Age	Modern human settlement in the UAE dates back to ca.7000BC
Bronze Age	Archaeological evidence of human settlements; the domestication of the camel boosts trade
Iron Age	The invention of falaj, an irrigation technology, takes place somewhere between 1300-300BC
630	Envoys from the Prophet Muhammad arrive, heralding the conversion of local people to Islam
1761	The Baniyas tribe discovers fresh water in Abu Dhabi and settles on the island; leading to the construction of Qasr Al Hosn
1790s	The pearl trade is booming off the coast of Abu Dhabi
1835	Maritime Truce signed between the Trucial States and Britain
1930s	The first oil concession in Abu Dhabi is granted to Trucial Coast Oil Development Company
1950s	Oil is discovered in the UAE, exports begin in 1962
1966	HH Sheikh Zayed bin Sultan Al Nahyan becomes ruler of Abu Dhabi
1971	Britain withdraws from the Gulf and The UAE is established, with HH Sheikh Zayed bin Sultan Al Nahyan of Abu Dhabi as the leader. The UAE joins the Arab League
1972	Ras Al Khaimah joins the UAE
1973	The UAE launches a single currency, the UAE dirham
1981	The Gulf Cooperation Council is formed, with the UAE as a founding member
1985	Emirates Airline is founded
1999	The doors of the Burj Al Arab, the tallest hotel in the world, open for the first time in Dubai
2001	Construction starts on Dubai's Palm Jumeirah
2003	Etihad Airways is founded
2004	Sheikh Zayed bin Sultan Al Nahyan dies and is succeeded as leader of the UAE by his son, Sheikh Khalifa bin Zayed Al Nahyan
2005	Emirates Palace, billed as the world's most expensive hotel, opens to the public
2007	The Sheikh Zayed Mosque, the eighth largest mosque in the world, opens during Ramadan. Work also begins on Yas Island and Saadiyat Island
2008	In the wake of global economic crisis, much of the UAE's property market crashes
2009	Abu Dhabi hosts its inaugural Formula 1 Grand Prix at Yas Marina Circuit; the Sheikh Khalifa Bridge opens, linking the new areas of Abu Dhabi directly to the Corniche; Dubai Metro, the region's first public mass-transit system, is launched
2010	The tallest building in the world, the Burj Khalifa, opens; Ferrari World Abu Dhabi, the world's largest indoor theme park, opens
2011	The first hotels on Saadiyat Island open their doors to the public; Capital Gate, the world's 'most leaning' tower also opens in Abu Dhabi
2012	Yas Waterworld is completed

dipped their oars into Arabian waters. They were attracted by the strategic advantages of the area's position between Europe and India, and keen to quash the rise of piracy in the local waters. By 1820, the British had exerted their authority and a general treaty was agreed by the local rulers, denouncing piracy. The following years witnessed a series of maritime truces, with Abu Dhabi and the other emirates accepting British protection in 1892. In Europe, the area became known as the Trucial Coast, a name it retained until the departure of the British in 1971.

Girl Power

Following elections back in 2007, a number of women were voted in to government positions. Today, over 40% of government employees are women, one of the highest rates in the world.

Despite opportunities for fishing and grazing, it was not until the discovery of freshwater, in 1761, that the ruling Al Nahyan family moved from the Liwa Oasis to Abu Dhabi island. By the 1800s, the town had developed considerably and, during the second half of the 19th century, led by Sheikh Zayed bin Khalifa (or 'Zayed the Great'), Abu Dhabi became the most powerful emirate along the western coast of the Arabian Peninsula. It was under Zayed's rule and great influence that Abu Dhabi and the northern emirates accepted the protection of Britain.

When Britain announced its withdrawal from the region, in 1968, the ruling sheikhs of Bahrain, Qatar and the Trucial Coast realised that, by uniting forces as a single state, they would have a stronger voice in the wider Middle East region. Negotiations collapsed when Bahrain and Qatar chose independence;

however, the Trucial Coast remained committed to forming an alliance and, in 1971, the federation of the United Arab Emirates was born. The new state comprised the emirates of Abu Dhabi, Dubai, Ajman, Fujairah, Sharjah, Umm Al Quwain and, by 1972, Ras Al Khaimah. Under the agreement, the individual emirates each retained a certain degree of autonomy, with Abu Dhabi and Dubai providing the most input into the federation. The leaders of the new federation elected the ruler of Abu Dhabi, His Highness Sheikh Zayed bin Sultan Al Nahyan, to be their president of the newly-founded country. The well-liked and much-respected Sheikh held this position until he passed away on 2 November 2004.

His eldest son, His Highness Sheikh Khalifa bin Zayed Al Nahyan, was then elected to take over the presidency. Despite the unification of the seven emirates, boundary disputes have caused a few problems. At the end of Sheikh Zayed's first term as president, in 1976, he threatened to resign if the other rulers didn't settle the demarcation of their borders. The threat proved an effective way of ensuring cooperation. The formation of the UAE came after the discovery of huge oil reserves in Abu Dhabi in 1958 (Abu Dhabi has an incredible 10% of the world's known oil reserves). This discovery dramatically transformed the emirate. In 1966, Dubai, which was already a relatively wealthy trading centre, also discovered oil.

GOVERNMENT & RULING FAMILY

The Supreme Council of Rulers is the highest authority in the UAE, comprising the hereditary rulers of the seven emirates. Since the country is governed by

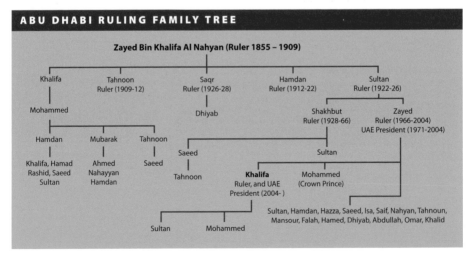

ABU DHABI RULING FAMILY TREE

Zayed Bin Khalifa Al Nahyan (Ruler 1855 – 1909)

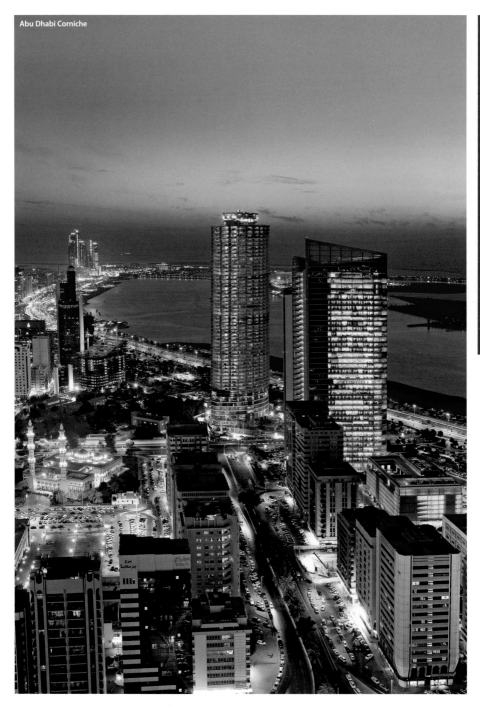

Abu Dhabi Corniche

hereditary rule, there is little distinction between the royal families and the government. The Supreme Council is responsible for general policy involving education, defence, foreign affairs, communications and development, and for ratifying federal laws. Each emirate has one single vote, and the rulers of Abu Dhabi and Dubai have power of veto over decisions.

Modern UAE

Trade and commerce are still the cornerstones of the economy, with the traditional manufacturing and distribution industries now joined by finance, construction, media, IT and telecoms. With so many world-class hotels, leisure and entertainment options, the UAE is becoming an increasingly popular and important tourist and sporting destination.

The Supreme Council elects the chief of state (the president) from among its seven members. The current president is the ruler of Abu Dhabi, Sheikh Khalifa bin Zayed Al Nahyan. He took over the post in November 2004 from his late father, Sheikh Zayed bin Sultan Al Nahyan. The Supreme Council also elects the vice president of the UAE, currently Sheikh Mohammed bin Rashid Al Maktoum, ruler of Dubai. The president and vice president are elected and appointed for five-year terms, although they are often re-elected time after time, as was the case with Sheikh Zayed. The president appoints the prime minister (currently Sheikh Mohammed bin Rashid Al Maktoum) and the deputy prime ministers (currently Sheikh Saif bin Zayed Al Nahyan and Sheikh Mansour bin Zayed Al Nahyan).

The Federal National Council (FNC) reports to the Supreme Council. It has executive authority to initiate and implement laws and is a consultative assembly of 40 representatives, half of whom are chosen for the post in the FNC Elections. In 2011, nearly 130,000 Emiratis were eligible to run and vote in the elections. The Council monitors and debates government policy but has no power of veto.

The individual emirates have some degree of autonomy and laws that affect everyday life vary between them. For instance, if you buy a car in one emirate and need to register it in a different emirate, you will have to export and then re-import it.

INTERNATIONAL RELATIONS

The UAE remains open in its foreign relations and firmly supports Arab unity. HH Sheikh Khalifa bin Zayed Al Nahyan is very generous with the country's wealth when it comes to helping Arab nations and communities that are in need of aid.

The UAE became a member of the United Nations and the Arab League in 1971. It is a member of the International Monetary Fund (IMF), the Organisation of Petroleum Exporting Countries (Opec), the World Trade Organisation (WTO) and other international and Arab organisations. It is also a member of the Arab Gulf Cooperation Council (AGCC, also known as the GCC), whose other members are Bahrain, Kuwait, Oman, Qatar and Saudi Arabia.

All major embassies and consulates are represented either in Abu Dhabi or Dubai, or both. See Embassies & Consulates on the last page of this book.

SHEIKH KHALIFA: A PROFILE

Sheikh Khalifa bin Zayed Al Nahyan is the president of the UAE and ruler of Abu Dhabi. Upon the death of his father, Sheikh Zayed bin Sultan Al Nahyan, in 2004, Sheikh Khalifa took over as Abu Dhabi's ruler and was quickly and unanimously elected by the seven members of the Supreme Council as the president of the country.

Sheikh Khalifa was born in Al Ain in 1948, the eldest son of Sheikh Zayed, and he was named Crown Prince of Abu Dhabi in 1969. Since then, he has held a number of high government positions and worked closely with Sheikh Zayed throughout his father's presidency in the development of infrastructure and basic human needs for the citizens of the UAE.

Sheikh Zayed is still enormously revered in the UAE and, so far, under his son, Sheikh Khalifa's leadership, the country, and especially Abu Dhabi, has witnessed astonishing growth. With his focus on the continuing development of the country's infrastructure, economic health and cultural contributions, he has laid the foundations for a prosperous UAE without sacrificing his goals of ensuring the country's security, furthering its international relations, safeguarding its environment, and promoting its heritage.

Recently, the Burj Khalifa, the world's tallest building, located in Dubai, was named after Sheikh Khalifa and he has remained generous with Abu Dhabi's oil wealth, ensuring that the other emirates aren't left behind. The most significant loan, of course, was the recent US$10 billion loan to Dubai, but Sheikh Khalifa is also known for his philanthropic commitments, such as the major gift in 2007 to Johns Hopkins Medicine, in honour of the late Sheikh Zayed.

FACTS & FIGURES

Population

The UAE population has grown rapidly in recent years as expat arrivals, robust economic expansion and high birth rates have continued to push up the total number. According to the World Bank, the UAE's population stood at 4.6 million in 2009 and, according to Abu Dhabi Statistics Centre, the capital's population stood at 1.64 million in that year.

However, at the end of 2011, that figure had risen to 7.2 million living in the UAE, and is expected to have increased by around 5.6% to 7.6 million by the end of 2012. Abu Dhabi's population, at the end of 2012, is expected to be around 3.1 million. Nearly nine out of ten UAE residents are expats, with Emiratis accounting for 11.5% of the population.

World's Richest City

In 2007, *Fortune Magazine* named Abu Dhabi the world's richest city. The emirate has 10% of the world's oil reserves and has invested its sovereign wealth wisely to create a healthy economy. Its global profile has increased in recent years as the emirate has become an economic powerhouse.

Local Time

The UAE is four hours ahead of UTC (Universal Coordinated Time – formerly known as GMT). Clocks are not altered for daylight saving in the summer, so when Europe and North America gain an hour, the time in the UAE stays the same. During this period the time difference is one hour less, so when it is 12:00 in the UAE it is 09:00 in the UK instead of 08:00, as it is during the winter. The table shows time differences between the UAE and various cities around the world (not allowing for any daylight savings in those cities).

Time Zones

City		City	
Amman	-2	Los Angeles	-12
Athens	-2	Manama	-1
Auckland	+8	Mexico City/Dallas	-10
Bangkok	+3	Moscow	-1
Beijing	+4	Mumbai	+1.5
Beirut	-2	Munich	-3
Canberra	+6	Muscat	0
Colombo	+2	New York	-9
Damascus	-2	Paris	-3
Denver	-11	Perth	+4
Doha	-1	Prague	-3
Dublin	-4	Riyadh	-1
Hong Kong	+4	Rome	-3
Johannesburg	-2	Singapore	+4
Karachi	+1	Sydney	+6
Kuwait City	-1	Tokyo	+5
London	-4	Toronto	-9
		Wellington	+8

Social & Business Hours, Weekends

Working hours differ greatly in the UAE, with much of the private sector working a straight shift (usually from 08:00 to 17:00 or 09:00 to 18:00, with an hour for lunch), while a minority work a split shift (working from 09:00 to 13:00, then taking a long lunch break before returning to work from 16:00 to 19:00). It's not uncommon for working hours in private companies in the UAE to be longer than in other countries.

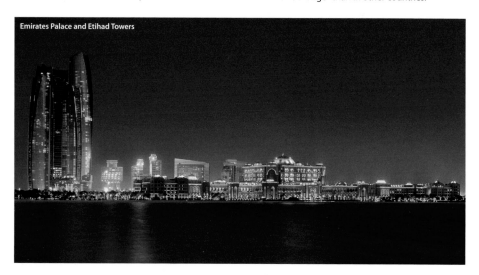

Emirates Palace and Etihad Towers

UAE: Facts & Figures

The UAE, and Abu Dhabi in particular, have witnessed huge growth as commerce, industry and tourism take a hold. Take a look at the main numbers affecting the country and its capital city.

UAE Free Zones

There are more than 30 free zones in the UAE. Designed to encourage investments from overseas, free zones allow 100% foreign ownership, 100% repatriation of profit and 0% tax.

Abu Dhabi GDP By Sector

Manufacturing 10% Public Administration & Defense 3% Real Estate & Business Services 4%
Education 1% Restaurants & Hotels 1%
Construction 5% Transport, Storage & Communication 3%
Less: Imputed Bank Services 1% Other 2%
Health 1%
Agriculture, Livestock & Fishing 1% Wholesale, Retail Trade & Repairing Services 3%
Electricity, Gas & Water 1%
Mining and Quarrying 64%

Source: Statistics Center – Abu Dhabi

UAE GDP By Emirate

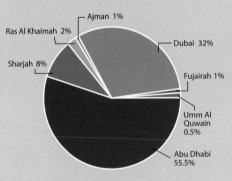

Ajman 1%
Ras Al Khaimah 2%
Dubai 32%
Sharjah 8%
Fujairah 1%
Umm Al Quwain 0.5%
Abu Dhabi 55.5%

Source: Ministry of Economy

UAE GDP By Sector

Mining and Quarrying 36% Agriculture, Livestock & Fishing 2%
Manufacturing 12% Transport, Storage & Communication 5%
Real Estate 8%
Electricity, Gas & Water 1% Restaurants & Hotels 2%
Financial Services 7%
Construction 7% Government Services 4%
Wholesale/ Retail Trade & Repairing Services 16% Social & Personal Services 1%

Source: UAE Yearbook 2010

Temperature & Humidity

Rainfall

Source: Meteorological Department, Abu Dhabi International Airport & National Center of Meteorology and Seismology

Population By Emirate

Source: Ministry of Economy

Education Levels

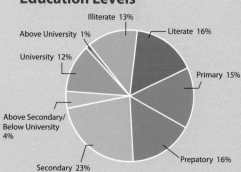

Source: Statistics Center – Abu Dhabi

Abu Dhabi Population Age Breakdown

Source: Statistics Center – Abu Dhabi

Facts & Figures

Government offices are generally open from 07:30 to 14:30, Sunday to Thursday. Embassies and consulates operate similar hours, but may designate specific times and days for certain tasks (such as passport applications), so it's best to call before you go. Most embassies take a Friday/Saturday weekend. All will have an emergency number on their answering service, website or on their office doors.

The majority of larger shops and shopping centres are open throughout the day and into the evening, generally closing at 22:00 or midnight. Traditional shops and smaller street traders often operate under split shift timings, closing for three or four hours in the afternoon. Some food outlets and petrol stations are open 24 hours a day.

Friday is the Islamic holy day and therefore a universal day off for offices and schools; most companies and schools have a two-day weekend over Friday and Saturday. Some companies still require a six-day week from their staff, while others operate on a five-and-a-half-day system. Consumer demand means that the hospitality and retail industries are open seven days a week.

Ramadan Hours

According to UAE labour laws, all companies are obliged to shorten the working day by two hours during Ramadan. Even though this is to assist Muslim employees who are fasting, the law makes no distinction in this regard between Muslim and non-Muslim employees. So, technically, even non-muslim expats are entitled to a shorter working day. However, many international companies do not follow this principle and labour lawyers would advise you not to make a fuss if you are not given a shorter working day during Ramadan. Some lucky expats do get to work shorter hours during Ramadan and many businesses, schools and shops change their hours slightly during this special period of the year.

Abu Dhabi's traffic has a totally different pattern during Ramadan; instead of being gridlocked in the mornings and quiet in the afternoons, the mornings are almost jam-free and you'll sail through any usual trouble spots, while in the afternoons the roads tend to get busy and sometimes totally clogged. Night-time activity increases during Ramadan, with many shops staying open later (until midnight or even 01:00) and the city's many shisha cafes and some restaurants stay open until the early hours.

Public Holidays

The Islamic calendar starts from the year 622AD, the year of Prophet Muhammad's migration (Hijra) from Mecca to Al Madinah. Hence the Islamic year is called the Hijri year and dates are followed by AH (AH stands for Anno Hegirae, meaning 'after the year of the Hijra').

As some holidays are based on the sighting of the moon and do not have fixed dates on the Hijri calendar, Islamic holidays are more often than not confirmed less than 24 hours ahead of time. Most companies send an email to employees the day before, notifying them of the confirmed holiday date in advance.

Some non-religious holidays are fixed according to the Gregorian calendar. It should be noted that the public sector often gets additional days off or holidays where the private sector may not (for example on National Day the public sector gets two days of official holiday, whereas private sector companies take only one day).

This can be a problem for working parents, as schools fall under the public sector and therefore get the extended holidays, so your children will usually have more days off than you do. This isn't a problem if you have full-time home help, but if not then you may have to take a day's leave.

Below is a list of the holidays and the number of days they typically last. The listed number of days (the length of holiday) applies mainly to the public sector, so if you work in the private sector you may get fewer days per holiday. The main Muslim festivals are Eid Al Fitr (the festival of the breaking of the fast, which marks the end of Ramadan) and Eid Al Adha (the festival of the sacrifice, which marks the end of the pilgrimage to Mecca). Mawlid Al Nabee is the holiday celebrating the Prophet Muhammad's birthday, and Lailat Al Mi'raj celebrates the Prophet's ascension into heaven.

Lunar Calendar

The Hijri calendar is based on lunar months; there are 354 or 355 days in the Hijri year, which is divided into 12 lunar months, and is thus 11 days shorter than the Gregorian year. There are plenty of websites with Gregorian/Hijri calendar conversion tools, so you can find the equivalent Hijri date for any Gregorian date and vice versa. Try rabiah.com/convert.

Public Holidays

New Year (1)	1 Jan 2013 (Fixed)
Mawlid Al Nabee	24 Jan 2013 (Moon)
Lailat Al Mi'raj (1)	06 Jun 2013 (Moon)
Eid Al Fitr (3)	14 Aug 2013 (Moon)
Arafat Day (1)	14 Oct 2013 (Moon)
Eid Al Adha (3)	15 Oct 2013 (Moon)
Islamic New Year's Day (1)	05 Nov 2013 (Moon)
UAE National Day (2)	2 Dec 2013 (Fixed)
New Year (1)	1 Jan 2014 (Fixed)
Mawlid Al Nabee	14 Jan 2014 (Moon)
Lailat Al Mi'raj (1)	27 May 2014 (Moon)

Currency

The monetary unit is the dirham (Dhs.), which is divided into 100 fils. The currency is also referred to as AED (Arab Emirate Dirham). Notes come in denominations of Dhs.5 (brown), Dhs.10 (green), Dhs.20 (light blue), Dhs.50 (purple), Dhs.100 (pink), Dhs.200 (yellowy-brown), Dhs.500 (blue) and Dhs.1,000 (browny-purple). The denominations are indicated on the notes in both Arabic and English. To see examples of the UAE's banknotes, visit the website of the Central Bank of the UAE (centralbank.ae) and click on 'currency' on the left. There are a total of six coins in circulation, but you typically only come across the three largest denominations: the Dhs.1, 50 fils and 25 fils. Distinguishing between the coins is tricky if you are not an Arabic speaker – the amount is written in Arabic only. The Dhs.1 coin is the largest, the 50 fils is smaller but seven-sided, and the 25 fils is of a similar size to the 50 fils but is circular. All are silver in colour. The dirham has been pegged to the US dollar since 1980, at a mid rate of $1 to Dhs.3.6725.

Exchange Rates

Foreign Currency	1 Unit FC = x Dhs	Dhs1 = xFC
Australia Dollars (AUD)	3.85	0.26
Bahrain Dinars (BHD)	9.74	0.10
Bangladesh Taka (BDT)	0.05	22.15
Canada Dollars (CAD)	3.69	0.27
Denmark Kroner (DKK)	0.64	1.55
Euro (EUR)	4.81	0.21
Hong Kong Dollars (HKD)	0.47	2.11
India Rupees (INR)	0.07	14.89
Japan Yen (JPY)	0.04	22.32
Jordan Dinars (JOD)	5.18	0.19
Kuwait Dinars (KWD)	13.05	0.08
Malaysia Ringgits (MYR)	1.21	0.83
New Zealand Dollars (NZD)	3.03	0.33
Oman Rials (OMR)	9.54	0.10
Pakistan Rupees (PKR)	0.04	26.28
Philippines Pesos (PHP)	0.09	11.13
Qatar Riyals (QAR)	1.01	0.99
Saudi Arabia Riyals (SAR)	0.98	1.02
Singapore Dollars (SGD)	3.02	0.33
South Africa Rand (ZAR)	0.42	2.41
Sri Lanka Rupees (LKR)	0.03	34.95
Sweden Kronor (SEK)	0.56	1.80
Switzerland Francs (CHF)	3.96	0.25
Thailand Baht (THB)	0.12	8.35
United Kingdom Pounds (GBP)	5.92	0.17
United States Dollars (USD)	3.67	0.27

Source: www.xe.com, Dec 2012

Exchange Centres

Al Ansari Exchange 02 610 8888, *alansariuae.com*
Al Fardan Exchange 02 622 3222, *alfardanexchange.com*

Al Rostamani International Exchange Company
02 643 0643, *alrostamaniexchange.com*
Habib Exchange Company 02 627 2656, *habibexchange.com*
Lari Money Exchange 02 622 3225
UAE Exchange 02 610 5555, *uaeexchange.com*

ENVIRONMENT

Flora & Fauna

While the variety of flora and fauna in the UAE is not as extensive as in some parts of the world, a number of plants and animals have managed to adapt to life in arid conditions. In addition, the Abu Dhabi Municipality has an extensive greening programme in place and areas along the roads are unusually colourful for a desert environment, with grass, palm trees and flowers being constantly maintained by an army of workers and round-the-clock watering. The city also boasts a large number of well-kept parks (see p.213).

The region has about 3,500 native plants, which is perhaps surprising considering the high salinity of the soil and the harsh environment. The most famous is, of course, the date palm, which is also the most flourishing of the indigenous flora. In mountainous regions, flat-topped acacia trees and wild grasses create scenery not unlike that of an African savannah. The deserts are unexpectedly green in places, even during the dry summer months, but it takes an experienced botanist to get the most out of the area.

Indigenous fauna include the Arabian leopard and the ibex, but sightings are extremely rare. Realistically, the only large animals you will see are camels and goats (often roaming dangerously close to roads). Other desert life includes sand cats, sand foxes, desert hares, gerbils, hedgehogs, snakes and geckos.

Recent studies have shown that the number of bird species is rising each year, due in part to concerted greening efforts. This is most apparent in parks, especially in spring and autumn, as the country is on the route for birds migrating between central Asia and east Africa. Al Wathba lake, some 30km south of Abu Dhabi city, attracts numerous species, but is currently inaccessible. The Ajban area to the city's north attracts twitchers (p.275) for its variety of bird species, while you can see flamingos at the Ras Al Khor Wildlife Sanctuary at the southern end of Dubai Creek.

Off the coast of the UAE, the seas contain a rich abundance of marine life, including tropical fish, jellyfish, coral, the dugong ('sea cow') and sharks. Eight species of whale and seven species of dolphin have been recorded in UAE waters. Various breeds of turtle are also indigenous to the region including the loggerhead, green and hawksbill turtles, all of which are under threat. Sightings by snorkellers and divers

Environment

off both coasts are not uncommon, particularly at places such as Snoopy Island (p.262) and Khor Kalba (p.261) on the East Coast.

Bu Tinah, a tiny archipelago which lies in Abu Dhabi waters, has received much attention of late. Its rich natural habitat of coral, seagrass, mangroves, flamingos, osprey, dolphins, hawksbill turtles and dugong saw Bu Tinah nominated as one of the seven wonders of the natural world; however, the area is protected and not open to visitors.

Environmental Issues

Environmental Initiatives & Organisations

On the positive side, the UAE government and local municipalities have started making significant efforts towards reducing waste and consumption and raising environmental awareness. Masdar City (masdarcity.ae), a cutting edge development in Abu Dhabi, is at the forefront of the emirate's efforts to emerge as a global leader in green technologies and sustainable development. Once completed, Masdar City will be the world's first waste-free, carbon-neutral development; already operational is the Masdar Institute of Science and Technology (p.150). During 2013, plastic carrier bags will be phased out across

the country. In 2011, Abu Dhabi Corniche won the international Blue Flag award, given to beaches that meet strict environmental criteria and water quality. Other programmes are in place to revitalise the coral reefs off the coast.

See Them For Yourself

Beyond the city, you'll find hardy creatures that survive in the sand dunes, mountains and wadis, despite harsh conditions. If you're camping in the desert, look out for trails on the dunes in the morning left by gerbils, camels, dung beetles and the elusive sand skink.

The government effort is being accelerated by various environmental organisations which aim to protect the environment, as well as to educate the population on the importance of environmental issues. The Environment Agency Abu Dhabi (ead. ae) assists the Abu Dhabi government in the conservation and management of the emirate's natural environment, resources, wildlife and biological diversity.

Sir Bani Yas Island, part of Abu Dhabi emirate, is home to an internationally acclaimed breeding programme for endangered wildlife. Created as a

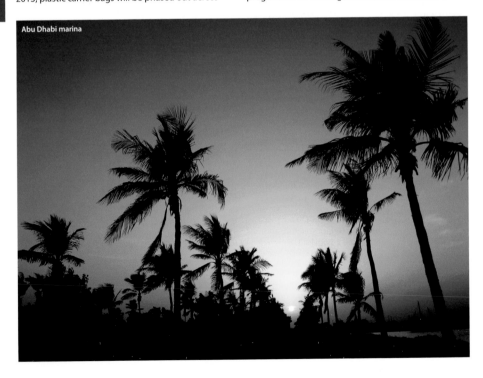

Abu Dhabi marina

Girls Gone Green

Abu Dhabi Eco-Chicks is a group of 'educated, empowered and eco-minded' ladies who get together to make a difference. Their website, abudhabiecochicks.wordpress.com, is a great resource for all the latest issues and campaigns affecting the environment and Abu Dhabi.

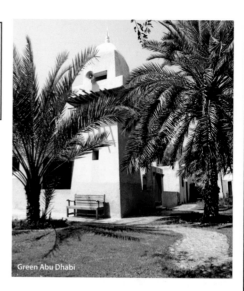
Green Abu Dhabi

private wildlife sanctuary by the late Sheikh Zayed, it is now an exclusive eco-resort (02 801 5400, anantara.com). Emirates Wildlife Society is a national environmental NGO that operates in association with the WWF (panda.org/uae). In addition, The Breeding Centre for Endangered Arabian Wildlife (06 531 1212) at Sharjah Desert Park, has a successful breeding programme for wildlife under threat, particularly the Arabian leopard. Al Ain Zoo (p.238, 283) has been equally instrumental in conserving species; its Arabian oryx breeding programme has been particularly successful. See also Environmental Groups (p.282).

Water Usage & Desalination

Abu Dhabi, naturally surrounded by saltwater, sand and not much else, seems an unlikely place to experience such rapid growth. The city has risen from the dunes in just over 50 years. Of course, this has taken a toll on the environment and, according to the WWF's Living Planet Report 2008, the UAE has the highest ecological footprint per person in the world, narrowly edging out perennial offender, the USA. Even more surprising, water usage in the UAE is the highest per capita in the world and the fresh water supply is being decimated by the ever-increasing population. This has forced the country to rely more and more on desalination and, in the next few years, production will need to be drastically ramped up to meet demand. Pair this with a negligible amount of arable land (meaning more imports) and a population of expats who invest less into the community than a long-term resident or citizen would, and the UAE will be hard-pressed to improve upon its poor environmental track record in the near future.

However, the late Sheikh Zayed was visionary in his respect for the environment, seeking to balance its health with that of the country's population and, with increasing awareness, Abu Dhabi is attempting to become a better steward to life, land and water.

The construction of the carbon-neutral Masdar City is an attempt to show what can be accomplished with human ingenuity and ambition, and Masdar's research university is constantly striving for and developing new green technology to combat business as usual.

Water Way To Save

As part of its water conservation initiatives, Abu Dhabi has recently launched a campaign to install water saving devices free of charge in every household in the emirate. The initiative will notably reduce residents' water bills and save as much as 75 billion litres of water annually. The 'Watersavers' campaign will be rolled out over the next few years. See watersavers.ae for more information.

In addition, there are a number of environmentally friendly initiatives and government-backed education programmes, such as Heroes of the UAE (heroesoftheuae.com). Its website outlines how individuals, schools and businesses can help to overcome the challenges the country faces.

Water Retention Habiba Al Marashi, Chairperson, Emirates Environmental Group

There is an urgent need for all sectors to save water. The solutions vary from simple to complicated ones like checking for leaks, turning taps off, using a pail of water for washing cars, using water saving fixtures and recycling water to name a few. However, saving water requires a conscious effort on all our parts to ensure that we are saving a precious and expensive resource.

Going Green

If everyone in the world was to live like the average UAE resident, calculations suggest that 4.5 planets would be needed to provide the natural resources. Indisputably, the UAE is living beyond its ecological means and habits have to change.

Responsibility

Perhaps it is a result of living in a nation inhabited by a huge number of expatriates, but the average UAE resident seems to feel very little responsibility towards their new country's environment. Expats from countries where 'green' initiatives, such as household recycling, are commonplace may be surprised by the lack of awareness and facilities for similar schemes in the UAE. Government efforts, such as the ban on plastic carrier bags, are firm steps in the right direction but they are slow to take effect. In the meantime, there is a pressing need for all residents to start making a personal contribution to reduce the impact of their presence.

Recycling

On the recycling front, UAE residents are becoming more proactive. The Emirates Environmental Group (p.283), for example, has reported a large increase in its school, corporate and community recycling drives which collect paper, plastic, glass, aluminium and toner cartridges. Schools and offices can contact Zenath Green Matters (zenath.com) who are experts in recycling paper and cardboard. Equally, mobile phones, broken computers and all kinds of electronic equipment can now be recycled through Enviroserve (enviroserve.ae/electronic-waste) or even at your nearest Plug-ins store (800 758 4467). Abu Dhabi National Energy Company (taqa.ae) has a programme which aims to place recycling centres into key areas, such as Al Hosn University and the American International School (see p.144). If your area doesn't have a recycling scheme, it can involve rather a lot of administrative wrangling with the developer or community management company, but it's worth bringing the issue to the attention of your residents' committee to try to build support and put pressure on the developers. In the meantime, you can always take your own waste to the recycling bins that are dotted around Abu Dhabi.

Abu Dhabi has many parks

"
Consider the three Rs – reduce, reuse and recycle. Look for a positive and practical change that you can make to a routine and make it a habit. Once you've done that, don't rest on your laurels – find the next change that you can make, and the next.
"

Small Efforts For Big Changes

The first step towards a greener life in the UAE is simply to consider the three Rs – reduce, reuse and recycle. Look for a positive and practical change that you can make to a routine – like switching off the lights when you leave a room – and make it a habit. Once you've done that, don't rest on your laurels – find the next change that you can make, and the next. You'll soon find that looking for ways to use the three Rs becomes habit in itself, influencing buying decisions, product consumption and usage levels. Changing the world may be a lofty goal, but changing yours and your family's personal habits is extremely achievable, makes a difference and sets an example. Here are a few suggestions to help get you started...

Getting Started

- The average UAE resident consumes more than double the amount of energy of citizens in France and the UK; more even than America, traditionally the worst ecological offender. Simple actions, such as turning air conditioning up a few degrees or using energy efficient light bulbs can have a big impact. A simple Watersaver device can save 550 litres a day per household. Find more ideas at heroesoftheuae.ae.
- Invest in reusable water bottles rather than buying bottled water for all your drinking needs, which sends a tremendous amount of waste to landfills. If you can't imagine drinking from the tap, invest in a water cooler and buy the big five-gallon containers.
- Take the bus or organise a carpool. When you drive to the shops, combine it with other errands to cut down on carbon emissions.
- Cover your pool in the summer. An uncovered pool loses up to 3,785 litres of water per month through evaporation.
- Unplug you phone charger. As much as 95% of the energy used by phone chargers is wastage caused by leaving them continually plugged in.
- Create your own desert oasis and choose native plants for your back garden to cut down on the volumes needed for daily watering.
- You often have to rip away several layers of bags and wrapping to get to your take-out order. Prepare your own meals more often to do away with the middlemen.
- Make the most of Abu Dhabi's arid climate and dry your laundry in the open air rather than using the tumble dryer.
- Plastic bags will be phased out during 2013; stay ahead of the trend by using reusable carriers or jute bags and help cut down on the millions of plastic bags that go into landfills every year.
- According to the Centre of Waste Management, recycling will soon be mandatory in the UAE capital. In the meantime, there are already workplace recycling programmes (contact the Environment Agency Abu Dhabi at customerservice@ead.ae for more details) and a few drop-off sites for individuals conveniently located at Spinneys supermarkets.
- If you're a thrift store junkie, check out the UAE's second-hand stores and markets (see Shopping, p.333), such as the thrift shop in the St. Andrew's Church compound (standrewauh.org).

BUSINESS & COMMERCE

Overview

The UAE is considered the second richest Arab country, after Qatar, on a per capita basis. The country has just under 10% of the world's proven oil reserves (most of it within Abu Dhabi emirate) and the fourth largest natural gas reserves.

The UAE GDP was growing at a rate of over 7% per year prior to the crash of 2009 and, after a temporary blip in that year, the economy reverted back to positive territory by registering 3.2% growth in 2010 (cia.gov). At an estimated $262.1 billion in 2011, the UAE economy is the second largest in the Gulf, after Saudi Arabia. In May 2012, the UAE was named the world's 16th most competitive economy by the World Competitiveness Yearbook (WCY), climbing 12 places year-on-year; however, the WCY conceded that the country's economy faced challenges in the shape of an oversupply of real estate, ongoing debt restructuring and bond repayments to face over the next couple of years.

Successful economic diversification means that the UAE's wealth is no longer solely reliant on oil revenue; services alone already account for more than half of the GDP. In mid-2011, the International Monetary

Fund forecasted that the UAE's non-oil sector would accelerate to 3.3% growth, up from 2.1% in the year before. Boosting Abu Dhabi's infrastructure and manufacturing sector is central to the UAE's plans to wean its economy off oil. The government aims to boost growth by creating jobs, lowering the costs of running businesses and by attracting more foreign investment.

The Abu Dhabi Economic Vision 2030 is a blueprint, created by Abu Dhabi Council for Economic Development, the Department of Planning and Economy and the General Secretariat of the Executive Council, which aims to lead the emirate's economy into a highly diversified future, focused on acquisitions, aerospace, energy and industry, healthcare, infrastructure, real estate and hospitality, communications and service ventures. Across the country, these sectors are playing an increasingly important part in the national economy. Other sectors, such as publishing, recruitment, advertising and IT, while not as developed in terms of size, have been steadily growing in Abu Dhabi and Dubai, aided in part by various free zones.

However, don't be fooled by the high national income into thinking that the average expat coming to work in Abu Dhabi will automatically be on a huge salary. The wealth isn't spread evenly and, even before the financial crisis, the salaries for most types of jobs, with the exception of highly skilled professionals, were dropping. This downward trend is attributed in part to the willingness of workers to accept a position at a lower wage. While the UAE GDP per capita income stands at around Dhs.95,000, this figure includes all sections of the community and the average labourer, of whom there are many, can expect to earn as little as Dhs.600 ($165) per month.

While the unemployment level of the national population in the UAE is lower than that of many other Arab states, there are still a significant number of Emiratis out of work (over 30,000, according to some estimates). This is partly due to a preference for public sector work and partly because of qualifications and salary expectations not matching the skills required in the private sector. However, the government is trying to reverse this scenario and reduce unemployment in the local sector with a 'Nationalisation' or 'Emiratisation' programme (which is common to countries throughout the region). The eventual goal is to rely less on an expat workforce, which will be achieved by improving vocational training and by making it compulsory for certain types of companies, such as banks, to hire a set percentage of Emiratis.

Trade

Abu Dhabi has come a long way since the days when the pearling industry was its primary source of trade. Now, with roughly one-tenth of the world's

Aldar HQ

oil reserves, as well as vast natural gas assets, it has become a major international player. But with a trade policy based on economic openness and liberalisation, both emirate and country continue to diversify, as non-oil and gas exports steadily rise. Even in light of the economic downturn of 2009, Abu Dhabi's foreign trade has grown significantly, including non-oil exports with particular emphasis on re-exports. Abu Dhabi has also made significant efforts over the past few years to attract foreign investment in order to increase opportunities for development and prosperity. With flexible and investor-friendly laws, availability of raw materials and funds, tax exemptions and low tariffs, the investment climate in the UAE, and Abu Dhabi in particular, is an ideal one for foreign investment. Qatar, Saudi Arabia, Japan, South Korea and the US are among the UAE's biggest trade partners for exports, while the US, China, India and Germany top the list of major import sources.

Tourism

The UAE is well ahead of many other countries in the Middle East in terms of travel and tourism. Boosting tourism plays a central part in the government's economic diversification plans and is a major driving force behind the array of record-breaking infrastructure and hospitality developments announced over the past few years. In Dubai, work on key tourism developments is going ahead, despite gloomy economic conditions and, in the past couple of years, major projects such as Dubai Metro (p.54), the Burj Khalifa (p.6) and the Meydan racecourse (p.227) have been completed. Others have fallen victim of the credit crunch and are either delayed, cancelled or on indefinite hold.

Abu Dhabi was previously viewed by many as Dubai's lesser-known sibling but, in recent years, the capital has set itself up to become a major tourist destination in its own right. The city has recently witnessed an unprecedented boom in both plans for and construction of new hotels, amusement and theme parks, shopping malls, sports and recreational facilities, and art galleries and museums. Luxurious tourist resorts, including the Emirates Palace hotel (p.201), have put Abu Dhabi on the global tourism map and outside the city, there's now a handful of classy resort hotels and attractions, such as Al Ain Zoo (p.238, 283), being developed to widen the offering. Other mega-projects such as Saadiyat Island, which will be home to the Sheikh Zayed National Museum, the Louvre Abu Dhabi and the Guggenheim – all three are slated to open in 2014. Until then, neighbouring Yas Island will continue to hog most of the limelight with its brand new hotels, its annual Formula 1 Grand Prix, big-name concerts and the joys of Ferrari World, the world's largest indoor theme park, and Yas Waterworld.

Even during the global downturn of 2009, Abu Dhabi experienced an 8% growth in its tourism sector. The following year, Abu Dhabi attracted more than 1.8 million visitors. Since then, a large number of new hotels and attractions have opened, with predictions of a 10% year-on-year increase taking annual visitor figures to well over 2 million.

But it's not just leisure travel that the emirate is going for. The Abu Dhabi National Exhibition Centre (ADNEC), which opened in 2007, has contributed greatly to the number of business events held in town. The centre now welcomes over one million visitors per year and in addition to trade fairs that attract an international audience, large-scale popular events like the Abu Dhabi International Book Fair (see p.28) and The Bride Show Abu Dhabi (see p.27), help keep the local public involved too.

Everyday there is news of upcoming events in the city and the Abu Dhabi Tourism Authority wants the world to know about it, working to attract more tourists to the emirate with a multimillion-dollar worldwide advertising campaign and initiatives.

Economic Growth

Abu Dhabi has undergone tremendous growth since the discovery of oil and the late Sheikh Zayed bin Sultan Al Nahyan took over as ruler of the emirate. However, compared to the Dubai of the late 1990s and early 2000s, Abu Dhabi grew at a snail's pace. That all changed at the beginning of Sheikh Khalifa's rule. Thanks to relaxed real estate laws and new free zones, foreign money started pouring in and driving a boom that lasted a good five years, bringing the luxurious Emirates Palace, the transformation of Yas Island (p.196) and Saadiyat Island (p.35), as well as huge residential construction projects on Reem Island (p.87) and off the mainland.

⌐ Really Tax Free? ─────────

Do taxes exist in the UAE? Yes and no. You don't pay income or sales tax, except when you purchase alcohol from a licensed liquor store – when you'll be hit with a steep 30% tax. The main tax that you will come across is the municipality tax of 5% on rent and 10% on food, beverages and rooms in hotels. The rest are hidden taxes in the form of 'fees', such as your car registration renewal, visa/permit fees and Dubai's Salik (road toll).

Abu Dhabi has undergone tremendous growth over the past decade. Huge development projects are either on the way or have been finished. However, despite its immense wealth and impressive progress, Abu Dhabi did not remain completely untouched by the financial crisis of 2009; progress on some of the most significant projects in Abu Dhabi slowed, and other projects were scaled back. Nevertheless, Abu Dhabi's oil wealth meant that the capital could afford to ride out the storm (and even extend Dubai a $10 billion loan to fight off its own creditors) before returning to growth in 2010. The outlook is positive: the International Monetary Fund (imf.org) has outlined expectations of steady economic growth through to 2016. With its sizable government-led projects and ambitious expansion plans, Abu Dhabi is positioned to benefit greatly as its transformation into an increasingly significant global hub continues.

CULTURE & LIFESTYLE

Culture

The UAE manages what some Arab cities fail to achieve: a healthy balance between western influences and eastern traditions. Its culture is still very much rooted in the Islamic customs that deeply penetrate the Arabian Peninsula and beyond. However, the country's effort to become modern and cosmopolitan is proof of an open-minded and liberal outlook.

Islam is more than just a religion; it is a way of life that governs even mundane everyday events, from what to wear to what to eat and drink. Therefore, the culture and heritage of the UAE is closely linked to its religion. However, the UAE is tolerant and welcoming; foreigners are free to practise their own religion, alcohol is served in hotels and the dress code is liberal. Women face little discrimination and, contrary to the policies of neighbouring Saudi Arabia, are able to drive and walk around uncovered and unescorted.

The rapid economic development over the last 30 years has changed life in the United Arab Emirates beyond recognition. However, the country's rulers are committed to safeguarding their heritage. They are therefore keen to promote cultural and sporting events that are representative of their traditions, such as falconry, camel racing and traditional dhow sailing. Arabic culture in poetry, dancing, songs and traditional art and craftsmanship is encouraged.

Courtesy and hospitality are the most highly prized virtues, and visitors are likely to experience the genuine warmth and friendliness of the Emirati people. Luckily, the negative view of Islam that has affected many Muslims living abroad has not had an impact on Abu Dhabi, where you'll find people of various nationalities and religions working and living side by side without conflict. In Islam, the family unit is very important and elders are respected for their experience and wisdom. It's common for several generations to live together in the same house. Polygamy is practised in the UAE, with Islam allowing a man to have up to four wives at one time, providing he has the financial and physical means to treat each

of them equally. However, a Muslim man taking more than one wife is more the exception than the norm, and most Muslim families resemble the traditional western family unit: mum, dad and kids.

Weddings are important cultural occasions; the men and women celebrate separately with feasting and music. They are usually very large affairs; however, the government has placed a ceiling of Dhs.50,000 on dowries, and overly lavish weddings can result in a prison sentence or Dhs.500,000 fine. The government-sponsored Marriage Fund, based in Abu Dhabi, assists Emiratis with marriage, from counselling and financial assistance (long term loans of up to Dhs.70,000 for a UAE national man marrying a UAE national woman) to organising group weddings to keep costs down. With so many UAE Nationals studying abroad, and so many expats in Abu Dhabi and Dubai, inter-cultural marriages are increasingly common. The Marriage Fund strongly encourages nationals to marry fellow nationals (in an effort to preserve the culture and reduce the number of UAE spinsters), but it is easier for a national man to marry a non-national woman than it is for a national woman to marry a non-national man.

Race Relations

Abu Dhabi is a diverse, multicultural society with many different nationalities living side by side. Even though most of the time this is a harmonious arrangement, there are times when where you come from does seem to be an important factor. For example, some job advertisements are very forthcoming about their racial requirements, asking for 'western candidates' or 'fluent Arabic'. And salaries in the city definitely reflect nationality, with employees from Asia sometimes getting paid less than their western colleagues, even when doing similar jobs. Unfortunately, this kind of racism spreads to other areas too – it is becoming increasingly common for landlords to refuse tenants of certain nationalities, and certain bars and nightclubs have been accused in the past of having racist door policies (usually strenuously denied by those outlets, of course).

When you first arrive, you may find many aspects of the local culture seem very strange to you. Take time to observe and understand before you pass judgement; you'll soon realise that the many different nationalities living here make Abu Dhabi a sometimes-frustrating but ultimately fascinating city.

Language

Arabic is the official language of the UAE, although English, Hindi, Malayalam and Urdu are all commonly spoken throughout the country.

Arabic is the official business language, but English is so widely used that you could conduct business here for years without learning a single word of Arabic. Most road signs, shop signs and restaurant menus are in both languages. The further out of town you go, the more you will find just Arabic, both spoken and on street and shop signs.

Arabic isn't the easiest language to pick up, or to pronounce. But if you can throw in a couple of words here and there, you're more likely to receive a warmer welcome or at least a smile – even if your pronunciation is terrible. See the opposite page for a list of useful Arabic phrases, and p.152 for Arabic language courses.

Religion

Islam is the official religion of the UAE, and is widely practised throughout the country. The Islamic holy day is Friday. The basis of Islam is the belief that there is only one God and that Prophet Muhammad is his messenger. The faith shares a common ancestry with Christianity and many of the prophets before Muhammad can be found in Christian as well as Muslim writings. There are five pillars of Islam that all Muslims must follow: the Profession of Faith, Prayer, Charity, Fasting and Pilgrimage. Every Muslim is expected, at least once in his or her lifetime, to make the pilgrimage (Hajj) to the holy city of Mecca (also spelt Makkah) in Saudi Arabia.

BASIC ARABIC

General
Yes	na'am
No	la
Please	min fadlak (m)
	min fadlik (f)
Thank you	shukran
Please (in offering)	tafaddal (m)
	tafaddali (f)
Praise be to God	al-hamdu l-illah
God willing	in shaa'a l-laah

Greetings
Greeting (peace be upon you)	
	as-salaamu alaykom
Greeting (in reply)	
	wa alaykom is salaam
Good morning	sabah il-khayr
Good morning (in reply)	
	sabah in-nuwr
Good evening	masa il-khayr
Good evening (in reply)	
	masa in-nuwr
Hello	marhaba
Hello (in reply)	marhabtayn
How are you?	
	kayf haalak (m) / kayf haalik (f)
Fine, thank you	
	zayn, shukran (m)
	zayna, shukran (f)
Welcome	ahlan wa sahlan
Welcome (in reply)	
	ahlan fiyk (m) / ahlan fiyki (f)
Goodbye	ma is-salaama

Introductions
My name is...	ismiy...
What is your name?	
	shuw ismak (m) / shuw ismik (f)

Where are you from?	
	min wayn inta (m) /
	min wayn inti (f)
I am from…	anaa min...
America	ameriki
Britain	braitani
Europe	oropi
India	al hindi

Questions
How many / much?	kam?
Where?	wayn?
When?	mataa?
Which?	ayy?
How?	kayf?
What?	shuw?
Why?	laysh?
Who?	miyn?
To/for	ila
In/at	fee
From	min
And	wa
Also	kamaan
There isn't	maa fee

Taxi Or Car Related
Is this the road to...	hadaa al
	tariyq ila...
Stop	kuf
Right	yamiyn
Left	yassar
Straight ahead	siydaa
North	shamaal
South	januwb
East	sharq
West	garb
Turning	mafraq
First	awwal

Second	thaaniy
Road	tariyq
Street	shaaria
Roundabout	duwwaar
Signals	ishaara
Close to	qarib min
Petrol station	mahattat betrol
Sea/beach	il bahar
Mountain/s	jabal/jibaal
Desert	al sahraa
Airport	mataar
Hotel	funduq
Restaurant	mata'am
Slow Down	schway schway

Accidents & Emergencies
Police	al shurtaa
Permit/licence	rukhsaa
Accident	haadith
Papers	waraq
Insurance	ta'miyn
Sorry	aasif (m) /
	aasifa (f)

Numbers
Zero	sifr
One	waahad
Two	ithnayn
Three	thalatha
Four	arba'a
Five	khamsa
Six	sitta
Seven	saba'a
Eight	thamaanya
Nine	tiss'a
Ten	ashara
Hundred	miya
Thousand	alf

Culture & Lifestyle

Arabic Family Names

Arabic names have a formal structure that traditionally indicates the person's family and tribe. Names are usually taken from an important person in the Quran or from the tribe. This is followed by the word bin (son of) for a boy or bint (daughter of) for a girl, and then the name of the child's father. The last name indicates the person's tribe or family. For prominent families, this has Al, the Arabic word for 'the', immediately before it. For instance, the President of the UAE is His Highness Sheikh Khalifa bin Zayed Al Nahyan. When women get married, they do not change their name.

Additionally, a Muslim is required to pray (facing Mecca) five times a day. Times vary according to the sun's position. Most people pray at a mosque, but it's not unusual to see people kneeling by the side of the road if they are not near a place of worship. It is considered impolite to stare at people praying or to walk over prayer mats. The modern-day call to prayer, transmitted through loudspeakers on the minarets, ensures that everyone knows it's time to pray.

Islam is the principle religion, but the UAE is tolerant of other denominations; the ruling family has, in the past, donated land for the building of churches. There is a vibrant Christian community in Abu Dhabi and there is even a Hindu temple in Dubai.

National Dress

On the whole, Emiratis wear traditional dress in public. For men, this is the dishdasha or khandura: a white, full length shirt dress, which is worn with a white or red checked headdress, known as a gutra or sifrah. This is secured with a black cord (agal). Sheikhs and important businessmen may also wear a thin black or brown robe (known as a bisht), over their dishdasha at important events, which is equivalent to the dinner jacket in western culture. In public, women wear the black abaya: a long, loose black robe that covers their normal clothes, plus a headscarf called a sheyla.

Dressing Down

Abu Dhabi is less strict than many of its regional neighbours. Women are not required to cover their hair, but you should avoid wearing anything too tight or revealing. In public, both men and women should wear garments that cover shoulders and knees. It's fine to wear shorts at sports clubs and swimwear at the pool or beach but don't forget hats and sunscreen. You'll quickly get a feel for what is and isn't acceptable, and it differs from emirate to emirate. Dubai is more liberal still, while Sharjah is a touch more conservative.

The abaya is often of sheer, flowing fabric and may be open at the front. Some women also wear a thin black veil hiding their face, and gloves. Older women sometimes still wear a leather mask, known as a burkha, which covers the nose, brow and cheekbones. Underneath, women traditionally wear a long tunic over loose, flowing trousers (sirwall), which are often heavily embroidered and fitted at the wrists and ankles. However, these are used more by the older generation and modern women will often wear the latest fashions under their abayas.

Food & Drink

The food in Abu Dhabi reflects the diversity of its culture, so pretty much every type of international cuisine imaginable is on offer. Regardless of the size of your budget, you can eat good food from virtually any part of the world. The many hotels have different internationally themed restaurants and the standard of the cuisine is what you'd expect from a top-notch establishment. From modern European to Asian fusion or Mexican, you can get pretty much anything you fancy. While restaurants located in hotels are licensed to serve alcohol (see Alcohol, p.313), some of the best places to eat are the small streetside cafeterias around town, where you can feast on a tasty meal for two and still get change from Dhs.50. All of the main fastfood chains have branches here, so you won't have to venture too far to find a McDonalds, Burger King or KFC.

In terms of food shopping there are several large supermarkets (p.336) that stock a variety of international brands. The largest is probably Carrefour (p.336) at Marina Mall which is reasonably priced and its shelves stock a variety of products from around the world. Spinneys (p.338) and Abela (p.336) are more expensive but sell an excellent range of British, South African and American foods. Australia's Jones the Grocer (p.337, 379) caters to gourmet tastes and there's now an increasingly good offering of organic food too (see p.330). There are co-operative societies in virtually every central district of the city; some are open 24 hours and offer great value. For local fresh fish and produce, the fish market down at Port Zayed (p.192) is definitely worth a visit but get there early for the freshest catch straight off the boat.

Arabic Cuisine

Arabic cuisine is very meat orientated and, with the exception of mezze, there is not much on the vegetarian menu. While modern Arabic cuisine comes from a blend of Moroccan, Tunisian, Iranian and Egyptian cooking styles, the term invariably refers to Lebanese food. Takeaway outlets selling shawarma (lamb or chicken sliced from a spit and served in pita bread with salad and tahina) and falafel (mashed chickpeas and sesame seeds, rolled into balls and deep fried) are worth a visit at least once. Mezze is a

A traditional minaret

The Grand Mosque

Men praying

Sheikh Zayed Grand Mosque

selection of dishes often served with Arabic bread, a green salad and pickles. Dishes can include hummus (a creamy dip made from ground chickpeas, olive oil and garlic), tabouleh (finely chopped parsley, mint and cracked wheat salad), fatoush (lettuce and tomato with small pieces of fried Arabic bread), and fattayer (small pastries filled with cottage cheese and spinach).

Charcoal grilling of meat and fish is popular. Khouzi is a Ramadan favourite (whole lamb served on a bed of rice, mixed with nuts), an authentic local dish also served at the mansaf, a traditional, formal Bedouin dinner with dishes placed on the floor in the centre of a ring of seated guests. Other typical dishes include kibbeh (deep fried mince, pine nuts and bulgur) and a variety of kebabs.

The meal ends with Lebanese sweets, which can be extremely sweet, but delicious. The most widely known are baklava (filo pastry layered with honey and pistachio nuts) and Umm Ali, a dessert with layers of milk, bread, raisins and nuts. And to accompany your meal, you must sample the extensive variety of wonderfully fresh juices.

Emirati Cuisine

There are also opportunities to sample the local Emirati food. The legacy of the UAE's trading past means that local cuisine uses a blend of ingredients imported from around Asia and the Middle East. Spices such as cinnamon, saffron and turmeric along with nuts (almonds or pistachios), limes and dried fruit add interesting flavours to Emirati dishes.

Dried limes are a common ingredient in Arabic cuisine, reflecting a Persian influence. They are dried in the sun and are used to flavour dishes, either whole or ground in a spice mill. They impart a distinctively musty, tangy, sour flavour to soups and stews.

Pork

Pork is taboo in Islam. Muslims should not eat, prepare or even serve pork. In order for a restaurant to serve pork on its menu, it should have a separate fridge, preparation equipment and cooking area. In restaurants, where bacon appears on a menu, you will usually be served beef or veal bacon. Supermarkets are also required to sell pork in a separate area and Spinneys and Choithram both have screened-off pork sections. As pork is not locally produced you will find that it's more expensive than many other meats. All meat products for Muslim consumption have to be halal, which refers to the method of slaughter.

Alcohol

Alcohol is only served in licensed outlets associated with hotels (restaurants and bars), plus a few leisure clubs (such as golf clubs and sports clubs) and associations. Restaurants outside of hotels that are not part of a club or association are not permitted to serve alcohol. Nevertheless, permanent residents who are non-Muslims can get a liquor licence (p.44) which allows them to obtain alcohol for consumption at home.

Dates

One of the very few crops that thrive naturally across the Middle East, date palms have been cultivated for around 5,000 years. It's said that in some countries the Bedouin way of life was sustained primarily by dates and camel milk up until as recently as the mid 20th century. High in energy, fibre, potassium, vitamins, magnesium and iron, with negligible quantities of fat, cholesterol and salt, dates are a cheap and healthy snack. Just five dates per day provide enough nutrition for one recommended daily portion of fruit or vegetables.

Shisha

Smoking the traditional shisha (water pipe) is a popular and relaxing pastime enjoyed throughout the Middle East region. It is usually savoured in a local cafe while chatting with friends. They are also known as hookah pipes, hubbly bubbly or nargile. Shisha pipes can be smoked with a variety of aromatic flavours, such as strawberry, grape, mint or apple. Unlike a normal cigarette or cigar, the smoke is softened by the water, creating a more soothing effect, although it still causes smoking-related health problems. Plans are being considered to ban shisha cafes in Abu Dhabi's residential areas, due to increasing awareness about the dangers of passive smoking and to ensure young people aren't being encouraged to take up smoking.

Even so, smoking shisha is one of those things that should be tried at least once during your time in the UAE, especially during Ramadan, when tents are erected throughout the city and filled with people of all nationalities. You can buy your very own shisha pipe from souvenir shops or from supermarkets, and once you get to grips with putting it all together you can enjoy the unique flavour anytime you want.

For the best shisha experience, try Mirage Marine Cafe (p.384) or Ma Wa Weel (02 639 1333).

Tipping

It is entirely up to the individual whether to tip for services and it is not a fixed expectation, as you may find in other countries. Some people in Abu Dhabi choose not to tip at all, but for those who feel that the service was worth recognising, the usual amount is 10% and tips are greatly appreciated. An increasing number of restaurants now also include a service charge on the bill, although it's not clear whether this ever sees the inside of your waiter's pockets, so some people add a little extra. Tips in restaurants and bars

Cultural Dos & Don'ts

You'll find that, in general, people in the UAE are patient when it comes to cultural etiquette and are keen to explain their customs to you. However, there are a few cultural dos and don'ts that you should be aware of to avoid causing offence to others.

PDAs

Not a reference to the once-cool handheld gadget, but to public displays of affection: these are a no-no in the UAE and anything more than an innocent peck on the cheek will at best earn you disapproving looks from passers by.

Appropriate Attire

While beachwear is fine on the beach, you should dress a little more conservatively when out and about in public places. If in doubt, ensuring that your shoulders and knees are covered is a safe bet. That said, when out at bars and clubs in the evening, pretty much anything goes. Always carrying a pashmina is a useful tactic, enabling you to cover up when necessary – whether that's for cultural reasons or the 'deep-freeze' mall airconditioning.

Photography

Abu Dhabi is full of snap-worthy sights and normal tourist photography is fine. Like anywhere in the Arab world, it is courteous to ask permission before photographing people, particularly women. In general, photographs of government and military buildings should not be taken.

Arabic Coffee

It's likely that you'll be served traditional Arabic coffee (kahwa) during formal business meetings. This is an important social ritual in the Middle East so be polite and drink some when offered. Cups should be taken in the right hand and if there is a waiter standing by, replenishing your cup, the signal to say that you have had enough is to gently shake the cup from side to side.

Meeting People

Long handshakes, kisses and warm greetings are common when meeting people in the Middle East. It's normal to shake hands with people when you are introduced to them, although if you are meeting someone of the opposite sex, be aware that a handshake may not always be welcome. It's best to take your cue from the other person and not offer your hand unless they first offer theirs. It's polite to send greetings to a person's family, but can be considered rude to enquire directly about someone's wife, sister or daughter. You may see men greeting each other with a nose kiss; this is a customary greeting in the Gulf region but is only used between close friends and associates and you should not attempt to greet someone in this way.

Out On The Town

Abu Dhabi has a good variety of nightlife and alcohol is widely available in the city's hotel bars, pubs and clubs (see Going Out, p.396). Remember, however, that you're in a Muslim country and drunken or lewd behaviour is not only disrespectful but can lead to arrest and detention.

Business Etiquette

Business meetings in the region will usually start with introductions and small talk before you get down to business. Business cards will be exchanged – you should treat them with respect; as an extension of the person who gave them. Punctuality to meetings is important and arriving late is considered to be very bad mannered. Do not assume, however, that your meeting will start at the appointed time or that once started it will not be interrupted.

Home Values

When visiting an Emirati home it is customary to remove your shoes; however, it's best to take your cue from your host. Traditionally, men and women dine separately and meals are eaten while seated on floor cushions. When you sit, be carefully not to point your feet at anyone or to show the soles of your feet. Mealtimes are long and leisurely and as a guest your plate will be heaped high. Try everything offered but if you're not sure you'll like something, take a small amount that you can finish. If you invite a Muslim to your home, you should not offer pork or alcohol, as this may cause offence.

are often shared with other staff. See Going Out for more information (p.353).

For taxi drivers, it is regular practice to round up your fare as a tip, but this is not compulsory, so feel free to pay just the fare, especially if the driving standards were poor. For tipping when collecting your valet-parked car at hotels, around Dhs.5 is average. At petrol stations, especially when you get your windows cleaned, it's common practice to give a few dirhams as a tip. In beauty salons, spas and hairdressers, tipping is at your discretion but around 10% of the treatment price is an acceptable amount.

LOCAL MEDIA

Newspapers & Magazines

The UAE has a number of daily English language broadsheets. The cream of the crop is definitely Abu Dhabi's *The National*, arguably the region's first national newspaper offering quality journalism, intelligent editorial and meaty lifestyle pieces. Other titles include *Gulf News*, *Khaleej Times* and *Gulf Today*. In most areas of Abu Dhabi, you can also pick up a free copy of *7Days*, a tabloid-size newspaper published five days a week that features local and international news, business and entertainment news, and a sports section. Whichever country you're from, chances are you'll be able to find copies of your favourite home paper in Abu Dhabi's supermarkets.

There are plenty of local magazines, including a range of Middle Eastern editions of international titles that are produced here (examples include *OK!*, *Grazia*, *Harpers Bazaar*, *Men's Fitness* and *Stuff*). Keep an eye out for expat titles like *Connector* and *Aquarius*, as well as for listings magazines such as *TimeOut Abu Dhabi* and *What's On*.

Censorship

International magazines are available in bookshops and supermarkets, at inflated prices. All titles are examined and, where necessary, censored to ensure that they don't offend the country's moral codes. You'll find much the same is true of international films and TV shows, the vast majority of which make it over to the UAE, although they are assessed before they hit cinema screens or are shown on TV.

Radio

The UAE has a number of commercial radio stations that broadcast in a wide range of languages. The leading English language stations operate 24 hours a day and, while most are physically based in Dubai, they can usually be picked up with a good reception throughout Abu Dhabi:

Satellite Radio

Depending on your satellite TV provider, you may get some radio stations through your decoder. Various channels are available, including Virgin Radio from the UK and the BBC World Service. You can also access a variety of music channels – from country to pop. You can get around 20 music channels on OSN (osn.com).

Dubai 92: current music, competitions and popular DJs, 92.00FM, dubai92.com
Dubai Eye: quality talk radio, 103.8FM, dubaieye1038.com
Virgin Radio: hit music along the lines of Virgin Radio in other cities, 104.4FM, virginradiodubai.com
Channel 4: contemporary music for a younger audience, 104.8FM, channel4FM.com
The Coast: middle of the road and classic hits throughout the day, 103.2FM, 1032thecoast.com
Radio 1: hit music broadcast across the country, 104.1FM, gulfnews.com/radio1
Radio 2: contemporary music broadcast throughout the UAE, 99.3FM, gulfnews.com/radio2
The BBC World Service can also be picked up in Abu Dhabi on 90.3FM.

Always On The Box

OSN offers a Showbox service, with which you can pause live television and record your favourite shows on a digital box. You can also watch special previews of forthcoming movies, or virtual 'boxsets' of popular series. See osn.com for more information on the services.

Television

Local TV is in a state of continuous improvement – gone are the days when all you could watch was early episodes of *ER* and *Mad About You*, with all the kissing scenes cut out.

Channels like Dubai One and MBC4, despite being free-to-air, are doing a good job of securing the rights to some fairly mainstream international shows, and Fox Movies, which is also a free-to-air channel, has often been the first Middle Eastern TV station to screen major Hollywood movies, not too long after they've been in cinemas.

Satellite or cable TV is a staple in most expat homes – although it can be a bit hit and miss when judged by international standards. Some shows are aired just a few days later than they are in the US or UK, while others are delayed by a few months.

In 2012, Sky News Arabia, a 24-hour Arabic-language news channel, started broadcasting from its studios in Abu Dhabi.

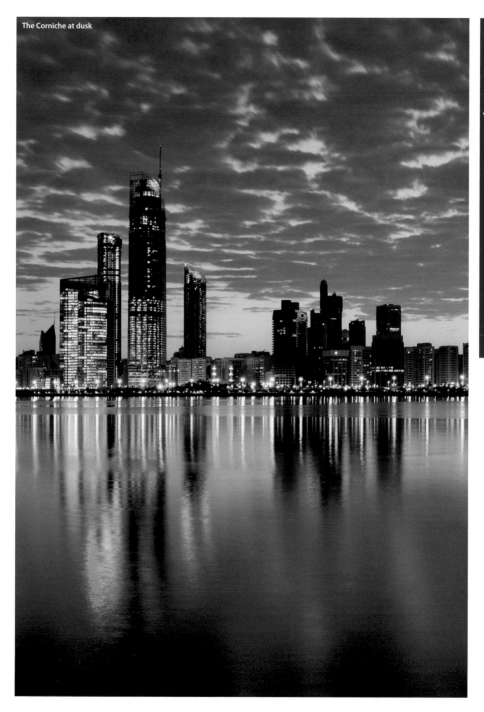

The Corniche at dusk

Internet & Directory Of Useful Websites

When compared to other Middle-East nations, the UAE is near the top for internet connectivity, but when you bring Europe and the US into the picture the country's offerings aren't exactly the best value in the world. That said, it's relatively easy to get hooked up if you live in the established areas of Abu Dhabi city.

Right away, you will probably find that using the internet while in Abu Dhabi has a few quirks that can take some getting used to, not least the much-despised proxy that blocks access to any sites deemed offensive. What is or isn't offensive is up to the Telecommunication Regulatory Authority (TRA), which supposedly applies the same rules to both Etisalat and du subscribers (See p.94) for how to get hooked up).

While living in a Muslim community, you can certainly expect sites containing pornography or dubious religious content to be blocked, and until recently VoIP (Voice over Internet Protocol) access was blocked. Regulators finally authorised VoIP phone in March 2010, but only existing licence-holders may offer VoIP, thus excluding popular services such as Skype. The TRA said it was making it legal for people to place international calls through the internet, but would allow only licensed operators to run such services; the four companies licensed to offer international VoIP services are Etisalat, du and the satellite firms Yahsat and Thuraya.

For consumers, that means the prices of any international internet calls will be set by those companies and it is not yet clear whether this will result in substantial cost savings. So, if you do want to speak to friends and family abroad, you either have to use the actual telephone or use authorised VoIP services (when they're made available). Messaging services like Skype and Google Chat still work computer-to-computer, although you may have to download Skype on your next overseas holiday. Of course, you can access Skype and other blocked sites with the help of a proxy blocker, but then you're technically breaking the law.

It's a frustrating conundrum, made even more so by the lack of any reasons other than financial, but rules are rules. Other sites that you will not be able to access include online dating sites, sites dealing with gambling or drugs, and, oddly, some photo-sharing sites as well.

UAE CALENDAR 2013

The UAE hosts a wide variety of public events. Whether you choose to chill out to tunes from world music, swot up at annual art fairs, raise money for charity or watch as the world's greatest golfers fight it out for titles and prize money, the UAE offers some unforgettable experiences.

Abu Dhabi HSBC Golf Championship January
Abu Dhabi Golf Club Madinat Khalifa A (Khalifa City A)
abudhabigolfchampionship.com
With US $2 million in prize money and some of the biggest names in golf appearing, the Abu Dhabi Golf Championship is one of the biggest sporting events.

USEFUL WEBSITES

Abu Dhabi Information
abudhabi.ae	Abu Dhabi government portal with tonnes of information
abudhabitourism.ae	Abu Dhabi Tourism Authority
abudhabiwoman.com	Forums and advice for women living in Abu Dhabi
adach.ae	Abu Dhabi Authority for Culture and Heritage
adnec.ae	Abu Dhabi National Exhibition Centre
adpolice.gov.ae	Abu Dhabi Police
askexplorer.com	Essential info on living in the UAE from Explorer Publishing
dubizzle.com	Great website for classifieds and community, Dubai and Abu Dhabi
sheikhzayed.com	Site dedicated to the life of the late UAE President
thenational.ae	Local newspaper
visitabudhabi.ae	Abu Dhabi tourism site

UAE Information
7days.ae	Local newspaper
ameinfo.com	Middle East business news
government.ae	UAE Government e-portal
gulfnews.com	Local newspaper
khaleejtimes.com	Local newspaper
weather.adac.ae	Weather information from the Department of Atmospheric Studies

The Bride Show Abu Dhabi   January
Abu Dhabi National Exhibition Centre (ADNEC)
Al Safarat
thebrideshow.com
This show brings the whole wedding industry together, showcasing dresses, entertainment, honeymoon destinations and wedding organisers.

Dubai Shopping Festival   January
Dubai 04 445 5642
dubaievents.ae
The month-long shopping extravaganza is a great time for bargain-hunters to visit the city.

Omega Dubai Desert Classic   January
Emirates Golf Club Dubai 04 380 2112
dubaidesertclassic.com
This longstanding PGA European Tour fixture has been won by legends such as Ernie Els and Tiger Woods, and is a popular event among the golfing community of the UAE.

Standard Chartered Dubai Marathon   January
Dubai 04 433 5669
dubaimarathon.org
This event attracts runners aiming to fundraise or work off that festive winter tummy in either the 10km road race or 3km charity run, as well as the more daring and elite marathon runners who take on the full 42km.

Dubai Duty Free Tennis Championships   February
The Aviation Club Dubai 04 282 4122
dubaidutyfreetennischampionships.com
Firmly established on the ATP and WTP circuits, this multi-million dollar tournament attracts the world's top men's and women's seeds.

Skywards Dubai International Jazz Festival   February
Dubai Festival City Dubai 04 391 1196
dubaijazzfest.com
This festival attracts a broad range of artists from around the world to the chilled and pleasant setting in Al Badia. Macy Gray, The Brand New Heavies and James Blunt have all taken to the stage.

Terry Fox Run   February
The Corniche Al Khubeirah
terryfox.org
Each year, thousands of individuals run, jog, walk, cycle and rollerblade their way around an 8.5km course for charity. The proceeds go to cancer research programmes at approved institutions around the world. For more information, email abudhabiterryfoxrun@gmail.com.

Al Ain Aerobatic Show

Abu Dhabi Desert Challenge   March
Empty Quarter Liwa 02 296 1122
abudhabidesertchallenge.ae
This high profile, well-established motorsport event attracts some of the world's top rally drivers and bikers to race on the Empty Quarter's challenging desert routes and take on its steepest dunes.

Abu Dhabi Festival   March
Emirates Palace Al Ras Al Akhdar 02 651 0300
abudhabifestival.ae
Hosts an impressive lineup of recognised musicians and orchestras from around the world. It is a strong advocate of cross-cultural understanding, playing a major role in reviving art and culture across the Gulf.

Abu Dhabi International Triathlon   March
The Corniche Al Khubeirah
abudhabitriathlon.com
With a prize purse of $250,000, the Abu Dhabi International Triathlon is one of the world's richest triathlons, attracting talent from all over the world.

UAE National Day

Every 2 December, the country turns green, black, red and white all over. In fact, the flag becomes as ubiquitous as traffic jams as residents throughout the Emirates celebrate the birth of the UAE. Cars, trucks and taxis are decorated with flags and pictures of the country's rulers to show their patriotism. And, especially along the Corniche and in public parks and markets, military bands and folklore exhibitions entertain the crowds. It wouldn't be an independence celebration without fireworks, and Emirates Palace hotel holds the city's biggest display, set to music.

UAE Calendar 2013

Abu Dhabi Yacht Show
March

Yas Marina Yas Island West **02 407 2770**
abudhabiyachtshow.com
The three-day event sees more than 150 yacht manufacturers, brokers, services and accessories attract thousands of sea loving guests to Yas Marina.

Al Ain Classics Festival
March

Al Ain
aacf.ae
Now in its second decade, the Al Ain Classics hosts some of the most distinguished musicians in their fields; the festival attempts to showcase music from both the Arab and Western worlds.

Art Dubai
March

Madinat Jumeirah Dubai **04 384 2000**
artdubai.ae
Now a truly international art exhibition, with over 75 galleries from 32 countries represented in the programme, running alongside is the Global Art Forum, a lecture and discussion board programme.

Exhibitions

With a steely focus on increasing MICE (meetings, incentives, conferences and exhibitions) tourism, Abu Dhabi has invested heavily in its state-of-the-art exhibition space, ADNEC (adnec.ae). The exhibition centre is also the venue for numerous musical and cultural events, as well as meetings and exhibitions, and has a number of outlets. The Aloft Hotel at ADNEC is already open while a Hyatt hotel will open soon in Capital Gate – the world's 'most leaning' building.

Dubai World Cup
March

Meydan Racecourse Dubai **04 327 0077**
dubaiworldcup.com
Billed as the world's richest horse race, the Dubai World Cup has certainly become one of the premier thoroughbred races of the year, and the new Meydan course and hotel are destinations in their own right. One of the biggest events in the UAE sporting and social calendar.

Emirates Airline Festival Of Literature
March

InterContinental Dubai Festival City Dubai **04 353 4002**
emirateslitfest.com
In its short history, this literary festival has grown to host more than 80 authors, with such heavyweights as Amit Chadhuri, Yann Martel, Martin Amis and Michael Palin having appeared to discuss their works to an international audience. On slate are readings, debates, panels and various workshops for adults and kids alike.

Abu Dhabi International Book Fair
April

Abu Dhabi National Exhibition Centre (ADNEC)
Al Safarat **02 657 6180**
adbookfair.com
A joint venture between Frankfurt Book Fair and the Abu Dhabi Authority for Culture and Heritage, the Abu Dhabi International Book Fair is the Middle East's largest book fair, attracting authors and publishing professionals from all over the world.

Al Gharbia Watersports Festival
April

Mirfa Public Beach Al Gharbia
algharbiafestivals.com
From kiteboards and surf ski kayaks among the waves to chilled-out camping and concerts on shore, the annual Al Gharbia Watersports Festival has it all for the UAE's water lovers.

Dubai Festival City Dragon Boat Festival
April

dubaidragonboat.com
Open to social, school and corporate groups, this fun, competitive and sociable team-building event takes place each spring.

Dubai Fashion Week
April

Dubai World Trade Centre Dubai **04 429 0916**
dfw.ae
One of the glitziest events on the annual calendar, in which regional fashion designers present their collections to the world's fashion media.

Gulf Film Festival
April

Dubai **04 391 0069**
gulffilmfest.com
Promoting the work of filmmakers from the GCC, the week-long festival also showcases a number of international movies and a competition for Emirati short films.

WOMAD Abu Dhabi
April

womadabudhabi.ae
Co-founded by Peter Gabriel, the three-day World of Music, Arts and Dance festival attracts nearly 100,000 spectators for the music and dance acts, art installations, workshops and food stalls from all over the globe. After skipping a year in 2012, WOMAD returns to Abu Dhabi in 2013.

Summer in Abu Dhabi
May

Various locations **800 555**
summerinabudhabi.ae
A family carnival held away from the sizzling streets in the air conditioned comfort of ADNEC. The exhibition halls are home to a host of games, sports and educational experiences to keep kids busy and active during the summer months.

Abu Dhabi Classics
October

Various locations
abudhabiclassics.com
A series of classical music concerts by international
artists and orchestras which takes placed at venues
across the capital and at Al Jahili Fort in Al Ain. The
festival runs from October to May and gets bigger,
lasts longer, and becomes even more adventurous
every year.

Abu Dhabi Film Festival
October

Various locations **02 401 1900**
abudhabifilmfestival.ae
This festival has gone from strength to strength to
become one of the region's premier film events. The
past few years have seen stellar line-ups and, with
more films, grants and awards, and more film stars
and celebrities making appearances, the future looks
promising. In 2012, Emirati filmmaker Ali Al Jabri took
over the directorship of the event.

Abu Dhabi Art
November

UAE Pavilion and Manarat Al Saadiyat
Saadiyat Island **02 657 5800**
abudhabiartfair.ae
This art fair boasts an impressively full programme of
exhibitions, lectures, debates and workshops.

Al Ain Aerobatic Show
November

Al Ain International Airport Al Ain **800 555**
alainaerobaticshow.com
A three-day annual air show which, from 2012, takes
place over National Day weekend, the event sees
flying daredevils from around the world performing
aerobatic stunts and amazing displays that truly wow
the crowds.

DP World Tour Championship
November

Dubai
dpworldtourchampionship.com
The world's best golfers converge on Dubai for the
prestigious final fixture of the PGA European Golf Tour
and a shot at their share of the multi-million dollar
prize fund.

Emirates Airlines Dubai Rugby Sevens
November

The Sevens Dubai **04 321 0008**
dubairugby7s.com
Over 130,000 spectators descend on The 7evens
stadium over the course of three days to watch top
international teams compete for the coveted 7s
trophy, while Gulf teams go head-to-head with local
competition, all of which tends to keep the party
atmosphere going into the wee hours.

Emirates International Date Palm Festival
November

Abu Dhabi National Exhibition Centre (ADNEC)
datepalmfestival.net
An annual celebration of the UAE's culture, history
and traditions and the significant role that the date
palm plays.

Formula 1 Etihad Airways Abu Dhabi Grand Prix
November

Yas Marina Circuit formula1.com
Racing fans delight in this big weekend in November;
as this is one of the last races of the F1 season,
excitement is guaranteed and the event usually
features a number of big name entertainers to top off
the experience.

Mubadala World Tennis Championship
December

Zayed Sports City Al Safarat **02 493 8888**
mubadalawtc.com
After years of hosting the world's number one and
two seeds and attracting record crowds of up to
15,000 fans, this three-day tournament has quickly
become a stellar way to end the year in Abu Dhabi.
The final takes place on New Year's Eve. In addition to
the matches, a series of tennis-based activities and
tournaments are organised in the run-up to the event,
including the popular Community Cup.

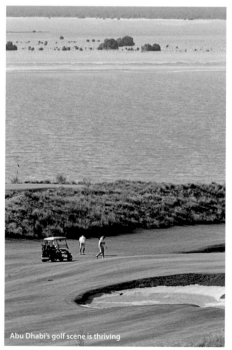
Abu Dhabi's golf scene is thriving

Supply, meet Demand

Abu Dhabi: Becoming A Resident

CITY PROFILE

Half a century ago, Abu Dhabi was small and undeveloped with no sealed roads and only a handful of permanent buildings. The economy was based around pearl diving, fishing and date palm cultivation; until the discovery of oil in 1958 which brought about radical change.

And In 78th Place...

Abu Dhabi ranked number 78 in the Mercer's 2011 Quality of Living Survey (mercer.com) and was the second ranking city in the Middle East region after Dubai (74). Abu Dhabi has the highest personal safety ranking in the Middle East, followed by Muscat and Dubai. According to Mercer's 2012 figures, Abu Dhabi is the 76th most expensive city in the world to live in, a fall of nine places from 2011 thanks to decreasing property prices.

While it's become cliched to talk about Abu Dhabi as a sleepy coastal village that transformed into a modern metropolis, tax-free expat haven and headquarters for luxury living, the truth is that, behind these cliches, Abu Dhabi is, for most people, a wonderful place to live with excellent career opportunities, a readily available network of social contacts, some unique activities and, apart from a few sweaty months in summer, brilliant weather.

Most expats will tell you that their standard of living is better here than it was back home; they can travel more, spend more time with family, enjoy outdoor living and make more friends.

This chapter is here to help you, whether you are making the decision to move or not, you've just arrived and don't know where to start, or you find yourself faced with an overwhelming amount of red tape. Just remember, procedures and laws do change regularly, sometimes in quite major ways. While these changes are generally announced in newspapers, they are often implemented quickly so it's a good idea to be prepared for the unexpected.

ABU DHABI'S ECONOMY & TRADE

In 2008, when the rest of the world saw economies crumble, Abu Dhabi's GDP actually rose by 30% and, after a temporary slow-down in 2009, the city's fortunes were once again on the up by 2010. Although property prices have fallen a little since then – good news for the capital's residents – on the whole, Abu Dhabi's economy continues to thrive and the service sector, in particular, has grown rapidly following the city's transformation into a modern metropolis.

However, oil is still a significant contributor to Abu Dhabi's economy, accounting for around half of the annual GDP.

But, knowing the oil will eventually run out, the ruling family and government has ploughed great sums into other industries and of particular note is the investment in tourism. This is best demonstrated by the developments on Saadiyat Island and Yas Island, which now includes the F1 circuit, numerous hotels, the Ferrari World theme park, a waterpark, and top-class golf courses. The construction, commercial and financial sectors are now also significant contributors to the economy.

While Abu Dhabi hasn't been completely immune to the globally challenging economic climate of late, a full blown recession was averted thanks mainly to the robustness of the property market. While neighbouring emirates, Dubai in particular, were hit hard by the crisis, with real estate plummeting by up to 50%, demand remained high in the Abu Dhabi property market with certain areas of the city boasting some of the highest rents per square metre of any city in the world.

Drinking In Abu Dhabi

While drinking alcohol is forbidden for Muslims, it is served in the many bars, clubs and restaurants throughout Abu Dhabi. You won't find a booze aisle in your local supermarket, although some people have made the mistake of stocking up on the 0% alcohol beers that line the shelves. To buy alcoholic beverages from specialist liquor stores, you'll need to apply for a licence; see p.44 for more on this process.

While many Abu Dhabi residents could feel as if the recession never really hit, certain projects did fall victim, resulting in redundancies and a noted departure of professionals from the construction sector in particular. Almost all the projects shelved or put on hold were still in the planning phase and there are still a large number of large, high profile developments going ahead.

Major Developments

Al Bateen Wharf

A complete regeneration of Abu Dhabi's oldest district to complement the heritage buildings and old dhow boatyards, the new Al Bateen Wharf (tdic. ae) will be a total facelift and include a fisherman's village, with a 400 room twin tower hotel, a boardwalk flanked by cafes and restaurants and a marina complex that will feature dry stacking. It will also have health clubs, spa facilities, a business centre and a range of apartments.

Green open spaces line the Corniche

City centre streets by night

The Corniche at dusk

Skyscrapers on Abu Dhabi island

Abu Dhabi's Economy & Trade

Arzanah

Arzanah (capitala.ae) is a 1.4 million square metre mixed-use development being constructed around Zayed Sports City at the eastern end of Abu Dhabi island. There will be a range of apartments and villas located amid a network of landscaped gardens complete with footpaths and cycle paths, although property cannot be bought by expatriates. Amenities for residents and visitors will include a two-kilometre stretch of beach and a canal, around which will be hotels, indoor and outdoor retail areas, a Carrefour hypermarket, restaurants and cafes, sports facilities including bowling, tennis and an ice rink, and an aquatic centre.

World Trade Center

One of the city's landmarks, the redevelopment of the World Trade Center (wtcad.ae) area has, at its core, three silver blade-like towers thrusting into the sky. Designed by famous architects Foster & Partners, the project houses an Arabian Souk, shopping boutiques and a choice of eateries; later, a string of offices, tower apartments and a number of luxury hotels will also open their doors. Already open since 2011, the charming World Trade Center Central Market (p.348, 380) has begun to revitalise the downtown area of the city with its mix of stores and F&B outlets.

Transport Projects

Abu Dhabi International Airport has grown with the city and the latest addition was Etihad's Terminal 3; now work is underway on the Midfield Terminal Complex, which will deliver a new passenger terminal and increase the airport's capacity to a whopping 40 million passengers per year. Initial work has also begun on a metro system that will run 131km throughout the city, with sections both above and below ground. The Abu Dhabi Metro is due for completion in 2016.

Masdar City

Once complete, Masdar City (masdarcity.ae) will be a dream eco-city in the desert: a zero-carbon, zero-waste $20 million city powered by renewable energy sources. The seven-year sustainable development project is being built in phases, and is attracting companies, scientists and entrepreneurs from around the world to live and work there. The high-density city will be car free, with no one living more than 200 metres from local public transport – light rail transit (LRT) and personal rapid transit (PRT) – and will be connected to Abu Dhabi by high-speed rail links. Currently the retail area includes an organic grocery store (p.337), cafes, a travel agency, bank outlets and a monthly community market.

World Trade Center Central Market

Qasr Al Hosn & Cultural Foundation

Qasr Al Hosn is the oldest building in the city, dating back more than 200 years. The Abu Dhabi Tourism & Culture Authority (abudhabitourism.ae) is working on an ambitious programme of conservation for Qasr Al Hosn and the neighbouring Abu Dhabi Cultural Foundation. The site will then be fully accessible to visitors as the nation's prime memorial and its principal historical site. The exhibits will include monuments, artefacts and antiquities belonging to the ruling family, and the site will also be home to the Natural History Museum, housing exhibits from the region.

Stare Wars

As annoying and infuriating as it is to have someone blatantly stare at you, it does happen here. The good news is that these stares are not really sexual or predatory in nature – they are more the result of curiosity. The bad news is that there is little you can do to stop this strange little quirk of living in the region. Your best defence is to avoid wearing tight or revealing clothing, particularly in certain areas such as Al Meena.

Saadiyat Island

Arguably Abu Dhabi's biggest and most important development, Saadiyat Island (saadiyat.ae) – which translates as 'island of happiness' – is being developed at a huge cost over the course of a decade. Once complete, Saadiyat Island will feature major cultural attractions, numerous hotels and stretches of pristine beach. The Cultural District will be the hub of the project with several museums and arts centres, including the Sheikh Zayed National Museum, the Guggenheim museum and a Louvre art museum. Two bridges and a tunnel link Saadiyat with Abu Dhabi island and Saadiyat will also eventually be home to over 145,000 residents. A couple of residential developments are already being lived in, while Manarat Al Saadiyat houses an excellent art exhibition space and a Saadiyat Island visitor centre, as well as a restaurant. The St Regis and Park Hyatt hotels are open, as are the Monte Carlo Beach Club and Saadiyat Beach Golf Club.

Shams Abu Dhabi

Shams Abu Dhabi (sorouh.com), a self-contained development, will include commercial and entertainment districts, a five-star hotel, a marina, and a residential area for 55,000 people, all surrounded by mangrove forests and the sea. Connected to the mainland by two bridges, the partially opened residential area is bisected by canals and pedestrian walkways. At the entrance to the development, The Gate District will be a breathtaking arch of eight towers.

CONSIDERING UNITED ARAB EMIRATES

Sunny days, great shopping, outdoor living and tax-free salaries sum up the Abu Dhabi dream. Of course, there are red-tape hassles and everyday annoyances, but for many expats these are far outweighed by the many positives.

Costs of living in Abu Dhabi reached a peak towards the end of 2008, when rents were sky-high, and prices for everything increased as a result. If there has been any positive side to the global recession, it's that prices have stabilised a little and you're actually better off now than you were before. While the rental market is still more expensive than other emirates, supply is finally catching up with demand, with several large residential developments having come on line at the end of 2012 and more set to follow.

Housing options to suit different lifestyles and incomes are increasingly available, with tenants even gaining some negotiating opportunities for cheaper rents and multiple cheque payments. The job market is still growing in most sectors, but before you jump on the first plane, make sure you test the waters by contacting potential employers, monitoring newspaper appointments pages and scouring international recruitment websites.

You should also consider how you will enter the city and stay here. To stay in Abu Dhabi long-term, you need a residency visa, and for this you need a 'sponsor'. Your sponsor is usually your company, or your spouse if you are not working (see p.39). If you don't have work lined up, you can enter on a visit visa, but will only be allowed to stay for a limited time (p.36).

BEFORE YOU ARRIVE

If you're coming to Abu Dhabi to work, or even just to look for work, you should have any qualification certificates and important documents (such as your marriage certificate, birth certificate and educational degrees) attested in your home country. This can be quite a lengthy process, and can involve solicitors and the UAE foreign embassy.

Property owners may consider selling up before the move, but don't be hasty. It may be wise to wait and give yourself a year before you commit long-term – although many people have come intending to stay 'for a year or two' and are still in the country five or 10 years later.

You also need to get your financial affairs in order, such as telling banks and building societies, and the tax office – tax rules differ from country to country, so check whether you have to inform the tax office in your home country of any earnings you accrue while

When You Arrive

in Abu Dhabi. Speak to your pension company too (see Work, p.114).

If you've got kids, you should start researching schools as soon as possible. There are fortunately a lot more schools in Abu Dhabi today than there were a few years ago, although it can still be very tough to get a guaranteed place at the school of your choice. The earlier you get your child's name on the waiting list, the better.

Customs

Before you fly into Abu Dhabi, be aware that several prescription medications are banned, especially anything containing codeine or temazepam. The UAE maintains a zero-tolerance policy on recreational drugs, and even microscopic amounts could land you in jail. Your bags will be scanned on arrival to ensure you have no offending magazines or DVDs. Each passenger is allowed 2,000 cigarettes, 400 cigars or two kilograms of tobacco. Non-Muslims are also allowed four 'units' of alcohol; a unit is either one bottle of wine, one bottle of liqueur or spirits, or half a case of beer.

When it comes to choosing an area of Abu Dhabi to live in, you should take your time to explore the different residential areas (see p.84 for a head start). It's a good idea to arrange temporary accommodation for when you first arrive (try to negotiate this with your employer), so that you can look for your perfect home. Speak to shipping companies (p.313) about bringing your stuff over, and try to book as far in advance as you possibly can.

If you're coming to Abu Dhabi on a 'look-see', do your homework before you arrive. Contact recruitment agencies in advance, sign up with online job sites, and visit agencies in your home country that specialise in overseas recruitment. Check also that your qualifications or industry experience are in demand here. See Work (p.100) for more information.

WHEN YOU ARRIVE

As you would expect during an international move to any new city, you're likely to arrive to find a long 'to-do' list waiting for you in Abu Dhabi. You'll be doing a lot of driving around, plenty of form filling, and a healthy smattering of waiting in queues in government departments. Just keep your sense of humour handy and soon all the boring red tape will be a distant memory.

The first thing you'll probably need to sort out is visas – you may be lucky enough to have a company PRO (personnel relations officer) who does this all for you; if not, see p.39.

egate Card

The eGate service allows UAE and GCC nationals, as well as expats with a valid residence permit, to pass through both the departures and arrivals halls of Abu Dhabi International Airport (as well as those of Dubai and Al Ain International Airports) without a passport. Swipe your smart card through an electronic gate and through you go, saving a great deal of time otherwise spent in long queues. Applications for a card are processed within minutes at Abu Dhabi International Airport. The eGate card costs Dhs.200 and is valid for two years. You'll need your passport containing the valid residence permit and you will be fingerprinted and photographed. Payment can be made by cash or credit card. For further information, see abudhabi.ae.

House-hunting will also be high up on your agenda – see p.70 for advice on finding your ideal home, and then dealing with all those tricky extras, like electricity, water, phones and furniture.

You're almost certainly going to need a car and while the bad news is that driving here can be a little scary at first, the good news is that cars and their upkeep are cheap. See Driving, p.56.

As for paperwork, you're going to need to get a driving licence, of course, but also the less obvious liquor licence if you're planning on buying alcohol to drink at home. See p.44.

And once you've got the administrative stuff out of the way, it's time to put your feelers out and start meeting your fellow expats – a task which some find challenging, but most find easier than expected. See How To Make Friends, p.42.

GETTING STARTED

Entry Visa

Visa requirements for entering Abu Dhabi vary greatly between different nationalities, and regulations should always be checked before travelling, since details can change with little or no warning. GCC nationals (Bahrain, Kuwait, Qatar, Oman and Saudi Arabia) do not need a visa to enter Abu Dhabi. Citizens from many other countries (including the UK, USA, Australia and many EU countries) get an automatic visa upon arrival at the airport (p.38). The entry visa is valid for 30 days, although you can renew for a further 30 days at a cost of Dhs.620.

Expats with residency in other GCC countries, who do not belong to one of the 33 visa on arrival nationalities but who do meet certain criteria (professions such as managers, doctors and

Our local experts
are happy to assist
you with your
relocation needs.

Go knowing
www.crownrelo.com

Tel +971 2 6733076
abudhabi@crownrelo.com

engineers), can get a non-renewable 30 day visa on arrival – check with your airline before flying.

People of certain nationalities who are visiting the Sultanate of Oman may also enter the UAE on a free-of-charge entry permit. The same criteria and facilities apply to UAE visitors entering Oman (although if you have Abu Dhabi residency you will pay a small charge).

Visa On Arrival

Citizens of the following countries receive an automatic visit visa on arrival: Andorra, Australia, Austria, Belgium, Brunei, Denmark, Finland, France, Germany, Greece, Hong Kong, Iceland, Ireland, Italy, Japan, Liechtenstein, Luxembourg, Malaysia, Monaco, Netherlands, New Zealand, Norway, Portugal, San Marino, Singapore, South Korea, Spain, Sweden, Switzerland, United Kingdom, United States of America and Vatican City.

All other nationalities can get a 30 day tourist visa sponsored by a local entity, such as a hotel or tour operator, before entry. The fee is Dhs.100, and the visa can be renewed for a further 30 days for Dhs.620.

Citizens of eastern European countries, countries that belonged to the former Soviet Union, China and South Africa can get a 30 day, non-renewable tourist visa sponsored by a local entity, such as a hotel or tour operator, before entry into the UAE. The fee is Dhs.100 for the visa and an additional Dhs.20 for delivery.

Other visitors can apply for an entry service permit (exclusive of arrival/departure days), valid for use within 14 days of the date of issue and non-renewable. Once this visa expires, the visitor must remain out of the country for 30 days before re-entering on a new visit visa. The application fee for this visa is Dhs.120, plus an additional Dhs.20 delivery charge.

For those travelling onwards to a destination other than that of the original departure, a special transit visa (up to 96 hours) may be obtained free of charge through certain airlines operating in the UAE.

A multiple-entry visa is available to visitors who have a relationship with a local business, meaning they have to visit that business regularly. It is valid for visits of a maximum of 14 days each time, for six months from the date of issue. It costs Dhs.1,000 and should be applied for after entering the UAE on a visit visa. For an additional Dhs.200, a multiple entry visa holder is eligible for the eGate service (see p.36). Many travel companies will be able to arrange visas on your behalf although they will likely levy up to Dhs.50 extra in processing charges for this service.

Fully Fledged Resident

After entering Abu Dhabi on an employment or residency visa, you have 60 days to complete all of the procedures involved in becoming a resident – although it's unlikely to take anywhere near that long. If you need to leave the country again before the process is completed, you should be able to do so as long as you have the entry visa that was stamped in your passport when you first entered. It's probably best though that you avoid booking any holidays in those first few weeks.

Residence Permit

In order to live in Abu Dhabi, you need to have a residence permit. There are two types of permit, both of which require the individual to be sponsored: one is for those sponsored for employment, and the other is for residence only (for example when you

Embassy Insight   Yacoob Abba Omar, South African Ambassador to the UAE

The main role of the embassy is to promote South Africa to our host country. Aside from consular services, we also deal with signing agreements, arranging for various delegations to visit SA, and meeting with industry and government representatives.

Despite the current economic climate, the business ties between South Africa and the UAE have been growing from strength to strength, with bilateral trade between the two countries reaching Dhs.6.14 billion in 2008. I believe that we will be seeing more South African initiatives in the future, as South African businesses are resilient and innovative and have the reputation of adhering to high standards and quality.

We encourage South African citizens to register with the Embassy. This would come in handy especially during emergencies, but we also connect citizens with the South Africa Business Council so they can network with fellow South Africans.

Our flagship event is the Freedom Day celebration on 27 April, which is aimed at key contacts of the Embassy. We also support SABCo in hosting the South Africa Family Day, which the South African community attends in droves to celebrate Freedom Day. My advice to first timers is to begin by learning some of the culture and traditions of our host country. Use the opportunity of being here to visit many countries in the region.

For a full list of embassies in Abu Dhabi, see the last page of this book.

are sponsored by a family member who is already sponsored by an employer). There was a property-owner visa issued for a while which fell into the latter category, with the developer acting as sponsor, but without employment rights. However, this law ceased to exist in 2008, meaning buying a property no longer entitles you to a residency permit – although certain property owners are still able to apply for investor-based residency and are entitled to a multiple entry visa (renewable for Dhs.2,000 provided the owner leaves and then re-enters the country within a fixed time frame).

Labour Card

Once you have your residency permit, either through your employer or family sponsor, you need a Labour Card for work. If you are on a family residency and decide to work, your employer, not your visa sponsor (usually your husband), will need to apply for a labour card. You'll need to give your employer the usual documents including a letter of no objection (NOC) from your sponsor (husband/father), your passport with residency stamp, attested certificates, passport photos, and a photocopy of your sponsor's passport. The Labour Card will cost your employer Dhs.1,000, and must, under current regulations, still be renewed annually, although the plan is for the Emirates ID (p.44) to eventually replace the Labour Card. See Work, (p.100).

The residency permits used to be valid for three years but, following a new ruling in late 2010, are now only valid for two years at a time, after which you are eligible to apply for renewal. To keep your residency valid, you cannot leave the UAE for a period of more than six months at any one time.

This is particularly relevant to women going back home to give birth, or children studying abroad. If the residency is cancelled, the original sponsor can visit the Immigration Department and pay Dhs.100 for a temporary entry permit which will waive the cancellation and allow the person to re-enter the UAE. You'll need their passport copy, and will have to fax them a copy of the permit before they fly back.

A couple of recent regulations have stirred up a little controversy and confusion. In June 2012, the general directorate of residence and foreigners affairs in Abu Dhabi stated that anyone looking to renew their visa would need to show a tenancy contract with their name on it. This would, effectively, have prevented anyone from subletting a room in an apartment or villa and, obviously, caused much consternation. The regulation was withdrawn although the government has described it as being 'shelved', implying that it may well be reintroduced in the future.

Sponsorship

Employer Sponsorship

If you have moved to Abu Dhabi to take up a job, your employer is obliged to sponsor you. Your new company's PRO should handle all the paperwork, meaning you probably won't have to visit the Immigration Department yourself. They will take your passport, employment visa (with entry stamp), medical test results, attested education certificates, copies of your company's establishment immigration card and trade licence, and three passport photos.

For a fee of Dhs.300 (plus typing fees) the Immigration Department will process everything and affix and stamp the residency permit in the passport. This may take up to 10 days, during which time you'll be without your passport, but for an extra Dhs.100 they can do it on the same day. Your company must pay these fees for you. When arranging your residency, the company will apply directly for your labour card (see left). The Ministry of Labour website (mol.gov.ae) has a facility for companies to process applications and transactions online.

To be accepted by the authorities here, your education certificates must be verified by the issuing institution, a solicitor or public notary in your home country and then by your foreign office to verify the solicitor as bona fide, and finally by the UAE embassy. It's a good idea to have this done before you come to Abu Dhabi; however, there are private companies offering attestation services in Abu Dhabi as well. The minimum turnaround time you can expect for this service is two weeks.

PROs & NOCs

In Abu Dhabi, a PRO is your company's 'man who can' who liaises with various government departments and carries out admin procedures. The PRO will take care of all visa, residency, health card and labour card applications. An NOC is a no objection certificate, and is essentially a letter stating that the person in question permits you to carry out a particular procedure. You'll find you need one of these in a variety of situations, whether it's from your employer, allowing you to switch jobs, or your own NOC permitting a family member to work.

Family Sponsorship

If you are sponsored and resident in Abu Dhabi, you should be able to sponsor your family members, allowing them to stay in the country as long as you are here. To sponsor your wife or children, you will need a minimum monthly salary of Dhs.3,000 plus accommodation, or a minimum all-inclusive salary of Dhs.4,000, although there are rumours that this

Getting Started

Sponsoring A Maid

To sponsor a maid you must have a salary above Dhs.6,000 per month and be able to provide the maid with housing, medical insurance and the usual benefits, which include an airfare back to their home country at least once every two years. The process is very similar to sponsoring a family member (see p.39), the main differences being the additional costs involved – you have to pay a 'maid tax' of around Dhs.5,200 per year.

When you are processing a health card for a maid, driver or cook, you will need to pay an additional fee (Dhs.60 – Dhs.100) to have him or her vaccinated against hepatitis. There will also be a small typing fee (see Domestic Help, p.95).

amount may rise to as high as Dhs.10,000 – see abudhabi.ae for the latest regulations. Only what is printed on your labour contract will be accepted as proof of your earnings, so make sure you're happy with this before starting the job.

To apply for residency visas for your family, you will need to take your passport, the passports of all your family members, and your labour contract to the Family Entry Permit counter at the Immigration Department (02 446 2244, 600 522 222). Your company PRO may help you with this process, but in most cases you will need to do it (and pay for it) on your own. After submitting all the relevant documents, you will be told to return after a couple of days to collect the visas. Once the visas are processed, your family members must apply for a health card and take a medical test (see right).

Older Children

For parents sponsoring children, difficulties arise when sons (not daughters) turn 18. Unless they are enrolled in full-time education in the UAE, they must transfer their visa to an employer. Alternatively, parents can pay a Dhs.5,000 security deposit (one-off payment) and apply for an annual visa. Daughters can stay on their father's sponsorship until they get married.

With the medical test out of the way, you then return to the Immigration Department with all the essential documents as before, plus the medical test result and the attested birth certificate (if sponsoring a child) or attested marriage certificate (if sponsoring your spouse).

For Dhs.300 (plus typing) the application will be processed and, around five days later, the passport – with the residency permit attached – will be ready for collection (for an additional Dhs.100, you can have the process completed on the same day).

If the family member is already in the UAE on a visit visa, you can still apply for residency as above. Once processed, the family member must, however, exit the country and re-enter with the correct visa, or, alternatively, you can pay Dhs.500 to have the visa swapped. If you have family sponsorship and then get a job, you don't need to change to employer sponsorship, but the company will need to apply for a labour card on your behalf.

It is common to hear that women can't sponsor their husbands unless they are doctors, nurses or teachers. While this used to be the rule, today it is possible for working women to sponsor their husbands and children, provided that they meet the minimum salary requirements (usually Dhs.10,000 per month). If you are in this situation you should speak to the Immigration Department and present your case.

The main disadvantage of a wife sponsoring her husband is that the spouse's visa must be renewed annually, while, on the other hand, if a husband sponsors his wife, the spouse's visa only needs to be renewed every three years.

There are constraints when UAE residents want to sponsor their parents – a special committee reviews each case individually. Usually, the committee considers the age and projected health requirements of the parents and will also need proof that you will be fully providing for them, that your accommodation is suitable for housing them and you will need to pay a deposit of around Dhs.5,000 per parent. They will need medical insurance and the visas will only be issued on an annual basis.

Medical Test

You need to take a medical test to get your residence visa – you will be tested for communicable diseases such as tuberculosis and HIV. Food handlers and domestic workers may require extra tests and vaccinations. To take your test, you will need the test form filled out in Arabic (there are typing offices near the screening centres that can do this for you for around Dhs.20), a valid passport copy and a copy of your entry visa, and the test fee of Dhs.250, plus Dhs.50 for immunisation costs.

Blood will be taken and, if your tests are positive for HIV, you will be deported to your home country. Therefore, if you are at all nervous about the possibility of testing positive, it may be a good idea to get tested by your doctor in your home country before you arrive in Abu Dhabi. You will also need to undergo a chest x-ray to test for TB, while female domestic workers are usually subject to a pregnancy test.

There are just four screening centres to serve the emirate of Abu Dhabi, so you will likely find the government testing centres chaotic, which can be a little bit scary if it's your first experience of Abu Dhabi's healthcare system.

Masdar City

How To Make Friends

Whether you are a social butterfly who usually flits from social group to social group, or someone who is more likely to keep themselves to themselves, it is very easy to make friends in Abu Dhabi. Meeting new people early on is one of the keys to dealing with culture shock and beginning the whole settling-in process. Remember, the vast majority of people living in Abu Dhabi are in the same boat. Most people are far from their friends and family, and the transient nature of the city means that even those who have been here a long time are keen to meet new people as other friends will have left. The best advice is to dive right in and make an effort to get involved in anything that interests you. Whether this be plucking up the courage to start a conversation in the supermarket or writing a post on a forum arranging an outing, everybody has to start somewhere. To help you get started, there are numerous nationality-based, sporting and social groups in Abu Dhabi, and these are handy for broadening your network of acquaintances and, ultimately, your circle of friends.

Getting to know new people is one of the most important things you can do to help you settle in when you move to a new city – here are just a few ways to get connected.

Social groups

Royal Society of St George: A society dedicated to raising money for charities through organising events and social evenings. rssgauh.com

Abu Dhabi Irish Society: The Abu Dhabi Irish Society is open to all Irish people and anyone wanting a taste of Irish culture in Abu Dhabi. Regular events include society outings, social evenings, Irish dancing classes and Gaelic games. The society also hosts the Irish Business Forum meetings. irishsocietyabudhabi.com

Scottish St Andrew's Society of Abu Dhabi: This group of expat Scots, joined by more than a few 'foreigners', enjoys getting together for social gatherings and Scottish cultural activities, including the Burns supper in January. adscots.com

Aussies Abroad: An organisation dedicated to the promotion of Australian culture in the UAE. Social and recreational events include regular drinks nights, annual Anzac Day functions and balls. aussiesabroad-abudhabi.com

St David's Society: Formed by a group of enthusiastic Welsh expats, the youngest of the British tribal societies now has over 120 members. A regular newsletter keeps members informed of monthly events, such as dhow trips, quiz evenings, weekend breaks or social gatherings. stdavidssocietyabudhabi.blogspot.com

The UAE has a liberal attitude to other religions. Even if you are not a regular church-goer, churches can act as good community hubs.

American Women's Networks: This informal group of women offers an informative and welcoming atmosphere to newcomers, and helps connect them to local interests. Mainly for North Americans, is also welcomes women with links to America. awnabudhabi.com

Leisure

A new start is the perfect opportunity to get involved with a new hobby or skill, while meeting like-minded people.
Duplays: A web-based sports network that lists all the teams for all the sports available in the city. If sport is your thing, then joining a team is one way of immediately meeting a whole bunch of like-minded people. duplays.com
Abu Dhabi Country Club: A popular choice for aerobics and fitness classes. Check the website for an up-to-date timetable. adhfc.com

Networking

Networking is one of the easiest ways to make new business contacts, so it makes sense that it is a good way to increase your social circle too. With strict laws against dating and matchmaking services here in Abu Dhabi, these social networking groups are purely for meeting like-minded people in a friendly, social setting. See Work, p.104, for details of business networking groups.
Meet-Up: meetup.com is a popular forum for finding friends with similar hobbies where you can arrange times for sessions in an easy-going manner, rather than having to stick to a rigid routine.
Women's Groups: There are many organisations set up purely for women to meet other women and make new friends. It may be daunting going along to your first coffee morning but, within minutes, you'll be surrounded by people who have all been in your shoes before and are willing to lend a hand. They also organise day trips and have online forums with updates on events, accommodation advice, furniture for sale and even job opportunities. Visit abudhabiwoman.com and expatwoman.com.
Mum's The Word: Abu Dhabi Mums is a non-profit social group for mums with pre-school children. Open to anyone who is expecting or has children up to the age of 5 years, members receive discounts at various outlets in the city and Christmas and Easter parties are organised. abudhabimums.ae

Churches

The UAE has a liberal and welcoming attitude to other religions. For example, there are several active churches established across Abu Dhabi. Even if you are not a regular church-goer, the churches here tend to also act as good community hubs, so it might be worth checking out any scheduled events or activities.
Arab Evangelical Church
Al Mushrif, 02 443 4350
Evangelical Community Church
Al Mushrif, 02 446 4563, eccad.org
St Andrew's Church Abu Dhabi
Al Mushrif, 02 446 1631, standrewauh.org
St George's Orthodox Cathedral
Al Mushrif, 02 446 4564
St Joseph's Cathedral Abu Dhabi
Al Mushrif, 02 446 1929, stjosephsabudhabi.org
St Mary's Catholic Church
Al Ain, 03 721 4417, stmarysalain.com
St Stephen's Syrian Orthodox Church
Al Mushrif, 02 446 0711, ststephensauh.org

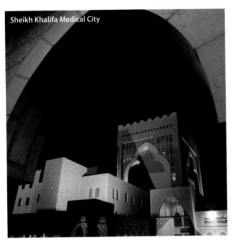

Sheikh Khalifa Medical City

Despite appearances, medical hygiene standards are followed and test results are processed efficiently. A good tip is to go wearing a plain, pale-coloured T-shirt: this way you should not have to remove your clothes or wear a hospital gown (which may have been used by someone else before you) for your x-ray.

Screening Centres

There are three screening centres in Abu Dhabi city. Mubadala's brand new Capital Health Screening Centre (02 496 9666) is located on Muroor Road at the Al Jazira Sports Stadium. Another facility is located on Airport Road near Sheikh Khalifa Medical City (02 633 1300), while the third one is located in the Musaffah area (02 552 8371).

ID Card

The UAE is well into the process of implementing an ambitious countrywide ID card programme. There were a few hiccups and false starts but it is now a legal requirement for all national and expat residents to register for and carry their Emirates ID card. The purpose is to secure personal identities and cut down on fraud and identity theft, although the card will eventually replace all other cards, such as health cards, labour cards and even driving licences.

UAE nationals must pay Dhs.100 for their ID cards; expat residents pay Dhs.100 per year of validity left on their residence visa (for example, if your residence visa expires in two years, you will pay Dhs.200 for your ID card) and a small delivery fee. ID cards for children under the age of 15 are necessary and are half the cost of adults' cards. To register for your card, take your passport to an authorised typing centre to get the forms processed. You will then receive a SMS confirmation of your appointment to get your

fingerprints and photograph taken, with your ID card delivery following a few weeks later.

For new residents just moving to the UAE, the process is even simpler and faster and is wrapped up in the visa application process. Your company PRO should be able to look after the whole process for you. You can find more up-to-date information, as well as a list of registration centres, at emiratesid.ae.

Driving Licence

If you are in Abu Dhabi on a visit visa and wish to drive a hire car, you need a valid international licence (although you can only do this if your nationality is on the transfer list on the right).

If you want to drive a private vehicle, you will need to get a temporary or permanent Abu Dhabi driving licence (except for GCC nationals who are allowed to drive on their existing GCC licences). You are not allowed to drive a privately owned Abu Dhabi car on just an international driving licence. As soon as your residence visa comes through, then you will need to switch to an Abu Dhabi driving licence, which is valid for 10 years. If you are not a citizen of one of the licence transfer countries, you will need to take a driving test. Obtaining a motorcycle licence follows the same procedure.

Traffic Police

Traffic & Patrols Departments – 02 419 6666
Traffic & Licensing Department – 02 419 5555

Liquor Licence

Abu Dhabi has a relatively liberal attitude towards alcohol. You can't buy alcohol in supermarkets, but you can buy it from licensed liquor shops for home consumption, if you have a liquor licence. Only hotels and sports clubs are allowed to serve alcoholic drinks in their bars and restaurants. Independent restaurants do not serve alcohol. To drink in a bar or restaurant you need to be 21 or older.

Applying for a liquor licence is straightforward, as long as you are non-Muslim and a resident of Abu Dhabi. Pick up an application form from any branch of A&E, Spinneys Liquor, GMP, ADMMI or High Spirits. You will need to return to the store with a completed form (employees at the stores should be able to complete the Arabic translation for you), a letter of no objection from your company/sponsor or your contract of employment (which must include salary information), a copy of your passport showing the visa resident page, and payment. Your monthly allowance is usually 10% of your monthly salary and the licence fee is usually 20% of that figure. However, several stores insist on a maximum permitted allowance of Dhs.2,000, making the fee Dhs.400. Many of the companies have special offers whereby they give you back the value of the licence fee in vouchers to spend in their outlets. The liquor store will then process your application through the police on your behalf. Once approved, you will get a specified amount (based on your monthly salary, and determined at the discretion of the police) to spend on alcohol each month. The limit is usually enough to last you a month, although if you've got a big party planned you might need to stockpile over a few months, since you can't overspend on your limit. It should take around 10 days to process your licence.

Once you have your licence, you can buy alcohol from any branch of A&E, Spinneys Liquor, GMP, ADMMI or High Spirits throughout Abu Dhabi. However, it can work out expensive, even though there is no additional tax at the till like in Dubai. The range and service, however, is excellent. You can also buy alcohol from shops in several neighbouring emirates, such as the Al Hamra Cellar in Ras Al Khaimah, the 'hole in the wall' near the Ajman Kempinski, and the Barracuda Beach Resort in Umm Al Quwain, which are usually much cheaper than the licensed stores. To buy from these shops you do not need to show your liquor licence, but you do need to have a licence on you when transporting alcohol. It is also illegal to buy alcohol for home consumption unless you have a licence, so it is wise to keep your licence updated, even if you only ever buy your alcohol from 'non-licence' shops.

BEFORE YOU LEAVE

Leaving already? Whether your time in Abu Dhabi lasts months, years, or longer, there are some things you should take care of before jumping on the plane. Ideally, when you leave, you should have wrapped up your financial affairs so you don't end up 'doing a runner' like many did in the wake of the global downturn that left many overspenders unable to service their debts. Things you will probably need to take care of include:

Getting electricity, water and other utilities disconnected – remember that most providers (ADDC and Etisalat) will need at least two days' notice to take a final reading and return any security deposits you have paid. You'll need to settle the final bill before you get your deposit, and make sure you keep hold of the original deposit receipt to smooth the process.

You'll also need to go through the official channels to close any bank accounts you have here. Banks (p.114) have been known to freeze an individual's account once they have been informed by the sponsor of a visa cancellation so it's a good idea to get your finances in order first.

Settle your debts – you can get into serious trouble if you try to leave the country without paying off all

Cancelling Your Visa

Your visa and how you cancel it will depend on the type of document you have. If you're on a residence visa that has been sponsored by your employer, as soon as your employment ends, so does your privilege to a work visa. Just as your employer would have been responsible for sorting out your paperwork, it is their responsibility to arrange visa cancellation.

There's not much paperwork involved. You'll have to submit your passport and sometimes sign a waiver or a memorandum of understanding clarifying that you have received all monies owed to you. Once your visa has been cancelled, you have a grace period of 30 days to leave the country, after which time you will be fined at a rate of Dhs.25 per day for the first 6 months, Dhs.50 per day for the next 6 months, and Dhs.100 per day after that.

If you are in Abu Dhabi on a spousal visa, and have, for example, separated or just need to leave, you will need the help of your husband or wife to cancel your status. The whole process takes about five days, whichever visa you happen to be on, and is reasonably smooth.

your loans and outstanding bills, so be sure to keep on top of payments to avoid large sums complicating your exit.

Leaving rented accommodation, make sure the place is spick and span so you can reclaim your entire security deposit. The landlord may also require a clearance certificate from ADDC to show you've paid all your bills, so leave enough time for all the red tape. If you own property, you may choose to either sell or rent out – see Housing, p.80, for more information.

Sell your car – this has been tricky recently, with many people owing more than they can sell the car for, but persevere and be prepared to take a financial hit if you need to offload to a dealer quickly – although this option is often the quickest and most practical. See p.26 for useful addresses.

Organise your shipping – shop around for good rates and give as much notice as possible to the shipping company. See p.90.

Sell the stuff you're not taking – have a garage sale, list items in supermarkets or on dubizzle.com or expatwoman.com, or check if a second-hand dealer will give you a fair price.

If you have pets – if you are taking them with you, you need to make sure their vaccinations are up to date, particularly the rabies vaccination. There are other procedures to be followed when exporting pets (p.138), and ideally you need around six months to prepare. If you can't take your pets with you, you should rehome them with a new family.

New Horizons

Even for the most laid-back of people, moving to a new country and new continent can be as strange as it is exciting.

Moving to a new country will likely turn out to be a wonderful experience which will broaden your mind in the years to come. In the beginning, however, it may take some time to settle into life in any new destination. For some, it's culture shock; for others, it's simply daily frustration. As you prepare to make the move, the prospect of weekly manicures and pedicures, remaining cool in an air conditioned 4WD while someone else stands at the petrol pump and refuels your car, and doing it all in a country of malls brimming with designer boutiques can be invigorating.

However, upon arriving, the reality is often different and, while many come to discover a higher quality of living, a taste for adventure and to take advantage of opportunities to experience things they never would have done in their home countries, there's no doubt that the first few weeks can be a little tricky for even the most stoic of expats.

Fortunately, there's plenty of help, advice and resources on hand to smooth the transition, and you'll even find many unexpected home comforts. While bright skies and endless sand ought to be enough to tell you that you're in the Middle East, the expat havens of restaurants serving up pork and bars pouring pint after pint could quickly have you forgetting. There's nothing wrong with enjoying these slices of home but bear in mind that, no matter how tolerant the UAE may be, you're in a Muslim country and need to behave accordingly.

Not that you should be scared to engage with the local Emiratis. You'll find comfort in discovering that most speak exceptional English, are extremely well educated and are keen to engage in conversation, particularly about sports and music. Take heed of a couple of cultural quirks and then dive into the local culture.

Women will encounter few problems, although you may sometimes struggle with a little unwanted interest if dressed in a revealing way. The best advice is to dress a bit more conservatively than you usually would, and you should avoid any problems.

Both expat men and women may attract extra looks or the occasional attempt to negotiate a higher cab fare, but this type of behaviour has grown increasingly rare in Abu Dhabi.

In fact, for most expats, the greatest culture shocks and frustrations come not from living in an Islamic country, but from living somewhere with a different pace and attitude to life: namely, for most new expats, the driving and the bureaucracy.

Although the situation is constantly improving, a popular topic of office discussion in the morning is the persistent lack of car parking in some parts of the city. The government is aware of this and trying to remedy the congestion. Parking is continually improving due to the Mawaqif paid parking programme but in heavily congested areas, such as Hamdan Street and Tourist Club Area, it may still be best to leave your car at home and catch a cheap taxi to save yourself a headache.

Adding to the frustrations, the driving standards of some residents leave a lot to be desired. Motorists drive fast, while tailgating and overtaking in the hard shoulder is a common sight on Abu Dhabi's highways, although the recent installation of frequent speed cameras has had a notable effect for the better. The best advice is to stay calm and alert, and drive within the recommended speed limits.

If the traffic is fast and busy, the opposite is true of the multitude of seemingly simple administrative tasks, such as visa processing, licences and contracts that you face in your first few weeks in the UAE.

Yes, many government offices, medical centres and banks are heaving with people, but unfortunately that can mean long queues rather than fast action. Allow a lengthy time frame to avoid disappointment. It is prudent to regularly (and politely) chase up the status of your pending paperwork, as it's not altogether rare for documents to go astray or be forgotten about. However, if you allow each setback and delay to get to you, you might not make it past the first few weeks.

Above all, however, be patient and accept that things may not be done exactly the same way as in your home country. Remember that you have arrived in a new country as a guest, and try to make the most of every opportunity to understand and appreciate another culture as you will ultimately end up learning a lot from it.

If homesickness does kick in, just imagine what you would be doing had you not made the move, which probably includes an umbrella, trashy TV and dreaming about your next holiday in the sun. Keep your free time packed, meet lots of new people, join lots of clubs and revel in the climate, conditions and even all the idiosyncrasies that make your new life so different. You'll soon be at ease with the new pace of life and, every now and then, an efficient process may even surprise and delight you.

Waterside living

THE 2013 JEEP® RANGE

Since the beginning, Jeep® vehicles have been synonymous with adventure and discovery. To this day, the Jeep brand continues to design and engineer vehicles for people who choose to take the road less traveled and spice up their every day by bringing a little adventure into their lives.

Please cut out this advertisement and bring it to our showroom for a free week-end test drive in your favourite Jeep.

mideast.jeep.com Join us at Jeep Middle Ea

Jeep

SOLE DISTRIBUTOR FOR JEEP IN ABU DHABI AND AL AIN

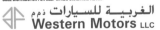
الغربية للسيارات ذمم
Western Motors LLC

New Airport Road Showroom : 02-5014566 / 02-6522510
Corniche showroom: 02-6676000
Al Ain: 03-7157477

www.jeepabudhabi.com

Getting Around

Getting Around

GETTING AROUND IN ABU DHABI

Private cars and taxis have long been the primary means of transportation for many of Abu Dhabi's residents and the government has made great strides in improving the city's infrastructure to accommodate all of the drivers. Traffic is still a major problem, but improvements such as the Sheikh Khalifa Highway have eased congestion a little. Abu Dhabi's public transportation options are also slowly getting better.

Many residents of Abu Dhabi are crazy about their cars and you'll see just about every make and model imaginable cruising down the wide highways. Buying, insuring, registering and maintaining your car is fairly easy and straightforward, but getting a driving licence can be a drawn-out nightmare for some. Abu Dhabi's roads can also be dangerous if you're not careful, but if you avoid speeding, pay attention at all times and learn how to drive a little defensively you will gain confidence in no time.

Abu Dhabi Road Network

Abu Dhabi's road network is excellent, and most main roads have at least three lanes. Streets are generally well-signposted with bilingual blue or green signs indicating the main areas or roads in and out of the city. Visitors should find Abu Dhabi's streets relatively easy to negotiate.

Abu Dhabi city is linked to the mainland by three bridges: Al Maqtaa Bridge, Mussafah Bridge and Sheikh Zayed Bridge. In addition, the Sheikh Khalifa Bridge and Expressway provide an alternative route to and from the city through Saadiyat and Yas Islands.

The streets on the main island are built on a grid system. Al Khaleej Al Arabi Street and Al Salam Street flank either side of the city, while Airport Road (2nd Street) runs in the middle from the Corniche to Al Maqtaa Bridge.

People often rely on landmarks to give directions; there is an official street name and numbering system, but the streets are often referred to by their colloquial names. For example, Sheikh Zayed the First Street is also known as Seventh Street, but the eastern section is popularly called Electra Street. Other confusing street names include: Al Bateen St (officially Hazaa bin Zayed The First St); Coast Rd (Al Khaleej Al Arabi St); New Airport Rd (East St); Nadja St (Bani Yas St); Eastern Ring Road (Al Salam St); Defence Rd (Hazaa bin Zayed The First St); Old Airport Rd (Shk Rashid bin Saeed Al Maktoum St) and Khalidiyah St (Sultan bin Zayed St).

Traffic Regulations

While the driving infrastructure is very good, the general standard of driving is variable. As a result, it is important that you pay extra attention and take a cautious approach. It is even more important to remember that you drive on the right side of the road in Abu Dhabi – and throughout the United Arab Emirates, of course – so a highway's right-hand lane is its slow lane and you should overtake on the left. People sometimes ignore this rule and drift into the centre lane or overtake on either side. If you are caught doing this, however, you could receive a traffic fine (see p.58).

Speed limits are usually between 60kmph and 80kmph around town, while on main roads and roads to other emirates they are 100 to 120kmph. The speed limit is clearly indicated on road signs. The number of fixed and mobile radar traps has increased in Abu Dhabi and the fines are hefty, so exercise caution. If you see the flash of the radar camera, you've been caught and will have to go online (adpolice.gov.ae) to check the amount of the fine, which will be due when you renew your registration (or sell your car).

Maps

With new roads popping up on a weekly basis, finding your way around Abu Dhabi can be difficult. Explorer Publishing produces several of the most up to date street maps available, including the fully indexed *Abu Dhabi Street Atlas*, the pocket-sized *Abu Dhabi Mini Map* and the handy *Abu Dhabi Tourist Map*. Visit askexplorer.com/shop.

Parking

In most cities of the UAE, parking is readily available and people rarely have to (or are able to) walk too far because of the oppressive heat during the summer months. In Abu Dhabi, the parking situation is improving, but it continues to be quite a big problem in the city centre.

Over the past few years, more underground pay-parking areas have appeared, particularly in the business district, and there are several more under construction. There is usually a small charge, but it is worth paying to return to a cool car – and to avoid driving around small, crowded street parking lots, trapped in a one way system for hours, waiting for a space to become available.

In order to improve the situation, the Department of Transport has introduced pay and display meters (see Mawaqif, p.51). The meters, which are all solar powered, have garnered a mixed response from residents and workers alike. All of the major shopping malls have ample car parking spaces and the new office and residential buildings springing up all over the city seem to have parking intelligently factored into their design plans.

If you are looking for a space on the street, don't be tempted to park illegally, as the police are quick to hand out tickets, which will set you back Dhs.200.

Road Signs

Signposting in Abu Dhabi is generally very good once you understand the system. Blue or green signs indicate the roads, exits or locations out of the city, while brown signs show heritage sites, places of interest and hospitals. Abu Dhabi's signage system now relies more heavily on street names and numbers, compared to the older system which relied more on local area names.

Mawaqif

The integrated parking management system, Mawaqif, has been introduced to ease parking in the city. Although it varies by neighbourhood, Mawaqif charges (Dhs.2-3 per hour) are generally not levied between 22:00 and 07:00. Fridays and official holidays are also exempt.

Residential permits are also available, allowing residents to park in any available standard parking bay in the area where they live. The annual fee for parking permits is Dhs.800 for the first vehicle and Dhs.1,200 for the second vehicle. To apply, you need a passport copy with residency visa, a lease or ownership contract, your last electricity bill or vehicle ownership documents. The verification and processing of resident permits takes a minimum of three working days.

For more information visit mawaqif.ae or visit the Customer Service Centre on the corner of Hamad Bin Mohamed Street and Al Salam Street (open 07:00-21:00 Sat to Thurs and 17:00-21:00 Fri), although you may want to catch a cab there as parking is a nightmare!

If the signage gets confusing, remember that Al Maqtaa, Al Mussafah, and Sheikh Zayed bridges all lie at one end of the island, while following any sign for the Corniche will lead you to the other end of the island; finally, look out for signs for Yas Island and you'll get onto the Sheikh Khalifa Highway, the giant ringroad that joins the Corniche with the Abu Dhabi-Dubai Road to the city's north.

Once you do get off the island, simply put, Dubai means north, Al Ain means east, and Tarif, Al Gharbia and Madinat Zayed all mean south.

Address System

All roads are numbered to aid navigation but, in general, numbers are being phased out and replaced with official road names. In the meantime, remember that the odd numbered streets run eastwards from First Street (the Corniche) to 31st Street, while the even numbered streets run south from Eighth Street (Al Salam Street) down to Second Street and then suddenly from 22nd Street down to 32nd Street. All of which is pretty confusing. Although all roads in

the capital city have an official name or number (or, in most cases, both), many roads are actually referred to by a different moniker by both individuals and companies. This lack of consistency makes locating an address difficult (post is delivered to PO Box numbers and not individual letterboxes, so official addresses don't really exist in the UAE).

You will find that companies often only list their building name, road and nearest landmark when giving their address. Hotels, mosques, shopping centres, parks and monuments, all of which are littered throughout the length of Abu Dhabi island, make useful reference points if you're trying to find a location or give directions to someone else. After a little time, you'll also get used to all the names given to roads and areas.

Explorer's *Abu Dhabi Street Atlas* makes locating particular buildings much easier with an index of almost 5,000 roads and buildings.

Cycling

Abu Dhabi is not the most bike friendly of places but, if you're willing to brave some crazy drivers, there are some areas where you can ride, including the Corniche that has cycle paths. Away from summer, exploring on two wheels is a good way of getting to know the city, especially its parks and some of the newer residential areas that have fewer cars and wide footpaths. Cycling does require a lot of care and a helmet is a must. Commuting by bike is extremely rare, especially once you factor in sweating, plus there are no lock-ups outside buildings and offices.

The Abu Dhabi government plans to make cycle lanes a key component of its new transport master plan, but the soaring summer temperatures are likely to prevent cycling from becoming the popular form of transport it is in European cities.

Walking

Cities in the UAE are generally very car-oriented and not designed to encourage walking. Summer temperatures of over 45°C are not conducive to spending any length of time walking through the city. The winter months, however, make walking a comfortable way to get around and people can be found strolling through the streets, especially in the evenings. The relative compactness of Abu Dhabi's main commercial area makes walking a pleasant way of getting around and, in general, the pavements are in good condition, although it can be quite a drop from the pavement to the road.

The biggest hindrance is haphazard parking, which can occasionally completely cover downtown pavements. Areas of construction or roadworks are marked, and those areas are best avoided, especially where they are demolishing older buildings. There are pedestrian crossings, although drivers tend to ignore

Public Transport

them and will seldom slow down. Crossing a main road anywhere but on a marked crossing is illegal and there are fines for jaywalking. Special pedestrian underpasses have been built under some major roads. Those along the Corniche are worth a visit just to see the beautiful mosaics covering the subway walls.

Strolling along the Corniche and Breakwater is a popular pastime, even more so in the winter when temperatures are perfect for enjoying the outdoors. There you will find retail kiosks, outdoor cafes and the new public beach, which are all best explored on foot. Abu Dhabi Municipality is doing a great job in keeping the public areas clean and pleasant and has even gone as far as recently introducing fines of up to Dhs.500 for spitting, dropping gum or cigarette butts or littering.

For other great places to meander in the city, see p.213 for the best parks and other recommended walking routes.

People With Disabilities

Most of Abu Dhabi's four and five-star hotels have adequate wheelchair facilities and the Abu Dhabi International Airport is well equipped for physically challenged travellers with a special check-in gate that has direct access from the car park, dedicated lifts and a meet and greet service. The service is known as 'Golden Class' (02 575 7466). Please note that it's always advisable to contact your airline prior to travel if you need a wheelchair on arrival.

In the rest of the city, in general, facilities for physically challenged people are limited, particularly at tourist attractions where wheelchair slopes are often little more than steep delivery ramps. Accessibility in pedestrian areas is also of varying standards, but there is some good news for Abu Dhabi residents with disabilities – things are starting to get better, with a few initiatives currently under way across the city. Abu Dhabi Municipality has pledged to install lifts on all the pedestrian bridges throughout the Salam Street and Tourist Club areas in order to assist children, the elderly and the physically challenged to cross those busy roads more safely.

In addition, Abu Dhabi has a fleet of limited mobility accessible buses and Tawasul Transport (02 673 4444) provides wheelchair accessible taxis on request. The UAE capital may be a little behind western cities in this regard but, to its credit, the municipality is determined to catch up – new hotels and offices now have to incorporate ramps and braille into their designs thanks to the recent tightening of construction legislation for public buildings, so the city is becoming much more accessible to those who have special needs.

There are specially designated parking spaces in most shopping malls and supermarkets – to use these spaces you will need to obtain a permit from the Abu Dhabi General Police Directorate (02 446 1461).

PUBLIC TRANSPORT

Abu Dhabi's government is currently working on overhauling the city's entire transport network to cater for the escalating number of both visitors and residents. The Surface Transport Master Plan (STMP) has been created as part of 'Plan Abu Dhabi 2030' and will eventually include an integrated rail, metro, tram, bus and ferry system along with an improved road network and special pavements and lanes for pedestrians and bicycles.

Meanwhile, however, the car is still the most popular and practical method of getting around Abu Dhabi. With the lack of trains and trams, and walking and cycling limited due to the searing summer heat, the population that uses public transport relies on the city's public bus service.

Air Travel

Abu Dhabi's location at the crossroads of Africa, Asia, and Europe makes it a popular hub and therefore an easily accessible destination from many corners of the world. London is less than seven hours away; Frankfurt, six; Hong Kong, eight; and Nairobi, four. Most European capitals and other major cities have direct flights to Abu Dhabi, many with a choice of operator.

The Abu Dhabi International Airport (code: AUH) is currently undergoing renovations as part of a multi-billion expansion plan. Upon completion of the Midfield Terminal, scheduled for 2014, the airport will have 58 gates, over 20,000 square metres for food and retail, and be equipped to handle upwards of 20 million passengers annually, with the potential to further increase capacity. For more information on the airport go to abudhabiairport.ae or contact the customer service desk (02 575 7818) or flight information line (02 575 7500).

Opened in 2009, Terminal 3 is exclusively for Etihad Airways, the national and award-winning airline of the UAE that is based in Abu Dhabi. Etihad is one of the fastest-growing airlines in the world, flying to 50 international destinations, including non-stop flights to London, New York, Hong Kong and Sydney.

On leaving the airport, you'll find that taxis are freely available outside the terminal. There is also an hourly round-the-clock bus service between the airport and Abu Dhabi's central bus station. It costs just Dhs.3 each way. Etihad also runs its own private bus service, which is free for those with a boarding pass and makes the journey between Abu Dhabi International Airport and Dubai.

Terminals 1 and 2 (Terminal 3 is adjacent to Terminal 1) have short and mid-stay parking, as well as a SKYPARK, while Terminal 2 has long-stay parking and a free shuttle bus to all other terminals. See abudhabiairport.ae for rates.

Getting Around

52

Abu Dhabi Explorer

For those departing Abu Dhabi and looking to check luggage and select seats ahead of time, there are two options for early check-in. Passengers can check-in to the City Terminal, located in the Tourist Club Area, up to 24 hours before a scheduled flight, depending on the airline. ADNEC, the Abu Dhabi National Exhibitions Company, also offers round-the-clock check-in services. Contact the City Terminal (02 644 8434) or ADNEC (02 444 9671) to see if you're eligible for early check-in.

Pack Carefully

When you arrive in Abu Dhabi, your bags are x-rayed. Be aware of any materials – books, DVDs, magazines, etc – that could be deemed immoral, sexually explicit, religious propaganda or potentially offensive, as they are strictly prohibited and will be confiscated if found. All narcotics (and even certain prescription and over-the-counter drugs containing codeine or temazepam) are banned items and possession could result in an immediate jail term. Contact drugreg.csc@moh. gov.ae or call the Ministry of Health and Drug Control on 02 611 7239 before you travel to check if your medication is on the controlled list.

Al Ain has its own international airport (code: AAN), which is about 20km west of the city centre. While the number of airlines operating out of here is not huge, the introduction of this airport has certainly eased the pressure on Abu Dhabi International Airport by redirecting some of the air traffic – particularly cargo planes. Most flights go to Mumbai, Karachi, Dhaka and Colombo. For more information on flights to and from the Garden City, contact the airport's customer service desk (03 785 5555).

The UAE's biggest airport is Dubai International Airport (code: DXB) which welcomes more than 150 airlines operating to and from nearly 200 destinations. Dubai's official airline, Emirates, operates scheduled services to almost 100 destinations in over 50 countries. Dubai-based low-cost carrier flydubai, flies to 13 mainly regional destinations. All three Dubai terminals have both short and long-term parking facilities, as well as busy taxi ranks. There are Metro stations at both Terminal 1 and Terminal 3, and Terminal 2 is accessible from a newly-opened station on the Green Line.

The vast new Al Maktoum Airport (also known as Dubai World Central, dwc.ae), located in the Jebel Ali area of Dubai, recently began freighter operations. It is likely that construction will continue until 2022, with passenger services gradually added. Upon completion, it will be capable of handling upwards of 100 million passengers annually.

In addition to the aforementioned, three more airlines are based in the UAE. Low-cost carrier Air Arabia is based in Sharjah and RAK Airways is the national operator of Ras Al Khaimah, a northern emirate (see Out Of The City, p.256). Rotana Jet now offers an internal service between Abu Dhabi, Al Ain, Fujairah and a number of Abu Dhabi's islands, and the carrier boasts that fares are even cheaper than taxis, with tickets available from Dhs.150 one way for the Abu Dhabi-Al Ain route.

Airlines

Air Arabia 06 508 8888, *airarabia.com*
Air Blue 02 645 4050, *airblue.com*
Air France 800 23823, *airfrance.ae*
Air India Express 02 632 2300, *airindia.in*
Air Seychelles 02 612 3470, *airseychelles.com*
Alitalia 02 611 8640, *alitalia.com*
Austrian Airlines 02 677 6621, *austrian.com*
Bahrain Air 02 633 4466, *bahrainair.net*
British Airways 02 611 8600, *britishairways.com*
Cathay Pacific 02 617 6000, *cathaypacific.com*
China Southern Airlines 04 221 8888, *flychinasouthern.com*
CSA Czech Airlines 02 491 5288, *czechairlines.ae*
Delta Airlines 02 671 3033, *delta.com*
Egypt Air 02 634 4777, *egyptair.com*
Emirates 600 555 555, *emirates.com*
Ethiopian Airlines 02 627 3333, *ethiopianairlines.com*
Etihad Airways 02 511 0000, *etihadairways.com*
flydubai 04 231 1000, *flydubai.com*
Gulf Air 02 651 6888, *gulfair.com*
Jazeera Airways 04 224 4464, *jazeeraairways.com*
Kish Air 02 6267 771 , *kishairlines.com*
KLM Royal Dutch Airlines 800 556, *klm.com*
Kuwait Airways 02 631 2230, *kuwait-airways.com*
Lufthansa 02 639 4640, *lufthansa.com*
Middle East Airlines 02 622 6300, *mea.com.lb*
Pakistan International Airlines 02 635 2600, *piac.com.pk*
Qatar Airways 02 621 0007, *qatarairways.com*
RAK Airways 02 491 0602, *rakairways.com*
Rotana Jet 02 444 3366, *rotanajet.com*
Royal Air Maroc 02 505 2024, *royalairmaroc.com*
Royal Brunei Airlines 02 622 6100, *bruneiair.com*
Royal Jordanian 02 627 5084, *rj.com*
Saudi Arabian Airlines 02 635 1400, *saudiairlines.com*
Shaheen Air 02 626 5111, *shaheenair.com*
Singapore Airlines 02 622 1110, *singaporeair.com*
SriLankan Airlines 02 633 7125, *srilankan.lk*
Sudan Airways 02 833 3967, *sudanair.com*
Yemen Airways 02 632 3675, *yemenia.com*

Boat

Despite being located on an island, opportunities for getting around by boat in Abu Dhabi are limited and there are currently no scheduled passenger services

Public Transport

from Abu Dhabi to other countries or even to Dubai. Boat trips for the public are mainly in the form of dinner dhows, tours and sightseeing day trips rather than for commuter travel; various companies offer popular trips by dhow or motorboat to explore the islands off the coast (see Tours and Sightseeing, p.230).

Dhow Do You Do?

The Bateen shipyards are among the oldest areas of Abu Dhabi and there you can see craftsmen practicing the ancient Arabian art of dhow building. As well as traditional working boats, racing dhows are built and stored here too.

If you know your bow from your stern, you could try hiring a fishing boat privately. Moreover, if you fancy being the captain of your own vessel, you could join the many expats here in Abu Dhabi who invest in a boat for regular weekend jaunts to one of the 200 different islands that are scattered offshore (see more information on The Islands, p.198). The ideal climate makes boating a popular hobby; check out uaeboats4sale.com for boat bargains.

Bus

The Abu Dhabi Department of Transport responded to the increasing need for public transport services by launching a two year bus initiative in 2008, and by the end of 2011, the Transport Department expects to have 123 routes in operation.

With bus routes all over the emirate, as well as inter-urban buses on the island, the service runs more or less around the clock and fares are inexpensive, costing as little as Dhs.2 for travel within the capital.

Big Bus Tour

If you're new to the city, try hopping onto a Big Bus Tour bus. Operating between 09:00 and 17:00 every day, tickets cost Dhs.200 for adults and Dhs.100 for under 15s, and are valid for 24 hours. The tour circumnavigates Abu Dhabi island and is ideal for learning where landmarks such as the Meena souks, the Corniche, Emirates Palace, ADNEC, Sheikh Zayed Mosque and Abu Dhabi Mall are all located before taking on the roads on your own. bigbustours.com

'Ojra' bus passes can be purchased at the central bus station next to Al Wahda Mall or at any Red Crescent kiosk on the island. An inter-urban pass costs Dhs.40 for one month of unlimited use. For more information on Ojra call 800 55555 or visit ojra. ae where comprehensive bus route maps can be found and easily downloaded in PDF format. Those without passes can simply deposit a Dhs.1 in the

silver box upon entering the inter-urban bus; drivers can't provide change, so be sure to have a coin handy. Buses are gender segregated with a special ladies' section in the front.

The main bus station in Abu Dhabi is on Hazza bin Zayed Road next to Al Wahda Mall and there are clearly marked bus stops on nearly every major road on the island. There are currently 80 air-conditioned bus shelters in the city, and there are plans to triple that number over the next couple of years.

The Abu Dhabi-Dubai Emirates Express is operated jointly by the Abu Dhabi and Dubai municipalities. The 150km route along Sheikh Zayed Road takes around two hours by bus. The route operates reliably every 30 minutes between 06:30 and 21:30 at the central bus station in Abu Dhabi. Return buses leave Dubai's Al Ghubaibah station from 06:20 until 23:40. The cost per person has recently increased to Dhs.20 for a one way ticket. There's an on-bus catering service available, and the RTA claims that onboard wifi could be rolled out soon.

Bus routes to the Western Region are also available at similarly inexpensive fares, if you don't mind spending a bit more time getting there as you would by your own car. An express service (the X90) was recently introduced between Abu Dhabi and Al Ain, leaving every 30 minutes between 04:30 and 00:00 with a single stop in Khatem. One-way tickets cost Dhs.15 and the journey takes 90 minutes.

Metro

Work is underway on Abu Dhabi's very own metro system (as well as the Etihad Rail project that will run throughout the whole country, from Ghweifat near the Saudi border in the west, to Oman and Fujairah in the east) but, for the moment, you can't go on the rails in the UAE capital. If you take a trip to Dubai, however, why not avoid all that stressful traffic, park up at Jebel Ali or Ibn Batutta and jump on the Dhs.28 billion Dubai Metro.

All of the Red Line stations are now open, so you can get on in the south of the city and travel all the way along Sheikh Zayed Road, passing Dubai Marina, Mall of the Emirates, the Burj Khalifa and Dubai Mall, the old areas of Bur Dubai and Deira, before ending up just past the airport in Rashidiyah. The Green Line opened in September 2011, running generally parallel to the Dubai Creek on both sides through Deira and Bur Dubai and sharing two interchanges with the Red Line. Trains run from around 06:00 to 00:00 every day except Friday (14:00 to 01:00) and Saturday (until 01:00) at intervals of 3 to 4 minutes at peak times. Each train has a section for women and children only, and a first or 'Gold' class cabin. One way fares in regular class start at Dhs.1.80 and go up to Dhs.5.80 – if you're hopping on and off all day, don't worry as the maximum daily fare is Dhs.14 by using the NOL card.

City roads

An Abu Dhabi taxi

Road sign

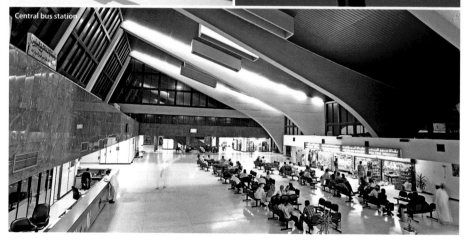
Central bus station

Taxi

If you don't have a car, taxis are the most common method of getting around and they are reasonably priced and plentiful. The city has a 7,000 strong taxi fleet that is overseen by TransAD (the centre for regulation of transport for hire cars, transad.ae). TransAD was established in 2007 to regulate the taxi service and establish an internationally recognised public transportation system in Abu Dhabi. It allows a few companies to run as franchise operations but has been regulating all taxi operations since the rather radical overhaul began.

Pretty In Pink

TransAD also operates a fleet of 70 women-only taxis. With pink roof lights and purple logos, they are driven by female taxi drivers and charge exactly the same fares as standard Abu Dhabi cabs.

TransAD imposes stringent rules on drivers, regularly fining those who commit offences such as demanding a fare higher than that on the meter, or even refusing to stop when hailed (all Dhs.500 fines). Some drivers will try to negotiate their fare with you, but keep in mind that this is totally illegal and you are within your rights to insist on the meter. Taxi drivers' English skills vary and, infuriatingly, they are often not familiar with street names or places, so it really helps to know where you are going. If you're new to the city, it's a good idea to take the phone number of your destination and a pocket map (such as Explorer's *Abu Dhabi Mini Map*) in case you get lost.

Dodgy Cabs

Finding a taxi in busy areas can be frustrating and many people turn to illegal cabs, particularly at the airport. Be warned that these unlicensed vehicles don't have to meet the safety standards that official taxis do – and if you're involved in an accident you may find yourself dragged into court. They are difficult to trace, and there have even been a few cases where drivers have been the victims or perpetrators of crimes.

Taxis can either be flagged down at the roadside or booked by phone; there's a booking fare of Dhs.3 during the day and Dhs.4 at night. If you're struggling to flag a cab your best bet is to get to a mall or a main hotel, as this is where you'll tend to find large groups of them.

All taxi companies service the airport and there are also specially registered airport taxis there; the journey into town costs Dhs.70-80.

The street taxis (which should have been phased out by the end of 2012) are easily recognisable thanks to their white and gold livery, as well as the green taxi sign on the roof. Those with silver livery and a yellow sign on the roof are the newer taxis.

Daytime (06:00-22:00) metered fares in the city start at Dhs.3.5 and increase by an additional Dhs.1.6 for every subsequent kilometre of a journey. Most trips around the city shouldn't cost more than Dhs.15. Nighttime fares are slightly more, with the starting fare at Dhs.4 and a minimal fare of Dhs.10 after 22:00

The fare chart must be in plain view inside every taxi and whilst tips are welcome, it's illegal for a driver to demand one. If you have any problems with a taxi driver call 600 535 353 – as part of its development, TransAD welcomes feedback.

Passenger Rights

Taxi drivers are obliged to accept any fare, no matter the distance. They are also obliged to drive in a safe manner, so don't be timid about asking them to slow down. If a driver refuses to pick you up because of your destination or refuses to drive responsibly, you can call TransAD and report the driver.

Taxi Companies

Al Ghazal Transport 02 444 7787, *adnh.com*
Al Ghazal Transport 03 751 6565, *adnh.com*
Arabia Taxi 800 272 242, *arabiataxi.ae*
CARS Taxi 800 227 789, *carstaxi.ae*
National Taxi 02 600 543 322, *nationaltaxi.ae*
Tawasul Transport 02 673 4444, *dasholding.ae*
Tawasul Transport 03 782 5553, *dasholding.ae*
TransAD 02 600 535 353, *transad.ae*

DRIVING

Getting A Driving Licence

Visitors, and people waiting for their residency permit to be processed, can apply for a temporary licence which is valid for six months and is issued by the Traffic Police Licensing Department (adpolice.gov.ae). To obtain one you will need to fill out the application form and take your essential documents along, including your full driving licence (paper counterpart and card if you're British). The licence is processed within a couple of minutes and costs Dhs.110. If you don't have a licence from your own country, then you will have to take a test. For further information, contact the Abu Dhabi Traffic & Licensing Department (02 419 5555).

Once you have your residence visa you may apply for a permanent UAE licence. Nationals of countries listed on p.57 can automatically transfer their driving licences, as long as the original licence is valid. To apply for a permanent driving licence, submit the necessary documents (your existing foreign licence, passport with visa page, letter of no objection from your employer or sponsor and a passport photo with Dhs.200) to the Traffic Police Licensing Department, where you will be required to take an eye test and will also have to provide proof of your blood group. Legal translation of your original licence may also be required; contact the Licensing Department for further information based on your home country.

Automatic Licence Transfer

Citizens with licences from the following countries are eligible for automatic driving licence transfer: Australia, Austria, Belgium, Canada, Denmark, England, Finland, France, Germany, Greece, Ireland, Italy, Japan, Netherlands, New Zealand, Norway, Poland, South Africa, South Korea, Sweden, Switzerland, Turkey, United States.

The licence is produced within minutes and is valid for 10 years, with renewal a straightforward process. Holding a passport and licence from separate countries can cause problems so, if possible, ensure that both are from the same issuing country before you arrive.

If you are from a country that falls under the automatic licence transfer list, but your licence has expired, you will have to sit the full driving test. The alternative is to return home, renew your licence, and save yourself the hassle. Citizens of other GCC countries do not need to apply for the licence transfer.

Always carry your licence when driving. If you fail to produce it during a police spot check, you will be fined. You should also ensure you have the car's registration card in the car.

Traffic Jam Session

Avoid getting stuck in annoying traffic jams for hours on end by tuning into any of the following radio channels, which provide regular updates about the Abu Dhabi traffic situation throughout the day.
Radio 1 – 100.5FM
Radio 2 – 106.0FM
Abu Dhabi FM – 90.0FM

If your nationality is not on the automatic transfer list, you will need to sit a UAE driving test to be eligible to drive in Abu Dhabi, regardless of whether you hold a valid driving licence from your home country or not. If you haven't driven in your country of origin and need to get a driving licence, the following information will apply to you as well.

The first step is to get a learning permit – start by picking up an application form from the Traffic Police. You will need your essential documents, the driving licence documents and Dhs.40. You will be given an eye test at the Traffic Police Department.

The Emirates Driving Company (02 551 1911, edcad.ae), a semi-governmental organisation part-owned by the Abu Dhabi Traffic Police, is the only government backed company providing driving lessons in Abu Dhabi. You can find a list of independent instructors on the website of the Abu Dhabi Chamber of Commerce (abudhabichamber. ae) and some of them will be recommended by The Emirates Driving Company. The list changes regularly, so the best thing to do is contact them directly and ask for up to date advice.

Some driving institutions insist that you pay for a set of pre-booked lessons and, in some cases, that package extends to 52 lessons and can cost as much as Dhs.3,000. The lessons must be taken on consecutive days and usually last 30-45 minutes. Other companies offer lessons on an hourly basis, as and when you like, for about Dhs.35 per hour. Women are traditionally required to take lessons with a female instructor at a cost of Dhs.65 per hour. If a woman wants to take lessons with a male instructor, she must first obtain an NOC from her husband or sponsor and the Traffic Police.

When your instructor feels that you are ready to take your test, you will be issued with a letter to that effect and can apply for a test date. You will need to fill out the necessary application form at the Traffic Police and to also hand in your essential documents, driving licence documents, and Dhs.35. The wait between submitting your application and the test date can be as much as two or three months.

The test actually consists of three different tests on different dates. One is a Highway Code test, another an 'internal' test, which includes parking

Busy interchange

Driving

and manoeuvres, and the third is a road test. When you have passed all three, you will be issued with a certificate within about five days. You take this to the Traffic Police (adpolice.gov.ae) to apply for your permanent licence.

The rules for riding a motorbike in the UAE are similar to those of driving a car, and if you have a transferable licence from your home country, you can get either a six-month temporary licence or a 10 year permanent one (see the list of nationalities).

The Abu Dhabi Police Traffic & Licensing Department (02 419 5555) is located on 23rd Street in Muroor, between Eastern Ring Road (Eighth Street) and New Airport Road (Second Street).

More information can be found on the Abu Dhabi Police website, adpolice.gov.ae.

Driving Schools

Al Harbi Driving School Tourist Club Area, 02 671 6177
Delma Driving School Delma Island, 02 878 1838
Emirates Driving Company Mussafah, 02 551 1911, edcad.ae

Renewing A Driving Licence

This follows much the same procedure as the initial licence transfer. When it's time to renew your licence, you will need to go to the Traffic Police Licensing Department with your expired licence, a letter of no objection from your employer or sponsor, a passport photograph and your Emirates ID card. You'll take another eye test and receive your new licence promptly.

Safe Driver

If you've had a drink, don't even think about getting behind the wheel of your car. Dubai's Safer Driver (04 268 8797, saferdriver.ae) currently does not have an internal Abu Dhabi service, but will send a driver to pick you up from either Dubai or Abu Dhabi and drive you and your car back to either other city for you. Rates vary depending on distance, but the minimum charge is Dhs.475. Money well spent.

Car Pooling

There is no official car pooling organisation in Abu Dhabi; however you may be able to find people with whom to share journeys. Try the community section of Dubizzle Abu Dhabi or one of the chat forums on abudhabiwoman.com or expatwoman.com.

Road Toll

Abu Dhabi doesn't levy an official road tax or toll for using its roads, although there is a car registration fee of approx Dhs.200 payable annually at which time your vehicle is inspected for safety and road worthiness (see Registering A Vehicle, p.66).

Dubai, however, has an automated toll system with four gates strategically placed around the city, known as Salik. Abu Dhabi residents need to be prepared for this when they visit Dubai so as not to incur the Dhs.50 fine each time they pass through a toll gate. Stickers, which can be purchased at most major Dubai petrol stations and registered online, are attached to the windscreen and read by radio frequency as you pass the toll spots. It's easy to top up your balance; see salik.ae or call 800 72545 (800 SALIK) for more information.

Traffic Fines & Offences

If you are pulled over by the police or are involved in an accident and don't have your licence with you, you could be fined there and then. You will be given a 24 hour grace period in which to present your licence to the police station; if you fail to do so, you risk having your car impounded and facing a court appearance.

Driving is on the right hand side of the road and it is mandatory to wear seatbelts in the front seats and advisable in the back. Children under 10 years old are no longer allowed to sit in the front of a car, although you may still see this happening. The ban is now countrywide and fines and penalties are issued to any one caught, including points on your licence. The maximum number of points which can be added to a licence before it is revoked is 24.

Keep Your Cool

Rude gestures and even small expressions of 'road rage' towards other motorists can get you into hot water leading to fines, imprisonment and even deportation – so it really is in your own best interest to remain calm at all times. Swearing is considered an extremely offensive act and you could be prosecuted. Of course it goes without saying, but you should exercise particular caution when dealing with police and officials.

Understandably, many people choose to block out the sun's glare by getting their windows tinted. The legal limit for window tint is 30% for both expats and locals alike, but you will find that exceptions are often made for Emiratis whose vehicles far exceed this limit.

Speed limits are usually 60-80km per hour around town, while on major roads they are 100-120km per hour. The speed is usually indicated on road signs, which are dotted at regular intervals along all main roads. There is no leeway for breaking the speed limit and there are a growing number of police-controlled speed traps, both fixed and mobile radar cameras, around Abu Dhabi with more popping up due to recent police initiatives.

The fine for speeding starts at Dhs.400 and increases depending on speed increments. The police also have discretionary power to confiscate vehicles and occasionally this does happen.

You do not receive any notification when you are caught on camera, so it can be quite a shock when you re-register your car and collect all the fines in one go. Keep a check on the number of fines against your vehicle by visiting adpolice.gov.ae and entering your vehicle registration. If you do, you can even pay online using a credit card. Fines can also be paid in the Traffic Fines section of the Traffic Police office.

Zero Tolerance

If you've had any alcohol at all, don't even consider driving. Abu Dhabi has a 100% zero tolerance policy and it will be straight to jail and in many cases deportation if you're caught by the police. There are plenty of taxis available so there's never any excuse to risk it.

Breakdowns

In the event of a breakdown, you will usually find that passing police cars stop to help, or at least to check your documents. Traffic Police recommendations are that you should pull your car over to a safe spot but, if you are on the hard shoulder of a highway, it is suggested that you pull your car as far away from the yellow line as possible and step away from the road until help arrives.

The Arabian Automobile Association (800 4900) offers a 24 hour roadside breakdown service for an annual charge. This includes help for minor mechanical problems, battery boosting, if you run out of petrol, get a flat tyre or lock yourself out. The more advanced service includes off-road recovery, vehicle registration and a rent a car service. It's a similar concept to the AA in Britain or AAA in the States. For more information go to aaauae.com.

In The Event Of An Emergency

Make sure, no matter how short your journey, that your mobile phone is with you and charged, and that you have a bottle of water in the car along with the number of a recovery service, your car registration documents, some fresh, bottled water and a blanket.

Other useful breakdown or recovery services include Abrat Al Sahraa Transport and Recovery (02 555 5848), Dana Auto Recovery Service (02 555 5555), International Automobile & Touring Club (02 632 4400) and Lucky Car Recovery (02 555 5522). Some dealers offer a free breakdown service for the first few years after buying a new, or even used, car. Be sure to ask the dealership about this option when purchasing a vehicle.

Traffic Accidents

All accidents must be reported to the police. In the city of Abu Dhabi, for minor collisions that do not require emergency services, call 02 446 2462 and wait for the police to arrive. For more serious accidents, dial 999 for emergency help. In other areas of the emirate, use 999 for all accidents, regardless of their severity. If there is only minor damage to the vehicles involved, the instruction from the Traffic Police (and a recent advertising campaign) is for drivers to move their vehicle to the side of the road. Once the police arrive, they will assess the accident and apportion blame.

Saeed

Saeed (saaed.ae)is a private organisation assisting the police. It responds to non-fatal traffic accidents in Abu Dhabi. In operation since 2008, Saeed staff are on the scene quickly in their three wheeled electric operated vehicles and they are now the first to respond to the majority of 999 traffic related calls. While usually much faster than the police, there is a Dhs.500 charge attached to Saeed's service, payable by the party at fault.

If you disagree with their judgement, it's tough luck. The police then document the necessary details and give you a copy of the accident report. Submit the paper to your insurance company to get the vehicle repaired. In Abu Dhabi a white accident report means you are at fault, and pink means you are not to blame. You will also have to pay Dhs.500 if you get the white slip.

The police may, in some circumstances, retain your driving licence until you obtain the necessary documentation from the insurance company saying the claim is being processed. Your insurers will then give you a paper that entitles you to retrieve your licence from the police.

Stray animals can be another hazard to avoid on the roads in the UAE. If an animal hits your vehicle and causes damage or injury, the animal's owner should pay compensation. However, if you are found to have been speeding or driving recklessly, you must compensate the owner of the animal, which can be expensive.

Petrol Stations

Petrol stations in Abu Dhabi are run by the Abu Dhabi National Oil Company's distribution division, ADNOC-FOD, and are usually open around the clock. There are plenty of gas stations on the main roads around Abu Dhabi emirate, but the ones on the island itself are mostly tucked away and can be difficult to find, though they are often signposted. Most offer extra services, such as car washing and even oil changes, with shops selling all those necessities that you forgot to buy at the supermarket. All ADNOC petrol stations now accept credit card payment for petrol.

Pumps are managed by attendants, who often clean your windscreen while filling up; although the price of petrol has fluctuated in comparison with other countries, and is expensive compared to other Gulf countries, most expats should still find it very cheap compared to their home countries. For example, you would expect to pay around Dhs.70 to fill up a small car, such as a Toyota Yaris, with unleaded petrol.

Help Yourself

ADNOC is currently considering the reintroduction of self-service pumps in Abu Dhabi with around half of the pumps in each petrol station being converted to automated self-service pumps. Self-service was attempted in 2008, but proved unpopular at the time, but ADNOC plans to implement a loyalty points system to those who opt for the self-service option (attendants will still be available) in order to encourage the system which, the company thinks, will be more convenient and speed up the filling-up process.

Petrol stations in the other emirates are numerous and run by the companies Emarat, EPPCO and ENOC. Pumps are also managed by attendants in the rest of the UAE and many stations will only accept cash.

GETTING A CAR

Hiring A Car

New arrivals to Abu Dhabi often find that they have no other option than to hire a vehicle until their residency papers go through. Others are perhaps unsure of how long they plan to stay in the UAE or simply prefer the relatively hassle-free option of renting over buying a vehicle. Most leasing companies include the following in their rates: registration, maintenance, replacement, 24 hour assistance and insurance.

All the main international car rental companies, plus a few extra, can be found in the UAE. It is best to shop around as the rates vary considerably. The larger, reputable firms generally have more reliable vehicles and a greater capacity to help in an emergency (an important factor when dealing with the aftermath of an accident). Find out which car hire agent your company uses, as you might qualify for a corporate rate. But do beware if you travel regularly to Dubai, as most rental companies will keep track of how many times you pass through the Salik toll gates (p.58) and charge you at the end of the month, along with a Salik service charge. If you are commuting between emirates also be aware that more companies are implementing a monthly mileage limit.

Leasing is generally available on a weekly, monthly or yearly basis. Monthly leasing prices start at around Dhs.1,500 for a small vehicle, such as a Toyota Yaris, and go up from there. As the lease period increases, the price decreases. So, if you're considering keeping the car for a long period, it may not work out that much more expensive than buying.

Before you take possession of your leased car, do a thorough check for any dents or bumps. To hire any vehicle, you will need to provide a passport copy, credit card (not debit card) and a valid driving licence. Those with a residence visa must have a UAE driving licence to drive a hired car, while those on a visit visa can use a licence from their home country as long as it is at least one year old. Comprehensive insurance is essential; make sure that it includes personal accident coverage and perhaps Oman cover if you're planning on exploring.

Car Hire Companies

Al Ghazal Rent A Car 02 634 2200, *adnh.com*
Al Ghazal Transport Company 02 444 7787, *adnh.com*
Al Raeed Rent A Car 02 446 9915, *alraeeduae.com*
Avis 02 575 7180, *avisuae.ae*
Budget Rent A Car > *p.61* 02 443 8430, *budget-uae.com*
Car Fare Rent A Car 02 643 7227, *carfarellc.com*
Diamondlease 02 622 2028, *diamondlease.com*
Dollar Rent A Car 02 641 9002, *dollaruae.com*
Europcar 02 626 1441, *europcar-middleeast.com*
Eurostar Rent A Car 02 645 5855, *eurostarrental.com*
Fast Limo 02 555 1441, *fastuae.com*
Fast Rent A Car 02 632 4000, *fastuae.com*
Hertz Rent A Car 02 672 0060, *hertzuae.com*
National Car Rental 800 3130, *national-me.com*
Payless Car Rental 02 599 8977, *paylesscar.com*
Sixt Rent A Car 02 550 3929, *sixt.com*
Thrifty Car Rental 02 634 5663, *thriftyuae.com*
United Car Rentals & Wafi Limousine 02 491 4450, *unitedcarrentals.com*

Buying A Car

Aside from the at-times horrendous traffic, the UAE is something of a motorist's dream. Petrol is cheap, big engines are considered cool and the wide highways stretching across the country are smooth and perfect for weekend drives. Buying a car is unlikely to cause a major headache either: the vast majority of the major car manufacturers are available through franchised dealerships in Abu Dhabi. Expat buyers are often pleasantly surprised by the low cost of new cars compared to prices in their home countries. For many, this lower initial cost, coupled with much cheaper fuel and maintenance costs, means they can afford something a little more extravagant than they might drive at home. The chaotic traffic, teamed with the open desert that covers most of the country, can be

Short-term Rental, Lease and International Reservations.

When it comes to getting more value for your money, there's just one name – Budget. Whether it is short-term rental, lease or international reservations, you can be assured of the quality of service that has earned us the vote as 'Best Car Rental Company in the Middle East'.

Car and Van Rental

For Reservations:

Toll-free: 800 2722 (24 Hrs.)
Abu Dhabi: +971 2 443 8430
Al Ain: +971 3 746 0989
Dubai: +971 4 295 6667
Jebel Ali: +971 4 881 1445
Sharjah: +971 6 533 7777
Ras Al Khaimah: +971 7 244 6666
Fujairah: +971 9 222 0172
Email: reservations@budget-uae.com
or book on-line at
www.budget-uae.com
An ISO 9001 certified company

A member of the UAE-based Liberty Investment Co. (Liberty Group)

Getting A Car

enough to persuade expats to turn to a 4WD or SUV – the extra bulk and height certainly makes you feel better protected.

There is a large second-hand car market in the UAE. Dealers are scattered around town, but the best area to start in is Mussafah, while Airport Road also has a decent selection of used car dealers. Expect to pay a premium of between Dhs.5,000 and Dhs.10,000 for buying through a dealer (as opposed to buying from a private seller), since they also offer a limited warranty, insurance, finance and registration.

Get A Check Up

Before buying a used car, it is advisable to have it checked by a reputable garage. This is especially necessary with 4WDs, which may have been driven off-road a lot. This service will set you back around Dhs.400, and it is best to book in advance. The major garages in Abu Dhabi are located out of the city, in Mussafah. To get to Mussafah, take the Coast Road out of the city over Mussafah Bridge and keep going.

Excitingly for car buyers, Motor World Abu Dhabi has now opened in Shamkah near Abu Dhabi Airport. The dedicated auto-trading venue has space for 100 showrooms, as well as easy parking. The complex is still in its infancy but more and more dealers are moving there all the time as all secondhand car dealerships have to find showrooms off the island in order to free up valuable parking space for residents.

Some Abu Dhabi residents venture up to Dubai to purchase second-hand cars from the Dubai Municipality Used Car Complex at Ras Al Khor, where all the cars have been thoroughly checked by EPPCO's Tasjeel service. It is certainly possible to find a bargain but be aware of the additional hassle involved when you try to register a vehicle from another emirate (see p.62, Importing A Car). This area is also home to Golden Bell Auctions (goldenbellauctions.com), with sales held every Wednesday evening. All cars up for auction have to undergo a test at the nearby EPPCO/Tasjeel garage, and all outstanding fines will have been cleared.

If you decide to buy a vehicle privately, check out the classifieds in Gulf News and Khaleej Times, or on the noticeboards at Abela and Spinneys supermarkets, St Andrew's Church and many of the sports clubs. You can also pick up a copy of Auto Trader UAE, which has a huge number of new and used cars advertised for sale. There are a number of websites which are worth searching too: Dubizzle (dubizzle.com) has a very good Abu Dhabi site, while Expat Woman (expatwoman. com) has all kinds of classifieds specific to Abu Dhabi and Al Ain; autodealer.ae is a used car website which covers all of the Emirates, and souq.com is an auction site which includes cars in its listings.

Importing A Car

It is possible to import or export your car, but be prepared for paperwork, paperwork and a bit more paperwork. Furthermore, given the amount of choice available locally, it hardly makes sense. Indeed, most people tend to take advantage of the bustling second-hand market available locally when they arrive and leave the region; however, if you're keen to hang onto your chosen four wheels, the best thing to do is to contact a car dealership who should be able to advise and assist you through the process. You could also contact Kanoo Shipping (kanooshipping.com) or Khalidia International Shipping (khalidiashipping.com) for more details. If you buy a car in one of the other emirates and want to register it in Abu Dhabi, then you have to officially export and import it. Exporting means going to the traffic department in the emirate in which the car is registered with copies of your passport and driving licence, along with around Dhs.450 to cover your export licence, export insurance and export plates, which are usually blue.

Gulf Spec

When buying a car – used and European or American marques in particular – check that it is 'Gulf Spec'. This means that the manufacturer has done things to reinforce the vehicle against the harsh climate, such as an electric fan over oil coolers, enlarged radiators, enlarged AC condensers and air filters better suited to dealing with the sand in the air.

New Car Dealers

Abu Dhabi Motors BMW 02 507 5800, *bmw-abudhabi.com*
Abu Dhabi Skoda 02 443 0772, *skoda-uae.com*
Al Futtaim Motors Toyota 02 419 9999, *alfuttaimmotors.ae*
Al Futtaim Motors Lexus 02 419 9888, *alfuttaimmotors.com*
Al Habtoor Motors Mitsubishi, Bentley, Aston Martin 02 642 3114, *alhabtoor-motors.com*
Al Masaood Automobiles Nissan 02 677 2000, *nissan-almasaoodautomobiles.com*
Al Otaiba Group Chevrolet 02 558 8777
Al Yousuf Motors Daihatsu 02 558 8890, *aym.ae*
Audi Abu Dhabi Audi 02 665 8000, *audi-abudhabi.com*
Bin Hamoodah Automotive Chevrolet 02 444 8888, *binhamoodahauto.com*
Central Motors & Equipment Fiat, Mercedes-Benz, Jeep 02 554 6262, *cmeuae.ae*
Elite Motors Mitsubishi 02 642 3686, *belbadi.com*
Emirates Motor Company Mercedes-Benz 02 656 7777, *emc.mercedes-benz.com*

Getting A Car

Galadari Automobiles Mazda 02 677 3030, *mazdauae.com*
Habtoor Royal Car Showroom Mitsubishi, Bentley, Aston Martin 02 698 9600, *habtoormotors.com*
Juma Al Majid Est Hyundai 02 644 0233, *hyundai-ae.com*
Liberty Abu Dhabi Automobiles Cadillac, Hummer 02 558 9988, *libertyautos.com*
Omeir Bin Youssef Group Peugeot 02 622 7777
Peugeot Peugeot 02 633 3000, *peugeotabudhabi.ae*
Porsche Centre Abu Dhabi 02 674 5600, *porscheabudhabi.com*
Premier Motors Ford, Jaguar, Land Rover, Ferrari, Maserati 02 558 8344, *premier-motors.ae*
Trading Enterprises > *p.63* Chrysler, Dodge, Volvo 02 633 3408, *tradingenterprises.com*
Trading Enterprises Honda 02 676 3300, *hondauae.com*
Volkswagen Abu Dhabi 02 681 7770, *volkswagen-abu-dhabi.com*
Western Motors > *p.48* Jeep 02 667 6000, *jeepabudhabi.com*

Tinted Windows

Currently, the government allows you to avoid the sun somewhat by tinting your vehicle's windows up to 30%. Some areas have facilities where you can get your car windows tinted, but don't get carried away – remember to stick to the limit. Random checks take place and fines are handed out to those caught in the dark. Tinting in Sharjah is allowed for a fee of Dhs.100 per year and Ajman residents may tint for Dhs.200 per annum, but only if they are women.

Used Car Dealers

501 Cars 02 666 6501, *501cars.com*
Al Ain Class Motors 03 763 3333, *alainclass.com*
Al Futtaim Automall 02 673 3504, *automalluae.com*
Al Hilal Auto 02 417 4720, *alhilalbank.ae*
Ali & Sons Used Cars Division 02 555 4411, *asusedcars.com*
Porsche Centre Mussafah 02 619 3911, *porscheabudhabi.com*
Prestige Cars 02 681 0111, *prestigecars.ae*
Princess Cars 02 558 5050, *princesscar.com*
Reem Automobile Showroom 02 446 3343, *reemauto.com*

Vehicle Finance

Many new and second-hand car dealers will be able to arrange auto finance for you, often through a deal with their preferred banking partner. Previously, this involved writing out years and years worth of post-dated cheques, but most official dealers and main financial establishments will now be able to set up monthly automatic transactions for you.

Always ask about the rates and terms of the auto loan, and then consider going directly to one of the banks to see if they can offer you a better deal. It is often easier to get financing through the bank that receives your salary. Also, the interest rates on personal loans are often a little lower than those on car loans. Ask your bank if you qualify for a personal loan.

Transferring Ownership

All transactions must be directed through the Traffic Police (see p.44). A Dhs.3,000 fine is imposed on both buyer and seller for cars sold unofficially. To register a used car in your name, you must transfer vehicle ownership. You will need to collect an application form from the Traffic Police (see p.44) and submit it, along with a no objection letter from the finance company, the original licence plates, the valid registration card, the insurance certificate and Dhs.200. The previous owner must also be present to sign the form.

Vehicle Insurance

Before you can register your car, you must have adequate insurance. Insurers will need to know the usual details, such as year of manufacture, value and chassis number. If you got a real bargain of a car and feel it's worth much more than you paid, make sure you instruct the insurance company to cover it at the market value. Take copies of your UAE driving licence, passport and the existing vehicle registration card.

Annual insurance policies cover a 13 month period (this allows for a one-month grace period when your registration expires). Rates depend on the age and model of your car and your previous insurance history, but very few companies will recognise any no-claims bonuses you have accrued in your home country. Rates are generally 4-7% of the vehicle value, or a flat 5% for cars over five years old. Fully comprehensive cover with personal accident insurance is highly advisable, and you are strongly advised to make sure the policy covers you for 'blood money'. For more adventurous 4WD drivers, insurance for off-roading accidents is also recommended. Young or new drivers might need to call a few insurance companies before finding one that is willing to insure them, especially if they own a sports car. If you have no claims for three years, you will probably qualify for a reduction in your insurance rates.

Pimp Your Ride?

The area between Al Salam and Al Falah Streets is the place to head for accessories. Small workshops can provide everything from new tyres and alloys to custom car covers and window tinting – you can even get your car seats reupholstered.

Breakdown?

With AXA car insurance, we'll be there within an hour. And, if we're not, we'll give you AED 150.

redefining / insurance

رؤية جديدة / للتأمين

Call 800-4845 or visit www.axa-gulf.com

Terms and conditions apply

Registering a Vehicle

All cars must be registered annually with the Traffic Police. Allow plenty of time; expect to be pushed from counter to counter, filling in form after form.

Before starting the registration procedure, check you do not have any traffic offences and fines against your car number because the registration procedure cannot be completed until these have been settled.

To Oman And Back

It is wise to check whether your insurance covers you for the Sultanate of Oman as, within the Emirates, you may find yourself driving through small Omani enclaves (especially if you are off-road, near Hatta, through Wadi Bih and on the East Coast in Dibba). Insurance for a visit to Oman can be arranged on a short-term basis, usually for no extra cost.

There is a one month grace period after your registration has expired during which time you can re-register your vehicle (hence, the 13 month insurance period). You must have your valid insurance papers ready before registering or re-registering your car.

In order to obtain licence plates for the vehicle, it must first be tested and then registered with the Traffic Police. If you have purchased your vehicle brand new from a dealer, they will probably do the registration for you; otherwise you will have to get it done yourself. A new vehicle does not need to be tested for the first two years, though it must be re-registered after the first year. Re-registration costs Dhs.100 plus Dhs.5 for a sticker that is placed onto your number plate. The test involves a technical inspection, checking lights, bodywork, fire extinguisher and emissions.

Once the car has been passed, you will receive a certification document. This will cost Dhs.120. Once your vehicle is insured, you must submit the insurance documents (valid for 13 months), the proof

Blood Money

As the law currently stands, the family of a pedestrian killed in a road accident is entitled to Dhs.200,000 diya (blood) money. The money is usually paid by the insurance company unless there's any evidence of the driver having been under the influence of alcohol. However, an amendment to the law is being considered to put a stop to the terrible trend among desperate lower-income workers of killing themselves to provide for their family. This will mean blood money is not automatically due if the victim was walking across a road not intended for use by pedestrians, such as the Abu Dhabi-Dubai Road.

of purchasing agreement and the vehicle 'passing' certificate to the Traffic Police, along with the essential documents and Dhs.325.

Vehicle Repairs & Maintenance

By law, no vehicle can be accepted for major 'collision' repairs without an accident report from the Traffic Police, although minor dents can be repaired without a report. Your insurance company will usually have an agreement with a particular garage to which they will refer you. The garage will carry out the repair work and the insurance company will settle the claim. Generally, there is Dhs.250-500 deductible for all claims, but check with your insurance company for details of your policy.

If you purchase a new vehicle, your insurance should cover you for 'agency repairs' – repairs at the workshop of the dealer selling the car – although this is not a guarantee and you may have to pay a premium. It's worth it though, as your car's warranty (two to three years) may be invalid if you have non-agency repairs done on it. Even if you buy a fairly new second-hand car (less than three years old) it may be beneficial to opt for agency repairs to protect the value of the car. When buying a used car, many shoppers like to see a history of agency maintenance, especially for relatively new vehicles. It may seem ridiculous to have an oil change at the dealership every 5,000km, but it often pays off when selling.

Besides accidents and bumps, common problems in this part of the world include the air-conditioning malfunctioning, batteries suddenly giving up and tyres blowing out. The aircon is likely just to need topping up, which is fairly straightforward. Car batteries don't tend to last too long in the hot conditions, and you may not get much warning (one day your car just won't start), so it's always handy to keep a set of jump leads in the boot.

If you get your car started, it's worth a trip to Mussafah, where there's a concentration of small workshops. Haggle hard for repairs, spares and even a new battery.

Vehicle Repairs
ADM Abu Dhabi Motors 02 507 5800, *bmw-abudhabi.com*
Al Habtoor Motors 02 555 3344, *habtoormotors.com*
Al Mazroui & Clevy Auto Services 02 555 4589, *mazautouae.com*
Ali & Sons Company 02 672 3900, *ali-sons.com*
Bosch Service Centre 02 681 9101, *cmeuae.ae*
Central Motors & Equipment 02 554 6262, *cmeuae.ae*
Elite Motors Workshop 02 558 3441
Trading Enterprises 02 698 4000, *tradingenterprises.ae*

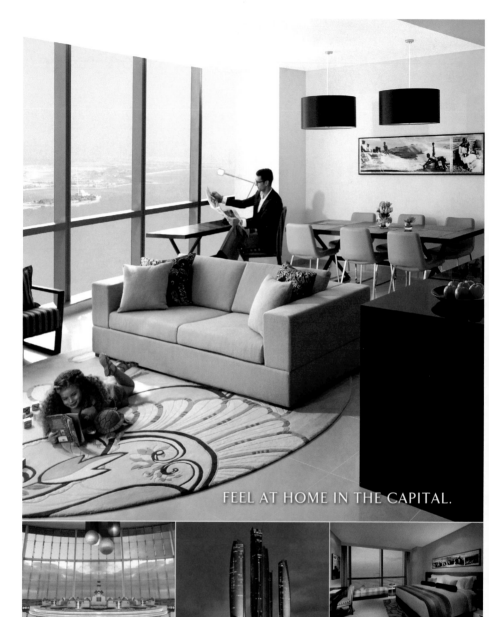

FEEL AT HOME IN THE CAPITAL.

Housing

Housing

HOUSING

Apart from securing your new job, getting your accommodation satisfactorily sorted out is probably the most crucial factor in making your move to Abu Dhabi a success. The first thing to decide is what type of accommodation you want (and can afford) to live in, and in what part of town. This chapter provides a detailed round-up on the different residential areas in Abu Dhabi (p.84), focusing on the type of accommodation available, the amenities, and the general pros and cons. There are sections on the procedures and practicalities involved in both the rental (p.72) and owning (p.75) markets too, discussing what you need to do to secure your dream pad. Once you've found somewhere to live, this chapter also tells you how to get settled in, covering everything from getting your TV and electricity connected to sprucing up the garden. Happy house hunting.

ACCOMMODATION OPTIONS

Hotel & Serviced Apartments

Hotel apartments are ideal if you require temporary, furnished accommodation, although they are a relatively expensive option. Apartments can be rented on a daily, weekly, monthly or yearly basis. They come fully furnished and serviced (with maid service), and usually have satellite TV and excellent leisure facilities. Water, electricity and sometimes internet are included in the rent. Rates vary hugely according to the area and facilities provided. They can also fluctuate depending on the time of year, but usually, if you take a yearly lease, your rate will be fixed for that year.

Al Diar Palm Hotel Apartments Nr Al Salat Plaza, Muroor St, Al Muroor, 02 642 0900, *aldiarhotels.com*
Al Maha Arjaan By Rotana Sheikh Hamdan Bin Mohammed St, Al Markaziyah, 02 610 6666, *rotana.com*
Al Manzel Hotel Apartments Sheikh Zayed First St, Tourist Club Area, 02 644 8000, *almanzel-hotelapartments.ae*
Al Rawda Arjaan By Rotana Nr Al Wahda Sports Club, Old Airport Rd, Al Wahdah, 02 403 5000, *rotana.com*
Beach Rotana Abu Dhabi Nr Abu Dhabi Mall, Tourist Club St, Tourist Club Area, 02 697 9000, *rotana.com*
Cassells Hotel Apartments Sheikh Zayed The First St, Markaziya East, 02 610 7777, *cassellshotelapartments.ae*
Century Hotel Apartments Al Salam St, Tourist Club Area, 02 644 7665, *aldiarhotels.com*
Corniche Towers Hotel Appartments Nr Volkswagen Service Center, Corniche Rd, Al Khalidiyah, 02 681 0088
Fortune Hotel Apartments Al Salam St, Tourist Club Area, 02 645 0666, *fortune-hotels.net*

Hilton Baynunah Corniche Rd East, Markaziya West, 02 632 7777, *hilton.com*
Ivory Hotel Apartments Nr KIA Motor Showroom, 9th Street, Tourist Club Area, 02 613 8500, *ivoryhotelapts.ae*
Jumeirah At Etihad Towers Residences > *p.68* Nr Emirates Palace, West Corniche St, Al Ras Al Akhdar, 02 811 5555, *jumeirah.com*
Mourouj Hotel Apartments Nr Madinat Zayed Shopping Mall, East Rd, Al Dhafrah, 02 641 3555, *mouroujhotelapartments.ae*
Murjan Asfar Hotel Apartments Nr ADNEC, Shk Rashid Bin Saeed Al Maktoom Rd, Al Musalla, 02 643 3330, *asfarhotels.com*
Platinum Hotel Apartments Khaled Bin Alwaleed St, Al Hosn, 02 634 4463, *platinumhotelapartments.com*
Rainbow Hotel Apartments Nr Crown Plaza, Sheikh Hamdan St, Markaziya East, 02 632 6333
Ramee Guestline Hotel Apartments I Nr Al Salama Hospital, Hamdan St, Tourist Club Area, 02 674 7000, *rameehotels.com*
Ramee Hotel Apartments Abu Dhabi Nr Al Falah Plaza, East Rd, Al Dhafrah, 02 642 2696, *rameehotels.com*
Royal Regency Hotel Apartments Nr Ahlia Hospital, Shk Hamdan Bin Mohammed St, Markaziya East, 02 626 6566, *royalregencyuae.com*
Sahara Hotel Apartments Shk Zayed Second St, Tourist Club Area, 02 631 9000
Staybridge Suites Abu Dhabi Yas Island Yas Island Golf Plaza , Yas Island West, 02 656 3333, *ichotelsgroup.com*
Vision Hotel Apartments Old Mazda Rd, Tourist Club Area, 02 699 2666, *visionhotel.net*
Vision Links Muroor Rd, Al Nahyan, 02 699 2666, *visionhotels.com*

Owning A Property

Since 2005, foreigners have been allowed to purchase freehold property in certain areas of Abu Dhabi. With new developments in Saadiyat, Yas, Al Reef and Reem Island coming to the market, there is an increasing amount of choice. Property prices soared for a few years and, while everything came crashing down in neighbouring Dubai, a shortage of supply coupled with consistent demand insulated Abu Dhabi from the worst. Prices have levelled out and, although they remain high, buying a house is a viable option for people planning on staying in Abu Dhabi for the long term. For more information on the procedures involved in buying a property, see p.75.

Standard Apartments

Abu Dhabi apartments come in various sizes, from studio to four-bedroom, with widely varying rents (and conditions) to match. Newer apartments usually have centralised air conditioning (C A/C) and older ones have noisier air conditioning units built into the wall. C A/C is normally more expensive, although in some apartment buildings, your air-conditioning costs are included in the rent. Many of the newest developments utilise district cooling, a system in which all of the buildings within an area receive cold water from a central cooling plant. Residents living in apartments with district cooling will need to sign an agreement with the local cooling company and pay that company monthly. The cost of chilled water can also creep up during the hotter months.

Top-of-the-range apartments often come semi-furnished (with a cooker, fridge and washing machine), and have 24 hour security, covered parking, a private gym and a swimming pool.

One downside to apartment living is that you'll have to do with less privacy than in a villa and will be at the mercy of your neighbours to a certain extent. Also, depending on the area, parking may be a problem too: some apartments do not have dedicated parking and others might come with just one dedicated space – check ahead.

Villas

The villa lifestyle is attractive, but it doesn't come cheap, and smart villas are snapped up pretty quickly. The good news is that, if you look hard enough and use the grapevine, you might find the

perfect villa that won't break the budget. Depending on the location, size and age of the property, a villa may be cheaper than some apartments, but be aware that air-conditioning costs will be higher. Villas differ greatly in quality and facilities. Independent ones often have bigger gardens, while compound villas are usually newer and may have shared facilities like a pool or gym.

No Place To Park?

Many apartments charge an additional rental fee for covered or underground parking. In some areas, this is essential, as finding parking outside your apartment can be nearly impossible, particularly if you live in the city centre although the Mawaqif paid parking programme is slowly easing this problem.

Villa Sharing

Sharing a large villa is a popular option with young professionals for economic and lifestyle reasons. The downside is the lack of privacy and the chore of finding new housemates when someone moves out. If you're looking to share an abode, dubizzle.com is the best place to start. See p.72 for information on the legality of accommodation sharing.

Corniche high-rises

RENTING A HOME

Employers are legally obliged to provide accommodation or an accommodation allowance, although no guidelines are given as to how much this should be. Some large organisations, like ADNOC, have their own compounds or residential complexes. Other companies have arrangements with particular apartment buildings or compounds and reserve a percentage of the properties for their employees. Your contract may offer you the option of choosing company facilities, or taking a cash amount. Accepting company facilities will save you a great deal of time, effort, and stress in finding a place to live, and it will probably be well-maintained. Some expats use the company facilities for the first year, until they are settled, and then look for something they are happier with.

In general, the rent for most property is paid annually, in advance. Some landlords may accept payment in more than one cheque, meaning that you provide them with an agreed number of post-dated cheques that will be cashed on their due date. Some employers will arrange to pay your rent payments directly from your salary, which can save a lot of hassle.

Rents in Abu Dhabi have been astronomically high in the last few years with supply vastly outstripping demand. The good news is that, the situation is getting much better for tenants as more housing stock is being released onto the market, increasing rental options and decreasing rents.

Finding A Rental Home

There are a number of ways to find suitable accommodation, the most obvious of which is via a real estate agent (see p.75). The advantage of an agent is that he or she will do the work for you. The downside, of course, is that agents charge a fee, usually 5% of the yearly rent or Dhs.5,000, whichever is higher. Agents will be able to show you several properties, but if that agent also represents the landlord, they might not have your best interests in mind. If you have the time, it is worth checking classified ads in local newspapers, although this works better when trying to find shared accommodation. Dubizzle (dubizzle.com) is another good option when looking for a place to call home (see p.74).

Sometimes an even better bet is to drive around a few areas and look out for 'To Let' signs displayed on vacant villas; these will display the phone number of either the landlord or the letting agent.

If you find a particularly attractive apartment building, try asking the security guard on duty if there are any vacant properties. Often this extra effort when looking for a home can result in a 'real find' and many proud barbecues to come. It also helps to ask colleagues and friends to keep an eye out for vacancies in shared villas.

Sharing

Sharing an apartment is an easy way to save money, but renters should be aware that groups of people living together in certain areas (for example, near schools and in areas deemed for families only) is frowned upon, and may even be illegal. The number of apartment and room sharing adverts pasted all over town implies that authorities have accepted it as a necessary part of growth and development, but the legality of sharing remains hazy.

While the law clearly stipulates that it is illegal for unmarried men and women to live together, it's doubtful that the Abu Dhabi authorities would come knocking on doors to check the marital status of tenants, as they did in Sharjah in 2010.

It is generally understood that limited numbers of unrelated singles of the same sex are allowed to share, as long as it's not in a neighbourhood specifically designated for families and the home is not overcrowded. Sharing should be approached with caution, as the local laws are subject to change at any time. Especially if the rules regarding visa

HOUSING ABBREVIATIONS

When looking for property to rent in newspaper classifieds or online, there's a whole new language to learn. Here's our guide to some of the most common abbreviations:

BR	Bedroom
C A/C	Centralised air conditioning (sometimes included in the rent)
C/port	Car port (usual in compounds)
D/S	Double-storey villa
Eff	Efficiency
Ensuite	Bedroom has private bathroom
Ext S/Q	Servants' quarters located outside the villa
Fully fitted	Includes appliances (oven, kitchen, refrigerator, washing machine)
Hall flat	Apartment has an entrance hall
HWS	Hot water system
L/D	Living/dining room area
M/a	Mature age (either you or the building)
Ns/prof	Non-smoking professional
OSP	Off-street parking
PWK	Per week
S/S	Single-storey villa
Shared pool	Pool is communal for all villas on compound
Spac	Spacious
W A/C	Window air conditioning (often indicates an older building)
W/robes	Built-in wardrobes (closets)

reapplications which were floated briefly in summer 2012 (before being quickly shelved) ever do see the light of day, as these would make it very difficult for anyone subletting a room to renew their residency visa (see p.39).

Dubizzle

Dubizzle (dubizzle.com) is a good starting point for house hunting. The site features listings by various real estate agents and private individuals alike and whether you're looking to buy or rent, browsing the ads will quickly give you an idea as to the current market prices. You can also find rooms being sublet and second hand furniture at bargain prices here.

The Lease

In order to process the lease for a rental, the estate agent will need a copy of your passport and visa, and a rent cheque or cheques. To rent through your company, you will need a copy of the company's trade licence, a photocopy of the passport of whoever is signing the rent cheque, and the cheque itself.

In addition to the financial terms, your lease will state what you are liable for in terms of maintenance and what your landlord's responsibilities are. Given that expenses such as water and electricity can quickly add up, it is important that you read the contract and discuss any points of contention before you sign on the dotted line.

You should check for the following:
- **Rent payment** – do you have to pay a whole year upfront or in regular instalments? If you can afford to provide fewer cheques, you can use that as a bargaining chip to lower the rent.
- **Maintenance** – who is responsible for day to day maintenance and repairs? Some rents may be fully inclusive of all maintenance and repairs, or you may be able to negotiate a cheaper rent if you carry them out yourself.
- **Water and electricity** – are these included? If not, will they be billed separately? Some apartments have a standard fee for electricity, some fees even include water and electricity. Most don't.
- **Parking** – landlords do not have to provide parking, so check first to see if there is an additional charge for underground or covered parking.
- **Security deposit** – is one required and if so, how much (usually between Dhs.3,000 and Dhs.5,000)?
- **Home improvements** – are DIY or decorating permitted?
- **Pets** – are they permitted and are there any restrictions on type of pet? In some apartments, cats are permitted but dogs are not; there are seldom such restrictions in villas.

Other Rental Costs

Extra costs to be considered when renting include:
- Water and electricity deposit of Dhs.1,000 paid to Abu Dhabi Distribution Company (ADDC).
- A one-off, fully refundable security deposit (usually between 2% and 5% of the annual rent, although some landlords stipulate a fixed amount of around Dhs.5,000).
- Real estate commission – 5% of annual rent (one-off payment).

If you are renting a villa, don't forget that you may have to maintain a garden and pay for extra water. With the arid climate, your water bill will quickly add up – especially in the parching summer months. To avoid massive water bills at the end of every month, some people choose to get a well dug in their garden for all that necessary plant and grass watering. Expect to pay around Dhs.1,500 to Dhs.3,000 to have a well dug and a pump installed.

Early Termination Penalties

Most leases are usually fixed for one year. If you leave before the year is up, you will probably have to pay a penalty. Rent is usually paid annually, although some landlords allow you to pay in two or three instalments (with post-dated cheques). If you really want to get out of your lease, you may be able to sublet it to new tenants, but this can only be done with your landlord's consent.

The Rent Committee

The Abu Dhabi Committee for Settlement of Rent Disputes (800 2353) was created to oversee rent disagreements between landlords and tenants. The committee also oversees rental prices and, where necessary, can impose increase caps. Any tenant that has a dispute regarding rent increases, eviction and breaches of contract, can take their case to the committee; in many cases, the committee rules in favour of the tenant.

If the case goes to court, the Arabic copy of your lease will be the version referred to, so make sure you get it translated before you sign your lease agreement, in case there are any hidden extras. In turn, landlords should register their properties and all rental contracts through the Tawtheeq programme that protects tenants but also protects landlords from brokers and agents. Tenants should demand a registered contract from their broker or landlord. Full details about settling rental disputes are available on the Abu Dhabi Government's website abudhabi.ae (under 'Land Transactions') or you can call the committee directly.

Alternatively, if your property is managed by Abu Dhabi Commercial Properties (adcp.ae) – and a surprisingly high percentage are – you can lodge a complaint with them.

Real Estate Agents

Al Jar Properties Nr National Bank of Abu Dhabi, ICAD 1, Mussafah, 800 25527

Asteco Property Management SJ Tower, Shk Rashid Bin Al Maktoum Rd, Al Karamah, 02 626 0068, *asteco.com*

Aztec Properties Various locations, 02 645 1672, *aztecproperties.ae*

Better Homes Various locations, 02 600 522 212, *bhomes.com*

Cassells Real Estate Corniche Towers, Al Khalidiyah, 02 681 7666, *cassellsrealestate.org*

Cluttons EMC Bldg, Shk Rashid Bin Al Maktoum Rd, Al Madina Al Riyadiya, 02 441 1225, *abudhabi.cluttons.com*

Finders & Keepers > *p.IBC* Al Batin Business Centre, Bainunah St, Al Bateen, 02 406 9428, *findersnkeepers.com*

Future View Real Estate Various locations, 02 627 2992

Hayatt Real Estate Al Nahyan, 02 4918 790 , *hayattrealestate.com*

Homestyle Property > *p.73* Nr Sheraton Hotel, Al Salam St, Tourist Club Area, 02 672 3220, *homestyle-property.co.ae*

LLJ Property Al Jazira Club, 02 495 0500, *lljproperty.com*

Sherwoods Gibca Tower, Nr Al Noor Hospital, Shk Khalifa St , Markaziya East, 02 626 6887, *sherwoodsproperty.com*

Silver Lake Property Management Seven Star Rent A Car Bldg, Off Hamdan Bin Mohammed St, Markaziya East, 02 676 2465, *silverlakeuae.com*

BUYING A HOME

Buying property in Abu Dhabi can be a little confusing at first. This is predominantly because owning a property in Abu Dhabi is a relatively new concept for non-GCC expatriates and, therefore, real estate laws are new and constantly changing. It was only in 2005 that Sheikh Khalifa passed the law that enables expatriates to buy property within designated investment areas of the city. Non-GCC nationals are not permitted to own land, but they can purchase properties on developed land on a 99 year leasehold basis (known as an Usufruct lease). Expats can also lease and build on undeveloped

land on a 50 year development lease (known as a Musatahah lease), but it is very uncommon for individual expatriates to do as so few undeveloped land plots are ever released for private ownership/leasing.

Abu Dhabi's Urban Planning Council (upc.gov.ae) has identified the following areas in which expats can currently invest in property: Sowwah Island, Reem Island, Raha Beach, Lulu Island, Al Reef, Yas Island, Saih as Sidirah, Saadiyat Island, Hydra Village and Masdar.

However, within these areas, most of the properties for sale are part of ongoing projects like Shams Abu Dhabi and Marina Square (both on Reem Island), Al Bandar (Raha Beach) and Al Reef Villas. Indeed, Al Reef was the first of these developments to be inhabited with most stages completed by the end of 2011.

Residential Developments

Until recently, due to only a handful of developments open to foreign purchases reaching completion, the main buying option for non-GCC expats has been off-plan bought directly from the developer. Abu Dhabi is undergoing massive growth and the main developers are taking a key role in the emirate's transformation. However, with more and more developments coming online, that situation may be about to change with completed villas and apartments being made available to expats too. Although the financial crisis slowed progress on some major developments, it hasn't caused problems to the same extent that it has in Dubai, and 2012 and 2013 will see a number of large-scale projects reach completion, such as on Reem Island, Al Maryah Island and Raha Beach. Abu Dhabi's developers are generally extremely reputable, but the level of finish and facilities management capability will vary from development to development. When considering buying, it is essential to research the development company thoroughly before jumping in and making a binding commitment.

The major developers in Abu Dhabi are:

Aldar Properties (aldar.com). Projects include Yas Island, Al Raha Beach, World Trade Center, the iconic HQ building, Al Gurm Resort and Al Raha Gardens.

Tourism Development & Investment Company (TDIC) (tdic.ae). Responsible for many of Saadiyat Island's cultural, residential, commercial and tourism projects; developer of Sir Bani Yas and Dalma islands, plus a number of Abu Dhabi's hotels and resorts.

Sorouh (sorouh.com). Developer for Shams Abu Dhabi – one of the biggest developments on the capital's horizon. The company also has big plans for Lulu Island.

Mubadala Development Company > *p.115* (mubadala.ae). Owned by the Abu Dhabi government, this company is developing Al Maryah Island, which will be part of the capital's central business district, and has impressive blueprints for Arzanah and the Mina Zayed Waterfront.

Tamouh (tamouh.com). Marine Square on Reem Island is a huge project; Tamouh is also involved with Danet Gateway and Meena Plaza.

Manazel Real Estate (manazel-re.com). Manazel's Al Reef Villas are nearly fully occupied, and its first properties in Mussafah are due to reach completion in phases through to 2016.

Islamic Mortgages

Shariah-compliant or Islamic mortgages are alternative financing options that are available to non-Muslims. The term 'home finance' is used as opposed to mortgages. Complying with Islamic beliefs, the bank purchases the asset on behalf of the buyer who then effectively leases it back from the institution at a marked-up price, but with zero interest. The bank owns the title deeds of the purchased property until the full amount is repaid.

Legal Issues

By law, there may be no requirement to have a solicitor act for you when buying property in Abu Dhabi, but doing so provides extra peace of mind. Inheritance laws should be considered before buying in Abu Dhabi and it is strongly advised that you have a local will in place (see Inheritance Law, p.122).

Lending A Hand

A mortgage consultancy or broker will conduct all the legwork for you. Upon assessing your circumstances, choice of property and financial eligibility, they will gain pre-approval on your behalf, cutting out the middlemen banks and all the running around that goes with dealing with them, essentially holding your hand until the keys are handed over. Your fee to the mortgage broker is either a percentage of the purchase price (approximately 0.5%) or a set price agreed at the outset.

House Hunting

Despite the recent slowdown, real estate is still big business in Abu Dhabi, so it's no surprise that the capital is crawling with agents. And because there are, on the whole, only a few developments offering properties to expatriate buyers, an agent can be indispensable when finding your dream home. The list of real estate agents on p.75 is a good starting point, but often it's just a case going through the property listings in Gulf News (gnads4u.com) or on dubizzle.com to find out which properties are listed with which agent.

Real estate agents in Abu Dhabi require neither qualifications nor certifications, and your experience with a particular company may come down to the specific person that you deal with. In many cases, it can help to ask for friends' and colleagues' recommendations. If you're already in touch with a real estate lawyer concerning potential property purchases, it might be worth asking for names of trustworthy agents.

In general, expect to pay a flat fee to the agent, usually 2% – 5% of the purchase price, upon

Seaside living

completion of the sale. Always ask for full explanations of the fees and associated costs of sale. Don't feel too shy to ask if there are hidden costs.

Going It Alone

Private sales are not very common in Abu Dhabi. It is extremely rare to see properties for private sale advertised and the majority of private sales are transacted between family, friends or business associates. Of course, there's nothing to stop you looking for a private sale as a way of cutting out the middleman and saving you agency fees. When they do crop up, private sales are usually advertised via notice boards in community centres or local supermarkets, listed as classified adverts in Gulf News, or featured online at dubizzle.com or gnads4u.com.

Maintenance Fees

Maintenance fees are payable by the owner and cover the developer's cost of maintaining all the facilities and communal areas. Fees are typically paid annually, although some developers are now accepting quarterly payments.

Potential purchasers should factor in maintenance fees when deciding where to buy. Not only do fees vary from developer to developer but also from one development to the next. These fees are rarely mentioned in any of the developers' contracts and, if they are, the fine print will nearly always read 'subject to change'.

If you live in an apartment, communal facilities may include a gym, changing areas, tennis courts, playground facilities and a swimming pool. Full-time security and cleaning personnel will also be employed to service communal areas. In a villa, communal responsibility will extend to security personnel manning the way to gated communities and all communal landscaping. Both will include rubbish collection, and villa communities may also enjoy pools and tennis courts.

Mortgages

The UAE mortgage industry is still in its relative infancy compared to other countries. The country is home to many of the world's international finance houses, as well as local banks and lenders, but although familiar names such as HSBC, Barclays, Standard Chartered and Citibank sit alongside local entities, sophisticated borrowing structures are difficult to secure and can take longer to complete than in other parts of the world. The financial crisis that began in late 2008 also saw a lot of banks in the region suspend or severely curtail their mortgage lending activities. Some banks began to lend again in 2009, but on a much more cautious basis than in the gung-ho pre-recession days. You may find a local mortgage now but you certainly shouldn't rely on doing so.

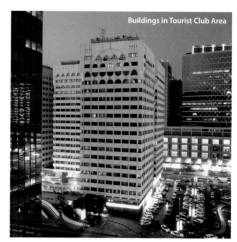

Buildings in Tourist Club Area

When considering buying property, you should be aware that many banks and lenders only provide mortgages for select developments, which vary from institution to institution. Additionally, each bank and lender has different acceptance criteria and mortgage processes, which change frequently.

Interest rates vary massively from approximately 6.5% up to 9.5%, which is significantly higher than in some parts of the world, and many lenders will insist on life insurance being taken on the loan amount. This is often a stumbling block if overlooked and not addressed before the transfer date. In addition, many lenders will only finance up to a maximum of 85% – and often less – of the property price (100% finance mortgages do not currently exist in the UAE and are unlikely to appear anytime soon). The amount financed by the lender also varies and depends on whether the property is a villa or an apartment, where they are and who built them.

Equity release and mortgage transfers have recently been introduced to the market, offering investors the opportunity to release equity and secure better rates. To combat price sensitive customers moving their loans, most banks have introduced exit fees but there are still completely flexible mortgages available. New innovations also include international mortgages, which offer loans in currency denominations other than dirhams. This offers clients the ability to structure their loan in a preferred currency, with the ability to switch.

Mortgage Application

It is possible for prospective buyers to seek a mortgage pre-approval, which can give the buyer confidence when entering the market. For a mortgage application, you need your passport plus copies, six months of bank statements, salary confirmation from your employer and six months of salary slips.

Buyer's Confidence

The property market may not be the get-rich-quick scheme it once was, but there are still plenty of reasons to own a home in the UAE. If you decide to take the plunge and snap up a home in the Emirates, just how do you go about it?

Location, Location, Location

The first step is choosing your location which, while always a major factor, becomes even more significant in the UAE. Which emirate do you want to buy in? This may sound a little broad and ridiculous but it's not as ludicrous a consideration as you may think. Dubai and Abu Dhabi are, for obvious reasons, the most popular options but Ajman is marketing itself as a Dubai commuter destination, with properties far cheaper than you'll find in the larger emirates. Due to high prices and limited availability in Abu Dhabi, many working in the capital have chosen to set up home in Dubai, with a property in Dubai Marina just an hour's drive from Abu Dhabi.

The question of freehold or leasehold depends hugely upon your location. 'Freehold gives non-GCC nationals the opportunity to own entirely, while leasehold offers a lease on the property which would usually run from a period between 30 and 99 years. Leasehold means that the land or the property is never entirely owned

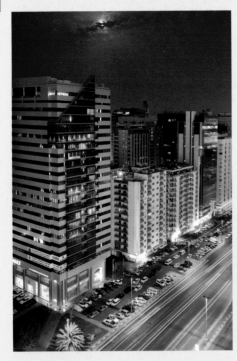

by the client in full,' explains Landmark Properties director of sales and leasing, Michael Michael.

Traditionally, non-GCC nationals could only buy on a leasehold basis but, since 2002, Dubai has introduced freehold property rights within designated zones. Now, the majority of purpose-built, community style developments in Dubai boast freehold units, with many in Abu Dhabi now following suit – especially the bigger off-island developments that are coming online over the next year or so.

That dealt with, buyers should consider the usual property purchasing factors and bear in mind that, unless your budget knows no bounds, willingness to compromise is a must. Think about your circumstances and lifestyle. How long will it take to get to work, do you have a young family that requires nearby schools and play areas, or is access to public transport a factor? Just as important is to have a firm top figure in mind and to not exceed it; if you see somewhere that will need some work, how much will that cost and do property and renovations come in on budget?

Another major consideration in this part of the world is whether you want to buy a pre-owned property, a brand new property, or even an off-plan property. 'Off-plan is a non-ready property that was a popular option for investors and end-users in the UAE during the pre-crash upswing, as it offered spread payment plans and affordable prices giving buyers an opportunity to get on the property ladder,' continues Michael.

The off-plan option still has certain advantages, but Michael adds that buying habits are changing. 'We are now noticing that clients are demanding completed to near-completed properties in freehold areas as they want to see the finished product before purchasing, to make sure the specifications are to their liking.

'Knowing they can move into their properties or rent them almost immediately is a massive draw, while buying in a freehold area also gives peace of mind for easier re-sale opportunities in the future.'

Securing Finance

Securing finance is one of the most worrying aspects of buying a property in the UAE as the process differs a little from those in most people's home countries. 'Rates are variable and, unfortunately, there aren't any fixed rate options like you find in Europe or the US,' explains Tamweel senior financial consultant, Dean Biddulph. 'Also, banks here have far fewer mortgage products on offer compared to many other locations around the world.'

The reality is that buyers have the choice between a refinance or equity-release mortgage for completed properties, or a new mortgage product for a complete or under-construction property. If buying directly from the developer, they'll often have a partner on board who can offer favourable rates and terms.

'Mortgages are available for both freehold and leasehold properties,' continues Biddulph, 'with up to 85% finance available on completed units and between 75% and 80% on properties still under construction. Interest rates typically range from 6.5% to 8.5% depending on the finance type, lender, project and your down payment, and the maximum loan tenor is up to 25 years.'

Before You Sign

Property found, offer accepted, mortgage secured… in most countries, that would be the end of the story, but there's a whole other area that you should consider before signing on the dotted line. As your dream pad is almost certain to be in a larger development or community, even if you have bought a freehold property, you can't do just anything you like with it, and there will still be several costs that need paying.

Service charges can differ greatly from one property to another, warns Place Strata Management's Jim O'Hare. 'That can affect re-sale chances and property values if there's little or no reserve cash in the sinking fund, or if service charges are considered too high.'

Dubai is leading the way in real estate regulation, such as Strata Law that governs responsibilities over common facilities among other things. The other emirates, Abu Dhabi and Ajman in particular, are already hatching plans to follow suit with similar systems to the Dubai model.

As a final point, there is no requirement to have a solicitor act on your behalf to buy a property in the UAE, although – for peace of mind, at least – you may wish to run any contracts past a real estate legal specialist.

There are certain issues not directly related to the buying process but important nonetheless – inheritance, for example – that can be legal minefields in the UAE and differ according to a whole range of factors.

So while the property buying process in the UAE differs from other places in the world and warrants careful planning and the consideration of several key elements, all involved in the industry are now subject to much more stringent rules regarding transparency, thanks in part to the economic downturn.

Buying A Home

A mortgage 'approval in principle' should only take up to four working days to come through upon submitting the correct paperwork. Generally, employed applicants can borrow a higher percentage of income than self-employed. Most lenders offer mortgages of up to 50% of disposable monthly income, based on the applicant's debt burden ratio – your realistic ability to service the monthly payments from your income, minus your other financial commitments. The larger the deposit placed, the better your terms are likely to be. Mortgage terms are usually for 25 years. Age restrictions are in place and vary, but lenders will normally finance individuals up to 65 years of age.

The next step is for the lender to provide an unconditional approval on the basis that any conditions noted in the pre-approval are satisfied. This is to assure you that no further requirements need to be fulfilled in order for you to get your mortgage. Finally, you can start house hunting. Once you've found your dream home, the lender will issue an offer letter, followed by the mortgage documentation, which states the terms and conditions of the mortgage. Once the paperwork is signed and sent back to the lender, the settlement process can begin. This is when the lender transfers the mortgage payment to either the seller or to the existing lender who has the first charge over the property. This usually occurs on the day of transfer or as per the conditions of the lender. Then it's time to collect your keys and call the removal van.

Other Purchase Costs

In addition to the purchase cost and deposit required, the charges incurred by the property purchaser securing a home with a mortgage are as follows:
- Real estate agents/brokers fee: 2% – 5% of the purchase price.
- Mortgage arranged via bank or lender: 1% to 1.25% mortgage processing fee based on value of loan.
- Land registry (see below): 1% of the purchase price.

Valuation

Your mortgage lender will arrange a valuation of your chosen property via an independent source. This is in order to determine the market worth against the selling price and the lenders loan to you. The cost to the buyer is between Dhs.2,500 and Dhs.3,000. Additional obligatory costs to the mortgaged property buyer equate to approximately an extra 6% on top of the purchase price, not including any cash deposit required.

Optional Costs

You are not legally required to engage a lawyer for property transactions in the UAE, but you may wish to employ legal help to see you through the process. Legal costs vary depending on whose services you use. See p.122 for a listing of law firms. If employing the services of a mortgage consultancy or broker, the typical cost is 0.5% of the property price.

Land Registry

The government of Abu Dhabi's Department of Municipal Affairs (dma.abudhabi.ae, 02 678 5555) is the emirate's land registry and transactions agency. Upon completion of a sale, a land registry fee is due (1% of the property price). Registering the property establishes legal ownership and provides the new owner with a title deed, safeguarding against future disputes.

Selling A Home

When selling your property, your first and most important task is to find yourself a preferred agent. Some real estate agencies charge 'marketing' fees of 1% to 2% of the sale price, so be careful. For a list of popular estate agents, see p.75. You can, of course, try to market and sell your property privately to avoid real estate fees. Advertising online is an increasingly common route to finding buyers, but be prepared for plenty of calls from bargain hunters offering significantly below the asking price. There is no legal need for a property survey, assessment or solicitor, so all of these fees are negated, although if you decide to go it alone, think carefully about engaging a solicitor.

Residential towers

Khalifa City

Al Mushrif

A city centre mosque

Villa living

Residential Areas Map

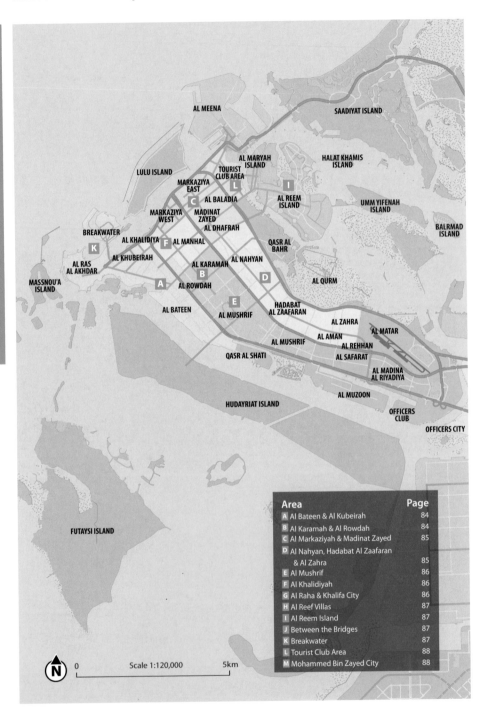

Area	Page
A Al Bateen & Al Kubeirah	84
B Al Karamah & Al Rowdah	84
C Al Markaziyah & Madinat Zayed	85
D Al Nahyan, Hadabat Al Zaafaran & Al Zahra	85
E Al Mushrif	86
F Al Khalidiyah	86
G Al Raha & Khalifa City	86
H Al Reef Villas	87
I Al Reem Island	87
J Between the Bridges	87
K Breakwater	87
L Tourist Club Area	88
M Mohammed Bin Zayed City	88

0   Scale 1:120,000   5km

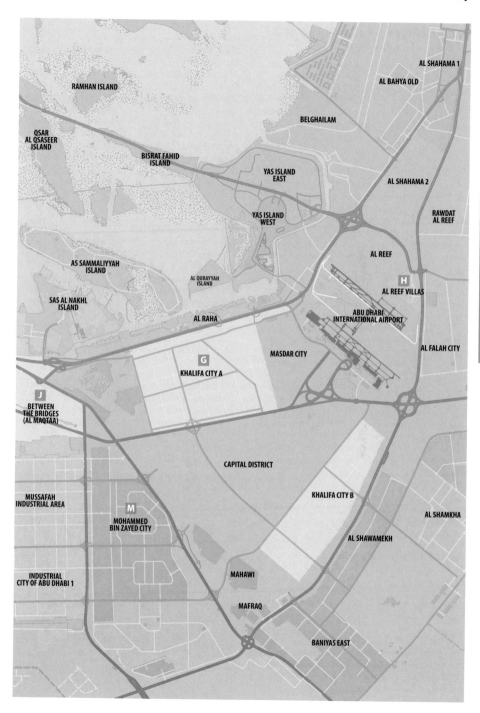

RAMHAN ISLAND

AL SHAHAMA 1

AL BAHYA OLD

BELGHAILAM

QSAR
AL QSASEER
ISLAND

BISRAT FAHID
ISLAND

YAS ISLAND
EAST

AL SHAHAMA 2

YAS ISLAND
WEST

RAWDAT
AL REEF

AS SAMMALIYYAH
ISLAND

AL QURAYYAH
ISLAND

AL REEF

SAS AL NAKHL
ISLAND

AL REEF VILLAS

AL RAHA

ABU DHABI
INTERNATIONAL AIRPORT

AL FALAH CITY

MASDAR CITY

KHALIFA CITY A

BETWEEN
THE BRIDGES
(AL MAQTAA)

CAPITAL DISTRICT

MUSSAFAH
INDUSTRIAL AREA

KHALIFA CITY B

MOHAMMED
BIN ZAYED CITY

AL SHAMKHA

AL SHAWAMEKH

INDUSTRIAL
CITY OF ABU DHABI 1

MAHAWI

MAFRAQ

BANIYAS EAST

RESIDENTIAL AREAS

Al Bateen & Al Kubeirah

A large and highly sought-after area of the island, occupied mostly by UAE nationals, complete with palaces, walled properties, decorative fountains and beautiful streetscaping. It's a quiet area, popular with families, and the tone is set by Baynunah Street, which runs from Al Bateen to the Corniche and is easily one of the most picturesque and well-kept roads in Abu Dhabi.

Accommodation

Even with a drop in rental prices throughout the city, rents remain expensive here. Expect to pay anything from Dhs.75,000 per year for the smallest of flats, to Dhs.400,000 and above for multi-bedroom villas. Most of the housing takes the form of villas, but there are some larger flats available in Al Kubeirah, which tend to get snapped up very quickly thanks to their relative affordability.

Shopping & Leisure

Residents of the northern third of the area can easily enjoy the Corniche and all that goes with that area – running, cycling, hanging out at the beach and the beachside cafes. For shopping, Al Bateen Mall (02 666 1222) provides the basics but, if you're looking for more substantial shopping, there's a branch of Spinneys in Al Kubeirah and Marina Mall (p.345) is a short drive away in Breakwater. The InterContinental (p.203) and Hilton Al Kubeirah offer a wide array of licensed establishments and the Marina Al Bateen Resort (p.194), with its restaurant and Waves Lounge Bar (02 665 0144), provides other options. For the big spenders, Emirates Palace (p.201) and Jumeirah at Etihad Towers are both close by and guarantee treatment fit for a sheikh.

Healthcare & Education

Healthcare facilities in the area are good, with both the popular Gulf Diagnostic Center Hospital (p.164) on Khaleej Al Arabi Street, and the Swedish Medical Centre (p.159) firmly entrenched. For teeth problems, the Advanced American Dental Clinic (p.171) on 13th Street and the Modern German Dental Centre on Baynunah Street have the area covered. The American Community School of Abu Dhabi (p.144) and the Al Bateen Science School, a private Arabic school, are both in the area.

Al Karamah & Al Rowdah

There's not very much to differentiate between these two areas, both of which have quiet, unassuming streets lined by date palms and leafy trees. These areas do offer a suburban lifestyle and are quite popular with western expats.

Accommodation

Housing options are mainly in the form of large, single-family villas and low-rise apartments, including two well-established compounds in Al Karamah, which are predominantly occupied by expat families. The closer you get to downtown, the easier it is to find relatively inexpensive flats – some even dipping under Dhs.100,000. That said, prices tend to fluctuate a lot, and villas can go for anywhere between Dhs.250,000 and Dhs.350,000 for three and four bedroom properties, and between Dhs.400,000 to Dhs.550,000 for seven, eight and nine bedroom places. The area's size and the age of different dwellings makes for large variations in prices, so it's worth viewing properties in different areas and price ranges to get an idea of what works best to your budget.

Shopping & Leisure

Al Wahda Mall (p.343) is the prime shopping spot with a Lulu hypermarket (p.337) and an extensive selection of name brand stores. There is also an Abu Dhabi Co-op (p.336) on the corner of Al Nahyan Street and Al Bateen Street. As is common all over the capital, small grocery shops and tiny restaurants and cafeterias are scattered about. The Grand Millennium Al Wahda hotel (p.202) offers several dining options but other than that, there's not a whole lot to do in the area – which is a draw in itself for many.

Healthcare & Education

The best bet for healthcare is Sheikh Khalifa Medical City (p.166) just off 11th Street, which incorporates the old Central Hospital, but Gulf Diagnostic Center Hospital (p.164) is relatively close by over in Al Bateen. As for education, the Sheikh Zayed Private Academy (02 446 9777, szpag.com) is an exclusive and prestigious girls' school offering an international

Villa living

curriculum. Abu Dhabi International Private School in Al Karamah (p.144) is an International Baccalaureate school, and closer still are Abu Dhabi Women's College (adwc.hct.ac.ae) and the relatively new Pearl Primary School (p.146).

Al Markaziyah & Madinat Zayed

The area boxed in by the Corniche, Al Salam Street, Al Falah Street and Old Airport Road is regarded as Abu Dhabi's downtown. This is the place for those looking to live in the heart of the city; virtually everything the capital has to offer can be found here, except possibly a parking spot. The traffic is generally terrible and the slow changing traffic lights can mean that even short journeys seem to take forever. The major roadworks that dominated Al Salam Street for years seem to have been completed, but the ongoing construction of the nearby Tourist Club Area can often affect this part of town.

Accommodation

Demand and location mean that this is some of the most expensive real estate around. However, the financial crisis, coupled with substantially increased supply, has brought the rents down significantly. One and two bedroom places are available for under Dhs.150,000, while the closer an apartment is to the Corniche, the higher the price. A three bedroom penthouse with a sea view goes for a solid Dhs.300,000.

Shopping & Leisure

With hotels like Le Royal Meridien (p.203) overlooking the Corniche, and the Crowne Plaza (p.201) on Hamdan Street, there's no shortage of licensed restaurants and bars in the area, and the array of small, independent restaurants offer almost everything else a person could hope for. There's a cinema in Al Mariah Mall (p.346) and, close by, the National (02 671 1700) and El Dorado (02 676 3555) cinemas specialise in Bollywood and other Indian flicks. In addition, there's a Lulu Centre on Al Salam Street, plus the Liwa (p.348) and Hamdan Centre (p.347) both on Hamdan Street. The Madinat Zayed Shopping Centre and Gold Centre (p.348) is a somewhat eclectic affair with stores selling everything from high-priced gold jewellery and kitschy desert-themed souvenirs to bedroom suites and home accessories.

Healthcare & Education

The area's high concentration of medical facilities offers plenty of choice to residents. The New Medical Centre Specialty Hospital (p.165) is just off Airport Rd and 7th Street, while Lifeline Hospital (p.165) is at the corner of 4th and 7th streets. The Dar Al Shifa Hospital (p.161) is on 11th Street, and Al Noor Hospital (p.161) is between Hamdan and 3rd streets, close to 4th

Street. Also nearby, at the Corniche end of 4th Street, is the Hospital Franco-Emirien (p.164). Schools are a little less profuse, but there are a couple of options nearby. Al Muna Primary School (p.144), which follows the British curriculum, is between Hamdan and 7th streets and is located behind the Liwa Center.

Al Nahyan, Hanabat Al Zaafaran & Al Zahra

Sandwiched between Muroor Road and the Eastern Ring Road, this area runs all the way from 11th Street down to Al Bateen Airport. Encompassing primarily low-rise residential and single-family housing in old villas, with new villa compounds such as Al Maqtaa village, the area has a decent mix of expats and locals and, in many parts, there's a nice community feel. The freshly revamped Eastern Ring Road now provides easy access.

Accommodation

As one might imagine, rental prices vary quite a bit over such a large area. Many of the villas are old or rundown, so there are some bargains available; however, if you want a nicely maintained two-bedroom flat, expect to pay Dhs.100,000 to Dhs.150,000, and for villas with three bedrooms and up, Dhs.200,000 marks the low end. Expect to pay more with reputable agents and in closer proximity to downtown. The best deals are to be found in Al Zahra, closest to Al Bateen Airport.

Shopping & Leisure

The northern end of Al Nahyan is close to Al Wahda Mall (p.343), and there are a couple of grocery stores dotted around the area; the nearby Carrefour (p.336) on Airport Road offers relief for those in Muroor. The Eastern Corniche (p.198) runs along the Eastern Ring Road and is a great place to jog, cycle and picnic, while the eastern mangroves are perfect for canoeing and kayaking. Sheikh Khalifa Park, south of Al Bateen Airport, is a large patch of greenery, complete with playground equipment. As far as restaurants go, there are endless options within easy reach by heading north to downtown or south to the Park Rotana (p.204) and the hotels and cafes around Souk Qaryat Al Beri (p.359).

Healthcare & Education

The Middle East Specialised Medical Centre (p.168) is in Hadabat Al Zaafaran and provides general medical and dental services. Heading north to 11th Street takes you to the Dar Al Shifa Hospital (p.161) and the Sheikh Khalifa Medical City (p.166). In terms of schools, American International School (p.144) and the Lycée Louis Massignon (02 444 8085) are both on 29th Street, just beyond Al Zahra. Abu Dhabi Indian School (adisuae.com) is in the centre of Hadabat Al Zaafaran.

Residential Areas

Al Mushrif

A sleepy area in the very centre of the island, Al Mushrif consists mainly of villas, which range from the palatial to the abandoned. It's close to the Churches Area, home to various Christian congregations, which goes some way to explaining why it's popular with many expats. There are definitely deals to be had, with two bedrooms starting at about Dhs.110,000 and three-bedroom villas starting at Dhs.150,000. Bigger places start from around Dhs.350,000 and go up significantly higher for the largest villas with seven bedrooms or more. Except for in the small shops along Airport Road, there's not a whole lot of shopping to be done in the area, but Abu Dhabi Equestrian Club (p.288) and the Abu Dhabi Country Club (p.178, 182) offer some leisure reprieve. As for education, the British School – Al Khubairat (p.145) in the Church Area is one of the most popular schools for expats in the city.

Al Khalidiyah

Definitely one of the most popular and upscale areas of the city, and in high demand for its proximity to the Corniche, Khalidiyah Garden and plentiful shopping opportunities. With such leisure destinations in easy reach, it's a very pedestrian friendly area. It's an attractive area for expats but there's a good mix of residents with lots of Arab expats and locals too. There's always plenty to do, but in a quiet, refined sort of way.

Accommodation

There are lots of options to choose from here, from luxury apartments overlooking the water, to inland compound villas. You might be able to find a bargain studio for under Dhs.60,000, but more common are two and three bedroom apartments that go for rents ranging from just under Dhs.150,000 to Dhs.200,000. Khalidiyah Village is a compound of about 150 villas and apartments; a three bedroom apartment here will set you back Dhs.180,000, while a six bedroom villa goes for up to Dhs.400,000. The area's popularity means that everything tends to get snapped up quickly.

Shopping & Leisure

Abela (p.336) and Choithram (p.337) are the main supermarkets in the area, both with hefty stocks of western brands. There's a Lulu (p.337) hypermarket in the Khalidiyah Mall (p.344), in addition to dozens of big name stores and a Cine Royal cinema (p.356). There's also the Khalidiya Centre that has a branch

of Paris Gallery and a handful of smaller stores. As far as entertainment goes, there are a number of restaurants in the Sheraton Khalidiya (p.206), as well as plenty of options just minutes away in Al Khubeira or, in the other direction, Madinat Zayed. For the active Abu Dhabian, there are cycling and jogging tracks along the Corniche, and volleyball nets on the public beaches.

Healthcare & Education

The Khalidiyah Urgent Care Centre (p.164) is located next to Khalidiyah Mall on 26th Street but, for more extensive services, head to Sheikh Khalifa Medical City (p.166). The Gulf Diagnostic Center Hospital (p.164) is not far away in Al Bateen. With very few schools in this area, the closest options, like the American Community School (p.144), are in Al Bateen as well.

Al Raha & Khalifa City

These areas are either for those who want the quiet life, those who are planning on putting down long-term roots or, increasingly, those who are drawn by the more affordable housing costs. Non-GCC expats are eligible to buy property in Al Raha, which is a long beachfront development with big plans. The Khalifa Cities (A and B) are inland with less going on, but more facilities are being opened including the new Raha Gardens retail village with cafes, a salon, pharmacy, money exchange and pet shop. The recent opening of the Al Forsan leisure complex is an additional draw for many.

Accommodation

Al Raha is one of the few places in Abu Dhabi where villas and apartments are for sale to non-GCC residents. However, the units get snapped up quickly. Two bedroom apartments go for Dhs.1.5 million and above, while four bedroom villas typically go for between Dhs.3 million and Dhs.4 million. Three bedroom townhouses start at around Dhs.190,000. Khalifa A is more affordable, with a four bedroom villa going for around Dhs.170,000. Khalifa B, meanwhile, offers some of the city's cheapest accommodation, with two and three bedroom apartments going for between Dhs.70,000 and Dhs.125,000.

Shopping & Leisure

Beyond the dining and shopping options at Al Raha Mall (p.346), there's an Abela and a good-sized Spinneys supermarket open in the area; Etihad Plaza also has a couple of cafes that can be popular with

Living In Khalifa City Rosana Salamey, Khalifa City resident of one year

Khalifa City is a great place to live for those looking to escape the crowded city life. Although the area is still partially under construction, the daily necessities are easily available at any of the nearby markets. Moreover, it's only a 10 minute drive away from Yas Island and Al Raha Beach, so there's always something to do if you're looking for a night out.

lunching office workers, but otherwise there's not too much going on here. Al Raha Beach Hotel and the 'between the bridges' hotels (the Shangri-La Qaryat Al Beri, Traders Hotel and the Fairmont Bab Al Bahr) are the best bets for entertainment, while Yas Island (p.196), with its clutch of hotels and growing entertainment venues, is a short drive away. For leisure pursuits, Abu Dhabi Golf Club (p.287) is located in Madinat Khalifa A, and the recently opened Al Forsan International Sports Resort (p.218) offers members pool, gym, shooting, equestrian, cable watersports, paintball and go-karting facilities.

Healthcare & Education

There are no real medical facilities in the area yet, but there are certainly some good schools with Raha International (p.146), Al Yasmina (p.144) and the Canadian International School (p.145) adding some decent alternatives to Abu Dhabi island's offerings. GEMS American Academy school (p.146) recently moved to a state-of-the-art facility in Khalifa City A.

Al Reef Villas

Al Reef Villas is one of the areas in which expatriates can buy property on a 99 year leasehold basis. Most villas quickly sold out when they first went on sale four years ago and, for any properties that become available, expect to pay in excess of Dhs.1 million for two bedrooms (perhaps even up to Dhs.1.3 million), and Dhs.1.6 million plus for a four bedroom. Located out in the desert beyond the airport, there's not much in the way of amenities or entertainment, but options are expanding dramatically on Yas Island, and the Sheikh Khalifa Highway offers a quick and direct route to Al Meena, the Tourist Club Area and the Corniche. Al Reef Villas also offer some of the best value rentals in Abu Dhabi, with prices for three bedroom starting from around Dhs.120,000.

Al Reem Island

With Tala Tower and the Sun and Sky Towers in Shams Abu Dhabi having already welcomed their first residents, Al Reem Island and the neighbouring Al Maryah Island are open for business, even if they're far from complete. These mega-projects suffered a number of setbacks caused by the financial crisis and, in the case of Tala Tower, a fire. One-bedroom apartments are for sale to expats in Marina Square, starting from Dhs.1 million, while two-bedroom apartments in Shams Abu Dhabi cost more than Dhs.2 million. Rents for one bedroom flats start around Dhs.100,000, while two bedrooms will set you back around Dhs.150,000 a year. Other than the Paris-Sorbonne University Abu Dhabi (p.150), there are few amenities, but big promises have been made, with schools, parks, restaurants and medical centres on the way.

Between the Bridges

Besides the Shangri-La Residences, which are prohibitively expensive, the only other developments to live in are Golf Gardens, Sas Al Nakhl Village and Officers' City with its Mangrove Village and Seashore Villas compounds. You'll need a decent amount of luck in finding a place and, if any do become available, expect to pay between Dhs.220,000 to Dhs.350,000 a year for a four to six bedroom villa. Residents of the area enjoy the quiet, family-friendly atmosphere and the built-in conveniences – a branch of Spinneys (p.338), plus gyms, pools and beach access, are all within easy reach of each compound. Also, with the Shangri-La Qaryat Al Beri (p.206), the Traders' Hotel (p.207) and the Fairmont Bab Al Bahr (p.201) nearby, there are plenty of restaurants and nightspots to bring a buzz to the otherwise quiet lifestyle. As far as healthcare is concerned, the closest facilities are the Mussafah Clinic (02 552 0777) and the New National Medical Centre (p.168), both in Mussafah. Again, you'll have to travel a little distance to find schools; Raha International (p.146) and Al Yasmina (p.144) are in Al Raha, the Canadian International School (p.145) and GEMS American Academy (p.146) are in Khalifa City A, and the GEMS Cambridge High School (p.145) is located in Mussafah.

Breakwater

Marina Village is an exclusive development offering the only residential properties in the Breakwater area. The view is inspiring, but the prices, at upwards of Dhs.500,000 for a four bedroom villa, are among the city's most expensive. However, for the well-to-do, this is a nice, quiet little corner of the island that comes with gyms and private pools as part of the deal. There's the Mirage Marine (p.384) restaurant

The Busy Buzz Of The Tourist Club Area

Sorcha Grisewood Tourist Club Area resident of two years

The unattractive, noisy, congested and overcrowded heart of downtown Abu Dhabi is a good location if you enjoy being close to hotels, shops and restaurants. Abu Dhabi Mall, Le Meridien Abu Dhabi and the Beach Rotana are all in walking distance, and there are several expat haunts in the area like The Captain's Arms, Brauhaus, and Trader Vic's. I love the huge variety of cheap Indian, Filipino and Lebanese restaurants, but I hate the parking situation – if you're new, expect to spend lots of time driving around trying to find a space until you become familiar with the area.

complex in the area and Marina Mall (p.345) is right next door. Also, Emirates Palace is a quick spin (or swim) away for a night of fine dining. For both medical facilities and schools, the most convenient options are in Al Bateen (p.84).

Mohammed Bin Zayed City

Mohammed Bin Zayed City lies opposite Khalifa City B near Mussafah and is also becoming extremely popular with residents looking for a bit more space for their money. The area still has a lot of building work underway and some streets have the appearance of construction sites, but it is well serviced with the Delma and Mazyad Malls including Carrefour and LuLu supermarkets close by. Three bedroom apartments can be commonly found for under Dhs.90,000 and four bedroom villas with a private garden can be snapped up for Dhs.150,000.

Tourist Club Area

Busy, noisy, lively and hectic, the Tourist Club Area is a good place to live if you want to be close to all the action. The location in the city centre is astonishing and there's a great mix of nationalities living here, providing great initiation for those new to Abu Dhabi. With several hotels within walking distance, there's never a shortage of things to do and the Corniche is nearby too.

Accommodation

This is mainly a high-rise neighbourhood where prices range from Dhs.50,000 for a slightly questionable studio right up to around Dhs.150,000 for a three bedroom flat. The high concentration of people here and quick turnover means that you can usually find something here, even if it's not your dream home.

Shopping & Leisure

With Abu Dhabi Mall (p.341), countless supermarkets and grocery stores, a couple of liquor stores and the old Abu Dhabi Co-op (p.336), shopping options are abundant. The restaurant choices seem infinite too. From hole-in-the-wall joints to the high-end offerings of five-star hotels, there are plenty of options, taking in everything from a Dhs.10 biryani to a thick porterhouse steak and bottle of cabernet. In terms of leisure activities, there are hotel health clubs, tennis courts and gyms, plus there's a bowling alley and the Grand Abu Dhabi cinema (p.356) at Abu Dhabi Mall.

Health & Education

Al Salama Hospital (p.161) is on Hamdan Street and the city's main maternity hospital, Corniche Hospital (p.161), is next to the Sheraton Hotel (p.206). Abu Dhabi Grammar School Canada (02 644 4703) is the only school in the area.

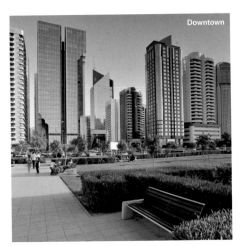

Downtown

SETTING UP HOME

Moving Services

When hiring from abroad, Abu Dhabi employers sometimes offer help (such as a shipping allowance or furniture allowance) but the city is also well served by relocation specialists. There are two options if you are looking to move your furniture and personal effects to or from Abu Dhabi: air freight and sea freight. Air freighting is fast but expensive, so it's a good option if you're only moving smaller amounts. If you have a larger consignment, sea freight will take longer (on average, six weeks from the UK to Abu Dhabi) but is comparatively cheap. If you decide to send your additional belongings by air, you can enquire with the airline you are flying with. Gulf Air (gfcargo.com) and Etihad (etihadcrystalcargo.com) have dedicated cargo handling departments and fly direct to Abu Dhabi from multiple destinations around the globe. If you have more goods than can reasonably, or affordably, be flown on the same plane as you, you will need to call in the services of a removal company. Companies with a wide international network are usually the best and safest option but, more importantly, it will mean you have a local contact in both your departure and arrival destinations. It's important to check that any removals company is not only competent in the country of origin, but that they have reliable agents in the country to which you are shipping your personal belongings, if they don't handle this part of the move themselves. Local freight specialists include Al Futtaim Logistics; see p.90 for more listings of removal firms and freight handlers. Most removal companies offer free consultations plus advice and samples of packing materials. It's worth contacting a number of companies as quotes can vary widely.

Setting Up Home

Once your belongings have arrived in Abu Dhabi and are ready for collection, you'll be notified by phone or letter. Some agencies carry out the customs clearing process for you, but with others you have to handle this part yourself.

Even if your agency handles your paperwork, you may be called to be present while the customs officers open your boxes to ensure nothing illegal or inappropriate (such as banned DVDs or books) is being brought into the country.

One Stop Shops

The larger international removals companies, such as Allied Pickfords (alliedpickfords.ae), Bishop's Move (bishopsmove.com) and Writer Relocations (writercorporation.com) can take a lot of the stress out of moving to Abu Dhabi. In addition to packing, shipping and storing your possessions (and even your car, if you're particularly attached to it), some firms can help speed up the visa process, find you rental accommodation in advance, organise travel for your pets and even find suitable schools for your children.

After this, depending on the agreement you have with the removal company, either their representative in Abu Dhabi will help you transport the boxes to your new home or you can make the arrangements locally.

You can find small removal companies advertised in the classifieds section of the newspapers. However, for a cheaper option, head for the Central Post Office in Madinat Zayed. In the car park next door, you will find a number of small trucks and drivers who will transport your goods for a fee (be sure to negotiate). You will need to pack the goods yourself. These drivers don't provide any insurance, so pack fragile items very carefully or transport them yourself.

When it's time to move on from Abu Dhabi, just carry out the process in reverse: weed out the things you no longer want or need, sell them or give them to charity, then call the removal company and have them ship everything home – don't forget the insurance. The cargo section of Omeir Travel (omeir.com) handles local freight and is a good place to start.

Relocation experts offer additional services to help you settle in quickly. Practical help ranges from finding accommodation and schools to getting your phone connected and sourcing medical care. In addition, a good relocation specialist can also put you in touch with social networks to help you get established.

Relocation & Removal Companies

Abu Dhabi Shipping Agency Salem Saif Saqer Al Mehairbi Bldg, Tourist Club Area, 02 644 9100, *adsa.ae*
Al Futtaim Logistics Mussafah, 02 555 9835, *logisticsuae.com*

Allied Pickfords Arab Tower, Shk Hamdan Bin Mohammed St, Markaziya East, 02 677 9765, *alliedpickfords.com*
Crown Relocations > *p.37* Mina Centre, Al Meena, 02 673 3076, *crownrelo.com*
Delight International Movers Nr KM Trading, Al Salam St, Markaziya East, 02 643 4733, *delightmovers.com*
Gulf Agency Abu Dhabi (GAC) Mina Zayed Free Port, 02 673 0500, *gac.com/abudhabi*
Move One Relocations Costa Coffee Bldg, Shk Rashid Bin Al Maktoum Rd, Al Karamah, 02 658 4696, *moveoneinc.com*

Furnishing Accommodation

Most properties, including rentals, are unfurnished, and don't even have basic white goods such as a cooker or fridge. Not all villas have fitted cupboards and wardrobes. However, Abu Dhabi is home to many furniture shops, ranging from Swedish simplicity at IKEA (p.324) to modern design at THE One (p.324), so you should have your new pad kitted out and feeling like home in no time. See p.323 for more information on where to buy furniture, and for white goods.

Smooth Moves

- Get more than one quote – some companies will match lower quotes to get the job.
- Make sure that all items are covered by insurance.
- Ensure you have a copy of the inventory and that each item is listed.
- Don't be shy about requesting packers to repack items if you are not satisfied.
- Take photos of the packing process to use for evidence if you need to make a claim.
- Carry customs-restricted goods (DVDs, videos or books) with you: it's easier to open a suitcase in the airport than empty a box outside in the sun.

Second-Hand Furniture

To save money, second-hand furniture is definitely an option, and Abu Dhabi has a wealth of used furniture and upholstery shops. Many of these are located in the Tanker Mai community, just off Muroor Road between 15th Street and Delma Street. In addition, it seems that on almost every corner, there's a skilled carpenter that will make furniture to order, often at very reasonable rates. With so many people constantly arriving and leaving Abu Dhabi, there is a busy trade in second-hand goods among the expat community. Check the busy listings and classifieds at dubizzle.com, websouq.com and expatwoman.com. Also check the message boards at supermarkets like Spinneys and Abela and newspaper classifieds for garage and car boot sales as many expats hold their own 'everything-must-go' sales when it's time to pack up and move on.

Furniture Leasing

If you're only planning to be in Abu Dhabi for a short time, acquiring all that furniture and all those appliances only to get rid of them in a couple of years, may not make sense in terms of hassle and cost. Furniture leasing is an alternative option. Some real estate companies, especially during the downturn, started branching out and offering newer services, so it's worth asking (see Real Estate Agents, p.75). Indigo Living (p.91) in Dubai offers short and long term leasing options across the UAE.

Curtains & Blinds

Year-round sunshine is a draw for many expats coming to Abu Dhabi, but not everyone can sleep with the sun beating through the window. Some properties have windows built to standard sizes, which means you can buy ready-made options from shops such as IKEA (p.324) or Pan Emirates (p.326). If these don't measure up though, there are several companies that will tailor and install curtains and blinds to fit your property, though usually for a higher price than pre-made ones. IKEA also has a fabric section and offers a tailoring service for basic curtains and Roman blinds at very reasonable prices. Alternatively, most tailors will be happy to run up a simple pair of curtains for you. Community notice boards and even online classifieds have adverts for second-hand blinds or curtains that were specially made to fit the strange window sizes found in many freehold developments.

Abu Dhabi Blinds 04 368 8759, *abudhabiblinds.com*
Al Hijad Furniture & Curtains Shk Hamdan Bin Mohammed St, Markaziya East, 02 678 0057
Areeca Furniture & Curtains Nr Al Diar Capital Hotel, Mina Rd, Tourist Club Area, 02 679 0010, *areeca.com*
Avenue Interiors Al Raha Mall, Al Raha, 02 556 6100, *avenueinterior.com*
Bin Husain Curtains & Decor Sanaiya 3, Mussafah, 02 555 1520, *binhusain.net*
Couture Interiors 406 Shk Zayed The First St, 800 268 8873, *couture.ae*
Gemaco Interiors Shk Rashid Bin Saeed Al Maktoom Rd, Madinat Zayed 02 633 9100, *gemacointeriors.com*
Royal Blinds Nr ADCB Bank, Shkh Zayed The First St, Markaziya East, 02 678 9877, *royalblinds.com*
Sedar Sheikh Zayed The First St, Al Manhal, 02 633 4477, *sedaremirates.com*

Interior Design

Moving into a new, empty apartment can be a hassle if you've arrived without any furnishings – but starting with a blank canvas can also be a great opportunity to create a home from scratch. Whether you need help with choosing colours for the walls, decorative art to hang on them, or the furnishings throughout, there are an increasing number of specialists just a phone

call away. The possibilities are endless and an interior designer's job is to sort out what fits you and your life best. It's a great option to help you get settled.

Areeca Furniture & Curtains
Nr Al Diar Capital Hotel, Mina Rd Tourist Club Area 02 679 0010
areeca.com
Map 2 R3
Offering high-end, bespoke soft furnishings, upholstery, furniture, plus full interior design services.

Gemaco Interiors
Gemaco Bldg, Shk Rashid Bin Saeed Al Maktoom Rd Madinat Zayed 02 633 9100
gemacointeriors.com
Map 2 L5
Specialist in modern, international furnishings with a track record for excellent customer service.

Indigo Living
Mall Of The Emirates Dubai 04 323 3370
indigo-living.com
Map 3 E2 Metro Mall of the Emirates
Along with interior design consulting, this Dubai-based store (the flagship showroom near Safa Park is excellent) offers furniture rentals.

Interiors & Fashion Consultant
Various locations 02 673 3305
style-made-easy.com
Offers complete home makeovers, looking after everything from room layout to which cutlery to buy.

Saraya Interior Design
Nr Hamdan Post Office, Shk Khalifa Bin Zayed St Markaziya East 02 674 7433
sarayaid.ae
Map 2 P3
An international firm with experience kitting out everything from homes to hotels.

Household Insurance

Though household theft is relatively uncommon in Abu Dhabi, insurance is the best way to guarantee your valuables are protected. There are a number of local and internationally recognised insurance companies operating in the UAE that offer coverage against theft, fire, natural disasters and water damage. To apply, you will need to submit a declaration estimating the value of your household contents. In the event of a claim, the provision of receipts is necessary. Good coverage will include periods while you are away, though insurers may stipulate minimum security requirements in the policy.

For a list of companies providing household insurance, see Insurance Companies, p.119.

UTILITIES & SERVICES

Electricity & Water

Electricity and water services are provided by the government and run by the Abu Dhabi Distribution Company (ADDC). The service is excellent and power cuts and water stoppages are rare. When you register, there is a deposit of Dhs.1,000. If the property has been leased through your company, they may arrange the deposits and settle the bills for you.

Water and electricity deposits, as well as monthly bills, can be paid at any ADDC outlet, online (addc.ae, 800 2332) or through various banks. Those offering this service are listed on the reverse side of the bill. ADDC charges a standard rate per unit, currently 15 fils a unit for electricity, 0.2 fils per unit for water for expatriates. Your bills will fluctuate quite significantly depending on the time of year; your electricity bill is higher in the summer when the air conditioning is on around the clock. If you have a garden, the sprinklers will also need to be on more frequently during the hotter months.

Electricity

The electricity supply in Abu Dhabi is 220/240 volts and 50 cycles. The socket type is identical to the three-point British system but most appliances here are sold with two-pin plugs. However, adaptors can be purchased at any grocery or hardware store.

─ Apartments Are Cool ─

You can expect a significantly higher A/C bill in a villa – not only are most villas bigger than your average apartment, but many apartment buildings include air conditioning costs in the rent.

Water Suppliers

Awafi Mineral Water Nr Toyota Bldg, Mussafah, 02 555 5762, *awafiwater.com*
Masafi Various locations, 800 5455, *masafi.com*
Nestle Pure Life Various locations, 800 4404, *nestle-family.com*
Oasis Water Various locations, 02 600 522 261, *oasiscome2life.com*

Gas

There is no mains gas supply in Abu Dhabi. Some newer apartment buildings supply gas for cooking from central storage tanks situated on the roof or underground, but for residents of older buildings and those living in villas, it is common to buy gas canisters for cooking. These generally cost Dhs.250 for a new canister from most local 'corner' shops. Each refill costs around Dhs.75, depending on the size of the canister.

If you live away from the centre of town, you can hear the gas delivery van's bell ringing in the morning and afternoon, as it goes on its rounds. Two companies that deliver are Al Ruwais Industrial Gases (02 555 9295) and Tarish Ateeq Al Qubaisi Gas (02 559 9477).

─ In Hot Water ─

The water in your cold taps can get so hot in summer that you have to turn off your water heaters – in fact this is often the only way to get cooler water, since your hot water unit is usually inside the house, away from the sun's glare. You know winter's coming when you have to turn the water heater on again.

Sewerage

The Mafraq Wastewater Treatment Works receives and treats the sewage and waste water from both industry and the municipality, for Abu Dhabi city and the surrounding areas. The treated water is reused for irrigation, landscaping and agricultural activities. This is part of the city's efforts to protect the environment from pollution. The sewage is collected on a regular basis from septic tanks by sewage trucks. It is then pumped to the plant through more than 15 pumping stations. The sewage undergoes complex treatments to free the water from bacteria and it is regularly tested by the Environment Agency (ead.ae).

Rubbish Disposal

If you live in an apartment, your rubbish will generally be disposed of down a garbage chute accessible from each floor. The rubbish is then transferred to a skip or dumpster. You will also find dumpsters by the roadside in residential areas, and all rubbish needs to be put inside them. They are emptied by the municipality on a regular basis and taken to a landfill in the Mussafah industrial area.

While dumpsters are emptied regularly (generally every night) they can be a bit of a nuisance, particularly if they don't have lids. They tend to attract street cats and the occasional rat. If you have a problem with your dumpster, a call to the municipality (800 555) will ensure it is taken care of – or call Feline Friends (p.283) if the cats are troubling you.

The number of recycling collection points throughout the city is increasing. You'll find collection points near government buildings, at supermarkets and at large hotels.

Also, once a year there is a big can-collecting competition between all the schools of Abu Dhabi. This is organised by the Environment Agency. Abu Dhabi Municipality has recently distributed recycling bins to many households as the start of an ongoing domestic waste recycling programme. The Emirates Environmental Group (eeg-uae.org) is an active organisation and is always looking for volunteers to help with clean-ups.

Telephone

There are two telecoms companies operating in the UAE, du (du.ae) and Etisalat (etisalat.ae). Both service providers offer mobile packages while at the moment, Etisalat is the sole provider of landline services in Abu Dhabi.

To install a landline you must apply directly to Etisalat with a completed application form, a copy of your passport, a residence visa (the Emirates ID should shortly replace the need to provide both of these) and an installation fee of Dhs.180. Once the application is submitted, it is wise to maintain close contact and politely request progress reports from Etisalat. Connection installation times vary widely from an efficient three days to several frustrating weeks. Quarterly rental for a standard landline (for all sockets) is Dhs.45. You then have to choose which Etisalat package you want for calls.

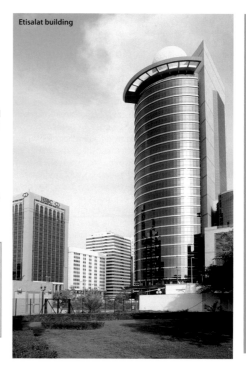

Etisalat building

Codes & Prefixes

Abu Dhabi	02	**Jebel Ali**	04
Ajman	06	**Ras Al Khaimah**	07
Al Ain	03	**Sharjah**	06
Dubai	04	**Umm Al Quwain**	06
Fujairah	09	**UAE**	
Hatta	04	**Country Code**	971

With Etisalat, all calls made locally (within the city) from one landline to another are free. Calls to anywhere else in the UAE cost Dhs.0.30 per minute. For international calls, the tariffs vary from country to country. Etisalat's off-peak timings for national calls are 14:00 to 16:00 and 19:00 to 07:00, Saturday to Wednesday; and at weekends from 14:00 on Thursday to 07:00 on Saturday. Discounted long distance rates are available all day Friday and on public holidays. See etisalat.ae for full details.

The other operator, du, offers a range of packages, but to route your call through the du network on your Etisalat landline, you need to dial the prefix 08888 before the number. To apply for a package, visit the du shop on Khalifa Street (02 622 0109), taking your passport or Emirates ID, and a copy of your tenancy contract. There is a Dhs.25 activation fee but there is no longer a monthly fee for the service. du charges for calls by the second, rather than per minute. Calls to other national landlines are 0.25 fils per second; calls to mobiles cost 0.5 fils per second. du offers round-the-clock off-peak international rates but tariffs vary depending on destination; calling the US is currently charged at 2.28 fils per second, while calling the UK will cost 3.18 fils per second. For national calls, off-peak timings are 14:00 to 16:00 and 19:00 to 07:00, Saturday to Wednesday; and at weekends from 14:00 Thursday to 07:00 Saturday. du also offers a prepaid service whereby customers buy pay-as-you-go recharge cards and top up the credit on their landlines, rather than being billed monthly.

Public payphones are all over the city; a few accept coins, but most require phone cards, which are widely available from many shops and supermarkets. They come in denominations of Dhs.30, but for international calls, beware… the units vanish at a truly amazing rate.

Cheap Calls Not Allowed

Downloading certain voice over internet protocol (VoIP) services, such as Skype, can be difficult within the UAE due to sites being blocked here. However, if you have downloaded the software in a different country, or within an area where the restriction is lifted, such as in certain free zones, it will still work when calling another computer but not when calling landlines or mobiles. See also Internet, p.94.

Mobile Phones

Mobile phone users can choose between du (prefix 055) and Etisalat (prefix 050 or 056). Both providers offer monthly or pay-as-you-go packages. You can register for a pay-as-you-go SIM card for either Etisalat or du from any of the company kiosks located in malls, or from any of the many mobile phone shops scattered throughout the city.

To get a pay-as-you-go line, you will need your passport (or Emirates ID) with a residency visa. A du pay-as-you-go line costs Dhs.55 and this includes Dhs.10 credit. An Etisalat pay-as-you-go line costs Dhs.165 and also includes Dhs.10 credit. Both du and Etisalat require you to renew your line every year – the renewal fee for a du line is Dhs.55 and Dhs.100 for an Etisalat line, although both frequently have special offers including free credit when you renew.

Both companies also offer monthly post-paid services. For a du post-paid, you will need your ID and residency visa, as well as either a UAE credit card, a recent utility bill with your physical address, your tenancy agreement, or a salary certificate that shows a minimum salary of Dhs.2,500 per month. For an Etisalat post-paid mobile line you will need your ID with residency visa as well as a salary certificate showing a minimum salary of Dhs.2,500 per month.

Missing Mobile?

Lost your mobile? For Etisalat, call 101, or du customer care 055 567 8155, to temporarily disconnect your number (you will need to know your passport number for security). Your SIM card can be replaced and you can keep the same number, but you'll lose all the numbers you had saved in your phone's memory. To replace the SIM, go to a branch of Etisalat or du with your essential documents and a fee of Dhs.50. If you need to cancel your mobile number permanently, you will need to fill out the cancellation forms.

Television

Local media in the UAE is improving dramatically and television is no exception. There are a number of free channels but non-Arabic speakers are limited in the number of channels they can actually understand.

Because of this, many expats opt for paid TV programming from one of the satellite services like the Orbit Showtime Network (OSN). However, if you don't fancy having a satellite dish installed or your rental arrangement doesn't allow it, Etisalat's E-Vision cable service has a number of packages that include channels from most satellite and paid providers in the area. For added convenience, Etisalat offers customers phone, internet and television bundles, and Yahsat (yahsat.ae), a satellite subsidiary of Mubadala Development, plans to offer the same three-way bundle across satellite connections.

There are an increasing number of HD channels launching in the UAE, including Abu Dhabi HD which shows sport and entertainment programmes, and OSN Movies & GE HD which broadcasts a 'best of' selection of OSN shows and movies. OSN customers can

purchase a Showbox (a recordable digital receiver), with which users can pause live television and record favourite shows. The box also allows viewers to watch special previews of forthcoming movies or virtual 'boxsets' of popular series. OSN customers can now also watch movies and series whenever they want online through OSN Play, which is free to subscribers. See osn.com for more info.

Spoilt For Choice

Far from being a TV backwater, you'll find most major series and films show on local satellite networks although they will generally be a month or two behind the UK or USA. OSN, for example, shows Boardwalk Empire, True Blood, Homeland, Glee and American X Factor. Abu Dhabi Media Company has the rights for Premier League football, and shows all 380 games a season live via a set-top box and Internet Protocol TV.

ART Dubai, 04 806 1111, *artonline.tv*
Emirates Cable TV & Multimedia (E-vision) Various locations, *evision.ae*
Eurostar Communications Nr Zania Bldg, Shk Zayed The Second St, Al Baladia, 02 634 7357, *eurostargroup.com*
Firstnet Arab Digital Distribution, Dubai, 04 806 1222, *firstnettv.net*
Global Direct Television Tawash Bldg, Nr Hamad Center, Shk Zayed The Second St, Madinat Zayed, 02 621 8382, *gdtvllc.com*
OSN Dubai Media City, Dubai, 04 367 7777, *osn.com*

Internet

All internet usage is regulated by the Telecommunications Regulatory Authority (TRA). This means that many sites that are deemed to be offensive, either religiously, culturally or politically,

VoIP

Regulators finally authorised VoIP (Voice over Internet Protocol) phone service in 2010, but only existing licence-holders may offer it. This means popular services such as Skype are excluded from the deal. Those companies that are licensed are Etisalat, du and the satellite firms Yahsat and Thuraya. However, if Skype is already downloaded to your computer, you can still use it to call other computers, and if you have a Virtual Private Network or some other type of proxy blocker, you can use it to call other phones. Just be aware that this is technically breaking the law. See also Internet (above).

Etisalat On The Go

When out and about, look out for Etisalat's wi-fi hotspots to get online. These are located all over town at various malls, cafes and restaurants, and you can connected by purchasing a prepaid access card at the venue. See izone.ae for listings.

international courier services deliver to Abu Dhabi, including DHL (800 4004), FedEx (800 33339), UPS (800 4774) and Aramex (02 555 1911), and all of them will deliver to your door. If you are expecting a package, make sure the person sending it has included the correct phone number, as that is often the only way for the courier to find your location.

Carpet Cleaners & Laundry Services

Wall-to-wall carpets are rare in this part of the world, but loose rugs and carpets are commonplace. When they're looking a bit grubby, the companies listed below can pay you a visit, give you a quote, and take the carpets away to be cleaned, returning them a couple of days later. All of the carpet services listed below will also come to your house to clean upholstery.

There are no self-service launderettes, but laundry shops are everywhere. As well as dry cleaning and laundry, they all offer ironing services. If you have specific instructions, make sure these are noted when you drop off your laundry – creases in trousers are standard, so if you don't want them, speak up.

Compensation policies for lost or damaged items vary, but losses are rare, even in the places that look most disorganised. Larger chains, such as Champion Cleaners (050 105 4972), normally have a free pick-up and delivery service. Expect to pay Dhs.12 for a shirt, Dhs.45 for a suit and Dhs.40 for a quilt.

Aroma Cleaning Nr KM Trading, Shk Hamdan Bin Mohammed St, Markaziya East, 02 671 5330
Delight Cleaning Services Nr KM Trading, Al Salam St, Markaziya East, 02 678 9216
Modern Cleaning Methods 02 645 2825, *modernmethodsco.com*

Domestic Help

Domestic help is readily available in Abu Dhabi, on both a full or part-time basis, and the affordability is likely to be better than in most expats' home countries. If you are looking for a bit of help on the home front, there are a number of options. Legally, a housemaid may only be employed by the individual who sponsors her, but in practice many maids take on cleaning or babysitting for other families; if caught, you can face a hefty fine, but the law is rarely enforced and it is a fairly common practice. If you are looking for someone part-time, but want to stay within the law, there are many companies and agencies in Abu Dhabi that provide daily, weekly or monthly cleaning services and maids on an hourly basis; for around Dhs.20 to Dhs.30 per hour, they'll take care of all your sweeping, mopping, dusting, washing and ironing. Most companies stipulate a minimum number of daily hours, usually two or three per visit.

are blocked and can't be accessed. Although both Etisalat and du provide internet services in the UAE, only Etisalat provides internet in Abu Dhabi at present. Prices start at Dhs.79 a month for dial-up internet and steadily rise for faster service, topping out at the 'Superior' service for Dhs.699 a month for 30Mbps broadband. There is a Dhs.200 installation fee, plus a one-off payment for the modem. Etisalat also has wi-fi hotspots around the city. You can purchase prepaid access cards that provide different increments of time depending on how much is spent. Etisalat also offers plans for unlimited access, and sell a number of different USB Wi-Fi modems that allow users to access the internet anywhere that mobile signals are available. Go to etisalat.ae for more details.

Postal Services

There is currently no postal delivery service to home addresses, and everyone has their mail delivered to a PO box. Mail is first delivered to the Central Post Office and then distributed to clusters of PO boxes in various areas. To get your own PO box, fill in the application form at your nearest post office and pay the annual fee (Dhs.200); you will be given a set of keys (Dhs.10 per key) to access your own box. Empost will send you notification by email when you receive registered mail or parcels in your PO box. For an extra Dhs.9 you can have the item delivered to your door. However, you might have to pay customs charges on international packages. Many people have mail delivered to their company's PO box instead of arranging a private one.

Gift Express

If you would rather not chance the post, Gift Express provides a selection of gifts that can be sent to most countries. See giftexpressinternational.com for more information.

Letters and packages do occasionally go missing and, if the item has not been registered, there's little that you can do apart from wait – some turn up months after they are expected.

Empost offers a courier service for both local and international deliveries. Delivery times are guaranteed and packages can be tracked. Registered mail is a relatively inexpensive alternative, and can also be tracked via a reference number. All of the major

Abu Dhabi Maids Various locations, 055 222 9800, *abudhabimaids.ae*
Exiles Maid Service Various locations, 02 557 1542, *exilesmaidservice.ae*

HOME IMPROVEMENTS

Maintenance

Whether you're a home owner or live in rental property, and whether you are responsible for your property's general maintenance or have an assigned company to take care of it, housing in Abu Dhabi requires constant maintenance – not in small part thanks to the climate. Air conditioning units can be temperamental and need regular servicing, plumbing problems aren't uncommon, electrics can go haywire and creepy crawlies like to pay a visit.

Most homeowners employ the services of a maintenance company. Annual contracts don't come cheap, but the benefit is that it will cover you for most of your maintenance needs. The contract should include regular scheduled servicing of air conditioning units and boilers, seasonal pest control protection, basic masonry works and 24 hour emergency call out services. Most companies offer extra services, such as swimming pool maintenance and gardening for an add-on fee.

Typical costs for such maintenance contracts go from Dhs.7,000 up to Dhs.11,000 per year. If you are renting, check whether your landlord has such a maintenance contract in place before hiring anyone. It's also worth checking if the development company responsible for your accommodation already employs maintenance services, and a recent trend has been for various developers to branch out into also providing maintenance themselves.

If it's up to you to get a problem fixed, there are plenty of companies around to help you. It's advisable to listen to the suggestions of friends and co-workers, especially if they have had positive experiences in the past with a particular company. For A/C problems, you can also try York Air Conditioning and Refrigeration Inc (02 641 4277) or Prime Central Air (02 672 4648). For pest control, try National Pest Control (02 563 1680). However, for any of these services, there are dozens of options, and it's always good to do your research before you decide.

If you live in a community development, your developer will have standard rules and regulations relating to noise, parking, and general upkeep of your property. These will be detailed on the developers' websites and local security guards perform regular checks. If you live in a villa, a dirty or messy garage may be frowned upon, and you could be fined for such things as parking on the street rather than in

a designated bay, so it's worth making yourself fully aware of what is required of you as either a tenant or homeowner.

Builders

As with so many of Abu Dhabi's property laws, alterations are a hazy issue. The first expats to own property in Abu Dhabi have only recently been given the keys to their finished homes and nascent laws are still changing regularly; even people involved in real estate law aren't always sure of specifics.

As an expatriate, any place of your own will be in a new development. If you wish to make alterations to your property, your first step would be to approach the developer to find out the changes they will allow. In master developments, for instance, there are strict rules regarding the consistency between properties, and any changes may have to remain within the general layout and design.

In Dubai, where the expat property market is slightly more mature, permission applications for alterations are submitted to the master developer of the complex, who must approve the plans and receive a deposit of Dhs.5,000 before any building work can start. An inspector makes a site visit during the works and carries out a final assessment on completion, after which your deposit is returned if you have met all the guidelines. Developers determine the colour of the paint you may use on the exterior of your property and the design and style of any doors, gates or decorative iron fencing. It's likely that a similar system will become the norm in Abu Dhabi in due course.

Many developers employ maintenance companies, contractors and subcontractors, so it's likely that, if you are given permission to carry out your alterations, you may be required to use one of the companies that your developer already works with. Often, for smaller projects, the contractor you hire can arrange approval itself, saving time and effort on your part. Just make sure you've got a reputable contractor on your side. Ask people you trust for references or start with these options: Dwellings Group (02 643 6431) and Abu Mohison General Maintenance & Contracting (050 622 9463).

Painters

Once you own a property, you are free to decorate the inside any style you choose. If you rent, the likelihood is that your landlord will not mind you painting or decorating as you please on the basis that he has your deposit, and will be happy to keep hold of it should you not leave the villa or apartment in its original state. It's often the case that landlords don't need much of a reason to hold back security deposits, so it's worth checking and getting something in writing before you get the roller out.

Modern villas offer style and comfort

An excellent range of paints and associated implements can be found at Jotun Paints (02 551 0300) and Ace Hardware (02 673 1665). Companies like Evershine (02 553 1851) offer painting services. The cost of internally painting a whole villa can vary between Dhs.3,000 and Dhs.8,000, depending on size, materials and contractor.

Gardens

Abu Dhabi, though not exactly blessed with ample yearly rainfall, has somehow managed to turn, and keep, its parks and lawns green. Irrigation is the city's saving grace, and anyone wanting a green garden must copy that blueprint. Lushness requires due diligence and, in the hot summer months, many plants will require watering as often as twice a day. If you're not up to watering by hand, it is worth considering hiring a gardener or even having a simple irrigation system installed.

If maintaining a grassy garden seems like too much hassle which, especially if you're only renting, is understandable, you can always opt for astroturf. Fake lawns are increasingly popular; they stay green throughout the year and there's no need for watering (although you do need to hose them down every few weeks). You can buy astroturf (in varying degrees of quality) in Ace Hardware, while Clearview (clearview.ae) installs fake lawns. Another option is to opt for block paving or decking. Again, you can purchase decking in Ace Hardware (aceuae.com), while Alomi (alomirealwoodflooringllc.com) is a specialist wood merchant that has carpenters with experience in laying decks.

If you are buying a brand new house, the developers may have left you with no more than a sandpit plot, so you will need to start your garden from scratch, and landlords are not obliged to landscape the gardens of new villas before they rent them to you either.

To cut down on watering bills, you could have a borehole dug, but because expats do not enjoy land rights, this will involve you getting permission from the landowner. In any case, the general rule of thumb is the further away from the sea you are, the deeper you will have to drill. On the other hand, the further you get from the sea, the less you have to worry about the salinity of the water. It's also worth planting hardy native species as this will greatly cut down on the quantities of water required.

Whatever greenery you decide to plant, the plant souk at Meena Port is the perfect starting point. It sells a wide array of plant types, ranging from lush and thirsty to the most desert-hardened, and there's plenty to inspire even the most amateur of gardeners. Many of the stores in the souk offer landscaping services at very reasonable rates as well.

A more upmarket alternative is Exotica (exoticaemirates.com) in the Tourist Club Area. In addition to a healthy selection of plants, it offers landscaping and irrigation services. Other places that sell plants are IKEA (p.324), Carrefour (p.336), Spinneys (p.338) and even the Abu Dhabi Co-op (p.336). All these stores also sell small selections of gardening tools, outdoor furniture and hoses, but to properly 'tool up' for large outdoor jobs, head to Ace Hardware which stocks almost anything you could ever need for sprouting an oasis in this desert. For information on buying garden furniture, see Shopping, p.323.

Swimming Pools

A lot of properties in Abu Dhabi have private pools or at least access to a shared development pool. If you don't have one in your villa, you can always pay to have one installed – but it doesn't come cheap. Another option is to have a custom-made, free-form fibre glass and ceramic tiled pool fitted. As tough and durable as a concrete version, these pools are effectively portable. Delivery of one of these usually takes around four weeks, with an on-site installation period of approximately 10 days. Prices for such a pool start at around Dhs.110,000, which does include all labour costs, pumps and filtration. Try Pools by Design (050 754 6852) or, if you want a more traditional pool, speak to Absolute Pools (absolute-pools.com).

Aside from cleaning, your pool will also require the water to be changed and chemical levels checked and balanced on a regular basis. Those Pool Guys (thosepoolguys.com) and Falcon Crest (fcstswimming.com) are both well-established companies in the UAE and can take care of all pool maintenance. Most pool maintenance companies will also be able to perform standard repairs to things such as broken lights and water filters.

Work, Finance & The Law

WORKING IN THE UAE

Expat workers come to Abu Dhabi for a number of reasons: to advance their career, for a higher standard of living, to take advantage of new opportunities or, most commonly, for the lifestyle and the experience of living and working in a new culture. Whatever the reason, there are various advantages to working here.

While the biggest bonus of working in Abu Dhabi may seem to be tax-free salaries, the cost of living (or your newly acquired lifestyle) can somewhat balance out this benefit.

In addition, the instability of the world's economy has had an effect on the job market in the UAE, and there has been a shift from the fervent recruitment drive of past years, with many previously employed in Dubai taking advantage of Abu Dhabi's increased stability by looking for work in the country's capital.

However, the situation is constantly changing. At the very senior end of the scale, there remain some idyllic opportunities and huge packages that attract the big players, predominantly in the construction, aviation and finance industries.

For less senior positions, the image of a cushy expat life in the Gulf is changing, with much more competition in all areas of the market and an increasing number of people looking for work in Abu Dhabi. Not so long ago, foreign expats could walk into jobs that they could only dream of back home, but these days the market is much more competitive, not least because of the effects of the global economic downturn. All-inclusive packages with accommodation and education allowances are also not as common, although basic benefits still apply (such as annual flights home and 30 calendar days leave).

Work-wise, Abu Dhabi is still a land of opportunities for skilled professionals. It is easier to change industries, as skill sets are less pigeonholed than in other countries and jobs in certain industries (such as construction) are more available.

One of the main differences about working in Abu Dhabi, as opposed to your country of origin, is that you or your spouse need to be sponsored (see p.39) by an employer, which often leaves people feeling tied or uncomfortably obligated to their employer. If you leave the company, your current visa will be cancelled and you will have to go through the hassle of getting a new residency permit (for you and your family, if they are on your sponsorship).

Labour Card

To work in the private sector in the United Arab Emirates, you are legally required to have a valid labour card (although the plan is for this, ultimately, to be replaced by the Emirates ID, p.44). The labour card can only be applied for once you have residency and is usually organised by the company PRO (see p.39). If you are recruited from your home country, your company will have to get approval from the Ministry of Labour. You will then enter on an employment visa, get a health card, take the medical test, and get the residency stamp in your passport. The company PRO then takes all of the relevant paperwork to the Ministry of Labour where the actual labour card will be issued (even though it has 'work permit' printed on the back).

The card features your photo and details of your employer. You're supposed to carry the card with you at all times but it is highly unlikely that you will ever be asked to produce it. The process can also be quite slow, and it's possible you may not receive your card for a few weeks, or sometimes even months, after starting work. The labour card costs Dhs.1,000 (paid by your company). Its expiration is linked to that of your residence visa, and is currently valid for two years. It must be renewed within 50 days of expiry. Failure to do so will result in a fine (which your company will be liable for) of Dhs.5,000 for each year the card has expired.

If your employer is arranging your residency, you will need to sign your labour contract before the labour card is issued. This contract is printed in both Arabic and English. It's not necessarily your agreed 'contract' as such – most employees will sign a more comprehensive contract. Unless you read Arabic, it may be advisable to have a translation made of your details, since the Arabic is the official version in any dispute. However, if there is any discrepancy, the judge would want to know why your company got the details wrong in the first place (see Employment Contracts, p.104).

Working Hours

Working hours differ dramatically between companies; straight shifts vary from 07:30 to 14:30 for government organisations to the common 09:00 to 18:00 for private companies. Most retail outlets tend to be open from 10:00 to 22:00 but often operate shifts. Teachers start early, at around 07:30, and classes finish around 14:00, although their hours aren't as predetermined as other roles.

Although less common nowadays, some offices and shops operate split shifts, which allow for a longer break in the afternoon (hours are usually 08:00 to 13:00 and 16:00 to 19:00).

The maximum number of hours permitted per week according to UAE Labour Law is 48, although some industries, such as hospitality and retail, have longer stipulated hours. Annual holiday allowance starts at one calendar month per year, or roughly 22 working days. Some employees, especially those in management, have more than this and long service usually adds to holiday allowance.

Friday is the Islamic holy day and, therefore, a universal day off for offices and schools. Consumer demand means that the hospitality and retail industries are open seven days a week, although most smaller shops will not open until Friday evening. Saturday is the second day of the weekend; some companies work five and a half days a week and some operate a six-day week, taking only Friday as a rest day.

Public holidays (see p.10) are set by the government, while the timing of religious holidays depends on the sighting of the moon. This can mean that it is difficult to plan holidays, as confirmation of public holidays can come just days before the event. The labour law states that all employees (even non-Muslims) are entitled to a shorter working day during Ramadan, although labour lawyers would advise you not to insist on this if you are non-Muslim or not fasting.

Business Culture

Like anywhere in the world, doing business in the UAE has its idiosyncrasies. Even if you work for a western company, the chances are that some of your business transactions will be with Emiratis, whether on a customer or client basis. While you're likely to find that Emiratis are open to different styles of business

and are generally keen to explain their customs, understanding some of the local business etiquette can help you keep one step ahead of the competition.

It's a good idea to dress conservatively for meetings, particularly if you are female, and it is advisable to cover your knees and arms. You may also have a meeting with a woman wearing a hijab (a veil which leaves the face uncovered), or some women choose to wear a niqab which covers the full face. Don't be surprised if greetings are more tactile in the UAE than in your home country; long handshakes, kisses and effusive compliments are common. While it's normal to shake hands with people of the same sex, if you are meeting someone of the opposite sex, it's best to take your cue from the other person and not offer your hand unless they offer theirs.

It's polite to send greetings to a person's family, but can be considered rude to enquire directly about someone's wife, sister or daughter. A nose kiss is a customary greeting in the Gulf region but is only used between close friends and associates and you should not attempt to greet someone in this way.

Business meetings will usually start with numerous greetings and an exchange of business cards – you should take the time to read the card as a sign of respect. Punctuality is important and arriving late to meetings is considered very impolite – however, don't

Aldar HQ

assume that your meeting will start at the appointed time or that it will not be interrupted. If you're attending a business meeting at an Arab-owned company, it's likely that you'll be served traditional Arabic coffee, or kahwa. Sharing coffee is an important social ritual in the Middle East so you should drink some when offered. Cups should be taken in the right hand and, if there is a waiter standing by replenishing your cup, there are two ways to signal that you have had enough: either leave a small amount of coffee in the bottom of your cup or gently tip the cup from side to side.

While not so much a matter of etiquette, patience is the ultimate virtue when doing business in the UAE. Things often move more slowly and decisions take longer than you may be used to. Keeping in regular contact with your clients and customers helps to maintain genial relations and picking up the phone rather than relying on email can make the world of difference.

Finding Work

Until the financial crisis hit, Abu Dhabi's economy was booming and, therefore, the recruitment market was more than buoyant. But even at the height of the crisis in 2009, Abu Dhabi suffered less than its neighbouring Dubai, for example, and far less than most the rest of the world's economies. By 2010, things were looking up once more, and in 2011 and 2012 there were plenty of reports of increased recruitment across the UAE. The newly rising oil prices are adding to the economic upturn and are as such likely to boost the job market too. However, the competition for good positions is greater which means there is a stronger focus on what skills employees will bring to the table.

There are numerous recruitment agencies in Abu Dhabi but employers also use local newspapers and headhunters to advertise job opportunities. It is undoubtedly easier to look for a job once you are in Abu Dhabi. Your first step should be to get your hands on the Gulf News appointments supplement (gnads4u.com), published daily except Fridays and Saturdays, or the Khaleej Times' Appointments (khaleejtimes.com) every day except Friday – also available online. The National has a careers section that is available to those who subscribe online.

It is also beneficial to check listings on online versions of international newspapers as companies within the UAE often post jobs on these sites. Websites for The Guardian (guardian.co.uk) and The Times (timesonline.co.uk) newspapers in the UK and The Washington Post (washingtonpost.com) in the US are often a good resource. You can also upload your CV to sites like monstergulf.com, naukrigulf.com, bayt. com and gulftalent.com. Job advertisements are also posted on Dubizzle (dubizzle.com). It is a good idea to register with a recruitment agency and to contact companies directly and start networking (p.104). Networking sites like linkedin.com can be useful too. Thanks to Abu Dhabi's relatively small size, the more people you meet, the more likely you are to bump into someone who just happens to work somewhere that has a vacant position that you might be able to fill. Many larger Abu Dhabi-based companies have vacancy listings on their websites, so if you have a company in mind, it's up to you to keep checking its site for updated listings. Advertisements in Abu Dhabi can be more direct than in other countries and, while it isn't always acceptable to specify candidate requirements like nationality in other countries, advertisements here will often detail whether they are looking for a 'western applicant', for example.

Hiring Again

Good news for job seekers. According to the September 2012 findings of a survey by Bayt.com, more than 50% of the UAE's employers expected to 'definitely' or 'probably' hire more employees in the next three months, while 29% said that they would 'definitely' be hiring within the year.

Most recruitment agencies accept CVs via email, but you can check whether they accept walk-ins. The agency will then set up an interview where you are usually required to fill out a form summarising your CV; you will also need a few passport photos. The agency takes its fee from the registered company once the position has been filled. It is illegal for a recruitment company to levy fees on candidates for this service, although some might try.

Headhunters (also known as executive search companies) will usually contact desirable candidates directly to discuss opportunities, but this is normally for more senior positions.

Should you be suitable for a job, a recruitment agency will mediate between you and the employer and arrange all interviews. However, don't rely too heavily on the agency finding a job for you. More often than not, agencies depend on candidates spotting one of their advertised vacancies. You can sign up with more than one agency but they may both try to put you forward for the same job. In this case, it is at your discretion which agency you want to represent you. Following is a list of recruitment agencies based in the UAE. Some of these agencies specialise in certain industries so do your research and register accordingly.

For additional information and tips n finding work in Abu Dhabi, grab a copy of *Working in the Gulf*, a career guide to all GCC countries with country and city-specific chapters and listings for recruitment firms, ministries of labour and more.

Flying Solo

With the gradually improving economy, more expats are taking the plunge to go into business on their own in the Emirates. If you'd like to try your hand at business, freelancing may be the way forward.

During the financial crisis, becoming a freelancer was often out of necessity rather than choice. Now, with the economy once more growing, choosing to go freelance can help you explore business opportunities created by the new upturn – while enjoying the other benefits of flying solo.

For some, like digital media professional Russell, the advantages of freelancing are clear: 'Freelancing offers freedom and the chance to earn a better living. You get to concentrate on work you enjoy and can pick and choose jobs once you're established.'

But it's not always easy: not knowing where your next pay cheque is coming from can be a source of anxiety, made worse by continual invoice chasing with unreliable clients.

Also, benefits such as medical insurance and holiday pay are funded from your own pocket, and there's no cover if you are sick or unable to work.

Solid contacts are important wherever you are in the world, so good networking skills are indispensable. They are even more vital in the UAE, says Russell, where being granted a contract or even just an opportunity to pitch 'really is all about who you know.'

Networking groups and business councils are both excellent places to widen your professional network, but it would be foolhardy to simply start freelancing without having at least one regular, reliable client already lined up.

It goes without saying that word of mouth can either make or break your reputation, so tread carefully and make sure you act professionally at all times. This is especially important in the UAE, where everyone seems to know everyone, and where social functions often double as professional networking opportunities and vice versa.

If you do decide to freelance, there are currently really only two options, both of which only cover media industries.

Dubai Media City (dubaimediacity.com) and spin-offs such as Studio City are the first and there is no issue with an Abu Dhabi resident setting up in a Dubai free zone.
- Only media professionals of the following categories are eligible: artists, editors, directors, writers,

engineers, producers, photographers, camera operators and technicians in the fields of film, TV, music, radio or print media.
- The permit includes a residence visa, access to 10 shared work stations, and a shared PO Box address and fax line.
- A minimum of three hours per week and no more than three hours per day must be spent at the hot desk.
- A business plan, CV, bank reference letter and portfolio must be submitted along with your application.

Costs at DMC include:
- Dhs.5,000 security deposit (refundable)
- Dhs.5,000 joining fee (one-off payment)
- Dhs.8,000 annual permit fee
- Dhs.4,000 annual membership fee

Alternatively, Abu Dhabi's twofour54 could be a possibility.
- Only media professionals of the following categories are eligible: broadcast graphic designers, post production sound editors, video editors, set designers, set riggers, camera operators, camera assistants, floor managers, gaffers, lighting operators, lighting assistants, production engineers, production sound engineers, production sound assistants, special effects technicians, vision mixers, gallery operators, grips, hairdressers, make-up artists and TV production stylists.
- The permit includes a residence visa
- A CV, high resolution passport photo and colour passport scan must be submitted along with your application.

Costs at twofour54 include:
- Dhs.2,500 annual licence fee
- Dhs.2,200 visa fee
- Dhs.5,000 security deposit, refundable upon termination of the licence
  On top of these, you'll also need to take desk or office space at twofour54 – there are various solutions available.

Working In The UAE

Recruitment Agencies

ABC Recruitment Al Ghahedi Tower, Nr Al Falah & Shk Rashid Bin Saeed Al Maktoum Sts, Madinat Zayed, 02 635 5656, *abcrecruitment.ae*

BAC Middle East Liberty House, Dubai, 04 439 8500, *bacme.com*

Charterhouse > *p.105* Regus Al Bateen Business Centre, 34 Bainunah St, Al Bateen, 02 406 9819, *charterhouseme.ae*

IMG Recruitment & General Services IMG Bldg, Corniche St, Markaziya East, 02 626 8885, *imgrec.com*

Jobscan Executive Search Nr KFC, Shk Hamdan Bin Mohammed St, Markaziya East, 02 627 5592, *jobscan.ae*

Manpower Professional Dubai Internet City, Dubai, 04 391 0460, *manpower-me.com*

Specialist Services Nr Abu Dhabi Municipality, Mussafah, 02 644 0879, *specserve.com*

Talent Partners Silver Wave Tower, Mina Rd, Al Meena, 02 667 2535, *talent2.com*

WTS Energy 3 Towers Bldg, Shk Zayed The Second St, Al Baladia, 02 6738 768, *wtsenergy.com*

Networking & Events

With Abu Dhabi still a relatively small city, made up of real business areas that are smaller still, networking is critical, even across industries. Everyone seems to know everyone and getting in with the corporate 'in-crowd' definitely has its plus points. Business acumen here can, at times, be more important than specific industry knowledge, so it pays to attend business events and trade shows. Make friends in government departments and this will often land you in the front line for opportunities. Likewise, bad news is rarely made public here, so staying in tune through the grapevine can help prevent wrong decisions. Social networking sites like LinkedIn (linkedin.com) and Xing (xing.com/net/lewa) are great resources when looking for new jobs or contacts. There are specific sub-groups within these sites for business professionals based in the UAE.

Business Councils

Abu Dhabi Business Women Council Abu Dhabi Chamber Of Commerce & Industry, Markaziya West, 02 617 7495, *adbusinesswomen.ae*

Abu Dhabi Chamber Of Commerce & Industry Corniche Rd, Markaziya West, 02 621 4000, *abudhabichamber.ae*

AmCham Abu Dhabi InvestBank Bldg, Off Shk Rashid Bin Saeed Al Maktoum St, Markaziya West, 02 631 3604, *amchamabudhabi.org*

Arab Business Club Pyramid Centre, Umm Hurair Rd, Dubai, 04 358 3000, *arabbusinessclub.org*

Australian Business Group Abu Dhabi Green Tower, Shk Khalifa Bin Zayed St, Markaziya East, 050 264 1134, *ausbg.net*

British Business Group Cert Technology Park, East Rd, Al Nahyan, 02 445 7234, *britishbusiness.org*

Canadian Business Council Abu Dhabi Cert Technology Park, East Rd, Al Nahyan, 02 446 7223, *cbcabudhabi.com*

French Business Group Nr Al Diar Regency Hotel, Al Salam St, Tourist Club Area, 02 674 1137, *fbgabudhabi.com*

German Emirati Joint Council For Industry & Commerce (AHK) Abu Dhabi Mall, Tourist Club Area, 02 645 5200, *ahk.de*

Iraq Business Council Abu Dhabi Green Tower, Shk Khalifa Bin Zayed St, Markaziya East, 02 627 1570, *ibcad.com*

Lebanese Business Council Green Tower, Shk Khalifa Bin Zayed St, Markaziya East, 02 626 6204, *lbcuae.ae*

Luxembourg Trade & Investment Office Luxembourg, Al Meena, 02 491 2446, *investinluxembourg.ae*

Philippine Business Council Of Abu Dhabi (PBC-AD) Nr Eldorado Cinema, Shk Zayed The First St, Tourist Club Area, 02 672 0288, *philippinebusiness.org*

South African Business Council University Of Wollongong In Dubai, Dubai, 04 390 0433, *sabco-uae.org*

Swiss Business Council Abu Dhabi Masdar City, 02 653 8181, *swissbcuae.com*

Trade Representative Of The Netherlands Netherlands Embassy, Markaziya East, 02 695 8000, *netherlands.ae*

Employment Contracts

An employment contract should list the full details of your employment, including the name of the employer, details of your salary and a breakdown of your responsibilities. Accepting an expat posting can have its pitfalls, so before you sign your contract pay special attention to things such as probation periods, accommodation, annual leave, education allowance, travel entitlements, medical and dental cover, notice periods, and repatriation entitlements.

There is often confusion over the offer letter and the contract. An offer letter should give details of the terms of the job you are being offered, such as salary, leave, hours and other benefits; if you accept the terms of this offer, it then becomes a legally binding contract. You may be asked to sign an additional Ministry of Labour contract that accompanies your residency application, but the initial offer letter remains, in effect, your contract. If you receive your employment contract in both English and Arabic, it is a good idea to have the Arabic version translated to ensure they match – the Arabic version will prevail in the UAE courts.

The UAE Labour Law mandates an end-of-service gratuity payment for employees to compensate for the lack of a pension system. The rules are a bit

convoluted, but basically, an employee on a fixed-term contract, who has completed one or more years of continuous service, will be entitled to 21 days' pay for each of the first five years of service, and 30 days' pay for every additional year, to a maximum of two full years' pay. If the employee is on an 'unlimited duration' (open-ended) contract and terminates it of his own accord, he will get a third of the gratuity for a service period of between one and three years, two thirds for three to five years, and the full amount if service exceeds five years.

Leaving before the end of your fixed-term contract, or being fired for breaking the UAE Labour Law, could result in the loss of your gratuity payment. Gratuity payments are worked out according to your basic salary. Bear in mind that your total monthly remuneration will be split into various categories (basic salary, plus housing, transport and utilities allowances). You will still get the same cash salary at the end of every month, but because your basic salary is much lower than your total salary, your gratuity payment is lower. Although employees are entitled to gratuity, companies in financial trouble have in the past not been able to pay the money out of their operating budgets, and the government is currently considering restructuring the gratuity system or introducing a pension plan.

Abu Dhabi offices

The UAE Labour Law states that probation periods can be set for a maximum of six months, although three months is more common. Some companies may delay the residency process illegally until the probation period is up, which can make settling in difficult – no residency means you can't sponsor family members, buy a car or get a bank loan.

By law, employees are not entitled to paid sick leave during their probation period and most companies do not permit annual leave to be taken during this time – you will continue to accrue annual leave over the course of the year. Discuss these matters with your future employer before signing your contract.

Free Zones

Free Trade Zones (FTZ) have been set up in Abu Dhabi to attract more investment from foreign companies. An independent Free Zone Authority governs each individual zone, and the major advantages for companies establishing themselves in a free zone is that they may have 100% foreign ownership, pay no corporate taxes for 15 years (renewable for additional years), are allowed 100% repatriation of capital and profits, plus there are no personal income taxes, and no currency restrictions.

For employees working in a free zone, one of the big advantages is the lack of red tape if you move jobs to another free zone company. This is because the free zone is your sponsor rather than the individual company, so if you change your employer, you won't actually be switching sponsors.

The free zones in the capital all have easy access to the main transit hubs, business districts and sea transport routes. The Industrial City of Abu Dhabi (ICAD I, II and III) is located off the island at Mussafah, next to Mussafah Industrial Area. Development is underway at the Khalifa Industrial Zone of Abu Dhabi (Kizad), which, upon its completion scheduled (expected by 2013) will be two-thirds the size of Singapore and eventually function as the primary port for the capital. In addition, the Abu Dhabi Airports Company is building Abu Dhabi Airport Free Zone at Abu Dhabi International Airport, Masdar City will be an environmental and scientific free zone, and plans exist to set up a free zone that will act as an international financial hub.

Labour Law

The UAE Federal Law Number 8 for 1980 on regulation of labour relations (otherwise known as the UAE Labour Law) outlines information on employee entitlements, employment contracts and disciplinary rules. The law is employer friendly, but it also clearly outlines employee rights.

You can download a copy of the document from the Ministry of Labour website (mol.gov.ae); the document has not been fully updated for some time now but amendments and additions are often posted on the MoL website.

Labour unions and strikes are illegal, although there have been some protests by labourers in the past. The labourers achieved some results and the employers concerned were forced to pay wages immediately or remedy living conditions, and a hotline was set up for other unpaid workers to report their employers. If you find yourself in the situation where you have not been paid, you can file a case with the UAE Labour Department who will take the necessary action. You could also get a lawyer to deal with the claim on your behalf (see p.122 for a list of law firms). Although lawyers are expensive in Abu Dhabi, the employer will have to bear the cost if the case is settled in your favour.

Maternity Leave

Under UAE Labour Law, women are entitled to 45 days maternity leave, on full pay, once they've completed one year of continuous service – fathers are not yet entitled to paternity leave.

Maternity leave can only be used directly before and after the birth. Those who have been with their employer for less than a year can claim 45 days on half pay (see p.129 for more information).

Changing Jobs

Until recently, anyone leaving a job and cancelling their visa faced the possibility of being 'banned' for six months. Fortunately, the banning rules have been relaxed and, effective January 2011, anyone on an unlimited contract who has completed at least two years of service with their employer can transfer to a new job without having to get a no-objection certificate or NOC.

Should you have less than two years under your belt and yet be looking to change jobs, there may still well be the possibility of negotiating with your current employer to arrange a transfer, particularly if you are leaving on good terms.

It is important to review whether a non-compete clause was added to your contract, particularly if your new role is with a direct competitor to your current employer. This clause could mean that you are restricted to taking an unrelated role before you can return to your current field. However, in practice this can be a tricky one for your employer to enforce, certainly if you have worked for the same firm for two years or more.

To change sponsors, pick up the relevant forms from the Ministry of Labour and get them typed in Arabic. Get the forms signed and stamped by both your previous and new employers, and submit them along with the trade licence and establishment

card of your new company. Everything goes to the Immigration Department who will amend your visa. In most cases, your new employer will take care of this procedure for you.

There are some exceptions where you can transfer your sponsorship without the approval of your current sponsor, such as death of your sponsor, change of company ownership, company closure and cancellation of your company's trade licence. If your company has closed, it is important to note that you will receive an automatic labour ban unless the company has cancelled its trade licence.

Regulations differ in the free zones, as you are technically sponsored by the Free Zone Authority (FZA) rather than the company. Therefore, if you move to another company within the free zone, there is no need to transfer your visa.

Banning

The notorious 'ban' is a topic of frequent discussion in Abu Dhabi; however, the details of when and for how long you can be banned change from case to case. There are two types of ban: an employment ban that restricts employment for a period (usually six months to a year), or a visa ban (which restricts entry or departure from Abu Dhabi).

A visa ban is often imposed if you have committed a serious criminal offence, or you have absconded from the UAE. Theoretically at least, it is possible for your employer to ban you from working with another company for a short period of time if you have served less than two years in the position, even if you have served the correct notice period and have left on good terms. However, this is far less likely these days since a new fee was introduced and employers now have to pay to ban an employee.

NOC

A No-Objection Certificate was once required to work for another employer, though laws were recently amended so that you won't need an NOC if you have spent at least two years with a current employer. If you're considering switching jobs, check with the Ministry of Labour or a lawyer to see whether you should seek an NOC.

A six-month employment ban can also be imposed by the Ministry of Labour, with no instruction from your previous employers, but this is indeterminate and can often be resolved. If you do receive a ban, all is not lost, it may be possible to pay for your ban to be lifted.

The laws regarding banning change frequently and revisions are occasionally posted online without any announcements to the general public; check the Ministry of Labour website (mol.gov.ae).

Exhibitionist Tendencies

With financial uncertainty still rocking businesses, but exhibitions still in the work diary, should you keep putting yourself out there? Is it better to conserve cash or continue to showcase?

The Middle East is becoming a hub for international conferences, trade shows and exhibitions. The economic shockwaves of the last couple of years, however, have prompted many local companies to question the merits of intense marketing. Budgets were slashed across the board, from in-house advertising costs and PR contracts to international travel and salaries, but could exhibiting be the outlay that brings the most worthwhile returns?

Exhibitions offer opportunities for businesses to interact with, talk (and listen) to new prospects, demonstrate products and services in real life instead of in a catalogue and check out the competition. By meeting a high volume of contacts in a short amount of time, exhibitions are actually a cost-effective way of boosting trade – providing you follow up on those many business cards you accumulate. Even better, with hotel occupancy down and airlines reducing prices, there are travel deals to be had; by sending more company representatives to attend, opportunities can be maximised further. If you can dominate in these times, you can prosper at the expense of competitors. If contacts are in place, your brand remains strong and you manage to retain staff, then you could be ideally placed to capitalise once the market shows signs of upturn. A recent survey by industry research company Exhibit Surveys Inc. revealed that up to 66% of trade show visitors plan to purchase one or more products as a result of attending an exhibition. Exhibiting may thus be the wisest spend in securing both long and short-term business goals.

Alex Heuff, PALME exhibitions director at IIR Middle East explains: 'Trade shows are still the most cost-effective route to market for local and international firms. In times of financial constraint, for companies big and small, taking part in a trade-related exhibition or event remains the best way of using tighter resources to stay directly in front of customers. I expect the events sector to play a critical role as the catalyst to stimulate the investment climate and boost economic growth, while playing a major role in driving up visitor traffic in the region. Some sectors will always do well in an economic downturn, such as IIR's Arab Health Show, Middle East Electricity and PALME, where secondary shows targeting hobbies and lifestyle may not weather the storm and personal buying habits shift. When times are good you should exhibit, when times are bad, you must exhibit.'

As many European trade shows and conferences shift their attention – and budgets – to Asia and emerging markets such as India, China and Russia, the Middle East is often the location of choice. Thanks to its unique position, excellent conference facilities, transport links, and the potential for a few, post-exhibition, relaxing days on the beach to celebrate a deal being done, the UAE finds itself in a prime position and is pushing to capitalise on this trend.

Major Exhibitions In Abu Dhabi & Dubai

January

Arab Health
arabhealthonline.com
Big Boys Toys
bigboystoysuae.com
The Bride Show Abu Dhabi
thebrideshow.com
International Water Summit
internationalwatersummit.com
World Future Energy Summit
worldfutureenergysummit.com

February

Gulf Education Supply Show
gesseducation.com

March

**Gulf Incentive, Business Travel &
  Meetings Exhibition**
gibtm.com
International Jewellery and Watch Show
jws.ae

April

Abu Dhabi International Book Fair
adbookfair.com
Careers UAE
careersuae.ae
Cityscape Abu Dhabi
cityscapeabudhabi.com
WETEX
wetex.ae

May

Abu Dhabi Telecoms CEO Summit
telecomsceosummit.com
Arabian Travel Market
arabiantravelmarket.com
Beautyworld Middle East
beautyworldme.com

September

GITEX Shopper
gitexshopperdubai.com
The Hotel Show
thehotelshow.com
**International Hunting & Equestrian
  Exhibition Abu Dhabi**
adihex.net
Middle East Pool & Spa Exhibition
mepool.com

October

Abu Dhabi Medical Congress
abudhabimed.com
Abu Dhabi Science Festival
abudhabisciencefestival.ae
Chic Lady Show
chiclady.al-hader.com
Cityscape
cityscapeglobal.com
Gifts & Premiums
premium-dubai.com
GITEX Technology Week
gitex.com
Power + Water Middle East
powerandwaterme.com

November

**Abu Dhabi International Petroleum
  Exhibition and Conference (ADIPEC)**
adipec.com
Big Five Exhibition
thebig5exhibition.com
Dubai World Game Expo
gameexpo.ae
Gulf Traffic
gulftraffic.com
International Automobile Show
int-autoshow.com
UFI Congress
ufi.org
Sharjah World Book Fair
sharjahbookfair.com
Sweets Middle East
sweetsmiddleeast.com
SIAL Middle East
sialme.com

December

Abu Dhabi International Motor Show
admotorshow.com
Middle East Business Aviation
meba.aero
World Green Tourism
worldgreentourism.ae
**The National Exhibition for Small &
  Medium Enterprises**
sme.al-hader.com

Absconding

Anyone leaving the country without cancelling their residence visa with their sponsor will be classed as 'absconding' and may receive a ban, though employers have to wait six months to report absconders who have left the country. Anyone who leaves their employment and remains in the country without notifying their employer can be reported as having absconded after a period of seven days. Absconders are reported to the Ministry of Labour, who then pass information on to Immigration and the police.

Under Article 120 of the Labour Law, if you leave the country or are unaccountable for seven days in a row or 20 days in total, your company can terminate your employment contract without awarding you gratuity pay or any outstanding benefits.

During the economic downturn, there were reports of residents leaving the city at short notice to avoid the ramifications of defaults on bank loans and debts. If you default on a loan and the bank files a case against you, you could receive a visa ban which restricts you from either entering or leaving the country. Details of this claim are filed with the Immigration Department, the police and the Ministry of Labour, which means you could be identified and detained when your visa is scanned at the airport on departure or arrival.

NOC

No-Objection Certificate is a letter of confirmation awarded by your former employer or the Ministry of Labour giving you permission to work for another employer. If you have an NOC from your previous employer, and the Ministry of Labour approves the move, your visa transfer should be hassle-free. But this is one area where laws change frequently so it's best to check with the Labour Department or a lawyer first.

Redundancy

Redundancy can be a serious blow in a city like Abu Dhabi where you may only remain for as long as you have a job. If you are unfortunate enough to be made redundant, try not to dwell on feelings of self doubt about your performance or likeability and instead focus on the financial ramifications.

Firstly, discuss with your employer whether they could be flexible with your visa status. If you have a good relationship, you should have room to negotiate the terms under which you leave, and it's worth requesting a few months' leeway so you have the opportunity to find a new employer and sponsor. If your company wishes to cancel your visa immediately, you have a 30 day grace period in which to leave the country or find new employment before incurring any fines for overstaying your visa. Similarly, if you're living in company accommodation, negotiate with the

company about when you need to move out. If the company has paid upfront, it's possible that they may let you stay for a fixed period.

As there are no overdraft facilities in Abu Dhabi, it is a good idea to plan for every eventuality and put money aside as a buffer should you lose your job unexpectedly; this money can help pay for key bills like rent and car loans.

Company Closure

Employees faced with the unfortunate situation of company bankruptcy or closure are entitled, under UAE Labour Law, to their gratuity payments and holiday pay, but you will need to speak to the Labour Department for the proper process as it is complex. An employee of a firm that has been closed can transfer sponsorship to a new employer if they find a new job, but, if not, their visa will be cancelled and they will have to leave the country.

If your company closes without cancelling its trade licence, you may receive a short time ban from taking a new role with a new employer, although this is unlikely for the majority of employees. Consult the appropriate government offices to get your paperwork right, or invest in the services of a lawyer (p.122) who specialises in labour issues.

Voluntary & Charity Work

There are a number of opportunities to do voluntary or charity work in the UAE with groups always looking for committed volunteers. If it's environmental voluntary work you're after, the Emirates Environmental Group (eeg-uae.org) runs regular campaigns. If you're unsure which group you'd like to support, check volunteerinabudhabi.com.

Volunteer Organisations

Abu Dhabi Animal Shelter

Abu Dhabi Falcon Hospital Al Shamkha
02 575 5155
abudhabianimalshelter.com
Map **3 D3**
Established by the government in 2010, this animal shelter picks up on the great work done by a number of smaller animal charities over the years. Managed by Abu Dhabi Falcon Hospital (p.216), it provides veterinary care for stray or abandoned dogs and cats, while also seeking out new homes for them.

All As One

Fairmont Dubai Dubai 04 311 6707
aaodubai.org
The Dubai branch of an international charity and NGO that raises money for housing, caring for, treating and educating orphaned children in Sierra Leone.

Environmental Agency Abu Dhabi
Al Mamoura Bldg, Muroor Rd Al Nahyan
02 445 4777
ead.ae
Map **2 M8**
As a non-profit entity, Environmental Agency Abu Dhabi (EAAD) is always keen to hear from and ready to welcome volunteers who are willing to get involved, particularly in work related to environmental education.

Ewa'a Shelter For Women & Children
Various locations **02 558 4812**
shwc.ae
A non-profit, non-governmental organisation operated under the UAE Red Crescent, Ewa'a Shelter offer help for female victims of human trafficking and other exploitation. If you would like to take part, you can volunteer to help provide education, health, and entertainment services.

Feline Friends
Various locations **050 582 2916**
felinefriendsuae.com
This organisation helps cats in the UAE. Volunteers rescue and re-home stray cats and kittens, promote street cat control and even provide care to sick and injured cats.

Gulf For Good
International Humanitarian City
Dubai **04 368 0222**
gulf4good.org
Organises a variety of once-in-a-lifetime challenges – from climbing Kilimanjaro or Everest Base Camp, to cycling, hiking and kayaking through the wilderness of Borneo – with challengers' sponsorship going to local charities based in the countries where the challenges take place.

The Little Wings Foundation
Dubai **050 281 2443**
thelittlewingsfoundation.org
This non-profit organisation provides medical assistance to children in the Middle East and North Africa who have musculoskeletal deformities, providing them with the tools they need to have a happy and successful life.

Make A Wish Foundation
02 666 5144
makeawish.ae
The local branch of the global foundation is dedicated to making a dream come true for children diagnosed with life-threatening illnesses, providing them and their families with hope and happiness.

Médecins Sans Frontières > *p.175*
**Villa 4/1, Nr Brazilian Embassy, Street #5,
Al Muroor St** Madinat Zayed **02 631 7645**
msf-me.org
Map **2 N4**
This is an international and independent non-profit organisation that provides emergency medical relief around the world and relies on volunteers to provide aid in any way possible. Volunteers can become involved locally, mainly through organising fundraising events or participating in awareness campaigns.

Red Crescent Society Of The United Arab Emirates
Nr Abu Dhabi Bus Station, Al Muroor Rd
Al Nahyan **02 641 9000**
rcuae.ae
Map **2 M8**
The Abu Dhabi branch of the wide-reaching charity helps provide medical and educational assistance, responds to aid appeals and also provides sponsorship for orphans.

Special Care Centre
Nr Al Wahda Mall Al Dhafrah **02 641 8418**
donateabrick.org
Map **2 M7**
A non-profit organisation which supports children with special needs. The centre is always in need of volunteers to help with activities and events. Register by filling in a form at the centre.

Working As A Freelancer/Contractor
The opportunities for freelance or contract work in Abu Dhabi have in the past been limited as, generally speaking, you could not legally work without a residence visa and a labour card, and you could not work for anyone who is not your sponsor. Due to the new part-time labour laws, however, the possibilities of working freelance or contract work seem to be expanding, as you can now accept such work if you are sponsored by your spouse.

It is also possible to work on a contract or consultancy basis for short-term contracts by being employed by a company or agency which then sub-contracts you to another firm. As yet, there is no proper Abu Dhabi equivalent of the 'freelance visa' available at Dubai's Media City, however media professionals can set up as freelancers at twofour54 (see Flying Solo, p.103.)

Other professions can work in a Free Trade Zone (FTZ) where you are sponsored by the particular FTZ and so can move around within the zone (see Free Trade Zones, p.106); as an individual freelancer however, the cost of setting up and maintaining a presence in a free zone can be prohibitive.

Work, Finance & The Law

High-rise offices

Setting Up A Small Business

The business climate in the United Arab Emirates has made a rapid recovery from the global downturn. Although the pre-crisis levels of absolute optimism and boundless investment are unlikely to be repeated any time soon, there certainly are opportunities for savvy entrepreneurs.

Starting a business requires meticulous market research, a strict, realistic business plan and responsive action to take advantage of fleeting openings in the market. Several high-profile cases have also made it clear that there are serious risks involved in doing business in the country; bankruptcy laws are not as defined as in other countries and mismanagement of funds could result in harsh repercussions, including deportation or even jail time.

The government and ruling families have passed legislation and formed organisations that aid the start-up process in the UAE. In August 2009, the UAE Ministry of Economy removed the minimum capital requirements for new businesses, which used to be Dhs.300,000.

One of the major hesitations that entrepreneurs have about starting a business here in the UAE is the requirement of having a local sponsor control a majority stake of the company. The increasing number of free zones (p.106) in the region, however, eliminate that rule and allow for full private foreign ownership. The licensing process for opening a business in a free zone is also more streamlined and helped by the free zone organisation.

Government and private sector-sponsored initiatives are also helping to spur business and educate potential business owners. Abu Dhabi University (adu.ac.ae) has a Centre of Excellence for Innovation and Entrepreneurship which enables and supports Emiratis, while the Khalifa Fund for Enterprise Development (khalifafund.gov.ae) encourages local business people with training and development. The annual Abu Dhabi Forum on Entrepreneurship provides discussion and ideas.

There are various business groups in Abu Dhabi that help facilitate investments and provide opportunities for networking with others in the community. Some business groups and councils (p.104) provide information on trade with their respective countries, as well as on business opportunities both in Abu Dhabi and internationally. Most also arrange social and networking events on a regular basis.

Before you set up, contact the Abu Dhabi Chamber of Commerce & Industry (abudhabichamber.ae) and the Ministry of Economy (economy.ae). Both can offer some excellent advice. Embassies or consulates can also be a good business resource and may be able to offer contact lists for the UAE.

Working Part-time

The laws governing part-time work were amended in early 2011, and while it's still a bit nebulous as the UAE government irons out the details, there are several important changes. Those sponsored by a husband or wife can seek part-time employment without the need for a permit. If you're looking to secure a part-time position, written permission from your sponsor spouse is all that's required.

In effect, this frees housewives or husbands to have greater flexibility and options when seeking a position, as they are already sponsored by their working spouse. There's good news for parents looking to get the teens out of the house, too; those on student sponsorship visas are permitted a one-year part-time work permit, as are teenagers between the ages of 15 and 18. The jobs available to teens are restricted to occupations not requiring heavy manual labour and working hours are limited to six daily, so you might want to rethink sending the kids off to work a summer in the oilfields.

The new labour laws stipulate that employers should give priority to UAE and GCC citizens, although it's unclear exactly how that will be enforced. Check with the Ministry of Labour (mol.gov.ae or 800 665) for further information.

Top Tips For Healthy Personal Finance

Don't Neglect Your Credit Cards: They are great to bail you out in emergencies, but unless you are disciplined when using them, credit cards can land you in trouble. Leave them in a secure place at home where you won't be tempted and always make the minimum repayments on time to avoid late fees.

Try To Live Off Half Your Salary: Really examine your expenses and be brutal when it comes to deciding what you can live without – manicures, double lattes, fancy restaurants and gym memberships are all luxuries, and cutting them out of your budget could mean surprising savings at the end of the month.

Entertain At Home: Eating out in Abu Dhabi's lavish restaurants is so alluring, but it doesn't come cheap. In tough financial times, master the art of 'cocooning' – staying in and inviting friends round for dinner or a movie night.

Shop Smart: Certain supermarkets may be convenient and stock all your favourites from back home, but they are much more expensive than other, more basic supermarkets. You'll save more if you buy your everyday items from a larger hypermarket (p.336). Decide on a grocery budget at the beginning of the month, and make it last.

Don't Pay Full Price For Anything: Shops in the city regularly offer promotions, sales and buy-one-get-one free promotions. Shop around to find the best bargains; you'll be amazed at what you can save. Get Packing: There's no such thing as a free lunch, but packing your own sandwiches is the next best thing. It's healthier and the savings you'll make do add up at the end of the month.

Take Advantage Of Exchange Rates: Certain items can work out much cheaper when buying from Amazon, even when you factor in the shipping, simply because of the exchange rate. You can get a current CD for over Dhs.10 cheaper than what you'd pay in a retail outlet here – so if you're ordering a few, you could save a bundle. If you've got visitors coming over, get your Amazon order delivered to them (most orders ship free locally), and get them to bring it with them.

Buy Second-hand: Visit Sarah's Flea Market in Officer's City (fleamarketuae.com) for a browse through other people's unwanted items or try the Dubai Flea Market at Safa Park (dubai-fleamarket.com). Supermarket noticeboards are cluttered with great pre-owned items looking for new homes, as is the Abu Dhabi section of Dubizzle (dubizzle.com).

Reduce Costs Over Summer: If you are planning to be away for some time over the summer, look into downgrading your satellite TV and internet packages for a few months. That way, you can usually upgrade again come September without having to pay any reconnection fees. Better yet, if you only have satellite TV so you can watch the Premier League football, cancel it completely over summer. You can always re-subscribe when the season kicks off again.

Cost Of Living

Bottle of wine (off-licence)	Dhs.40
Burger (takeaway)	Dhs.12
Can of soft drink	Dhs.1.5
Car rental (per day)	Dhs.100
Cigarettes (pack of 20)	Dhs.7
Cinema ticket	Dhs.30
Cleaner (per hour)	Dhs.25
Dozen eggs	Dhs.8
House wine (glass)	Dhs.25-40
Loaf of bread	Dhs.4.5
Milk (1 litre)	Dhs.5.5
Mobile to mobile call (local, per minute)	30 fils
New release DVD	Dhs.85
Newspaper (international)	Dhs.15
Petrol (gallon)	Dhs.6.25
Pint of beer	Dhs.20
Six-pack of beer (off-licence)	Dhs.25
Taxi (10km journey)	Dhs.20
Text message (local)	18 fils
Water 1.5 litres (supermarket)	Dhs.1.5

FINANCIAL AFFAIRS

Bank Accounts

There are several reputable banks in Abu Dhabi, including names well-known globally, such as HSBC, Citibank and Barclays Bank. However, banks that operate internationally rarely actually have connections with their counterparts in other parts of the world, so you won't be able to view or manage accounts held in other countries through your Abu Dhabi account.

Bank Opening Hours

Banking hours are generally 08:00 to 13:30, Saturday to Wednesday, and 08:00 to 12:00 on Thursday. Some branches, especially those in malls, remain open later in the evenings, even as late as 22:00; all banks are closed on Fridays.

Most banks offer online banking, so you can check your balance, transfer money and pay bills online. There are plenty of ATMs (cash points) around Abu Dhabi and most cards are compatible with the Central Bank network (some also offer global access links). You may pay a small fee for using another bank's ATM but it should never be more than a few dirhams.

To open an account in most banks, you need a residence visa or to have your residency application underway. To apply, you will need to submit your original passport, copies of your passport (personal details and visa) and an NOC from your sponsor. Some banks set a minimum account limit – this can be around Dhs.2,000 for a deposit account and as much as Dhs.10,000 for a current account. This means that, at some point in each month, your account balance must be above the minimum limit; many people avoid this complication by having their monthly wage deposited into their accounts. If you don't have a residence visa, Emirates NBD can organise an account for you that will provide an ATM card, but not a chequebook or access to overdrafts or credit cards.

Although credit cards are widely available, banks are currently still exercising more caution than they have been in the past, due to the recent global credit crisis, particularly where loans are concerned.

A number of laws have been introduced to combat money laundering. The UAE Central Bank monitors all incoming and outgoing transfers, and banks and currency exchanges are required to report transfers over a certain limit. Additionally, if you need to send more than Dhs.2,000 by international transfer you may have to show a valid passport.

Main Banks

Abu Dhabi Commercial Bank (ADCB) Al Salam St, Tourist Club Area, 02 696 2222, adcb.com

Abu Dhabi Islamic Bank 02 610 0600, adib.ae

Al Hilal Bank 02 499 4444, alhilalbank.ae

Al Masraf Al Masraf Tower, Shk Hamdan Bin Mohammed St, Tourist Club Area, 02 672 1900, arbift.com

Bank Of Sharjah Al Mina St, Tourist Club Area, 02 679 5555, bankofsharjah.com

Barclays Bank Al Jazeera Tower, Shk Hamdan Bin Mohammed St, Markaziya East, 02 495 8555, barclays.ae

Citibank Corniche Plaza Bldg, Al Salam St, Markaziya East, 02 698 2206, citibank.com

Commercial Bank Interantional Shk Srour Bldg, Corniche Rd, Al Khalidiyah, 02 681 8448, cbiuae.com

Commercial Bank Of Dubai Baniyas Tower, Corniche St, Markaziya East, 02 626 8400, cbd.ae

Crédit Agricole Corporate & Investment Bank Al Muhairy Centre, Al Manhal, 02 631 2400, ca-cib.com

Dubai Bank IMG Bldg, Corniche Rd, Markaziya East, 800 5555, dubaibank.ae

Dubai Islamic Bank Nr Etisalat, Shk Rashid Bin Saeed Al Maktoum St, Madinat Zayed, 02 634 6600, alislami.ae

Emirates Islamic Bank Shk Rashid Bin Saeed Al Maktoum St, Al Musalla, 02 446 4000, emiratesislamicbank.ae

Emirates NBD Al Baluchi Tower, Shk Zayed The Second St, Tourist Club Area, 800 456, emiratesnbd.com

First Gulf Bank Shk Zayed The First St, Al Khubeirah, 600 52 5500, fgb.ae

HSBC Omeir Bin Yousuf Bldg, Nr Etisalat building, Shk Rashid Bin Saeed Al Maktoum St, Madinat Zayed, 600 55 4722, hsbc.ae

Mashreq Bank Blue Tower,Sheikh Khalifa Bin Zayed St, Markaziya East, 02 612 7248, mashreqbank.com

National Bank Of Abu Dhabi Nr Sheikh Khalifa & Baniyas Sts, Markaziya East, 02 611 1111, nbad.com

RAK Bank Nr Abu Dhabi Mall, Tourist Club Area, 02 644 8227, rakbank.ae

The Royal Bank Of Scotland 235 Shk Rashid Bin Saeed Al Maktoum St, Al Karamah, 02 408 4005, rbsbank.ae

Standard Chartered Crystal Tower, Khalidiyah Financial Centre, Shk Zayed The First St, Al Khalidiyah, 02 60052 2288, standardchartered.ae

Union National Bank UNB Bldg, Salam St, Markaziya East, 02 674 1600, unb.co.ae

Sowwah Square > p.115

This development is at the heart of Al Maryah Island, Abu Dhabi's new business district. Sowwah Square (sowwahsquare.ae) is home to the new HQ of Abu Dhabi Securities Exchange and a number of other major businesses. If you're in the area, don't miss breakfast at Jones The Grocer (p.379).

Pension Planning

Many expats come to Dubai to advance their career and the city's advantageous tax climate makes it an appealing choice financially as well. But what about pensions and securing your financial future?

Ask the expert

Robert Palmer Senior Pensions Advisor, Expatriate Pensions

What considerations should expats bear in mind when considering the impact that working in Dubai will have on their pensions?
Planning for your financial future is a topic not to be taken lightly no matter where you live; however, this is especially the case for expats and in my opinion, the answer is exceptionally straight-forward: it's simply always best to take advice from an expert who specialises in pensions.

For expats in general, what's the single most important characteristic to look for in a pension plan?
The key word here is 'flexibility'. Basically, you can never know what's going to happen next. It can be amazing career prospects one minute and redundancy the next. Choose something that can take account of a sudden change in your circumstance

Are pension products available locally or should expats look into making arrangements in their home country?
All of the large international assurance companies have offices here and offer easy-to-understand retirement planning products. Tax status can influence advice here in the UAE, but the rule of thumb is to take advantage of solutions using one of the world's traditional offshore centres. These include the Isle of Man, Jersey and Guernsey in the UK.

How about any pensions expats may have been saving for in their home countries or elsewhere before making the move here?
This is an important consideration and it's crucial to understand your options fully. For example, not everyone is aware that it's now possible to take advantage of new legislation initiated in most EU countries, which allows expats to transfer their existing pension plans with them.

Why should expats transfer their existing pension plans? What are the main benefits of doing this while working in Dubai?
Transferring your existing pension during the time you're working here in Dubai offers a number of benefits, which can be summarised under the following three areas:

1) Tax advantages
2) Investment control
3) Easy-to-understand solutions

Planning Ahead

New to Dubai? The tax-free lifestyle is a great opportunity to advance your financial standing. However, if you have a pension scheme in your home country, it may not be worth continuing your contributions once you come to Dubai, but rather to set up a tax-free, offshore savings plan. It's always advisable to speak to your financial adviser before you make any big move – after all, it may have a huge impact on your future.

Financial Planning

Many expats are attracted to Abu Dhabi for the tax-free salary and the opportunity to put a little something away for the future. However, Abu Dhabi's alluring lifestyle can quickly steer you away from your sensible goals. It is often necessary for residents to get credit cards and bank loans to finance their life and lifestyle – especially as start-up costs such as accommodation (often paid a year upfront) and buying a vehicle kick in quite soon after arrival – and it is easy to slip into debt.

You'll find there is little or no support if you do (see Debt, p.120). It is therefore extremely important to plan your finances straight from the off, and arrange a safeguard in case your finances take a turn for the worse or you're hit by an unexpected cost or setback. Expenses as innocuous as home or vehicle repairs, dental or medical treatments, or even unforeseen flights home can very quickly put a strain on the bank account.

When choosing a financial planner in Abu Dhabi, you should ensure that they are licensed by the Central Bank of the UAE (04 665 2220, centralbank. ae), so that you have some recourse in the event of a dispute. You should also consider the company's international presence – you'll still want the same access to advice, information and your investments

Freezing Funds

In the past, banks have frozen funds when you have left your place of work (until you obtain another residency visa and NOC or salary transfer certificate from your new employer), leaving many people without access to their accounts for several weeks or months as the paperwork was being dealt with or they were legally job hunting. Banks have now been encouraged to work with account holders in order to keep the account open; however, the freezing only ever took place when there were loans (credit cards or auto loans, for example) against the account.

if you return home. It may also be better to use an independent company or adviser who is not tied to a specific bank or savings company and, therefore, will objectively offer you the full range of savings products on the market.

Financial Advice

There seems to be an overabundance of financial advisers in the city who may contact you over the phone and advertise their services. Most advisers won't ask for money initially, however they may ask you for contact details of your friends and family members so that they can continue to spread the word.

Before leaving your home country, you should contact the tax authorities to ensure that you are complying with the financial laws there. Most countries will consider you not liable for income tax once you have proven that you are a UAE resident (a contract of employment is normally a good starting point). However, you may still have to fulfil certain criteria, so do some research before you arrive (if you are already here, check with your embassy). You may still be liable for tax on any income you receive from your home country (for example, if you have rented out your property).

If you have a pension scheme in your home country, it may not be worth continuing your contributions once you come to Abu Dhabi, but rather to set up a tax-free, offshore savings plan. It is always advisable to speak to your financial adviser about such matters before you make any big move.

Financial Advisers

Holborn Assets Al Shafar Tower, Dubai, 04 457 3800, *holbornassets.com*
KPMG Falcon Tower, Al Nasr St, Markaziya West, 02 634 3318, *kpmg.com*
Mondial (Dubai) > *p.117* Pinnacle Bldg, Shk Zayed Rd, Dubai, 04 399 6601, *mondialdubai.com*

S t a y i n g   I n   T h e   B l a c k   G r a h a m   B e n t l e y   PIC de Vere Group

Abu Dhabi is one of the best places to be right now, financially speaking. There are amazing opportunities for getting out of debt, staying out of debt and saving for your future, providing you know how. You need to get organised, make a list of all your monthly repayments and prioritise them. Get rid of the credit cards with the extortionate interest rates first. Work out how much you need to spend on debt repayments each month, then half of what you have left over you should be saving, and the other half for living on. It may not sound feasible but this is why it is important to speak to a financial adviser; together you can look at how to offset certain debts by finding ways of making your money work harder for you, which is a lot easier than it sounds in a tax-free environment. The most important thing is to live within your means. Don't get sucked into the expensive lifestyle, make going for a meal in an expensive restaurant a treat rather than the norm. It's easy to fall down the slippery slope and end up in more debt than when you first arrived, just remember to stay level-headed.

PIC Middle East Villa 213/4, 25th Street, Shk Rashid Bin Saeed Al Maktoum St, Al Mushrif, 02 676 5588, *pic-uae.com*

Prosperity Offshore Investment Consultants Bayswater Tower, Dubai, 04 454 2530, *prosperity-uae.com*

Insurance Companies

Abu Dhabi National Insurance Company (ADNIC) ADNIC Bldg, Shk Khalifa Bin Zayed St, Markaziya East, 02 408 0100, *adnic.ae*

Abu Dhabi National Takaful Company Al Bateen, 02 410 7700, *takaful.ae*

Al Ain Ahlia Insurance Company Shk Rashid Bin Saeed Al Maktoum St, 02 445 9900, *alaininsurance.com*

Al Khazna Insurance Company Villa 51, East of Al Nahyan Camp, Delma St, Al Nahyan, 02 696 9700, *alkhazna.com*

Alliance Insurance Ghanam Al Mazroui Bldg, Madinat Zayed, 02 632 6067, *alliance-uae.com*

Allianz SE Dubai International Financial Centre (DIFC), Dubai, 04 702 6666, *allianz.com*

Arab Orient Insurance Company New Honda Showroom Bldg, Zayed The First St, 02 676 3222, *insuranceuae.com*

AXA Insurance (Gulf) > *p.65* National Consultative Council Complex, Delma St, Al Nahyan, 02 495 7999, *axa-gulf.com*

Daman National Health Insurance Company Millenium Tower, Nr Hamdan Centre, Shk Hamdan Bin Mhd St, Markaziya East, 02 614 9555, *damanhealth.ae*

Emirates Insurance Company Emirates Insurance Co Bldg, Tourist Club Area, 02 644 0400, *eminsco.com*

Guardian Insurance Brokers Abu Dhabi University Tower, Muroor Rd, Al Nahyan, 02 491 3777, *gib-uae.com*

Lifecare International Khalid Al Attar Towers, Shk Zayed Rd, Dubai, 04 331 8688, *lifecareinternational.com*

MedNet UAE Dubai Internet City, Dubai, 04 390 0749, *mednet-uae.com*

MetLife Alico Dubai International Financial Centre (DIFC), Dubai, 04 360 0555, *metlifealico.ae*

Nasco Karaoglan Al Muroor, 02 642 2255, *nascodubai.com*

National General Insurance Co (NGI) Al Sahel Tower, Old Passport Rd, Al Khalidiyah, 02 667 8783, *ngi.ae*

NEXtCARE UAE Business Avenue Bldg, Shk Rashid Rd, Dubai, 04 209 5200, *nextcare.ae*

Nexus Al Ghaith Towers, Shk Hamdan Bin Mohammed St, Markaziyah East, 02 6266669, *nexusadvice.com*

Oman Insurance Company Blue Tower, Shk Khalifa Bin Zayed St, Markaziya East, 02 612 8444, *tameen.ae*

Qatar Insurance Company ADCB Bldg, Nr Shk Hamdan Bin Mohammed & Salam Sts, Markaziya East, 02 676 9466, *qatarinsurance.com*

RSA Habib Bank Bldg, Shk Hamdan Bin Mohammed St, Markaziya East, 02 635 1800, *rsadirect.ae*

Zurich International Life Al Otaiba Bldg, Shk Rashid Bin Saeed Al Maktoum St, Markaziya West, 02 627 5777, *zurich.com*

Credit Cards

The process for obtaining a credit card is fairly straightforward and is usually offered by the bank connected to your payroll account. If you are eligible, in facy, you'll often receive phone calls from your bank offering credit cards – and, if you do opt for one, a representative will usually offer to meet you to set up the account. Banks will normally ask that you have a minimum salary (dependent on the credit amount), a salary certificate, which details your earnings (this should be provided by your employer), and a copy of your passport with your residence visa and work permit.

Most shops, hotels and restaurants accept the major credit cards (American Express, Diners Club, MasterCard and Visa). Smaller retailers are sometimes less likely to accept credit cards due to the extra processing fees, however, the Supreme Committee for Consumer Protection passed a resolution prohibiting them from charging customers for these extra processing fees. Check economy.ae for details or to report a violation. If you are paying in cash, you may sometimes be allowed a discount – it's certainly worth enquiring.

If you lose your credit or debit card, you must contact the bank as soon as possible and report the missing card. Once you have reported the loss, it is highly unlikely that you would be held liable for any further transactions made on the card. As a consequence of ATM fraud, banks have now set a limit on the amount of cash you can withdraw per day in order to limit the financial damage of stolen credit cards (the amount varies from card to card). Although, if you expect you'll need more, you can pre-arrange to have these limits extended temporarily or permanently. In addition to these measures, banks also advise the public on how to prevent credit card crime. A frequent problem is that people do not change their pin when they get the card. This is vital for secrecy, and banks also suggest you continue to change your pin on a regular basis.

Cash For Gas

Although credit cards are accepted at Abu Dhabi petrol stations, strangely, you are no longer able to use your credit card to buy petrol at garages in most the other emirates. Garages in Dubai and Fujairah, for example, only accept cash at the petrol pumps and some at their convenience stores too, so make sure you have cash at hand.

Financial Affairs

Offshore Accounts

While offshore banking used to be associated with the very wealthy or the highly shady, a lot of expats now take advantage of tax efficient plans.

An offshore account works in much the same way as a conventional account, but it can be adjusted specifically for you. Money can be moved where it will produce the best rewards, and cash accessed whenever and wherever you need it, in your desired currency. Offshore accounts allow for management through the internet and over the phone, in a range of currencies (most commonly in US dollars, euros or pounds sterling).

If you are travelling outside the UAE, try to make sure that your account comes with 24 hour banking, internationally recognised debit cards, and the ability to write cheques in your preferred currency. To open an account, there is usually a minimum balance of at least $10,000. Do some thorough research before opening an account, and check the potential tax implications in your home country.

It is important to seek independent financial advice, and not just the opinion of the bank offering you an account. Lloyds TSB (lloydstsb.ae) and HSBC (hsbc.ae) both offer good offshore services but will, of course, only advise on their own products. To open your account, you may have to produce certain reports or documents from your chosen country. However, for those willing to do the research and undertake the admin, offshore banking can prove to be a lucrative investment.

Taxation

The UAE levies no personal income taxes or withholding taxes, but there are rumours that income tax and VAT may be introduced in the future. There are no firm dates for implementation at present, and it would no doubt be unpopular and possibly hamper attempts to attract foreign investment, but the IMF is advising Middle Eastern governments to introduce tax reforms in order to diversify their resources.

Taxing Issue

You may need to register your residency in the UAE with the government in your home country to avoid paying income tax or capital gains tax. It's best to check with your consulate for exact details. There are also rumours that income tax will be introduced in the UAE, however, at present, nothing concrete has been announced by the government.

The only noticeable taxes you pay as an expat are a 5% municipality tax on rental accommodation, a 30% tax on alcohol bought at licensed liquor stores and 50% tax on tobacco (although cigarettes are still comparatively cheap). The municipality tax is included in your ADWEC bill, and if you don't pay, your utilities will be cut off.

There is also a 6% Abu Dhabi Tourism Authority tax and a 10% service charge in hotel food and beverage outlets; sometimes this is included in the display price, but be sure to read the small print at the bottom of the menu to avoid any surprises. Independent food and beverage outlets will not charge the Tourism Authority tax, but may still have the service charge.

Cheques

Cheques aren't commonly used as a method of payment in Abu Dhabi and most residents will only have to organise them when handing over post-dated cheques for rental agreements. The most important thing to remember is that issuing a cheque when you have insufficient funds in your account to cover the amount is considered a criminal offence. If your cheques bounce and a complaint is filed with the authorities, you could be arrested; even if the complaint isn't filed, banks now have the right to close a customer's account if they bounce four cheques over the course of a year.

When writing a post-dated cheque, it is important that you are sure of your finances; you should also encourage the beneficiary to deposit the cheques as soon as possible (if that is best). A cheque cannot be cancelled, unless it is mislaid or stolen, so a cheque you wrote several months ago could land you in big trouble, if cashed unexpectedly.

Debt

In a city that seems to run on credit cards and post-dated cheques, it can be quite a shock (and a major inconvenience) to find that severe penalties are dealt out for late or missed payments. While you may be forced to take large loans to purchase vehicles or for annual rent, it is important to note that, if you are suddenly made redundant and your finances spiral out of control, there is no safety net.

Unlike some countries, where you will receive several reminders for missed payments, if you are late paying for basic household bills such as electricity or water, your services may be disconnected without much warning – even if you regularly pay your bills. Missed payments on credit cards bills will often incur fines or restrictions to services, and it is also considered a criminal offence to write a cheque when you have insufficient funds to cover the balance (see Cheques). In some cases, failure to meet payments can lead to prosecution, a visa ban (p.107) and jail time.

The economic downturn highlighted this issue when several residents, who were made redundant, made a swift departure from the UAE to avoid prosecution. Banks are subsequently more cautious about who they offer loans to. There are also rumours that debt collectors are increasingly being employed

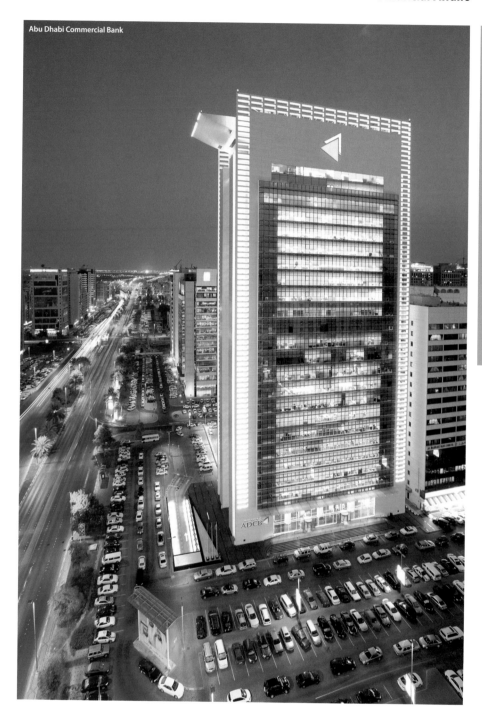

Abu Dhabi Commercial Bank

to recover outstanding debts from residents who have returned back to their home countries. The best way to avoid any unpleasant situations is avoid getting into debt in the first place – plan well, and always keep some money in reserve.

Don't Bank On It

There are no bankruptcy laws in the UAE, so individuals who fall into financial difficulties are fully liable for their debt. If you are unable to keep up with repayments for your bank loans and your bank files a complaint against you, you may be faced with a visa ban or an extended term in jail.

LEGAL ISSUES

Shariah Law

The country's constitution permits each emirate to have its own legislative body and judicial authority. Abu Dhabi has retained its own judicial system, including appellate courts (courts of appeal), which are not part of the UAE federal system. There are three primary sources of UAE law, namely federal laws and decrees (applicable in all emirates), local laws (laws and regulations enacted by the individual emirates), and Shariah (Islamic law). Generally, when a court is determining a commercial issue, it gives initial consideration to any applicable federal and local laws. If these do not address the issue, Shariah may be applied. Moreover, Shariah generally applies to family law matters, particularly when involving Muslims.

Afridi & Angell Al Ghaith Tower, Shk Hamdan Bin Mohammed St, Markaziya East, 02 627 5134, *afridi-angell.com*
Al Tamimi & Company Al Sila Tower, Al Sowwah Square, Al Maryah Island, 02 813 0444, *tamimi.com*
Clyde & Co West Tower, Abu Dhabi Mall, Tourist Club Area, 02 644 6633, *clydeco.com*
Consolidated Consultants (Jafar Tukan & Partners) Nr City Terminal & Saba Hotel, Tourist Club Area, 02 644 2955, *ccjo.com*
DLA Piper Middle East Penthouse C2 Bldg, Al Bateen, 02 494 1500, *dlapiper.com*
Emirates Advocates Abu Dhabi Islamic Bank, Al Najda St, Markaziya East, 02 639 4446, *emiratesadvocates.com*
Habib Al Mulla & Company Alia Tower, Shk Khalifa Bin Zayed St, Markaziya East, 02 676 6003, *habibalmulla.com*
Hadef & Partners Blue Tower, Shk Khalifa Bin Zayed St, Markaziya East, 02 627 6622, *hadefpartners.com*
International Advocates & Legal Consultants Bin Hayai Bldg, Shk Zayed The First St, Al Khalidiyah, 02 633 5000, *alalamyalawyers.com*

Kudsi Law Firm Falcon Tower, Al Nasr St, Markaziya West, 02 633 6500, *kudsilawfirm.ae*
Reed Smith Golden Falcon Tower, Shk Hamdan Bin Mohammed St, Markaziya East, 02 622 2636, *reedsmith.com*
Simmons & Simmons ADNIC Bldg, Shk Khalifa Bin Zayed St, Markaziya East, 02 651 9200, *simmons-simmons.com*
SNR Denton Al Ghaith Tower, Shk Hamdan Bin Mohammed St, Markaziya East, 02 626 6180, *snrdenton.com*
Trowers & Hamlins Tower C1, Al Bateen Towers, Bainuna St, Al Bateen, 02 410 7600, *trowers.com*

Wills & Estate Law

Having a valid will in place is one of those essential things that everybody should do. It is especially important to seek legal advice when drawing up your will if you become a property owner in Abu Dhabi. This is one area where the law is rather complicated – under Shariah law, the basic rules for who inherits property after someone's death differ from those in other countries. For example, in the event of your death, it may be the case that your sons (or brother, if you don't have any sons) are first in line for inheritance and your wife could end up with nothing. Therefore, it is better to make sure that you have a clear last will and testament in place. An Abu Dhabi-based lawyer will be able to assist you with a locally viable will. See p.122 for a list of law firms, or contact Just Wills (just-wills.net), part of a UK-based estate planning organisation that has a presence in the UAE.

Family Law

In accordance with the UAE constitution, family law (which governs matters such as divorce) will either be governed by UAE law – Shariah law – or by the laws of the individuals' originating country. If the parties are from different countries, the law applicable will be the law under which their marriage was solemnised.

Normally, the court will look into the possibility of reconciliation before granting a divorce. This means that, before filing for divorce, you can approach the Family Guidance and Reformation Centre which functions under the Abu Dhabi Judicial Department (02 651 2222, adjd.gov.ae). Anyone experiencing marital problems or any family dispute is able to approach this organisation. The other party in the dispute will be called in and the counsellors will try to help you reach an amicable settlement. If the matter is not resolved, the Guidance Centre may refer the matter to the court for legal proceedings to take place.

In deciding on the custody of children, the court's paramount concern will be the child's welfare. In Shariah law, custody of the child will be the mother's right while the child is a minor, unless there are compelling reasons to decide otherwise.

Crime

Abu Dhabi is known for having a low crime rate – in fact, for many expats, it is one of the key benefits of living here. However, it would be naive to think that there is no crime, as there are cases of theft, rape and even murder, but these occur on such a small scale that they rarely affect the quality of life of the average expat. The most common reason for expats getting on the wrong side of the law is driving under the influence of alcohol. In the UAE, there is a zero-tolerance policy toward drinking and driving. If even a sip of alcohol has passed your lips, you are not allowed to drive. While there are few spot checks, if you have an accident, even a minor one in which you were not at fault, you might be breathalysed and the consequences can be serious. Driving the morning after a heavy night is risky, since you will still have alcohol in your system. You will be arrested, and the usual penalty is a minimum 30 days in prison, although it can vary from case to case. You should bear in mind too that your insurance company is likely to refuse to pay the claim if you were in an accident, even if you were not to blame. It's just not worth the risk – cabs are cheap and there are plenty of them.

It also pays to keep your cool if you are involved in any altercation; obscene gestures can result in a prison sentence or a fine and even deportation. Even using profane language on the phone can lead you in serious trouble, so if you feel yourself getting frustrated, it's probably best to hang up. The bottom line is that harming others, whether verbally or physically, will get you into trouble. If the other party is injured, a jail term may be in order, though if the victim chooses to drop the charges then you will be released. If you are detained for being drunk and disorderly, you may spend a night in the cells but, if you are abusive, you could be looking at a fine or longer sentence.

In 2010, two vacationing Britons were sentenced to a month in prison followed by deportation after an Emirati woman alleged they kissed and embraced in a restaurant. This high-profile case should serve as a reminder that the authorities may extend the full arm of the law if you are caught breaking it.

Police

Abu Dhabi has a large, active, and highly respected police force who take community involvement seriously. The uniforms are easily identifiable: the standard uniform is ash-grey but traffic police wear white sleeves and a white belt to differentiate themselves. Police vehicles are generally red and white with blue and red lights on the roof, but you will also see brown SUVs and pick-ups, as well as some unmarked vehicles. The police are approachable; most speak some English and they are generally helpful if you need to ask simple questions or for directions.

They will also respond promptly if there is a problem. The emergency telephone number is 999 and you can use it if you are involved in a traffic accident or to report a crime or criminal behaviour.

In the event of a road accident, call 999 immediately. In the case of non-serious accidents, if no one is hurt and vehicle damage is minor, drivers are recommended to move their vehicles to the side of the road to avoid blocking traffic. In some cases, the first vehicle to respond may not be a police vehicle but one of a new group of vehicles that is white with black and orange markings from Saeed (see p.59).

Jaywalking

In an attempt to cut pedestrian casualties on Abu Dhabi roads, the police are cracking down on jaywalkers. Crossing the street at an unauthorised point could land you a Dhs.200 fine, so do the smart thing and cross only at marked intersections, bridges, or subways.

If the accident is serious, the vehicles should not be moved. When the police arrive, have your vehicle registration card, driver's licence and insurance papers ready for them and follow their instructions. They will ask for your opinion of what happened and then decide who was at fault. If the police decide you were at fault, you will be given a pink form. If the police determine you are not at fault, you will be given a green form. The form allows you to have your vehicle repaired. A garage cannot repair accident damage without a form.

Rather than dismissing minor crimes, the police deal quickly with 'nuisance' problems, such as rowdy neighbours and the harassment of women. They can also direct other emergency services (fire, ambulance and rescue), though the fire department can also be called directly on 997. Community policing has been found to be very successful and is being expanded to other regions. The Abu Dhabi police website has plenty of useful information.

If You Are Arrested

If you are arrested, you will be taken to a police station and questioned. If it is decided that you must go to court, the police will pass the case to the public prosecutor who will then set a date for a court hearing. If the offence is a minor one, you may get bail and the police will keep your passport and often the passport of another UAE resident who is willing to vouch for you. Police stations have holding cells, so, if you don't get bail, you'll be held until the hearing. All court proceedings are conducted in Arabic, so you should try to make sure you have secured the services of a translator. If sentenced, you'll go straight from court to jail.

Legal Issues

Upon being arrested, you are advised to contact your embassy or consulate (see inside back cover for contact details) as soon as possible. They will be able to liaise with family, advise on local legal procedures and provide a list of lawyers, but they will not pay your legal fees. The consulate will try to ensure that you are not denied your basic human rights, but they cannot act as lawyers, investigators, secure bail, or get you released. Also worth remembering is the fact that anyone arrested and detained on a Thursday evening will languish in a cell until the courts reopen after the weekend – if it's a holiday (such as Eid) you'll be inside even longer. The main prison is in Al Watba, between Abu Dhabi and Dubai, and there is a small local prison located at the police station in Khalidiyah.

Victim Support

There are some support services available to those who have been victims of crime. Women and children, who are victims of domestic violence, can contact the

Tips For Women

The following general tips are useful for women in Abu Dhabi:
- Stick to the dress code; tight, revealing clothing equals unwanted attention.
- Be careful when out alone at night, especially after a few drinks.
- Never get into an unmetered taxi; and always take down the taxi number.
- As long as you exercise due care and attention, Abu Dhabi is a safe place for women.

Family Development Foundation (fdf.ae) which is in the process of setting up a shelter for family violence victims; the organisation also offers counselling and advice for women and their partners. The UAE Red Crescent also operates the EWA'A women's shelters in Sharjah, Ras al Khaimah, and Abu Dhabi.

The National Committee to Combat Human Trafficking (nccht.gov.ae) assists those who are victims of sexual abuse. Its website also provides information on other support services in the UAE. Abu Dhabi Police (adpolice.gov.ae) offers a social support centre.

Prohibited Items

Taking illegal narcotics is an absolute no-no – even the smallest amounts of marijuana or hashish could earn you a prison sentence of four years or more, which would almost certainly be followed by deportation. Even airport passengers in transit with drug residue on clothing or luggage can face stiff penalties. If you're found guilty of dealing or smuggling, you could be looking at a life sentence, or even the death penalty (although this is uncommon).

Some medications that are legal in your home country, such as codeine, Temazepam and Prozac, may be banned here – check with the UAE embassy in your home country before leaving and, if you are in any doubt, try to find an alternative. If you must bring the medication with you, keep a copy of the prescription and obtain a medical report from your doctor – this may help explain your case if you are questioned. There is a list of approved drugs on the Ministry of Health website (moh.gov.ae) but it is not known how frequently this list is updated or how reliable it is.

Abu Dhabi National Exhibition Centre

Laws To Remember

Licence To Drink: There are several places you can go to buy alcohol if you don't have a liquor licence, but the fact of the matter is that, if you want to enjoy a few drinks in Abu Dhabi, you should really have a 'little black book'. The good news is that it is relatively easy to get a licence: just head down to any bottle shop, grab the application form and then follow the instructions on p.44.

Crimes Of Cohabitation: You would have to be pretty unlucky to get pulled up on this – especially given just how many people disregard this rule – but the UAE law states that men and women who are not related to each other can not live together. If you are worried about the risk, however low it may be, the choice is to get married, or live apart.

Illegitimate Bumps: Getting pregnant if you are not married is a big no-no here. If you are having your prenatal check-ups at a government hospital, you will be asked for your marriage certificate when you register. If you are at a private clinic, you won't have to show your marriage certificate until the baby is born. Either way, you need to have that crucial piece of paper before giving birth here, or you could be looking at a spot of bother that transcends sleepless nights and dirty nappies.

Remain Orderly: Drinking in public view (unless you are at a licensed venue or event), is illegal. Being drunk and disorderly in public is against the law, no matter where you are. Be careful when you are ordering that seventh cocktail – if that's the one that's going to make you lose your decorum, think about the consequences and make sure there is someone responsible for getting you home safely (apart from the taxi driver).

Keep The PDAs In Check: Holding hands won't land you in any trouble, but think twice before kissing, hugging and other public displays of affection. It may be acceptable in some places (like in airport lounges), but it has been known to get people into trouble, particularly if the kissing and hugging is on the more amorous side. Beware in nightclubs: a seemingly innocent kiss, even between married couples, can result in a bouncer giving you a rather firm warning.

Bounce Into Jail: It is a criminal offence to bounce a cheque in the UAE and can result in jail time, so make sure you have enough money in your account to honour it. And don't rely on post-dating here: there are many reports of funds being cleared from your account long before the date that is written on the cheque.

Don't Have One For The Road: It goes without saying that drinking and driving is illegal. But what many people fail to understand is that there is no such thing as a safe, legal limit when it comes to drinking and driving here. Even a sip of wine or a strong brandy pudding can put you over the limit, because the limit is zero. If you are driving, you should stick to soft drinks, and only soft drinks, all night. If you are drinking, it's best to leave the car keys at home and get a cab.

Over The Counter But Outside The Law: Codeine is widely available in over-the-counter medications in countries like the UK, and Temazepam is a commonly prescribed sleep aid. However, they are illegal substances in the UAE, and possessing them could result in arrest. You can't buy them here, and it's a good idea to tell your overseas visitors not to stock up on the Tylenol or Restoril before they arrive. If they do need these medications, they should carry a doctor's prescription, translated into Arabic if possible.

Respect Ramadan: In the UAE, it is illegal to eat, drink or smoke in public view during Ramadan fasting hours. 'In public view' includes your car, the beach, and even the gym. You should not chew gum either. Many restaurants have closed off sections where you can eat lunch out of sight, and most offices set up a little area where non-Muslims can eat and drink during the day. If these options are not available to you, then you should wait for Iftar (the breaking of the fast) before eating, drinking or smoking.

Look Mum, No Hands: It's one of the most widely flouted laws in the history of the legal system, but it is absolutely, completely and utterly illegal to drive while talking on your mobile handset. Apart from being dangerous, not just for you but for your fellow road users, it is punishable with hefty fines and black points. Invest in a hands-free kit, or better yet, switch your phone off while driving – it may be one of your few opportunities to enjoy some peace and quiet in the midst of a typical busy day.

Family &
Education

FAMILY

Family is a huge part of life in Abu Dhabi, as well as an integral part of Emirati culture. From birth to higher education, bringing up your family here is a rewarding and enjoyable experience. The facilities, from the practical to the pleasurable, are world-class and Abu Dhabi has so much to offer families of all nationalities. However, while the nurseries, play centres and facilities for babies and toddlers are very good, and the primary and secondary schools of extremely high standard, older children may have more of a struggle settling into life in the Emirates.

With improved education facilities, especially at university level, and an ever-expanding leisure industry, teens have a lot to keep them occupied, but the challenge is often transport. An overhauled bus system and cheap taxis have to be relied upon as driving your teenagers to and from malls can be a bit of a chore. Also, chores need to be enforced for older kids in order to avoid 'expat brat' syndrome – in spite of the changes to laws that now allow children and spouses to work part time, there are still relatively few options for Saturday jobs in Abu Dhabi, so you may want to encourage your older children to volunteer (p.110).

Children are rarely expected to be seen and not heard in Abu Dhabi and many restaurants are abuzz with kids running around. There are, however, places where kids will be less welcome, so you should always call before you turn up. Cinemas also seem to have a pretty open-door policy – although often to the annoyance of other patrons. Parks (p.213), beaches (p.215) and amusement centres (p.218) keep families happy and childcare options are available, although more in the form of paid babysitters than parent-run babysitting circles.

Whether you come with your family or have a family here, Abu Dhabi is a great place to call home.

Getting Married

Many expats choose to return to their country of origin in order to get married; however, it is possible to get married in Abu Dhabi, as long as you adhere to certain legal criteria.

┌ Shotgun Weddings ─────────────

It's illegal to have a baby out of wedlock in the UAE. If you are unmarried and fall pregnant, you have two choices: get married quickly or leave the country. You'll be asked for your marriage certificate when you give birth and if there is a significant discrepancy in your dates you will face many questions and a lot more paperwork.

To marry before a Shariah court in Abu Dhabi, the man must be a Muslim while the woman can be a non-Muslim. A Muslim woman cannot marry a non-Muslim man in the UAE. Even if you get married at the Shariah court, the church or a temple, you will still need to register your wedding in your home country.

Wedding blessings aren't limited to churches and embassies; many people choose to get married in one of the hotels but you could also consider a beach wedding or a ceremony aboard a yacht.

There are plenty of hotels (see p.198) to choose from for your reception and your chosen venue will be able to assist you with everything from layout to music, menus to recommended florists. For those with limitless budgets, you could marry on the beach in front of the Emirates Palace (p.201) or Park Hyatt (p.204), or even in the stunning ballroom at the Park Rotana (p.204). If you fancy having the Grand Mosque as your photo backdrop, you can't beat the Shangri-La hotel (p.206). The eco-conscious creative team at Millennium Hotel Abu Dhabi will even come up with globe-friendly concepts for your special day.

┌ Tailor-Made ─────────────

There are many talented tailors in Abu Dhabi (p.334) and you may wish to have your wedding dress tailor-made. The off-the-rack selection is limited, but you may find what you want at the recently opened boutique store Alice Temperley in Marina Mall (p.345). If you can't find what you're looking for here, many of Abu Dhabi's brides and couples choose to scoot up the road to Dubai where the choice is more expensive.

You may find that a wedding planner is just what you need, especially when your family support network is miles away. C'est La Vie (clvweddings.com), Wedding.ae (wedding.ae) or Fonoon (fonoon-uae. com) are good options.

Wedding photographers Lisa Lundqvist (lisalundqvistphotography.com) and Jonathan Gibbons (jgibbonsphotography.com) are both based in Abu Dhabi, while local florists Exotica (02 644 4416) and Petals (02 443 9880) pride themselves on their spectacular wedding arrangements. Most spas (p.181) offer special services for brides and Lina of linasmakeup.com promises to make you feel like a princess on the day. For further inspiration, visiting the Abu Dhabi Bride Show (see p.27) is a must. This annual exhibition covers the full spectrum of what you'll need for your big day.

The Paperwork

While bright sunshine on your Abu Dhabi wedding day is almost guaranteed, rules and regulations are not; they often vary between venues so it's best to do plenty of research to ensure you know what to expect.

As a Muslim marrying another Muslim, for example, you should apply at the marriage section of the Shariah Court, Sheikh Zayed Court. For further information, the Shariah Court can advise (800 2353). You'll need two male witnesses and the bride should ensure that either her father or brother attends as a witness. In terms of paperwork, you must hold a valid residence visa, plus you'll need your passports along with copies, proof that the groom is Muslim and the Dhs.50 fee.

If you are not Muslim, you must contact your embassy for advice, and all couples, regardless of where they get married, must register the marriage with their embassy afterwards. In all cases, you need to produce an original or legalised birth certificate, and a certificate of marital status. In the majority of cases, a marriage performed in Abu Dhabi is legally recognised worldwide, but it's still best to check with your embassy; the passport division will also be able to assist you with changing your name after you are married.

Christians can choose to marry at one of the churches in Abu Dhabi. The cost of the ceremony and church fees for an Anglican ceremony (Anglican Church of St Andrews, 02 446 1631, standrewauh.org) is Dhs.1,500, while marrying at the Catholic St Joseph's Cathedral (02 446 1929, stjosephsabudhabi.org) costs Dhs.200, and before you start on your table plan, you should first contact the chaplain of your particular denomination for a prenuptial enquiry appointment.

Each denomination's requirements differ, although it's worth noting here that if you're not concerned about sticking to a particular doctrine but would like a church wedding, the Anglican ceremony is somewhat simpler to arrange than the Catholic equivalent. For ceremonies in hotels or unusual venues, contact the Evangelical Community Church for advice, eccad.org.

Filipino citizens are required to contact their embassy before the court will authenticate the marriage certificate and Hindus can be married through the Indian embassy (further information can be found on the Indian Embassy website, indembassyuae.org).

Having A Baby

In many ways, having a baby while you are living in Abu Dhabi as an expat is very easy. The standard of maternity healthcare, whether you choose to go private or government, is excellent and, as long as you have insurance or the means to pay for healthcare, there is absolutely no reason to return to your home country to give birth (more on maternity healthcare on p.169).

There is a better chance that you can get away with one income in Abu Dhabi, meaning that one parent (in practice, usually the mother) has the opportunity to stay at home after having a baby rather than having to return to work for financial reasons. And you will have access to cheap childcare and babysitting services here, so you may find that you can be a little more independent than your counterparts back home.

Babies Born Back Home

Babies born abroad to expatriate mums with UAE residency are required to have a residence visa or a visit visa before entering the UAE. The application should be filed by the father or family provider, along with the essential documents, a salary certificate (for the provider, not the baby) and a copy of the birth certificate.

Of course, there are some disadvantages too. If you are pregnant and working, then you've got some pretty paltry maternity leave to look forward to: just 45 days' paid leave and absolutely nothing for dads. You can take another month unpaid, as long as your employer agrees; and, if you need some extra time for medical reasons, you can take up to 100 days, although this is only granted upon production of a medical certificate from your doctor. Having an understanding employer can obviously result in these maternity leave rules being slightly more flexible.

Another disadvantage to living here and having a baby is the absence of the family support network you may have had back home – grandparents and other family members, who would normally muck in

Planning The Big Day Suzie Jackson, 26, newlywed

The events team at the Hilton Abu Dhabi assisted us with pretty much all the organising and created a package deal for us which was really useful. I met with them monthly in the run-up and they kindly threw in lots of free added extras for us, including extra dishes on the buffet, a free wedding cake and even the honeymoon suite! The ceremony took place in the Hilton's garden by the lake and was just beautiful. We kept out of the sun by starting everything at 16:30. Finding cravats and waistcoats for the guy's outfits proved impossible, so my sister brought them from the UK and I managed to get my whole outfit, dress, veil, the lot, from The Wedding Shop in Dubai. On the day, we gave everyone little Arabic scrolls printed with the order of service as our wedding favours and, to keep our budget from spiralling out of control, we saved on printing by emailing our invites, used a photographer buddy of ours to take the pictures and our friends kindly loaned us their cars.

Family

to help you with mundane tasks like cooking, cleaning and babysitting are now thousands of miles away. Fortunately, there are strong networks of other parents who meet up regularly and offer plenty of support to each other; for example, abudhabimums.ae.

Pregnant Out Of Wedlock

If you fall pregnant but are not married, then there is no reason to panic, but there are several decisions that you will need to make fairly quickly. It is illegal to have a baby out of wedlock while you are a resident in the UAE and if you deliver your baby at any hospital here, private or public, and can't produce a marriage certificate, you will most likely face a prison sentence. Therefore, as soon as you see the blue lines on the pregnancy test, you need to sort a few things out. The easiest solution is to have a quick wedding, after which you can go on to have antenatal care in a government or private hospital without any fear of punishment. If this is not an option, you can stay in Abu Dhabi until a reasonable time before you are due to give birth, and even have your antenatal check-ups in a private hospital, but you will need to ensure that you return to your home country to actually deliver the baby. Once you have delivered, you can return to Abu Dhabi with the baby: there are no rules against being a single mother here (see p.131 for more information on single parents).

Birth Certificate & Registration

The hospital that delivers the baby will prepare a 'notification of birth' (which will be in Arabic) upon receipt of hospital records, photocopies of both parents' passports, your marriage certificate and a fee of Dhs.50.

Take the notification certificate for translation into English at the Preventative Medicine Department of Sheikh Khalifa Medical City (p.166) or Al Ain Hospital (p.160), where you will be issued with an application form. The certificate then needs to be attested at the Ministry of Health (Dhs.20) and the Ministry of Justice & Foreign Affairs (Dhs.150) – procedures for which the baby's father must be present.

Every expat child born in the UAE should be registered with their parents' embassy. If parents are from different countries, you will probably be able to choose which nationality your child adopts and, in some cases, they may be able to take on dual nationality. Check with your embassy for further details. Remember, your baby needs a UAE residence visa within 120 days of birth and to do this, you need to have received his or her passport, so you should start the process as soon as possible. If you don't get the residency within that time, you will be fined Dhs.100 for every day you go over the limit. If you feel like you've got enough on your plate with your new arrival, MEDI-Express (mediexpress.ae) offers a service, for a fee, that will take much of the administration and hassle out of arranging the birth certificate for your baby.

More Maternity?

The UAE's Federal National Council is considering plans that will see maternity leave for the country's working mothers increase to 100 days, with the possibility of reducing the working day by two hours for up to four months after delivery.

Adoption

While you can't adopt a UAE National baby, many couples in Abu Dhabi adopt children from Africa, Asia and the Far East. Adoption regulations vary according to which country the child is from, but once you clear the requirements of that country and complete the adoption process, you'll have no problems bringing your new child into the UAE on your sponsorship. Check with your embassy about the procedure for applying for citizenship of your home country for your new child. If you're considering adoption, a good place to start is the Adoption Support Group (p.134).

Getting Divorced

Statistics show that the UAE has one of the highest divorce rates in the Arab world. To counter this, bodies such as the State Marriage Fund have launched

Baby No. 3 Jenny McDougall, 38, housewife

This is the third baby I've had abroad. Being pregnant overseas can be nerve-racking with the obvious communication challenges combined with confusion over where the best place to go for appointments is, but it's perfectly possible and the Corniche Hospital has some of the best expertise I've come across in Abu Dhabi. However, there were some operational struggles – it would sometimes take six hours to complete a 20 minute appointment due to the backlog of people waiting. When I discovered the new Al Noor Hospital, I went there for my check-ups – their expertise was fine and the turnaround was so much more efficient. My advice to anyone having a baby here is never be afraid to ask for a second opinion and to build up your support network group ASAP. You'll need friends who understand what you're going through when the baby is born. I'd highly recommend investing in the help of a doula – you'll find their support absolutely invaluable.

schemes offering education and counselling services to National couples. Expats can get divorced in Abu Dhabi and, in some cases, the procedure can be relatively straightforward.

However, expat couples wishing to divorce may also be governed by the laws of their home country (if the couple has mixed nationalities, the home country of the husband applies), so it is advisable to seek legal advice. A husband who sponsors his wife has the right to have her residence visa cancelled in the event of divorce. See p.122 for a list of law firms.

It can be challenging getting divorced while living abroad, especially if the situation isn't amicable. If you are the one filing for divorce and you have legal representation in your home country, it is likely that you will also need a solicitor here to serve the divorce papers to your spouse.

In addition, whilst you may be living in Abu Dhabi and, therefore, think custodial issues are not relevant, it may still be a good idea to arrange for a residence and access order or similar through the courts in your home country in order to clarify your parental rights for when you do intend to return. If the relationship between you and your spouse has deteriorated somewhat, it would be a good idea to try and meet with a mediator. You can approach the Family Guidance and Reformation Centre which functions under the Abu Dhabi Judicial Department (800 2353, adjd.gov.ae).

Single Parents

It is possible to live in Abu Dhabi and sponsor your children as a single parent here. There will be extra requirements that you need to meet, including a minimum salary level and a letter of no objection from the other parent (or a death certificate, in the case of a deceased spouse). You may also need to show your divorce certificate, but it is best to visit the Immigration Department to find out the exact requirements, as these may change from time to time.

Do You Doula?

A doula can be hired to provide support and advice during pregnancy, childbirth and after the birth of your child. This can be vital as there is very little in the way of post-partum care in Abu Dhabi. Fully trained, they can help take a lot of the stress out of the experience, for mothers in particular. Visit expatdoula.com or dubaidoulas.com.

Being a working single parent in Abu Dhabi may seem daunting for a number of reasons. Firstly, as an expat, your support system may not be as great as back home, where friends and family can help out and, secondly, in a country where marriage and family

are so important, you may feel a little like the 'odd one out'. However, once you get used to people enquiring where your husband is (if you have a child with you people assume you're married), there are actually lots of advantages of living in Abu Dhabi as a working single parent.

The nurseries (p.140) in Abu Dhabi are very good and a few offer full day care, plus they are generally much more affordable than in your home country. There is also the option of having a live-in nanny (see Sponsoring a Maid, p.40), which means that you can not only work as a single parent but you can maintain a social life.

Babysitting & Childcare

Although there is not a registered network of childminders in Abu Dhabi, there are quite a few options available. Many parents hire a full-time maid who will clean and cook along with taking on babysitting duties but, if you do choose this option, be very clear about any childcare expectations from the very beginning.

A few local domestic help agencies offer babysitting services but may not wish to look after very young babies. Exiles (exilesmaidservice.ae), a maid service available in Khalifa City and Al Raha Gardens, for example, provides childcare services to their existing clients. Bear in mind that First Aid and childcare qualifications are not legally required for babysitters or childcare workers, but you can always request that a suitable person be found. If you are unsure, always ask to interview the babysitter before first stepping out without the kids.

If you're looking for a live-in nanny, try Majestic Nannies (majesticnannies.com), established in Abu Dhabi in 2003. The company specialises in providing qualified, internationally trained and experienced childcare staff for 'discerning' parents.

Networking and word-of-mouth can pay huge dividends, as many parents with young children will be in the same boat as you. Abu Dhabi Mums (abudhabimums.ae) provides a wide variety of activities and services and, whilst they don't specifically offer childcare services, becoming involved with their activities is a great way to build up your network of 'pre-approved' babysitters. It is possible that you may even meet another parent who is willing to take care of your child for a fee or perhaps, at least, trade evenings.

Most four and five star hotels will happily organise childcare for guests and there are plenty of creche facilities around Abu Dhabi but be warned that they are of varying standards. You'll need to investigate further in order to find one you're comfortable with and you can expect to pay anything between Dhs.15 to Dhs.40 per hour (See Nurseries and Preschools, p.140).

Activities For Kids

Abu Dhabi is a veritable playground for kids with so many different activities on offer. In the cooler months, take advantage of the great outdoors with a trip to the kid-friendly parks (p.213) that are great for running, playing and eating alfresco. You could also try playing Frisbee on the beach (see p.215) or get them learning how to sail (see p.298).

It is a good idea to keep an eye on the local press as, most months, there's something going on for kids, from a roaming theatre group coming to town to a visiting circus and, as the weather heats up, you'll find that there's still plenty to keep the young ones occupied with everything from pottery to yoga, bowling, ice skating and martial arts – all of which are on offer all year round.

┌ Edutainment & Fun Zones ───

Just about every mall in the capital has play areas for kids. Some are little more than glorified video game arcades while others have small rollercoasters and other rides to bring a smile to small faces. Marina Mall's Fun City (p.218) is one of the largest. Likewise, Sparky's (p.220) in Khalidiya Mall boasts room to move and plenty of options. FunZone (p.220), Kidoos (p.220) and Wanasa Land (p.220) are all sure to get the kiddies worked up in a frenzy of excitement. See also Discover Abu Dhabi, p.188.

There are plenty of well-equipped indoor play centres around town offering all sorts of fun play and learning opportunities. Many of these centres are conveniently placed within one of the city's numerous shopping malls. Check out Fun City at Marina Mall (p.345), Kidoos at Abu Dhabi Mall (p.341), Sparky's at Khalidiyah Mall (p.344) and My Playground (02 634 0035) which can be found on the first floor of the Marks & Spencer building in Al Markaziyah and hosts great facilities, such as a bouncy castle, cinema, library, sandpit and maze to keep the younger kids occupied.

There are various other clubs that run after-school activities (p.134) and summer camps (p.133), with most hobbies covered.

Abu Dhabi International Sailing School

Abu Dhabi International Marine Sports Club
Breakwater **02 681 3446**
Map **2 E1**
Children must be confident swimmers to join this school which offers sailing lessons for children over 8 years old. Children are taught the basic techniques by professional instructors.

Abu Dhabi Pottery

Nr Khalidiya Garden, 16th Street, Shk Zayed The First St Al Khalidiyah **02 666 7079**
abudhabipottery.com
Map **2 G4**
Classes are available for adults and children over 5 years old, giving you the chance to try hand building and the wheel technique. Classes cost Dhs.185 for adults and Dhs.100 for children; there are supportive, knowledgeable instructors on hand who can help your child create something original to take home.

Bodytree Studio

Shk Hazaa Bin Zayed St Al Karamah **02 443 4448**
bodytreestudio.com
Map **2 J7**
Offering a variety of classes for adults and children, Yoga Tree provides a good opportunity for kids to be introduced to yoga in a fun and relaxed environment. The classes run for 30 minutes and a package of four classes can be purchased for Dhs.140.

Noah's Ark Art & Music Institute

Nr KFC, Shk Rashid Bin Saeed Al Maktoum St, Nr KFC Markaziya West **02 641 9793**
noahsarkjingles.com
Map **2 L4**
This school has been offering classes for adults and children since 2008. A wide range of art and music classes are available, from Singing Juniors (for kids aged between 3.5 years to 6 years) to Jingles instrument lessons (piano, guitar, drums, keyboard).

Royal Institute Of Music & Arts

National Printing Centre Bldg, Shk Khalifa Bin Zayed St Markaziya East **02 622 5410**
Map **2 L3**
Classes of varying level are on offer here, from theory to practical coaching by experienced and certified music teachers in guitar, piano, keyboard, drums, violin and vocals. The institute is recognised by the Ministry of Education and it also prepares students for the music examinations conducted by Trinity Guildhall and ABRSM Colleges of Music, London.

Whiz Kidz

Jumbo Electronics Bldg, Hazza Bin Zayed St Al Dhafrah **02 641 7450**
Map **2 P7**
Whiz Kidz offers a range of activities, including classes on drawing, cooking, painting, arithmetic training, calligraphy, public speaking and etiquette. The monthly fee to join the kids' club costs Dhs.250 to Dhs.400. The club opens from 9:00 to 18:00 every day except on Fridays.

The Young Musician Music Institute
Al Raha Mall Al Raha 02 556 2080
theyoungmusician.com
Map **1 R7**
For the budding rock guitarist or concert pianist in the family, The Young Musician Music Institute offers music lessons, including guitar, piano, and voice tuition. The Institute works with the Trinity College of London curriculum, and examinations and certificates are available twice a year. There is also a branch at Al Raha Mall.

Mother & Toddler Activities
There is very much a community spirit among expat mums in Abu Dhabi that is well worth tapping into. A number of mother and baby or toddler groups offer support and camaraderie for new mums feeling a million miles from friends and family. It's quite unusual to find a stay-at-home dad here, as they tend to be the primary earner in Abu Dhabi, but most groups should also welcome dads to the fold. Abu Dhabi Mums (abudhabimums.ae) is a fantastic resource and lists a variety of mother and toddler activities available in the emirate including day outings, music groups and various arts and crafts. It also organises regular social activities for its members, provides information on useful services and allows members access to its toy library and stock of baby equipment. As a new mother, you will find that a group like this is an invaluable way to meet other mums and it's an easy way to quickly establish a much needed support network.

Summer Camps
The summer holidays are longer in the UAE than in many other countries and, due to the hot weather, children can find themselves cooped-up indoors for the majority of their holidays. Fortunately, Abu Dhabi has a good variety of activities to keep children occupied over the sticky summer months. For starters, there are summer camps run by various organisations, while several nurseries also offer summer day care for younger children. You'll likely find that it is necessary to book in advance, as places for the best summer

Family Festival
Abu Dhabi Tourism Authority hosts an annual festival of family activities (summerinabudhabi.ae) at the Abu Dhabi National Exhibition Centre (p.28) and shopping malls right across the city. Shows, sporting events and educational activities are organised to keep both kids and parents entertained.

Urban Park

schemes tend to fill up quite quickly. Little Smarties (p.142) in Khalifa City and The Butterfly Montessori (p.141) both offer summer day care for preschoolers. For slightly older kids, Libra Summer Camps (libra-uae. com) is a professionally run company that prides itself on only using highly experienced and qualified coaches or teachers, all of whom have been fully screened. Run by British expats, it provides a varied, fun and educational experience in a safe environment with an emphasis on team sports, crafts and music. Camps are run at multiple venues across Abu Dhabi and cater for children aged 5 to 14.

Some hotels in Abu Dhabi also cater for the kids during the holidays. The Sheraton Abu Dhabi (p.206) and Beach Rotana Abu Dhabi (p.200), for example, both run fun-packed summer programmes that include swimming lessons, ball games, treasure hunts, island trips and tournaments.

As ever, word-of-mouth is usually the best way to find out about new camps and activities in the emirate and learn which one might best suit you and your kids – for updates, check out forums on sites such as expatwoman.com and abudhabiwoman.com.

After-School Activities

Most schools pride themselves on offering a broad spectrum of after-school activities in addition to their set academic curriculum and they often see these extracurricular activities as important parts of a child's overall development. Activities vary but they can include anything from sports teams, drama and computer clubs to dance lessons, singing or even gardening classes.

Local sports clubs in Abu Dhabi also provide a range of children-friendly activities and, whether your kid dreams of bending it like Beckham at the Abu Dhabi Football Academy or your little one fancies taking centre stage at Turning Pointe (p.279), you will find plenty to keep them occupied; check the Activities Finder on p.274 to see which sports

Dib Dib

Brownies, Guides, Cubs and Scouts Groups are all well established in the region, having been in Abu Dhabi since 1967. All children, from 5 year olds through to 18 year olds and older, can join the groups, which are based on the UK Guide and Scout movements. Parents who want to get more involved should feel free to volunteer as they're always looking for adults to help run the units. For more information on Brownies and Guides, contact abudhabi.dc.bgifc@gmail.com; for more information on Cubs and Scouts contact Geir Johnsen, Group Scout Leader (geirkj@broadpark. no, 050 613 3912) or Ade Waite, Group Scout Leader (adewaite@hotmail.com, 050 815 6537).

are on offer in the capital. The Libra Group (libra-uae.com) also runs a wide range of exciting after-school activities around and throughout Abu Dhabi – with academies in swimming, football, rugby, basketball, tennis and martial arts offering training to young athletes.

Support Groups

Life in Abu Dhabi can sometimes be challenging, and with many residents leaving behind loved ones, there is often a lack of the family support network that many people are used to. Making the first step of reaching out for help can be tough; however, there are groups out there that are more than willing to help ease you through the difficult patches.

Check out the list below, or look for updates of support groups on askexplorer.com, or in any of the monthly health magazines such as Connector or Aquarius. Online forum Abu Dhabi Woman (abudhabiwoman.com) may also provide fruitful leads: there are discussions covering all aspects of life in the UAE, and various informal support groups and coffee groups can also be found here.

Be aware that, if a suitable support group does not exist in Abu Dhabi, you're more than likely to find it in Dubai.

If possible, follow personal recommendations as standards can vary enormously, especially if a group or workshop is linked to a business. Be wise and use your discretion.

Abu Dhabi Ladies
Various locations
abudhabiladies.ae
A support group open to ladies of all ages who want to find new friends. The group offers lots of activities on an informal basis. Abu Dhabi Ladies meet every Wednesday at the Hilton Hotel Jazz Bar between 10:00 and 12:00.

Abu Dhabi Mums
Various locations
abudhabimums.ae
A voluntary but well-run organisation that provides support and offers a range of activities for parents and children. It also arranges events and member discounts, while supplying vital information to the capital's mothers.

Adoption Support Group
Dubai **04 360 8113**
groups.yahoo.com/group/asgdubai
Meetings are held once a month for parents who have adopted children or who are considering adoption. For more information on the meetings, call Carol on the number listed above.

Alcoholics Anonymous

Various locations **050 414 3042**
aauae.net
Anyone needing help can contact this organisation 24 hours a day for advice. Meetings are held daily from Monday to Saturday at St Andrew's Church Centre at various times. There are also four meetings a week held in Al Ain's Oasis Hospital. See the website for details of times.

Dubai Dyslexia Support Group

Dubai **050 652 4325**
This group holds occasional meetings for people with dyslexia and may be able to assist you if you suspect that your child is suffering from the condition.

Future Centre For Special Needs

Nr Mazyad Mall Mohammed Bin Zayed City
02 5533 506
future-centre.org
Map **2 E6**
A non-profit organisation that educates and supports people with special needs as well as carrying out research. The centre offers therapy-based sessions to those who do not attend classes or who are awaiting placement.

Ladies Of Courage

Sheikh Khalifa Medical City Al Dhafrah **02 819 4495**
skmc.ae
Map **2 K7**
A breast cancer support group that meets every third Thursday of the month at Sheikh Khalifa Medical City. Meetings are organised by staff at the centre and are open to everyone – call for timings.

Multiplied UAE

Various locations **050 658 1338**
multiplieduae.com
This is an online support group offering a forum for parents of multiples to exchange advice and ask questions. Also, many parents get together for play dates and activities with their children.

Narcotics Anonymous UAE

ECC Offices, Villa 8/2, Nr Al Khubairat School, 8th Street Al Mushrif **050 131 0055**
nainarabia.com
Map **2 L13**
A non-profit organisation that offers advice and support for those suffering from drug addiction. Classes are conducted in both English and Arabic. Narcotics Anonymous holds weekly meetings on Fridays at 19:00 at the Al Mushrif centre. Call Lisa (050 416 2857) or Wessam (050 268 7890) for directions or further information.

Overeaters Anonymous

Danat Towers, Nr Holiday Inn Al Rehhan (Dubai)
056 743 0514
oaindubai.net
An organisation that helps individuals deal with the emotional and physical stress of various compulsive eating disorders. Meetings are organised on Wednesdays at 17:00 – call Sally (056 743 0513) or email oaabudhabi@gmail.com for more information on the location (a short drive away in the neighbouring emirate, Dubai) and on how to join.

Stillbirth & Neonatal Death Society

Dubai **04 348 2801**
dubai-sands.org
This is a UK-based charity that offers support for those families experiencing pregnancy loss, either through stillbirth, neonatal death or late miscarriage. Contact Angela on 04 382 2801, Anita on 050 644 7903 or Jo on 055 158 0967. SANDS also offers hospital and home visits.

Death

In the event of the death of a friend or relative, the first thing to do is to notify the police by dialling 999. The police will fill out a report and the body will be taken to a hospital where a doctor will determine the cause of death and produce a report. The authorities will need to see the deceased's passport and visa details. Abu Dhabi Police will investigate in the case of an accidental or suspicious death, and it's likely that an autopsy will be performed at a government hospital. If you're unhappy with the outcome of an investigation, you could hire a private investigator, but this is a bit of a grey area so seek advice from your embassy or consulate (see the last page of this book).

Certificates & Registration

The Abu Dhabi authorities will also need to see the deceased's passport and visa details. The hospital will issue a death certificate declaration on receipt of the doctor's report, for a fee of Dhs.50. Make sure that the actual cause of death is stated, then take the declaration of death and original passport to the Al Asima police station, next to the Spinneys in Al Khalidiya. The police will give permission to release the body in a letter which, along with the death declaration, original passport and copies, should be taken to the Department of Preventative Medicine. In Abu Dhabi, this is at Sheikh Khalifa Medical City (p.166); in Al Ain, you will need to go to the Al Ain Hospital (p.160). The actual death certificate will be issued here for a small fee. If you are sending the deceased home, you should also request a death certificate in English or have the certificate translated into the appropriate language. Then take the certificate to the Ministry of Health and the

Family

Ministry of Foreign Affairs for registration. Notify the relevant embassy or consulate of the death so it can be registered in the deceased's country of origin. Although this is not always obligatory, for legal purposes, a death certificate from the home country, or a consular report of death, may be mandatory. They will also issue their own death certificate that could cost up to Dhs.700. You will need to take the original passport and death certificate along for the passport to be cancelled. The deceased's visa must also be cancelled by the Immigration Department. You should take with you the local death certificate, original cancelled passport and the consulate death certificate.

Returning The Deceased To Their Country Of Origin

To return the deceased to their country of origin, contact the cargo section of Omeir Travel Agency (omeir.com, 02 612 3456). The company has experience in making such arrangements and will give you all the necessary information, along with the procedure to follow. The body will also need to be embalmed, for which you must get a letter from the police. Embalming can be arranged through the Sheikh Khalifa Medical City for Dhs.1,000, which includes the embalming certificate (there should be no charge if a copy of the deceased's medical card is supplied). The body must be identified before and after embalming. The following documents should accompany the deceased overseas: the local death certificate, a translation of the death certificate, the embalming certificate, NOC from the police, the consulate death certificate and NOC and the cancelled passport.

Local Burial Or Cremation

More often than not, the deceased is repatriated to their country of origin; however, Abu Dhabi does have mortuary, cremation and burial sites all equipped with modern and proper facilities. Cremation is available only to Abu Dhabi residents and, for more information, you should contact New Medical Centre (02 633 2255). Further details and assistance can be obtained from consular officials at your embassy. Local burial is also possible in Abu Dhabi and takes place at the Abu Dhabi Christian Cemetery with all arrangements for the funeral made with St Andrew's Church (02 446 1631).

Al Foah Funeral Services (alfoahfuneralservices. com), with offices in Abu Dhabi and Al Ain, runs a multi-faith crematorium and can take care of all funeral arrangements, including repatriation of human remains, thanks to a partnership with Etihad Cargo.

Middle East Funeral Services, a company based in Dubai but operating throughout the UAE, can handle all funeral-related procedures in Abu Dhabi offering guidance wherever needed. More information can be found on its website, mefs.ae, or you can phone 04 273 0313 (available 24 hours a day).

Pets

The attitude towards pets in Abu Dhabi is mixed so it is sensible to keep your pet under control at all times. Pets are prohibited from parks and beaches, so your options to walk your dog are limited to the streets in your neighbourhood. Even in these areas, dogs must always be on a lead and certain breeds (call 800 555 for complete details of which breeds) must be muzzled. However, the desert is an excellent place to walk your pooch, with big wide open spaces for Rover to run around without leash or muzzle.

Sleek Salukis

The saluki is the breed of dog most commonly associated with the region; they are used in traditional forms of hunting. The Arabian Saluki Centre (02 575 5330) offers a wealth of information and if you'd like your own desert dog, contact K9 Friends (p.283) or Abu Dhabi Animal Shelter (p.110).

You should check with your landlord what their pet policy is before you move in. It is almost always stated in contracts that pets are not allowed but, if you talk to the landlord, there may be some leeway. If your landlord seems unreliable, it is definitely worth having your contract amended.

Be sure to keep your pet indoors or within your garden to avoid contact with strays or nervous neighbours. Abu Dhabi has a significant problem with strays, although Feline Friends (p.111), K9 Friends (p.283) and Abu Dhabi Animal Shelter (set up by the municipality itself) are hard-working animal charities that take in as many as they can.

You should inoculate your pet and register it with the municipality who will microchip cats and dogs, and provide plastic neck tags. If the municipality picks up an animal without a tag and microchip, it is treated as a stray and will be kept for a short time before being put down. Officially, vets should not provide treatment for your cat or dog if it has not been microchipped, although this may not always be the case.

Looking For A Pet?

Open since 2010, the Abu Dhabi Animal Shelter (abudhabianimalshelter.com) houses stray dogs and cats looking for a new home. Check the website for details on the adoption process.

Aside from rabies, dogs have to be vaccinated against distemper, canine hepatitis, leptospirosis and parvovirus; cats have to be vaccinated against rabies, feline rhinotracheitis, calicivirus and panleukopenia. While rare, there have been reports of dogs being

ADFH Pet Care Center

Your excellent one-stop center
for all your pet's needs

ADFH Pet Care Center
your pet's health
and happiness
is important to us!

To make a booking or for more information
P.O.Box 45553, Abu Dhabi, United Arab Emirates, Phone: +971-2-5755155, Fax: +971-2-5755001

stolen, either to be sold to unscrupulous pet shops, or for dog fighting. Ensure your garden is secure and don't let your dog roam around on the street.

Animal Hospital

The Abu Dhabi Falcon Hospital, located out near the Abu Dhabi Airport, is also home to the Abu Dhabi Animal Shelter, as well as a pet care centre which boasts a cat and dog 'hotel' facility with 100 large, air-conditioned rooms. Smaller animals such as parrots, rabbits and turtles are looked after too. The pet centre features a dog-training area, a cat and dog-grooming salon and a pet clinic, but the facility often gets booked up quickly. You can find out more about its services on p.216.

Bringing Your Pet To Dubai

Pets may be brought into the UAE without quarantine as long as they are microchipped and vaccinated with verifying documentation, including a government health certificate from the country of origin. Bear in mind that certain breeds are banned and that dogs that are crossed with any of those breeds will also not be allowed in the UAE.

Pets must also have an import permit and an additional RNATT (rabies) blood test is required for pets entering the UAE from many countries (visit petimport.moew.gov.ae and create an account). However, you cannot import cats and dogs under 4 months old and all pets must arrive as cargo. Bear in mind also that rabies injections must have been done more than 21 days prior to applying for the import permit. The companies mentioned in Taking Your Pets Home (below) also deal with importing pets.

Taking Your Pet Home

The regulations for 'exporting' your pet depend on the rules of the country to which it is going. Basic requirements are a valid rabies vaccination, not older than one year but not less than 30 days old, and a health certificate that can be obtained from the Ministry of Environment & Water (cost Dhs.100, moew.gov.ae). It is normally issued one week before departure. You'll also need an export certificate and a travel box, normally wooden or fibreglass, which meets the airline regulations.

The airline you are travelling on should be able to inform you of specific regulations pertaining to your destination, such as blood tests and quarantine; in reality, however, airlines are rarely aware of all requirements and you're better off talking to your vet or a pet relocation expert based either here in the UAE or in the country you're moving to.

The British Veterinary Centre (p.138), American Veterinary Clinic (p.138), the German Veterinary Clinic (p.138) and Dubai Kennels and Cattery (p.138) all provide complete international travel services, and can assist with importing and exporting your pet.

Pet Grooming & Training

Standards of care at Abu Dhabi's veterinary clinics are reasonably high, and prices do not vary dramatically. Kennels are generally of a good standard, although spaces are limited during peak times (summer and Christmas). An alternative is to use an at-home pet-sitting service – someone will come into your house at least once a day to feed and exercise your pet for a reasonable fee (for a bit extra, they might even water your plants). Try forums such as abudhabiwoman. com to be pointed in the direction of someone who can help.

In terms of grooming, there are a number of companies that offer everything from basic shampooing, medicated baths and nail clipping to more indulgent options, such as pet fashion.

Pet Boarding

Aside from Abu Dhabi Animal Shelter (p.110) which also has kennels and catteries, there is little by way of niche offerings for pet lovers in Abu Dhabi. It's likely that, once you find a vet that you like, you'll use that company for boarding and grooming too. All of the establishments below offer veterinary services, as well as having kennels and catteries and offer full grooming services for your all precious pets. If you want a wider range of services, then head for Dubai where several more expansive companies, such as Dubai Kennels & Cattery (dkc.ae), can be found.

Pet Boarding

Abu Dhabi Falcon Hospital > *p.vii, 137, 186*
Nr Abu Dhabi International Airport, Off Sweihan Rd, Al Shamkha, 02 575 5155, *falconhospital.com*
American Veterinary Clinic Al Falah St, Al Khalidiyah, 02 665 5044, *americanvet.ae*
The British Veterinary Centre Khaleej Al Arabi St, Al Khalidiyah, 02 665 0085, *britvet.com*
Cloud9 Pet Hotel & Care Madinat Khalifa A (Khalifa City A), 050311 9929, *cloud9pethotel.com*
Dubai Kennels & Cattery > *p.139* Street 34, Off Al Rebat St, Dubai, 04 285 1646, *dkc.ae*
German Veterinary Clinic 39th Street, Madinat Khalifa A (Khalifa City A), 02 556 2024, *germanvet.ae*
National Veterinary Hospital Shk Rashid Bin Saeed Al Maktoum St, Al Mushrif, 02 446 1628, *nationalvet.com*
New Veterinary Clinic Al Raffedeeyam Laundry Bldg, Baniyas St, Tourist Club Area, 02 672 5955

EDUCATION

There is no cause for concern that your child's education will suffer as a result of going to school in Abu Dhabi; on the contrary, many parents report satisfaction with the way a multicultural upbringing results in well-rounded, worldly wise children.

Something you can't escape, unfortunately, is paying high school fees – as an expat, your child will have to go to private school, and it will cost you a pretty penny. So, before you hand over wads of your hard-earned cash, it is really worth doing your research and picking a school that best suits the needs of your child.

Have a chat with other parents for word-of-mouth recommendations, or ask your company's HR departments which schools they are used to dealing with. And as Abu Dhabi traffic can be a nightmare, it makes sense to look at schools near your home or office as a starting point.

Although prices are high, there is legislation in the offing that will control how much schools can hike their prices each year, with any increases related to performance and facilities.

School terms run to a similar calendar to education systems in the UK and USA, with the academic year starting in September after a long summer holiday.

Nurseries & Pre-Schools

Some nurseries accept babies from as young as 3 months, although most prefer to take on children who have started walking (around 12 months). Fees and timings vary dramatically, so it's best to call around and visit a few nurseries to get an idea of what's available. As a general rule of thumb, most nurseries are open for four or five hours in the morning and charge anything from Dhs.3,000 to Dhs.12,000 per term.

The more popular nurseries have unbelievably long waiting lists, so, if you're after a particular establishment, it may be necessary to enrol your child before he or she is even born just to make sure they get a spot.

Some of the bigger primary schools also have nursery sections – if you've got a primary school in mind for your child, it is worth checking to see if they have a nursery, as this may help you secure a place in the school itself a few years down the line.

The Ministry of Social Affairs is currently developing a nursery rating system but, for the time being, parents will have to make the decision based on their own research. There are a number of factors to consider when you are looking for a nursery and it is always a good idea to take your time to visit several schools to get a hands-on feel of the place and the quality of the facilities and training before making a decision.

Try to drop in during the day so that you can have a look at the facilities while there are children around. Many of the nurseries in Abu Dhabi operate morning hours which may rule them out if you are working full time. However, many will also run late classes for an extra fee and a number of them have early-bird drop-offs. They may also organise sessions during the holiday periods.

Another factor worth thinking about when selecting your child's nursery is whether or not they provide meals – having to make a packed lunch every morning when you're trying to get ready for work may not be suitable for you.

Blooming Buds Nursery
Off Saeed Bin Tahnoon St Al Bateen **02 491 8908**
bloominbudsnursery.com
Map **2 F13**
Open most the year round, and operating from 07:00 to 14:00 Sunday to Thursday, Blooming Buds is a high-tech yet charming villa-nursery, with classes spread over two floors. Based on the UK's early Years Foundation Stage curriculum, there's equal focus on learning through playing, creativity, activities and interacting with learning tools. The nursery also runs a summer holiday programme that is popular with Abu Dhabi parents.

Bright Beginnings Nursery
Villa 22/2, Al Khaleej Al Arabi St, Al Mehairba Al Bateen **02 445 5339**
brightbeginnings.ae
Map **2 F11**
Bright Beginnings accepts children from just 4 weeks old, and follows a broad-based curriculum that will prepare children for both the American and British school systems. It has a lovely covered outdoor play area that includes a splash pond, and excellent art and learning facilities. Parents can opt for a two, three or five-day week. It is also open during the summer, while an afternoon programme is available at an additional cost. Another branch operates in Al Mushrif (02 449 2840).

British Orchard Nursery
Nr Aramex, Shk Rashid Bin Saeed Al Maktoum St Al Nahyan **02 443 9893**
britishorchardnursery.com
Map **2 N8**
Having gained an excellent reputation for being one of Dubai's best and best-equipped British curriculum nurseries, British Orchard has now extended its nurseries to Abu Dhabi, bringing its highly-qualified team and activity-packed programme with it. Open to children from 6 months to 4 years old, there are also all sorts of extras (holiday camps, kids' parties) available to kids who attend.

Busy Bees Nursery

12th Street Madinat Zayed **02 621 9492**
busybeesnursery.org
Map **2 M5**
Formerly known as Sesame Street Private Nursery, Busy Bees Nursery follows an American curriculum. Its focus is on learning through social play. English is spoken by all teachers and a 30 minute Arabic lesson is given daily. Busy Bees is open from 08:00 until 13:00. Age: 18 months to 4 years old.

Butterfly Montessori Pre-School

28th Street Al Bateen **02 665 8611**
admont.ae
Map **2 H6**
Butterfly Montessori Pre-School follows an American nursery curriculum and uses the Montessori education method, encouraging learning through exploration, expression and play. It is open daily between 07:15 and 13:00. Age: 18 months to 4 years.

The Montessori Way

Montessori is a popular teaching method that encourages a more flexible approach to learning than a strict academic curriculum. Children are encouraged to discover new things through imaginative play, social interaction and physical activity. The method is also used to help children to develop their own instinct to learn and is a good foundation for the International Baccalaureate curriculum. Several nurseries mentioned in this chapter offer Montessori based teaching methods including: International Montessori Nursery, Butterfly Montessori, Radiant Montessori Nursery, Kotwals Nursery and all four Stepping Stones nurseries.

First Steps School & Nursery

Off Al Karama St Al Karamah **02 446 0960**
firststeps.ae
Map **2 K8**
A popular nursery and pre-school, the atmosphere is extremely friendly and the excellent staff combine fun and creativity with expression. Its classes are based on the British curriculum and it also features a basic introduction to Arabic. Both three-day and five-day weeks are offered. Age: 24 months to 4 years old.

Giggles English Nursery

Al Meena Rd Tourist Club Area **02 673 4226**
Map **2 S2**
Giggles is a well-established nursery, having opened its doors in 1987. It welcomes all nationalities although it follows the British curriculum. A first aid expert is always on site and bus transport is available

at an additional cost. Two Giggles nurseries are now in operation: one on Meena Road and one at Giggles English School on Airport Road (02 641 6255). Age: 18 months to 4 years old (Al Meena Road); kindergarten to grade six (Airport Road).

Humpty Dumpty

Villa 3, 11th Street Al Bateen **02 666 3277**
humptynursery.com
Map **2 F8**
There are two Humpty Dumpty nurseries in Abu Dhabi, one in Al Bateen and one in Madinat Khalifa A (02 556 1068). The nurseries teach children to learn through play, social interaction, self discovery and self expression. They have 'ready beds' for children's rest and relaxation. They are open from 07:30 to 14:00, Sunday to Thursday; there is also an afternoon club which runs from 14:00 to 15:00. Age: 1 to 4 years.

International Montessori Nursery

Off 31st Street Al Rehhan **02 449 4680**
imn.ae
Map **1 H7**
The Montessori system promotes learning through experience and interaction, and as such, the classes at the International Montessori Nursery are mixed in age with a high teacher to child ratio. It offers a flexible drop-off and pick-up system, between 07:30 and 09:00 and 12:00 and 13:45. Children can attend two, three or five days a week. Age: 18 months to 5 years old.

Jigsaw Nursery & Creche

Nr Karama & Delma Sts Al Karamah **02 445 5222**
jigsawnurseryad.com
Map **2 K9**
Another nursery based on the British curriculum for the full age range of pre-schoolers, Jigsaw Nursery and Creche promotes balanced development. Infants are well catered for, while older children can take their learning on a little further and receive regular basic music lessons and Arabic lessons. Age: 12 months to 4 years.

Kotwals Nursery

Villa 79A, Off 63rd Street Mohammed Bin Zayed City **02 559 0068**
kotwalsmontessori.net
Map **1 Q11**
This is a Montessori nursery that has created a 'school within a house' approach. Its dedicated programme uses an innovative approach to learning using linguistics, non-competitive study and encourages children to make their own decisions. It also offers afternoon care and other care programmes. Age: 6 weeks to 4 years old.

Education

Leens Nursery
Nr Al Falah Plaza, Muroor Rd Al Dhafrah
02 642 2350
Map **2 N6**
This long-established nursery school for kids has been teaching the Indian curriculum for 35 years. Age: 18 months to 4.5 years old.

Little Smarties Nursery School
21st Street Madinat Khalifa A (Khalifa City A)
02 556 5500
littlesmartiesnursery.com
Map **1 R7**
Located in Madinat Khalifa A, Little Smarties is an international nursery that prepares students for the British school system. The applied curriculum is based on Letterland and Jolly Phonics. The nursery's priority is to create a safe environment where children's confidence, creativity and curiosity can be nurtured. Hours are 08:00 to 14:00 daily. Age: 2 months to 4 years old.

Noah's Ark Nursery & Day Care Centre
Al Najda St Madinat Zayed **02 635 1035**
noahsarknurseryad.com
Map **2 P4**
For infants aged between 20 months and 4 years, this bright and friendly nursery and day care centre is open 07:00 to 18:30, Sunday to Thursday and 07:00 to 13:30 on Saturdays. Its curriculum takes a 'learning through play' approach. It also has a branch in Musaffah (same contact number as above).

Radiant Montessori Nursery
Nr Gate B Sheikh Zayed University Al Nahyan
02 445 5576
rmn4me.com
Map **2 M9**
This school provides a Montessori nursery education to children for three, four or five days per week. It also has optional afternoon sessions and transport is available. Facilities are varied and of a good standard. Age: 3 months to 4.5 years old.

Stepping Stones Nursery
Villa #22, Off 2nd Street Al Bateen **02 681 5583**
steppingstones.ae
Map **2 D5**
Stepping Stones encourages children to learn through play, themed activities, crafts, cooking and 'pretend play'. Options are available for three-day or five-day weeks. The school has three branches, with Al Rawda (02 445 2260) and Bain Al Jasrain (02 558 8318) offering the British curriculum and Al Bateen following the American curriculum; both include aspects of the Montessori learning system. There is a late class until 14:00. Age: 18 months to 3.5 years.

Teddy Bear American Nursery
Nr 16th & 33rd Streets Madinat Khalifa A
(Khalifa City A) **02 556 8566**
teddybearnursery.net
Map **1 R7**
An excellently equipped American nursery with a curriculum based on the intellectual, physical, social, moral and emotional development of children. The nursery offers plenty of creative activities and also runs a summer camp. Age: 12 months to 4 years.

The Club Creche
Open to pre-schoolers, The Club's (p.179) very own creche is open between 08:00 and 12:30 every day. Members can attend a fitness class, sunbathe by the pool or play tennis safe in the knowledge that their children are being fully and expertly supervised.

Twinkles Nursery
Baniyas St Al Dhafrah **02 445 5950**
twinklesnursery.com
Map **2 P7**
One of the newer nurseries, having opened in early 2012, Twinkles is a full and colourful nursery, ideal for those living in downtown areas, which caters for children from 1 to 4 years old.

Primary & Secondary Schools
As an expatriate in Abu Dhabi, you most likely have no choice but to enrol your child in private education – although expat kids can attend government schools provided there is space, they must speak Arabic and you'll most likely end up paying tuition fees too. In practice, private schools are pretty much the only option for most expat families.

When planning your child's education, there are several golden rules that will help ease the process: firstly, if you have a school in mind, get your child's name on the waiting list as soon as possible, since the demand for spaces at the more popular schools is high. Secondly, consider the 'school run' when choosing your school – Abu Dhabi's rush-hour traffic can turn a short journey into a tedious hour-long trek every morning. Thirdly, pick a school that offers the best curriculum for your child: if you are British and are planning to return home after a couple of years, it might be best to find a school that offers the English National Curriculum; similarly, if you think you might end up elsewhere on another expat assignment after you leave Abu Dhabi, it might be better to choose the International Curriculum, which will help your child slot into a wide range of curriculums.

Kids here start school as early as 3 years old (in schools that offer a foundation or reception year), and usually graduate from secondary school at around

18 years. Most schools are open from 08:00 to 13:00 or 15:00, from Sunday to Thursday. Ramadan hours are shorter – usually starting an hour or so later and finishing an hour earlier.

School fees are a contentious issue: private education doesn't come cheap. For a good school, you can expect to pay Dhs.25,000 plus per year for KG years, Dhs.30,000 and up for the middle primary years, and as much as Dhs.60,000 per year for secondary school. Ouch! If you're lucky, your company may offer school fees as part of your package. On top of this, you will usually need to pay around Dhs.500 to put your child's name on a school's waiting list, and a registration fee (around Dhs.2,000), which comes off your fees.

Be prepared to accept that there are a lot of school holidays here in Abu Dhabi. The summer holidays stretch for 10 long weeks over the hottest months of July and August, when many kids return to their home countries for extended holidays, or attend summer camps. There are also holidays in April and December. Schools close for at least a week twice a year for Eid Al Fitr and Eid Al Adha, and will most likely also open for reduced hours during the month of Ramadan. If one of you is a stay-at-home parent, then this poses few problems in terms of childcare; however, if both of you work, you will need to make sure that you have alternative arrangements for childcare during school holidays and random days off.

School Inspections

Education standards in private schools are high and it is controlled and maintained by the Abu Dhabi Education Council (adec.ac.ae). Visit ADEC's website to see the criteria by which the council judges private schools. In addition to quality inspections, ADEC also regulates school fees; all annual increases must be pre-approved and are currently capped at 20%.

Abu Dhabi's family focus

Which Curriculum?

Choosing the right curriculum for your child can be obvious – for example, if you're planning on being in Abu Dhabi for a year or two before returning to your home country, it makes sense to pick the curriculum that is offered back home, such as the English National Curriculum or the American Curriculum. However, if you are not sure what your future plans are, you may want to consider the International Baccalaureate Programme (IB), which is compatible with most curriculums worldwide.

There are distinct differences between each curricula; it is a good idea to do plenty of research before deciding which one is best for your child.

┌─ School Rehaul ─

In mid-2011, the Abu Dhabi Education Council (ADEC) announced a major rehaul of the schooling system. Part of the Abu Dhabi 2030 vision, ADEC said that 40 schools will be merged, 23 new will open, 11 will be renovated and 19 relocated. ADEC also announced the closure of six villa schools and plans to set up affordable private schools. None of the schools listed in this guide are subject to the rehaul, which is predominantly aimed at improving the public schooling sector.

School Uniforms

Most private schools in Abu Dhabi will insist on students wearing the official school uniform. Each school will use a particular uniform supply shop and this will be the only place where you can buy official school items. Before heading out and spending a fortune on uniforms, check with the school and with other parents which items are compulsory and which are not: a sturdy pair of black school shoes and a pair of non-marking trainers are usually essential items, whereas a branded school bag is often not.

School Transport

If, for whatever reason, you are not able to do the school run every morning and afternoon, you can make use of the bus services offered by most schools. The advantages are that the bus driver will get to deal with the traffic every day and, since school transport has to abide by some strict regulations, you can rest assured that your child will reach school safely.

The disadvantages are that it can be a very expensive option: you will pay the same fee whether you live 500 metres up the road or 15 kilometres from the school. Also, if your child is one of the first on the pick-up roster, it will mean a particularly early start and then a very long ride on the bus as it drives round to pick up all the other kids headed for the same facility – followed by the same all over again on the way back in the afternoon.

Education

Still, for parents who work or don't drive, school transport is a god-send given the limited public transportation options. You should speak to your school directly about the costs and arrangements.

Abu Dhabi International Private School
Al Karamah St Al Rowdha **02 443 4433**
aisuae.com
Map 2 J8
Abu Dhabi International Private School follows an excellent international programme that allows students to graduate with the relevant American, British or International Baccalaureate qualifications. It has a capacity for more than 3,000 co-ed students ranging in age from kindergarten to grade 12, with a set percentage of slots reserved for children with special needs. The multinational staff are predominantly native speakers from various English-speaking countries. The school offers sports and activities such as soccer, volleyball, basketball, badminton, tennis, hockey, cooking, arts and crafts and dance.

Developing The Future

The Pearl, Al Yasmina and Al Muna schools have all been developed and are being run by Aldar Academies, a recent subsidiary of the government-backed developers behind Yas Island. Aldar also opened its first secondary school in Al Bateen in September 2011 and the company says it hopes to open many more schools across the UAE capital in the years to come. Schools currently teach the British International Curriculum and there are plans to also introduce the International Baccalaureate. See aldaracademies.com for more information.

Al Bateen Secondary School
Khalifa Bin Shakhbout St Al Bateen **02 813 2000**
albateen.sch.ae
Map 2 H7
One of the most recent additions to Abu Dhabi's education offering, Al Bateen Secondary School provides a high-quality, British-style education to students aged 11 to 18. As a new school, the facilities are top notch.

Al Rabeeh School
21st Street Madinat Khalifa A (Khalifa City A)
02 448 2856
alrabeeh.sch.ae
Map 1 F6
Al Raheeb is a well-established junior school that educates some 800 co-ed students between the ages of 3 and 11. The curriculum is a varied and

international one, although all classes are given in English.

Al Yasmina School
Al Raha Gardens Al Raha **02 501 4888**
alyasmina.sch.ae
Map 1 P7
This is a large international school catering mainly to families living off the island. Al Yasmina has a capacity of over 2,000 students, ranging from kindergarten to 18 years old and it follows the English National Curriculum. It will eventually offer A-levels. The school has excellent facilities and a comprehensive extra-curricular programme.

American Community School
Off Sultan Bin Zayed St Al Bateen **02 681 5115**
acs.sch.ae
Map 2 F5
The American Community School serves over 1,000 students of many nationalities. It offers the American curriculum, although it also offers the International Baccalaureate (IB) curriculum as well. Learning is encouraged through a diverse mix of activities, and there is a full extra-curricular programme available. With a kindergarten, elementary school, middle school and high school, students from 4 years to grade 12 (usually age 18) are accepted.

American International School
29th Street, Off Sheikh Rashid Bin Saeed Al Maktoum St Al Rehhan **02 444 4333**
aisa.sch.ae
Map 1 H7
This school is one of the largest in Abu Dhabi, with over 1,200 students, from pre-school to grade 12 (typically, age 4 to 18). It was founded in 1995 and serves both expat and local children. The school offers both the American and IB curriculums. Facilities include a library, music rooms, art rooms, science labs, computer labs and a gym.

The Australian School Of Abu Dhabi (ASAD)
Nr 32nd & 40th Streets Madinat Khalifa B (Khalifa City B) **02 586 6980**
aia.vic.edu.au
Map 1 V12
Located in Khalifa City, the school caters for a full range of students from kindergarten through to year 12 (17 or 18 year olds). Its curriculum is based on Australian and International Baccalaureate programmes, with Arabic language and Islamic classes also available to Muslim students. Sports and extracurricular activities are a major part of school life; there are football fields, a 25-metre swimming pool, a gym and basketball courts.

Belvedere British School

Nr Al Safeer Mall, 31st Street Mohammed Bin Zayed City **02 559 5525**
belvederebritishschool.com
Map **1 N12**
Another new opening (September 2012), this school is a spin-off from the highly-rated independent British school that has been one of the UK's best since 1880. Covering all age groups, from 3 to 19, the curriculum is based on aspiration and wide-ranging skills.

Homeschooling

One of the main reasons for homeschooling in the UAE is to avoid the hefty private school fees. K12 (k12.com/int/arabian_gulf) in Dubai's Knowledge Village offers some online courses, but schools in your home country will be able to provide you with the curriculum, materials and online testing, for a fee. For excellent additional support and organised group outings, log on to the Abu Dhabi Home Schoolers Association website (abudhabihomeschoolers.org), where you'll find information on membership and homeschooling resources. The Ministry of Education do offer homeschooling for all nationalities but the curriculum is only in Arabic. Many expats who have multiple children find that, whilst nurseries tend to be more affordable than in their home countries; when it comes to schooling, it makes more financial sense to return home where education is often offered by the government for no fee.

Brighton College Abu Dhabi

Bloom Gardens Al Matar **02 815 6500**
brightoncollegeabudhabi.net
Map **1 J7**
New in 2011, Brighton College Abu Dhabi is an offshoot of the successful Brighton College in the UK; it follows the British Curriculum and accepts enrolment requests for ages 3 to 16.

The British International School Abu Dhabi (BISAD)

Abu Dhabi University Madinat Khalifa B (Khalifa City B) **02 586 0340**
bisabudhabi.com
Map **1 Q11**
The British International School offers the English National Curriculum and caters for students from 3 to 18 years of age. The impressive purpose-built site has state-of-the-art facilities for sport, technology, culture and the arts. At capacity, the school will have 2,000 students (it is currently 'growing through' to the last few year groups), but it promises small class sizes and low student-teacher ratios. The school is operated by Nord Anglia Education.

The British School Al Khubairat

Off Shk Rashid Bin Saeed Al Maktoum St Al Mushrif **02 446 2280**
britishschool.sch.ae
Map **2 K12**
This popular, not-for-profit school was established in 1971 and is one of the best-known schools in Abu Dhabi. It follows the British curriculum, which is taught by multinational teachers. Children aged 3 to 18 can attend the school. Facilities include an auditorium, sports pitch, libraries and a swimming pool.

The Cambridge High School Abu Dhabi

63rd Street Mohammed Bin Zayed City **02 552 1621**
gemscis-abudhabi.com
Map **1 N12**
Another school based on the British curriculum, Cambridge High School educates children between kindergarten and year 13, guiding them through GCSEs, AS Levels and A levels. The school has playgrounds, a swimming pool, science lab, multimedia labs, music and art studios, a library and courts for various sports. Extra-curricular activities play an important role in school life. It also has a fleet of school buses picking up and dropping off all over Abu Dhabi.

Canadian International School

Off 20th Street Madinat Khalifa A (Khalifa City A) **02 556 4206**
cisabudhabi.com
Map **1 T8**
The Canadian International School is a new school located in Madinat Khalifa A. It follows the Alberta programme of study and inquiry-based learning. All teachers are educated and certified in Canada. Boasting all-new facilities, including a new 25 metre pool, primary and secondary students are based in two different buildings on the property, with classes available for KG1 through to grade 12.

Emirates National Schools

Mohammed Bin Zayed City **02 559 0000**
ens.sch.ae
Map **2 N9**
Emirates International is a multicultural school for students from KG1 through to grade 12 (around 18 years old), offering American diploma and International Baccalaureate programmes. English is the main language, although Arabic children are offered language and culture lessons, while western children have the opportunity to learn Arabic and French. Sports and arts play important roles. There is also an Al Nahyan Campus (02 642 5993) covering KG and primary, and it has a girl's school. A primary and a girl's school are located at its other campus in Al Ain (03 761 6888).

Education

GEMS American Academy

3rd Street Madinat Khalifa A (Khalifa City A)
02 557 4880
gemsaa-abudhabi.com
Map **1 R7**
GEMS American Academy used to be located in the heart of Abu Dhabi, but as of September 2011, the school has been operating in a purpose-built facility in Khalifa City A. While fees are on the expensive side, they include textbooks and supplementary materials. The school also operates a bus service for an additional cost.

GEMS World Academy Abu Dhabi

Najda St Al Nahyan **02 641 6333**
gemsworldacademy-abudhabi.com
Map **2 P6**
Part of the GEMS global school network, this school is conveniently located for families living in the heart of Abu Dhabi and offers kindergarten and elementary education, with highly-qualified western staff and facilities that include playgrounds, artificial fields, music rooms, a climbing wall and a health clinic.

The Glenelg School Of Abu Dhabi

Nr Petroleum Institute & Abu Dhabi Golf Club
Madinat Khalifa A (Khalifa City A) **02 599 2001**
gsad.sch.ae
Map **1 M8**
Run by the Glenelg School of the US, this branch follows the American school curriculum. English is the main language of teaching, but both Arabic and Islam arguably play a more significant role here than at several of the other international schools. Arabic language and social studies, Islamic studies and world languages are all offered. The school caters for the full age range from KG1 to grade 12.

Horizon Private School

20th Street Madinat Khalifa A (Khalifa City A)
02 556 0811
horizonprivateschool.com
Map **1 S8**
Open since 2008, this is a highly sought after option for those living off the island due to its reputation for tough entrance exams and high grades. The school educates around 900 international students from KG1 right up to Grade 10, offering a varied curriculum and good facilities.

The International School Of Choueifat Abu Dhabi

Off Shk Rashid Bin Saeed Al Maktoum St Al Mushrif
02 446 1444
iscad-sabis.net
Map **2 L11**
The nine International Schools of Choueifat that are located throughout the GCC run almost as

if one school, sharing knowledge, expertise and encouraging interaction between students. The Choueifat curriculum is an individual one based around learning 'points' although sports and activities play an important part. The school covers all ages from KG1 upwards.

Our Own English High School Abu Dhabi

Al Salam St Al Dhafrah **02 642 5990**
gemsoo-abudhabi.com
Map **2 Q7**
Operated by global school giant GEMS, the curriculum comes from the National Council of Educational Research and Training, New Delhi. It covers the full range of age groups and has excellent educational, artistic and sporting facilities, as well as a full extra-curricular programme.

The Pearl Primary School

Nr East & Hazaa Bin Zayed The First Sts Al Dhafrah
02 641 8887
pearlprimary.sch.ae
Map **2 N7**
Offers studies based on the UK's Whole School Curriculum Plan. The Pearl is part of the Aldar Academies umbrella, providing classes from foundation stage (kindergarten) to Year 6 (usually aged 10 to 11). It is a fairly new school with top-class facilities that include a 25 metre swimming pool, grass playing fields, a library and a technology lab.

Raha International School > p.147

Al Raha Gardens, Off 3rd Street Al Raha **02 556 1567**
ris.ae
Map **1 R7**
Raha International School offers the International Baccalaureate organisation's Primary Years Programme and Middle Years Programme. Facilities include a swimming pool, a learning pool, a large sports hall, a library and an art and design studio. For those interested in sports, there are tennis courts, sports fields and recreation play areas.

University & Higher Education

In the past, the vast majority of expat teenagers have returned to their home countries when moving from secondary to tertiary education. However, a growing number of institutions within Abu Dhabi and the other emirates now entice more people into studying in the UAE. Degrees and diplomas are now offered in the arts, sciences, business and management, and engineering and technology. Furthermore, there are a number of government projects underway to improve and expand Abu Dhabi's higher education facilities. Zayed University has been upgraded and relocated, and there will be a new University City constructed in the next couple of years. The Abu Dhabi Vocational

RAHA
INTERNATIONAL
SCHOOL

Nurturing
Fresh Perspectives

Raha International School is situated on 94 acres of beautifully landscaped property located in Khalifa City A, Abu Dhabi.

The campus is unique in that buildings are constructed to reflect traditional Arabic architecture. It features several large piazzas and wide walk areas lined with palm trees with an abundance of open space and play areas.

The school is equipped with visual arts, music and performance rooms, ICT labs, libraries, two well-equipped gymnasiums, four tennis courts, a 25-metre swimming pool and beginner's pool, dance studio, football pitch and dining hall.

At Raha International School (RIS), we believe that a successful education is all about inspiration; inspired teaching to drive academic achievement and to encourage emotional intelligence. RIS is an International Baccalaureate World School catering for all grades from Pre-K to Grade 12, and offers the internationally acclaimed IB curriculum respected for its relevance to today's multicultural and increasingly global society. A strong sense of common purpose pervades our learning community.

ecis
REGULAR
Member

Come and meet us to discuss how your child can play a leading role in guiding the next generation with intelligence, an insightful world view and thoughtful ambition.

T +971 2 556 1567   **E** admissions@ris.ae
www.ris.ae

táaleem
inspiring young minds

Education

Education and Training Institute (p.148) opened in late 2007, providing vocational training and qualifications in industry sectors such as health, law and tourism. The New York Film Academy Abu Dhabi (p.150) opened in 2008, offering both two-year and shorter term courses and workshops in acting and film making, while the Masdar Institute of Science & Technology now provides cutting-edge programmes within sustainable development.

Destination Education

With the growing number of leading education providers now based in Abu Dhabi, more and more students will find a suitable degree on offer close to home. Should you wish to broaden your options, Dubai's Knowledge Village (kv.ae) and Academic City (diacedu.ae) both offer a number of other options for further study. Knowledge Village groups a number of leading international universities and colleges together in the same area and encourages students and faculty members to interact, creating a unique learning environment. In addition, it provides access to student housing and a number of other useful services.

Education UK Exhibition

Organised annually by the British Council, the Education UK exhibition is part of an initiative to enhance educational relations between the UK and the UAE. Students from across the UAE can attend the event in order to gather information on British universities, whether they have campuses here in the UAE or in the UK. The 2011 event was held in January and November and took place in both Abu Dhabi and Dubai. Check britishcouncil. org for details of future events.

Current academic options include American University in the Emirates (aue.ae), Birla Institute of Technology and Science (bits-pilani. ac.in), Cambridge College International Dubai (cambridgecollegeinternational.nsw.edu.au), Esmod Dubai (esmod-dubai.com), Heriot-Watt University Dubai (hw.ac.uk), Mahatma Gandhi University (mgudxboc.com), Manchester Business School (mbs. ac.uk), The British University in Dubai (buid.ac.ae), University of Wollongong in Dubai (uowdubai.ac.ae), European University College Brussels, Royal College of Surgeons in Ireland (rcsileadership.org) and the Canadian University of Dubai (cud.ac.ae).

Some universities, including several of the ones listed above, offer students the opportunity to study part-time, or via e-learning. International correspondence courses are also available. The UK-based Open University (open.ac.uk) is popular, as is the South African-based UNISA (University of South Africa). UNISA recently opened an office in Dubai

(unisa.ac.za). Gulf News' classifieds section carries adverts for the numerous other study options for short courses.

Abu Dhabi University

Abu Dhabi-Al Ain Rd Madinat Khalifa A (Khalifa City A) **800 23968**
adu.ac.ae
Map **1 Q11**
The Abu Dhabi University has campuses in both Abu Dhabi and Al Ain. Any student, regardless of nationality, is encouraged to apply. Its courses include business administration, computer science and information technology, and education. Contact the admissions office for more information.

Abu Dhabi Vocational Education & Training Institute

Mohammed Bin Zayed City **02 508 2700**
adveti.abudhabi.ae
Map **1 M8**
Abu Dhabi Vocational Education and Training Institute (VETI) opened at the start of the 2008/2009 academic year. It provides vocational diplomas in areas such as information technology, fashion design, finance, hotel management, property development, paralegal studies and graphic design. Facilities include smart board technology, Wi-Fi and a sports hall. Other campuses are located in Al Ain (03 715 7640) and Al Gharbia (02 894 3001).

Centre Of Excellence For Applied Research & Training

CERT Technology Park Al Nahyan **02 404 8501**
certonline.com
Map **2 N12**
This establishment offers courses in a variety of fields, including engineering, business and health sciences, some of which are through online tuition. Specialised courses such as advanced diplomas in professional training, business English, food inspection and highway maintenance, and the University of Strathclyde MBA, are also available.

Emirates College Of Technology

Millennium Tower, Shk Hamdan St Markaziya East **02 626 6010**
ectuae.com
Map **2 N2**
There are two locations in Abu Dhabi, its male-only campus on Hamdan Street and a campus for women (02 642 0420) on Defence Street. Emirates College of Technology offers diplomas in business administration and computer information systems, HR management, e-commerce and marketing, banking and finance, accounting, computer design and animation, and mass communication and public relations.

Education

European International College

Off 31st Street Al Matar **02 449 1450**
eic.ac.ae
Map **1 J7**
An institution focused on hotel management and tourism; however, several courses are on offer under this umbrella including a bachelor's degree in hospitality. The college is affiliated with prestigious western hospitality institutions and offers a full and diverse student experience.

Masdar Institute Of Science & Technology

Nr Abu Dhabi Airport, Masdar City 02 810 9333
masdar.ac.ae
Map **1 U7**
Open since 2009, this institute provides cutting-edge education and research into renewable energy solutions, advanced technologies and sustainable development. The 2009 intake consisted of 88 graduate students but within a couple of years the institute had 170 students. Seven two-year long, graduate level degrees are currently on offer.

New York Film Academy Abu Dhabi

Muroor Rd Al Nahyan **02 446 6442**
nyfa.edu
Map **2 M9**
This film school offers full-time and part-time courses in everything from on-camera acting to documentary and feature filmmaking. The courses cover a broad range of necessary disciplines, including writing, directing, editing and cinematography; which should be perfect for any budding Spielbergs.

New York Institute Of Technology

Centre Of Excellence For Applied Research & Training Al Nahyan **02 404 8523**
nyit.edu
Map **2 N12**
The Abu Dhabi branch of the well-known higher education institute. Principal academic offerings are in architecture and design, the arts, science, engineering, and computer science. Students also have the chance to spend time studying at its other locations, like Canada, China, Jordan and, of course, Manhattan.

New York University Abu Dhabi

Nr ADIA Tower, Off Al Nasr St Markaziya West
02 628 4000
nyuad.nyu.edu
Map **2 L3**
The relatively new branch of this well-regarded American institution is primarily a research university, with a liberal arts and science college. Undergraduate education here is based on a vast and varied curriculum that results in full NYU degrees. Appealing to international students, the university is looking to

give students the full, traditional college experience, including an exceptional extra-curricular and sporting programme.

Paris-Sorbonne University Abu Dhabi

Al Reem Island **02 656 9555**
sorbonne.ae
Map **1 G4**
The legendary Sorbonne arrived in Abu Dhabi in 2006. The university is based in a cutting-edge educational campus on Al Reem, offering top facilities and teaching for undergraduate and masters degrees in law, business, languages, philosophy, history of art and more. New masters' programmes were added in 2011, including human resource management, performing arts management, tourism, banking and finance and multimedia publishing.

The Petroleum Institute

Nr Al Maqta & Sheikh Zayed Bridges Al Maqtaa
02 607 5100
pi.ac.ae
Map **1 M8**
This institute is dedicated to education and research in areas significant to the engineering, geoscience and general oil and gas industries. The institute is supported by many of the world's biggest oil-producing companies. There's a wide portfolio of undergraduate and graduate programmes available.

Zayed University

Madinat Khalifa B (Khalifa City B) **02 599 3111**
zu.ac.ae
Map **1 R9**
Located in a massive, brand-new and purpose-built university complex with separate colleges offering arts, science, business science, communication & media, education studies, languages and information technology. Also has postgraduate and masters courses, predominantly in business and management.

Special Needs Education

The available support for children with special needs is increasing by the year in Abu Dhabi. Some of the establishments based in the city are listed below; turn to p.154 for more information.

Abu Dhabi Centre For Autism

Nr Al Mafraq Hospital Mafraq **02 582 1621**
zho.ae
Map **1 T13**
The largest centre of its kind in the UAE, the non-profit organisation helps autistic children and their families. It deals with the medical side of the condition in terms of diagnosis, therapy, psychiatry and neurology, while also working on a holistic approach to increasing children's comfort and social interaction.

MFA.DESIGN.
————
The only graduate design
program in the Gulf region

www.qatar.vcu.edu/mfa

Shared Glass collaboration with Fabrica 2011

vcuqatar | virginia commonwealth university in qatar
جامعة فرجينيا كومنولث في قطر

مؤسسة قطر
Qatar Foundation

Education

Al Noor Speech Hearing Capacity Day Centre

Nr Fatima Bin Mubarak School Al Zahra **02 449 3844**
Map **1 H6**
Run partially as a charity, this centre takes in young students who cannot afford to go to other centres in the UAE. Students of all ages and all types of disabilities are accepted, with the centre providing both formal and informal education, as well as vocational training. The aim is for students to become fully self-dependent.

British Institute For Learning Development

22nd Street Madinat Khalifa A (Khalifa City A) **02 556 6078**
british-ild.com
Map **1 S8**
Specialist school for children with sensory deprivation and learning difficulties. Run by British experts and supported by St Andrew's College International, the school takes a thorough approach encompassing speech therapy, educational psychology, reading development, play therapy, therapeutic listening and an 'astronaut programme' that aims to increase learning capacity and intelligence.

Future Centre For Special Needs

Nr Mazyad Mall Mohammed Bin Zayed City **02 5533 506**
future-centre.org
Map **2 E6**
A non-profit institution for youths between the ages of 3 and 14. Classes cater to those with ADHD and behavioural disorders, Down's syndrome, cerebral palsy and traumatic brain injury; there's also an autism unit. The combination of education, therapy and care enables specialised and holistic services to be offered to children and young adults with complex needs, degenerative conditions and additional sensory impairments, while also supporting their families.

Language Courses

Alliance Francaise Abu Dhabi Choitram Bldg, Al Khalidiyah, 02 666 6232, *af-aboudabi.net*
American Language Center Marjan Plaza Bldg, Shk Hamdan Bin Mohd St, Nr Hamdan Centre, Markaziya East, 02 627 2779
Berlitz Bin Haiyai Bldg, Shk Zayed The First St, Al Khalidiyah, 02 667 2287, *berlitz.ae*
British Council Khalidiya Tower, Shk Zayed The First St, Al Manhal, 02 600 529 995, *britishcouncil.org*
Circolo Italiano 050 6223 258, *cicer-abudhabi.com*
English Language Services Villa 9, Nr Dar Al Shifa Hospital, Al Najda St, Al Dhafrah, 02 642 6640, *elsmea.org*
Goethe-Institut Gulf Region Shk Zayed The Second St, Tourist Club Area, 02 672 7920, *goethe.de*

International English Institute For Language Studies
Nr Bus Station, Hazza Bin Zayed St, Al Nahyan, 02 642 2407

The Mother Tongue Arabic Language Center

Bin Fardan Bldg, Shk Zayed The First St Al Manhal **02 639 3838**
mothertongue.ae
Map **2 G4**
A centre that specialises in teaching Arabic to non-Arabic speakers at levels from absolute beginner to advanced. The highly-acclaimed courses typically run for around 12 weeks with three classroom hours per week at a cost of Dhs.1,800 to Dhs.1,950 per course. Both the facilities and teachers are of excellent quality.

Teaching English

If you're interested in a career move, would like to expand your skill set or are just looking to earn a little extra cash on the side, you might like to consider a TEFL (Teaching English as a Foreign Language) or TESOL (Teaching English to Speakers of Other Languages) course. Abu Dhabi Men's College (hct.ac.ae) offers courses, as do the British Council (britishcouncil.org) and Abu Dhabi Higher Colleges of Technology (hct.ac.ae). If you can't find anything to suit in Abu Dhabi, plenty of institutions within Dubai's Knowledge Village (kv.ae) also offer courses. The four-week courses cost around Dhs.9,000.

Libraries

The National Library, established in 1981, carries over 300,00 titles in Arabic and around 100,000 in foreign languages. A separate children's library was established in 1996, with 15,000 kids' volumes available, predominantly in Arabic, French and English. The National Library soon plans to place 'lending dispenser' machines, containing around 250 books across all languages and genres, across the whole of the emirate. In addition, several private establishments and associations run libraries at their facilities.

Al Shaheen Library Nr Al Adil Trading, Off Shk Hamdan Bin Mohammed St, Markaziya East, 02 676 8995, *booklovers.8k.com*
Alliance Francaise Abu Dhabi Choitram Bldg, Al Khalidiyah, 02 666 6232, *af-aboudabi.net*
The Club Mina Zayed Free Port, 02 673 1111, *the-club.com*
Daly Community Library St Andrew's Church Abu Dhabi, Al Mushrif, 02 447 8386, *standrewauh.org*
National Library Shk Sultan Bin Hamdan Al Nahyan Bldg, Corniche, Markaziya East, 02 651 5464, *adach.ae*

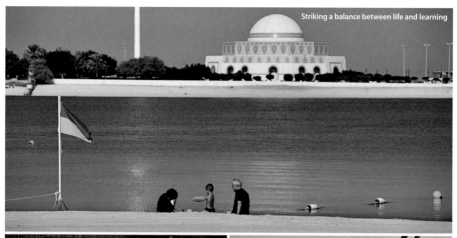

Striking a balance between life and learning

Special Needs & Learning Support

The UAE boasts an excellent private school system for expats; however, it is sometimes more difficult to find quality education for children with special needs.

If your child has physical or learning difficulties, there are several organisations that can help. In 2009, the Ministry of Education announced that private schools in the UAE would be required, by law, to provide adequate facilities for children with special needs. While this ruling is still being implemented to a degree, recognising that less able children deserve the same quality of education as other children can surely be seen as a positive step – and one which is long overdue.

There are schools that seem to be leading the way in terms of opening doors to children with special needs, while certain other private schools in Dubai and Abu Dhabi will offer places to children with mild dyslexia or Down's syndrome.

Dr Lesley P Stagg, principal of Greenfield Community School, believes that as long as the school is able to meet the specific needs of a particular child in terms of facilities, curriculum and staffing, then there is no reason to turn away a child with special needs. 'We assess each case individually, and our main decider is whether the child will benefit from being educated at our school,' says Dr Stagg. 'In terms of special facilities and services, we offer in-class and withdrawal support, we have a therapy room where visiting therapists can work with students with special needs, and we request parents to employ personal assistants ('shadows') in cases where this helps the child remain focused in the classroom.'

Delice Scotto, principal at the Al Mizhar American Academy for Girls, implements a similarly broad-minded approach. 'All children who require learning support work in small groups and individually with learning support teachers according to Individualised Education Plans (IEPs),' she explains. 'With these support systems in place, learning support students at our school can be successfully integrated into mainstream school activities. 'Students are assessed at the admissions stage, and undergo a psycho-educational evaluation,' continues Scotto. 'Out of this assessment come recommendations that serve as a basis for that child's IEP, and as long as that child's needs are able to be met by our learning support department, they will be offered a place.'

There are currently three full-time learning support teachers at the Academy, all of who have master's degrees in special education from the United States, as well as extensive experience in dealing with students with a variety of special needs, from dyslexia and ADHD to emotional disabilities and the Autism spectrum. At Greenfield Community School, there is a similarly progressive approach to ensuring staff can meet the needs of all children: 'several of our teachers have specialist training in all aspects of special educational needs, including gifted and talented children, and we offer ongoing professional development to raise skills further,' says Dr Stagg.

Dubai Dyslexia Support Group, a non-profit support group that holds regular meetings for families affected by dyslexia, are also a great resource outside of the schooling system. The group is run by Anita Singhal, who is well aware of the difficulties facing such families here: 'not all schools offer support,' she says. 'The main problem is finding a school with a learning support unit or specialist help and, unfortunately, awareness is lacking in many schools.'

However, it's not all bad news – according to Singhal, nearly all dyslexic children, bar those with severe dyslexia, can integrate fully into mainstream education with the correct support; and parents have a huge role to play in helping their children overcome learning challenges. 'One of the key things a parent can do is to develop a dyslexic child's self esteem,' says Singhal. 'Never compare them with other siblings or their peers, and encourage their strengths rather than focusing on weaknesses'.

Unfortunately, the picture is not so bright for children with more severe learning difficulties or special needs. While in an ideal world it may be desirable for these children to attend 'normal' schools, the truth is that the majority of private schools in the UAE do not have sufficient facilities or support to cope with severe disabilities or meet the special needs of some children. While this may result in, for example, a child with a physical disability not being able to attend a mainstream school despite not having any cognitive impairment, some parents feel that there is little point pushing the issue.

Children with Down's syndrome are among those who find inclusion in mainstream schools a challenge. Although more and more schools are opening their doors to children with Down's syndrome, there are still many schools and nurseries that refuse to allocate places to these children, according to Ingeborg Kroese, co-ordinator 0-5 years, All 4 Down Syndrome Support Group. 'Even those children with Down's Syndrome who are in mainstream schools require part-time or full-time learning support assistants who help them access the curriculum,' she says. 'These learning support assistants are funded by the parents, and so financial constraints are a very real problem.' One of the key mandates of the All 4 Down Syndrome group is to encourage early intervention activities (physiotherapy, speech and language therapy and occupational therapy), which can stimulate the development of children with Down's syndrome under the age of 5. The group also holds regular talks with Dubai's Knowledge and Human Development Authority (KHDA) to discuss ways to increase inclusion of less able children in mainstream education organisations.

Organisations such as the British Institute for Learning Development aim to bridge a gap between private schools that may lack adequate facilities and more extreme solutions in the form of centres for children with severe disabilities. Although it focuses more on learning support and sensory therapy than on helping children with physical disabilities, the institute seeks to address children's learning and behavioural problems through occupational therapy and neuro-developmental therapy (Sensory Integration). Students are supported through work with speech therapists, psychologists and specially qualified teachers. With this approach, Dr Chris Reynolds, who established the institute in 2002, believes that both 'slow learners' and 'gifted learners' can make great progress.

See the list of Special Needs schools and groups on p.150.

Revolutionary Cancer Treatments.
First. Attentive. Precise. Effective.

The Regional Center for Cancer Care at American Hospital Dubai

Cancer not only affects your health, but also your family and lifestyle. Understanding this, the American Hospital Cancer Care Facility offers a range of current Medical Oncology and Hematology services for adults and children. Our specialists are American Board Certified (or equivalent) and are supported by a team of expert staff trained in advanced cancer treatment techniques in the region.

We are here to ensure that you are never alone in your fight against cancer. Because when you are treated at American Hospital, you are with family.

Clinical Offerings: Medical Hematology Oncology • Pediatric Hematology Oncology Chemotherapy • Radiation Oncology • Surgery • Palliative Care • Multidisciplinary Approach

For more information, contact +971 4 377 6369

Our team of specialists (from left to right):

Dr. Shah Numani: Consultant PET/CT Physician, **Dr. Maroun El Khoury:** Consultant Hematology/Oncology,

Dr. Faraz Khan: Consultant Oncologist/Hematologist, **Dr. Nidal Mahgoub:** Consultant Pediatrician Hematology/Oncology,

Dr. Salim Chaib Rassou: Consultant Radiation Oncology, **Dr. Aaron Han:** Consultant Pathologist

المستشفى الأمريكي
AMERICAN HOSPITAL
D U B A I دبــــي

Delivering better health in the Middle East

Organization Accredited
by Joint Commission International

www.ahdubai.com

The first hospital in the Middle East to be awarded Joint Commission International Accreditation (JCIA)

The first private laboratory to be certified by the College of American Pathologists (CAP)

Health, Fitness & Well-Being

HEALTH

Both private and public healthcare services are available in the UAE. General standards are very high, with English-speaking and internationally trained medical staff in most facilities but, as in most countries, private healthcare is seen as preferable as you are much more likely to experience shorter waiting times and generally more comfortable inpatient facilities.

Under UAE Labour Law, an employer must provide access to healthcare for all of its employees. This can take one of two forms: either the employer pays for a private medical insurance policy, or it pays contributions towards government healthcare and covers the costs of obtaining a health card for each employee (p.158).

Government Healthcare

The Abu Dhabi Health Services Company (seha.ae) owns and operates 12 hospitals with 2,644 beds, 62 ambulatory care, family care and urgent care centres and two blood banks. These hospitals include: Al Mafraq, Sheikh Khalifa Medical City, Corniche and Al Rahba. SEHA also operates Al Ain Hospital and Tawam Hospital in Al Ain, as well as the Western Region's Al Gharbia Hospitals umbrella which includes smaller primary healthcare providers in Madinat Zayed, Ghiathy, Marfa, Al Sila, Delma and Liwa.

With the exception of emergency care, which is available for free unless you require any follow-up treatment, you will need a health card to access government health services. In order to see a doctor, you will need to present your health card and a form of ID (ID card, labour card, driving licence or passport) and will be charged a nominal fee (usually Dhs.50) for a consultation. Additional charges may apply for further tests, treatment and medication.

Health Card

Employers in Abu Dhabi must pay for health cover for all of their employees. An employer can decide whether to provide health cards for its staff or pay for a private insurance policy. If your employer provides you with a health card, you are entitled to subsidised healthcare at government-run hospitals and clinics.

The health card must be renewed each year, but you only need to take a new medical test when your residence visa is due for renewal.

Your employer should start the process for you, by telling you which of the city's three Disease Prevention and Screening Centres to go to (there are two more in Al Ain and the Western Region).

The process requires you to complete blood tests and a chest x-ray for prevention of communicable diseases; see Becoming A Resident, p.31 for details of the process.

Accidents & Emergencies

Sheikh Khalifa Medical City (p.166) and off-island Al Rahba Hospital (p.161) have the best equipped accident and emergency (A&E) departments in Abu Dhabi, although Al Mafraq (p.165) and Al Noor Hospitals (p.161) also have good, general A&E departments. Part of Sheikh Khalifa Medical City, the Khalidiyah Urgent Care Center (p.164) in the heart of the city treats minor emergencies, such as abdominal pains, cold and flu, minor bone breaks, ear, nose and throat issues, asthma attacks, rashes, vomiting and diarrhoea.

In Al Ain, Al Ain Hospital (p.160) deals with general accidents and emergencies, while Tawam Hospital (p.166) specialises in emergency trauma cases. The A&E departments at both these hospitals are very efficiently managed and, even if you have a relatively minor injury, you rarely have to wait very long to see a doctor.

While finding a place to get emergency treatment is easy, getting there can be more problematic as Abu Dhabi's paramedic services have only just started to develop. Abu Dhabi Police receives all 999 calls, although you can dial 998 to be put straight through to ambulance services. An ambulance will be dispatched to take the patient to the relevant hospital depending on the type of medical emergency. Private medical firms, such as NMC (nmc.ae), also run fleets of ambulances, although be warned that you'll need to subscribe to the services or pay for one-off use.

General Medical Care

For general non-emergency medical care, there are a few different options available. Most hospitals have a walk-in clinic where you can simply turn up, present your health or insurance card, register and queue to see a general practitioner. It's common to be seen by a triage nurse who will take down the details of your medical history and ailment before you see a doctor. These departments usually operate on a first-come-first-served basis, so waiting times can vary dramatically. Early evening, at the end of the working day, is generally a busy time and best avoided, if possible. It's advisable to call the hospital prior to visiting to make sure that they operate a walk-in service and to check opening times. If you are on a private healthcare plan, make sure in advance that the hospital is on your insurer's network.

Most hospitals and smaller clinics offer family medicine as part of their outpatient services. You can usually call to make an appointment, but there's no guarantee that you'll get an appointment on the same day. If your usual family medicine department has no available appointments but you need immediate non-emergency medical care, they may admit you through the A&E department, but they will advise you of this when you call.

Finding A General Practitioner

While some people prefer the convenience of walk-in clinics, others would prefer to register with a practice where they are familiar with the administrative procedures and they can see the same doctor on return visits. There are a number of clinics in Abu Dhabi that offer general practice and family medicine, and it's worth asking friends and colleagues for recommendations. Most areas of the city have a local medical centre, so if proximity to your home or place of work is important, you should be able to find something nearby.

Stay Calm, Act Fast

In the event that you're faced with a medical emergency, try to stay calm, call for an ambulance and, while waiting, follow these instructions:

- Clear a path to the patient – move furniture and unlock doors.
- If possible, have someone waiting to meet the ambulance, especially if your villa or apartment number is not clearly visible from the street.
- Do not move the patient unless their life is threatened by external factors, such as fire, falling debris or electricity.
- Be prepared to answer the following questions related to the patient's condition: are they conscious; are they breathing; are they bleeding?

General Practice Clinics

Al Aahed Medical Centre Suhail Salam Al Khaily Bldg, Hilton Rd, Al Ain, 03 764 2791
Al Dhahery Clinic Saeed Hillal Abdulla Al Kuwaiti Bldg, Main St, Al Ain, 03 765 6882
Al Maqtaa Healthcare Center Off Al Khaleej Al Arabi St, Al Maqtaa, 02 558 4611, *ahs.ae*
Bani Yas Primary Health Care Centre Nr Mafraq Hospital, Bani Yas, Mafraq, 02 583 5599, *mafraqhospital.ae*
Dawn Medical Centre Shk Hamdan Bin Mohammed St, Markaziya East, 02 621 6900, *ahaliagroup.com*
Dr McCulloch Clinic Al Noor Hospital, Markaziya East, 02 626 2677, *dr-mcculloch.com*
Family Medicine Centre Al Ain Hospital, Al Ain, 03 763 5888, *alain-hospital.com*

Gulf Diagnostic Center Hospital Al Khaleej Al Arabi St, Al Bateen, 02 417 7222, *gdc-hospital.com*
Hamdan Medical Centre Khaleej Pharmacy Bldg, Hilton St, Al Ain, 03 765 4797
Ibn Sina Medical Centre New Al Manara Pharmacy Bldg, Shk Zayed The Second St, Al Khalidiyah, 02 681 6400, *ibnsinauae.com*
New Al Ain Medical Clinic 225 Main St, Mina Bazaar, Al Ain, 03 764 1448
Swedish Medical Centre Khalidiya St, Al Bateen, 02 681 1122

Private Healthcare

Private healthcare facilities in Abu Dhabi are expanding dramatically and standards are very high. Many employers opt to provide their staff with private insurance policies that gives access to a network of private hospitals and clinics. Waiting times are generally shorter in private clinics.

If you have private health insurance, it's worth checking what you are entitled to as levels of cover vary depending on the policy. Dental care, maternity and screening tests aren't usually covered as standard, and you may need to have been on the policy for a year before you can receive maternity cover. Before making an appointment to see a healthcare professional, always check whether the clinic or hospital is part of your insurer's network to avoid being landed with the full costs yourself. Your insurer will also provide details about its payment policy; some companies offer direct billing, which means the insurer pays the hospital or clinic directly and you only pay a nominal fee each time you access medical services, while others require you to pay the cost of the consultation, treatment and medication up front and then file a claim to the insurer.

If your employer is paying for your medical insurance, your employment contract will state whether your spouse and dependents are included in the policy. If you plan to cover the cost of insuring your family yourself, you may need to purchase a separate policy for them as it's not always possible to extend existing policies.

For a list of companies providing healthcare insurance, see Insurance Companies, p.119.

Q u i c k & E a s y Stuart Griffiths, British expat, 61

I've been living in the UAE for over 20 years, and have visited doctors and specialists on a number of occasions and noticed big improvements in recent years. There are some good doctors and clinics, and some that are not so good. It's really down to trial and error to find one you like, as different doctors and practices suit different people. You can get access to health professionals very quickly and easily, and you'll find getting tests done and results back is a much quicker process in the UAE than some other countries; in the UK, for example, it can take a long time, but here you can often walk in off the street and have tests done straight away, with the results back in a day or two. Seeing a specialist is also easier.

Pharmacies & Medication

The UAE has a more relaxed policy on prescription drugs than many other countries and most can be bought over the counter. If you know what you need, it cuts out the hassle of having to see a doctor just so that you can get a prescription. Pharmacists are willing to offer advice, but bear in mind that they don't know your medical history. Always tell the pharmacist if you have any pre-existing conditions and allergies or are taking other medications, and make sure that you understand the administration instructions in case these aren't available in English.

You might find it frustrating that certain common medications from your home country are not available here (such as Gaviscon for infants and Pepto Bismol); you can however bring these into the country for your own personal use and often you can find a locally available equivalent. You may find that there are similar products (such as Infacol instead of infant Gaviscon) so it is worth taking the medications to the pharmacy and asking if they have something that does the same thing.

There are pharmacies all over the city and a number are open 24 hours a day, such as Urban Pharmacy (02 445 8584), Lifeline (02 633 2255), Al Noor (02 613 9101) and Al Ain Pharmacy (03 765 5120). Supermarkets and petrol station convenience stores sell basic medications and first aid equipment. It's worth checking if your local pharmacy offers deliveries as this is often an unadvertised service. Deliveries can be handy if you need regular medication, such as blood pressure medication or diabetic supplies, and can be useful for those days when you wake up feeling too poorly to get out of bed. There is not normally a delivery charge but be sure to tip the driver.

Prohibited Medications

Certain medications do require a prescription, and some medications (such as codeine, Diazepam and temazepam) are banned in the UAE, even though they are widely available in other countries. It's a crime to have these medicines in your possession, unless you can produce an official prescription from your doctor in your home country, but even then you might end up at the police station while it is translated into Arabic. Unless it is absolutely necessary and there's no locally available alternative, it's best to avoid medications that are banned in the UAE. The list of banned drugs changes regularly, so it's best to check with the Registration & Drug Control Department at the Ministry of Health (moh.gov.ae) before travelling with any medication.

Main Hospitals

In general, both private and government hospitals deliver high standards of care in Abu Dhabi. Most hospitals offer a comprehensive range of inpatient and outpatient facilities, so if you like a particular hospital but need to see a specific specialist, the chances are the hospital will be able to cater to your needs. Once you have registered with one hospital it is easier to return there for further treatment. For very specialist treatment, you'll be referred to somewhere else in the city. Many of the services offered in hospitals are also offered in clinics and small practices, so if you have a hospital phobia, then this might be a better option for non-emergency treatment. See Specialist Clinics & Practitioners, p.166. It is worth having a look around the main hospitals before deciding which one suits you – especially if you are intending to have a baby in Abu Dhabi. For more information on having a baby in Abu Dhabi, see p.129.

Dubai Healthcare City

There are plans to create a medical district for Abu Dhabi, while the developer Mubadala is working on a separate medical area known as the Arzanah Medical Complex. The Singaporean-run complex will feature a number of top healthcare facilities, although specialist centres have already opened their doors there. Dubai Healthcare City adds plenty more facilities to the UAE. The aim of the development has been to create a global hub for medical treatment, prevention and research. City Hospital (ehl.ae) and a range of private clinics and research institutes are already open, including Boston University Institute for Dental Research & Education Dubai (budubai.ae), American Academy of Cosmetic Surgery Hospital (aacsh.com), Dubai Gynaecology & Fertility Centre (dha.gov.ae), Dubai Bone & Joint Center (dbaj.ae), Imperial Healthcare Institute (imperialhealth.org) and Moorfields Eye Hospital Dubai (moorfields.ae). See dhcc.ae.

Ahalia Hospital

Shk Hamdan Bin Mohammed St Markaziya East
02 626 2666
ahaliagroup.com
Map **2 M3**
The flagship facility of the large Ahalia group has 24 hour casualty and ambulance services, along with specialists in cardiology, homeopathy, neurology, radiology and many other medical disciplines.

Al Ain Hospital

Shakhboot Bin Sultan St Al Ain **03 763 5888**
alain-hospital.ae
Map **4 D2**
One of the two major government-run hospitals in the city of Al Ain (the other being Tawam Hospital), the Al Ain Hospital has 30 different departments, including cardiology, orthopaedics, paediatrics, urology and ENT. The focus is on emergency and acute care.

Al Noor Hospital

Shk Khalifa Bin Zayed St Markaziya East **02 626 5265**
alnoorhospital.com
Map **2 N3**
One of the best known private hospitals, with specialists in cardiology, gynaecology, paediatrics, dermatology, dental and more. There are less traditional departments, such as the Chinese medicine clinic, a Lasik centre and a sleep laboratory. Another branch is located on Airport Road (02 444 6655).

Al Raha Hospital

Hyper Market Bldg, Bani Yas St Madinat Zayed
02 633 0440
alrahahospital.com
Map **2 P4**
A private general hospital in the centre of the island. The excellent facilities cover urology, gynaecology, ENT, dentistry, internal medicine, paediatrics, anaesthesia, radiology and pathology disciplines.

Al Rahba Hospital

Abu Dhabi-Dubai Rd Al Rahba **02 506 4444**
alrahba.ae
Map **3 D2**
Another government hospital, Al Rahba is just off the island on the Abu Dhabi-Dubai highway. Outpatient departments include dermatology, diabetic education, dialysis, ENT, endocrinology, nephrology, neurosurgery, obstetrics and gynaecology. Al Rahba also has a neonatal intensive care unit.

Al Salama Hospital

Shk Hamdan Bin Mohammed St Tourist Club Area
02 671 1220
alsalamahospital.com
Map **2 R3**
This private hospital is located in the Tourist Club Area and provides inpatient and outpatient treatments in various fields including obstetrics, infertility, cardiology, neurosurgery, pathology, sports medicine and physical therapy.

American European Medical Center

Shk Rashid Bin Saeed Al Maktoum St Al Nhayan
02 445 5477
aemcare.com
Map **2 L10**
Established in 2006, the American European Medical Center has emerged as one of the city's top outpatient clinics with wide-ranging health services and specialities. In addition to general & internal medicine, the clinics and faculties include cardiology, dental surgery, gastroenterology, general surgery, obstetrics and gynaecology, pediatrics and radiology. House calls can also be arranged through the American European Medical Center Home Healthcare service.

Behavioral Sciences Pavilion

Sheikh Khalifa Medical City Al Dhafrah **02 610 4962**
skmc.gov.ae
Map **2 K7**
This government-run specialist psychiatric hospital, located within Sheikh Khalifa Medical City, provides across-the-board psychiatric diagnosis, treatment and support for adults, adolescents and children.

Burjeel Hospital

Al Najdah St Al Markaziyah **02 222 2332**
burjeel.com
Map **2 P7**
Having opened to patients in 2012, this new tertiary care centre is Abu Dhabi's biggest private hospital and covers more than 30 specialties in total. Among Burjeel special areas of expertise is reproductive health and IVF: the facility is linked to Brussels University, an acknowledged leader in research and treatment for reproductive science, and the services available in Abu Dhabi include the latest developments in a wide range of reproductive ailments, including IVF.

Corniche Hospital

Al Salam St Markaziya East **02 672 4900**
cornichehospital.ae
Map **2 Q2**
The government-owned Corniche Hospital is a purpose-built obstetrics and gynaecology facility that is also home to the largest maternity department in the city – if you're pregnant during your time in Abu Dhabi, chances are you'll come through the doors here at some point or another. The hospital is run by the renowned Johns Hopkins Medicine group.

Dar Al Shifaa Hospital

Bani Yas St Al Dhafrah **02 641 6999**
daralshifaa.net
Map **2 P7**
The extensive facilities here include emergency, neonatal intensive care, paediatric and neonatology, obstetrics and gynaecology, maternity and delivery, ENT, urology and lithotripsy, dermatology, internal medicine, cardiology, as well as physical medicine and rehabilitation.

Delma Island Hospital

Delma Island, Western Region 02 878 1888
Map **3 A2**
This government facility may be small, but the health services on offer are comprehensive to serve the Delma Island community. The hospital provides emergency services, internal medicine, paediatrics, obstetrics and gynaecology, general surgery, and dialysis to residents and tourists on the 45 sqkm island off the coast of Al Gharbia.

To Your Health

Piling On The Pounds

While many people in Abu Dhabi spend the greater portion of their time in outdoor pursuits during the winter months, the heat of the summer means that, for four months of the year, it's easy to fall into lazy ways. In general, people have a more sedentary lifestyle here, and the city's car culture, all-you-can-eat-and-drink brunches and fastfood outlets at every turn see many new expats gaining a few extra pounds. Fortunately, there are a number of weight loss groups and nutritionists on hand to help (p.176), as well as ample fitness centres and gyms (p.177) and opportunities to take part in sports (see Activity Finder, p.274) to keep you active and help shift the extra weight.

Diabetes

Obesity is also a major contributing factor to the UAE's high incidence of diabetes. Recent figures from the Imperial College London Diabetes Centre in Abu Dhabi (icldc.ae) show that nearly 20% of the UAE's population suffer from diabetes, with the majority of them being Type 2, a preventable form of diabetes that is strongly linked to lifestyle and eating habits. The government is aggressively promoting awareness campaigns headed by organisations, such as the Imperial College London Diabetes Centre in Abu Dhabi itself, to educate the population about preventive measures, healthy eating and the benefits of an active lifestyle. If you suffer from diabetes or think you may be at risk, you can speak to your doctor or contact a specialist diabetes clinic. There are also a number of nutritionists who can help you manage Type 2 diabetes through diet (see Nutritionists & Slimming, p.176).

New Germs

The UAE is a transitory place and, with so many people coming and going and bringing new germs with them, you may find that bugs and colds are more common. With the stresses involved in moving to a new place, you may also find that your immune system is impaired for a while and you are not as resilient to germs as you normally are. Generally speaking though, if you maintain an active lifestyle and a good diet, your immune system will fight off any unwanted allergies before you even know about it. It's worth keeping a closer eye on your kids and if any strange symptoms appear, a trip to the doctors is best, even if it's just to put your mind at rest.

While you're likely to enjoy a generous slice of the good life in Abu Dhabi, all-you-can-eat brunches and the party lifestyle will eventually take their toll. Living in hot, dry, dusty conditions can also have an effect on your well-being. Here are some of the common health complaints you should be aware of.

Sun Safety

It goes without saying that extra sun care needs to be taken when out and about in the UAE. The hot sun and high temperatures are recipes for sunburn and heat stroke if you are not prepared. Sun block is widely available in supermarkets and pharmacies. Sun hats, light, loose clothing that covers your limbs, sunglasses and seeking shade are recommended when out and about in the hotter parts of the day and during the summer months. With high temperatures throughout the year, you should also ensure that you drink enough water to remain hydrated; this is particularly important when you exercise and during summer months. It's wise to keep a couple of bottles of water in the car in case of emergencies. If you have a breakdown in busy traffic during the summer, you may be faced with an uncomfortable wait while the police or recovery truck comes to the rescue. You should also be aware of any changes to your skin, such as new moles or ones that change shape, colour or bleed. Contact your doctor or a dermatologist if you have any concerns.

Other Ailments

If you suffer from asthma, you may find that the dusty outdoor environment and the dry, air-conditioned indoors aggravate your symptoms and you may need to rely on your inhaler more often than you would at home. A number of medical practices offer asthma clinics, including NMC (nmc.ae). Sinusitis can also be triggered by the dust, although this is more common among people who have lived in the city for a number of years. Ear, nose and throat (ENT) specialists can advise the best course of treatment and arrange surgery if necessary (see Specialist Clinics, p.166). The average working week in the UAE is longer than in many other countries. Spending longer hours in the office can take its toll on your body, making you more susceptible to bugs and colds; it can also make you prone to suffering from stress injuries such as repetitive strain syndrome.

Mosquito Prevention

Finally, while the WHO declared the UAE malaria-free in 2007, mosquitoes are common at the beginning and end of winter, particularly around the water, and the perfect alfresco evening can be ruined by bites from these tiny critters. Mild mosquito-repellent sprays and lotions are usually effective enough to keep the mozzies at bay, so you shouldn't need to resort to DEET-based or tropical strength products. If you prefer natural remedies, citronella oil is reportedly an effective mosquito-repellent and is available in health food stores (p.330). To save yourself from being bitten while you sleep, plug-in mosquito repellers are available from most supermarkets (p.336) and pharmacies (p.160).

Health

Emirates Hospital
Nr Delma & Karama Sts Al Karamah **02 446 6422**
emirateshospital.ae
Map **2 K9**
A specialty hospital offering all the usual disciplines, as well as plastic surgery, a foot and hand hand clinic, asthma treatment and an anti-ageing clinic.

Emirates International Hospital
Nr Al Ain Civic Centre Al Ain **03 763 7777**
Map **4 D2**
This private facility in Al Ain has specialist departments including accident and emergency, physiotherapy, dermatology, venereology, cardiology, cardiovascular, ENT, internal medicine, obstetrics and gynaecology, ophthalmology, general surgery, laparoscopy and urology, plus extensive maternity facilities, including a special care baby unit.

Ghayathi Hospital
Silla Rd, Ghayati Ruwais **02 874 1666**
Map **2 B3**
Government-run Ghayathi Hospital provides basic medical services for people in the small towns of Ghiathy, Bida Mutawa and Seer Bani Yas, located in the far west of the emirate.

Gulf Diagnostic Center Hospital
Al Khaleej Al Arabi St Al Bateen **02 417 7222**
gdc-hospital.com
Map **2 G10**
Well-established private hospital in Al Bateen. In addition to specialist areas including tropical medicine, pathology, psychology and a range of surgeries, the hospital offers a full range of outpatient medical services including general practice and dentistry.

Hospital Franco-Emirien
Corniche Rd Markaziya East **02 626 5722**
hfe.ae
Map **2 N3**
Surgeons at the large, private Hospital Franco-Emirien specialise in abdominal, orthopaedic and gynaecological operations. The hospital also has a maternity ward and a delivery suite, in addition to an outpatient clinic, an emergency ward and a large dental centre.

Khalidiya Urgent Care Center
Nr Khalidiyah Mall Al Khalidiyah **02 417 0100**
skmc.gov.ae
Map **2 H5**
A 24/7 emergency care centre linked to Sheikh Khalifa Medical City. The centre takes some of the

Sheikh Khalifa Medical City

strain off SKMC's A&E facility, by dealing with minor emergencies such as cold and flu symptoms, vomiting and diarrhoea, minor breaks and sprains, ENT problems and rashes.

Lifeline Hospital

First Aid

Abu Dhabi presents the perfect opportunity to try outdoor pursuits such as dune bashing, stand-up paddle boarding and other activities that you might not have considered at home. With new physical activities comes the potential for injury, often a long way from medical access. If your first aid skills are non-existent or rusty, you can brush up on your general CPR and other techniques in a short course or even attend a tailor-made paediatric first aid course for parents and nannies. Licensed medics at LifeStartME (050 702 0236) can arrange training.

Lifeline Hospital
Shk Zayed The Second St Markaziya East
02 633 5522
lifelineauh.com
Map **2 N4**
A top-class and extremely well-equipped private hospital in the city centre, Lifeline Hospital offers a 24 hour emergency department (with ambulance service), a diagnostics clinic, maternity ward and an in-house pharmacy, plus specialist MRI and mammography departments.

Madinat Zayed Hospital
Tariq Rd Madinat Zayed **02 884 4444**
seha.ae
Map **3 C3**
A mid-sized government hospital serving the Al Gharbia western region of Abu Dhabi emirate. Given its remote location, this facility offers surprisingly extensive medical services that include an emergency department, general medicine and an advanced ophthalmology department.

Mafraq Hospital
Sheikh Rashid Bin Saeed Al Maktoum Rd Mafraq
02 501 1111
mafraqhospital.ae
Map **1 T13**
One of the UAE's biggest and busiest hospitals, the Al Mafraq hospital is located off the island, some 35 kilometres from the city centre. It has more than 500 beds, 36 clinical and non-clinical departments, as well as a whole host of tertiary and day-visit medical facilities. In the UAE, however, Al Mafraq is best known for its expertise in complex surgery. It does also have a well-equipped emergency department.

National Hospital
Nr Honda Showroom Al Baladia **02 671 1000**
nh.hcmena.com
Map **2 P5**
This state-of-the-art, private hospital offers general medicine and surgery, in addition to a wide range of specialised medical disciplines including IVF treatment, sports physiotherapy and holistic health.

NMC Speciality Hospital Al Ain
Nr UAE University Al Ain **03 755 5999**
nmc.ae
Map **4 D2**
The Al Ain branch of this hospital has extensive outpatient and inpatient facilities. There are also several family doctors based out of the hospital, as well as a dental surgery, an in-house pharmacy and a state-of-the-art diagnostics centre.

NMC Specialty Hospital Abu Dhabi
Shk Zayed The Second St Madinat Zayed
02 633 2255
nmc.ae
Map **2 M4**
One of the UAE capital's largest private facilities, offering a comprehensive range of medical services, plus a general outpatient unit which operates 24 hours a day. Specialist departments include

paediatrics, cardiology, orthopaedics, dentistry, neurology, gastroenterology, urology, eye care, psychiatry, dermatology and ENT. A private ambulance service is also available.

Oasis Hospital
Nr Al Ain & Khalid Bin Sultan Sts Al Ain
03 722 1251
oasishospital.org
Map **4 D2**
A small, private hospital in Al Ain, which is locally renowned for its maternity and specialist baby care units. Outpatient services include a diabetes clinic, physiotherapy, infectious diseases and pre-natal care.

Sheikh Khalifa Medical City
Al Karamah St Al Dhafrah **02 610 2000**
skmc.gov.ae
Map **2 K7**
Encompassing several 'Centres of Excellence', Sheikh Khalifa Medical City (SKMC) is the flagship institution for Abu Dhabi's public health system. Sheikh Khalifa Medical City consists of a 568 bed acute care hospital, 14 specialised outpatient clinics and the blood bank, which is accredited by the Joint Commission International. SKMC also manages a 125 bed behavioural sciences pavilion, six family medicine clinics, two walk-in clinics, an urgent care centre, and two dental centres within Abu Dhabi. SKMC operates under the management of Cleveland Clinic of the USA, and is owned by the Abu Dhabi Health Services Company (also known as SEHA), which oversees operations of all public hospitals within the emirate.

Specialized Medical Care Hospital
Al Ain St Al Ain **03 755 2291**
Map **3 C4**
A private facility in the Al Jahili area, the Specialized Medical Care Hospital offers 24 hour hospital care with a particular emphasis on minor and one-day surgical procedures, plus an outpatient care manifesto that includes paediatrics, dentistry, cardiology, obstetrics and gynaecology.

Tawam Hospital
Khalifa Bin Zayed St, Al Bateen Al Ain **03 767 7444**
tawamhospital.ae
Map **4 B3**
This private hospital is best-known for its expert maternity clinic. Affiliated with the prestigious American Johns Hopkins Medicine group, its specialised clinics include an oncology department, an emergency trauma department, a diabetes centre, an infertility clinic providing treatments such as IVF, and a pain clinic that delivers pain-relief treatments such as acupuncture.

Specialist Clinics & Practitioners
Whatever your ailment, the chances are you will find a relevant specialist at one of the many hospitals or medical clinics. At a push, you can make appointments without referral, but it is usually recommended that you discuss your condition with your regular doctor before seeking specialist help, as they will be able to offer advice on who the best specialist is for your particular ailment.

Most places will advise you over the phone or by email to save you the hassle of making an appointment, but a face-to-face consultation is recommended to ensure you get the best possible advice. Most hospitals also offer a range of outpatient medical specialities; the NMC Speciality Hospital (p.165) prides itself on providing the highest possible care for an extensive range of medical conditions.

If you prefer a more personal environment, there are numerous small, specialist practices dotted throughout the capital. These offer diagnosis and treatment of a range of medical conditions. In addition, many general practice clinics have resident specialists; Dr McCulloch's general practice clinic (p.159), for example, offers a maternity clinic, screening for childhood diseases, treatment for acute illness and occupational medicine (specialising in aviation), and it is a specialist in medical care for divers. It is well worth checking what your local clinic (see p.159) can offer before seeking specialist services elsewhere.

Advanced Cure Diagnostic Centre
Nr Al Bateen Mall Al Bateen **02 667 5050**
cure.ae
Map **2 F6**
Diagnosis and treatment for a wide spectrum of illnesses, with specialists covering cardiology, ENT, hepatology, obstetrics and gynaecology, paediatrics, immunology, pulmonary care, critical care, sleep medicine, neurology, orthopaedics and dermatology.

Al Rawdah German Medical Center
**Nr Abu Dhabi International Private School,
Al Karamah St** Al Karamah **02 652 0200**
argmc-uae.com
Map **2 J8**
Cutting-edge centre for paediatrics, physiotherapy, radiology, osteopathy, dermatology and diabetology.

Fakih IVF
Emirates Hospital Al Karamah **02 446 6422**
fakihivf.com
Map **2 K9**
A top IVF and fertility clinic, that deals with all manner of reproductive health and fertilisation issues, and has an impressive success rate.

Serious Medical Conditions

Medical facilities for chronic medical conditions are continually improving in Abu Dhabi. Here's the lowdown on the most prevalent serious illnesses in the UAE and where to go to receive treatment for them.

If you suffer from a serious medical condition, you'll find a good range of services available in Abu Dhabi and most clinics will help you seek treatment overseas or in your home country if services aren't available here.

Heart Disease

Heart disease is the highest cause of death in the UAE with over 40% of UAE fatalities linked to heart problems, according to Ministry of Health figures. The MoH promotes heart disease awareness with regular campaigns to educate people about contributing factors such as smoking, obesity, stress, high blood pressure, diabetes and sedentary lifestyles, most of which have an above-average prevalence in the UAE. Care for heart disease patients has improved dramatically in recent years thanks to Sheikh Khalifa Medical City which holds a Cardiac and Vascular Disease Conference.

Stroke

Stroke is the third biggest killer in the UAE, after heart disease and accidents and, worldwide, is the most common cause of lifelong disability. Most major hospitals have a neurosciences department offering neurological screening, treatment and rehabilitation; Al Ain Hospital (p.160) has a dedicated stroke unit, as does the Neuro Spinal Hospital (nshdubai.com) in Dubai.

Cancer

Tawam Hospital (p.166), in Al Ain, runs a cancer care centre and maintains the UAE's only cancer registry. On occasion, the hospital runs campaigns offering women free breast cancer check-ups. It also has a full oncology department, offering radiotherapy, chemotherapy, haematology, counselling and diagnostics. American Hospital (ahdubai.com), in Dubai, has both a cancer care centre and a paediatric oncology unit. Safe & Sound (safeandsound.ae) is a UAE-wide breast cancer awareness campaign and its website is packed with information on the disease, self examination and fund-raising activities. Life Diagnostic Centre (p.168), among others, has a dedicated breast cancer clinic.

Early Detection & Prevention

With all chronic diseases and serious illnesses, it is imperative to seek medical attention as early as possible to improve the chances of survival and minimise any lasting effects. Some insurance policies do not cover pre-existing or chronic medical conditions, so check your paperwork carefully and consider taking out additional cover if you have a family history of a disease or are particularly at risk through contributing factors.

Freedom Medical Clinic
East Rd Markaziya East **02 652 0200**
Map **2 N4**
A well-respected general medicine practice with medical, laboratory, radiology and ultrasound facilities.

Golden Sands Medical Center
Al Falah St Madinat Zayed **02 642 7171**
Map **2 N6**
General medicine, ophthalmology and radiology are available at this clinic.

Imperial College London Diabetes Centre
Nr Zayed Military Hospital, Al Khaleej Al Arabi St
Al Safarat **02 404 0800**
icldc.ae
Map **1 G8**
The world-renowned specialist centre for research, training, diagnostics and treatment. Offers diabetes management including dietetics, podiatry, radiology, endocrinology, non-invasive cardiology, metabolic and endocrine disorder management.

Life Diagnostic Centre
Marine Plaza Tower, Lulu St Markaziya East
02 633 2300
albadiegroup.com
Map **2 N4**
This clinic houses a specialist breast cancer and mammography department.

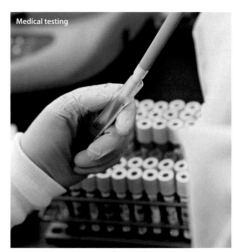

Medical testing

gynaecology, obstetrics, dermatology, ENT, ophthalmology and urology. In addition, an ambulance and house-call service are available.

Wooridul Spine Centre
Arzanah Medical Complex Al Madina Al Riyadiya
wsc.ae
Map **1 J8**
The region's first facility dedicated to minimally invasive spinal care is scheduled to open in early 2013. The centre is partnered with Wooridul, the renowned Korean spine specialists.

⌐ Skin Sense ¬
The strong sun in Abu Dhabi means you should be especially wary of any new moles or irregular marks that appear on your skin, or if existing moles change or grow in size. Dermatologist clinics specialise in looking after your skin, including Dr Menon's Laser Med Clinic (drsmenon.com) and Dr Ahmed Kamel Clinic (02 626 0040).

Middle East Specialised Medical Centre (MESMC)
Nr Emirates Media, East Rd Al Nahyan **02 446 7446**
mesmc.com
Map **2 M9**
Private city centre facility with doctors dealing with general and internal medicine, dentistry and ENT.

New National Medical Centre
Nr Cambridge School Mussafah **02 552 0100**
nnmc.hcmena.com
Map **1 N12**
The centre's departments include a 24 hour emergency unit, internal medicine, paediatrics,

Obstetrics & Gynaecology

Most hospitals and general practice clinics in Abu Dhabi offer gynaecologic and obstetric medical services. In your home country, you may be used to receiving reminders from your doctor when you are due for a smear test or mammogram; in the UAE, however, you will need to be more proactive, and while a gynaecologist can advise you on how frequently you should have check-ups, it will be up to you to remember when you are due for a test and to schedule an appointment. If you are looking for a long-term gynaecologist, then it's worth checking out some of the specialist clinics listed below. 'Well Woman' check-ups can be done on a regular basis (usually annually) and offer the chance to get your regular check-ups out of the way in one go, at the same time as having a general health check.

The majority of contraceptives are available in Abu Dhabi (although the morning-after pill is not) and a gynaecologist will be able to advise you on the most suitable form of contraception for you. If you take oral contraceptives, a variety of brands are available over the counter in pharmacies without prescription. Because of the risk of thrombosis, you should make a point of going to your doctor to have your blood pressure checked every six months, just to make sure everything is ok. It's worth noting that, although rarely enforced, the law states you should be married in order to be prescribed or purchase contraceptives.

Maternity Care

If you are having a baby, the level of maternity care in Abu Dhabi is very good. Among expats, the most popular maternity hospitals are Al Noor and Corniche (see Main Hospitals, p.160). Before you decide on a government hospital, it's worth checking their policy regarding husbands and family members being present in the labour ward. Certain hospitals may not allow your husband to be with you in the labour ward, although he can be present at delivery if it is not by caesarean; if you are persuasive and there are no local ladies admitted, your husband may be allowed access to the ward. However, if this is a deal-breaker, it's best to know upfront.

All government hospitals now charge expatriates for maternity services, and delivery and costs vary quite notably according to the package you choose. Private hospitals will be more expensive, although, if you shop around a little and speak to friends who have been through it all before, you may be surprised to find that, in some cases, the difference between government and private maternity care is not as great as you might think. No matter which you opt for, if you have medical insurance, check that it covers maternity costs – some have a limitation clause (you may need to have been with the insurer for at least 12 months prior to conception) and some may not cover any costs at all. Some insurers also require prior written advice of your expected delivery date and method as well as the last scan before birth: for hassle-free reimbursement, it is best to check your insurer's requirements well before your due date.

Most private hospitals offer tailored maternity packages that include prenatal care, delivery and postnatal care for you and the baby. Be aware that the price the hospital quotes is for the most basic 'best case scenario' delivery, and if you have any additional requirements, such as an epidural or an assisted delivery, you will be charged extra.

If you give birth by caesarean section, the cost is usually significantly higher and the hospital stay is also longer. If you go to an independent gynaecologist for your prenatal care, you will usually be offered a choice of hospitals and delivery packages, where your doctor can attend for the birth.

Waterbirths are now possible at the Al Ain Cromwell Hospital (alaincromwell.com), a brand-new facility specialising in services for women and children. Corniche (p.161), Al Rahba (p.161) and Dar Al Shifa (p.161) hospitals all have neonatal intensive care units and Oasis Hospital (p.166) has a special care baby unit.

For more information on having a baby in Abu Dhabi see Having A Baby, p.129.

Obstetric & Gynaecology Clinics

Prenatal care and maternity services are offered at many main hospitals (p.160) and specialist clinics (p.166); the medical facilities and practitioners listed below are those which exclusively offer or specialise in obstetrics, gynaecology and pre and postnatal care. In addition, B4Baby and Beyond is the first and only private midwife clinic in Abu Dhabi and offers antenatal care, lactation advice and a well-baby clinic. The clinic is located in the Swedish Medical Centre (02 681 1122) which also has an on-site obstetrician and gynaecologist. A number of gynaecology clinics offer fertility testing, but only a few clinics offer assisted reproductive technology and IVF treatment; National Hospital (p.165) and Tawam Hospital (p.166) are two of the few facilities that offer IVF.

The British Clinic

Al Hamra Centre Bldg, Shk Zayed The Second St
Tourist Club Area **02 677 1252**
thebritishclinic.net
Map **2 R4**
A specialised clinic offering fertility techniques and minimally invasive therapy, as well as general obstetric services, maternity care and antenatal counselling.

Mum's The Word   Jennifer Simon, mother of two

There are lots of options for paediatric care in Abu Dhabi and the doctors are generally very friendly and helpful. I've taken my daughters to a few different places. Doctors in general here seem to be quick to prescribe medication, and this is true for paediatric care as well. I think it's important to shop around a bit until you find a paediatrician that you like, feel confident taking advice from and who will not prescribe drugs unnecessarily, to ensure you get the best possible care and attention for your child. The Gulf Diagnostic Centre Hospital is good, but can get very busy at times. The Advanced Cure Diagnostic Centre also provides a good service – you don't need a referral from your regular doctor to see a specialist paediatrician, but you are supposed to make an appointment in advance. If your child becomes ill suddenly you can turn up and see a doctor quite quickly, although you may have to wait a while if your child isn't seriously ill.

Dr Amal Al Biely
Damas Jewellery Bldg, Khaled Bin Al Walid St
Markaziya East **02 632 4934**
Map **2 M4**
Well-regarded, independent gynaecology and obstetrics specialist.

Dr Wafa Gyn & Fertility Centre
Al Noor Hospital Markaziya East **02 626 9444**
wafafertility.com
Map **2 N3**
A very highly-regarded private specialist based at – although not associated with – Al Noor Hospital.

HealthPlus Women's Health Center
Hazaa Bin Zayed The First St Al Karamah
02 643 3494
hplus.ae
Map **2 J8**
A newly opened centre of excellence covering general obstetrics and gynaecology, maternal-foetal medicine, minimally invasive surgery, urogynaecology and reproductive medicine. It is the first of 20 such centres set to open across the emirate.

Paediatrics
The majority of the government and private hospitals and general medical centres have full-time paediatricians. A growing number of these hospitals have devoted paediatric departments (see Main Hospitals, p.160 and General Practice Clinics p.159). Abu Dhabi is quite well-served for neonatal care with

the Corniche (p.161), Al Rahba (p.161), Dar Al Shifaa (p.161) and Oasis (p.166) hospitals all having facilities to care for newborns with health problems but, for issues occurring after the newborn stage, you will need to find another paediatrician.

Your kids deserve the best, so don't be afraid to ask questions to determine the best choice. Call around and request the experience and qualifications you need, or you think your child may need. Ask other parents for recommendations. Dr McCulloch Clinic (p.159), Gulf Diagnostic Center Hospital (p.164) and Advanced Cure Diagnostic Center (p.166) are all popular with expat parents. There are also specialists, such as paediatric surgeons and neurodevelopment therapists, and doctors that care for children with special needs and learning difficulties. Your paediatrician should be able to give you the appropriate referrals.

Dr Abdullah Azzam Paediatric Clinic
Grand Store Bldg, Shk Zayed The First St
Al Khalidiyah **02 634 4185**
Map **2 K4**
An independent paediatrics clinic located conveniently in Al Khalidiyah.

Dr Ahmed Al Hilfi Clinic
City Seasons Hotel & Apartments, Shk Zayed The Second St Markaziya East **02 674 4438**
Map **2 P4**
A friendly and professional independent outfit in the city centre. Dr Al Hilfi specialises in paediatric surgery.

Child Health In The UAE Dr Maurice Khoury, paediatrician, Advanced Cure Diagnostics

Abu Dhabi does not have a Child Heath Record like the one available in the UK or France, which gives advice and guidance to parents and includes compulsory check-ups at specific ages. Paediatricians in Abu Dhabi do, however, perform these check-ups as part of routine early-years examinations. Close follow-up is recommended during the first year, with monthly examinations for the first six months, then every two to three months until 12 months, then every three to six months until your child is 4 years old. After then, a yearly check-up is a minimum recommendation. Check-ups will assess growth and psychomotor development and a quick exam of major systems – ears, neurological, eyes, mouth and teeth, heart sounds and breathing, abdomen, genital inspection and skin assessment.

The Ministry of Health in the UAE follows an immunisation calendar which is based mainly on the US calendar. Immunisations in the first year of life are actually almost identical in all countries around the world. The main difference is with the timings of the different shots and the number required for full immunity. Any child immunised in the UAE will be fully compliant with the UK or the US schedule when they reach 18 months.

The UAE still recommends immunisation for tuberculosis (BCG) at birth, although the routine use of this vaccine in Western Europe and North America has been discontinued. Exposure, however, might be higher in the UAE. The country is a travel hub and this definitely increases risk of exposure.

Children growing up in the UAE are not at a higher risk of contracting any particular 'exotic' diseases; however there is a notably higher incidence of allergy-related disease, especially asthma, which is probably due to the combination of local climate factors in association with individual predisposition. No specific measures of prevention need be taken. If your child should be diagnosed with asthma, proper treatment can be given to allow for a normal active lifestyle.

Dr Ghiath Sandouk
Gulf Diagnostic Center Hospital Al Bateen
02 417 7222
gdc-hospital.com
Map **2 G10**
A paediatric allergist based at Gulf Diagnostic Center Hospital.

Dr Jazia
Gulf Diagnostic Center Hospital Al Bateen
02 417 7222
gdc-hospital.com
Map **2 G10**
A well-known privately practising paediatrician.

Dr Raad Al Khayyat
Aster Medical Centre Tourist Club Area **02 645 6100**
Map **2 R4**
An independent general paediatrician.

Dr Sami Kanderian Clinic
City Seasons Hotel & Apartments, Shk Zayed The Second St Markaziya East **02 678 7846**
Map **2 P4**
A general paediatrics clinic.

┌─ Troubled Minds ─────────────

If your child is having trouble adjusting to life in Abu Dhabi, finding it hard to fit in at a new school or missing friends and family back home, an outside perspective can sometimes help. The American Center For Psychology and Neurology offers child counselling and psychology services which are useful for children with emotional difficulties and can help kids cope with family issues, such as parents going through divorce. The NMC Specialty Hospital (p.165) deals with psychiatric disorders in children and offers a range of therapies, including counselling and family therapy.

Ghaleb Khalayli Paediatric Clinic
Al Hamiri Bldg, Shk Khalifa Bin Zayed St, Aflaj Hazza Al Ain **03 766 3998**
Map **4 D3**
A general paediatrics clinic in Al Ain.

Dentists & Orthodontists
Dentistry in Abu Dhabi is, like most other medical services, of a very high standard but with prices to match. Standard health insurance generally doesn't cover dentistry, unless it's for emergency treatment brought about by an accident. You may be able to pay an additional premium to cover dentistry, but the insurer may first want proof that you've had regular check-ups for the previous two or three years.

If you have a health card, you're entitled to dentistry at your assigned hospital and, if your hospital does not have a dental section, it will refer you to another public hospital that does. Service is generally very good, but the rates may not actually be any lower than those of a private dental clinic. It is well worth speaking to friends, neighbours and colleagues to find a dentist that provides good service at reasonable prices, as a standard filling could set you back anywhere between Dhs.50 and Dhs.1,000. If it is root canal treatment that you need, expect to part with anything from Dhs.600 to Dhs.3,000.

As well as routine and surgical dental treatment, cosmetic dentistry is also big business in Abu Dhabi, so if you're looking for a smile makeover, there is plenty of choice. The clinics listed below are specialist dental clinics. For a wider choice, many general practice clinics (p.159), specialist clinics (p.166) and main hospitals (p.160) also offer dental services.

Advanced American Dental Clinic
Nr American Community School Al Bateen
02 681 2921
americandentalclinic.com
Map **2 E5**
A well-known dental practice that offers everything from orthodontic dentistry and periodontal treatments to endodontic treatments, teeth whitening, neuromuscular dentistry as well as cosmetic dentistry.

Al Ain International Dental Clinic
Nr Clock Tower, Commercial Bank Of Dubai Bldg Al Ain **03 751 1660**
alainden.ae
Map **4 D2**
This Swedish-run dental clinic offers laser dentistry, preventive treatment, child and adolescent dental care, cosmetic dentistry and prevention of gum and jaw disease.

Barbara Orthodontic & Dental Polyclinic
Al Manara Pharmacy Bldg, Shk Khalifa Bin Zayed St Markaziya East **02 626 9898**
barbaradc.ae
Map **2 N3**
Well-known practice with GP, offering implants and orthodontic treatment.

British Dental Clinic
Shk Hamdan Bin Mohammed St Markaziya East
02 677 3308
Map **2 Q3**
Expert dental surgeons provide emergency, preventative, general dental care and cosmetic dentistry at this friendly, well-known clinic.

Health

Canadian Dental Clinic
Shk Khalifa Bin Zayed St Al Ain **03 766 6696**
Map **4 D2**
Experienced dentists offer full range of procedures to Al Ain residents.

City Dental & Medical Centre
Main St Al Ain **03 764 2252**
Map **4 C2**
Provides a full range of dental procedures and treatments.

Dr Elisabeth Dental Clinic
Hilton Corniche Hotel Apartments, Shk Khalifa Bin Zayed St Markaziya East **02 626 7822**
Map **2 N3**
General dentistry and dental care in a friendly city centre environment.

Dr Firas Dental Clinic
Marina Mall Breakwater **02 633 5990**
drfirasclinic.com
Map **2 D1**
Offers everything from cosmetic dentistry, veneers, fillings, crowns and bridges, to root canals, gum treatment, teeth cleaning, extractions and emergency care to patients of all ages.

Gulf Dental Clinic
Nr Al Ain Oasis Al Ain **03 765 4373**
Map **4 D2**
A general dental and orthodontic clinic that is popular and well-regarded among expats living in Al Ain.

International Dental Clinic
Arabian Home Pharmacy Bldg, Shk Rashid Bin Saeed Al Maktoum Rd Al Manhal **02 633 3444**
Map **2 L6**
High quality dental clinic providing all general dentistry services.

Maher Medical Centre
Mercedez Benz Bldg, West Corniche Rd Al Khalidiyah **02 666 3588**
Map **2 H4**
Part of a larger general medicine facility, the dental clinic provides a full spectrum of dental check-ups and treatments.

Modern German Dental Center
C6 Tower, Bainuna St Al Bateen **02 667 3235**
Map **2 D6**
General dentistry, with dentists specialising in outpatient surgery, such as root canal treatment, tooth bleaching, crowns and implants.

Paris Dental Clinic
Abu Dhabi Coop Bldg, Shk Hamdan Bin Mohammed St Markaziya East **02 677 3373**
Map **2 R3**
A well-regarded team of specialists providing general dental care, including endodontic treatment, cosmetic procedures, implants, as well as orthodontic treatment.

Petra Dental Care Centre
Euro Hotel Apartment Al Dhafrah **02 641 1899**
Map **2 M7**
Extremely good dental clinic offering a wide range of treatments and services, including general orthodontic work.

Royal London Dental Clinic
Al Bhadi Bldg Al Ain **03 755 7155**
Map **4 C2**
Dental examinations, preventive treatments, restorative dentistry, gum disease treatment, root canal treatment, children's dentistry and cosmetic dentistry from an experienced and qualified team.

Swedish Dental Clinic
Nr American Community School Al Bateen
02 681 1122
Map **1 C5**
Expert care and treatment in a well-equipped city centre general dental clinic.

Opticians & Ophthalmologists
You are never far from an optician in Abu Dhabi, with a store in most shopping malls. Prescription frames, sunglasses and contact lenses are readily available, with many larger opticians also offering eye examinations. Some have their own facilities to make your glasses on site, and you should only wait around 30 minutes for them, unless you have specific requirements. In addition, most opticians also offer contact lens fitting, stocking everything from standard lenses to disposable and coloured lenses.

The dry, dusty environment of Abu Dhabi can cause problems for eyes, even if you haven't experienced problems with your eyes before. Natural tear or refresher eye drops can increase eye comfort and these are available from most opticians and pharmacies. Spending lengthy periods in air-conditioned environments can also cause problems for contact lens wearers. Opticians can advise on the most suitable lenses and additional eye drops if required. Sunglasses are an essential accessory in Abu Dhabi, to protect your eyes from the strong sun, and prescription lenses are widely available.

For eye problems requiring specialist treatment, several hospitals and clinics, including the Sheikh Khalifa Medical City (p.166), Magrabi Eye & Ear Center (p.173) and the Madinat Zayed Hospital (p.165), have well-equipped ophthalmology departments catering for patients of all ages. A branch of the world-renowned Moorfields Eye Hospital (www.moorfields. ae) has also opened in Dubai, providing optometric, ophthalmic and orthoptic (relating to eye movement) care from simple eye tests to complex surgical procedures. Both Moorfields and Maghrabi Eye & Ear Centre have specialist paediatric ophthalmology units.

If you have concerns about your eyesight or the eyesight of your child, you can make a direct appointment with a specialist, or speak to your local doctor who will be able to offer a quick check-up and referral to a suitable specialist. If you want to ditch the glasses, there are several hospitals and clinics offering various laser eye surgery procedures, including LASIK eye surgery. Prices start from around Dhs.4,000 per eye, rising to around Dhs.7,500. All good laser surgery packages should include a complete year's follow-up care. Even if you have never had problems with your eyes, you will need to have an eye test done in order to get a UAE driving licence. This will take place, free of charge, at the licensing centre and only takes a minute or two to complete.

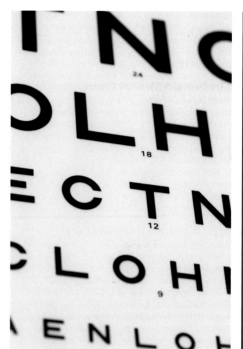

Ophthalmologists & Vision Correction Clinics

Magrabi Eye & Ear Center
Al Nakheel Tower, Bani Yas St Markaziya East
02 634 5000
magrabihospitals.com
Map 2 N3
This centre offers refractive surgery, as well as having departments specialising in cataracts, vitreo-retina, glaucoma, cornea and external eye disease, paediatric ophthalmology, ocular oncology, neuro-ophthalmology and ophthalmic investigation. It can also advise on and prescribe low-vision aids and contact lenses.

Opticians
Elite Optic Shk Zayed The First St, Al Khalidiyah, 02 666 6019, eliteoptic.com
Kattan Opticians Al Mullah Bldg, Shk Hamdan Bin Mohammed St, Markaziya East, 02 678 0818
Magrabi Eye & Ear Specialized Hospital Al Khaleej Al Arabi St, 02 444 6565, magrabihospitals.com
Magrabi Optical Al Jimi Mall, Al Ain, 03 763 0680, magrabioptical.com
Moorfields Eye Hospital Dubai Healthcare City, Dubai, 04 429 7888, moorfields.ae
Vision Express Al Wahda Mall, Al Dhafrah, 02 443 7015, alshaya.com
Yateem Optician Various locations, 02 627 7022, yateemgroup.com

Alternative Therapies
The UAE Ministry of Health grants licences to and administrates qualified practitioners of alternative medicine through its dedicated department for Traditional, Complementary & Alternative Medicine. Natural medicine can be specialised, so when consulting with someone make sure that you ask questions and explain your needs and expectations to ensure practitioners can help with your situation. Prices vary but are generally comparable to western medicine, and most insurance companies will not cover the costs. As always, word-of-mouth is the best way of establishing who might offer the most appropriate treatment.

In addition to the clinics listed below, some of the main hospitals have departments offering alternative medical treatments:

National Hospital (p.165) has a holistic health clinic offering alternative and complementary therapies for disease prevention and cure, utilising drugless therapies such as hydrotherapy, mud therapy, dietetics, fasting therapy, acupressure, acupuncture and yoga therapy.

Al Noor Hospital (p.161) has a Chinese medicine clinic, and Tawam Hospital (p.166) offers acupuncture.

Ahalia Hospital (p.160) has a homeopathy department which can devise alternative therapies

Health

or complementary treatments to a wide range of conditions. Homeopathic doctors arrive at their diagnosis by considering not only your illness or condition but your body and your lifestyle; remedies are created using plant and mineral elements.

In addition, although not medical disciplines in their own right, both yoga and Pilates are effective forms of complementary therapy recommended for a wide range of conditions. Both are available at a number of studios and health clubs across Abu Dhabi, and there are classes with a focus either on the fitness aspect or on the classic, meditative form of yoga. See Yoga, p.306.

Well-being treatments, such as aromatherapy and colour therapy, are offered by various spas and salons. See Health Spas & Massage (p.181) for details and listings of addresses in Abu Dhbai.

Al Falah Natural Treatment Centre

Ahmed Al Fahim Bldg, Shk Khalifa Bin Zayed St
Markaziya East **02 622 2708**
Map **2 M3**
Based on the principles of Ayurveda – a system of medicine that dates back to 3,000BC – Al Falah has Ayurvedic departments dealing in general medicine, surgery, ENT, gynaecology, toxicology, psychology, rejuvenation and sexology. There is also a wellness spa, dealing in thermotherapy, acupressure, Thai massage, body cleansing and slimming. Another branch is located in Al Ain (03 766 5315).

Gulf Chinese Medical Centre

Mohd Bin Butti Bldg, Al Nasr St Markaziya West
02 634 3538
gulfchinesemedical.net
Map **2 L3**
One of the most accomplished alternative medicine centres in town, this clinic uses traditional Chinese treatments, such as acupuncture, acupressure, reflexology and therapeutic massage to address conditions like headaches, insomnia, arthritis, asthma, gastrointestinal problems, diabetes, hypertension and prostatitis. The facility also has a herbal centre.

Homeopathic Medical Specialized Clinic

Nr Lifeline Hospital, Off Shk Zayed The Second St
Markaziya East **02 621 0400**
hmcuae.com
Map **2 N4**
A clinic dedicated to homeopathy that offers curative and preventive treatments based on the healing properties of plants, animals and minerals.

Sports Injuries

Many Abu Dhabi residents lead an active lifestyle, working hard and playing harder. But accidents and injuries do happen, so whether you got roughed up

playing rugby, pulled something in the gym or put your back out moving a wardrobe, you'll be pleased to hear that the city has some excellent facilities with specialists from all around the world to help you on the road to recovery.

Physiotherapy is perhaps the most well-known form of sports injury rehabilitation but it can also help with neurological disorders, musculoskeletal pain and cardiopulmonary disorders, and is an effective means of preventing further injury. Chiropractic and osteopathic treatments are non-invasive and aim to improve the functioning of the nervous system, or blood supply to the body, through manipulation of the skeleton. Chiropractic therapy focuses on realigning the joints, especially those of the spinal column, while osteopathy combines skeletal manipulation with muscular massage.

Orthopaedics concerns the repair of damaged bones and joints, whether sustained through injury, disease or genetics. Pilates is said to be the safest form of neuromuscular reconditioning and back strengthening available and is becoming increasingly popular. Classes are offered by a number of gyms as part of their group exercise schedules. Bodytree Studio (p.306) at Al Bateen, is a dedicated pilates studio offering reformer and mat classes (soma.ae).

The majority of the main hospitals in Abu Dhabi (p.160) have a rehabilitation or physical medicine department of some description, offering a variety of therapies, and some general practice clinics (p.159) also have resident specialists. Al Mafraq Hospital (p.165), for example, has a physical medicine department with all the facilities and expertise for all manner of physiotherapy and rehabilitation. Al Noor Hospital (p.161) boasts a state-of-the-art physiotherapy and rehabilitation department, specialising in sports injuries, spinal injuries and ligament injuries. The latest techniques are employed, including short wave and microwave diathermy, ultrasonic massage, magnetotherapy, paraffin therapy, hydrotherapy and suspension therapy.

In addition to chiropody, chiropractic expertise and acupuncture, the Gulf Diagnostic Center Hospital (p.164) has dedicated physiotherapy, orthopaedic and sports medicine departments.

In Al Ain, the NMC Specialty Hospital (p.165) offers a back and neck pain clinic, as well as neuro rehabilitation, occupational therapy and speech therapy clinics, plus routine physical therapy. Also available are electro-acupuncture treatment, Thai massage and more traditional yoga classes. Oasis Hospital (p.166), meanwhile, has a highly recommended physical therapist who uses a combination of manual therapy, massage, ultrasound, electric current, and heated or cooled compresses to treat all manner of sporting or muscular injuries, pains and conditions.

174

© Ton Koene. Victims of severe floods in Pakistan (2010).

unconditional **medical care**
where needed, when needed

Médecins Sans Frontières/MSF is an international medical humanitarian organization that provides emergency aid to people affected by armed conflicts, epidemics, healthcare exclusion and natural disasters. Everyday 27,000 MSF aid workers offer assistance to people based only on need and irrespective of race, religion or political affiliation.

MSF works in 65 countries around the world.

MSF is independent: 90% of its funding comes from private donations.

In 1999, MSF was awarded the Nobel Peace Prize.

MEDECINS SANS FRONTIERES
أطـبّــاء بـلا حـدود

www.msf-me.org

MSF Regional Office +971 2 631 7645 PO Box 47226 Abu Dhabi, UAE

Health

Abu Dhabi Knee & Sports Medicine Centre
Al Saif Tower, Shk Zayed The Second St
Tourist Club Area **02 631 7774**
sportsmedicine.ae
Map **2 N4**
The first specialised orthopaedic centre in the MENA region, this facility deals solely in knee, shoulder and musculoskeletal sports injuries. It can deal with everything from surgical grafts and rebuilding joints, to the full range of physiotherapy and rehabilitation programmes.

Canadian Medical & Chiropractic Center
Nr Shk Rashid Bin Saeed Al Maktoum & Delma Sts
Al Karamah **02 446 9006**
chiropracticabudhabi.org
Map **2 L9**
Offers chiropractic adjustment, physiotherapy, sports rehabilitation, naturopathy, iridology, reflexology, orthotics customisation, as well as Swedish, Chinese, shiatsu and aromatherapy massage.

Chiropractic Specialty Clinics
Fotouh Al Khair Centre Markaziya East **02 634 5162**
chiropracticuae.com
Map **2 L4**
This clinic provides chiropractic care for all ages, including postural training, strength and conditioning programmes, rehabilitation, and massage therapy.

KKT International Spine Centre UAE
Villa 5, West 39 Al Bateen **02 681 5550**
kktuae.com
Map **2 E5**
A specialist in non-invasive spinal treatments for conditions including spinal misalignment, injury and degeneration and general back pain.

Nutritionists & Slimming
With such a wide variety of dining options in Abu Dhabi, and with much emphasis on lounging and relaxing without sufficient physical exercise, it's easy to let your diet suffer and pile on the pounds. Thankfully, a number of slimming clubs and nutritionists are on hand to help. There are dietary and nutrition experts in many of the region's hospitals; both Al Falah Natural Treatment Centre (p.174) and Ibn Sina Medical Centre (p.159) have expert departments dealing in clinical nutrition and medical weight loss programmes, while Imperial College London Diabetes Centre (p.168) has a nutrition team who can help you manage the condition through diet.

Eating advice for digestive disorders such as reflux, IBS and coeliacs, plus for allergies and the menopause is becoming more common – contact the main hospitals (p.160) or your local clinic for recommendations. NMC Specialty Hospital (p.165)

specialises in individual health care plans. The hospital also launched BiteRite Cafe (p.372) which opened just opposite the Al Wahda Mall. You can either eat a meal in the restaurant or choose its tailor-made healthy eating delivery service. Low-fat, low-calorie and low-cholesterol meals are devised by dieticians, freshly prepared and delivered direct to your door. It is located between Defence Road and Muroor Road. A similar holistic nutrition-health approach is taken by Live'ly (lively.ae) which has packages targeted at everything from shifting a few pounds to getting chiselled abs.

While there is not an official Weight Watchers franchise in the UAE, plenty of people follow the online version (weightwatchers.com) and, if you find you're struggling to stick to a new regime, you'll discover plenty of support in the online forums (see Useful Websites, p.26). Personal trainers are available at most gyms and fitness centres (p.177) to help you balance exercise regimes with sensible foods.

Cosmetic Treatment & Surgery
The UAE is becoming established as a luxury healthcare destination. This is in part due to a concerted marketing effort by the government in attracting the best renowned names in the medical industry to centres like Sheikh Khalifa Medical City (p.166), Dubai Healthcare City (p.160) and Abu Dhabi Healthcare City which is to be constructed on Reem Island over the next few years.

Cosmetic surgery is at the heart of this growth and the city now boasts several establishments that specialise in reducing, reshaping, removing and enlarging various parts of your anatomy. As well as exclusively cosmetic practices, many of the private hospitals and independent clinics offer cosmetic services, including aesthetic and reconstructive surgery (see Main Hospitals, p.160, General Practice Clinics, p.159 and Specialist Clinics, p.166). As is the case across all medical facilities, standards are generally high, but it is worth checking out a few different clinics before you go under the knife. If you want a bit of sprucing and don't fancy slicing, a lot of the cosmetic clinics will also offer Botox and other non-surgical alternatives. Cosmetic and plastic surgery are still young industries in Abu Dhabi and, if you are unable to find exactly what you are looking for, head straight for Dubai where a multitude of cosmetic facilities await.

Cosmetic Treatment Clinics

CosmeSurge & Emirates Clinics For Day Surgery
Nr Delma & Karama Sts Al Karamah **02 446 6648**
cosmesurge.com
Map **2 K9**
A team of experienced sub-specialist cosmetic surgeons offer surgical and non-surgical cosmetic

procedures, non-invasive beauty therapy and cosmetic dentistry. A branch has recently opened in Khalifa City A (02 557 2220).

Kaya Skin Clinic
Al Karama St Al Karamah **02 445 9923**
kayaskinclinic.me
Map **2 K8**
This specialist skin clinic offers a range of aesthetic treatments including laser hair removal, Botox, anti-ageing therapies and chemical peels.

Obagi Dermatoloy & Cosmetic Centre
Hazaa Bin Zayed The First St Al Karamah **02 445 7100**
obagi-uae.com
Map **2 K8**
Skincare experts provide surgical and non-surgical skin and cosmetic treatments, including fillers, Botox, laser, weight control, cosmetic enhancements and reductions, and aesthetic medical spa treatments.

Counselling & Therapy

Starting a new life in a different country can be a stressful process and, whether you are new to the city or not, sometimes it can help just to talk through whatever issues and anxieties you are facing. Mental health services are not as developed as in some other countries; private counsellors and therapists are uncommon. One option is to first see a general practitioner or family doctor who will be able to offer advice, and is well-placed to recommend or refer you to a suitable service; however, the limited scope of mental health services here means that medication is often the preferred treatment over other forms of psychological treatment, therapy or counselling.

There are, however, a growing number of psychiatric and neurology specialist facilities which have sprung up in Abu Dhabi in the past few years. These offer services ranging from counselling and family and couple therapy, to paediatric psychiatry, addiction support, treatment of mental health disorders and learning difficulties support. For many of these clinics, you do not need a referral, so if you are struggling with psychological issues and prefer to try alternative treatments before resorting to medication, it's worth getting in touch with them directly.

At the forefront, is the American Center for Psychiatry and Neurology (02 666 4866, americancenteruae.com). Located near Al Khalidiyah Mall, it is a dedicated mental health facility offering psychiatric evaluation, assessment and treatment for adults and children. It offers therapy on an individual basis for adjustment disorders, post-traumatic stress disorder, eating disorders, panic disorders, anger management and alcohol abuse, plus couple and marital counselling, child, adolescent and family counselling, and school and academic assessment

and treatment. In addition, it offers a corporate employee assistance programme, plus seminars, workshops and in-house consultation, and it comes highly recommended.

Gulf Diagnostic Center Hospital (p.164) has a specialist mental health department offering psychiatric and psychological care and treatment, including the treatment of eating disorders. For a softer touch to mental well-being, Anahata Wellness Spa (p.182) offers positive thinking meditation classes. For those coping with major psychiatric problems, the Behavioral Science Pavillion (p.161), at Sheikh Khalifa Medical City, is dedicated to the assessment, management and treatment of those with psychiatric disorders, and the NMC Specialty Hospital (p.165) has a dedicated psychiatric department and offers emergency evaluation and treatment, including crisis intervention and resolution. It offers a wide range of outpatient and inpatient units for adults, adolescents and children and, with a team of international experts, can offer treatment for schizophrenia, mood disorders, depression, anxiety, phobia, panic and adjustment problems, eating disorders, compulsive disorders, emotional problems, psychosexual dysfunctions and developmental disorders. It also offers student counselling and motivational courses.

The National Rehabilitation Centre has recently opened the Khalifa Rehabilitation Clinic (KRC) for recovering addicts, aimed at treating substance addiction. Currently based in Khalifa City A, KRC will move to a new centre in Mafraq City in 2014.

As with all medical issues, check your insurance policy to see what you are covered for, and be aware that most insurers will not cover anxiety or stress-related illnesses.

FITNESS
Gyms & Fitness Clubs

Abu Dhabi is quickly becoming a hub for some of the major sporting events that take place each year in the UAE. The Abu Dhabi Tourist Authority has been tasked with turning the world's sporting eyes on the emirate and with the first Abu Dhabi International Triathlon, the Club World Cup, Formula 1 Grand Prix, UFC and European Tour golf events all making an appearance, they are well on their way to succeeding in their goal. See Spectator Sports, p.226, for more information.

As a result of greater awareness of sports in the emirate, more emphasis is being placed on government-run healthy living initiatives and school sports, with new activities being introduced into both government and international schools.

Finding accommodation with its own gym facilities is difficult in Abu Dhabi. Many of the new housing complexes and tower buildings have been designed

Fitness

to include fitness facilities, or access to them, but the majority of tower buildings or villas on the island are too old for this.

There are, however, many options if you want to sign up for gym membership. Most of the larger hotels offer beach or health club membership. Hiltonia Health Club & Spa (p.183) and Monte-Carlo Beach Club memberships give you access to the properties' excellent gym facilities and full use of their beach and swimming pools to boot. The Fairmont Bab Al Bahr (p.201) opens its doors to gym-goers, with separate men's and women's gyms and access to their outdoor terrace pools, while anyone out on the islands might want to look to the fitness complex at St Regis Abu Dhabi (p.207).

If you would rather avoid hotel guests, but would still like access to a beach, The Club (p.179) offers a family and non-family beach, swimming pool, tennis courts and a well-equipped gym; however, membership can be steep and waiting lists long.

There are also several independent gyms and fitness centres. Most charge monthly or yearly membership fees although they usually also have daily rates or visitor passes for Dhs.100 to Dhs.250. If you're deciding which gym is right for you, bigger establishments will often offer a free day of access to get your business. Try several – signing up for a full year is a hefty, if worthwhile, investment.

Hiltonia Gym

To find like-minded team-mates, check out the Activity Finder on p.274.

If you need serious motivation, try one of the boot camp courses on offer from Original Fitness Co (p.179). It runs challenging, yet rewarding boot camp style group and individual training classes for all fitness levels and ages, focusing on everything from running and kickboxing to yoga and mixed martial arts. Women's only courses are also available. The Abu Dhabi Country Club also has personal trainers who offer tailored gym programmes, plus squash, tennis and swimming coaching is available should you wish to brush up on your strokes (Activities, p.274).

Abu Dhabi Country Club
Al Saada St Al Mushrif **02 657 7777**
adcountryclub.com
Map **2 J13**
Extensive facilities here include two gyms (one women-only), as well as nine tennis courts, two squash courts and a basketball court. There's a swimming pool and two Jacuzzis, several outdoor all-weather football pitches; personal trainers and coaches are on hand for group and private lessons. Classes are free to members and Dhs.50 for non-members. Membership is Dhs.10,000 per year for men and Dhs.5,000 for women.

Al Forsan International Sports Resort
Nr Abu Dhabi Golf Club & Resort Madinat Khalifa A (Khalifa City A) **02 556 8555**
alforsan.com
Map **1 P8**
In addition to all the other activities on offer at Al Forsan (p.218), there is a gym and swimming pool with memberships available, as well as single day access for Dhs.120 per day.

Quick Fit

If you can't stand the thought of going to the gym, try Hypoxi therapy. The training system is said to maximise cellulite and fat burn by combining exercise with vacuum suction. The method is non-evasive and painless and can be directed at those problem areas. Visible results can be noticed after a couple of sessions and the treatment is gaining in popularity. Try it at Abu Dhabi Country Club (p.178) or The Officer's Club (p.296). Find out more at hypoxi.net.

Group exercise classes are another great way to get in shape. The high energy levels, group motivation and fun attitude of group classes offer the perfect antidote to bunnies who are weary of the gym. Most fitness clubs, health clubs and hotel gyms offer some form of group class, and some are open to non-members, so it's worth calling around to find out what's on offer and trying out a few different classes until you find one that you really enjoy. There are a couple of studios that now only offer group sessions.

Whether you're a kicker, winger, fielder, striker or a hooker, there are numerous sports clubs in Abu Dhabi offering opportunities to get involved with your favourite sport at both friendly and competitive levels.

The Club
Mina Zayed Free Port **02 673 1111**
the-club.com
Map **2 V3**
Since opening way back in 1962, The Club has been an Abu Dhabi institution. Open to private members only, it has a private beach, various swimming pools, tennis, squash, badminton and a well-equipped gym. It is also home to Abu Dhabi Sailing Club (p.298) and Abu Dhabi Sub Aqua Club (p.280). Classes are reserved for members only, with body pump, spinning, stepping and yoga on offer. Annual adult membership starts at Dhs.3,450 although it is subject to a Dhs.3,750 joining fee, plus extras depending on which facilities you want to use.

Crowne Fitness
Crowne Plaza Abu Dhabi Markaziya East
02 616 6166
ichotelsgroup.com
Map **2 N4**
Much more than your bog standard hotel gym, the fitness centre here offers a full fitness studio, personal trainers, and several treatment rooms, which have attracted a large membership.

Fit Studio
Al Mamoura B, Muroor Rd Al Nahyan **02 445 3395**
fitstudio.ae
Map **2 N10**
A great option if you prefer social classes to going it alone in a gym, Fit Studio offers the full range of Les Mills disciplines (Bodyattack, Zumba, Bodycombat, Bodystep, TRX, RPM, Yogalates etc) from around Dhs.50 per class. You can see timetables and book classes online.

Haddins Fitness
Zayed Sport City Al Madina Al Riyadiya **02 403 4233**
haddins.com
Map **1 J8**
Haddin's Fitness at Zayed Sports City offers a broad range of group fitness classes, gym, tennis lessons and personal training, as well as their popular boxing programme. Tiered access memberships and package deals offer good value.

Original Fitness Company
C6 Tower, Baynunah St Al Bateen **02 406 9404**
originalfitnessco.com
Map **2 D6**
This company's claim to fame is its fitness boot camps. The four-week military-style training programmes are guaranteed to jump-start you on the road to fitness by combining cardiovascular, strength and mental conditioning. The company offers individual, group and corporate training sessions.

Six P Gym
Jumeirah at Etihad Towers Al Ras Al Akhdar
02 811 5622
jumeirah.com
Map **2 B3**
Although part of the Jumeirah at Etihad Towers hotel, the Six P Gym is almost a complete and separate health club, with state-of-the-art equipment, personal trainers and excellent amenities on offer.

WELL-BEING

Whether your definition of well-being is pampering at a luxury health spa, limbering up with an invigorating massage, getting a new look for your hair or nails, or being kicked into shape by your own fitness guru, Abu Dhabi has a whole host of facilities on offer that will have you feeling relaxed and rejuvenated in body and mind in no time.

Personal Grooming

Beauty is big business in Abu Dhabi. Salons are everywhere and, with certain services such as manicures, pedicures and waxing costing less than in many other international cities, you may find that a trip to the beauticians becomes a more regular diary fixture than at home. Fridays are usually the busiest day, so make sure you book ahead; on other days, many places accept walk-ins or bookings at short notice. In hotels, you'll find both male and female stylists working alongside each other, but in establishments located outside hotels, only female stylists are permitted to work in ladies' salons. These salons are very private and men are not permitted inside – even the windows are covered. There are also numerous salons aimed primarily at Arabic ladies, which specialise in henna designs, so look out for a decorated hand poster in salon windows. The traditional practice of painting henna on the hands and feet, especially for weddings or special occasions, is still very popular with UAE nationals. For tourists, a design on the hand, ankle or shoulder can make a great memento – it will cost about Dhs.40 and the intricate brown patterns fade after two to three weeks.

There are plenty of options for male grooming, with barbershops and salons to suit all budgets, and a growing number of specialist men's spas. So whether you're after a short back and sides, a traditional shave, a chest wax or a facial, there's something for all.

Many beauty salons, nail bars and hairdressers offer a combination of services, but as the quality, prices and service vary greatly, trial and error and word of mouth are the best ways to find a dependable salon. The listings below are a good starting place if you're new to the city. For a full listing of hairdressers, beauty salons and nail bars, visit askexplorer.com.

Beauty Salons & Nail Bars

Beauty salons and nail bars pop up thick and fast in Abu Dhabi, so whether your nails are in need of a polish or your skin is desperate for revitalising, you'll only need to make a quick dash down the road to your nearest shopping mall or hotel.

Many beauty salons in Abu Dhabi will offer a combination of services, from manicures and pedicures, to facials, body scrubs, Moroccan steam baths, massage, waxing, haircuts and styling. The quality of treatments and services can differ greatly so word of mouth recommendations and trial and error are probably the best ways to find a salon that is right for you. Kaya Skin Clinic (p.177) is a popular choice, with clinics based in Abu Dhabi and Dubai. They provide wonderfully rejuvenating treatments for skin dried out by the hot Abu Dhabi sun; their 'everyday radiance' treatment will have your skin feeling soft and perky again in no time. They recommend three sessions, which will set you back Dhs.1,950. If you're after something that is a little lighter on your pocket, try a 90 minute herbal facial at the Zari Spa & Beauty Centre (p.185). It'll zap life back into tried, sun-dried skin for just Dhs.175.

With the year-round sunshine holding endless possibilities for strappy shoes, flip-flops, sandals and summery wedges, there's no excuse for having less-than-perfect pinkies. It's worth trying out a few different nail bars to find one you really like as chances are you'll be making regular appearances there. Mosaic Nails (p.180) comes highly recommended for a top quality manicure and pedicure; they'll make your fingers and toes lovely and colourful for Dhs.110. In addition to sparkling and polished nails, Mosaic Nails offers hot and cold waxing, threading and tweezing, as well as Oriental and Moroccan bath treatments, massages and facials. Bridal and Shahrazad packages are also available. Nails (p.180) in Abu Dhabi Mall, and the Al Muhairy Centre and the Shangri La Souk is a firm favourite with the ladies of Abu Dhabi and you'll always find branches busy. A manicure costs Dhs.50, while a pedicure will be Dhs.60; add an extra Dhs.10 if you want a French polish.

If you fancy trying the traditional henna designs, Beautiful Henna Centre (p.180) offers a huge selection of Indian and Arabic patterns to choose from. If you'd rather relax in the comfort of your own armchair while one of their experts decorates your hand, ankle or shoulder, they also offer a home service.

Beauty Salons & Nail Bars

Al Lailak Beauty Saloon Corniche Towers A, Al Khalidiyah, 02 681 2612, *allailak.com*
Beautiful Henna Centre Shk Rashid Bin Saeed Al Maktoum Rd, Al Dhafrah, 02 634 3963, *noqooshaljameela.com*

The Beauty Spot Salon Eastern Mangroves Hotel & Spa By Anantara, Al Zahra, 02 656 1149, *beautyspot.me*
Dashing Nails Delma St, Al Nahyan, 02 441 0777, *dashingllc.com*
Glow Beauty Salon One To One Hotel – The Village, Al Nahyan, 02 495 2150, *uglow.ae*
Harmony Beauty Salon At The Club The Club, Mina Zayed Free Port, 02 673 1111, *the-club.com*
La Reine Beauty Center Al Mansoury Plaza, Shk Hamdan Bin Mohammed St, Markaziya East, 02 677 7090, *lareinebeautycenter.com*
Madonna Beauty Spa Porsche Showroom Bldg, Al Salam St, Tourist Club Area, 02 674 0666
Man/Age Luxury Men's Spa Marina Mall, Breakwater, 02 681 8837, *managespa.com*
Mosaic Nails & Spa Nr Delma & Al Karamah Sts, Al Karamah, 02 445 9660, *mosaicnailsandspa.com*
Nail Lounge Marina Mall, Breakwater, 02 681 6333
Nails Various locations, 02 644 4188
Shampoo Beauty Salon Marina Mall, Breakwater, 02 681 5898
Shamsa Beauty Salon Nr BHS Bldg, Shk Hamdan Bin Mohammed St, Madinat Zayed, 02 631 7063
Tips & Toes Villa 365-1, Al Khaleej Al Arabi St, Al Bateen, 02 445 8834, *tipsandtoes.com*
Zari Spa & Beauty Centre NMC Specialty Hospital Abu Dhabi, Madinat Zayed, 02 617 9150, *zarizardozi.com*

Hairdressers

You'll find ladies and gents hairdressers dotted throughout Abu Dhabi, and almost all shopping malls and hotels have salons. There are many small salons in the Tourist Club Area and Madinat Zayed areas of the city. In general, hairdressing in Abu Dhabi still has a long way to go until it reaches the standard you would find in most international cities, but there are a number of well-respected international salons. Finding a hairdresser you like and trust can be tricky business, but recommendations from friends and colleagues are a good place to start.

If you are looking for a simple trim and tidy-up, there are plenty of options for men and women in the city centre where you'll find a hairdresser or barber on just about every corner. Some of the smaller places are very reasonably priced and you could pay as little as Dhs.30 for a simple cut. The larger, branded salons are more expensive, with haircuts starting from around Dhs.100. For a style and a full head of highlights, prices are Dhs.300 and upwards, and you can expect to pay more for a higher quality cut and colours. Changes (02 634 1147) is a favourite amongst many of Abu Dhabi's expat ladies, as is Hairworks (02 681 6678) upstairs in Spinney's in Al Khalidiyah. Both have experienced hairdressers who offer highlights, colour and styling at reasonable prices. The newly opened Glamour Salon in Al Markaziyah has provided salvation to the blondes of Abu Dhabi with British and Australian stylists providing modern and professional cuts and colours (02 626 3002).

Unbeweavable

You can find a few salons that do afro hair, braiding, relaxing and extensions in and around the city centre and Tourist Club Area, such as Dalla Beauty Saloon. However, you may find that expertise differs greatly and, for that reason, many ladies head for Elyazia Beauty Center (elyaziabeautycenter.com) in Dubai's International City, which has gained something of a reputation for its afro hair care, weaves, extensions and colouring.

Barbers and gents salons offer decent, simple haircuts, traditional style shaves and, in some cases, men's facials. Men are likely to pay around Dhs.15 for a basic cut, though at upmarket salons, prices are around Dhs.60 or more. At the very high end, male spas such as The Lounge (p.184) and Man/Age (p.184) offer a range of pampering treatments for the modern male in addition to stylish haircuts.

Children are catered for too, and there are a number of specialist children's hairdressers in Abu Dhabi offering fun-shaped chairs to sit in or videos to watch while they have their hair done. Kids often receive a sweet, a balloon or a hair clip too.

Aziz Men's Salon Marina Mall, Breakwater, 02 681 8899
The Beauty Spot Salon Eastern Mangroves Hotel & Spa By Anantara, Al Zahra, 02 656 1149, *beautyspot.me*
Family Beauty Salon Habib Exchange Bldg, Shk Hamdan Bin Mohammed St, Madinat Zayed, 02 626 0939
Fringe Benefits At The Club The Club, Mina Zayed Free Port, 02 673 1111, *the-club.com*
Glamour Salon Al Nielin Bank Bldg, Nr East & Corniche Sts, Markaziya East, 02 626 3002, *glamoursalonuae.com*
Hilton Abu Dhabi Hair Salon Hilton Abu Dhabi, Al Khubeirah, 02 681 2754
Kids Land Salon Marina Mall, Breakwater, 02 681 6316

Health Spas & Massage

Soothing the body, mind and soul with a relaxing massage, cleansing facial or invigorating body scrub could be a weekly treat, a gift for someone special, or a way to de-stress after a trying time at work; whatever you're looking for, Abu Dhabi has a wide choice of luxury spas, day spas, beauty salons and massage parlours that will leave you or that special someone feeling pampered and rejuvenated.

Numerous massage and relaxation treatments are available at the various spas and health clinics. However, it's useful to bear in mind that prices, quality standards and the general style of treatment can vary enormously, so it's worth doing your research into what's on offer. The options vary from five-star luxury hotel spas to small and friendly independent establishments, which usually offer fewer bells and whistles but better value for money. To give an idea of the variety on offer, the following two spas represent the opposite ends in terms of how much you'll need to fork out and what you can expect to receive in exchange: at the top end of the spectrum, the Shangri-La's luxurious spa, Chi, has a wonderful range of Asian massage treatments, for which you can expect to pay around Dhs.700 for a 90 minute treatment (includes access to the spa's facilities); on the other hand, smaller day spas, such as Sharanis Wellness Spa, offers 60 minute signature treatments for around Dhs.270. If you're looking for something a little different, Abu Dhabi has numerous spas offering authentic massage and relaxation treatments from around the world; Eden Spa at Le Meridien specialises in the ancient Indian practice of Ayurveda massage, Footprint Spa focuses on reflexology and the traditional Arabian hammam (p.182) is offered by many of Abu Dhabi's spas.

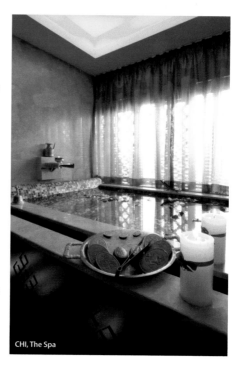

CHI, The Spa

Well-Being

Abu Dhabi Country Club
Al Saada St Al Mushrif **02 657 7777**
ww.adcountryclub.com
Map **2 J13**
The on-site beauty salon at this club offers a variety of services including neck, back and shoulder massages, deep tissue and hot stone massages and reflexology. There are two basic treatments and, for a full pampering session, you can also get your hair and nails done here.

Anahata Wellness Spa
Street 35 Madinat Khalifa A (Khalifa City A)
02 5577 722
anahataspa.ae
Map **1 R8**
Anahata Wellness Spa offers a huge range of treatments, from massage and Ayurveda to hair, nail and beauty care. Located in a spacious converted villa, the salon also holds Vinyasa Flow and Kundalini yoga classes, plus Pilates and positive-thinking meditation classes. It's truly a one-stop shop and the therapists are well-trained in their particular treatments. The location in Khalifa City A makes the spa a popular choice for ladies living off-island.

Anantara Spa
Emirates Palace Al Ras Al Akhdar **02 690 9000**
spa.anantara.com
Map **2 B2**
Expect the epitome of luxury at the Emirates Palace Anantara spa. This beautiful Moroccan-influenced spa only has seven treatment rooms, but each is spacious and elegantly kitted out with everything you need for some indulgent me-time. With two steam rooms, two Jacuzzis and a unique ice cave, plus a Moroccan hammam, the facilities are excellent. Treatment highlights include a caviar facial, Elemis treatments and the royal hammam ritual. The other branches at Eastern mangroves (p.201), Qasr Al Sarab (p.245) and the Desert Islands resort (p.244) offer a similar service for guests looking for a bit of luxurious pampering in these remote spots.

Anantara Spa
Eastern Mangroves Hotel & Spa By Anantara
Al Zahra **02 656 1000**
anantara.com
Map **1 H6**
Although the spa doesn't play quite the role it does in Anantara's other two UAE properties, it's still a key part of the offering at Eastern Mangroves and is the equal of all the other high-end spas in Abu Dhabi. Levels of luxury cannot be faulted, and the 10 self-contained treatment rooms (two of which can be used by couples) as well as the stunning hammam, sauna and steam rooms, all offer Thai relaxation with

Middle Eastern indulgence. Aside from the beautiful hammam, there are all manner of wraps and scrubs on offer (many using organic local Shiffa products), while the Thai massage is, of course, particularly good. The Shiffa Cleansing Emerald Ritual is about the most indulgent set of treatments you'll find anywhere.

Body & Soul Spa & Recreation Club
Al Raha Beach Hotel Al Raha **02 508 0486**
danathotels.com
Map **1 R7**
There's a range of massages, facials, body polishes and wraps to choose from and the prices are very reasonable in comparison to many other hotel spas; complimentary use of the pool, sauna, steam room and jacuzzi adds to the value. The small but cosy treatment rooms come complete with twinkling candles, sweet aromas and relaxing music. Check the website for regular seasonal promotions.

The Touch Of Arabia
For an Arabian pampering experience, opt for an Oriental Hammam. This treatment is traditional in the Middle East region and shares similarities with Turkish baths. The name refers to the bath (the room) in which the treatment takes place – typically an elaborate affair in Abu Dhabi's five-star spas. A hammam involves a variety of different experiences, including being bathed, steamed, washed with black soap, scrubbed with a loofah and massaged on a hot marble table; some treatments also involve mud masks and henna. While this may sound a little invasive, and more than a tad vigorous, it's a wonderfully invigorating experience which leaves your skin feeling as soft as cream. Absolute must-dos while in Abu Dhabi are the Moroccan Hammam at the Anantara Spa at Emirates Palace and the Moroccan bath at The Oryx Hotel (02 681 0001).

Bodylines
Yas Island Rotana Yas Island West **02 656 4000**
rotana.com
Map **1 T4**
You receive a warm welcome at the Bodylines fitness centre and, whilst the menu is limited to full body, hot stone or area-specific massage, the facility is spa-like in appearance with its cool slate walls, aromatherapy scented air and serene, spacious layout. Enjoy the option to relax in the steam, sauna and Jacuzzi facilities before your fully qualified therapist offers you the massage pressure of your choice and the option to choose from a selection of fragrant oils. Particularly nice touches include hot towels on your feet before and after your treatment and the chance to relax on

one of the day beds prolonging your feeling of Zen. There is also a gym on-site which boasts great views over the Gulf and can be enjoyed by club members.

Bodylines Health & Fitness Centre
Park Rotana Abu Dhabi Al Matar **02 657 3333**
rotana.com
Map **1 K7**
The treatment menu is limited to full body or area-specific massages as well as heavenly hot stone treatments. Cool slate walls, aromatic air and the serene layout make for a wholly relaxing experience – top it by enjoying the steam room, sauna and Jacuzzi facilities before your treatment, then finish off by chilling out on one of the sumptuous day beds.

CHI, The Spa
Shangri-La Hotel, Qaryat Al Beri Bain Al Jessrain **02 509 8900**
shangri-la.com
Map **1 L8**
The Shangri-La's CHI spa is a sanctum of Zen and relaxation. Arrive early to make the most of the spa pool, steam room, sauna and Jacuzzi and ready yourself for your treatment. Then choose from the extensive range of luxurious scrubs, massages, facials, signature treatment journeys and regionally inspired relaxation rituals, and sink into a state of bliss.

Corpofino Spa & Slimming Center
Villa 3/2, Nr Al Wahda Mall, Shk Rashid Bin Al Maktoum St Al Nahyan **02 445 2800**
corpofino.me
Map **2 L8**
Corpofino means 'fine body', and for over a decade, this spa, located in a villa near Al Wahda Mall, has been offering clients not only relaxing and rejuvenating traditional beauty treatments, but also tailor-made slimming programmes – including state-of-the-art equipment to tackle stubborn fat and cellulite. Nutritional advice is also available and once the hard work has been done, clients of this ladies only centre can reward themselves to a selection of beauty therapies from facials to Minx nails.

Cristal Spa
Cristal Hotel Abu Dhabi Madinat Zayed **02 652 0000**
cristalhotelsandresorts.com
Map **2 M4**
The Cristal Spa is nothing overly fancy but that's where its main advantages lie. There are three treatment rooms and a lounge area where guests can relax with water or tea. There's a temperature controlled pool, a sauna and Jacuzzi and clean, modern changing rooms, but it's the no-frills quality of the treatment that will have you returning again and again. You could even fit the superb Express Facial into your lunch break.

Eden Spa & Health Club
Le Meridien Abu Dhabi Tourist Club Area **02 644 6666**
lemeridienabudhabi.com
Map **2 S4**
The spa reception area may not be the most opulent in town, but the extensive treatment menu is very impressive – with an array of massages, facials, body wraps and body scrubs to choose from. Also on offer is balneotherapy, a hydro massage bath. The therapists know their stuff and the service is personable and to-the-point. Ayurveda therapies are also available.

ESPA At Yas Viceroy Abu Dhabi
Yas Viceroy Abu Dhabi Yas Island West **02 656 0862**
espaonline.com
Map **1 T5**
UK brand ESPA has become something of a byword for luxurious indulgence and the ESPA at Yas Viceroy is almost the dictionary definition of a modern, urban spa. From welcome to goodbye, it's a classy and professional operation, but not at the cost of personalised relaxation. The treatments on offer are vast – signature treatments, facials, dedicated male treatments, a ladies' hammam, and more than 30 massages, wraps and scrubs, while the range of combination journeys and 'escapes' offer good value – in fact, for a top-notch five-star spa, prices at ESPA remain fairly reasonable. Therapists make a spa and here they're every bit as professional and relaxing as their surroundings; relaxation areas certainly tempt and, if you've a little spare time, try the Metronap – 20 minutes in the recliner pod is equal to an eight hour sleep, apparently.

Footprint Spa
Al Wahda Mall Al Dhafrah **02 443 7375**
footprint-spa.com
Map **2 M7**
This independent day spa specialises in hand and foot reflexology, and offers a range of relaxing, revitalising and pampering scrubs, soaks, massages and reflexology treatments for your fingers, toes and head. The spa takes an entirely holistic approach towards treatments and therapists discuss various benefits to meet your mind and body requirements prior to starting the treatment.

Hiltonia Health Club & Spa
Hilton Abu Dhabi Al Khubeirah **02 692 4205**
hilton.com
Map **2 C3**
The Hiltonia Spa is a blissful haven of tranquillity set in beautiful surroundings. Cool marble floors and ethnic decor make a soothing setting and the spacious treatment rooms come complete with private showers. As well as the popular aromatherapy and reflexology treatments, the spa also offers signature

Well-Being

Indian head massages and an intriguing range of hydro treatments, some of which soothe the muscles and others detox. Alternatively, you can opt for one of the special packages, which combine body treatments with facials and nail care, and include the use of the sauna, eucalyptus steam room and Jacuzzi.

Iridium Spa
The St Regis Saadiyat Island Resort Sadiyat Island **02 498 8888**
stregissaadiyatisland.com
Map **1 G1**
The whites, beiges and browns, along with the natural stone and wood finishes, give Iridium Spa a feeling of rustic perfection. The treatment menu is fairly expansive (and expensive) but rather than provide a one-size-fits-all therapy, each massage, scrub and wrap is tailored to the client's wants and needs. Therapists are knowledgeable and do a great job at making you feel relaxed.

The Lounge
Al Khaleej Al Arabi St Al Bateen **02 667 7377**
thelounge.ae
Map **2 E6**
Men-only spa where there is nothing girly whatsoever about the pampering on offer. The spa is decorated in masculine earthy tones and gents can opt for a traditional shave, haircut, hair and scalp treatments, massage or steam, Moroccan and Turkish baths. The Lounge also offers IPL (intense pulsed light) which removes unwanted body hair in a similar way to laser hair removal. Facials, nail care, tanning and temporary tattoos are also available, and the service is fit for a king. The Lounge has plenty of streetside parking but, if you're too busy or shy to visit the spa, stylists and therapists are happy to come to your home or office.

Man/Age Luxury Men's Spa
Marina Mall Breakwater **02 681 8837**
managespa.com
Map **2 D1**
Pampering at the spa need not be just for the girls: this luxurious, one-stop men's spa offers male grooming including haircuts and shaving, manicures, massages and facials. There are also a number of signature combos that offer good value for money.

Mizan
Rocco Forte Hotel Abu Dhabi Al Madina Al Riyadiya **02 617 0000**
roccofortehotelabudhabi.com
Map **1 J7**
Rocco Forte hotels aren't renowned for their spas in the way that some brands are and business hotels often offer functional rather than overwhelming spa experiences, so Mizan is a real surprise. The huge spa is one of Abu Dhabi's biggest and best equipped, with the usual wet zones, saunas and Jacuzzis appearing alongside experiential showers, lovely plunge pools, a Vichy shower suite and a deluxe hammam area. The decor throughout wet areas, ladies' and gents' separate relaxation areas and the private treatment rooms is soft, airy and spacious, creating a nice, relaxed mood that differs from the standard 'chill out'. The usual treatments are covered although the basic Thai and Swedish massages are hard to look past.

Oriental Spa & Fitness
Sultan Bin Zayed St Al Bateen **02 665 5707**
This small spa in a converted villa has a homemade feel to it but offers a good range of treatments, like massage, beauty, hair care and nail treatments. Make-up courses are also available, as are a small swimming

Anantara Spa at Emirates Palace

pool, a fitness room, aerobics classes and a range of slimming and body-conditioning machines.

Rayana Spa
Hyatt Capital Gate Abu Dhabi Al Safarat **02 596 1100**
hyatt.com
Map **1 H8**
When you're located on the 19th floor of a record-breaking tower, it'd be a crime to hide the surroundings under dark spa blinds and candlelight. The five treatment rooms at Rayana embrace the location, with some nice Arabian touches added to focus on the spa's Middle East location. Each treatment room has the full range of facilities, including private changing and showers, and the atmosphere here is relaxing and adult – a professional but laid-back look at relaxation. As you'd expect at a Hyatt, therapists are very good and the range of treatments covers the usual facials, massages, scrubs and longer treatments. Fully aware of the ADNEC location, there's a great range of male-specific treatments and express treatments; busy executives can be rejuvenated during their one hour lunch break.

The SPA At Radisson Blu, Yas Island
Radisson Blu Hotel, Abu Dhabi Yas Island Yas Island West **02 656 2494**
radissonblu.com
Map **1 S5**
A high percentage of Abu Dhabi's spas reach exceptional levels, so factors like organisation, comfort and customer service take on extra importance. The SPA has them all down to an art. Arrive early and enjoy the Jacuzzi, steam room or sauna then give your body over to the capable hands of expert therapists who make you feel like a million dollars. The aromatherapy massages and Anne Semonin facials are all a cut above, but if you've a couple of hours to spare, try the signature Radisson Blu Formulation which is about as luxuriously pampering as spa treatments get and leaves you feeling like a whole new person.

Talise Spa
Jumeirah At Etihad Towers Al Ras Al Akhdar **02 811 5888**
jumeirah.com
Map **2 B3**
Talise is Jumeirah's own spa brand. Having won praise for its offerings at Dubai's Jumeirah Madinat and Zabeel Saray, expectations for the first Talise in Abu Dhabi were high. As you'd expect of a luxurious, pampering brand born in the world's capital of luxury pampering, Talise at Jumeirah at Etihad Towers doesn't disappoint. It's cavernous but the decor maintains a feeling of intimacy, throughout both the relaxation areas and the private treatment rooms – the Asian feeling from the hotel is carried into the spa. There's

a hammam – almost par for the course in Abu Dhabi these days – while indulgent scrubs, wraps, baths and massages are available from excellent therapists. Prices are at the higher end of the scale but, if you're able to splash out or preparing for a special occasion (hint hint, brides-to-be), try one of the signature rituals – they cost the earth but will make your year.

Zari Spa & Beauty Centre
NMC Specialty Hospital Abu Dhabi Madinat Zayed **02 617 9150**
zarizardozi.com
Map **2 M4**
A longstanding favourite among Abu Dhabi ladies, Zari has been in the business of pampering for over two decades. Initially a hair salon, the spa now offers a broad range of reasonably priced beauty treatments including facials, massages, threading, eyelash extensions, pedicures and hydrotherapies. Shahnaz, an Indian range of beauty products for the skin, face, body and hair is used in all treatments. While the treatment rooms with their trio of semi-private cubicles might not be everyone's cup of tea, the spa offers excellent value and membership packages are available to pick and choose from several treatments.

Zayna Spa
Grand Millennium Al Wahda Al Nahyan **02 495 3822**
millenniumhotels.com
Map **2 M7**
For head-to-toe pampering, this spa offers a relaxing journey. Gentle music, peppermint aroma and warm south-east Asian hospitality set the scene and each of the 10 treatment rooms is equipped with bath and changing facilities. The treatments range from luxurious caviar facials to a delightful hot stone massage. With packages available from 30 minutes up to five hours, Zayna Spa is a perfect haven for an after-work treatment or full blown indulgence day. Treatments are available for both men and women.

Zen The Spa At Rotana
Beach Rotana Abu Dhabi Tourist Club Area **02 697 9000**
rotana.com
Map **2 S5**
Spacious and comfortable, descending into Zen is like disappearing down a rabbit hole of relaxation. If it can be scrubbed, wrapped, hydrated, treated or massaged, then it's on the menu, and signature treatments, such as pregnancy, rejuvenation and immune boosting massages are excellent value. Each room has character, and the tranquillity suites with private changing rooms, showers and colossal baths are luxury defined. Options include signature men's treatments, a rasul four mud ritual, a range of teen treatments and couple's massage lessons.

Event facilities of
Abu Dhabi Falcon Hospital
the unique event venue in Abu Dha[bi]

Falcon World Tour
Your Exclusive Tourist Destination
Abu Dhabi Falcon Hospital

To make a booking or for more information call Mr. Amer Abu Aabed, mobile 050-6660739
P.O.Box 45553, Abu Dhabi, United Arab Emirates
Phone: +971-2-5755155, Fax: +971-2-5755001
Email: info@falconhospital.com Web: www.falconhospital.com

Discover Abu Dhabi

DISCOVER ABU DHABI

Although it has taken a while for Abu Dhabi to emerge from the shadow of neighbouring Dubai, the city has well and truly put itself on the global map over the past few years as one of the top places in the region to visit. Its desire to attract some of the globe's biggest sporting events has, as planned, captured the world's attention. Its ever-changing skyline, audacious re-imagining of desert islands, vast hotels, inspired buildings and permanently sunny weather have combined with its position as an increasingly important airline hub to transform it into an international destination and the region's sporting capital.

All this is good news for expats lucky enough to have relocated to this headline-grabbing emirate – but there's more to Abu Dhabi than just the high-living holiday highlights.

Scratch the surface and you'll discover plenty of cultural delights, multicultural attractions, traditional gems and even simple, sedate everyday leisure activities. As an adopted Abu Dhabi local, there are plenty of ways to fill your leisure time. Start by exploring the city and the divide between the old and new parts of town. Head to Al Bateen and its boatyards or Heritage Village for a flavour of what Abu Dhabi used to be like before the economic boom turned it into a modern, international metropolis.

Souks, forts, local restaurants and beautiful mangrove-packed waterways provide a contrast to the mind-boggling modern developments that are replacing older buildings on the island and popping up off the island and in newly created areas. Reem Island, Yas Island, Between the Bridges, Al Raha, Capital Gate, Saadiyat, World Trade Center – new Abu Dhabi is a mix of spectacular buildings, high-living hotels, shopping delights and more besides.

The city's art and culture scene is starting to bubble up into something interesting too, with galleries attracting major local and international artists and several high profile festivals drawing crowds to the emirate. There's a full calendar of international events to keep sports fans happy (p.26). During the cooler months, there are some excellent outdoor options for get-togethers with family and friends; Abu Dhabi's parks (p.213) are superbly maintained, while the beaches draw crowds of sunbathers and swimmers at the weekends (p.215). There's family fun to be had too at the various amusement centres scattered around town (p.218).

You're not likely to tire of enjoying the urban attractions anytime soon but, if you do, Abu Dhabi has one of the world's biggest adventure playgrounds just beyond its city limits and it's waiting to be explored. Head off road (p.220) to make the most of the awe-inspiring desert sands and wadi beds, hike in the mountain peaks (p.224), go camping (p.221) or take to the sea for some excellent diving (p.224), snorkelling (p.225) and sailing (p.298). And that's just Abu Dhabi – there are six other emirates to get to know too (see Out Of The City, p.236).

PLACES OF INTEREST

Al Bateen

The Al Bateen area (not to be confused with Al Bateen Airport) is on the western side of the island, stretching along the coast between the InterContinental hotel (p.203) and 19th Street. It is one of the capital's most affluent areas and has a pleasant, sought-after residential neighbourhood feel. Even its well-known marina has a waiting list; mooring space is in high demand and fees have trebled in the last few years. The district feels a world away from the city centre; the sprawling suburban streets have an air of tranquillity, and there are plenty of green, open spaces.

The Bateen dhow yard is well worth a visit, with its evocative smells of freshly cut African and Indian teak. Craftsmen use traditional skills to build the dhows and racing hulls that can be seen in competitions off the Corniche. If it's not too busy, the craftsmen will happily share the intricacies of their art. The yard is open every day except Friday. The best time to visit is around 17:00. The Bateen jetty is a popular launching spot for boats, and the area around the jetty has a number of marine supply stores; if you need anything for your boat, this is the place to start. The Emirates Heritage Club's sailing department is housed here too.

After strolling around and admiring the yachts you can visit one of the marina's restaurants and cafes which have scenic views across the Arabian Gulf. There are a number of diving clubs based in the marina, such as the Arabian Divers and Sportfishing Charters (p.230). However, be warned that this area is currently all change as the whole marina is being redeveloped to create the new Al Bateen Wharf (p.32). Although being developed in phases, it does mean that what's open one week may not be there the next.

The InterContinental Hotel is one of Abu Dhabi's landmark hotels, with the renowned Fishmarket (p.376) seafood restaurant overlooking the beach and the always-popular Chamas Churrascaria and Bar (p.374). You can reach the Breakwater area (p.87) in less than five minutes and the city's flagship hotel, Emirates Palace (p.201), is just at the bottom of the picturesque Baynunah Street. There isn't much in the way of shopping in the area, apart from the odd local store and Al Bateen Mall (02 666 1222), which sounds grander than it is, with some basic grocery shops and a post office.

Al Bateen has several public gardens and parks, popular for picnics and ball sports when the weather is cooler. There's a special green and pink running/

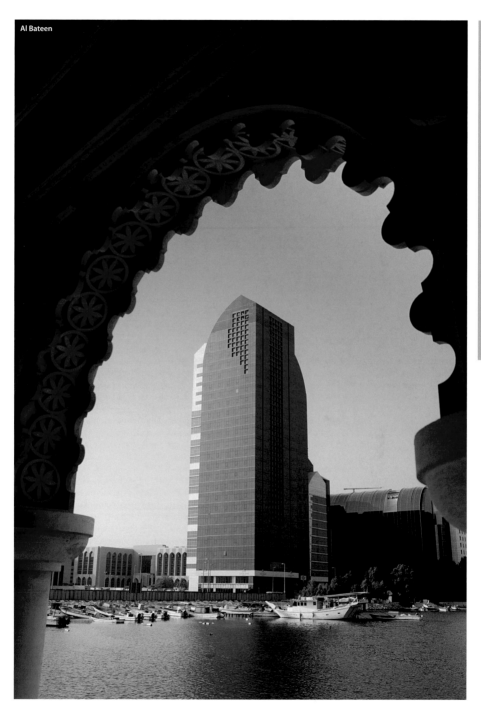

Al Bateen

Places Of Interest

cycle track along parts of 32nd Street. Wedged in between the mangroves surrounding the palace, Al Bateen Beach is usually one of Abu Dhabi's most tranquil public beaches. However, there is currently no public access due to the construction around the new sewage treatment station and the massive new bridge out to Hodariyat Island, with no word on when the beach will be reopened.

Al Hosn Palace

Al Karamah, Al Mushrif & Al Rowdah

Defined by 11th Street to the north, 30th Street to the east and 2nd Street to the west, the south of the area consists of wide leafy boulevards surrounding the Abu Dhabi City Golf Club and the Abu Dhabi Country Club, some small parks, and the Al Mushrif and Al Bateen Palaces. Predominantly a residential area, it is a pleasant, family neighbourhood close to a number of international schools, open parks and green playing fields. The Women's Handicraft Centre (210) on Al Karamah Street is well worth visiting – a government-sponsored initiative where traditional handicrafts such as weavings, hand-made souvenirs and local artefacts are made, displayed and sold (at fixed prices). It is always best to ask before photographing the veiled women in their workshops. There's also a lovely cafe on the premises where you can sample all manner of traditional fare.

The Abu Dhabi City Golf Club (p.286) is located in the Mushrif area, in the heart of Abu Dhabi. Evening race meetings take place during the winter months, including the million dirham President's Cup race. Entrance is free and it makes for a fun night out. The international racecourse has a spectacular show-jumping area and riding school adjacent to the track. A nine-hole, par 70 floodlit course is set in the middle of the racetrack, offering golfers a novel series of challenges on some of its holes. Next door is the busy Abu Dhabi Country Club (p.178), where you can sign up to attend individual fitness classes if you don't want to pay the full membership fees.

Al Khalidiyah

Al Khalidiyah is the area between 26th and 32nd Streets, stretching up to the Corniche from 11th Street. It is one of the most upmarket areas in the city and its leafy green suburban streets lead to high-rise towers and built-up local shopping areas. There are wide-open spaces filled with beautiful public parks, bustling, busy streets with traditional shops, and eye-catching modern buildings.

The Corniche marks the boundary of Al Khalidiyah, and the Corniche Beach Park (p.214). The expanded walking area around here makes it a popular destination for local residents.

The best access to the Corniche from this area is at the end of 30th Street, but watch out for the traffic

when entering. Close to the Corniche are Qasr Al Hosn (p.210), the oldest building in the city, and Abu Dhabi Cultural Foundation but, unfortunately, both are currently under development to create a heritage and culture centre for Abu Dhabi that will draw tourists from across the region.

Mention Khalidiyah to most local residents and they immediately think of the Khalidiyah Mall (p.344) on 26th Street, in front of one of the area's newer residential compounds. The attractive building, with its traditional Arabic design, houses 160 shops, a number of food outlets, a children's play area, and a well-stocked hypermarket.

More traditional food can be found at the multiple shawarma stands and this area has some of the best examples of these tasty, greasy joints: try Seashell Cafeteria behind Khalidiyah Tower, Zawak Al Sham near Fit Workz, Al Ramla Coast near Baskin Robbins, or Jabel Al Noor behind ADIB bank. After scoffing that down, The Folklore Gallery (p.212) on Khalidiya Street is a great place to head to for some browsing, with displays of local pottery and art. The gallery is also a good place for having any framing done: there's a wide range of frames and the craftsmanship is of a good quality.

The area between 7th Street and 9th Street is full of cafes and local shops, offering everything from tailoring services to laundry, and chocolate to stationery. It's a great place to get lost and explore on foot at the weekend.

This area has two large public parks in Al Khalidiyah Public Park (p.213) and the Al Khalidiya Kid's Park (p.213), which is actually in Al Khubeirah, and is for ladies and children only. Both are bustling with families during the cooler weather; they are great for evening and weekend picnics, and for keeping the children entertained.

Al Maqtaa & Al Matar

These areas form the main gateway to Abu Dhabi island, lying at the southern edge of the island, just before the mainland. One of the capital's most used and well-known flyovers linking the mainland to the city, Al Maqtaa Bridge, cuts through this district.

The opening of Sheikh Zayed Bridge has eased much of the congestion. The 842 metre long rollercoaster-style structure was designed by world famous Iraqi-born architect Zaha Hadid, and is another stunning addition to Abu Dhabi's increasingly rich architectural offering.

The most distinct landmark here is the heavily renovated Al Maqtaa Fort (p.208), one of the few remaining examples of its kind in Abu Dhabi. The 200 year old fort was originally built in the shallow channel of water at the entrance to the city as a checkpoint for those entering Abu Dhabi Island.

On the island, hidden away on a small road just before the Mussafah Bridge, is the Armed Forces Officers' Club (p.296). What makes this an interesting find is not only that it houses the best swimming pool in Abu Dhabi (one of only two 50 metre pools in the emirate), but that the rest of the sports and leisure facilities are all excellent, and include one of the best gyms around. It also has two Olympic-standard shooting ranges, three squash courts and a bowling centre. For families, Khalifa Park (p.303), just off 2nd Street, has gardens, fountains, party halls and a dedicated area for women and children; it is busy at weekends, although quiet midweek. On occasion, the park has played host to attractions, such as circuses and a community market, although simply heading there for an evening picnic is pleasant enough.

Also providing perfect picnicking in the cooler months or evenings is the long stretch of coast beside 30th Street which is very popular, despite a lack of parking. There are a few dedicated areas for picnicking but most people seem to just pull over, unload the family, and fire up the barbecue right there.

Zayed Sports City is open seven days a week and has an ice rink (p.290), bowling alley, tennis courts, gym as well as bumper cars, video games and a cafe. Sheikh Zayed Sports City is home to the UAE's largest stadium. The landmark structure was recently

Airport Road

Airport Road is like the backbone of the island, running its entire length. Its official name is Sheikh Rashid Bin Saeed Al Maktoum Street but, like most of Abu Dhabi's main roads, residents rarely use that, opting for the far simpler Airport Road or Old Airport Road.

It starts at the Al Maqtaa Bridge and leads through the centre of the island, ending at the Corniche. It is one of the most well-used, well-known roads in the capital and the majority of Abu Dhabi's districts are accessible from it. Local, independent stores are scattered all along Airport Road between the Corniche and 27th Street and the road is also popular for its used car lots, although these are starting to move off the island to the new Motor World (aldar.com) development (p.62).

The 16 kilometre road passes many of the city's landmarks: the spectacular Sheikh Zayed Grand Mosque (p.210), Al Bateen Airport, Sheikh Zayed Sports City, the Diplomatic Area and the Churches Area. As you reach 11th Street, you pass Sheikh Khalifa Medical City, followed by the iconic Etisalat building, Cannon Square and Qasr Al Hosn, before the road meets the Corniche.

Al Maqtaa bridge and fort

Places Of Interest

refurbished and is now the home ground of Abu Dhabi Harlequins Rugby Club; in addition, it plays host to major international events, as does the nearby ADNEC, the National Exhibition Centre. ADNEC is now home to the captivating Capital Gate or 'The Leaning Tower of Abu Dhabi' which defies gravity with its record-breaking 18 degree lean. Just as surprising is the ADNEC grandstand which looks onto the Coast Road. It seems an odd place for it, with a prime view of passing traffic, but it does serve a practical purpose – it is used for military parades and for the International Defence Exhibition (IDEX), which is held every year.

Al Markaziyah, Madinat Zayed & Tourist Club Area

This area, bounded by the Corniche, 2nd Street and 9th Street, is an area of superlatives. Here, you'll find the oldest areas, plus the amazing recent rise of Reem Island, with at least a dozen huge towers having gone up since 2008. It has the narrowest streets, the busiest traffic, the most roadworks, the most ambitious highway construction projects, the most hospitals, the biggest mall, some of the best restaurants, and the most interesting and artistic development projects on the island. It is the centre of downtown and offers the visitor and resident alike the true taste of cosmopolitan Abu Dhabi.

Al Markaziyah is regarded as the city centre and the main business district and when you walk through the streets you will feel the unmistakable ambience of the city's heritage and history. This district is a real fusion of residential and commercial, with well-known hotels and apartments, high-rise business towers, embassies and the Al Noor Hospital, surrounded by local and international shops. Two of the busiest roads in the capital, Hamdan Street (5th Street) and Electra Street (officially called Sh Zayed The Second St or 7th Street but rarely referred to as anything but Electra Street), run through the district. It's a haven for shoppers, as the local, traditional shops share the streets with big name international stores and smaller malls.

To escape the mass of buildings, you can head to Capital Park (p.214), which is a refurbished public park on Khalifa bin Zayed Street. You'll find a large pond with fountains, a children's play area, a small amusement arcade and an enclosed cafeteria. The area also has its share of the city's five-star hotels with the Crowne Plaza (p.201), Sands Hotel (p.206), Millennium (p.204), and Le Royal Meridien (p.203) all within walking distance.

The Tourist Club Area got its name from the now long-gone Abu Dhabi Tourist Club and is today an area in transition, as road projects, underpasses, bridges and expressways combine with the construction work on The Quay development. Older buildings are making way for newer high-rise towers; the old marina area is also due to be razed and replaced

by a collection of marinas, hotels and residential apartments. In this corner of the city, tradition meets modernity, with luxury five-star hotels neighbouring small local shops, cafes and bakeries.

When the construction work is finished in the next couple of years, it will make cross-town traffic much smoother, but, until then, you just have to accept that even taxi drivers will complain about going into this area. Nevertheless, the Tourist Club Area is buzzing with activity and is one of the most vibrant parts of Abu Dhabi. It's the perfect place to visit if you want to experience busy city life and the capital's social scene. It is located at the eastern end of the Corniche, with a cosmopolitan mix of residents and visitors. The Abu Dhabi Mall (p.341) with its 220 outlets and the Beach Rotana Abu Dhabi (p.200) with a great members only beach club and some of the best restaurants in town are the two main attractions in this part of Abu Dhabi.

Madinat Zayed is centred on the shopping centre of the same name, which is the place to go for colourful fabrics, Indian and Arabian gifts, and of course jewellery – something the next door Gold Souk (p.348) also excels in. The back streets between here and the NMC Speciality Hospital (p.165) are full of interesting shops selling the things that you can't find in the malls: musical instruments such as oudhs, bizarre electrical appliances and plastic buckets, and you'll even find the odd Ethiopian restaurant.

Al Meena

Al Meena is Abu Dhabi's main port area and an excellent place for visitors and residents to stroll around and explore.

Located on the north-eastern tip of the island, the area is dominated by low-rise apartments and quite old single-family houses, although many of the oldest buildings are being pulled down to make way for sleek modern blocks. Once you leave the residential area behind, you'll arrive at the Port Zayed area, which is best known for its souks.

This working port is home to the fish, fruit and vegetable market, the carpet souk, and the Iranian souk (p.340). The Iranian souk, in particular,

---

In The Club

The Meena area is where you'll find The Club (p.179), a real Abu Dhabi institution that has been going for nearly 50 years. This leisure facility is one of the most successful expat clubs in the capital, but there's a waiting list for those who want to join and guests must be signed in by a member. It has excellent facilities, including watersports, a library, a pool, a beach and an assortment of racquet and other sports. It often puts on plays and concerts not found anywhere else.

is a treasure trove to discover, selling all sorts of knickknacks. Shipments from Iran come over on dhows every three weeks or so – sometimes you'll be lucky and catch a new consignment of intricately detailed pots and plates; at other times there will be no one around. The souks offer an entirely different shopping experience to the malls, and you can utilise your bartering skills to good effect.

The dhow harbour, off Port Road, is a contrast of past and present with several hundred dhows resting in their berths. It is a fascinating place to explore early in the morning when the fishermen return from sea with their local delicacies. Try out the nearby restaurants, which offer an authentic selection of local cooking – mainly grilled meats and seafood. The harbour is also worth a visit at sunset when the dhows return. A number of dinner cruises also set sail from here.

Market Place

The Carpet Souk is on the port end of Al Meena Road and offers some great bargains on carpets and cushions. Discover old and modern carpets from Iran, Afghanistan, Pakistan, Turkey, China and Central Asia, all in an exquisite array of designs and colours. Look out for the hand-made carpets and don't forget to bargain – it's all part of the fun!

Between The Bridges

Just off the island, on the city's outskirts and spanning the area between Mussafah Bridge and Al Maqtaa Bridge, this area is noted for large independent villas and compounds, the nearby Abu Dhabi Golf Club (p.287) and the cluster of new hotels. Its Arabic name is Bain Al Jessrain but, to just about everybody now, it's known as 'Between the Bridges'.

This new area is defined by the Shangri-La (p.206), Traders Hotel (p.207) and Fairmont Bab Al Bahr (p.201), which provide the main entertainment focus in the area. Sharing the same stretch of creek and beachfront, the hotels have some of the UAE's very best restaurants, plus a wide range of facilities including spas, gymnasiums and more swimming pools than you can shake a lilo at.

The hotels are part of the larger Qaryat Al Beri (p.348) development, a Disney-esque recreation of a traditional souk in a modern setting, offering a variety of shops and restaurants under one roof and connected by a waterway on which Arabic gondolas, or abras, slowly meander through the unique architecture, under arches and past restaurant terraces.

For more traditional architecture, look across the road from Qaryat Al Beri and you'll see one of the most ornate Persian-influenced mosques in the city. This small turquoise blue gem is not open for tours but you can admire the craftsmanship from outside.

Just across the water, looking back at from the island side is the new Ritz-Carlton Grand Canal hotel, which add four signature restaurants, a couple of bars and other poolside dining options to the area's attractions.

Breakwater & Al Ras Al Akhdar

Breakwater is an area of reclaimed land which is entirely man-made and connected by a causeway to the western end of the Corniche. Development is almost complete now, with a community of luxury villas spread across a separate promontory. The beachfront walkways are an extension of the recent Corniche development and offer some of the best spots to admire and photograph the city's superb skyline. Along the waterfront there are a number of Arabic restaurants and cafes, and the Heritage Village (p.208) which features aspects of Abu Dhabi's past,

Breakwater at sunset

Places Of Interest

with displays of the ancient Bedouin lifestyle and an interesting collection of traditional folklore treasures.

The Abu Dhabi International Marine Sports Club (02 681 5566, adimsc.ae) was initially set up to provide a base for the city's power boat racing, but it now offers some of the best watersports facilities in the capital. The Abu Dhabi Theatre building is also worth a look: its shape led to speculation that it was either a mosque or an observatory – regardless, it has now fallen into disuse. Next to it stands an enormous flagpole which was, for a time at least, the tallest unsupported flagpole in the world at 123.1m (until it got pipped by Jordan, then Turkmenistan).

Al Ras Al Akhdar is the area on the north-western tip of Abu Dhabi dominated by the beautiful, and massive, Emirates Palace hotel (p.201). It is a quiet, picturesque part of the city that was, until recently, surrounded by popular, long, sandy beaches. However, the entire area is now being redeveloped.

The Emirates Palace (p.201) hotel is still the city's most iconic landmark and should be at the top of every visitor's list of 'must sees' in Abu Dhabi. It is a stunning property set in more than 85 hectares of landscaped gardens, surrounded by a pristine stretch of white-sand beach and a new yacht marina. Palatial in every sense, luxury and opulence oozes from every inch of the hotel, from the huge gold domed roof in the reception area to the massive hand-woven carpets displayed on the walls. An overnight stay in one of the stunning rooms grants you access to the tranquil outdoors areas, but you can visit the public areas indoors without a reservation; the afternoon tea is one of the draws here. The hotel is also home to some exceptional restaurants, a couple of excellent galleries and a 1,500 seat auditorium that hosts a variety of shows throughout the year, including films during the Abu Dhabi Film Festival (p.29) and concerts during the Abu Dhabi Classics series (p.29).

The Corniche & Al Khubeirah

The Corniche, seen as the face of the city, runs east to west across the top of the island. The area has undergone a massive, multi-million dirham redevelopment in recent years, and now provides plenty of opportunities to get out and enjoy the open air. Home to some of the city's most impressive buildings, Corniche Road is lined with the high-rise towers that make up Abu Dhabi's spectacular skyline.

Both sides of the road have been developed to complement the paved waterfront and the inland side has been beautifully landscaped with parks, picnic grounds, small gardens, fountains, covered-seating areas lining the pavements, and cafes. All areas are easily accessible, with parking and safe (and surprisingly attractive) pedestrian underpasses.

At the western end, towards the Emirates Palace, a multimillion dirham project to modernise and expand

the swimming beaches is now completed and there's a range of cafes and restaurants along the undulating shoreline. A casual stroll along the Corniche is a favourite part of many residents' evening routine and experience of the capital. The waterfront section is fully paved, making it ideal for rollerblading, jogging and walking, while the special cycle path draws both enthusiastic amateurs and more serious cyclists.

Marina Al Bateen Resort

Catering predominantly for high-end clientele, this popular resort and club, just south of Al Khubeirah, features a range of leisure facilities. There's a members' gym, an attractive swimming pool area as well as a lounge bar and an Italian restaurant (p.388). The resort also has berths for 160 boats in the marina, while watersports and boat trips can be arranged (marinaalbateen.com).

The grassed area next to the Hilton Hotel is perfect for picnics; it is particularly popular during winter weekends when families gather and spend the day playing on the grass or swimming in the water. To explore these areas from a different perspective, visitors can cruise along by the Corniche on a traditional wooden dhow or cabin cruiser, enjoying the changing vistas of the skyline, parks and fountains. Cruises generally last for an hour, and can be booked through a tour operator (see Boat Tours, p.230).

Towering Achievements

Marina Mall is one of the most popular malls in Abu Dhabi, with hundreds of outlets housing a variety of western high street brand-names. In the centre of the shopping centre is the 100 metre high tower, at the top of which you can enjoy a cappuccino with incredible views at Colombiano Coffee House (02 681 5533) or get 360 degree views of the city teamed with a la carte cuisine at the revolving restaurant, Tiara (02 681 9090).

Between the apartment buildings, there are several luxury hotels. The Hilton Abu Dhabi is frequented by visitors and residents alike, and is renowned for its top class eateries such as Bocca (p.373), and the beachfront restaurant Vasco's (p.394). The Sheraton Abu Dhabi is on the recently refurbished eastern part of the Corniche and the hotels attractions include many trusted restaurants to choose from. The nearby commercial buildings are occupied by many of the city's big investment banks, oil companies, and governmental departments. The skyline is ever-changing and the next few years will see the continued construction of architectural masterpieces, including hotels and residential developments.

Yas Marina

Downtown park

Mosque near The Corniche

Heritage Park

Island Life

The islands off the coast of Abu Dhabi have long promised to transform the capital, and now Yas and Saadiyat are destinations in their own right.

Ground was broken on Yas Island, a natural island to the east of the Abu Dhabi city centre, in 2007 and, since then, the island has been radically transformed through hotels, infrastructure and the Yas Marina Circuit, which hosts the Abu Dhabi Formula 1 Grand Prix.

The 5.6 kilometre track stands out for its unique design which actually runs right through the island's flagship hotel, The Yas Viceroy, giving about 250 very lucky VIPs envious views of the proceedings from the bridge on race weekends. What's more, the marina is incorporated into the circuit, so that the yachting crowd can not only make grand entrances but can view the race from their boats.

Other F1 fans – those of more modest means – can still enjoy thrilling racing moments. The grandstand was designed to offer the best views of any F1 venue. Some 50,000 people, including celebrities, dignitaries and hardcore fans, jam into the Yas Marina Circuit come November each year.

However, racing is only one part of the draw of Abu Dhabi's F1 weekend: the end of each racing day brings performances from A-listers that have included Kylie, Beyoncé, Aerosmith, Prince, Kanye West, Eminem and Kings of Leon over the years. Elsewhere, other venues on the island hold smaller concerts and DJ events, while free concerts from big name singers and bands take place on the Abu Dhabi Corniche beach.

Although the very biggest acts come thickest and fastest during the F1 weekend, the Yas Island Show Weekends (thinkflash.ae) is a series of concerts that continues throughout the cooler winter months; Shakira, Madonna and Snoop Dogg have all played on the island.

Equally, Yas Marina Circuit is a year-round venue for petrolheads too; they can put their driving skills to the test, or take high-speed driving lessons. The possibilities include karting, drag racing, as well as a host of other options from supercar driving to passenger experiences. If petrol-power isn't your thing, the circuit is thrown open to cyclists, runners, rollerbladers and walkers every Tuesday night – a great way to experience the bends and challenges of an F1 circuit from asphalt-level.

In 2010, Ferrari World (p.219) opened on Yas Island. The world's largest indoor theme park has enough attractions to keep motorsports enthusiasts of all ages entertained. Kids can learn to drive in a miniature Ferrari, while grown-up fans get to take a glimpse into the F1 paddock or experience race driving in a simulator. For thrillseekers, there's the world's fastest rollercoaster and the G-Force tower. And if all that speed makes you break out into a sweat, you can now head to neighbouring Yas Waterworld (p.216) which opened at the end of 2012. Featuring more than 40 rides and attractions, there are several loops, thrills and high speed chases, as well as simulated surfing waves and the Al Raha lazy river.

For those who like their leisure time to be spent in a slightly more sedate (or child-free) fashion, there's the Yas Links golf course and an assortment of hotels offering pools, spas, restaurants and bars to enjoy.

Further along the Sheikh Khalifa Highway, the giant bypass road that connects the Abu Dhabi-Dubai road with the Corniche, you'll find Saadiyat Island, just 10 minutes to the east of downtown Abu Dhabi. If Yas is all about thrills and spills, Saadiyat is set to be the calming, cultural capital of the Middle East, with the local branches of the world-famous Louvre and

Guggenheim on the way in 2014, as well as other impressive attractions like the Zayed National Museum, the Maritime Museum and The Performing Arts Centre. If the main venues are still a year or two away, there are still plenty of reasons to head to Saadiyat now. If you're eager for a taste of what's in store, then head to Manarat Al Saadiyat which doubles as a visitor centre, full of information on Abu Dhabi and the islands, as well as a bona fide art space in its own right, with plenty of top exhibitions showing. There's also an onsite restaurant.

The two main hotel openings so far, St Regis (p.267) and Park Hyatt (p.204), are both beautiful, sprawling properties that are quite unlike anything else in the UAE, backing up on to wild stretches of beach that look more California than Gulf. Elsewhere, the Monte-Carlo Beach Club (p.215, 02 656 3500) is a taste of the European jetset lifestyle; as well as granting access to a lovely stretch of Arabian Gulf and the swimming pools, there are Jacuzzi and spa facilities, private cabanas and bungalows, and a handful of restaurants and bars to choose from. Day passes are available from Dhs.400

With such varied options available, it's hardly surprising that island hopping has become an increasingly popular weekend activity for many Abu Dhabi residents.

Yas Marina Circuit and The Yas Viceroy

The New Corniche

The Corniche should not be confused with the New Corniche (or Eastern Corniche), which runs along the eastern side of the island and is also known as the Eastern Ring Road (or, in fact, Al Salam Street or 8th Street). A popular place for barbecues, picnics and a spot of fishing, the area is now undergoing a huge facelift, with resort hotels, cafes and restaurants on the way, creating another outdoor area for Abu Dhabi's residents to enjoy.

The Islands

Exploring Abu Dhabi needn't mean being confined to the streets of the capital. You can also take to the seas and view more than 200 islands that are scattered in the waters around the main island. Many of these hidden treasures are just a short boat ride away; they vary in size and the majority are flat, sandy and uninhabited.

Getting There

There are no organised tours to the islands but Net Tours (p.233) can tailor a trip for you. You can choose which islands you would like to sail by or visit and enjoy a personalised island-hopping programme. Prices start from Dhs.1,800 to hire a speedboat for two hours, which accommodates up to seven people, or Dhs.2,400 to hire a larger boat for two hours which will take up to 19 people. The cost includes land transfers.

Arabian Divers & Sports Fishing Charters (p.230) has nearly two decades of experience sailing around the islands and can organise private charters. Prices start from Dhs.900 for a two hour trip in a small speedboat that carries up to six passengers. It also has large touring boats which can accommodate up to 19 people, plus a 23 metre luxury yacht.

The waters around the islands are rich in marine life and you may be lucky enough to spot the local population of humpbacked dolphins or the endangered dugongs on your trip. Between March and July, head farther out and there is the possibility of catching a glimpse of the migrating whale species found in the region, including the blue whale, Bryde's whale and Risso's dolphin. Several of the larger islands are currently closed to the public, as they are in the hands of developers in the middle of creating a variety of tourism destinations.

You can hire a fully staffed boat for a couple of hours and sail around the Arabian Gulf, observing the natural beauty of these unspoiled islands. There are still plenty of islands where you can stop off and enjoy the fantastic opportunity to explore, barbecue or simply relax in absolute peace.

The large, man-made Lulu Island can be seen directly opposite the Corniche, and is protected from the sea by a breakwater. Once a day trip retreat open to the public, Lulu Island is currently off limits due to planned redevelopment work, with no date for reopening available.

Situated 12 kilometres north-east of Abu Dhabi is Al Sammaliah Island, where plans are underway to develop the heritage and environmental aspects of island life for educational purposes, and a habitat restoration programme is in progress. The island covers 35 square kilometres and is home to one of the world's largest artificial mangrove plantations, covering some eight square kilometres.

You can moor your boat at Bahraini Island and spend the day on its unspoiled beaches or visit the wildlife sanctuary. It is a 40 minute trip, but a worthwhile journey as you may be able to spot dolphins swimming in the waters, and you pass by many of the other islands in Abu Dhabi's archipelago. You will need to take supplies with you as there are no facilities on the island.

Futaisi Island is five kilometres – or a 10 minute boat ride – to the south of Abu Dhabi. The island's history dates back hundreds of years; its inhabitants used to supply sweet water and stone for building forts and rulers' houses to the main Abu Dhabi island. It covers an area of around 50 square kilometres and part of this land is currently being turned into an eco-tourism destination. The rest of the island will remain quiet and undisturbed, creating a very effective wildlife sanctuary. Gazelles run and jump across the flats and spiny-tailed lizards roam the sands. The island is also an important transit point for migrating birds, and flamingos are commonly seen on the shores. Sightings of the endangered green sea turtle, as well as dolphins, are evidence of the rich marine life in the waters. There is a regular boat service that takes you to the island in the morning and brings you back to Abu Dhabi at the end of the day; alternatively, rent one of the beachfront chalets at the Futaisi Country Club (see futaisi.com for details of boat and accommodation).

Horseshoe Island is a small, flat and sandy isle, 25 minutes away from Abu Dhabi's east coast. It is home to a number of desert foxes and offshore is Surf Reef – a great spot for windsurfing. The island has been inaccessible to the public of late, so check ahead.

ABU DHABI HOTELS

One thing you'll discover quickly is that much of the social scene revolves around the city's many hotels. Whereas in, say, Europe, where generally a city hotel's main purpose is to provide accommodation and host the odd corporate function, in Abu Dhabi, hotels also act as places for residents to go for a drink, for dinner, to a nightclub, for a workout and to relax at the weekend.

There are dozens of the world's leading hotel brands to be found here, many of them housed in some of the city's most interesting buildings. Your first encounter with them may be when you come to Abu Dhabi on a reconnaissance mission before you make the decision to move permanently. You might also find yourself staying in one when you first move out, often hosted by your new company, while you find your feet and look for some accommodation of your own.

Once you're settled in, you'll soon become familiar with many of the places listed in this section. Whether you're going out for Friday brunch, after-work drinks or a romantic dinner, the UAE's licensing laws – alcohol can only be served in hotels or sports clubs – mean that it's likely to take place in a hotel.

Putting your visitors up in a hotel (should lack of space dictate and budget allow) is also something you may need to do; Abu Dhabi's popularity as a tourist destination means that most hotels are excellently geared up for holidaymakers, with several located on the beach or near to some of the main attractions.

There is a vast array of hotels, ranging from one of the most superlative and opulent in the world, the Emirates Palace (p.201), with a rack rate in the region of Dhs.6,000 for a night in a standard suite, right down to the cheapest digs in areas such as those in Al Salam Street costing under Dhs.250 a night. While the hotels at the higher end of the market offer superb surroundings and facilities, those at the cheaper end vary – and you certainly get what you pay for.

Get Away

If you'd like to escape the city for a day or two, there are a number of excellent desert, beach and mountain resorts within the UAE that are worth checking out. See Out Of The City, p.235 for full details.

For people arriving in Abu Dhabi on a holiday package, hotels are normally five or four star, but if you are looking for cheaper accommodation at the lower end of the market, make sure you check out the hotel and have a look at one of the rooms before checking in. Remember that, as with anywhere else in the world, you can usually get a discount on the rack rate or published price if you negotiate.

Many hotels also offer seasonal discounts to GCC residents, particularly in the hot summer months when prices can be 50% lower than at peak times, providing a great opportunity for a bargain break.

The Abu Dhabi Tourism & Culture Authority (ADTCA) oversees a hotel classification system that gives an internationally recognised star rating to hotels and hotel apartments so that visitors can judge

more easily the standard of accommodation they will receive. See abudhabitourism.ae for more details.

For restaurants and bars that operate in Abu Dhabi's hotels, refer to the index at the back of this book. Just look up the hotel name and all of its outlets that are featured in the book will be listed underneath.

Other Options

Quaint is not a word that readily comes to mind when describing Abu Dhabi. The area is not exactly known for cute little B&Bs or guesthouses nestling in the woods or on a secluded patch of beach. And hostels? Forget about it. However, Dubai, Sharjah and Fujairah all have youth hostels if you're in the market for a budget weekend. There's even a UAE Youth Hostel Association (uaeyh.com for more information).

Emirates Palace In Numbers

Emirates Palace cost approximately $3 billion to build. It took 20,000 construction workers three years. The hotel sits on 100 hectares of land and, wing to wing, covers a kilometre. The hotel has 128 kitchens and pantries which use up 5kg of pure edible gold and 200 tonnes of fresh oranges each year. The building features 114 domes and 1002 chandeliers. No wonder it was the first hotel in the world to feature a vending machine selling gold bars.

What Abu Dhabi is known for is grand, luxurious, palatial hotels. Probably the closest thing to a guesthouse would be the hotel apartments. In addition to catering to residential clientele, many of these places rent rooms by the night, complete with a kitchen if you're into fixing your own meals. Obviously, these are good for extended stays, giving the traveller a bit more autonomy and flexibility in day-to-day affairs.

The Abu Dhabi Tourism Authority has a hotel and apartment search engine at visitabudhabi.com. Approach the list with caution, however, as many places listed as having gardens, gyms and pools have nothing of the sort. The closest thing to a pool at some of the places is a puddle in the pavement in front of the entrance.

Abu Dhabi Airport Hotel
Abu Dhabi International Airport
02 575 7377
abudhabiairporthotel.ae
Map 1 V7

This convenient stopover is a godsend for weary travellers who have long transit times at the airport. Alternatively, you could check in the night before and just walk to the boarding gates having had a good night's sleep in this comfortable hotel.

Abu Dhabi Hotels

Al Ain Palace Hotel
Corniche Road East Markaziya East 02 679 4777
alainpalacehotel.com
Map 2 P3
The Al Ain Palace (fondly known as Ally Pally) is one of Abu Dhabi's more established hotels. It offers international restaurants and a well-known British-style pub which serves great food. Situated close to the Corniche with 110 deluxe rooms and suites, plus self-contained studios and chalet-style rooms, it's a good base from which to discover Abu Dhabi.

Al Diar Capital Hotel
Al Meena St Tourist Club Area 02 678 7700
aldiarhotels.com
Map 2 R3
Well-positioned in the centre of Abu Dhabi, close to both the business district and some of the city's major attractions. It has 200 rooms, 80 of which are suites and studios, and guests have access to the modern gym, swimming pool and beauty salon. The property also boasts six bars and restaurants making it a popular hangout for residents as well as visitors.

Al Diar Dana Hotel
Shk Zayed Second St Tourist Club Area 02 645 6000
aldiarhotels.com
Map 2 R4
Located in the Tourist Club Area, near Abu Dhabi Mall, this hotel has 112 spacious rooms, each with its own kitchenette for self-sufficiency, coupled with the perks of a hotel. On the dining front, those perks include a choice between a European pub, a pizzeria, a coffee shop and 49er's The Gold Rush (p.366), a Wild West themed rooftop restaurant and bar.

Al Diar Regency Hotel
Al Meena St Al Meena 02 676 5000
aldiarhotels.com
Map 2 Q3
A stone's throw from the business district, guests here have the option of rooms and suites with sea or city view balconies and all are equipped with kitchenettes. There is a business centre, a conference hall and a health club, while the in-house restaurant and popular pubs make for ideal retreats from busy city life.

Al Jazira Club Hotel
Al Jazira Sports & Cultural Grounds, Street 17, Al Madina Al Riyadiya 02 443 3966
azuae.com
Map 2 M12
The 75 room hotel is a modern and luxurious affair located right next to the Sports City stadium. The fitness and spa facilities are, as you'd imagine, exceptional, with an Olympic size swimming pool and two indoor playing fields.

Al Raha Beach Hotel
Nr Al Raha Mall Al Raha 02 508 0555
danathotels.com
Map 1 R7
In a city known for its big, brash, luxurious hotels, Al Raha was Abu Dhabi's first boutique resort and, although it is located just 20 minutes from the airport and is next door to a large shopping mall, it is rapidly becoming known as a retreat to escape to. The rooms enjoy sea views and there is a selection of excellent dining outlets. Leisure facilities at the resort include a health club, spa, two pools, squash courts, watersports and a children's playground.

Aloft Abu Dhabi > p.iv
Abu Dhabi National Exhibition Centre (ADNEC)
Al Safarat 02 654 5000
aloftabudhabi.com
Map 1 H8
Part of the Starwood group, Aloft Abu Dhabi is a true designer offering located at the Abu Dhabi National Exhibition Centre (ADNEC). Aloft is a modern, trendy 408 bedroom hotel with full business and events facilities, a state-of-the-art gym and rooftop splash pool, and a range of bars and restaurants, from Dine, the all-day buffet option, to the cool rooftop lounge bar Relax@12 (p.402) which is a popular hangout among local expats. Check the website for regular special offers.

Beach Rotana Abu Dhabi
Nr Abu Dhabi Mall, Tourist Club St Tourist Club Area 02 697 9000
rotana.com
Map 2 S5
An Abu Dhabi landmark, the hotel boasts a conference centre and luxury suites with 414 sea-facing rooms. It offers some of the most popular dining options in Abu Dhabi (such as Rodeo Grill, p.388) as well as direct access to the Abu Dhabi Mall. The Rotana's many leisure facilities include a private beach, a covered children's play area, tennis and squash courts, and swimming pools. In addition, the large Zen Spa is another major draw to both tourists and local residents alike.

Centro Yas Island
Golf Plaza Yas Island West 02 656 4444
rotana.com
Map 1 S5
One of the crop of seven Yas Island hotels that opened in time for the 2009 F1 GP, Centro is a modern and luxurious business hotel with 259 bedrooms, conferencing facilities, plus a fitness centre with gym, pool and steam rooms. F&B offerings are simple but stylish, with a buffet style restaurant, a deli for takeaways or room service, and a modern but informal lounge bar.

Cristal Hotel Abu Dhabi
Muroor Rd, Off Electra St Madinat Zayed 02 652 0000
cristalhospitality.com
Map 2 M4

This 192 room and suite hotel is right in the heart of the action, next to the downtown banking district. It has state-of-the-art conferencing facilities, a couple of decent F&B offerings in the shape of a cafe and an all day restaurant, and the Cristal Club Lounge is a popular venue for informal business meetings. The 19th floor spa and fitness club are both excellent.

Crowne Plaza Abu Dhabi
Shk Hamdan Bin Mohamed St Markaziya East
02 616 6166
ichotelsgroup.com
Map 2 N4

Situated in the heart of the city and only a few minutes' walk from the shopping district and beach, the Crowne Plaza is another well-established landmark hotel, ideal for both business and leisure travellers. The hotel has a lobby cafe and four restaurants – including popular Asian and Italian offerings – two bars, a health and fitness centre, and the rooftop has stunning views of the city. The hotel is a good venue for business with 13 meeting rooms, three executive floors and an excellent business centre.

Crowne Plaza Abu Dhabi Yas Island
Golf Plaza Yas Island 02 656 3000
ichotelsgroup.com
Map 1 S5

Sitting right next to Yas Links Abu Dhabi golf course, this 428 room hotel has a fully-equipped health and fitness centre that includes squash courts and a 25 metre swimming pool. Four excellent restaurants and two bars are also on hand to tempt guests and visitors.

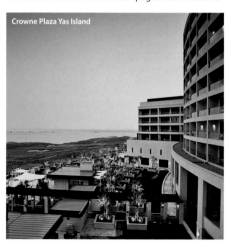
Crowne Plaza Yas Island

It boasts excellent conferencing facilities and, for sports and leisure fans, is just a five minute walk from both the Yas Marina Circuit, Ferrari World and Yas Waterworld.

Eastern Mangroves Hotel & Spa By Anantara
Al Salam St, Eastern Mangroves District Al Zahra
02 656 1000
anantara.com
Map 1 H6

Usually, Anantara focuses on exotic destination hotels – its other two UAE properties are the Desert Islands hideaway and Qasr Al Sarab desert resort – but Eastern Mangroves, located on the east coast of Abu Dhabi island just 10 minutes from the Corniche in one direction and the airport in the other, is definitely a city property and aimed more at business travellers. Not that you can tell, really. From the elegant but elaborate fixtures and fittings (check out the huge doors) to the views out over the mangroves (with not a city skyscraper in sight), this is definitely something of an oasis of calm – a business hotel for those who want to leave work at the door and relax. Rooms are luxurious but unfussy while, both in terms of service and style, it's a delightful mix of the Arabian and the Far Eastern.

Emirates Palace
West Corniche Rd Al Ras Al Akhdar 02 690 9000
kempinski.com
Map 2 B2

Arguably Abu Dhabi's most famous and instantly recognisable landmark, the $3bn Emirates Palace – reported to be the world's most costly hotel – boasts 392 opulent rooms and suites, all decked out with the latest technology and sumptuous decor. Operated by the exclusive Kempinski group, there are several outstanding food outlets offering seven-star service and some of the most indulgent dishes the city has to offer. The afternoon high tea is a must. Guests can enjoy the 1.3km stretch of private beach, two amazing pools and the exclusive Anantara spa, not to mention several galleries, exhibits and boutiques.

Fairmont Bab Al Bahr > p.355
Nr Al Maqta & Mussafa Bridges Bain Al Jessrain
02 654 3333
fairmont.com
Map 1 L8

Located next to the creek in the Souk Qaryat Al Beri area, the 369 room hotel is every bit as luxurious as you'd expect from a Fairmont. It has two pools and great views over the creek to Abu Dhabi island. The hotel's bars and restaurants have proven popular among locals, with Frankie's (named after owner and champion jockey Frankie Dettori, p.376), Marco Pierre White's Steakhouse and Grill (p.383)

Abu Dhabi Hotels

and The Chocolate Gallery (p.375) arguably the pick of the bunch.

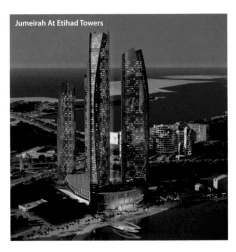

Jumeirah At Etihad Towers

Golden Tulip Al Jazira Hotel & Resort
Dubai – Abu Dhabi Rd Ghantoot 02 562 9100
goldentulipaljazira.com
Map 3 D3
Located on a large, quiet canal that encircles the hotel in Ghantoot – a quiet resort around 45 minutes north of Abu Dhabi island – the 80 room hotel is a stone's throw from the Ghantoot Racing and Polo Club, and offers a large pool area to chill out in, direct marina access, varied watersports facilities and four cafes and bars. Please note that Plastik, the resort's St Tropez style beach club, is now closed.

Grand Continental Flamingo Hotel
Shk Hamdan Bin Mohd Markaziya East 02 690 4000
Map 2 P3
This intimate hotel is centrally located in the business and commercial district. It has 155 rooms, all of which offer good views of the city. There are three restaurants, including the popular Peppino Italian restaurant (p.386). The hotel has a host of handy business facilities and a well-equipped gym.

Grand Millennium Al Wahda
Al Wahda Complex, Hazaa Bin Zayed St Al Nahyan
02 443 9999
millenniumhotels.com
Map 2 M7
In a great location next to Al Wahda Mall and almost slap-bang in the middle of downtown Abu Dhabi, The Grand Millennium Al Wahda is a giant testament to high-end hospitality. Its 844 rooms, suites and apartments are bright, modern and even more spacious than you'll find in most luxury hotels; the second floor spa and fitness areas are among the city's very best; while the rooftop pool, sunbathing area, juice bar and relaxation beds are the cherry on the cake. Its F&B outlets – Toshi and Porto Bello in particular – are excellent.

Hilton Abu Dhabi
West Corniche Rd Al Khubeirah 02 681 1900
hilton.com
Map 2 C3
Conveniently located between Abu Dhabi's financial district and Marina Mall, the Hilton is one of the capital's landmark hotels and has 350 beautifully decorated rooms and suites. The Hiltonia Beach Club is one of the city's most popular, with a private beach, swimming pools and a luxurious gym and spa. The restaurants and bars are also among Abu Dhabi's top entertainment options, particularly Hemingways (p.400), renowned Italian restaurant Bocca (p.373), and the funky Jazz Bar (p.400).

Holiday Inn Abu Dhabi
Nr East Rd & Shk Rashid Bin Al Maktoum Rd
Al Rehhan 02 657 4888
holidayinn.com
Map 1 H7
Located near to both Al Bateen Airport and ADNEC, the recently opened 203 room hotel has an excellent, fully staffed business centre and a roof level fitness centre with gym, pool, sauna and steam room. The fitness centre even offers a smattering of reasonably priced spa treatments, such as Swedish, Thai and aromatherapy massages to help take the edge off a busy working day. Food and drink options are limited but of good standard, with a restaurant, a cafe and a lounge bar.

Hyatt Capital Gate Abu Dhabi
Capital Gate Al Safarat 02 596 1234
hyatt.com
Map 1 H8
A business hotel quite unlike any other, Hyatt Capital Gate towers over the sprawling ADNEC complex, providing easy access to conference facilities, as well as being just 15 minutes from the airport in one direction and 20 minutes from the Corniche in the other. What truly sets this hotel apart, however, is that it is located in a 160m tall building that leans 18°, making it the world's 'most leaning' building. The individuality of the structure is beautifully highlighted throughout the hotel, from the incredible and hypnotic atrium that connects the 189 rooms and 22 suites to the overhanging pool. Plus, the entire hotel has breathtaking views. Service is understated and friendly, while the modern decor does its best to match those views. A business hotel, but should also be considered by leisure tourists in search of something different.

InterContinental Abu Dhabi
Bainouna St Al Bateen 02 666 6888
ichotelsgroup.com
Map 2 C4
This landmark hotel provides 390 modern rooms and suites in a prime location overlooking the Arabian Gulf and a lovely marina. There is a choice of superb eateries, including the always popular Fishmarket (p.376) and Belgian Beer Cafe (p.396), state-of-the-art business facilities, and, for relaxation, there is a 24 hour gym, outdoor pool, squash court and tennis courts. The beach area is being extensively redeveloped until early 2013, although guests still have full access to the beach and sea.

Jumeirah At Etihad Towers > p.68
Nr Emirates Palace, West Corniche St
Al Ras Al Akhdar 02 811 5555
jumeirah.com
Map 2 B3
Towering above Emirates Palace and offering some of the best views in town, this is the Dubai-based Jumeirah group's first venture in the UAE capital. Everything is on a grand and luxurious scale. The huge windows in the giant lobby offer an incredible panorama over the beaches, mangroves and channels behind the hotel – a lovely backdrop to check-in. Both public areas and the lovely rooms have a touch of Asian inspiration behind them; the 382 rooms and 199 serviced apartments all offer incredible views too – try to get a room looking out over the Corniche and Breakwater. Finding a balance between business hotel (13 meeting rooms, conference capacity of 1,400) and leisure resort (number of excellent hotels, Talise Spa, stand-alone gym), this vast property has something for everyone.

Khalidiya Palace Rayhaan By Rotana
Corniche Road West Al Ras Al Akhdar 02 657 0000
rotana.com
Map 2 A3
Situated at the west end of the Corniche and has the double benefit of still being within the city, yet giving the impression when inside of being situated at a more recluse location. A sense of grandeur and traditionalism meet you upon arrival. The large open aired space in the foyer is decorated with Arabic seating and furniture while looming above are grand chandeliers and the open plan centre of the hotel. With an offering of standard rooms, suites and apartments, the rooms are spacious and have all the standard amenities, with some offering balconies and sea views of the hotel's pool and private beach. Three restaurants are available for dining through the day or alternatively 24-hour room service is an option. The hotel also offers a fitness club, inclusive of spa, and six sea view conference rooms.

Kingsgate Abu Dhabi
Nr Abu Dhabi Mall Tourist Club Area 02 499 5000
millenniumhotels.ae
Map 2 R5
The 108 room Kingsgate Hotel is located near to the Abu Dhabi Mall (p.341) in the busy Tourist Club Area. Smaller and quieter than some of the area's bigger hotels, it is an understated but classy affair with nicely appointed but simple conference and banqueting facilities, sports and leisure offerings and one tasteful restaurant-cafe concept.

Le Meridien Abu Dhabi
Nr Old Abu Dhabi Co-Op Society Tourist Club Area 02 644 6666
lemeridienabudhabi.com
Map 2 S4
A recent facelift has rejuvenated this landmark hotel's 234 guest rooms and suites. There are plenty of leisure facilities, including a private beach, kids' and adults' swimming pools and a health club and spa. The European-style courtyard houses many of the hotel's food and beverage outlets, including a popular traditional pub, The Captain's Arms (p.397), and upmarket French, Thai and Italian restaurants which are all popular with local residents.

Le Royal Meridien Abu Dhabi
Shk Khalifa Bin Zayed St Markaziya East 02 674 2020
leroyalmeridienabudhabi.com
Map 2 P3
This hotel – one of the city's best known and most visited – has 277 beautiful rooms and suites, most with spectacular views of the Corniche and Arabian Gulf. There are 13 restaurants and bars, all of which are excellent and perennially popular among local expats. The hotel's revolving rooftop restaurant, Al Fanar (p.367), is among the favourites. Leisure facilities include both indoor and outdoor swimming pools, and a fitness centre.

Mafraq Hotel > p.234
Nr Mafraq Hospital, Al Mafraq Airport Area 02 659 6666
mafraq-hotel.com
Map 2 U13
Originally opened in 1996, this hotel has been going through renovations; call in advance to enquire about availability. Conveniently located just 10 minutes from Abu Dhabi International Airport, the hotel features 121 rooms and four suites with an excellent choice of leisure facilities that include a swimming pool and a recreation club. The Mafraq's revamp will also see an adjoining 129 room wing and chalet block added. Other facilities will include larger swimming pools, a ballroom and a new conference centre.

Abu Dhabi Hotels

Mercure Abu Dhabi Centre Hotel

Nr Liwa Centre, Shk Hamdan Bin Mohd St
Markaziya East 02 633 3555
mercure.com
Map 2 M4

Located in a central spot near the Liwa Centre in Markaziya East, this hotel has 215 nice rooms and suites, comprehensive meetings facilities and enough facilities to sate the appetite of most fanatical fitness freaks, in the form of a gym, swimming pool, sauna and Jacuzzi. There's also an array of decent F&B outlets, including a poolside sports bar, a piano lounge, a cafe, a Chinese restaurant and a popular French restaurant.

Millennium Hotel Abu Dhabi

Shk Khalifa Bin Zayed St Markaziya East 02 614 6000
millenniumhotels.com
Map 2 P3

The modern Millennium Hotel, located near the Corniche, offers great city panoramas. It has 305 elegantly decorated rooms and three restaurants serving Moroccan, Italian and International cuisine. The hotel is best known for its champagne and cigar bar, Cristal (p.398). The business and leisure facilities are comprehensive with boardrooms, a business centre, a fitness club and a swimming pool.

One To One Hotel – The Village

Al Salam St Al Nahyan 02 495 2000
onetoonehotels.com
Map 2 Q8

The One to One Hotel differs from many establishments in that it resembles a small, European boutique hotel. The One to One group seeks to redefine the region's notion of hospitality, so expect a more personal experience than you're likely to get from the big chains. The hotel is a little way from downtown, but is close to the airport and exhibition centre. It is becoming increasingly popular with the city's younger residents who are drawn to its stylish but relaxed cafes, bars and restaurants.

Oryx Hotel

7th Street Al Khalidiyah 02 681 0001
oryxhotel.ae
Map 2 F4

There are 96 luxurious rooms and 32 suites at this boutique-style hotel in Al Khalidiyah, just five minutes walk from the Corniche. It has a spacious and well-equipped gym, a soothing spa and a rooftop pool, as well as a range of services that are aimed specifically at the business traveller. The hotel has two restaurants, while a drink in the top floor Blue Bar is a must, if only to take in (and to take photos of) the panoramic views of Abu Dhabi's skyline.

Park Hyatt Abu Dhabi Hotel & Villas

Saadiyat Beach Sadiyat Island 02 407 1234
hyatt.com
Map 1 H1

The Saadiyat beach hotels are unlike anything else in the UAE and the Park Hyatt raises the bar on what to expect of a resort location. Laid-back, elegant and with a sense of luxury that floats effortlessly around rather than ever being forced, this is a true getaway. Sat in the lobby and looking out over the four swimming pools, the landscaped grounds or the private stretch of wild, wave-swept beach, it'd be easy to think that you were in Hawaii, California or Australia, when in fact central Abu Dhabi is just 20 minutes away. The sea-view rooms are perfection, although if you can stretch to one of the suites, you may never want to leave. With 306 rooms, suites and private villas, you could certainly never claim that the Park Hyatt is a boutique hotel, but the sprawling u-shaped layout makes it feel far smaller and more intimate, while giving guests the benefits of a larger resort, such as the two-storey Atarmia Spa with Jacuzzi and relaxation areas, a large fitness centre, two great restaurants as well as an all-day cafe concept, and a discreet bar.

Park Inn By Radisson Abu Dhabi, Yas Island Hotel

Golf Plaza Yas Island West 02 656 2222
parkinn.com
Map 1 T5

A modern and affordable offering on Yas Island, the Park Inn has a particular eye for business travellers and those visiting Yas Marina Circuit, Ferrari World and Yas Waterworld. There are 204 rooms, two modern meeting rooms, a pool bar and two very good restaurants with the Mexican, Amerigos (p.368), gaining a reputation as a fun venue for groups. Swankier restaurant, bar and spa offerings are available just next door at Yas Island's other hotels.

Park Rotana Abu Dhabi

Nr Khalifa Park, Al Salam St Al Matar
02 657 3333
rotana.com
Map 1 K7

Located in the new government-backed business area near Khalifa Park, the bridges off the island, the Grand Mosque and ADNEC, its 318 rooms and suites are lavishly laid out, while there are all the usual leisure and business facilities you'd expect from a five-star establishment. Its food and drink outlets, Teatro restaurant (p.394) and Cooper's gastro pub (p.398) in particular, have gained popularity among those living just off the island, thanks to the hotel's convenient location.

Yas Viceroy

Beach Rotana Abu Dhabi

Khalidiya Palace Rayhaan By Rotana

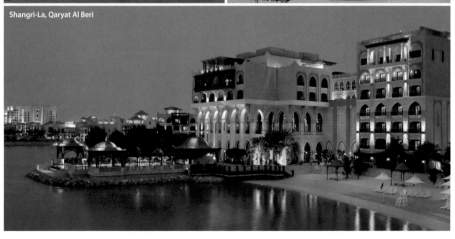

Shangri-La, Qaryat Al Beri

Abu Dhabi Hotels

Radisson Blu Hotel, Abu Dhabi Yas Island
Golf Plaza Yas Island West 02 656 2000
radissonblu.com
Map 1 S5
With views over both the marina, the F1 circuit and the Yas Links Abu Dhabi golf course, the Radisson Blu is located in the hotels complex on the western side of Yas Island. It is a large, comfortable and well-equipped hotel with excellent meeting, pool, fitness and spa facilities. However, it is the hotel's F&B that is getting the most attention; Filini (p.376) is already considered one of the city's best Italians, while Assymetri (p.368) draws the Friday brunch crowds in.

The Ritz-Carlton Abu Dhabi, Grand Canal
Nr Maqtaa Bridge Al Maqtaa 02 818 8888
ritzcarlton.com
Map 1 L8
This vast and sprawling property is the latest addition to Abu Dhabi's impressive list of resorts. It features more than 500 guest rooms, suites and private villas, laid out in a Renaissance style around landscaped gardens and large pool and beach areas. Sat beneath the Sheikh Zayed Grand Mosque (p.210) and opposite the Souk at Qaryat Al Beri (p.348), the Ritz-Carlton boasts a great location for tourists visiting Abu Dhabi. It has a huge number of outlets, with three signature restaurants, pool and beach bars all on offer. There's also a cavernous spa, with 15 private treatment rooms, plunge pools and its own stretch of beach.

Rocco Forte Hotel Abu Dhabi
Shk Rashid Bin Saeed Al Maktoum Rd
Al Madina Al Riyadiya 02 617 0000
roccofortehotelabudhabi.com
Map 1 J7
The Rocco Forte name is synonymous with luxury and the Abu Dhabi hotel is no different. The stunning wave-like glass building is home to almost 300 rooms and suites that share state-of-the-art facilities and great views. The Sports City location (restaurants look back out towards Sheikh Zayed Grand Mosque) makes this predominantly a business hotel thanks to the close proximity to ADNEC, but with one of Abu Dhabi's largest spas and fitness centres, a delightful pool area and several excellent outlets, it also has plenty to offer the leisure visitor.

Sands Hotel
Shk Zayed The Second St Madinat Zayed 02 615 6666
danathotels.com
Map 2 N4
Centrally located, this hotel is a popular option with business travellers. Offering quick access to the commercial and financial districts, it has excellent conferencing amenities, including secretarial services and meeting and banqueting capacity for up to 1,000

people. It also has some fantastic food and drink outlets, including the lively Harvester's English Pub. There is a rooftop pool, a sundeck and a good gym.

Shangri-La Hotel, Qaryat Al Beri
Qaryat Al Beri Complex Bain Al Jessrain 02 509 8888
shangri-la.com
Map 1 L8
This luxury resort hotel overlooks the creek that separates Abu Dhabi island from the mainland. The 214 spacious rooms and suites all have private terraces with stunning sea views. Its two gyms, kilometre of private beach and five swimming pools make it one of the most popular and luxurious holiday retreat in the capital. The spa and outlets – particularly Bord Eau (p.373) and Pearls and Caviar (p.401) – are extremely popular with the city's well-to-do residents looking for an atmospheric night out by the water's edge. The Shangri-La also has direct access to Souk Qaryat Al Beri (p.348), an Arabian style souk with shops, cafes and restaurants connected by waterways. The souk has emerged as one of Abu Dhabi's favourite dining destinations so you will not be short of options here even after you've covered all of the hotel's own dining outlets.

Sheraton Abu Dhabi Hotel & Resort
Corniche Rd Markaziya East 02 677 3333
sheratonabudhabihotel.com
Map 2 Q2
The recently refurbished 272 room Sheraton Abu Dhabi is situated on the revamped area of the Corniche. The hotel is a long-standing favourite dining venue for many Abu Dhabi expats. There are 11 restaurants and bars to choose from; these include a wide range of cuisines to please most culinary tastes. In addition, there's a popular English pub, which is good for watching sports. As for leisure activities, the facilities are varied: there are climate controlled outdoor pools, squash and tennis courts, a fitness centre and a private beach offering watersports and volleyball.

Sheraton Khalidiya Hotel Abu Dhabi
Shk Zayed The First St Markaziya West
02 666 6220
Map 2 J4
This downtown hotel is in the upmarket Al Khalidiyah area, close to Abu Dhabi's business and commercial districts in the heart of the city. There's a state-of-the-art business centre with well-equipped meeting rooms to lure business travellers. The hotel has 285 guest rooms and its other facilities include a rooftop gym, a sundeck and a pool. There are also two solid restaurant offerings, while The 3rd Avenue bar is proving to be a welcome addition to the expat social scene in this part of town.

The St Regis Saadiyat Island Resort
Saadiyat Beach Sadiyat Island 02 498 8888
stregissaadiyatisland.com
Map 1 G1

Quite unlike any other hotel in Abu Dhabi – or the UAE for that matter – the St Regis looks more like a California beach retreat, with the vastly proportioned public spaces and stunning colonial style rooms all offering views over the beautiful central pools, restaurant and private windswept, sandy beach (and one hole of the neighbouring Saadiyat Beach Links course). A true beach resort, with leisure facilities and dining (55 and 5th The Grill is particularly recommended) worth travelling for, the St Regis feels a million miles from the city.

Traders Hotel, Qaryat Al Beri
Qaryat Al Beri Complex, Nr The Bridges
Bain Al Jessrain 02 510 8888
shangri-la.com
Map 1 L8

Part of the large and picturesque Souk Qaryat Al Beri (p.348) complex that peers over the creek between the mainland and Abu Dhabi island, Traders offers 301 luxurious rooms and suites, a private beach and very well appointed gym and relaxed pool area. The hotel has just the one restaurant, a lobby lounge and a pool bar, but it also has direct access into Souk Qaryat Al Beri, where a maze of cafes, shops and restaurants await to be explored. Guests also have access to the neighbouring Shangri-La hotel's facilities, including one of the city's most highly regarded spas and a myriad of other options.

Tulip Inn Al Rahba
Shk Zayed Rd Al Rahba 02 563 8557
tulipinnalrahba.com
Map 3 D2

Half an hour from the city centre along the Abu Dhabi-Dubai highway, this 52 room hotel offers good value with regular offers on its website. It has a tennis court, a basketball court, swimming pools for adults and children and a Jacuzzi, with work to add a fitness club with spa underway. It has two bars, a shisha bar and a cafe, with one main restaurant specialising in Arabian cuisine.

Yas Island Rotana
Golf Plaza Yas Island West 02 656 4000
rotana.com
Map 1 T4

A superb hotel on Yas Island, The Yas Island Rotana has 308 rooms and suites which ooze modern luxury, while there are also more sports, fitness and spa facilities than you can shake a tennis racquet at. Another of the city's popular meetings and conferences venues, its F&B outlets are also starting to make a splash, particularly Blue Grill (p.372) and Rangoli (p.388).

Yas Viceroy Abu Dhabi
Nr Yas Marina Yas Island West 02 656 0000
viceroyhotelsandresorts.com
Map 1 T5

Originally opened for the first Abu Dhabi F1 GP, in November 2009, this hotel, which actually spans the race track (half the hotel is on either side, and the two halves are connected by a bridge over the track), became an instant architectural classic and Abu Dhabi icon. However, the space-age interiors were more modern art museum than five-star hotel for some. The luxurious Viceroy Group recently took over and has smoothed many of those edges to create a property that is now at once utterly modern but equally tactile, functional, sumptuous and welcoming. Rooms and suites are vast and all enjoy incredible views over the race track and surrounding Yas Island. The seven restaurants – spanning high-end seafood to luxury Middle Eastern and sushi – are all individually worth a visit. The two rooftop pools and pool bars are otherworldly locations, and the roof is also home to the amazing Skylite lounge and club, while the Rush cocktail bar is housed in the bridge that spans the race track. Spa duties here are performed by the UK's renowned ESPA.

ART & CULTURE
Heritage & Cultural Sites
Abu Dhabi has a good smattering of interesting attractions and places to visit, offering glimpses into a time not so long ago when the city was nothing more than a small fishing, pearling and trading port. Many of the pre-oil heritage sites have been or are currently being carefully restored, with close attention being paid to traditional design and the use of original building materials.

Abu Dhabi Tourism & Culture Authority
Nr Khalifa St, Al Salam St Al Matar 02 444 0444
abudhabitourism.ae
Map 1 K7

Previously housed in a remarkable building next to Qasr Al Hosn (p.210) that had become the heartbeat of the city's thriving community arts scene, Abu Dhabi Tourism & Culture Authority (the foundation in charge of Abu Dhabi's culture, heritage and leisure offerings) is now based near Zayed Sports City and ADNEC. Meanwhile, the entire city centre block that contains the foundation and heritage site Qasr Al Hosn is undergoing major renovations with the aim of creating the UAE's foremost cultural visitor attraction. The ABTCA continues to oversee the emirate's culture and heritage and organises exhibitions, screenings, performances and lectures all over the city. See the website for a full calendar.

Al Maqtaa Fort

Nr Maqtaa Bridge Al Maqtaa

This heavily renovated fort is one of the few remaining examples of its kind in Abu Dhabi city. Your first glimpse of the monument will likely be as you approach the Al Maqtaa Bridge towards Abu Dhabi island. The 200 year old fort, standing on the edge of the island, was built to fend off bandits and provides a wonderful contrast to the modern bridge right next to it. Be careful when taking photographs here as it is a sensitive military zone and there are often police patrols.

Bateen Dhow Shipyard

Nr InterContinental Abu Dhabi Al Bateen

Map 2 B6

Connected to the island via a short causeway over Khor Al Bateen, the Bateen Shipyard is a cluttered, busy and charmingly atmospheric area where proud boat builders continue to craft vessels in the way they have done for decades. Visit early in the morning or late in the afternoon and you'll be rewarded by friendly workers who are happy to explain their craft and be photographed.

Emirates National Auto Museum

E65 Rd/Hamim Rd, South of Abu Dhabi 050 829 3952

enam.ae

Map 3 D3

Located 45 kilometres south of Abu Dhabi, this impressive pyramid houses an assortment of cars from one dedicated collector: Sheikh Hamad bin Hamdan Al Nahyan, aka the 'Rainbow Sheikh'. After officially opening to the public in 2005, the museum has recently undergone development and is now home to almost 200 cars, including a vast collection of off-road vehicles, classic American cars, the Sheikh's rainbow collection of Mercedes and the largest truck in the world. Some exhibits were showcased in the BBC television programme Top Gear. Even if you're not particularly interested in cars, this is a fascinating collection and a great place to stop on the way to or from Liwa. Opening times are currently 09:00 to 18:00 seven days a week, but this can change. Entry, formerly free, is now Dhs.10 per adult with kids still free.

Heritage Village

Nr Marina Mall Breakwater 02 681 4455

Map 2 F2

The picturesque Heritage Village is situated on the Breakwater near Marina Mall, facing Abu Dhabi's waterfront. Run by the Emirates Heritage Club, it

Heritage Village

Where For Art Thou?

With big and bold new developments, Abu Dhabi is aiming to become the cultural capital of the Middle East – but what of its current art scene?

Since the capital is gearing up to become the cultural centre of the UAE, one might think the art scene would be buzzing. Well, not quite yet. But (and it's a big but) the best is yet to come. In typical UAE style, when they do it, they tend to go all out; that's the attitude for the upcoming Guggenheim and Louvre Abu Dhabi museums, both slated to open on Saadiyat Island in the next couple of years. The plans for these buildings (designed by Frank Gehry and Jean Nouvel, respectively) suggest buildings that will be works of art themselves, while the art housed inside promises to take viewers to new levels.

In the meantime, there are options. Foremost of these is the Abu Dhabi Art Fair, held in November. The exhibition, held in the Emirates Palace Ballroom, has previously showcased work from 50 galleries in 19 countries to thousands of attendees during the four-day event. When names like de Kooning, Richter and Basquiat are tossed around, the art world listens; Jeff Koons even made an appearance at the 2010 fair. The next edition is again scheduled for November and, as is often the case with these events in this neck of the woods, expect each year to show notable growth and improvement (abudhabiartfair.ae).

Other events at the Emirates Palace have included a Picasso exhibition, previews of both the Louvre and Guggenheim, and a sprawling display of Islamic art.

Of the bigger venues, the Manarat Al Saadiyat (p.212) has been an exciting addition. A multi-purpose venue, it houses lecture theatres, an auditorium and acts as a visitors' centre to the Saadiyat project. It also contains three galleries and, although it is still early days for Saadiyat Island, exhibitions here have shown a tiny glimpse of the potential that this huge island of culture holds, with some fascinating exhibitions examining the notion of Middle East unity organised by guest curators from around the region one of the definite highlights to date.

Although there are still only a handful of independent galleries in Abu Dhabi, the capital does have a burgeoning gallery scene. One of the premier spaces in Abu Dhabi is the Ghaf Art Gallery (p.212). The oldest contemporary art gallery in the capital, Ghaf concentrates on showcasing contemporary local and regional artists, as well as solo and mixed exhibits featuring international names.

Qibab Art Gallery (artslant.com) specialises predominantly in Iraqi art but as a gallery it is also dedicated to showing both local and foreign contemporary artists, often including handicrafts and traditional bazaars along with the artwork to give the viewer a real cultural experience.

Acento Gallery (p.212), strangely enough, specialises in Mexican and Spanish art but, in recent years at least, it has shown artists from New York as well as locally-based artists originally hailing from places like New Zealand, Uganda and Pakistan. Newcomer, Salwa Zeidan Gallery (p.212) shows international and Middle Eastern contemporary masters, as well as emerging artists from varied backgrounds. The gallery also shows a wide range of mediums, from painting, photography and sculpture to installation and performance art.

Finally, the Abu Dhabi Festival, billed as the UAE's premier classical arts event, takes place during March and April each year. Though concentrating on music, the festival showcases works by a couple of artists each year and often commissions new works. The festival often includes exhibits from Middle Eastern modern masters, with works by Parviz Tanavoli and Adam Henein having been shown. In addition to showing the artists' works, the festival featured lectures by the artists as well as panels about art in the UAE.

What The Future Holds

Although the incredible structures themselves will take a lot of the plaudits, both the Guggenheim and Louvre Abu Dhabi will be genuinely exciting spaces of international note. Guggenheim has already named its curators and says the gallery will exhibit a collection focused on international post-war art. The Louvre meanwhile – the first ever outside the original Paris location – will feature global works with particular focus on those creating a dialogue between east and west. Other than that, Louvre chiefs have said that the museum's location in a Muslim country will have no effect on the pieces that will go on show.

offers an interesting glimpse into the country's past. Traditional aspects of the Bedouin way of life, including a camp fire with coffee pots, a goats' hair tent, a well and a falaj irrigation system, are attractively displayed in the open museum. There are workshops where craftsmen demonstrate traditional skills, such as metal work and pottery, while women sit weaving and spinning. The craftsmen are happy to share their skills and may occasionally give you the chance to try them out. The little spice shop is a treat – you can get a range of dried herbs, handmade soap and plenty of chatter. It's a great place to buy saffron; the world's most expensive spice is available in the shop at far less than you would pay in major supermarkets. After visiting the village, sample some typical Arabic cuisine at the waterside restaurants with great views of the Corniche. Close by is a pleasant kids' play area. Entry is free.

Petroleum Exhibition
Nr Commercial Bank, Corniche Rd East
Markaziya East 02 444 6900
adnec.ae
Map 2 L2
The recently revamped Petroleum Exhibition covers Abu Dhabi's phenomenal development from a desert oasis to a thriving cosmopolitan city. Spread across three rooms, there are scale models, photographs and maps charting the earliest oil exploration in the desert and the Gulf, to the first oil export from Das Island in 1962. Interactive displays, like giant drill bits and documentary films (in English, French and German), give a fascinating insight into one of the world's largest oil and gas producers. Entrance is free.

Qasr Al Hosn
Shk Zayed First St Markaziya West
Map 2 K4
Qasr Al Hosn (also known as the Old Fort or the White Fort) is the oldest building in Abu Dhabi, dating back to 1793. It was the official residence of the rulers of Abu Dhabi when they moved from the Liwa Oasis to the island. Unfortunately, Qasr Al Hosn, along with the neighbouring Cultural Foundation, is closed for major renovations: the area is being redeveloped by the government and there are plans to reopen the fort as a museum and public monument.

Sheikh Zayed Grand Mosque
Shk Rashid Bin Saeed Al Maktoum St Al Maqtaa
02 441 6444
szgmc.ae
Map 1 K8
The stunning Sheikh Zayed Grand Mosque opened in 2007 and has captivated worshippers and visitors ever since. This architectural work of art is one of the largest mosques in the world, with a capacity for an astonishing 40,000 worshippers. The mosque's first event was the funeral of its namesake, Sheikh Zayed, who is buried at the site. It features 80 domes, over 1,000 columns, 24 carat gold-plated chandeliers and the world's largest hand-woven Persian carpet. Unlike other mosques in Abu Dhabi, Sheikh Zayed Mosque is very much open for non-Muslims to tour. One hour tours start at 10:00, 11:00 and 17:00 daily, but not on Fridays. For more information or to book a tour, call the number above or visit the website. This is one not to be missed.

Culture Reigns In Al Ain
As the UAE's birthplace – the oasis where the Emirates' tribes originally settled before heading to the coast – Al Ain is the country's most culturally rich city and area. Located 140km inland from Abu Dhabi, it is home to many heritage attractions such as the National Museum (p.237), the Palace Museum (p.237), Al Jahili Fort and Park (p.238). See Out Of The City, p.235 for more information about Al Ain.

Women's Handicraft Centre
Women's Association Complex, Al Karamah St
Al Mushrif 02 447 6645
Map 2 K11
This creative and arty initiative is government sponsored and run by the Abu Dhabi Women's Association as a showcase for local art and crafts. The museum within may be a little on the small side but it does offer the chance to examine the handiwork of local artists and learn something about the work on display. There is also a shop onsite where you can buy some of the items which are produced, making for an original and interesting keepsake. The round buildings near the museum are workshops where female artists display distinctive Arabian oils, handmade souvenirs, incense, local dress, silver thread work and weaving. It is suggested you remove your shoes before entering each hut and note that photography is not encouraged. This is an excellent place to experience the traditional art of henna. For just Dhs.10 you can get a small henna design painted on your hand, which will last about two weeks.

Art Galleries
While there's nothing of real international acclaim in Abu Dhabi yet, there are a number of galleries that have interesting exhibitions of art and traditional Arabic artefacts; plus, as the city matures, more and more are springing up. Most operate as a combined shop and gallery, but some also provide studios for artists and are involved in the promotion of art within the UAE.

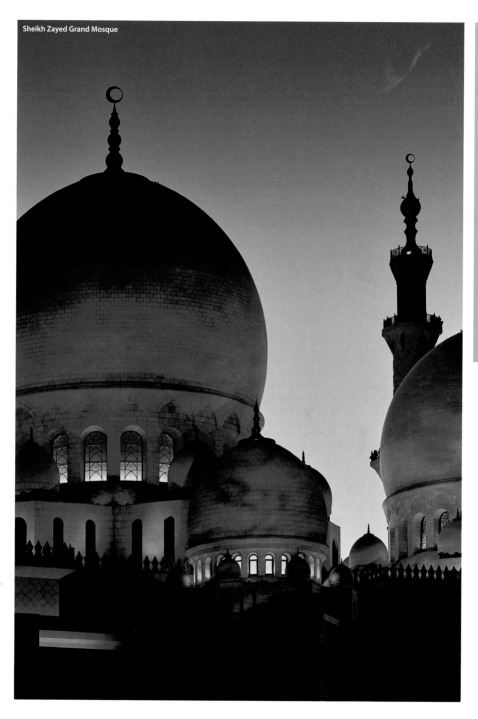

Sheikh Zayed Grand Mosque

Art & Culture

Abu Dhabi Tourism & Culture Authority
Nr Khalifa St, Al Salam St Al Matar 02 444 0444
abudhabitourism.ae
Map 1 K7

Abu Dhabi Tourism & Culture Authority hosts art exhibitions throughout the year. As a government organisation, it is charged with preserving and promoting local artistic expression, and does so successfully and enthusiastically. In addition to the regular art displays, the authority also hosts performing arts shows, poetry readings, lectures and film screenings. The foundation is currently based in a temporary location while the area around its original Khalidiyah Street home is being developed into a major heritage site; regardless, it continues to organise all manner of cultural activities throughout the city.

Ramadan Timings

During Ramadan, timings for many companies in Abu Dhabi change significantly. Museums and heritage sites usually open slightly later in the morning, and close earlier in the afternoon. Check before you go.

Acento Gallery
Warehouse 6, Street 13 Al Meena 050 847 6772
acentogallery.com
Map 2 U1

A modern, warehouse-loft style gallery in the old port area of the city, Acento is the city's largest art space and represents a roster of international artists, covering everything from paintings and etchings to sculptures. The gallery displays functional and decorative art, as well as more subjective pieces and exhibitions showcasing talent from all over the world which changes regularly.

The Barakat Gallery
Emirates Palace Al Ras Al Akhdar 02 690 8950
barakatgallery.com
Map 2 B2

Located in Emirates Palace Hotel, this recently opened and dynamic addition to Abu Dhabi's developing art scene has branches in London and Los Angeles. Barakat specialises in ancient art and has on display a multitude of antiquities from China, Egypt, the Near East, Africa, Greece and Rome. Items vary widely and include statues, jewellery, coins, necklaces and pottery.

Folklore Gallery
Shk Zayed The First St Al Khalidiyah 02 666 0361
folkloregallery.net
Map 2 G4

A simple but welcoming art and exhibition space, this gallery focuses on local artistic and craft offerings,

with traditional Bedouin ceramics and jewellery available at reasonable prices. Art comes in the form of prints and paintings that have been inspired by the country's landscape.

Gallery One
The Souk At Qaryat Al Beri Bain Al Jessrain
02 558 1822
g-1.com
Map 1 L8

Gallery One at Souk Qaryat Al Beri has become a significant player on the Abu Dhabi art scene. It regularly hosts exhibitions of international note, the most prominent to date being Art of Islam and Picasso Abu Dhabi. Exhibitions also bring together diverse works from across the Middle East and UAE. Gallery One usually runs a series of lectures alongside each exhibition, and entry to all shows and events is free.

Ghaf Art Gallery
Al Khaleej Al Arabi St Al Khalidiyah 02 665 5332
ghafgallery.blogspot.com
Map 2 G5

The funky Ghaf Art Gallery opened its doors to art lovers in 2006, intent on presenting local artists to Abu Dhabi residents. It hasn't disappointed, with Ghaf becoming a notable player in the city's arts scene. Exhibitions are both mixed and individual, showcasing local and also sometimes international artists, with new artists regularly exhibiting their work. The gallery is open from 10:00 to 21:00, but is closed on Fridays.

Manarat Al Saadiyat
Saadiyat Cultural District Sadiyat Island 02 6575 800
saadiyat.ae
Map 1 G1

Although the most eagerly anticipated elements of Saadiyat Island – the Guggenheim, Louvre and the Zayed National Museum – may still be a few years away from completion, the first of the island's new artistic offerings opened its doors a year or so ago. Manarat Al Saadiyat is a 15,400 square metre visitor centre that is home to the Arts Abu Dhabi Gallery, the Contemporary Art Gallery and the Universal Art Gallery, a restaurant as well as several auditoriums and other interesting display spaces. With an impressive programme of exhibitions, this exciting addition to Abu Dhabi's art scene is already exhibiting some fascinating works and collections.

Salwa Zeidan Gallery
Al Khaleej Al Arabi St Al Khalidiyah 02 666 9656
salwazeidangallery.com
Map 2 G5

Showcasing not just painting, sculpture and photography, but also works of installation and performance pieces, Salwa Zeidan's works are fresh and thought-provoking, and many provide an interesting comment on the current state of Islam. The gallery has hosted many exhibitions and been the driving force behind an annual sculpture symposium; at the moment, however, the gallery is about to relocate with the newly-constructed venue not named at the time of going to print. Visit the website for the new location and opening hours.

PARKS, BEACHES & ATTRACTIONS

Parks

Abu Dhabi has a number of excellent parks, most of which have lush green lawns and a variety of trees and shrubs, creating perfect escapes from the concrete and construction jungle of the city. During the winter months, the more popular parks can get very busy at weekends. Most have a kiosk or a cafe selling snacks and drinks, and some even have barbecue pits – just remember to bring your own wood or charcoal.

Regulations among the parks vary, with some banning bikes and rollerblades, or limiting ball games to specific areas. Pets are not permitted and you should not collect plant cuttings either. Some parks have a ladies' day when entry is restricted to women, girls and young boys, and certain smaller ones actually ban anyone other than ladies through the week, while allowing families only at the weekends.

Four new small neighbourhood parks (Al Bateen, Al Zaab, Al Rawdah and Al Karama) were opened during 2012, with as many as 20 playgrounds and play areas following suit. Three large parks with facilities including cafes, playgrounds and sports courts will open off the island in Khalifa City A soon too. The government's aim is to provide 25 square metres of open space for every resident of Abu Dhabi, while no resident should live more than 400m from a park or open space. Entrance to the smaller parks is generally free, while the larger ones charge up to Dhs.5 per person. The opening hours of most parks change during Ramadan.

Al Khalidiya Kids Park
Nr THE One Al Khubeirah adm.gov.ae
Map 2 F4
This is one of the more popular parks in the city with the area's residents flooding here during the cooler months. Costs of the various rides and play equipment vary, but the standard entry fee remains at Dhs.1.

Al Khalidiya Public Park
Al Khaleej Al Arabi St Al Khalidiyah
adm.gov.ae
Map 2 G4
Taking up a whole block, this large city park is popular with families. It has a variety of safe play areas for

DUBAI'S ART DELIGHTS

While Abu Dhabi's art scene is growing, an hour down the road in Dubai, it's positively flourishing, especially in the Al Quoz industrial area, where galleries, artists' spaces and cultural communities have popped up consistently over the past few years. Art Sawa (artsawa.com), The Third Line (thethirdline.com), Total Arts Gallery (courtyard-uae.com), Gallery Isabelle Van den Eynde (ivde.net) and Meem Gallery (meemartgallery.com) are some of the best; if you're looking for an artsy community, then head for The Jam Jar (thejamjardubai.com) or Shelter (shelter.ae). At the other end of the spectrum, Dubai International Finance Centre (DIFC) has top notch galleries, such as Artspace (artspace-dubai.com), The Farjam Collection (farjamcollection.com), The Empty Quarter (theemptyquarter.com) and Cuadro (cuadroart. com), which house quality pieces from masters such as Picasso and Matisse.

Art Dubai (artdubai.ae) is an annual get-together of industry people from across the Middle East and Asia. Held in March at Madinat Jumeirah, one of the main events is the Global Art Forum, which attracts artists, curators, museum groups and international media. Several exhibitions and events also run alongside the forum, drawing thousands of visitors. During Art Dubai, the ArtBus (04 341 7303, artinthecity.com) ferries culture vultures between Dubai's best venues. For major arts festivals or exhibitions, the ArtBus links Dubai-based art lovers with the country's capital to get a taste of what Abu Dhabi has to offer.

Ayyam Gallery, Al Quoz

Parks, Beaches & Attractions

toddlers and older children. Its lovely grassy areas are great for picnics, with a number of large trees providing excellent shade. A branch of the Abu Dhabi Cooperative Society operates on the south side of the park, allowing for the shopping to be done once the children have let off steam.

Al Nahyan Garden
Shk Zayed The First St Al Khalidiyah
Map 2 H4
One of a number of small children's parks found throughout the city, this well-maintained and compact park located near the Sheraton Khalidiya (p.206) ensures your little ones can't get up to too much trouble. Simple play equipment helps the kids let off steam. Entrance is just Dhs.1 but single men without their children or family will not be allowed entry.

Capital Park
Nr NBAD Markaziya East adm.gov.ae
Map 2 N3
This refurbished park is a welcome patch of green in the middle of the city centre. Each little cove of the garden has a small selection of climbing frames, swings and slides. A large pond in the middle erupts periodically with bursts from the stunning fountains, taking visitors by surprise. Vending machines and an enclosed cafeteria provide refreshment – and there is a popular takeaway pizza place right across the road. There is also a small mosque and a municipal plant shop.

The Corniche
Off Corniche Rd Al Khubeirah
Map 2 J3
Extensive land reclamation and park development along the Corniche has created an expansive series

Park on The Corniche

of lush green spaces for everyone to enjoy. Corniche Road now boasts an impressive six kilometres of parks that include children's play areas, a separate cycle and pedestrian path, cafes and restaurants, and Corniche Beach, a life-guarded beach park. There is the Family Park near King Khalid bin Abdul Aziz Street (26th Street), noted for its creative climbing structures; the Urban Park near Sheikh Rashid bin Saeed Al Maktoum Street, with its beautiful garden; the Lake Park near Muroor Street, known for its 'lake'; and the Formal Park by Baniyas Street, noted for its architecture and maze. There is plenty of parking on the city side of Corniche Road, and pedestrian underpasses at all the major intersections connect to the waterfront side.

Khalifa Park
Nr Al Bateen Airport Al Matar 02 449 0346
adm.gov.ae
Map 1 K7
Located in Al Matar, off the Eastern Ring Road, Khalifa Park is one of the city's largest parks and is now a major landmark. The inspiration for the designs of the gardens has been drawn from Arabic and Islamic architecture, as well as from some of the great gardens around the world, including Chatsworth House in England and the Al Hambra Palace in Spain. The gardens are set in a landscape of canals, fountains, lakes and waterfalls, and mini train tours of the park are available. With play equipment for children, picnic facilities and an outdoor auditorium, it's a popular spot in the cooler evenings and at weekends. During cooler months, a community market sees stalls set up in the park every evening. A host of activity programmes for kids are regularly run at the park as well.

Mushrif Central Park
Nr Al Karamah & Mohammed bin Khalifa Sts
Al Mushrif
Map 2 K11
This large park near Airport Road has been going through renovations for a couple of years and the result is that it is now a sprawling people's park with something for everyone. There is a jogging track, and future plans include a museum and a petting zoo.

Old Airport Garden
Nr Zayed Sport City Al Madina Al Riyadiya
Map 1 J8
This is a quiet park and an ideal place if you want to relax after taking the kids ice skating at the adjacent rink. One side of the park has swings and small tidy gardens, while the other side is more ornamental, with plenty of trees offering shade. Maintenance takes place in the mornings, so be prepared to move quickly if the sprinkler system is switched on. If the hunger pangs strike, there's a KFC right on the edge of the gardens. And for any unfortunate injuries, Al Noor

Hospital's (p.161) newest facility has opened near the park's southern boundary.

Tourist Club Park

Shk Hamdan Bin Mohd St Markaziya East
adm.gov.ae
Map **2 R4**

Also known as Electra Park, this is yet another serene retreat in the heart of the city. Like most other parks, it offers swings and slides for children to play on. It's rarely busy and therefore ideal for families. The park is located on Electra Street, between 4th and 5th Streets.

Beaches

A visit to one of Abu Dhabi's beaches is a perfect way to spend the day – warm turquoise waters, white sandy beaches and stretches of lush greenery will transport you a hundred miles from the stresses of city life. Swimwear is not the norm on the public beaches so prepare for a few stares if you decide to strip off.

An upside to the public beaches in Abu Dhabi is that, unlike in other places in the UAE, vehicles can't get onto the beaches, so you won't find 4WD enthusiasts churning up the sand. These beaches are there to be enjoyed by everyone, so keep them clean and beautiful by remembering to take your litter away with you.

Monte-Carlo Beach Club

For a taste of something a little more exclusive than the usual public beaches, look no further than Monte-Carlo Beach Club (02 656 3500), a shiny new European-style boutique beach club that has emerged as one of the main attractions on Saadiyat Island. In addition to a lovely stretch of Arabian Gulf and swimming pools, there are spa facilities, private cabanas and bungalows, and a handful of restaurants and bars to choose from. Day passes are available from Dhs.400.

Like the parks, the beaches are busiest during the cooler months and at weekends, and are very popular for barbecues and picnics, as well as perfect settings for a casual stroll.

The largest beaches can be found along the Corniche, and have loads of facilities as well as being flanked by all manner of outlets that serve up refreshments.

Located on the north-western tip of Al Ras Al Akhdar, Abu Dhabi Public Beach was the city's most popular public beach for years. Prior to the construction of Emirates Palace, the beach used to extend across to the Marina Mall causeway. Now smaller, it is pretty basic, with no facilities, and is currently closed due to the building of a new presidential palace opposite. Al Bateen Beach, popular with locals and used for fishing and swimming is

also currently closed due to nearby construction of a bridge. Once it's re-opened, head west on 19th Street (Saeed bin Tahnoon St) and turn left onto 16th Street when it ends. After 200 metres, you'll see the beach in front of Sheikh Sultan bin Sayed Playground.

Two new women-only beaches are set to be completed and opened in 2013. For other options to tip your toes in the warm waters of the Gulf, see Hotels, p.198.

Swim Safely

Although the waters off the coast generally look calm and unchallenging, very strong rip tides can carry the most confident swimmer away from the shore very quickly and drownings have occurred in the past. Take extra care when swimming off the public beaches where there are no lifeguards.

Waterparks

With the opening of Yas Waterworld, Abu Dhabi now has its own huge, game-changing waterpark that delights and enthrals kids of all ages. There are also small indoor waterparks in Khalifa Park (p.214) and Mushrif Mall (p.348) which are a nice option for younger kids. For a day out of the city, head north to Dubai, Umm Al Quwain and Ras Al Khaimah to get wet and wild. Wild Wadi, Aquaventure and Ice Land Water Park are all worth the journey from Abu Dhabi if more water fun is what you're after.

Aquaventure

Atlantis The Palm Dubai **04 426 0000**
atlantisthepalm.com
Map **3 E2** Metro **Nakheel**

Aquaventure is the ultimate destination for wet and wild thrill seekers. To get the adrenaline pumping, head straight to the Leap of Faith, a 27.5 metre near-vertical drop that shoots you through a series of tunnels surrounded by shark-infested waters. Alternatively, The Rapids will take you on a tumultuous 2.3 kilometre river journey around the whole park, complete with waterfalls and wave surges. For the little ones, there is Splashers, a giant water playground, while those looking for more tranquil pursuits can lounge on the park's beach where chairs are provided. Open daily from 10:00 until sunset. Entrance for those over 1.2m is Dhs.225, and Dhs.180 for those under that height. Children younger than 2 years old and Atlantis hotel guests get in for free. Special promotional rates for residents are frequently offered during summer. On selected Thursdays throughout the warmer months, Aquaventure holds its Cool Summer Nights parties, when the park stays open until midnight, with music and entertainment also on offer.

Parks, Beaches & Attractions

Dreamland Aqua Park

Dreamland Aqua Park
RAK Highway (E11) Umm Al Quwain 06 768 1888
dreamlanduae.com
Map 3 E1
Over 25 water rides spread across 250,000 square metres of green, landscaped grounds. Adrenaline junkies will not be disappointed with rides such as the Black Hole, the Kamikaze, and the four 'twisting dragons'. For a more leisurely experience, there's the lazy river, a wave pool, and a high-salinity pool for floating about. The Aqua Play area has 19 games and attractions for the whole family and, if you prefer not to get wet, you can burn rubber on the 400 metre go-kart track. There's a variety of cafes and restaurants, as well as a licensed pool bar and shisha majlis. Overnight accommodation is also available, either in a tent (provided for you) or a 'cabana' hut. Admission costs Dhs.135 for adults and Dhs.85 for children under 12, while children under 3 go free. The park is open all year round (check the website for timings). Fridays, Saturdays and holidays are reserved for families only.

Iceland Water Park
Al Jazeera, Al Hamra Ras Al Khaimah 07 206 7888
icelandwaterpark.com
Map 3 F1
Located in Ras Al Khaimah, this brand-new, gigantic waterpark opened in mid-2011.The park has a capacity to welcome 10,000 guests per day and the attractions include Penguin Falls (the world's tallest man-made waterfall), Penguin Bay (a rain dance pool), Arctic Slides and Tundra Baths. In addition, you'll find aqua games fields and a coral bay reef for snorkelling. General admission costs Dhs.150 for adults and Dhs.100 for kids, while annual and quarterly membership plans start from Dhs.750 per adult.

SplashLand
WonderLand Theme & Water Park Dubai 04 324 1222
wonderlanduae.com
Map 3 E2 Metro Dubai Healthcare City
The waterpark within the WonderLand amusement park offers fun for kids or adults, with nine rides including slides and twisters, a lazy river, an adults' pool and a children's activity pool with slides, bridges and water cannons. Alternatively, you can just relax by the pool and sunbathe.

Wild Wadi Water Park
Jumeirah Rd Dubai 04 348 4444
jumeirah.com
Map 3 E2 Metro Mall of the Emirates
Spread over 12 acres beside Jumeirah Beach Hotel (p.251), the park has 23 aquatic rides and attractions to suit all ages and bravery levels. One of the first you'll encounter is Wipeout, a permanently rolling wave giving you the chance to show off your body-boarding skills. Admission is Dhs.225 for adults and Dhs.175 for children under 1.1m in height. There is also a 'sundowner' rate (for the last two hours of opening), when adults pay Dhs.185 and children pay Dhs.145.

Yas Waterworld Abu Dhabi > p.217, 295
Nr Ferrari World Abu Dhabi Yas Island West
yaswaterworld.com
Map 1 T4
The latest waterpark in a country that has some of the best in the world has managed to raise the bar even higher. Based on an Arabian tale involving a lost pearl, Yas Waterworld combines touches of the traditional (the architecture and souk-style shopping and refreshment areas) with the very latest in water entertainment and technology. As well as kids' pools, a lazy river and an interactive pearl diving attraction, the park has some white-knuckle fun in the form of a suspended rollercoaster with integrated water guns, a six-person hydromagnetic tornado ride, a mammoth 'watercoaster', the region's first aqualoop and many more. A fantastic day out.

Wildlife

Abu Dhabi Falcon Hospital > p.vii, 137, 186
Nr Abu Dhabi International Airport,
Off Sweihan Rd Al Shamkha 02 575 5155
falconhospital.com
Map 3 D3
Abu Dhabi Falcon Hospital opened in 1999. Affiliated with the Environment Agency – Abu Dhabi (ead.ae/en), the team of specialists here provide diagnosis, treatment and disease prevention for falcons, other bird species and even poultry. Renowned for its work in the field, ADFH provides training opportunities to veterinary practitioners, students and technicians

WORLD'S BIGGEST FASTEST TORNADO

Live the ultimate water adventure

The UAE's first mega waterpark brings you 43 exhilarating rides, slides and attractions including 4 world-exclusives. Raise your heartbeat on the world's biggest tornado ride, float down the lazy river, or shop in the souk. Bring the whole family for a day of mega thrills, entertainment and fun.

YAS ISLAND

Yas Waterworld
ABU DHABI

yaswaterworld.com

Parts, Beaches & Attractions

from around the world. Responding to keen interest from the general public, the hospital also offers guided two hour tours on weekdays (these must be booked in advance). Contact the hospital on the number above or see the website for more information. Also on this site is the Animal Shelter (abudhabianimalshelter.com).

Abu Dhabi Wildlife Centre
Al Ain Rd Mussafah 050 7218 169
Map 3 D3
Abu Dhabi Wildlife Centre was created with a vision of caring for sick and orphaned animals – specifically cheetahs. It is now a fully fledged rehabilitation and breeding centre for endangered species and rare animals. Entrance costs Dhs.65 for adults, while kids under the age of 12 get in for Dhs.35; the prices are inclusive of an informative and entertaining 60 minute long tour of the facilities. The centre is open for educational visits too – call to arrange in advance.

Wild Times
Although the animal offerings in Abu Dhabi itself may be limited to Emirates Park Zoo, there are several high quality offerings beyond the city limits that are well worth a visit for wildlife lovers. Al Ain Zoo (p.238) is undoubtedly the best, with tie-ins with the world-renowned San Diego Zoo. However, Sharjah has the Arabian Wildlife Centre and Children's Farm (p.254) and there's also Dubai's Ras Al Khor wildlife sanctuary (04 606 6822) which is a stopping-off point for thousands of migrating birds each year, including more than 1,500 flamingos.
　　Head out to the islands off Abu Dhabi's coastline to see more of Mother Nature's best work. Arabia's biggest nature reserve, the Arabian Wildlife Park, is out on Sir Bani Yas (Out Of The City, p.243), while there are several other sanctuaries that can only be accessed by boat (p.198).

Emirates Park Zoo
35km from Abu Dhabi, Al Bahya 02 563 3100
emiratesparkzoo.com
Map 3 D2
The Emirates Park Zoo is located 35 kilometres outside the city on the road to Dubai. The zoo offers children the chance to get up close to their favourite animals, combining learning with touch. There are a number of interactive attractions, while the five acre zoo houses peacocks, ostriches, ibex, camels, horses, raccoons, ferrets, and exotic fish and birds, with anacondas and hippos soon to be added to the 2,000 species already on display. The zoo is a good option for kids' parties, while children can even volunteer at the zoo, helping

to take care of the animals. An equestrian school is also set to open on site in the near future. The park is open every day; see the website for more details.

International Fund For Houbara Conservation > p.v
Off East Rd Al Nahyan 02 693 4513
houbarafund.org
Map 2 M10
The International Fund for Houbara Conservation is a global organisation dedicated to the restoration and preservation of the Houbara bustard, an endangered bird which has migrated past the Arabian Peninsula for centuries. The centre in Abu Dhabi focuses on the breed and release programmes, and the organisation organises tours of its facilities or can go into schools or other groups to explain all about the Houbara bustard, its importance and the role the IFHC plays.

Amusement Centres

Action Zone
Mina Centre Al Meena 02 673 4577
actionzoneuae.com
Map 1 D2
Action Zone is big, bright and noisy – a kid's paradise. There are themed carousels, amusement rides, a bungee trampoline, video games and a climbing maze. Food is served and birthday parties hosted. To play, you purchase a swipe card (Dhs.3) and load it with credit. Games are Dhs.3 to Dhs.20. Open weekdays from 10:00 to 23:00 and 00:00 on weekends.

Al Forsan International Sports Resort
Nr Abu Dhabi Golf Club & Resort Madinat Khalifa A (Khalifa City A) 02 556 8555
alforsan.com
Map 1 P8
Al Forsan is the ultimate amusement and activity centre for those who like the great outdoors, with go-karting, off-road buggying, a variety of paintball grounds, rifle and clay pigeon shooting, archery, a complete equestrian centre and a cable ski watersports lake. There are also tennis and basketball courts, swimming pools and a handful of restaurants. Enough to keep the whole family busy for a year or two, then!

Fun City
Marina Mall Breakwater 02 681 5527
funcity.ae
Map 2 D1
Themed as a tropical forest, the park has a dramatic entrance built into a rock with the sound of thunder crashing all around. An array of computer and video games, carousels and other funfair facilities await. This is certainly not a 'learning through play' centre, but

Under Starter's Orders...

Ferrari World has thrillseekers, fans of Italian performance cars and motorsports addicts all purring in delight.

The UAE has made catching up an art form. Where once there were sleepy fishing villages, vast sandy expanses and shipyards full of dhows, we now see majestic towers, sprawling communities and cutting-edge marinas.

Resorts, restaurants and attractions have all risen from the desert sands but the one thing that was strangely lacking until late 2010 – a top quality theme park. Amazing waterparks, yes (and another one has been added since, right next to Ferrari World), but due to the long delays affecting the mammoth Dubailand project, fans of white-knuckle rides, roaring rollercoasters and high speed rushes had to look elsewhere for their kicks. Not so any more. Ferrari World is slated as 'the world's biggest indoor theme park' and we certainly wouldn't challenge the claim. Part theme park, part simulator and part museum/learning centre for the legendary Italian brand, Ferrari World has won the hearts of UAE petrolheads and visitors alike.

Out-and-out theme park fans should be impressed by the Formula Rossa – billed as the world's fastest rollercoaster, it reaches speeds of up to 240km/h. It's so fast riders have to wear safety goggles. The G-forces an F1 driver experiences are imitated by a 62m high ride that drops vertically through the park's roof, while a flume style water ride leads visitors through a series of twists, turns, rises and falls based on the workings of a Ferrari 599 engine.

State-of-the-art simulators used to train Ferrari drivers give a realistic experience of being in the breakneck hustle and bustle of a real Grand Prix, while young wannabe Schumachers and Alonsos can attend a driver school.

If fast paced thrills and spills aren't your thing, there are also plenty of more demure and educational attractions – especially for those with an interest in cars and Italy. Bell'Italia is an aerial tour of a miniature Italy, where all manner of traditional Italian foods and flavours are on offer. And anyone who has ever wanted, well, just about anything adorned with the famous 'prancing horse' logo won't go home disappointed after a visit to the flagship store.

Ferrari World Abu Dhabi is open Tuesday to Sunday from 11:00 until 20:00 and general admission tickets cost Dhs.225. For further details and current news and event, log onto ferrariworldabudhabi.com.

a high-tech, bright lights amusement outlet – and a good option for keeping kids busy while you shop. To get started, you need to purchase a play credit card (Dhs.3) which is then loaded with as much credit as you like. Games and rides cost Dhs.10 to Dhs.12.

Fun World
Al Muhairy Bldg, Shk Hamdan Bin Mohammed St
Al Manhal 02 632 2255
Map 2 K4
Fun World has a range of computer games that are intended to encourage kids to draw, paint and solve puzzles; they can also thread beads and try their hand at sand art. There's a soft play area for the little ones (Dhs.15), a coffee shop and a children's hairdresser all on the same floor. You need to purchase a Fun World credit card (Dhs.3) that you load with credit so your child can access the games (Dhs.3.50 to Dhs.8 each).

FunZone
Al Mariah Mall Markaziya East 02 677 1741
almariah.com
Map 2 P3
This indoor family entertainment centre has popular arcade games from bumper cars to video games and virtual reality simulators.

Kidoos Entertainment
Abu Dhabi Mall Tourist Club Area 02 645 9070
kidoosentertainment.com
Map 2 S5
Kidoos is a good and busy play club for younger children. There is plenty for youngsters to do with a large, soft play area, a sand pit, an art centre, numerous computers and even a small climbing wall. Refreshments are also available. Operating hours are 10:00 to 22:00 daily except Thursday (10:00 to 23:00) and Friday (14:00 to 23:00). Admission costs Dhs.35 on weekdays, and Dhs.45 from Thursday to Saturday.

Murjan Splash Park
Khalifa Park Al Matar 050 878 1009
adm.gov.ae
Map 1 K7
Located inside Khalifa Park, this is like a mini waterpark, with lots of water-based games and rides aimed at kids aged 11 and under. Being indoors, it's a good option for those warm summer months. Tuesdays and Wednesdays are ladies' days.

Play & Learn
Marina Mall Breakwater 02 681 5990
Map 2 D1
Located near to the cinema at Marina Mall, Play & Learn offers computer and PlayStation games for older children, along with a soft play area, a sand pit, an art centre and kitchen facilities for younger family

members, who will enjoy the crafts and dressing-up, while parents tend to take heart from the fact that there's an emphasis on learning and development through play. Entrance is Dhs.45. There is also a branch at Al Raha Mall (02 556 5777).

Sparky's
Khalidiyah Mall Al Khalidiyah 02 635 4316
Map 2 H5
A large, shiny and brand new family fun centre that takes up a large section of Khalidiyah Mall's top level, Sparky's has a kids' roller coaster, bumper cars, a 4D cinema, a bowling alley, a football striker zone and a soft play area, as well as arcade games. Another Sparky's (02 559 1744) operates from Mazyad Mall.

Wanasa Land
Al Wahda Mall Al Dhafrah 02 443 7654
Map 2 M7
For younger children, this new centre has a large, soft play area and animal themed carousels and amusement rides. The older children have a choice of 45 high-tech computerised games, an electronic shooting range and five hair-raising funfair rides. The food court is next door and has nine restaurants and fastfood outlets. There is no entrance fee; rides start from Dhs.5 or you can buy a swipe card for your child and put a set amount of money on it.

OUT & ABOUT

The UAE has much more to offer than its headline-grabbing, metropolis-based attractions. Beyond the city limits, in all directions, is a varied and fascinating landscape that has great potential for exploring and leisure-time activities. Getting out into the deserts and wadis by 4WD is a must-do while you're an Abu Dhabi resident and, once you're out there, there are some super hiking and camping spots to take advantage of too. The sea that surrounds the country is also a great adventure playground, and the warm Gulf waters provide a wonderful opportunity to try snorkelling, diving and sailing.

Off-Roading
Al Ain: The oasis town (p.236) is worthy of a visit in its own right, while nearby are the imposing Jebel Hafeet and Hanging Gardens, a great trekking spot.

Liwa: A trip to Liwa (p.243) is one you'll never forget – it's one of the few remaining chances to experience unspoiled dunes. The drive from Abu Dhabi is long, more suitable for a two or three day camping trip, but the journey is worth it. Prepare for the most adventurous off-road driving the UAE has to offer, and some of its most incredible scenery.

Northern Emirates: For a full day out or weekend away, with some of the best driving in the Emirates, combine the mountains around Wadi Bih, near Ras Al Khaimah (p.256), with one of the interesting wadi routes on the east coast.

East Coast: From Abu Dhabi, the east coast (p.260) can be reached in about three hours. The mountains and beaches are fantastic spots for camping, barbecues and weekend breaks, as well as various other activities. There are some great wadi and mountain routes here, and the area is also renowned for its diving and snorkelling opportunities, particularly around Snoopy Island.

Hatta: The Hatta (p.246) region is home to the popular Big Red sand dune, a huge draw and a must-do challenge for off-roaders and quad bikers, as well as the Hatta Pools, a great swimming spot in the Hajar Mountains. For further information and tips on driving off-road, check out both the *UAE Off-Road Explorer* and *Oman Off-Road Explorer*. These books feature a multitude of detailed routes and give advice on how to stay safe, where to camp and things to do along the way.

If you want a wilderness adventure but don't know where to start, contact any of the major tour companies (see Tour Operators, p.231). All offer a range of desert and mountain safaris.

If you're really keen to learn, OffRoad-Zone (04 339 2449, offroad-zone.com), located in Jebel Ali on the way to Dubai, runs a driving centre at the Jebel Ali Shooting Club where you can practise tackling various obstacles that you might find while off-roading, including deep water, loose rocks and steep descents.

Camping

Constant sunshine and an awe-inspiring array of locations make camping a much-loved activity in Abu Dhabi and the UAE. In general, warm temperatures and next to no rain mean you can camp with much less equipment and preparation than in other countries, and many first-timers or families with children find that camping becomes their favourite weekend break.

For most, the best time to go is between October and April, as in the summer it can get unbearably hot sleeping outside. Choose between the peace and tranquillity of the desert, or camp among the wadis and mountains next to trickling streams in picturesque oases. Many good camp sites are easily accessible from tarmac roads so a 4WD is not always required. You can camp just about anywhere, but there are some stand-out spots that are super places to pitch up.

Jebel Yibir is the UAE's highest (named) peak and, as such, camping out on the mountain (there's a road

up to the summit) is a good option for the warmer months as the temperatures up there are much cooler than down below.

The Wadi Sidr off-road route leads to a plateau that offers some good places to camp, with great views, while both Fossil Rock (p.259) and the drive from Madam to Madah provide terrific, accessible dune driving and camping spots. On the outskirts of Al Ain, close to the border with Oman, camping near the mountains can be just as spectacular. The ground is rockier, and some of the driving can be questionable, with rocks the size of footballs scattered throughout the gravel tracks. Upon reaching a camping spot, however, the adventurous camper is blessed with solitude, amazing rock formations, wadis, and a sky bursting with stars. There are even waterfalls and pools to be found in this area of the country.

The ultimate camping experience is, without doubt, to be found in the sea of dunes at Liwa, where you can go to sleep beneath a perfect starry sky and then wake up in the morning completely surrounded by one of the world's most mesmerising dunescapes (see Out Of The City, p.243). For more information on off-road adventuring and places to camp, refer to the *UAE Off-Road Explorer*.

CARRY WHEN CAMPING

Although the UAE has low rainfall, care should be taken in and near wadis as flash floods can and do occur. Remember, it may be raining in the mountains, kilometres away from where you are, but the effects are no less risky. You should consider taking the following equipment:

- Tent
- Lightweight sleeping bag (or light blankets and sheets)
- Thin mattress (or air bed)
- Torches and spare batteries
- Cool box for food
- Water (always take too much)
- Camping stove, or BBQ and charcoal if preferred
- Firewood and matches
- Insect repellent and antihistamine cream
- First aid kit (including any personal medication)
- Sun protection (hats, sunglasses, sunscreen)
- Jumper/warm clothing for cooler evenings
- Spade
- Toilet rolls
- Rubbish bags (ensure you leave nothing behind)
- Navigation equipment (maps, compass, Global Positioning System)
- Mobile phone (fully charged)

Beginners' Guide To Desert Driving

Off-road driving is exciting and adventurous, but it shouldn't be undertaken lightly; it requires skill, the correct equipment and a little planning before venturing out for the first time.

The key to driving on sand is maintaining controlled momentum and always looking ahead so you can plan for obstacles before you reach them. Most of the tracks on routes such as Fossil Rock (see the feature in Out Of The City, p.259) shouldn't present any problems, but they will get you used to how your car handles on sand and the different style needed to driving on hard surfaces. Before you start driving, deflate your tyres to 15-18psi. This increases the surface area of the tyre in contact with the sand, providing added traction for the soft conditions and saving your engine from being overworked. Make sure you are in 4WD (high range), and use the lower gears at higher than normal revs. You will find you use first and second a lot, but on more open and flatter tracks, you will get into third and even fourth, and at times it will feel very similar to driving on the road. When the track becomes undulating or you head into the dunes, slow down, keep a steady

Don't worry too much about getting stuck – it happens to everyone. Clearing a little sand from around the wheels and getting a few people pushing will get most cars out of minor problems.

pace and stay alert for obstacles. You should try to use the accelerator more than anything else, barely touching the brakes or clutch. If you do brake, do so lightly and smoothly to avoid sinking into the sand.

At first, even small dunes can seem quite extreme, so take things carefully. Plan your ascents to take the smoothest route and try to reduce your speed so that you coast over the top of a rise or a dune at close to walking pace so you will be in control for the descent. Go easy on the gas – it is far better to fail to make a climb because you were going too slowly than to end up jumping over the top of a dune.

When you get over the top, brake gently and, if you decide to stop, do so just on the downward slope. This will allow you to start going again easily. You will often not know what the slope is like until you are right on it; point your car straight down the dune and let your engine do most of the controlling of your speed. Drivers of automatic cars can do the same using the accelerator; pressing down hard will change down gears, but you may need to use the gear stick to ensure the car doesn't change back up before you want it to, robbing you of the momentum and power you need to climb dunes. Descending, you will need to change into first or second so the car doesn't race away from you.

Don't worry too much about getting stuck, it happens to everyone. If you do, don't keep revving the engine – chances are it will just dig you in further. Get out of your car to assess the situation, and try to work out how it happened so you can learn for next time. Usually, clearing a little sand from around the wheels and getting a few people pushing will get most cars out of minor problems. If you are in deeper, you may need to dig the car free, lower the tyre pressures more or get someone to tow you out.

Essential Equipment

There are some basic technical requirements for anyone driving in the desert. A well-maintained and fully serviced vehicle, a spare tyre in good condition, a jack, a tool kit including everything to change a tyre, a sturdy plank or block of wood in case you need to change wheels in sand, a tow rope and shackles, a pressure gauge, and a shovel are all essential. And, as with any other time you venture out into the desert, you should always have at least one other car with you – even on the simplest routes you might get stuck deep enough to need towing out. Remember to make sure you have plenty of fuel in the tank too.

Other things that can help get you out of sticky situations include sand mats or trays (or your floor mats if you are not too attached to them), a compressor to re-inflate tyres, heavy duty gloves, jump leads, a fully charged mobile phone, and a GPS, which can help take the guesswork out of navigation. Also make sure everyone in your car has plenty of water, sun cream and a hat, and shoes rather than sandals, as the sand can still get very hot.

Hiking

Despite Abu Dhabi's flat terrain, spectacular hiking locations can be found just a few hours outside the city limits. In the very north of the UAE, the Ru'us Al Jibal Mountains contain the highest peaks in the area, standing proud at over 2,000 metres, while the impressive Hajar Mountains stretch from Musandam in the north all the way down to the Empty Quarter desert in the south. Inland, Al Ain provides some excellent hiking routes, with plenty of mountains, including the imposing Jebel Hafeet, teamed with seven lush oases. Routes range from short, easy walks leading to spectacular viewpoints, to all-day treks over difficult terrain, and can include major mountaineering. Some hikes follow centuries-old Bedouin and Shihuh mountain paths, a few of which are still being used. One of the easiest places to reach is the foothills of the Hajar Mountains on the Hatta Road, near the Oman border. After passing through the desert, the flat, stark, rugged outcrops transform

ADRENALINE SPORTS

Adrenaline junkies don't need to head out to sea or jet across to distant shores to get a taste of extreme adventure; there may not be any actual jumping out of a plane or stomach-in-chest feelings, but Spacewalk, located in the Abu Dhabi Country Club (p.178), is an indoor skydiving centre that uses a vertical wind tunnel to keep thrill-seekers flying for minutes at a time.

If driving extremely fast sounds more exhilarating, Yas Marina Circuit (p.294) holds periodic track days that allow drivers to try out the performance and handling of their own cars on the Grand Prix circuit before the Formula 1 racers take to the track again in November. Or, for a hefty fee, professional drivers take passengers along for the full F1 experience. Check out the website yasmarinacircuit.com or call 02 446 0384 for details.

For those who need to feel the rush more often, there's always the Dubai Autodrome (dubaiautodrome.com), where racers can rent different types of cars or just wheel around in go-carts, in addition to the regular track days.

Finally, if you're hankering after cooler climes and are missing your fix of powder and mountains, head to Ski Dubai (p.250) – the indoor piste in the heart of the city, complete with its very own 'black run'. Lessons for beginners are available, while experienced downhillers can go on Freestyle Night to get some serious air on the jumps, kickers and rails.

the landscape. Explore any turning you like, or take the road to Mahdah, along which you'll find several options. Other great areas for hiking and exploring include the mountains in and around Musandam, and the mountains near the east coast. The mountains in the UAE don't generally disappoint, and the further off the beaten track you get, the more likely you are to find interesting villages where residents live in much the same way as they did centuries ago.

For somewhere a bit further afield see *Oman Trekking*, a guide book from Explorer Publishing with pull-out maps covering major signed routes in Oman. As with any trip into the UAE 'outback', take sensible precautions. Tell someone where you are going and when you should be back, and don't forget to take a map, compass, GPS equipment and robust hiking boots. Don't underestimate the strength of the sun – take sunscreen and, most importantly, lots of water. For most people, the cooler and less humid winter months are the best season for serious mountain hiking. Be particularly careful in wadis (dry riverbeds) during the wet season as flash floods can immerse a wadi in seconds. Also note that there are no mountain rescue services in the UAE, so anyone venturing out should be reasonably experienced or accompanied by someone who knows the area. See Activities, p.277, for companies that offer organised hikes.

Diving

The UAE offers diving that's really very special; the lower Arabian Gulf and the Gulf of Oman will satisfy all tastes and levels of experience for divers and snorkellers alike. You can choose from over 30 wrecks in relatively shallow water, tropical coral reefs and dramatic coastlines that are all virtually undived. Better still, they're bathed in comparatively warm water all year round. Water temperatures range from a cooler 20°C in January to a warmer 35°C in July and August. Although the land temperatures can be in the high 40s in the summer months, it is rarely too hot when out at sea for dipping into the water. While the visibility is not quite as spectacular as in the best dive sites in the tropics, it's rarely a problem.

The UAE's coastal waters are home to a variety of marine species, coral life and quite a few shipwrecks, so you won't run out of stuff to see. You'll see some exotic fish, like clownfish and seahorses, and possibly even spotted eagle rays, moray eels, small sharks, barracuda, sea snakes and stingrays. Most of the wrecks are on the west coast, while the beautiful flora and fauna of coral reefs can be seen on the east coast.

There are many dive sites on the west coast that are easily accessible from Abu Dhabi. Cement Barge, Mariam Express and the MV Dara wrecks are some of the more popular dive sites. Off the east coast, a well-known dive site is Martini Rock, a small, underwater mountain covered with colourful soft coral, with a depth range of three to 19 metres. North of Khor Fakkan is the Car Cemetery, a reef that has thrived around a number of cars placed 16 metres below water. Visibility off both coasts varies by the time of the year; generally, it ranges from five to 20 metres.

DRIVE WITH CARE

To protect the environment from damage, you should try to stick to existing tracks rather than create new tracks across virgin countryside. While it may be hard to deviate from the track when wadi bashing, dunes are ever-changing, so obvious paths are less common. Although the sandy dunes may look devoid of life, there is a surprising variety of flora and fauna that exists.

The main safety precaution to take when wadi bashing is to keep your eyes open for rare, but not impossible, thunderstorms – the wadis can fill up quickly and you will need to make your way to higher ground pretty quickly to avoid flash floods.

Another option for diving enthusiasts is to take a trip to Musandam (p.263). This area, which is part of the Sultanate of Oman, is often described as the 'Norway of the Middle East' due to the many inlets and the way the sheer cliffs plunge directly into the sea. It offers some spectacular dive sites. Sheer wall dives with strong currents and clear waters are more suitable for advanced divers, while the huge bays, with their calm waters and shallow reefs, are ideal for the less experienced. Visibility here is between 10 and 35 metres. If you plan to travel to Khasab, the capital of the Musandam peninsula, you may not be able to take your own air tanks across the border and will have to rent from one of the dive centres there. You may also require an Omani visa. Alternatively, from Dibba on the UAE east coast, you can hire a fast dive boat to take you anywhere from five to 75 kilometres up the coast. The cost ranges between Dhs.150 and Dhs.500, for what is usually a two-dive trip.

There are plenty of dive companies in the UAE that can help you should you want to try diving for the first time, or improve on your existing diving skills (see Activities, p.280). Padi training is available from beginner level through to instructor qualifications. Most companies offer both tuition and straightforward dive outings, with equipment.

Snorkelling

Snorkelling is a great hobby and, with conditions in the UAE creating relatively calm waters for most of the year, this is the perfect place to get into it. Whatever your age or fitness levels, snorkelling will get you into the sea and the minute you get your first glimpse of bright reef life, you'll be hooked.

Snorkelling offers a different experience to diving, with many interesting creatures such as turtles, rays and even sharks all frequently seen near the surface. It's a great way for the family to enjoy an activity together and all you need is some basic equipment and you're ready to go.

You can pretty much snorkel anywhere off a boat – all you need is a mask and fins, and you'll likely see something swimming around – but there are certain areas where you're guaranteed to enjoy greater marine action. The east coast is a plum area for snorkelling and has the most diverse marine life. Most dive centres take snorkellers out on their boats (along with divers, and the trip lasts for about two hours in total). Some centres can make arrangements to take you to Shark Island (also called Khor Fakkan Island) where you can spend the day. They'll come and collect you at the time you agree on. If that's what you'd like to do, it's best to arrange this with your dive centre in advance. Depending on your swimming ability and the water conditions, you can go to Sandy Beach Hotel (p.262) and spend the day on the beach and swim out to Snoopy Island, just a short distance from shore. In winter time, the water recedes a long way and the distance you have to swim is even less – but the water temperature will be considerably cooler too.

The west coast is not so great, with the best places for seeing fish being the waters by harbour walls, but take care: on the outside of harbour walls the waves tend to bash against the rocks and you may get caught off guard by a rogue wave (created by boats in the construction areas). You can snorkel on the inside of the harbour walls, but the water there is rather still and tends to silt up. The fish also prefer the outside walls.

Water Choice

As well as boating, diving and snorkelling, there are plenty of other water-based activities to fill your leisure time with. Windsurfing, jet skiing and waterskiing are all available from various beachfront hotels and sports clubs (p.304), while canoeists and kayakers can take advantage of the mangroves and lagoons on both sides of Abu Dhabi island for some first-class exploring (see p.276). Kitesurfing (p.290) is a growing pastime worldwide, and there are a couple of good spots in town, with more out on the islands, down in Al Gharbia or up in Dubai, while surfing (p.304) is possible in the UAE, although the waves are a far cry from Hawaiian tubes. Stand up paddle boarding (p.304) is a relaxing way to view the coast of Abu Dhabi from a new vantage point and get fit at the same time. You can get inspiration watching the very best in action at the Al Gharbia Watersports Festival (p.28).

Musandam offers good snorkelling too, but the waters there can have strong currents so it's a good idea to go with a tour company and have a guide to point out the best sites. The best fish life is to be found between the surface and 10 metres below, so try to snorkel along the side of rocks and islands. There are a number of tour companies that offer dhow trips for dolphin watching and snorkelling, and the boats usually moor in areas that are safe to snorkel in (see Boat Tours p.230).

Boating

With calm waters and year-round sunshine, the UAE offers ideal conditions for those wishing to sample life on the ocean waves. A number of companies provide boat charters, offering everything from sundowner cruises of a couple of hours and overnight trips with snorkelling stopovers, to scuba diving excursions to remote destinations such as Musandam.

Large sailing yachts, speedboats and other motorboats can be hired for private charter and corporate events; other companies offer outings on dhows and also cater to weddings and birthday parties. Fishing trips and watersports packages are also available. If you're on the east coast and fancy a traditional boating experience, large independent groups can charter a dhow from the fishermen at Dibba. If you haggle you can usually knock the price down substantially.

Respected UAE charter companies operating out of Abu Dhabi include Belevari Marine (belevari.com), ART Marine (artmarine.net), Croatian Emirates (pyc. hr), Ocean Active (oceanactive.com) and Arabian Divers & Sportfishing Charters (fishabudhabi.com). See Activities, p.298, for more details and, if you're a boating enthusiast, pick up Explorer's *UAE Boating & Yachting* book.

SPECTATOR SPORTS

For eight months of the year, Abu Dhabi residents can enjoy a calendar packed with top-class sporting events, many of which attract world-class names from sports ranging from tennis to Formula 1 and sailing.

The UAE's sunny winter climate, its location within easy reach of Europe and Asia, its development of some excellent sporting facilities, and its ability to stump up monstrous sums as prize money mean the country is growing ever more attractive as a venue for international sporting associations to include on their schedules. All of this is great news for sport fans. From big headline events, such as the Grand Prix and FIFA Club World Cup, to regular tennis and golf tournaments, and even local horse and camel racing meets, there's an awful lot going on.

Boat Racing

With both the Abu Dhabi Grand Prix in November and then the Dubai Grand Prix in December, the UAE is the only country with two stops in the Class 1 World Power Boating Championship (class-1.com). These boats are something to behold, reaching speeds of 250km/h and sometimes barely even touching the water. In addition to Class 1 events, there is the F1 Abu Dhabi Grand Prix, the Wooden Power Boats Championship, the UAE Jet Ski Championships (see adimsc.ae for all those events), sailing competitions and dhow races throughout the year at the Abu Dhabi International Marine Sports Club.

Dubai International Marine Club (dimc.ae) is just as busy, if not more so, with many events planned in partnership with the ADIMSC. For something completely different, however, every year there's the Dubai Dragon Boat Festival (dubaidragonboat.com) in April, with teams from all over competing in the races.

Sailing is a sport that is really on the up in Abu Dhabi and the world's biggest sailing event, the Volvo Ocean Race (volvooceanrace.com), stopped in town during January 2012. The event saw racing teams, including the new Team Abu Dhabi, sail over 39,000 nautical miles of the world's most treacherous seas via ports around the world. Abu Dhabi was the first Middle East port ever to host the racers, and there was enormous excitement surrounding the event, which brought huge crowds to the capital.

Camel Racing

Camel racing? Seriously? This popular local sport is actually very serious business with racing camels changing hands for as much as Dhs.10 million each, while as much as Dhs.25 million in prizes is won each year. A camel owner with a star racer can do very well for himself, and it shows at the races as the owners drive alongside the track, keeping up with the animals. The Al Wathba Camel Race Track is 45km from Abu Dhabi, on the road to Al Ain. There are two tracks; the main one is grandstanded and the secondary track is out towards the Endurance Racing Center. If you run out of direction signs, just follow the herds of camels going to the tracks to train. Morning races take place throughout the winter on Thursday and Friday from as early as 06:30 to 08:30. Periodically, major races are held on public holidays like National Day. Admission to the track is free.

Racing Robots

Racing camels used to be ridden by children, but this practise has since been outlawed – and robotic jockeys have taken over. The operators follow the race in 4WDs while directing the jockeys by remote control – quite a bizarre sight.

Cricket

Sheikh Zayed Cricket Stadium, near Khalifa City A on Airport Rd, is host to many international matches of cricket. This is a popular sport in Abu Dhabi, largely thanks to the big number of expats from several cricket countries. In addition to recent test matches held at the venue, Pakistan has made the stadium its second home because of foreign teams' refusals to play in Pakistan due to security concerns. In fact, Pakistan has played all its 'home' one day internationals and Twenty20 games in Dubai or Abu Dhabi for over a year. There's almost always something going on at the stadium, with England training there last year in preparation for their series in India and other teams regularly using it for pre-season preparation. See emiratescricket.com.

Football

Football is as popular in the UAE as it is the world over and, in recent years, there has been plenty of action for fans of the game to watch. Abu Dhabi was awarded the honour of hosting the FIFA World Club Cup in 2009 and 2010, a tournament which saw the champions of each continent competing in a knock-out competition. Matches were held at Zayed Sports City and Mohammed bin Zayed Stadium. There's a strong domestic competition too – the UAE Football League – and attending one of these games makes for a really colourful experience. Emirati supporters are fanatical about their teams and there are some strong local rivalries. There are plenty of stars on display, with Fabio Cannavaro (Italy's 2006 World Cup winning captain and World Player of the Year) currently plying his trade at Dubai's Al-Ahli, while Argentinian legend Maradona was coach of Al Wasl. For information, see uaefa.ae.

Golf

Golf fans have plenty to keep them entertained throughout the year, with three major tournaments taking place in the UAE. First, the Abu Dhabi Golf Championship (abudhabigolfchampionship.com) is staged each January at the National Course at Abu Dhabi Golf Club, near Khalifa City A. The championship is the opening event on the European PGA Tour's Middle East-based Desert Swing Trio, with over $2 million in prize money given away each year.

Dubai, too, has become a major golf destination, with two world-class events held each year. The Dubai Desert Classic (dubaidesertclassic.com), held each February, has previously been won by the likes of Tiger Woods and Ernie Els. In addition, the Dubai World Championship (dubaiworldchampionship.com), held in November or December each year, is a major event: no fewer than 50,000 golf fans have turned up in previous years to witness the culmination of the European Tour's Race To Dubai.

A golfer's paradise

Horse Racing

Horse racing is extremely popular in the United Arab Emirates and is accessible to everyone through free admission to many race meetings. These are held in the afternoons or evenings throughout the cooler months (the season runs from November to early April). Emirates Racing Authority (emiratesracing.com) is the internationally recognised governing body for horse racing in the UAE and oversees all aspects of the sport. With four tracks spread among Abu Dhabi, Dubai and Sharjah, there are plenty of places to catch the action.

Abu Dhabi Equestrian Club (adec-web.com) in Al Mushrif hosts races on Sunday evenings beginning at 18:00 during the racing season, with show jumping and endurance events also taking place. Sharjah's Equestrian and Racing club holds a handful of events each year, but Dubai's tracks, Jebel Ali and the brand new supertrack Meydan, host the big races. The culmination and the highlight of the racing season is the Dubai World Cup (dubaiworldcup.com), the world's richest horse race, held every year in March at Meydan Racecourse.

Gambling is not allowed in the UAE, but everyone can take part in various free competitions to select the winning horses, with the ultimate aim of taking home prizes or cash.

It may be a fair drive from the city, lying up next to the Dubai border, but Ghantoot Racing & Polo Club (grpc.ae) is definitely worth a visit. It is the only club in Abu Dhabi that is dedicated to this equine sport that is growing rapidly in popularity throughout the region. The club has a modern infrastructure for sports and events, and the polo calendar is full of regular chukka tournaments and high profile international games that can be fun to watch. For a bit of a chuckle, look out for games of camel polo.

Tours & Sightseeing

Discover Abu Dhabi (side tab)

Motorsports

The Yas Marina Circuit (p.294) has been a boon to motorsports fans in the capital. Ever since the facility opened for the Grand Prix in 2009, announcements of new events just keep pouring in. In addition to the Grand Prix, easily the UAE's headline motor racing event, the circuit has held endurance races, drag racing, a GT1 battle of the brands and a leg of the Australian V8 Supercars. Check the website yasmarinacircuit.com for information on upcoming events.

Dubai Autodrome also hosts events of various categories all year round. The website dubaiautodrome.com lists a full calendar of events.

For fans of more rugged terrain, the Abu Dhabi Desert Challenge (abudhabidesertchallenge.com), which has stages right across the whole emirate, is the opening round of both the FIA and the FIM Cross Country Rally World Cups.

Desert Slickers

As well as the Abu Dhabi Desert Challenge (p.27), there are numerous other desert rally events that take place throughout the year right across the emirate and deep into the Liwa desert, like the dune drag races that see motors storm up the almost sheer face of Moreeb Dune. See emsfuae.org for the latest events.

Rugby

Although amateur club matches take place in Abu Dhabi, Al Ain and Dubai throughout the year (see Abu Dhabi Harlequins, p.297), the big rugby event takes place every December in Dubai, when fans and party-goers from the UAE and far beyond head to The Sevens Stadium on the Al Ain road for the Emirates Airline Dubai Rugby Sevens (dubairugby7s.com).

This 'light' version of the sport is fast paced and competitive, with young, up-and-coming international stars taking centre stage in the knock-out format. As much about the atmosphere as the sport, as evidenced by the hugely popular 'Rugby Rock' concert held on the final night of the event, The Sevens is without doubt one of the region's biggest parties and sporting spectacles.

However, rugby fans based in Abu Dhabi are now increasingly treated to one-off matches, such as the first round of the Asian 5 Nations Rugby tournament in April 2011.

Tennis & Squash

The UAE's tennis fans are blessed with a couple of stellar tournaments that help get the year off to a good start. First is the Abu Dhabi Mubadala World Tennis Championships (p.29), usually kicking off around the New Year's celebrations at the

International Tennis Complex at Zayed Sports City. For the past few years, the three-day tournament has attracted six of the top players in the world, including Roger Federer and Raphael Nadal, to the capital.

February sees the Dubai Duty Free Tennis Championships (p.27), which is held at the Aviation Club. It is a great opportunity to catch some of the top male and female players on the tour, such as previous winners Novak Djokovic and Caroline Wozniacki.

Endurance Racing

For those who like to watch athletes pushing their bodies to mind-altering limits, there's the Abu Dhabi International Triathlon (abudhabitriathlon.com) in March. Including a 3km swim in the lagoon at the Emirates Palace, a 200km bike section that travels the length of the island before zipping around the Yas Marina F1 circuit and a 20km run up and down the Corniche, spectators are sure to catch sight of plenty of iron men and women, including some of the biggest names in the sport, attracted by the early season race, exotic scenery and large prize purse.

Endurance athletes are also on show at January's Dubai Marathon (dubaimarathon.org) which, thanks to its flat, fast course and generous prize money, has also become one of the biggest in the calendar over the past few years, with spectators able to cheer on the likes of world record holder Haile Gebrselassie.

TOURS & SIGHTSEEING

What better way to experience Abu Dhabi than customised land, sea or sky tours? As exhilarating for those who are in the city for just a short time as they are for longtime residents, desert safaris or dhow cruises allow you to take in the beauty of the area while also getting a feel for the traditional culture. Abu Dhabi's spectacular geographic location makes for an ideal touring site and indeed, with the city's tourist numbers growing rapidly every year and millions of dirhams being pumped into promotional marketing for the emirate, the different types of tours and thrills will only continue to multiply in the years to come. Already, most tour companies offer desert safaris and dhow cruises, but some offer helicopter tours, as well as diving and snorkelling trips. Many tour companies will work with adventurers who want to customise their own experience.

The most classic option, however, is the desert safari. Expert drivers blast 4WD vehicles up, down and around massive dunes while passing old Bedouin villages and pointing out beautiful natural attractions. Mountain safaris lead passengers through the narrow wadis and steep passes of the Hajar Mountains. This tour makes for an exhilarating experience not to be missed. Most driving safaris include pick-up from your place of residence and lunch. Some end the day of wild driving at a replica Bedouin camp where passengers can watch a belly dancer, eat Arabic delicacies and smoke shisha. Many operators even run overnight safaris that combine desert and mountain safaris. When booking, it is often advisable to reserve spaces three or four days in advance.

Sick Of Safari

Even the milder, shorter safaris involve some fairly vigorous off-road driving and, if you tend to experience motion sickness in cars, the chances are that you won't enjoy the ride, especially as, in the middle of the desert, you can't really just get out. Equally, pregnant women, and anyone with back or neck problems, should probably avoid 4WD safaris.

Bus Tours

For a tourist wanting a quick peek at the main attractions of the city, a bus tour is the way to go and the Big Bus Tours (bigbustours.com, 800 244 287) has a fleet of London-style double decker buses that provide a hop-on hop-off service, with commentary for attractions across Abu Dhabi and Dubai. In Abu Dhabi, Marina Mall is the main starting point, but riders can get on or off at any of the 11 stops that include Sheikh Zayed Mosque, Abu Dhabi Mall, the Meena souks, the Corniche, the Public Beach and Heritage Village.

Desert & Mountain Tours

Desert safaris are by far the most popular variety of tours available, perhaps because a good safari offers many activities in one day. Starting with an exciting

ride up and down some of the desert's biggest dunes, you can try sand skiing before watching the sun set over the dunes. After driving a short distance further to a permanent Bedouin-style camp, you are treated to a sumptuous barbecue, followed by shisha, belly dancing, camel rides and henna painting.

You can vary the length of your safari, choosing to stay overnight or combine it with a trip into the mountains, if desired. A safari trip into the mountains is highly recommended, if only to see just how much the landscape changes from orange sand dunes to craggy mountains within the space of a couple of short kilometres.

The approximate cost for a desert safari is Dhs.150 to Dhs.350 (overnight up to Dhs.500). Many companies offer these types of tours (see Main Tour Operators, p.231); following is a selection of typical itineraries you can choose from.

Don't Forget Your Camera

The UAE is absolutely stacked with picturesque sights, so keep your camera handy and don't forget to use it to capture your memories and keep them forever. See p.320 of Shopping for information on where to purchase or repair camera equipment.

Dune Dinners

Enjoy some thrilling off-road desert driving before settling down to watch the sun set behind the dunes. Starting around 16:00, tours typically pass camel farms and fascinating scenery that provide great photo opportunities. At an Arabian campsite, enjoy a delicious dinner and the calm of a starlit desert night, returning around 22:00.

Exploring the desert

Tours & Sightseeing

Full-Day Safari

This day-long tour usually heads out into the vast expanses of desert dunes, passing the occasional traditional Bedouin villages or camel farm in the desert on the way. Between taking on sand dunes of varying colours and heights, a cold buffet lunch may be provided in the wide open expanses before the drive home.

Hatta Pools Safari

Hatta is a quiet, old-fashioned town nestled in the foothills of the Hajar Mountains, famed for its fresh water rock pools that you can swim in. The full-day trip usually includes a stop at the Hatta Fort Hotel, where you can enjoy the pool, landscaped gardens, archery, and nine-hole golf course. Lunch is served either in the hotel, or alfresco in the mountains.

Mountain Safari

Normally, a full-day tour takes you to the east coast, heading inland at Dibba and entering the spectacular Hajar Mountains. You will travel through rugged canyons onto steep winding tracks, past terraced mountainsides and ancient stone houses that offer a glimpse of life as it used to be. The journey homewards can often take in Masafi Market on the way.

Overnight Safari

This 24 hour tour starts at about 15:00 with a drive through the dunes to a Bedouin-style campsite. Dine under the stars, sleep in the fresh air and wake to the smell of freshly brewed coffee, before heading for the mountains. The drive takes you through spectacular rugged scenery, past dunes and along wadis, before stopping for a buffet lunch and returning to Abu Dhabi.

Boat Tours

There's nothing like a breezy evening under the stars just off the Corniche while taking in Abu Dhabi's arresting skyline. Dinner cruises range from hearty affairs to more romantic versions, and most companies offer private charters. Alternatively, book a daytime tour to soak up the sun while gliding through the sparkling, turquoise waters of the Gulf, admiring Abu Dhabi's stunning coastline with its countless islands and beautiful mangroves. In addition to organised sightseeing tours, there are also catamaran rentals and the inflatable speedy crafts of The Yellow Boats (p.231).

Al Dhafra

Nr Meena Fish Market Al Meena 02 673 2266
aldhafra.net
Map 2 S1
As well as dinner cruises, Al Dhafra has several traditional Arabic dhows available for charter. Most clients take their own equipment as there is only a

limited amount on board. Food can be supplied at additional cost. Charters cost from Dhs.600 per hour for a dhow that can take 20 people. For more details on Al Dhafra, see the review on p.367 in Going Out.

Arabian Divers & Sportfishing Charters > p.281

Nr UAE Central Bank, Marina Al Bateen Resort
Al Bateen 050 614 6931
fishabudhabi.com
Map 2 C6
As well as sport-fishing, scuba and snorkelling, this firm offers sightseeing trips and chartered tours that you can tailor, from island hopping to cruises and dolphin watching.

Dhow & Out

Large, independent groups can charter a dhow from fishermen at Dibba on the east coast to travel up the coast to Musandam (p.263). Be prepared to haggle – around Dhs.2,500 per day for a 20-25 person dhow, or Dhs.100 per hour for a smaller one is standard. Take your own food and water, as there's nothing onboard except ice lockers. Conditions are basic, but you'll have the freedom to plan your own route to see the Musandam's fjord-like scenery. Turtles and dolphins can often be seen from the boat. It's also possible to arrange stops along the coast and take camping equipment, although you can sleep on board.

Belevari Marine

Emirates Palace Marina Breakwater 02 659 4144
belevari.com
Map 2 A1
A full-service company that charters luxury yachts, speed boats, dhows and sailing boats and can provide a wide range of services, from captains to on-boat catering.

Noukhada Adventure Company

Al Meena St Al Meena 02 650 3600
noukhada.ae
Map 2 S2
Offers fantastic sailing and kayaking adventures along the coastline and through the mangroves. Options start with two-hour kayak tours and go through to full moon tours and sailing trips to wildlife rich Belghailam Island.

Sea Cruiser

050 800 9495
seacruiser.ae
Map 3 D3 Halat Al Bahraini / Al Maya Island
The Sea Cruiser boats are tourist vessels that have large air-conditioned interiors with huge wrap-

Boating off the Corniche

the amazing F1 track, taking in Al Raha Beach, Sheikh Zayed Mosque and Emirates Palace on the way back. Prices vary depending on the tour.

Seawings

Jebel Ali Golf Resort Dubai **04 807 0708**
seawings.ae
Map **3 E2** Metro **Jebel Ali**
Offers aerial tours all over the UAE, including Abu Dhabi, in its fleet of seaplanes. Tours last 35-45 minutes, depending on take-off point, and up to nine people can fly at a time. Head over to the Yas Marina Circuit or check out the Bu Tinah nature reserve.

Main Tour Operators

Almost all tour operators offer the main types of excursions: city tours, desert safaris and mountain safaris. Some, however, offer more unique activities, such as fishing or diving trips, expeditions to see the Empty Quarter in Liwa (p.243), helicopter tours and desert driving courses. The main tour companies and those that offer something a little bit different are listed in this section, along with some of their highlights – contact them directly for full programmes.

around windows, as well as plenty of space out on deck. Private chartering is possible, while there are a range of packages, such as Corniche, Al Maya island, watersports, Yas Island and a family package.

The Yellow Boats

Marina Mall Breakwater **800 8044**
theyellowboats.com
Map **2 D1**
These high speed RIBs offer tours of Abu Dhabi waters and the nearby islands and are not for the faint of heart. The 30 minute rides where the skipper shows off the boat's abilities cost Dhs.150. The boats can also be chartered by the hour or hired for corporate events.

Aerial Tours

With views as varying as towering skyscrapers and shifting sand dunes, rocky peaks and turquoise waters, Abu Dhabi reveals plenty of its wonders from the air. Swoop over the cityscape in a helicopter or take in the serenity of the desert from a graceful hot air balloon. Either option will make memories to last a lifetime.

Falcon Aviation Services

Al Bateen Executive Airport Al Matar **02 444 8866**
falconaviation.ae
Map **1 J7**
Take off from Marina Mall in a luxurious six-seater Eurocopter EC130 for a bird's eye view over Abu Dhabi, Saadiyat and Yas. A 20 minute tour costs Dhs.625.

Hala Abu Dhabi

Etihad Bldg, Muroor St Madinat Zayed **02 617 7811**
halaabudhabi.ae
Map **2 M5**
Helicopter tours in an EC130 or a Bell 206 sweep the Corniche before heading out over Saadiyat and Yas to

Absolute Adventure

Al Diyafah Centre Dubai **04 345 9900**
adventure.ae
Metro **Al Jafiliya**
Organises a host of activities, including mountain biking, trekking, climbing, kayaking, watersports, 4WD safaris and motorised hang glider flights. Also offers training for outdoor pursuits instructors, and can organise treks, safaris and travel to far flung places like Nepal and Mongolia. The activity centre, located directly on Dibba's beach, can accommodate 14 people for group stays with a barbecue on the beach.

Tour Tips

If you are booking a tour, make sure you call around to get the best price. Abu Dhabi is dedicated to discounts, particularly at this point in time, and you can often get a better rate as a full-time resident. Just remember, it is all about putting on the charm – not being a cheeky customer. Also, keep an eye on local newspapers and magazines throughout the year for some great sightseeing discounts.

Abu Dhabi Travel Bureau

Nr Chamber of Commerce, Corniche Rd
Markaziya West **02 622 1100**
abudhabitravelbureau.com
Map **2 L2**
One of the UAE's biggest travel and tour operators with 40 years of experience in the UAE and 14 offices

Tours & Sightseeing

throughout Abu Dhabi alone, with another in Al Ain. Organises all manner of travel, including desert safaris, cruises, cultural trips and educational visits.

Advanced Travel & Tourism
Nr Qatar Airways, Shk Hamdan Bin Mohammed St Markaziya East **02 634 7900**
advancedtravels.net
Map **2 N3**
General agent offering tour packages and family trips throughout the UAE, and the greater region.

Al Badeyah Eyes Tourism
Nr Al Safeer Center Mohammed Bin Zayed City **02 559 6155**
abet-uae.com
Map **1 N12**
Based close to Al Raha Beach, this tour company offers desert safaris, dhow cruises and city tours.

Al Badie Travel Agency
Al Badie Tower, Al Nasr St Markaziya West **02 632 2775**
albadietravel.com
Map **2 K3**
Large, general travel agency that can organise everything from golf trips and F1 stays to off-roading in the Empty Quarter, culinary tours and Bedouin style desert safaris, with sand skiing and falconry thrown in for good measure.

Fascinating Falconry

Falconry is a national sport in the UAE and the two hour guided tour available at the Abu Dhabi Falcon Hospital provides a unique opportunity to learn about these impressive creatures. The guided tour, which needs to be booked online (falconhospital. com), is conducted twice daily from Sunday to Thursday. Also on site is the Animal Shelter (abudhabianimalshelter.com). Alternatively, contact the International Fund for Houbara Conservation (houbarafund.org) which is an organisation dedicated to the protection and conservation of the Houbara bustard. Groups can tour the fund's Abu Dhabi facility, or experts can head to groups and schools to explain all about this important bird.

Arabian Adventures
Emirates Travel Shop, Corniche Rd Al Khalidiyah **02 691 1711**
arabian-adventures.com
Map **2 P2**
One of the big tour operators in the country, Arabian Adventures offers a range of tours and itineraries including desert safaris, city tours, sand skiing, dhow cruises, camel riding, and wadi and dune bashing.

Cyclone Tours & Travels
Omeir Holidays Bldg, Shk Khalifa Bin Zayed St Markaziya East **02 627 6275**
cyclonetours.com
Map **2 N3**
Offers everything from urban city tours of Abu Dhabi and Al Ain to overnight desert safaris in remote locations. Desert driving courses, fishing trips and dinner cruises on traditional dhow boats are also available to arrange on request.

Desert Adventures
Al Raha Beach Hotel Al Raha **02 556 6155**
desertadventures.com
Map **1 R7**
This Dubai-based company (with an Abu Dhabi office) is well-known for organising tours throughout the Emirates and the wider Gulf region. From cultural city tours to culinary tours, safari adventures and cruises in traditional dhows, the company is experienced in organising specialist experiences.

Desert Rangers
Nr American Hospital, Street 18 Dubai **04 357 2200**
desertrangers.com
Metro **Oud Metha**
Desert Rangers offers one of the most comprehensive ranges of tours and safaris, including a number of special interest trips such as dune buggy safaris, rock climbing, deep sea fishing. Different activities take place across the Emirates; see the website for details.

Emirates Adventures
Al Salam St Tourist Club Area **02 644 5117**
eatours.ae
Map **2 R3**
Offers city tours of Abu Dhabi, Dubai and Al Ain, as well as several desert safari options, with dune buggy tours and wadi treks.

Emirates Travel Express
Nr Clock Tower Signal, Main St Al Ain **03 765 0777**
eteholidays.ae
Map **4 E2**
With 30 years of experience in the United Arab Emirates, Emirates Travel Express offers the usual range of city tours, safaris and dhow cruises, but also caters for those with a taste for adventure further afield, offering cruises and safaris in India, the Masai Mara and more.

Hala Abu Dhabi
Etihad Bldg, Muroor St Madinat Zayed **02 617 7811**
halaabudhabi.ae
Map **2 M5**
A part of the massive Etihad travel group, Hala organises a wide range of tours and sightseeing

activities, from desert safaris and dhow dinner cruises to helicopter tours and Hatta treks, city highlights tours and helicopter trips.

Kurban Tours

Nr Arab Bank, Al Nasr St Markaziya West
02 555 0566
kurbantours.com
Map **2 K3**
Tour company specialising in the UAE, Lebanon and Oman, with trips including golfing experiences, cultural sightseeing, Bedouin-style desert safaris, east coast wildlife tours, deep sea fishing and intrepid Hatta adventures.

Net Tours

Sheraton Abu Dhabi Hotel & Resort Markaziya East
02 679 4656
netgroupauh.com
Map **2 Q2**
Covers all the main tour types with both half day and overnight desert safaris, Liwa desert adventures, tours of all the UAE's main cities, helicopter tours, dhow cruises and adventure sports breaks, including cycling, hiking, dune buggying, sand skiing and camel riding. It also has a branch in Al Ain (03 768 7400).

Omeir Travel Agency

Airlines Tower, Shk Khalifa Bin Zayed St
Markaziya East **02 612 3456**
omeir.com
Map **2 N3**
One of the UAE's largest general travel agencies with 50 years' experience in the region, Omeir Travel Agency offers all the usual tours – desert, city and cruises – as well as some extremely good offers on local accommodation, should you wish to flesh out your tour with an overnight stay away from home one weekend. The company has a second branch in Al Ain (03 711 4000).

Orient Tours

Nr Sheraton Kalidiyah Markaziya West **02 667 5609**
orienttours.ae
Map **2 J4**
Orient Tours provides the usual gamut of city tours, desert and mountain safaris, 4WD adventures and cruises. The company also caters for corporate events and private parties on request.

Safar Travel & Tourism

Liwa St Markaziya East **02 418 0888**
safar.ae
Map **2 N3**
Safar Travel & Tourism has a dedicated adventure arm looking after tours and sightseeing. Island tours, desert safaris in a 4WD or driving quads, cultural city

tours, wadi trekking, wildlife adventures, outdoor shows, dhow dinner cruises, fishing and watersports trips are all on the menu.

Salem Travel Agency

Muroor Rd Madinat Zayed **02 621 8000**
salemtravelagency.com
Map **2 N5**
The agency operates Arabian Odyssey – a tour operator that is dedicated to themed trips throughout the United Arab Emirates. The tours, trips and experiences on offer include falconry tours, city tours, cruises, treks, desert safaris and hot air ballooning. The company also has an Al Ain branch (03 766 2915) for excursions departing from the UAE's Garden City.

Sunshine Tours

Various locations **02 444 9914**
adnh.com
Sunshine Tours offers a wide range of tours from heritage site visits to scenic helicopter rides and dhow cruises on Abu Dhabi's turquoise waters. Desert safaris and overnight trips can also be booked through the operator, while excursions to some of the most popular destinations in other emirates can be arranged on request.

Mangroves surround Abu Dhabi

Out Of The City

OUT OF ABU DHABI

Abu Dhabi may have everything from mangroves and marinas to boutiques and beaches, but there are a number of interesting and varied areas outside the city and country that deserve a place in your weekend plans. There are six other emirates in the UAE and five other countries in the GCC, all of which warrant exploration.

All six of the other emirates in the UAE – Dubai, Sharjah, Ras Al Khaimah, Umm Al Quwain, Fujairah and Ajman – are within a few hours' drive of the centre of the capital. From the sleepy streets of Umm Al Quwain and the rugged mountains of Ras Al Khaimah to the cultural grandiose of Sharjah, each emirate has something different to offer, and each can be explored, at least in part, over a weekend. The country's vast deserts and harsh-looking mountains are equally accessible with a copy of the *UAE Off-Road Explorer* and can be reached easily and quickly if you need to escape civilisation for a while.

With Abu Dhabi and Dubai both being international travel hubs, it's easy to find quick, cheap flights to the neighbouring GCC countries of Oman, Saudi Arabia, Qatar, Bahrain and Kuwait, none of which are more than an hour and a half flight away. Oman is considered by many to be one of the most beautiful and culturally interesting countries in the region, and it can easily be reached and explored by car – Muscat is only a five hour drive from Abu Dhabi.

Like the UAE, the countries in the GCC are growing at a phenomenal rate and are trying to attract more tourism. Many hotels in the GCC, including in the UAE, regularly hold promotions or offer discounted rooms, especially in the summer months. It's a good idea to sign up for the mailing lists of regional travel agencies, such as Salem Travel (salemtravelagency.com) and Dnata (dnata.ae), to find out about any weekend getaway packages they offer.

ABU DHABI – REST OF THE EMIRATE

Al Ain

Al Ain is the capital of the eastern region and Abu Dhabi emirate's second city. Its greenery and the fact that it is the birthplace and childhood home of Sheikh Zayed bin Sultan Al Nahyan, the former (and much-loved) ruler of the UAE, gives it special status in the hearts and minds of the people.

In the days before the discovery of oil, the journey from Abu Dhabi to Al Ain took five days by camel. Today, it only takes an hour and a half by car and most tour companies offer excursions to this fascinating Garden City that straddles the border with the Sultanate of Oman; the UAE side is known as Al Ain

and the Oman side as Buraimi. The fortresses around the city, 18 in all, illustrate Al Ain's importance as part of the ancient trade route from Oman to the Arabian Gulf, and there is evidence of the area having been inhabited for at least the last 7,000 years. Indeed, the city's archaeological legacy is of such significance that Al Ain is now a Unesco World Heritage Site.

Throughout his life, Sheikh Zayed pursued his vision of creating an oasis of greenery in the desert by initiating a series of 'greening' projects. As a result, Al Ain's seven natural oases are now surrounded by tree-lined streets and beautiful urban parks. The main Al Ain Oasis is home to palm plantations, many of which are working farms. The palms provide welcome shade and a haven from the noise and bustle of the city. Most of the farms still use the ancient falaj system of irrigation, which taps into underground water. If you do go exploring in the palm plantations, it is best to stick to the paved areas that weave between the walled-in farms. On the outskirts of the city, you will also find a Camel & Livestock Souk (p.237) which is worth a visit.

Jebel Hafeet

Jebel Hafeet is unmissable – in more ways than one. Rising abruptly from the surrounding countryside, it dominates the area, and the views from the top are stunning. On a clear day you can see the surrounding desert plains, oases, wadis, and the Hajar Mountain range in the distance. At 1,240 metres, the mountain provides a dramatic backdrop to the city, which itself is 300 metres above sea level. The winding road to the top is regularly referred to by international motoring magazines as one of the world's best driving roads. It is in excellent condition with a number of strategically placed viewpoints, all with plenty of parking spaces (and portable toilets). It snakes its way to the top through a series of twists, turns and hairpins. The more energetic could try cycling – a gruelling hour or so up, then 10 minutes down. The five-star Mercure Grand Hotel (p.240) is set in a commanding position, at 915 metres, with splendid views of the surrounding area.

The hot springs at the base of Jebel Hafeet are reputed to have healing properties – although the water temperature may be just too hot in the summer – and the facilities at the striking Green Mubazzarah Park (03 783 9555) include chalet accommodation and a boating lake. There's also the Al Ain Al Fayda Resthouse (03 783 8333) which has a really lovely setting and provides a brilliant green contrast to the starkness of Jebel Hafeet towering above.

Buraimi

Visitors from the UAE don't need a visa to enter the Oman side of the Buraimi Oasis, as long as you are an official resident in the UAE. In 2008, the Al Mudeef border was closed to non-GCC traffic, but the Al Hili

Al Ain Attractions

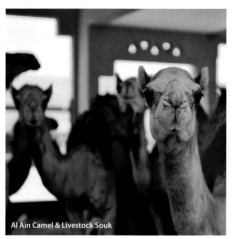

Al Ain Camel & Livestock Souk

Al Ain Camel & Livestock Souk
Nr Bawadi Mall, Zayed Bin Sultan St Al Ain
adach.ae
Map **4 E3**
Conditions in the souk have improved dramatically with spacious pens for the animals and ample parking for visitors. A visit to the market is a fantastic way to mingle with locals and witness camel and goat trading like it's taken place for centuries. The locals arrive in pick-ups laden with animals and settle in to do some hard bargaining. Arrive early, preferably before 09:00, to soak up the true essence and atmosphere.

Al Ain Ladies Park
Zayed Al Awwal St Al Ain
Map **4 D2**
Commonly known as Basra Park, this quiet garden is for women and children only (boys under the age of 10). There are plenty of benches under the shady trees. Play areas with swings, slides and climbing frames are sure to keep the kids busy.

Al Ain National Museum
Nr Sultan Fort, Zayed Bin Sultan St Al Ain
03 764 1595
adach.ae
Map **4 E2**
Divided into three main sections – archaeology, ethnography and gifts – the presentations include photographs, Bedouin jewellery, musical instruments, weapons and a traditional majlis.

Al Ain Oasis
Nr Al Ain National Museum Al Ain **03 763 0155**
adach.ae
Map **4 E2**
This impressive oasis in the heart of the city is filled with palm plantations, many of which are still working farms. The cool, shady walkways transport you from the heat and noise of the city to an otherworldly, tranquil haven. You are welcome to wander through the plantations, but it's best to stick to the paved areas. The farms have plenty of working examples of falaj, the traditional irrigation system which has been used for centuries to tap into underground wells. There are eight different entrances, some of which have arched gates, and there is no entry fee.

Al Ain Palace Museum
Al Ain St Al Ain **03 751 7755**
adach.ae
Map **4 D2**
The museum was originally a palace belonging to Sheikh Zayed bin Sultan Al Nahyan, dating back to 1937. Now, it tells the story of its previous owner and

checkpoint is still open, either for a trip through to Buraimi and back (with only passport and residence visa checks), or you can get stamped out of the UAE here if you are planning on entering Oman.

The entry point to Oman is about 50 kilometres from the centre of Al Ain, along the road to Sohar. The only real problem you should have in getting from Al Ain to Buraimi is finding it: there are almost no signs to Buraimi in Al Ain. As a general guide, once you are on Khalifa bin Zayed Street, keep going until you get to the large roundabout, then turn left (heading north) and go past the university (on your left). As you look to the right, everything you see is Oman. The border crossing is ahead on your right.

If you are not travelling with your own car, transport in and around Buraimi will need to be by one of the local orange and white taxis. You'll also see UAE taxis, but once they've crossed the border their meters all magically stop working, so know where you are going and agree a price beforehand. Drivers usually accept payment in both Omani riyals and UAE dirhams, and a trip within the township of Buraimi will generally cost no more than Dhs.3 or 300 baisa (OMR 0.3). If you are driving yourself and decide to enter this part of the oasis, make sure your car insurance covers Oman as this is not always the case.

The Buraimi Souk is worth a visit for the local atmosphere and colour – along with more mundane household goods, there are a few souvenir shops selling pottery, silver jewellery and woven crafts. Behind the souk is Al Hili Fort, a good starting point from which to explore the oasis. Al Khandaq Fort, located in Hamasa town in Welayat Buraimi, is believed to be about 400 years old. Like many of Oman's forts, it has been extensively restored, and it is great to wander around and admire the views from the battlements.

his remarkable achievements turning the desert state into a wealthy, popular and thriving country. The museum is a lovely, quiet place to stroll and explore.

Al Ain Paradise
Nr Zakher R/A, Zakher District Al Ain 03 782 0788
alainparadise.com
Map 4 C3
This public park appears in the Guinness Book of World Records thanks to having the largest number of hanging flower baskets. The colourful park is a must-see. Families only on Fridays.

Al Ain Public Garden
Zayed Bin Sultan St Al Ain
Map 4 D2
As the main park in the city of Al Ain, the Public Garden is a tranquil spot amid the hustle and bustle. Walkways wind their ways under shady trees, fountains are attractively lit up at night and areas for younger children offer a variety of fun and safe play equipment. For older kids, there's a small amusement arcade tucked away near the back entrance.

Al Ain University Natural History Museum
University of Al Ain Al Ain 03 767 7280
Map 4 D2
Aimed at those interested in the flora and fauna of the UAE, this museum is a small but informative centre run by the university. It includes a herbarium and collections of various species of animals and birds. An assortment of rocks, minerals and fossils is on display.

Al Ain Zoo
Public Institution Zoo & Aquarium, Nhayyan Al Awwal St Al Ain 03 782 8188
alainzoo.ae
Map 4 D3
Stretching over 900 hectares, this is one of the largest and best zoos in the Gulf region. With ample greenery, a casual stroll through the paths that criss-cross the park makes for a wonderful family day out. As well as seeing large mammals, reptiles and big cats, you can get up close to some rare and common local species such as the Arabian Oryx and sand gazelle, or pay a visit to the fantastic birdhouse. Since its founding, the zoo has been a centre for endangered species' conservation and visitors can look forward to spotting true rarities. Nearly 30% of the 180 species are endangered and the park is even home to a stunning pair of white tigers and white lions. Family nights with activities from sports games to cartoon screenings take place on Wednesdays. A park train regularly departs from the central concourse, providing a whirlwind tour of the zoo. The park is open daily from 09:00 to 20:00 in winter and from 16:00 to 22:00 during summer. Entrance is Dhs.15 for adults, Dhs.5 for children and it's free for those under 2 years.

┌───┐

Camel Safaris

Al Ain Golden Sands Camel Safaris offers a selection of tours that include a camel ride over the dunes of Bida Bint Saud. The rides usually last one to two and a half hours and include transfers from Al Ain. Call 050 447 7268 for the details.

└───┘

Al Jahili Fort
Nr Central Public Gardens Al Ain 03 784 3996
adach.ae
Map 4 D2
Celebrated as the birthplace of the late Sheikh Zayed bin Sultan Al Nahyan, the picturesque fort was erected in 1891 to defend Al Ain's precious palm groves. It is set in beautifully landscaped gardens and visitors are encouraged to explore the exterior. It's also the stunning venue for a number of concerts in the Abu Dhabi Classics series.

Hili Archaeological Park
Mohammed Ibn Khalifa St Al Ain
adach.ae
Map 4 E1
Located 10 kilometres outside Al Ain on the Dubai-Al Ain highway, the gardens are home to a Bronze Age settlement (2,500 – 2,000BC), which was excavated and restored in 1995. Many of the artefacts found during the excavation are now on display in the Al Ain National Museum (p.237).

Hili Fort
Nr Date Farm & Hili Oasis Al Ain
Map 4 E1
Across the border in Buraimi, the Hili Fort is located at the edge of a date palm plantation near the Buraimi Souk. The area features several delightful mud-walled paths that lead out from the back into the oasis.

Hili Fun City > p.239
Off Emirates St Al Ain 03 784 5542
hilifuncity.ae
Map 4 E1
This 22 hectare spacious, leafy park is perfect for family outings. There are plenty of spaces for picnics and barbecues, with arcade games and refreshment stands nearby. The park is being gradually updated and there are now more than 30 attractions – with even more rides on the way. The park has an amphitheatre where various singing, dancing and circus shows are put on throughout the day. The park is open 16:00 to 22:00 (Monday to Thursday), 12:00 to 22:00 (Friday and Saturday), with Wednesdays reserved for ladies and children only. The park is closed on Sundays and for Ramadan. Special opening hours apply for the June-August period. Entrance

costs Dhs.50; free for kids up to 89cm tall. Located on the eastern side of the park is a mammoth 60 by 30 metre ice rink. The Dhs.25 admission fee to the ice rink includes the rental of skates for one hour.

Muraijib Fort
Al Jimi St Al Ain **03 621 5300**
adach.ae
Map **4 D2**
Built in 1816, the Muraijib Fort is the oldest fort in Al Ain. It is located on Al Jimi Street and the restored remains of the fort are situated within beautifully landscaped gardens, which are reserved for women and children only.

Silmi Garden
Mohammed Ibn Khalifa St Al Ain
Map **4 D2**
Silmi Garden is a popular spot with locals. Like all other parks in Al Ain, it is well cared for with plenty of trees, shrubs, flowers, fountains and a play area with swings and slides. Unfortunately, you have to park on the street and all the signs are in Arabic. You needn't worry if your Arabic isn't great; the park is quite easy to locate, especially at night as the walls are lit with multi-coloured lights.

Al Ain Hotels

Al Ain Rotana
Zayed Ibn Sultan St Al Ain **03 754 5111**
rotana.com
Map **4 D2**
Located in the centre of the city, the hotel's rooms, suites and chalets are extremely spacious and modern. The other facilities include a beautiful garden pool and good fitness facilities. In addition, the hotel is also a nightlife hub with six dining venues, including the ever-popular Trader Vic's and a highly recommended Lebanese restaurant.

Al Massa Hotel
Nr Hamdan Bin Mohd & Al Baladiah Sts Al Ain
03 763 9003
almasahotels.com
Map **4 D2**
This city centre establishment has 50 rooms and 12 suites, along with a cafe and Lebanese-style restaurant. It is a little dated but clean and welcoming if you're simply looking for a place to stay in the centre of town.

Ayla Hotel
Khalifa Bin Zayed Al Awwal St Al Ain **03 761 0111**
aylahotels.com
Map **4 D2**
A new hotel near the town centre, the rooms are practical and tasteful, while there's a modern gym,

indoor pool, sauna, Jacuzzi and basic spa offerings. Dining options are simple but adequate, but Ayla is aimed mainly at an Arabic market (and a business one at that) and outlets are not licensed. Western tourists shouldn't be put off – the hotel has a local flavour that creates a welcoming, relaxed atmosphere.

City Seasons Hotel Al Ain
Khalifa Bin Zayed St Al Ain **03 755 0220**
cityseasonsgroup.com
Map **4 D2**
This hotel has 77 lovely rooms and suites with excellent facilities. Executive suites have a separate living room and kitchen facilities. The hotel has a fitness centre, swimming pool and sun deck.

Danat Al Ain Resort
Nr Khalid Bin Sultan & Al Salam Sts Al Ain
03 704 6000
danathotels.com
Map **4 E2**
One of the most enjoyable inland resorts in the UAE, this hotel has landscaped gardens, swimming pools, luxurious guestrooms, deluxe villas and a Royal Villa with a private Jacuzzi. It also has great facilities for families and a delightful spa.

Green Mubazzarah Chalets
Nr Green Mubazzarah Park Al Ain **03 783 9555**
mubazzarah.150m.com
Map **4 D4**
Situated among the lush and picturesque foothills of Jebel Hafeet, accommodation consists of fully-furnished two and three bedroom chalets, ideal for enjoying the Green Mubazzarah natural springs and parkland.

Hilton Al Ain
Nr Khalid Bin Sultan & Zayed Bin Sultan Sts Al Ain
03 768 6666
hilton.com
Map **4 E2**
Located near the heart of Al Ain, this ageing hotel is a key landmark and sits in lush, landscaped gardens that contain a nine hole golf course, tennis and squash courts, a health club and a nice pool area. It is particularly convenient for visiting the wildlife park and Jebel Hafeet. The Hiltonia Sports Bar and Paco's Bar are both popular haunts.

Mercure Grand Jebel Hafeet Al Ain
Jabel Hafeet Al Ain **03 783 8888**
mercure.com
Map **4 D4**
Situated in a spectacular location near the top of Jebel Hafeet, the Mercure offers incredible views of Al Ain from all of its simply decorated rooms and terraced

Al Ain Oasis

Al Jahili Fort

Al Ain Zoo

Al Ain Palace Museum

restaurants. There are also three swimming pools, and a water slide. There is a pub, buffet restaurant and poolside cafe serving excellent evening barbecues.

Al Gharbia

Located way west of Abu Dhabi, and further than most people usually venture on or off-road, Al Gharbia (or the Western Region) actually makes up over two-thirds of the UAE. Along its hundreds of kilometres of coastline can be found some stunning beaches, as well as a number of islands, which are increasingly being developed and promoted for visitors. But the main reason to make the drive is Liwa – a destination that will blow you away with massive expanses of awesome desert and the biggest dunes this side of the Sahara.

Delma Ferry

A new car ferry travels between Jebel Dhanna and Delma Island. It leaves Marsa Jebel Dhanna at 09:00, 13:30 and 18:00 Saturday to Thursday, and 10:00 and 18:00 on Friday. It makes the return trip from Delma Island at 06:00, 11:15 and 15:45 Saturday to Thursday, and 07:00 and 15:45 on Friday. There is currently no booking website or number, so you just need to turn up.

Prepare for the most adventurous off-road driving the UAE has to offer, and some of its most incredible scenery. For an overview of what you can find in the area, read on; for detailed routes and information, get a copy of *UAE Off-Road Explorer* or the *UAE & Oman Ultimate Explorer*.

The Pearl Coast

If you head west along the coast from Abu Dhabi, the first port of call is Mirfa. A long-established fishing port and pearling centre, Mirfa has a rather quiet feel these days, but this is all set to change following the inauguration of the Mirfa Corniche development in March 2011. The project is part of Abu Dhabi's 2030 development plan for the whole region. While the works are under way, new life has recently already been blown into the area by the opening of the refurbished Mirfa Hotel. Developed by Al Marfa Pearl, the resort now consists of 114 rooms and wide-ranging leisure facilities designed to attract a growing number of visitors to this part of the emirate. For now, the biggest annual draw remains the Al Gharbia Watersports Festival (p.28), held on the beach opposite the hotel. Each year the event wakes up Mirfa with a weekend of crowds, fireworks and competitive kitesurfing, wakeboarding and kayaking.

A hundred kilometres further along is Jebel Dhanna, another stopping point for history's pearl divers. With a great beach and the clear, shallow sea, the two hotels are among the region's best kept secrets. The Dhafra Beach Hotel (p.244) has been there for 30 years now, home to long-term residents that work in the area, and to the late Sheikh Zayed's ornate presidential suite, which is now available to visitors and popular with honeymooners at a cost of around Dhs.3,000 a night. Just along the beach, the Danat Jebel Dhanna Resort (p.244) is a real find. A good-value, five-star resort with a country club feel, it has great facilities and its bars and restaurants are particularly impressive. Both hotels are popular with international expats based in industrial outposts in the region, but at just a two-hour drive from the capital, they make for great weekend getaways for Abu Dhabi residents too.

Nearby, Ruwais is a purpose-built town, inhabited entirely by ADNOC employees from all over the world. It has a small stretch of shops, a pool and a recreation club, but holds little interest for visitors.

The last stop before you hit the Saudi Arabia border is Sila, a true frontier town. With sleepy streets and wide empty vistas, there is little happening in Sila today, but there is great potential for change as the proposed GCC railway network will stop here. Until then, visitors should head down from the town to the quiet harbour, where at the Abu Dhabi Fishermen's Cooperative Society (02 673 0888) you can buy some fresh catch. For a beach barbecue, pick up extra provisions at Al Rahi Home Grocery next to the Fishermen's Cooperative. Drive north, with the quarry-scarred embankment on your left, along the beach track, and find a spot away from the beach houses.

Arabian Wildlife Park

The Arabian Wildlife Park (desertislands.com) houses thousands of animals; the species include the endangered Arabian oryx, sand gazelle and mountain gazelle, as well as cheetahs, hyenas, Barbary sheep, Arabian rock hyrax, Arabian hares, northern ostriches and Ethiopian hedgehogs. Research and conservation play leading roles in the park's development, which has been an unprecedented success. Since the early 1960s, when the Arabian oryx was declared extinct in the wild, more than 500 born on Sir Bani Yas have been released back into the wild. Human interference has been removed from the park, but tourism and education are key to the park's success, and visitors are encouraged to take part in game drives, nature trails, mountain biking or even opt for an exclusive outdoor dining experience. Only those staying at The Desert Islands Resort & Spa by Anantara (p.244) can enter the park and, even then, you have to do so with an official guide provided by the resort.

This is one of the few spots along the coast where you can camp; two headlands further west, you'll find an even more pristine spot. It is there that you will find the powder white sand, calm turquoise sea and bobbing pink flamingos.

Desert Islands

As part of the plan to develop Al Gharbia for tourism, this huge, eight island project is one of the most exciting developments in the whole emirate. The islands include the larger Sir Bani Yas and Delma islands, and the six Discovery Islands, which will provide eco-tourism accommodation on small islands modelled after those in the Maldives.

Sir Bani Yas Island was once Sheikh Zayed's personal retreat and is now becoming a noted wildlife reserve, green energy champion and internationally renowned holiday resort. The Desert Islands Resort & Spa (p.244) has received accolades for its sensitive and stylish luxury. Located off the coast from Jebel Dhanna, it has succeeded in bringing tourists to the area to enjoy region-specific activities from safaris to snorkelling, and kayaking to mountain biking.

Far beyond Sir Bani Yas lies Delma Island. A two-hour ferry ride from Jebel Dhanna, this was the most important island in the Gulf for all but the most recent history. With rare and precious fresh water reserves, it was a favourite stopping point for traders, fishermen and pearlers, and has been inhabited for over 7,000 years. Important archaeology, fascinating history and fertile plantations are expected to appeal to future visitors too.

The volcanic landscape literally sparkles and big ospreys watch over fields of ostrich, but even with two new car ferries plying the route from the mainland, Delma's attractions are still very much under construction and the barren island is scarred with quarrying, construction and watchtowers. It feels like a deserted service station, which in marine terms it is. Currently the only accommodation available is at the Delma Motel (02 878 1222); another option is to camp – either up in the hilly moonscape interior or on a quiet stretch of beach.

Something Fishy

Perhaps the most unusual place to visit in the Liwa area is the fish farm near Khanur, where the water arrives from underground sources. There are pools and breeding tanks filled with tilapia, bulti, catfish and even some carp. To get there, and to learn about other off-the-beaten-track adventures in the region, pick up the UAE Off-Road Explorer.

Liwa

For most visitors to Al Gharbia, all roads lead to Liwa. On the way, they pass through tumbleweed towns like Ghayathi (good for stocking up on authentic Bedouin souvenirs) and the regional capital Madinat Zayed. The land here is ancient; at Bu Ghar, eight million year old fossils have been found. There are oases dotted throughout the region, and occasional farmsteads. Modern Bedouin, with entire bungalows on the back of big-wheeled trucks, criss-cross the interior all the way to Liwa.

Liwa Oasis is one of the largest oases on the Arabian Peninsula. This fertile crescent stretches over 150km and is home to the Bani Yas tribe, ancestors of the ruling family of Abu Dhabi. Dotted with date plantations, small towns and ancient forts, it's a quiet area, visited for traditional falconry, camel racing and trading, and because Liwa is the gateway to the great desert.

The Rub Al Khali is the biggest sand desert on the planet and is one of the world's great attractions with

The Empty Quarter

its unsurpassed majesty and scale. Covering parts of Oman, Yemen, the southern UAE and almost all of southern Saudi Arabia, the Rub Al Khali was historically regarded as the edge of civilisation by people living in the region.

There is an extraordinary beauty to this landscape, despite it being so harsh and inhospitable. Even today man has been able to make little mark on it. Desert driving in this area is more of an expedition than just a spot of dune bashing, so go prepared for the adventure of a lifetime.

The opportunities for camping in the region are endless, and sleeping under the stars is a great way to experience the peace and tranquillity of the desert. If you don't feel like roughing it, a clutch of stunning hotels have recently been added, ensuring that you need not go without your home comforts. Qasr Al Sarab (p.249) is the easily the most scenic and atmospheric choice: managed by Anantara, the luxurious resort sits in the midst of stunning red sand dunes and features Arabic-themed, spacious rooms and villas. Other alternatives include the Liwa Hotel (p.249), a comfortable resort with great leisure facilities; the Tilal Liwa Hotel (p.245), between Madinat Zayed and Liwa, and styled like a traditional fort; or the Liwa Resthouse (p.245) in Mezaira'a, although the main reason for stopping here is to stock up on fuel and provisions before heading into the brilliant wilderness.

Arabian Nights Under The Stars

An essential part of any Liwa adventure, camping in the desert is a truly unforgettable experience. The expanses of sand rolling into the distance at early dawn and the snaking silvery dunes in the moonlight are quite magical. This area provides some of the best desert views in the UAE. You can camp just about anywhere, so take any of the roads and tracks into the desert off the main road through the oasis. Find somewhere near to where you'd like to be for the next day's driving, but just make sure that you drive far enough from roads, habitation and activity to find a peaceful spot. Try to get settled in your campsite long before the sun goes down, both for safety reasons and to prevent getting stuck in the dark (and of course, to allow you to enjoy the sunset). One particularly good area is on the road to Moreeb Hill passing the Liwa Resthouse. This minor, paved road heads into the desert for 11.5km, leading you into some of the best dunes, and crossing plenty of sabkha flats – any one of which allows you to get off-road and into some sheltered areas, far from disturbances, in quite a short time.

Al Gharbia Hotels

Danat Jebel Dhanna Resort
Jebel Dhanna **02 801 2222**
danathotels.com
Map **3 B3**
Sitting on 800 metres of private, picturesque beach, this undiscovered treat of a hotel offers 109 luxurious rooms and suites including six waterfront villas. It has a health club and a spa that includes beach massage huts and a nice pool area with swim-up bar. The five dining venues at the hotel include an Italian restaurant, an all-day buffet restaurant, cafe and a shisha bar.

Desert Islands Resort & Spa By Anantara
Sir Bani Yas Island **02 801 5400**
desertislands.anantara.com
Map **3 B2**
Probably one of the most unique resorts found anywhere in the world, the Desert Islands Resort is accessible only by boat or the hotel's private aircraft (from Abu Dhabi International Airport). Once you arrive, luxurious and jaw-dropping leisure awaits – from stylish rooms and private beach villas to the wonderful beachside restaurant Samak, and the soothing treatments at the adjacent Anantara Spa. Surrounding the hotel is the Arabian Wildlife Park (p.242), with dedicated nature and wildlife drives, kayaking, snorkelling, trekking, hiking, archery and guided game walks. New, boutique style villas have recently opened too, some of them located directly inside the wildlife park.

Dhafra Beach Hotel
Jebel Dhanna Ruwais **02 801 2000**
danathotels.com
Map **3 B3**
A very pleasant and reasonably priced hotel with a variety of rooms and suites to choose from, as well as a handful of dining options, a fitness centre with a sauna, and two swimming pools. A good option if heading west.

Liwa Hotel *> p.234*
Mezaira Liwa **02 882 2000**
almarfapearlhotels.com
Map **3 C4**
With its raised location giving spectacular views of the Rub Al Khali desert, the green oasis and the neighbouring palace on the hilltop opposite, Liwa Hotel is a good option if you're not keen on camping in the dunes. The hotel has spacious rooms and green, landscaped grounds with an attractive pool. The quality of the facilities and the service in the hotel are good, and there's also a choice of dining options and evening venues.

Liwa Resthouse

Mezaira Liwa **02 882 2075**
Map **3 C4**

One of a number of resthouses in Abu Dhabi, Liwa Resthouse is a little past its prime and has been eclipsed by the nearby Liwa Hotel. Its (mainly Arab) clientele includes visiting business travellers, government officials and families on holiday. Although the accommodation and facilities are pretty basic compared to local hotels, it is clean and functional, and for the cheapest alternative to camping, it's worth a look.

Mirfa Hotel > *p.234*

Dubai – Sila Highway, Al Mirfa
02 883 3030
almarfapearlhotels.com
Map **3 C3**

Located in the quiet town of Mirfa, 160 kilometres from Abu Dhabi, this hotel is perfect for a weekend break or as a stopover if you're driving to Saudi Arabia. The hotel has just been renovated and now features 114 comfortable rooms and suites, and lush gardens that include a fantastic range of regional flora and attract plenty of local fauna. Leisure facilities consist of two pools, floodlit tennis courts, a volleyball court, a fitness centre and a kids' playground.

Qasr Al Sarab Desert Resort By Anantara

1 Qasr Al Sarab Rd Liwa **02 886 2088**
anantara.com
Map **3 D4**

The Qasr Al Sarab Desert Resort By Anantara offers five-star, Arabian-style, luxury accommodation on the edge of the vast Rub Al Khali desert near Hamim. The hotel has 150 rooms, plus one, two and three bedroom villas and a tented village. As well as a sensational pool area with a swim-up bar, it offers desert excursions, and there's an observatory from where guests can gaze into the desert night skies. Unsurprisingly for an Anantara resort, the spa, which features hammam baths amid peaceful courtyards, fountains and aromatic plants and flowers, is every bit as stunning as the endless dunes beyond.

Tilal Liwa Hotel

Nr Madinat Zayed, Rub Al Khali Liwa **02 894 6111**
danathotels.com
Map **3 C3**

One of the newest hotels in Al Gharbia, this four-star desert hideaway stretches around a charming pool area and offers a range of rooms and suites which blend old and new design elements, and look out over the endless sands. There are a few options for eating and drinking, and the gym, sauna and steam rooms keep guests busy, although desert safaris in the dunes should be at the top of all visitors' activity itineraries.

UAE – THE OTHER EMIRATES

Dubai

Cliches tend to trip off the tongue when describing Abu Dhabi's little brother – the city of gold, sleepy fishing village transformed into modern metropolis, the Vegas of the Middle East, and so on. The truth is that, while the emirate boasts an incredible number of attractions claiming to be the tallest, biggest or longest, it's not all bright lights – the atmospheric old town around the Creek, and the restored Bastakiya area are musts for any visitor wanting to scratch Dubai's cultural surface, and the beautiful Jumeira Mosque (p.247) is one of the few mosques in the region open to non-Muslims, offering a rare chance to learn about the impact of Islam on the local people.

Dubai is also a great place for families and, from amusement parks and aquariums to child-friendly hotels and restaurants, you'll find plenty of ways to keep the kids busy while in town.

Beyond the city, the desert opens up further possibilities and many visitors choose to combine a city break with a couple of nights camping with a tour group, or relaxing at a luxury desert resort such as Al Maha (p.248) or Bab Al Shams (p.248). That said, if it's bright lights you're after, Dubai outshines the rest of the region. The emirate has been successful in its quest for economic diversification, and its focus on tourism revenues has resulted in a fantastic array of superlative-laden attractions for tourists and residents alike. From skiing on real snow at Ski Dubai (p.250) and plunging through shark-infested waters at Aquaventure (p.215), to shopping till you drop at Dubai Mall (p.246) and surveying the entire city from the world's tallest building, Burj Khalifa (see below),

Downtown Dubai

HATS OFF TO HATTA

Out of the city, but not strictly out of Dubai, is the mountain town of Hatta. It lies within Dubai emirate, about an hour's drive south-east of the city, but makes for a great addition to any out-of-town trip to Dubai.

The Hatta Fort Hotel (04 809 9333, jaresortshotels.com) is a perfectly secluded mountain retreat in tranquil gardens. The hotel is fully equipped with numerous facilities and activities, including two swimming pools, a children's pool, a bar and restaurant, the Senses Beauty Salon, a driving range and chipping green, floodlit tennis courts and archery. The 50 spacious chalet-style rooms and suites all come with patios overlooking the impressive Hajars.

There are several good off-road options for those who want to do some 4WD exploring, including the nearby Hatta Pools, which you can swim in. They're fairly accessible from the town along an unpaved road, and there signs to guide you there. Pick up a copy of UAE Off-Road Explorer for other great routes in the area. Back in town is the Hatta Heritage Village. It is constructed around an old settlement and was restored in the style of a traditional mountain village. Explore the tranquil oasis, the narrow alleyways and discover traditional life in the mud and barasti houses.

Hatta's history goes back over 3,000 years and the area includes a 200 year-old mosque and the fortress built by Sheikh Maktoum bin Hasher Al Maktoum in 1896, which is now used as a weaponry museum. Entry is free.

a weekend trip to Dubai promises an action-packed break. Its selection of five-star hotels, restaurants, bars and clubs will ensure a well fed and watered stay, and luxury spas and clean beaches provide ample opportunities to relax.

For more help on planning a trip to Dubai, log on to askexplorer.com where you can find listings of forthcoming events and further information about Dubai hotels and attractions, and where you can order a copy of *Dubai Mini Visitors' Guide* or *Dubai Tourists' Map* – the essential guides for your weekend break.

Dubai Attractions

Adventure HQ
Times Square Dubai **04 346 6824**
adventurehq.ae
Map **3 E2** Metro **First Gulf Bank**
In addition to stocking up on active wear and outdoors goods, adrenalin addicts will find indoors thrills from the Cable Climb to the Chill Chamber.

At The Top
Burj Khalifa Dubai **04 888 8124**
burjkhalifa.ae
Map **3 E2** Metro **Burj Khalifa/Dubai Mall**
In less than 60 seconds, a high-speed lift whisks visitors up to the 124th floor of the world's tallest tower. From the Burj Khalifa observation deck, you can survey a 360° view of the city. Advance bookings are Dhs.100 for adults and Dhs.75 for children; tickets bought on the day cost Dhs.400.

Dubai Aquarium & Underwater Zoo
The Dubai Mall Dubai **04 448 5200**
thedubaiaquarium.com
Map **3 E2** Metro **Burj Khalifa/Dubai Mall**
Located, somewhat bizarrely, in the middle of The Dubai Mall, this aquarium displays over 33,000 tropical fish to passing shoppers free of charge. For a closer view of the main tank's inhabitants, however (which include fearsome looking but generally friendly sand tiger sharks) you can pay to walk through the 270° viewing tunnel. Also well worth a look is the Underwater Zoo, which includes residents such as penguins, piranhas and an octopus. If you're feeling really adventurous, you can even go for a scuba dive in the tank (call ahead to book), ride a glass-bottomed boat or feed the sharks.

The Dubai Mall
Nr Interchange 1, Financial Centre Rd Dubai
04 362 7500
thedubaimall.com
Map **3 E2** Metro **Burj Khalifa/Dubai Mall**
One of the world's largest shopping malls, The Dubai Mall is a shopper's paradise housing some 1,200

stores, including the famous New York department store, Bloomingdales. Even if you're not in town to shop, you should make a trip to the mall anyway to view the many attractions within. There is an Olympic sized ice rink, an indoor waterfall, a 22 screen cinema, Sega World indoor theme park, KidZania edutainment centre, the Dubai Aquarium and Underwater Zoo and some great alfresco dining venues with views of the spectacular musical displays of the Dubai Fountain.

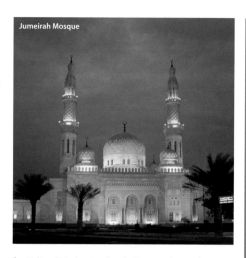
Jumeirah Mosque

Dubai Museum
Al Fahidi Fort Dubai **04 353 1862**
definitelydubai.com
Map **3 E2** Metro **Al Fahidi**
Located in Al Fahidi Fort, this museum is creative, well thought-out and interesting for all the family. The fort was originally built in 1787 as the residence of the ruler of Dubai and for sea defence, and then renovated in 1970 to house the museum. All aspects of Dubai's past are represented. You can walk through a souk from the 1950s, stroll through an oasis, see into a traditional house, get up close to local wildlife, learn about the archaeological finds or go 'underwater' to discover the pearl diving and fishing industries. There are some entertaining mannequins to pose with too. Entry costs Dhs.3 for adults and Dhs.1 for children under 6 years old. Open daily 08:30 to 20:30 (14:30 to 20:30 on Fridays).

Heritage & Diving Village
Nr Shk Saeed Al Maktoum House Dubai **04 393 7139**
definitelydubai.com
Map **3 E2** Metro **Al Ghubaiba**
Located near the mouth of Dubai Creek, the Heritage & Diving Village focuses on Dubai's maritime past, pearl diving traditions and architecture. Visitors can observe traditional potters and weavers practising their craft the way it has been done for centuries. Local women serve traditionally cooked snacks – one of the rare opportunities you'll have to sample genuine Emirati cuisine. It is particularly lively during the Dubai Shopping Festival and Eid celebrations, with performances including traditional sword dancing. Open daily 08:30 to 22:00 (Fridays 15:30-22:00). The village is very close to Sheikh Saeed Al Maktoum's House, the home of the much-loved former ruler of Dubai, which is a good example of a traditional home and houses a number of interesting photographic exhibits.

Jumeirah Mosque
Jumeira Rd Dubai **04 353 6666**
cultures.ae
Map **3 E2** Metro **World Trade Centre**
This is the most beautiful mosque in the city and perhaps the best known, as its image features on the Dhs.500 banknote. The Sheikh Mohammed Centre

for Cultural Understanding (cultures.ae) organises mosque tours for non-Muslims on Saturday, Sunday, Tuesday and Thursday mornings at 10:00. Visitors are guided around the mosque and told all about the building, and then the hosts give a talk on Islam and prayer rituals. The tour offers a fascinating insight into the culture and beliefs of the local population, and is thoroughly recommended. You must dress conservatively – no shorts and no sleeveless tops. Women must also cover their hair with a head scarf or shawl, and all visitors will be asked to remove their shoes. Cameras are allowed, pre-booking is essential and there is a registration fee of Dhs.10 per person.

KidZania
The Dubai Mall Dubai **04 448 5222**
kidzania.ae
Map **3 E2** Metro **Burj Khalifa/Dubai Mall**
This new addition to Dubai Mall offers kids the chance to become adults for the day. Billed as a 'real-life city' for children, youngsters can dress up and act out more than 75 different roles, from policeman to pilot and doctor to designer. The KidZania city even has its own currency, which children can earn and spend. It's intended to be both fun and educational.

The Lost Chambers
Atlantis The Palm Dubai **04 426 0000**
atlantisthepalm.com
Map **3 E2** Metro **Nakheel**
The ruins of the mysterious lost city provide the theme for the aquarium at Atlantis. The maze of underwater halls and tunnels provide ample opportunity to get up close to the aquarium's 65,000 inhabitants, ranging from sharks and eels to rays and piranhas, as well as multitudes of exotic fish. The entrance fee is Dhs.100 for adults and Dhs.70 for 7 to 11 year olds.

Just Deserts

With thousands of square kilometres of desert and a little sprinkling of luxury, the sands of the UAE make the perfect place for a short break from city life.

Bab Al Shams

If there are two things that the UAE does better than most other international tourist destinations, it is five-star luxury and the desert experience. Holidaymakers fly across the globe to indulge in the unique blend of opulence and landscape, but UAE residents have all this on their doorstep. From the mountains of RAK to the endless sea of sand two hours from Abu Dhabi, there are several excellent locations for a memorable desert getaway. Here are the highlights:

Al Maha, A Luxury Collection Desert Resort & Spa

Dubai-Al Ain Rd **04 832 9900**
al-maha.com

The Al Maha Desert Resort & Spa is the definitive place to get away from it all. Accessible only by a 4WD driven by your own field guide, the resort is congruously set on the slopes of a rising dune in the form of a Bedouin camp and blends into the desert as if it has been there as long as the sands. Rooms resemble a traditional Bedouin tent but are the epitome of luxury. Surrounded by colourful gardens and accessed by golf buggy, every one of the 42 suites has a private wooden-decked terrace and infinity plunge pool.

Inside, circular suites are full of gloriously decadent touches, including two chaise-longues, regal drapes, an array of fascinating artefacts and a vast, luxurious

bathroom bigger than most hotel rooms. Panoramic windows look out over the desertscape and doors open onto the patio area, which comes complete with a pair of powerful binoculars to spot the wild Arabian oryx (maha) that wander the resort.

Activities include a sunrise falconry display, horse riding, dune safaris, nature walks, archery, a sunset camel ride and champagne toast on the dunes, and there's the Timeless Spa for a full range of pampering. Eat in Al Diwaan restaurant with its great wine list or on your private terrace.

Should you fancy a spot of night swimming, there are pool lights to help you see where you are going, and the water temperature is adjustable.

Bab Al Shams Desert Resort & Spa

Nr Dubai Endurance Village **04 809 6100**
themeydan.com

Like a desert mirage come to life, Bab Al Shams is a Bedouin fantasy escape away from the hectic streets of the cities. Bamboo torches guide you to the low-rise building which blends into the imposing dunes that surround it. Your welcome, marked with the traditional ritual of dates and kahwa, is one of the many personal touches that infuse Bab Al Shams with Arabian hospitality and warmth.

The rooms, although luxurious, have been designed to evoke a feeling of Bedouin living; walls seem to be made of clay, furnishings are crafted from dark wood, and curtains are made of hessian. The bathroom is similarly designed and features clay pots, rustic tones and a large bath that looks like it could have been carved straight from the earth.

Camel rides on the dunes are available or, if you prefer relaxation, you can chill out in one of the holistic swimming pools. The infinity pool's horizon drops off into the sand dunes. Swim up to the in-pool bar for a cocktail or an icy cold beer and enjoy the splendour of the sunset over the dunes – you really do feel as though you are in an isolated world of tranquillity. You can take the pampering up a notch by heading to the Satori Spa, which offers a range of signature treatments.

As the evening sets in, head to the Al Sarab Rooftop Lounge for shisha and a selection of drinks. For dinner, you could choose to eat in the hotel's Al Forsan restaurant which serves an international buffet for breakfast, lunch and dinner, but the highlight is Al

Hadheerah, which offers not just a dinner but a full-on Arabian experience, including a huge buffet, horse and camel displays, belly dancing and traditional music.

Banyan Tree Al Wadi
Ras Al Khaimah **07 206 7777**
banyantree.com
Hidden in the undulating desert of Ras Al Khaimah emirate, from the access road, the impressive resort appears out of the sand like a mirage. Guests have a choice of either the traditional mudbrick inspired Al Rimal villas with mighty wooden doors and high ceilings, or the spacious nomad-style tented villas (over 250 sqm). All villas have their own pool, and luxury is around every corner.

The resort is set in 100 hectares, 60 of which are a nature reserve where Arabian gazelles, camels and oryx roam. There's even a watering hole for the wildlife strategically located under the balcony of one of the restaurants. Activities include archery, cycling and horse and camel rides, and there is a kids' club and falconry centre too. The spa is immense, with treatment pavilions (the word 'room' isn't enough) offering the ultimate in sublime pampering and state-of-the-art hydrotherapy treatments. The restaurants are equally opulent and there are great views from the roof-top bar. For a memorable romantic getaway with a touch of exotic desert scenery, Banyan Tree Al Wadi fits the (large) bill.

Liwa Hotel > p.234
Nr Mezzaira Village, Mezaira'a **02 882 2000**
The Liwa Hotel was originally conceived as a sheikh's palace, but prior to occupation was converted into a hotel. While it may not quite match royal standards, a stay here makes for an enjoyable weekend break with a difference, thanks to the stunning setting: the hotel offers beautiful, peaceful views of the desertscape. Rooms all have large terraces, so you can relax and enjoy the scenery, with five suites and three villas available. The decor is fairly basic, but it fits in with the calm, minimalist surroundings, only interrupted every now and then by the occasional revving of a 4WD or quad bike on its way back from a jaunt on the dunes. The restaurant serves buffet breakfast and dinner. Leisure-wise you'll find a large swimming pool and surprisingly lush grounds, perfect for relaxing. There is also a sauna, Jacuzzi and steam room, tennis and volleyball courts and a separate kids' pool and play area. But the real star of the show is the stunning landscape.

Qasr Al Sarab Desert Resort By Anantara
1 Qasr Al Sarab Rd **02 886 2088**
qasralsarab.anantara.com
Set on the edge of the Empty Quarter, at the birthplace of the Al Nahyan family, this palatial hotel's graceful windtowers and traditional Emirati architecture rise out of the impressive dunes in hues that blend the new

with the age-old desert. Luxurious, five star touches make it a true retreat from Abu Dhabi life.

Each spacious room is lavishly adorned, with decor in earthy tones contrasting with cutting edge lighting, sound and entertainment facilities. Extravagant bathrooms with rain showers and circular bathtubs, and expansive terraces and balconies, all with views across the Empty Quarter, provide endless opportunities for rest and relaxation. The luxurious Anantara spa and excellent restaurants provide the finishing touches for a truly relaxing escape from city life.

For those looking to dig a little deeper into Liwa's heritage, more than 2,500 cultural artefacts are on display throughout the resort, culminating in a stunning library stocked with literature about the region. Guests can enjoy a host of cultural and experiential activities from archery practice and dawn desert hikes to hamman spa treatments, sampling Emirati cuisine in a traditional Bedouin tent, and star gazing to a backdrop of oud music.

For a full range of regional getaway options, from desert to city to coast, get hold of a copy of Weekend Breaks Oman & UAE by Explorer, or the UAE & Oman Ultimate Explorer.

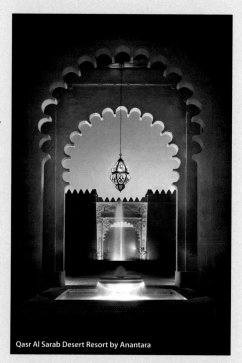

Qasr Al Sarab Desert Resort by Anantara

UAE – The Other Emirates

Out Of The City

SEGA Republic

The Dubai Mall Dubai 04 448 8484
segarepublic.com
Map 3 E2 Metro Burj Khalifa/Dubai Mall
This indoor theme park located in Dubai Mall offers
a range of thrills and spills, courtesy of the nine
main attractions and the 150 arcade games. A Power
Pass (Dhs.150) gets you all-day access to the big
attractions, which include stomach-flipping rides
like the Sonic Hopper, the SpinGear and the Halfpipe
Canyon. Unlike many other shopping mall amusement
centres, SEGA Republic is for all ages, and features
some truly unique thrills.

Ski Dubai

Mall Of The Emirates Dubai 800 386
skidubai.com
Map 3 E2 Metro Mall of the Emirates
Ski Dubai is the Middle East's first indoor ski resort,
with more than 22,500 square metres of real snow.
The temperature hovers around -3°C, even when it's
closer to +50 outside, to make for a cooling excursion
from city life. Competent skiers and boarders can
choose between five runs and a freestyle area, skiing
and snowboarding lessons are available for beginners,
and there is a huge snowpark for the little ones. Slope
pass and lesson prices include the hire charge for
jackets, trousers, boots, socks, helmets and either skis
and poles or a snowboard, but it's worth bringing
your own gloves as these are charged extra on top of
everything else. Freestyle nights are held every other
week on Mondays from 20:00 to 23:00.

Souk Al Bahar

Nr The Dubai Mall Dubai 04 362 7011
soukalbahar.ae
Map 3 E2 Metro Burj Khalifa/Dubai Mall
With atmospheric passageways, Souk Al Bahar is
designed to resemble a traditional souk. It houses a
host of designer boutiques and shops selling Arabian
wares such as carpets, paintings, jewellery, clothes and
perfumes, but its main attractions are the restaurants
and bars, many of which have terraces with views of
the Dubai Fountain and Burj Khalifa.

Souk Madinat Jumeirah

Al Sufouh Rd Dubai 04 366 8888
jumeirah.com
Map 3 E2 Metro Mall of the Emirates
This modern shopping mall is a recreation of
a traditional souk with confusingly winding
passageways, authentic architecture and
interconnecting waterways traversed by motorised
abras (traditional boats). It houses a collection of
boutique shops, galleries, cafes and bars and the
alfresco dining venues are always buzzing during the
evenings of the cooler months.

Dubai Hotels

The Address Downtown Dubai

Emaar Blvd Dubai 04 436 8888
theaddress.com
Map 3 E2 Metro Burj Khalifa/Dubai Mall
Even at over 300 metres in height, The Address is
dwarfed by its neighbour, the Burj Khalifa – but
breathtaking views, beautiful interiors and eight
dining outlets (including Neos, the panoramic bar
on the 63rd floor) make this one of the most popular
spots in town. There are also two more The Address
hotels, located at Dubai Mall and Dubai Marina, while
The Address brand runs the small boutique hotel at
The Montgomerie golf course and The Palace – The
Old Town in Downtown Dubai.

> ### Take A Tour
> Why not view the city from the upper floor of
> a doubledecker bus, learning some fascinating
> facts about Dubai along the way? The Big Bus
> Company (bigbustours.com) allows you to hop
> on and off as you like at various attractions, while
> the amphibious Wonder Bus even takes to water
> (wonderbustours.net).

Atlantis The Palm

Crescent Rd Dubai 04 426 0000
atlantisthepalm.com
Map 3 E2 Metro Nakheel
With a staggering 1,539 rooms and suites, all with
views of the sea or the Palm Jumeirah, Atlantis is
certainly one of Dubai's grandest hotels. It has no
less than four fancy restaurants featuring the cuisine
of Michelin-starred chefs, including a branch of
the world-famous chain Nobu. It is also home to
Aquaventure, the biggest water park in the Middle
East, and the Lost Chambers aquarium.

Bonnington Jumeirah Lakes Towers

Nr Almas Tower Dubai 04 356 0000
bonningtontower.com
Map 3 E2 Metro Jumeirah Lakes Towers
This British five-star institution made its Dubai debut
in Jumeirah Lakes Towers. Containing both hotel suites
and serviced apartments, as well as six restaurants and
bars, and a leisure deck with infinity pool, it has great
connections to Dubai Marina, as well as the rest of the
city via the nearby Metro stop.

Burj Al Arab

Nr Wild Wadi, Jumeira Rd Dubai 04 301 7777
jumeirah.com
Map 3 E2 Metro Mall of the Emirates
Standing on its own man-made island, this dramatic
Dubai icon's unique architecture is recognised around

the world. Suites have two floors and are serviced by a team of butlers. To get into the hotel as a non-guest, you will need a restaurant reservation.

Desert Palm Dubai

Al Awir Rd Dubai 04 323 8888
desertpalm.peraquum.com
Map 3 E2
Located outside the bustle of the city, Desert Palm is so tranquil you'll never want to leave. Overlooking polo fields, guests can chose from suites, or private villas with a pool. The extensive spa menu features massage and holistic therapies including reiki. Signature restaurant Rare is a must for meat lovers, while Epicure is a lovely gourmet deli and a great breakfast venue.

Dubai Festival City

Al Rebat St Dubai 04 2136 213
dubaifestivalcity.com
Map 3 E2 Metro Emirates
DFC has two hotels to choose from. The InterContinental (04 701 1111) has extensive spa facilities and great views from all its rooms and suites; next door is the Crowne Plaza (04 701 2222) with the ever-popular Belgian Beer Café.

Jumeirah Beach Hotel

Nr Wild Wadi, Jumeira Rd Dubai 04 348 0000
jumeirah.com
Map 3 E2 Metro Mall of the Emirates
Shaped like an ocean wave, with a fun and colourful interior, the hotel has 598 rooms and suites and 19 private villas, all with a sea view. It is also home to some excellent food and beverage outlets, including Uptown for happy hour cocktails and a great view of the Burj Al Arab. Kids and families will love Wild Wadi Water Park, which is located here.

Kempinski Hotel Mall Of The Emirates

Mall Of The Emirates Dubai 04 341 0000
kempinski.com
Map 3 E2 Metro Mall of the Emirates
Located in Mall Of The Emirates, this chic hotel's 400 deluxe rooms enjoy direct access to the shopping extravaganza of the iconic mall and Ski Dubai, the indoor ski slope. Check into one of the 15 exclusive ski chalet rooms, remove your boots, put your feet up to the (fake) fire and tuck into an apres-ski afternoon tea while watching the world slide by.

Madinat Jumeirah

Nr Burj Al Arab, Jumeira Rd Dubai 04 366 8888
jumeirah.com
Map 3 E2 Metro Mall of the Emirates
This extravagant resort has two hotels, Al Qasr and Mina A'Salam, with no fewer than 940 luxurious rooms and suites, and the exclusive Dar Al Masyaf summer houses, all linked by man-made waterways navigated by wooden abra boats which whisk guests around the resort. Nestled between the two hotels is the Souk Madinat, with over 95 shops and 44 bars and restaurants to choose from.

The Meydan Hotel

Meydan Racecourse, Al Meydan Rd Dubai
04 381 3333
themeydan.com
Map 3 E2
There's no better place to watch the racing action at The Meydan horserace track than from the rooftop infinity pool of this decadent, five-star, landmark hotel, but the striking modern design, spa and excellent outlets including Prime and Shiba make this hotel a deluxe destination in itself. Guests can make use of free shuttle buses to destinations around Dubai.

Aquaventure at Atlantis

One&Only Royal Mirage

Al Sufouh Rd Dubai **04 399 9999**
royalmirage.oneandonlyresorts.com
Map **3 E2** Metro **Nakheel**
This stunningly beautiful resort is home to three different properties: The Palace, Arabian Court and Residence & Spa. The service and dining (opt for the Beach, Bar & Grill for a romantic evening out; try delectable Moroccan cuisine in the opulent Tagine; or enjoy cocktails with a view in The Rooftop and Sports Lounge) are renowned, and a luxury spa treatment here is the ultimate indulgence.

The Palace – The Old Town

Emaar Blvd Dubai **04 428 7888**
theaddress.com
Map **3 E2** Metro **Burj Khalifa/Dubai Mall**
Palatial indeed, The Palace faces the mighty Burj Khalifa and the spectacular Dubai Fountain. Styled with traditional Arabic architecture, this opulent hotel boasts 242 luxurious rooms and suites, a beautiful spa and some excellent restaurants, including Argentinean steakhouse Asado, and majlis-style shisha tents arranged around the stunning pool.

Park Hyatt Dubai

Nr Dubai Creek Golf & Yacht Club Dubai **04 602 1234**
dubai.park.hyatt.com
Map **3 E2** Metro **Deira City Centre**
Enjoying a prime waterfront location within the grounds of Dubai Creek Golf & Yacht Club, the Park Hyatt is Mediterranean in style with low-rise buildings, natural colours and stylish decor. The hotel has 225 rooms and suites, all with beautiful views, as well as some great dining outlets and a luxurious spa. Excellent restaurants inside the hotel include The Thai Kitchen and Traiteur.

The Ritz-Carlton, Dubai

Nr The Walk, Jumeirah Beach Residence Dubai **04 399 4000**
ritzcarlton.com
Map **3 E2** Metro **Dubai Marina**
Even though it is the only low-rise building amid the sea of Marina towers behind it, all 138 rooms have beautiful views of the Gulf – the Ritz-Carlton was, after all, here years before the rest of the marina was built. Afternoon tea in the Lobby Lounge is a must, and there are several other excellent restaurants and a very good spa onsite. A huge extension is due online any time now. The Ritz-Carlton has also added another property to its offerings, with a new 341 room hotel in the DIFC area.

The Westin Dubai Mina Seyahi Beach Resort & Marina

Al Sufouh Rd Dubai **04 399 4141**
westinminaseyahi.com
Map **3 E2** Metro **Nakheel**
Set on 1,200 metres of private beach, The Westin has 294 spacious rooms and suites with all the luxury amenities you would expect of a five-star hotel, including the aptly named Heavenly Spa. There are plenty of dining venues, including perennially popular Italian Bussola, Senyar for cocktails and tapas, and wine and cheese bar Oeno.

Sharjah

Despite being eclipsed by its close neighbour Dubai in terms of international spotlight, Sharjah has substantially more culture and heritage to offer visitors. So much so that it was named the cultural capital of the Arab world in 1998 by Unesco, thanks to its eclectic mix of museums, heritage preservation and traditional souks. Sharjah is built around Khalid

Sharjah Corniche (image courtesy SCTDA)

Lagoon, also known as the Creek, and the surrounding Buheirah Corniche is a popular spot for an evening stroll. From various points on the lagoon, small dhows can be hired to see the city lights from the water. Joining Khalid Lagoon to Al Khan Lagoon, Al Qasba (p.253) is home to a variety of cultural events, exhibitions, theatre and music – all held on the canal-side walkways or at dedicated venues. There's also the Sharjah Fountain, a recent addition to the area's tourist attractions (almajaz.ae).

The city's main cultural centres, The Heritage Area (p.254) and The Arts Area, are two of the most impressive collections of museums and heritage sites in the country. The ruling Al Qassimi family are renowned collectors of historical artefacts and art, and in an emirate known for its conservatism, many of the works held within the Arts Area are surprising in their modernity. Sharjah's cultural worth is indeed so great that visitors should avoid trying to absorb it all in one trip.

Shoppers will have a blast as well, searching for gifts through Sharjah's souks. Souk Al Arsah has recently been renovated and is the oldest souk in the emirate, while the Central Souk is known for its well-respected carpet shops. There's also high-street shopping at Sharjah Mega Mall (megamall.ae, 06 574 2574) for days when culture and curiosities aren't on the agenda.

Sharjah Attractions

Al Hisn Kalba
Nr Bait Sheikh Saeed Bin Hamed Al Qasimi
Kalba **09 512 3333**
sdci.gov.ae
Map **3 E1**
Located in the East Coast town of Kalba, this complex consists of the restored residence of Sheikh Sayed Al Qassimi and Al Hisn Fort, which houses the town's museum and contains a limited display of weapons. It won't take long to get round but luckily there's also a collection of rides for children. Entrance is Dhs.3 for individuals and Dhs.6 for families.

Al Mahatta Museum
Nr Al Estiqal St Sharjah **06 556 6002**
sharjahmuseums.ae
Map **3 E1**
Home to the first airfield in the Gulf, opened in 1932, Sharjah played an important role as a primary stop-off point for the first commercial flights from Britain to India, and the museum looks at the impact this had on the traditional way of life in Sharjah and this part of the world overall. Four of the original propeller planes have been fully restored and are on display. Located behind Al Estiqlal Street, entry is Dhs.5 for adults and Dhs.10 for families.

Al Qasba
Nr Al Khan Lagoon Sharjah **06 556 0777**
alqasba.ae
Map **3 E1**
With an ever-changing events calendar that includes Arabic poetry readings, film viewings and musical events, the emphasis at Al Qasba is clearly on culture, but there's more on offer. The complex's shops, event spaces and restaurants are laid out between Sharjah's two lagoons and are packed on cooler evenings with window shoppers, diners and families. Motorised abras provide tours up and down the canal, but the biggest and most visible draw is the Eye of the Emirates – a 60 metre high observation wheel with air-conditioned pods offering amazing views over Sharjah and across to Dubai.

Sharjah Aquarium
Nr Sharjah Martime Museum Sharjah **06 528 5288**
sharjahaquarium.ae
Map **3 E1**
Although somewhat eclipsed by the two aquariums that opened in Dubai in recent years, Sharjah Aquarium is the city's newest attraction and draws big crowds, especially at the weekends. Situated next door to Sharjah Maritime Museum at the mouth of Al Khan Lagoon, its location allows visitors to view the Gulf's natural underwater life. There are over 250 species in the aquarium, as well as many interactive displays to educate visitors. Opening hours are 08:00 to 20:00 Monday to Thursday, 16:00 to 21:00 on Fridays and 08:00 to 21:00 on Saturdays; closed Sundays. Admission is Dhs.20 for adults, Dhs.10 for children and Dhs.50 for families.

Sharjah Archaeology Museum
Shk Rashid bin Saqr Al Qasimi Rd Sharjah
06 566 5466
archaeologymuseum.ae
Map **3 E1**
This hi-tech museum offers an interesting display of antiquities from the region. Using well-designed displays and documentary film, the museum traces man's first steps and progress across the Arabian Peninsula through the ages, and one area features the latest discoveries from excavation sites in the UAE. The museum is closed on Sunday, and for part of the afternoon on other days, so it is best to call before you visit to check times.

Sharjah Art Museum
Sharjah Arts Area Sharjah **06 568 8222**
sharjahmuseums.ae
Map **3 E1**
The Arts Area centrepiece, the Art Museum was originally built to house the personal collection of over 300 paintings and maps belonging to the ruler, HH Dr

UAE – The Other Emirates

Sheikh Sultan bin Mohammed Al Qassimi. Permanent displays include the work of 18th century artists, with oil paintings and watercolours depicting life in the Arab world, while other exhibits change frequently. There's an art reference library, bookshop and coffee shop, and the museum hosts various cultural activities. The museum is closed on Friday mornings, while Wednesday afternoons are for ladies only.

Sharjah Desert Park
Interchange 9, Al Dhaid Rd, Al Sajaá Sharjah
06 531 1999
sharjahtourism.ae
Map 3 E1
Located 25 kilometres outside the city, the Sharjah Desert Park complex comprises the Natural History Museum, the Arabian Wildlife Centre, the Childrens' Farm and the recently opened Sharjah Botanical Museum. The Natural History and Botanical Museums feature interactive displays on the relationships between man and the natural world in the UAE and beyond, while at the Arabian Wildlife Centre you get the chance to see many reptiles, birds, creepy crawlies, and mammals, including the rare Arabian leopard. The facilities are excellent and the animals are treated well. There is also a Children's Farm with animals that can be fed and petted. Picnic areas are available, plus cafes and shops. Closed on Tuesdays, entry costs Dhs.5 for children, Dhs.15 for adults and includes access to everything.

Sharjah Discovery Centre
Nr Sharjah International Airport, Al Dhaid Rd
Sharjah 06 558 6577
discoverycentre.ae
Map 3 E1
The Discovery Centre is a great family day out and children of all ages, including toddlers, can explore the many themed areas and experiment and interact with the exhibits. The underlying aim is to teach youngsters about the biological, physical and technological worlds in a practical, and interesting, way. There is good pushchair access, an in-house cafe for light bites, and ample parking. Entrance is Dhs.5 for children and Dhs.10 for adults. The centre is open from 08:00 to 14:00 Sunday to Thursday, and 16:00 to 20:00 Friday and Saturday. Be aware it can get busy at weekends.

Sharjah Heritage Area
Nr Sharjah Arts Area, Al Merraija Sharjah
06 569 3999
sharjahtourism.ae
Map 3 E1
The beautifully restored heritage area is a cultural treasure trove that includes a number of old buildings, such as Al Hisn Fort (Sharjah Fort), Sharjah Islamic Museum, Sharjah Heritage Museum (Bait

Al Naboodah), the Maritime Museum, the Majlis of Ibrahim Mohammed Al Midfa and the Old Souk (Souk Al Arsah). Traditional local architecture and life from the past 150 years is described, depicted and displayed throughout this extensive area. Toilets can be found at each venue and, when the time comes for a rest, there's an Arabic coffee shop in the shaded courtyard of Souk Al Arsah.

Sharjah Maritime Museum
Nr Sharjah Aquarium Sharjah 06 522 2002
sharjahmuseums.ae
Map 3 E1
With the goal of documenting the development of seafaring in the Middle East, the museum's displays feature fishing, trading, pearl diving and boat construction methods native to the UAE. Each room in the museum informs visitors about a different aspect of the marine industry. The museum also houses several real examples of traditional seafaring boats.

Sharjah Museum Of Islamic Civilization
Nr Sharjah Creek, Corniche St Sharjah 06 565 5455
islamicmuseum.ae
Map 3 E1
With vaulted rooms, and impressive galleries and halls, the architecture of this recently-opened museum alone makes a visit worthwhile, but with over 5,000 Islamic artefacts, and reams of information, this is one of the best places to learn about Islam and Islamic culture. The museum is organised according to five themes: the Islamic religion, Islamic art, artefacts, craftsmen and weaponry, each in its own gallery; the Temporary Exhibition Gallery hosts a programme of visiting exhibitions. Entry for adults is Dhs.5; children enter free.

Sharjah Science Museum
Nr Cultural Square Sharjah 06 566 8777
sharjahmuseums.ae
Map 3 E1
The interactive museum's exhibits and demonstrations cover subjects such as aerodynamics, cryogenics, electricity and colour. There's also a planetarium and children's area where the under 5s and their parents can learn together. The Learning Centre offers more in-depth programmes on many of the subjects covered in the museum. Entry costs Dhs.5 for children aged 3 to 17 years; and Dhs.10 for adults.

Sharjah Hotels

Coral Beach Resort
Nr Al Muntazah & Al Nuamia Sts Sharjah 06 522 9999
coral-international.com
Map 3 E1
Sitting on a perfect white beach, this resort boasts a convenient location and wide-ranging sports facilities.

Lou' Lou'a Beach Resort
Shk Sultan Al Awal Rd Sharjah **06 528 5000**
loulouabeach.com
Map **3 E1**
Beach resort situated on the Sharjah coast. Offers watersports and spa facilities.

Radisson Blu Resort, Sharjah
Corniche Rd Sharjah **06 565 7777**
radissonblu.com
Map **3 E1**
Located on the Sharjah Corniche, close to the city's main cultural attractions, the hotel has its own beach.

Sharjah Rotana
Al Arouba St Sharjah **06 563 7777**
rotana.com
Map **3 E1**
Located in the centre of the city, the Rotana caters mostly to business travellers.

Ajman
The smallest of the emirates, Ajman is around 10 kilometres further up the coast from Sharjah city centre, and the two cities almost merge with each other along the coast. There is a nice stretch of beach and a pleasant corniche to walk along. The Ajman Kempinksi Hotel & Resort is a grand offering for those who want a luxurious stay, while there are some other cheaper options along the beach.

Ajman Museum (p.255) houses a variety of interesting displays in a restored fort that is worth visiting as much for the impressive and atmospheric building itself as for the exhibits. The tiny emirate is known for being one of the largest boat building centres in the region, and while it is unfortunately mainly modern boats that emerge from the yards these days, you may still catch a glimpse of a traditionally built wooden dhow being worked on or sailing out to sea. The emirate's main souk is a reminder of the once customary slower pace of life, while Ajman City Centre (06 743 2888) represents the more frantic-paced modern shopping experience, with plenty of shops and a cinema.

Ajman Attractions

Ajman Museum
Nr Clock Tower R/A, Al Bustan Ajman **06 742 3824**
acm.gov.ae
Map **3 E1**
Ajman Museum's interesting and well arranged displays have descriptions in both English and Arabic. The museum has a variety of exhibits, including a collection of Ajman-issued passports and dioramas of ancient life, but it's the building itself that will most impress visitors. Housed in a fortress dating back to

around 1775, the museum is a fascinating example of traditional architecture, with imposing watchtowers and traditional windtowers. Entry is Dhs.5 for adults. Morning opening times are 09:00 to 13:00 then 16:00 to 19:00 in the evening. Closed on Fridays.

Ajman Hotels

Ajman Beach Hotel
Nr Kempinski Hotel Ajman Ajman **06 742 3333**
ajmanbeachhotel.com
Map **3 E1**
The Ajman Beach Hotel is a decent budget hotel with rooms facing both the sea and the creek. This location is excellent for visiting Ajman's principal sites, and you can practically fall out of bed and on to the white, sandy beach.

Kempinski Hotel Ajman
Shk Humaid Bin Rashid Al Nuaimi St Ajman
06 714 5555
kempinski.com
Map **3 E1**
Visitors to Ajman can relax on half a kilometre of the Kempinski's private beach or around its superb pool facilities. The hotel has 185 seaview rooms and a diverse range of international restaurants, cafes and bars, as well as a grand ballroom. The Laguna Spa offers a comprehensive spa menu, including an outdoor Balinese massage.

Umm Al Quwain
Nestled on the coast between Ajman and Ras Al Khaimah, not much has changed in Umm Al Quwain of late. The main industries are still fishing and date cultivation. The emirate has six forts, and a few old watchtowers surround the town.

With plenty of mangroves and birdlife, Umm Al Quwain's lagoon is a popular weekend spot for outdoors enthusiasts. In addition to bird watching, it's possible to come here for boat trips, windsurfing and other watersports. North of the lagoon is known for being a regional activity hub. The Emirates Motorplex (06 768 1166) hosts all types of motorsport events, including the Emirates Motocross Championship which takes place here on a specially built track.

One of the emirate's best-known and most visited attractions is Dreamland Aqua Park (p.216). Another favourite is the adjacent Barracuda Beach Resort (p.256) which is particularly popular thanks to its well-stocked duty-free liquor store.

The emirate has not escaped the attention of the developers completely and a project currently underway will see over 9,000 homes and a marina emerge on the shore of the Khor Al Beidah wildlife area. What impact this will have on the abundant plant and animal life remains to be seen.

Umm Al Quwain Attractions

Dreamland Aqua Park
RAK Highway (E11) Umm Al Quwain 06 768 1888
dreamlanduae.com
Map 3 E1
With over 25 water rides, including four 'twisting dragons', Dreamland Aqua Park is massive. If extreme slides aren't your thing, there's the lazy river, a wave pool, an aqua play area, and a high-salinity floating pool. Overnight accommodation in provided tents or huts is also available. Admission is Dhs.135 for adults and Dhs.85 for children under 1.2m, while children under 2 go free. The park is open all-year-round; Fridays, Saturdays and holidays are for families only.

Umm Al Quwain Hotels

Barracuda Beach Resort
Nr Dreamland Aqua Park, Khor Al Baida
Umm Al Quwain 06 768 1555
barracuda.ae
Map 3 E1
Known throughout the UAE for its popular tax-free booze emporium, Barracuda is also a pleasant resort for quick weekend getaways. Aside from the main hotel, the resort offers several lagoon-side one-bedroom chalets that can each accommodate up to five people. The chalets come with kitchenettes and barbecues – perfect for private overnight parties. There's also a large pool and Jacuzzi.

Flamingo Beach Resort
Nr Horsehead R/A Umm Al Quwain 06 765 0000
flamingoresort.ae
Map 3 E1
Cheap and cheerful, this resort is surrounded by a shallow lagoon interspersed with green islands that attract birdlife including migrating flamingos. Evening crab hunts are available for non-guests.

Imar Spa
Nr Palma Beach Hotel Umm Al Quwain 06 766 4440
imarspa.com
Map 3 E1
This five-star ladies-only spa haven is in the heart of Umm Al Quwain, in a peaceful, seaside setting. The hotel has a small private beach and terrace, a fabulous temperature-controlled pool and a saltwater aqua therapy pool. There are only two twin rooms and three singles so booking in advance is advised.

Ras Al Khaimah > p.257
With the majestic Hajar Mountains rising just behind the city, the Arabian Gulf stretching out from the shore and the desert starting just to the south near the farms and ghaf forests of Digdagga, Ras Al Khaimah

(RAK) has possibly the best scenery of any emirate in the UAE. The northern-most emirate in the country, a creek divides the main city into the old town and the newer Al Nakheel district.

In the past couple of years, Ras Al Khaimah has witnessed a real transformation into a prominent weekend destination, and several new resorts have opened to welcome the overworked residents of Abu Dhabi and Dubai in search of respite. If you're visiting for the day, you should definitely make time to visit the souk in the old town as well as the National Museum of Ras Al Khaimah, which is housed in an old fort.

Manar Mall (manarmall.com) is a large shopping and leisure facility, housing a cinema complex, family entertainment centre, a watersports area and dining options overlooking the creek and mangroves. Other shopping destinations include Al Hamra Mall (alhamramall.com) and Safeer Mall (mysafeer.com) and RAK Mall (rak-mall.com).

The town is also a good starting point for exploring the surrounding mountains, visiting the ancient sites of Ghalilah and Shimal, the hot springs at Khatt and the camel racetrack at Digdagga. Ras Al Khaimah boasts several archaeological sites, some dating back to 3000BC. Take the Al Ram road out of the Al Nakheel district towards the Hajar Mountains to discover some of the area's history, including the Dhayah Fort, Shimal Archaeological Site and Sheba's Palace. The bare ruins of the Dhayah Fort can be spotted from the road, but you might need a 4WD to access them. Further inland is the Shimal archaeological site and Sheba's Palace. Both are a little obscure, but worth the difficulty of finding them. Shimal includes a tomb from the Umm An Nar period, roughly 5,000 years ago. Further down the same road is another tomb, which dates back to the Wadi Suq period (2000BC). Many of the artefacts from these locations can be found at the National Museum at Ras Al Khaimah (see p.258).

RAK has really become something of an outdoor hotspot in recent years, with loads of sports, activities and adventures on offer. Golfers can choose between the Tower Links Golf Course (towerlinks.com) and Al Hamra Golf Club (alhamragolf.com). The former, a popular weekend haunt, is laid out among the mangroves around the creek and features a clubhouse, restaurant and gym. The latter has a gym, three dining options and a seaside sundeck.

Stellar Cellar
The Al Hamra Cellar, owned by MMI (mmidubai.com), is a tax-free liquor store that is well worth the trip. You won't find dodgy booze past its sell-by date; instead, you can browse a wide range of fine wines, spirits and beers at competitive prices. Call 07 244 7403 for more info.

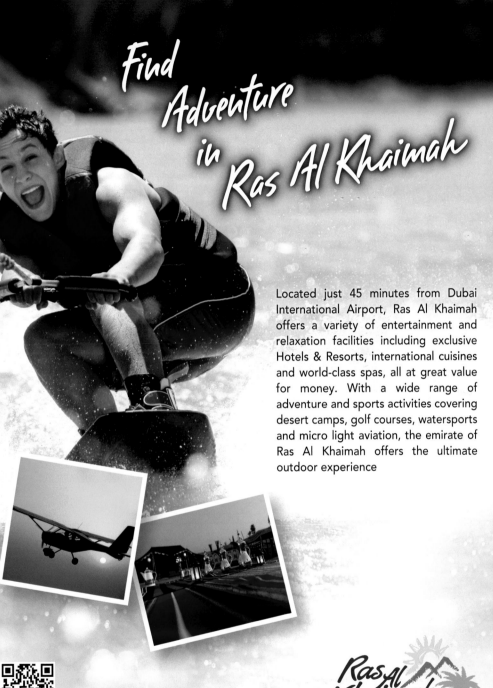

Find Adventure in Ras Al Khaimah

Located just 45 minutes from Dubai International Airport, Ras Al Khaimah offers a variety of entertainment and relaxation facilities including exclusive Hotels & Resorts, international cuisines and world-class spas, all at great value for money. With a wide range of adventure and sports activities covering desert camps, golf courses, watersports and micro light aviation, the emirate of Ras Al Khaimah offers the ultimate outdoor experience

www.rasalkhaimahtourism.com

Ras Al Khaimah

A RISING EMIRATE

The emirate is ideal for hiking and mountain biking, and outdoors activities from mountaineering to kayaking can be arranged by Al Shaheen (alshaheenme.com). Al Hamra Marina (alhamramarina. com) offers boat excursions, waterskiing and fishing trips, as well as jetski rentals while the Prince of the Sea (07 205 9555) sailing excursion combines a lovely boat trip (with lunch and dinner cruises possible) with a taste of tradition. Al Hamra Fort Hotel (p.258) and Banyan Tree Al Wadi (p.249) provide loads of activities for those staying the night and not, such as riding, archery, desert safaris and falconry experiences. Elswhere, Ice Land Water Park (p.216) provides cooling water fun.

There are also several chances to get into the mountains up the coast, as well as south of RAK in places like Jebel Yibir – the tallest mountain in the country, where a new track takes you nearly to the top for spectacular views.

Ras Al Khaimah Attractions

Dhayah Fort
Al Rams Ras Al Khaimah **07 233 8998**
rasalkhaimahtourism.com
Map **3 F1**
Built in the 16th century as a strategic military castle, Dhayah Fort stands proud on a mountainside overlooking the Gulf. It was the site of a battle between local tribes and British troops and the towers were set alight in 1819. The fort was restored in the 90s.

Ice Land Water Park
Al Jazeera, Al Hamra Ras Al Khaimah
07 206 7888
icelandwaterpark.com
Map **3 E1**
The first major attraction to open in the giant WOW RAK tourist destination, the polar-themed Ice Land has more than 50 rides and attractions, including Penguin Falls, Snow River and Mount Cyclone. Open from 10:00 every day; adult entry costs Dhs.150 while entry for children under 1.2m tall is Dhs.100.

National Museum Of Ras Al Khaimah
Nr Police HQ Ras Al Khaimah **07 233 3411**
rasalkhaimahtourism.com
Map **3 F1**
Housed in an impressive fort that was once the home of the present ruler of Ras Al Khaimah, this museum focuses on local natural history and archaeological displays, including a variety of paraphernalia from pre-oil, Bedouin life. Look out for fossils set in the rock strata of the walls of the fort – these date back 190 million years. The building has battlements, a working windtower and ornate, carved wooden doors. Entrance is only Dhs.2 for adults and Dhs.1 for children;

directions can be found on the museum website. Open every day except Tuesday and public holidays.

RAK Pearl Museum
Al Qawassim Corniche, Ras Al Khaimah
050 198 0480
rakpearls.com
Map **3 F1**
This museum presents visitors with a glimpse into the history of the pearling industry in the Arabian Peninsula. Displayed are collections of ancient equipment, diving suits, as well as a plethora of pearls in all different shapes and colours.

Ras Al Khaimah Hotels

Al Hamra Fort Hotel & Beach Resort
Al Jazeerah St Ras Al Khaimah **07 244 6666**
alhamrafort.com
Map **3 E1**
With traditional Arabic architecture set among acres of lush gardens and along a strip of sandy beach, this hotel offers a peaceful getaway. A range of watersports and activities, including two floodlit golf courses and an onsite dive centre, will keep you entertained, and the eight themed eateries offer a wide variety of international cuisines and atmosphere.

Al Hamra Palace Beach Resort
Al Hamra Village Ras Al Khaimah **07 206 7222**
casahotels.com
Boasting 147 rooms and suites, this beach resort is geared towards sports, activities and recreational time, with a long stretch of private beach, a lovely pool, tennis courts, kids' playing areas, a gym, golf course and watersports centre.

Desert Camps
A fun alternative to a night in a hotel can be a night at one of RAK's amazing desert camps. The Bedouin Oasis camp (arabianincentive.com), for example, was built using only traditional and natural materials, while the Bassata Camp (07 205 9555) offers the complete Arabian experience, with a barbecue, belly dancers and a spot of dune bashing.

Banyan Tree Al Wadi
Al Mazraa Ras Al Khaimah **07 206 7777**
banyantree.com
Map **3 F1**
Banyan Tree Al Wadi combines superior luxury with exclusive spa facilities, desert activities and a wildlife conservation area. Set within Wadi Khadeja, the villas are designed for optimum relaxation with private pools and views of the desert.

Exploring Fossil Rock

A brief guide to the perfect route for first-timers.

Fossil Rock is the UAE's easiest desert route to access, and to drive, with some superb and varied scenery along the way. Starting at Al Awir, off the E44 Hatta Road about 20 minutes outside the city of Dubai, it is the perfect drive for absolute beginners and novices to cut their teeth on in the desert and gain some valuable lessons. It provides a slightly more rugged landscape than the oceans of dunes that accompany all off-road adventures nearer to Abu Dhabi. As with anywhere, it's definitely better to accompany an experienced driver the first couple of times you head out.

The route is pretty straightforward to navigate – the driving starts along a sandy track then graduates to rolling through some easy medium-sized dunes later on. Making its way to the starting point in the fertile oasis town of Al Awir, the road weaves through a surprising amount of greenery, trees and farms, and many palaces and stately homes. Keep a look out for the estate that's home to herds of gazelle and deer, race horses that can often be spotted training, and the long wall of the summer palace belonging to the Al Maktoum family.

Existing tracks normally define the best path to take, especially on this route. They offer the easiest route, with only gentle inclines and descents, and limit damage to flora and fauna. However, when you start to get the hang of it, there are some places where

Off-Road Expert

For more information on all to do with driving off-roading and exploring all corners of the country, pick up a copy of the *UAE Off-Road Explorer*. Fossil Rock is one of 26 routes featured in full detail, with annotated satellite images and detailed descriptions of the route, along with attractions and activities along the way.

you can climb up to the top of the dunes following alongside the track to weave your way along the ridges. The first half of the route finishes in sight of a main road, where it turns and follows the sandy river bed of Wadi Fayah along the bottom of the dunes. This fast and fun track weaves through bushes, trees, dunes and some rocky outcrops to a short gravely climb out onto the road.

After crossing the road, sticking with the main undulating sandy track heading up into the dunes will take you quite smoothly and easily towards Fossil Rock, clearly visible ahead. If you are feeling confident with your new skills, there is plenty of adventurous terrain just off the main track to test your driving among the dunes and bowls on either side, including in the area around the rock known as Camel Rock.

The striking Fossil Rock is always there as a landmark to avoid getting lost, and whenever you have had enough, just pick up the track again and head towards the rock. When you reach the hard track under the pylons with Fossil Rock directly in front of you, the quickest and easiest exit route is to turn right and head back past the village of Maleihah and the main road. It is possible to head straight on for even more challenging driving and the climb up to Fossil Rock (or Jebel Maleihah as it is officially called) itself, but this is more one for expert drivers. If you do make it up to the top, whether on foot or behind the wheel, it is a fun place for a scramble, and for the views and a poke around to see if you can spot a fossil or two.

After leaving the desert, don't forget to re-inflate your tyres as soon as possible, as driving on tarmac with soft tyres can cause blowouts. To get to the nearest petrol station, when you meet the tarmac road turn left and it is roughly two kilometres along the road on the right. If you carry on a little further, you will reach the S116 – the fastest way back to civilisation.

Banyan Tree Ras Al Khaimah Beach

Al Jazirah Al Hamra Ras Al Khaimah **07 206 7777**
banyantree.com
Map **3 E1**
The sister property of Banyan Tree Al Wadi, this stunning beach resort offers 32 beachfront villas built in the style of the nomadic Bedouin's tents – but far more luxurious. A lovely hideaway, or great for thrill seekers, with snorkelling, sailing and watersports all on offer.

The Cove Rotana Resort

Off Shk Mohd Bin Salem Rd, Arcoob Ras Al Khaimah **07 206 6000**
rotana.com
Map **3 F1**
Built into the hills overlooking the Arabian Gulf, The Cove's sprawling layout of 204 rooms, 72 private villas and winding pathways is reminiscent of an old Mediterranean hill town. The resort revolves around an immaculate lagoon, protected from the sea by 600 metres of pristine beach. A Bodylines spa and several impressive restaurants round out the package.

Golden Tulip Khatt Springs Resort & Spa

Nr Hajjar Mountains, Khatt Ras Al Khaimah **07 244 8777**
goldentulipkhattsprings.com
Map **3 F1**
Simple and subdued, Golden Tulip Khatt Springs Resort & Spa relies on mountain views, uninterrupted tranquillity and incredible spa packages to attract weekend visitors. Next to the hotel, you can take a dip in the public Khatt Hot Springs – piping hot water which, it is claimed, has curative powers. Men and women have separate pools and a variety of massages are also available. It's a good idea to visit the hot springs in the morning and avoid Fridays as it can get very busy with families.

Hilton Ras Al Khaimah Resort & Spa

Al Maareedh St, Al Mairid Ras Al Khaimah **07 228 8411**
hilton.com
Map **3 F1**
Tucked away on an exclusive bay, out of sight of the city, the resort's many guest rooms and villas are perfect for a beach break. The pool bar, spa and laid-back dining options make this one of the most relaxing destinations in the region. Guests of the older Hilton Ras Al Khaimah (07 228 8888, hilton.com), located in the city, can use the facilities.

Fujairah

A trip to the east coast is a must for any west coast resident. Made up of the emirate of Fujairah and several enclaves belonging to Sharjah, the villages along the east coast sit between the rugged Hajar Mountains and the gorgeous Gulf of Oman.

The two or three-hour drive from Abu Dhabi (depending if you take the old route or the new highway through the mountains) passes through some of the UAE's most scenic mountain passes. Fujairah city has seen little development compared to west coast cities, but the real draw here is the landscape. Mountains and wadis stretch west of the coast, offering some of the country's best and most accessible camping spots. The beaches, reefs and villages attract visitors throughout the year.

East Coast Made Easy

To reach the UAE's east coast from Abu Dhabi takes about three hours by road. The most popular route is to pick up the E611 outside of Dubai, turning onto the E88 that runs from Sharjah to Masafi, and then turn left to Dibba or right to Fujairah. A quieter alternative is the S116, which heads south-east out of Sharjah, past Fossil Rock and through the Hajar Mountains, hitting the coast at Kalba. It's faster than the E88, it's smooth, it's got tunnels, great scenery, and is so quiet you'll wonder why no-one else seems to know about it yet.

Bidiyah

The site of the oldest mosque in the UAE, Bidiyah is one of the oldest settlements on the east coast and is believed to have been inhabited since 3000BC. The mosque is made from gypsum, stone and mud bricks finished off with plaster, and its original design of four domes supported by a central pillar was considered unique, but the shape was changed to stepped domes during the recent renovation. The building is believed to date back to the middle of the 15th century. The mosque is still used for prayer, so non-Muslim visitors can't enter. Built next to a low hillside with several restored watchtowers on the ridge behind, the area is now lit up at night with coloured light.

Dibba

Located at the northern-most point of the east coast, on the border with Musandam (p.263), Dibba is made up of three fishing villages. Unusually, each part comes under a different jurisdiction: Dibba al Hisn is part of Sharjah, Dibba Muhallab is Fujairah and Dibba Bayah is Oman. The three Dibbas share an attractive bay, fishing communities, and excellent diving locations – from here you can arrange dhow trips to take you to unspoilt dive locations in the Musandam. The Hajar Mountains provide a wonderful backdrop, rising in places to over 1,800 metres. There are some good public beaches too, where your only company will be the crabs and seagulls, and where seashell collectors may find a few treasures.

Fujairah City

The town of Fujairah is a mix of old and new. The surrounding hillsides are dotted with ancient forts and watchtowers, which add an air of mystery and charm. Most of these also appear to be undergoing restoration work, too. Fujairah is also a busy trading centre, with its modern container port and a thriving free zone attracting major companies from around the world. Off the coast, the seas and coral reefs make a great spot for fishing, diving and watersports. It is also a good place for birdwatching during the spring and autumn migrations as it is on the route from Africa to Central Asia. Since Fujairah is close to the mountains and many areas of natural beauty, it makes an excellent base from where to explore the countryside and discover wadis, forts, waterfalls and even natural hot springs.

Kalba

Just to the south of Fujairah you'll find Kalba, which is renowned for its mangrove forest and golden beaches. It's a pretty fishing village that still manages to retain much of its historical charm. There is a road through the mountains linking Kalba to Hatta which makes for an interesting alternative when returning.

Khor Kalba

Set in a beautiful tidal estuary (khor is Arabic for creek), Khor Kalba is a fascinating mangrove forest and home to a variety of plant, marine and birdlife not found anywhere else in the UAE. The mangroves

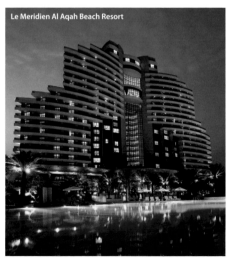
Le Meridien Al Aqah Beach Resort

flourish in this area thanks to a mix of seawater and freshwater from the mountains. The delicate wetlands are receding due to the excessive use of water from inland wells, but there is still plenty to see. For birdwatchers, the area is especially good during the spring and autumn migrations when the routes of migratory birds mean rare species can be spotted. The bird species frequently seen include the resident reef heron and the area is also home to a rare subspecies of white collared kingfisher, which breeds nowhere else in the world (except nearby in Oman). A canoe tour by Desert Rangers (p.232) is ideal for reaching the heart of the reserve. Furthermore, there's also the possibility of seeing one of the region's endangered turtles.

Fujairah Attractions

Dibba Castle
Dibba
Map **3 F1**
Hidden away in the Omani part of Dibba (aka Daba), next to vast farms and plantations, Dibba Castle is an interesting place to have a poke around. Built over 180 years ago, it has been restored, and while there aren't a lot of artefacts on show, you can access all the rooms and climb up the towers, where you'll get views over the castle and its surroundings. It is signposted off the road past the UAE border check post.

Fujairah Fort
Nr Fujairah Heritage Village, Al Sharia Fujairah
Map **3 F2**
Part of the east coast's rich heritage, Fujairah Fort has recently undergone a major renovation programme. Although you cannot enter the fort itself, the surrounding heritage buildings are open for viewing. Carbon dating estimates the main part of the fort to be over 500 years old.

Fujairah Heritage Village
Nr Fujairah Fort, Al Sharia Fujairah **09 222 6662**
Map **3 F2**
Situated just outside Fujairah city, this collection of fishing boats, simple dhows and tools depicts life

Bull Butting

On Friday afternoons during winter, crowds gather between the Hilton Hotel and the Khor Kalba area to watch 'bull butting'. This ancient Portuguese sport consists of two huge bulls going head to head for several rounds, until after a few nudges and a bit of hoof bashing, a winner is determined. It's not as cruel or barbaric as other forms of bullfighting, but animal lovers may still want to avoid it.

in the UAE before oil was discovered. There are two spring-fed swimming pools for men and women and chalets can be hired by the day.

Fujairah Museum
Nr Fujairah Heritage Village, Al Sharia Fujairah **09 222 9085**
Map **3 F2**
This interesting museum offers permanent exhibitions on traditional ways of life, including the not-so-distant past nomadic Bedouin culture. There are also several artefacts on display that were found during archaeological excavations throughout the emirate. Some of the items displayed include weapons from the bronze and iron ages, finely painted pottery, carved soapstone vessels and silver coins. The museum is open from 07:30 to 18:00 from Saturday to Thursday and from 14:00 to 18:00 on Friday. Entry fee is Dhs.5.

Fujairah Tennis & Country Club
Nr Rd 89, Halefaath Fujairah **09 224 4880**
fujairahtennisclub.ae
Map **3 F2**
The recently renovated sporting and leisure complex makes a great destination for a weekend away. In addition to six flood-lit hard courts and a centre court, the general sports and fitness facilities are fantastic, and overnight stays are possible at the adjacent boutique hotel which features 14 cosy rooms.

Fujairah Hotels
Fujairah is home to several great beach hotels, many of which offer scuba diving. In addition to the below, overnight stays are possible at the Fujairah Tennis & Country Club (p.262).

Fujairah Rotana Resort & Spa – Al Aqah Beach
Al Aqah Beach Fujairah **09 244 9888**
rotana.com
Map **3 F1**
Each of the 250 guest rooms and suites has its own balcony and view over the sea. The hotel offers some of the best dining options on the east coast, as well as an indulgent spa, a private beach and a huge pool.

Golden Tulip Resort Dibba
Mina Rd Dibba **+968 2 683 6654**
goldentulipdibba.com
Map **3 F1**
Simple, clean and with a great beach, this is a good option for an affordable getaway. From the nearby Dibba Port you can take a dhow cruise and the hotel is also in a great location for snorkelling in the pristine waters of the Gulf.

Hilton Fujairah Resort
Al Ghourfa Rd Fujairah **09 222 2411**
hilton.com
Map **3 F2**
Set at the northern end of Fujairah's corniche, just a stone's throw from the foothills of the Hajars, this relaxing resort has all facilities needed for a wonderful weekend away and is a regular haunt for most expats living and working in Fujairah. If you get tired of lounging by the swimming pool, or trying your hand at activities like tennis, snooker and basketball – or even watersports on the private beach – you could always head out to explore the rugged splendour of the surrounding mountains. The hotel is particularly good for families, and there are a number of safe play areas for children.

Le Meridien Al Aqah Beach Resort
Dibba – Khor Fakkan Rd Fujairah **09 244 9000**
lemeridien-alaqah.com
Map **3 F1**
All of the rooms at Le Meridien Al Aqah have views over the Indian Ocean, and the grounds are covered by lush foliage. It is particularly geared up for families, with a kids' pool and outdoor and indoor play areas. There's an extensive spa, a dive centre, and entertainment options include a cinema, bars and restaurants serving a range of Thai, Indian and European cuisine.

Radisson Blu Resort, Fujairah
Al Faqeet, Dibba Fujairah **09 244 9700**
radissonblu.com
Map **3 F1**
Its pastel exterior might be an acquired taste, but the modern, business-like interior and wonderful restaurants that lie within make this hotel a bit of a treat for the senses. The whole place is reminiscent of a spa, with clean lines and wholesome colours. There is, in fact, a wonderful Japanese spa and plenty of private beach.

Sandy Beach Hotel & Resort
Dibba – Khorfakkan Rd Fujairah **09 244 5555**
sandybm.com
Map **3 F2**
Snoopy Island has long been recognised as one of the best diving spots in the United Arab Emirates and the island is right off the coast from the Sandy Beach Hotel, making it a firm favourite with UAE residents. Day trippers can purchase a day-pass to the hotel to access the temperature-controlled pool, watersports and beach bar services. There is also a five-star Padi Dive Centre within the hotel that rents diving and snorkelling gear for exploring the reefs around Snoopy Island.

Out Of The City

GCC

Over the past decade, the countries that make up the Gulf Cooperation Council (Bahrain, Kuwait, Oman, Qatar, Saudi Arabia and the UAE) have been building their tourism industries in an effort to diversify their oil-based economies. Several international brands have opened hotels in the region and the respective governments have made a real effort to promote their heritage and culture. To learn more about the region's history, see the UAE chapter on p.245.

Oman

The most accessible country in the GCC for residents of Abu Dhabi, Oman is a peaceful and breathtaking place, with history, culture and spectacular scenery. The capital, Muscat, has enough attractions to keep you busy for a good long weekend, including beautiful beaches, some great restaurants and cafes, the mesmerising old souk at Mutrah, and the Sultan Qaboos Mosque. Out of the capital you will find many historic old towns and forts, and some of the most stunning mountain and wadi scenery in the region. Salalah (p.266) in the south has the added bonus of being cool and wet in the summer.

A flight from Abu Dhabi to Muscat takes 60 minutes, but when you factor in check-in times and clearing customs it's not much quicker than driving. There are daily flights from Abu Dhabi, Dubai and Sharjah with Etihad, Emirates, Oman Air and Air Arabia (p.264). Regular flights direct to Salalah are also available.

There is also a daily bus service between Abu Dhabi and both Muscat and Salalah, taking seven and 17 hours respectively, and costing from Dhs.50 for the Abu Dhabi to Muscat trip (ontcoman.com).

For further information on Oman check out the *Oman Residents' & Visitors' Guide*, *Oman Off-Road*

Visas

Visas for Oman are required whether entering by air or road, and different regulations apply depending on your nationality and how long you want to stay. Nationalities are split into two groups – check out the Royal Oman Police website, rop.gov.om, for full lists (click on 'Directorates', then 'DG of Passports'). People in group one can get a visit visa at the border for a nominal fee. Residents from group two, however, will need to get a visa from the Oman consulate or embassy in advance, which may take a few days to process so check before you head out for the border to avoid being stuck. Oman does have a common visa facility with the UAE, meaning people on an Abu Dhabi visit visa will not need a separate visa to visit Oman.

Explorer and the *Oman Trekking Explorer* – see askexplorer.com/shop.

Musandam

The UAE's northern neighbour, Musandam is an isolated enclave belonging to Oman. The region is dominated by the same Hajar Mountains that run through the eastern UAE. As the peninsula juts into the Strait of Hormuz, it breaks up into a myriad of jagged, picturesque fjords. Spending a day exploring the fjords on a wooden dhow is a must for any Dubai resident. Most trips originate from the region's capital, Khasab, and day trips from Khasab Travel & Tours (04 266 9950) cost around Dhs.200 per person and include lunch, soft drinks and an informative guide. Alternately, you can access the famous Wadi Bih off-road route from Dibba and spend a weekend camping atop some of the region's most magnificent mountains. See the *UAE Off-Road Explorer* for information about the route.

The Chedi Muscat

LONG WEEKEND TRIPS

Make the most of a long weekend by heading off to one of many great travel destinations within easy reach of the UAE.

Abu Dhabi's central location makes it an ideal base for exploring the region beyond the GCC countries. If you can't find a cheap flight from Abu Dhabi International Airport, don't hesitate to look for better deals departing from either Dubai, Sharjah or even Al Ain. The country now has two low-cost carriers, Air Arabia at Sharjah Airport and flydubai at Dubai Airport. Both offer some incredible deals. If you'd rather fly in style, both Etihad and Emirates fly to enough locations to keep you planning for years to come.

Kerala

Cyprus

It's hard to believe that this idyllic Mediterranean island is such a short flight from Abu Dhabi. Three main towns, Larnaca, Limassol and Paphos, each offer unique accommodation and leisure options, and capital city Nicosia is great for shopping and nightlife. Whether you choose to rent a self-catering apartment or stay in a luxurious hotel on full board, a holiday in Cyprus is a huge change from the Gulf. You can drive up mountains for crisp, cool air and some awesome views, and explore quiet local villages off the beaten track.

Flights:
Air Liban – Abu Dhabi to Larnaca, Dhs.4,400
Emirates – Dubai to Larnaca, Dhs.3,700
Etihad – Abu Dhabi to Larnaca, Dhs.2,200

Egypt

Egypt is an ideal trip for history fans. It's one of the oldest civilisations in the world and home to famous historical sites such as the Pyramids and Sphinx. It also has some amazing scenery: there is the moon-like White Desert and the isolated Siwa Oasis in the west, the Red Sea and the vast Sinai Peninsula in the east, and, of course, the Nile, which flows south to north through the country, past the incredible ruins between Aswan and Luxor. Cairo's chaotic streets are a constant adventure and the city has an active nightlife.

Flights
Etihad – Abu Dhabi to Cairo, Dhs.1,700
flydubai – Dubai to Alexandria, Dhs.1,700
Air Arabia – Sharjah to Luxor, Dhs.1,600

India

India is a land of many guises, from the beautiful beaches of Goa and the vibrant city of Mumbai to the imposing mountains of Kashmir and lush coastline of Kerala. It's best to avoid the summer monsoon, but if you do get caught in the rain, you can take advantage of good off-season deals. Some areas such as Ladakh in northern India and the desert state of Rajasthan receive very little, if any, rain all year.

Flights
Air India Express – Al Ain to Kozhikode, Dhs.1,600
Jet Airways – Abu Dhabi to Delhi, Dhs.3,000
Air Arabia – Sharjah to Kochi, Dhs.1,700
   Sharjah to Jaipur, Dhs.1,800
   Sharjah to Hyderabad, Dhs.1,800
Jet Airways – Dubai to Delhi, Dhs.2,400

Jordan

Jordan is packed with religious and historical sites, incredible architecture, and friendly, welcoming people. The capital, Amman, offers enough dining and cultural attractions to fill up a few days, but to truly experience the country, you'll need to get out of the city. Head south to feast your eyes on Petra, the ancient city built into solid rock canyons. On your way, don't miss the opportunity to float atop the waters of the Dead Sea. History and religious experts will be fascinated by the many holy sites that dot the country, and movie buffs shouldn't miss a trip to Wadi Rum, where Lawrence of Arabia was filmed.

Flights
Etihad – Abu Dhabi to Amman, Dhs.1,300
Air Arabia – Sharjah to Amman, Dhs.1,300
flydubai – Dubai to Amman, Dhs.1,500

Lebanon

Lebanon's blossoming development as a vibrant tourist destination has suffered some knockbacks with conflicts both internally and externally. But never a nation to take things lying down, it is doing everything possible to rebuild itself. Beirut's nightlife is considered by many to be the best in the Middle East, and its culinary excellence is well-known. Outside of Beirut is just as interesting; the massive Roman temples in Baalbek are not to be missed, and the many villages scattered throughout the country hold the key to Lebanon's incredible hospitality. Come the winter, you can enjoy a spot of skiing at Mzaar-Kfardebian (skimzaar.com).

Flights
Etihad – Abu Dhabi to Beirut, Dhs.1,600
Air Arabia – Sharjah to Beirut, Dhs.1,100
flydubai – Dubai to Beirut, Dhs.1,200

Sri Lanka

The beauty of Sri Lanka, apart from the short flight time from the UAE, is that you can either have a fantastic holiday on a small budget or indulge in luxury of a lifetime. Colombo has several attractions, but most holidaymakers choose to spend their time in the lush mountains or at the untouched beaches.

Flights
Sri Lankan Airlines – Abu Dhabi to Colombo, Dhs.1,300
Air Arabia – Sharjah to Colombo, Dhs.1,200

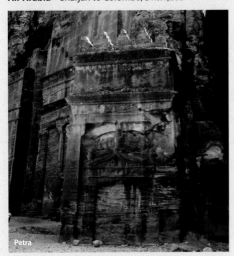
Petra

Emirates – Dubai to Colombo, Dhs.1,400
Qatar Airways – Dubai to Colombo, Dhs.2,600

Syria

With Damascus, the oldest continuously inhabited city in the world, Aleppo, the food capital of the world, and untouched countryside, Syria is a traveller's dream. However, in mid-2011 there was a period of civil unrest which resulted in many countries issuing warnings against all travel here – at the time of writing it is unclear whether the situation will resolve itself quickly, so check with your embassy before booking your trip. Once it is safe once more, the old part of Damascus is a joy to explore on foot thanks to the many souks and unique architecture. The ancient city of Palmyra (known as Tadmor in Syria) is only a four-hour bus ride from Damascus and a must for anyone interested in the country's incredible past. Syria is a great choice for budget-minded travellers, as flights to and from the UAE are cheap and you could spend an entire week eating only the delicious street food.

Flights
Etihad – Abu Dhabi to Damascus, Dhs.1,500
Air Arabia – Sharjah to Damascus, Dhs.1,500
flydubai – Dubai to Damascus, Dhs.1,600

Turkey

Perfectly placed between contrasting cultures of east and west, Turkey is a popular holiday destination with beautiful landscapes, great weather, sun, sea and mountains. Istanbul is an amazing city – full of history, great food and vibrant nightlife. Alternatively, take a road trip to the capital, Ankara, for a taste of Turkish student life and a glimpse of the country's most modern city. If you need a break from big-city life, head south to the equally impressive Bursa, where you'll find the iconic Ulu Cami mosque and huge, communal thermal baths.

Flights
Etihad – Abu Dhabi to Istanbul, Dhs.2,500
Turkish Airlines – Abu Dhabi to Istanbul, Dhs.1,600
Air Arabia – Sharjah to Istanbul, Dhs.1,600
Emirates – Dubai to Istanbul, Dhs.2,000

DIRECTORY:

Air Arabia – airarabia.com
Air India Express – airindiaexpress.in
Emirates – emirates.com
Etihad – etihadairways.com
flydubai – flydubai.com
Jet Airways – jetairways.com
Sri Lankan Airlines – srilankan.aero
Turkish Airlines – turkishairlines.com

Nizwa

Having driven for several hours, deep into the Hajar Mountains, you'll find yourself at Nizwa, the largest city in Oman's interior. This oasis city offers fascinating sights and heritage, including the 17th century Nizwa Fort and the Jabrin Fort, notable for the secret passageways that run throughout.

Salalah

Home to several museums and several souks, Salalah is best known for its lush landscape that is quite unlike anywhere else on the Arabian Peninsula. The scenery is especially attractive during the summer months, when the area catches the Indian monsoon. Salalah is also a major frankincense producer and you can visit the farms along the Yemen border to witness how it is extracted. A 16 hour drive from Dubai (flying is a much more attractive option), you should plan on spending a few days here to make the most of the relatively long journey over.

Oman Hotels

The Chedi Muscat

18th November St, Way No 3215, North Ghubra 32 Muscat **+968 24 524 400**
chedimuscat.com

This beautiful boutique hotel on the shore is famed for its clean lines, luxury and an impressive sense of calm. The stunning spa and outstanding restaurant don't hurt either. With an infinity pool, private beach and library, this is a destination for a break from bustle and perhaps isn't an ideal choice for families.

Crowne Plaza Muscat

Off Al Qurm St Muscat **+968 24 660 660**
ichotelsgroup.com

This established hotel boasts cliff top views over Al Qurum and the beach below. Many of the 200 guest rooms benefit from the striking vistas and several of the restaurants also boast outdoor terraces. There's a large swimming pool, gym, spa and dolphin watching trips available, making this hotel a great choice for those looking for relaxation and for visitors who want an action packed break.

InterContinental Muscat

Al Kharjiya St Muscat **+968 24 680 000**
intercontinental.com

An older hotel that has recently undergone a major facelift, the InterContinental continues to be popular for its outdoor facilities, international restaurants and regular entertainment in the form of dinner theatres and visiting bands. Alfresco restaurant, Tomato, is a must-try. Trader Vic's, with its legendary cocktails, is perennially popular. All of the rooms have views of Qurum Beach, landscaped gardens or the mountains.

Oman Dive Center

Nr Qantab & Barr Al Jissah, Bandar Jussa Muscat **+968 24 824 240**
extradivers-worldwide.com

Just south of Muscat, a stay here is an amazing and sociable experience; and one that is highly enjoyable whether you're a diver or not. You can book a barasti hut (they are actually made of stone, with barasti covering) for an average of RO.66 for two people (depending on season). The room price includes breakfast and dinner in the centre's licensed restaurant. For keen divers, the centre offers dive training and excursions, as well as boat tours in the surrounding area.

Hoota Cave

This cave has a large chamber with some amazing rock formations, an underground lake and a fascinating ecosystem. Facilities include a train that transports you into the cave, knowledgeable guides, a restaurant and a natural history museum. Photography is not allowed. Visitors must book at least 24 hours in advance, as there are only a limited number of people allowed in at any time. (+968 24 490 060, alhootacave.com).

Shangri-La's Barr Al Jissah Resort & Spa

Off Al Jissah St Muscat **+968 24 776 666**
shangri-la.com

With three hotels catering for families, business travellers and luxury-seekers, the Shangri-La is one of the most gorgeous resorts in the region. The hotels have several swimming pools and enough play areas to keep children occupied for days. The exclusive, six-star Al Husn is incredibly luxurious and perfect for a weekend of out-of-town pampering.

Six Senses Zighy Bay

Zighy Bay, Musandam Daba **+968 267 355 55**
sixsenses.com

Located in a secluded cove in Musandam, the resort has been designed in true rustic style and is made up of individual pool villas. Like all Six Senses resorts, the focus here is on relaxation. The spa treatments available are of the highest quality and expertly prepared dinners can be enjoyed from the comfort of your own villa, or from the mountainside restaurant with breathtaking views of the bay.

Bahrain

Just a 40 minute flight from Abu Dhabi, Bahrain has been a popular destination since the 1970s thanks to a mix of architecture, miles of souks, excellent shopping and some truly outstanding bars and restaurants. However, in early 2011, there was a period of civil unrest, which resulted in some countries issuing travel warnings on the island nation. At the time of writing, it remains unclear whether the situation will resolve itself quickly, so check with your embassy.

Bahrain Attractions

Bahrain Fort
Nr Karbabad Village, Karbabad Manama
bahraintourism.com
This impressive 16th century Portuguese fort is built on the remains of several previous settlements, going back to the Dilmun era around 2800BC. There are several large, informative notices dotted around the area, and some information booklets are available in English. Entry is free and the fort is open from 08:00 to 20:00 every day including Friday. The village at the entrance to the fort is worth a visit on its own. Nearly every square inch of the place, from walls to satellite dishes, is covered in brightly coloured murals.

Bahrain National Museum
Nr Al Fatih Highway Manama
bahraintourism.com
Situated on the corniche, this museum documents Bahraini life before the introduction of oil. Children will love the Hall of Graves and the museum often hosts impressive international exhibits.

Beit Al Qur'an
Nr Diplomat Radisson Blu Hotel Manama
+973 1729 0101
bahraintourism.com
The building may not look like much from afar, but a closer inspection reveals walls covered in beautiful Arabic calligraphy. The museum displays examples of historical calligraphy and Islamic manuscripts. Entrance is free, but donations are welcome.

The Burial Mounds
South of Saar Village & West of A'ali Village Manama
bahraintourism.com
One of the most remarkable sights in Bahrain is the vast area of burial mounds at Saar, near A'ali Village, at Hamad Town and at Sakhir. The mounds were built during the Dilmun, Tylos and Helenistic periods and are anything from 2,000 to 4,000 years old. The largest burial mounds, which are known as the Royal Tombs, are found in and around A'ali Village.

La Fontaine Centre Of Contemporary Art
92 Hoora Avenue Manama **+973 1723 0123**
lafontaineartcentre.net
This place is a true architectural gem. There are wind towers, cool corridors, a Pilates studio that has to be seen to be believed, a world-class restaurant, an extensive spa, regular film screenings and art

exhibitions. These make La Fontaine a unique jewel in Bahrain's crown. The enormous fountain in the courtyard is worth a visit.

Bahrain Hotels

Al Areen Palace & Spa
Nr Bahrain International Circuit, Umm Jidr Manama
+973 1784 5000
alareenpalace.com
Located close to the F1 International Circuit, this all-villa resort offers an extensive spa, outstanding restaurants and good conference facilities.

Al Bander Hotel & Resort
Nr Bahrain Yacht Club, Maámeer Sitra
+973 1770 1201
albander.com
Located at the southern end of Sitra, this resort has a wide range of facilities including swimming pools and watersports at their private beach. Rooms are either cabana style or in chalets, and there are activities for kids and a variety of food and dining options.

The Diplomat Radisson Blu Hotel, Residence & Spa
Nr King Faisal Highway & Shk Hamad Causeway Manama **+973 1753 1666**
radissonblu.com
Overlooking the Gulf, on the edge of the Diplomatic area and close to the National Museum, this is a five-star property with a spa, a large lagoon pool and a range of dining and drinking venues.

The Gulf Hotel Bahrain
Al Fateh Ave Manama **+973 1771 3000**
gulfhotelbahrain.com
Just five minutes from the city centre, the popular Gulf Hotel has 352 rooms including eight suites. Its facilities include an outdoor swimming pool, a gymnasium, a beauty salon, shops and babysitting services. It has several popular restaurants and bars.

Race To Bahrain

Long before Abu Dhabi hosted its first GP, Bahrain was welcoming the F1 circus to its own desert racetrack. After a break in 2011 (due to civil unrest, see p.266), the race returned in 2012. In the meantime, there are are other regular races, running through the winter months, or you can take to the track yourself in a single-seater Caterham Xtreme. The karting zone is a real rush, as is testing a monster 4WD across a range of obstacles at the off-road experience – one of just two anywhere in the world. See bahraingp.com for details of all of these activities.

MUSCAT

Sandwiched between spectacular rocky mountains and beautiful beaches, Muscat is one of the Middle East's most striking cities.

Muscat is one of the most attractive and charismatic cities in the Middle East, and once you've visited you'll understand why many count it as their favourite regional city. It is visually striking and hugely varied, set out between the Gulf of Oman and the Hajar mountains. While generally characterised by white, low-rise buildings, Muscat has many separate areas nestling between the low craggy mountains and the ocean. This is because the city is actually formed by three smaller towns that have grown together over history to form what is now known as Muscat. Indeed, there is no one area that defines Muscat on its own – each part has its own distinctive character and charm.

Great care has been taken to ensure that, while it is definitely a modern city, there is a cohesive and traditional Arabic element which has been retained. Visit the old town of Muscat or the Mutrah Souk for an idea of what life has been like for decades for the people that still live in the area. Muscat is clean and features a lot more greenery than you may be used to in Abu Dhabi. With beautiful beaches, bustling souks, a collection of great restaurants and cafes, and some fascinating museums, you'll need at least a few days to fully discover this friendly city. The main areas worth exploring are around the old town and the fishing port of Mutrah, although taking long walks along the beach in Qurum or exploring the natural lagoons in Qantab are also worthwhile activities.

The Old Town Of Muscat

The old town of Muscat is situated on the coast at the eastern end of the greater Muscat area between Mutrah and Sidab. It is quiet and atmospheric, based around a sheltered port that was historically important for trade. The area is home to some very interesting museums. Muscat Gate Museum is located in one of the fortified gates of the old city walls, and illustrates the history of Muscat and Oman from ancient times right up to the present day. The view from the roof over the old town is worth the visit alone. Bait Al Zubair is in a beautifully restored house and features major displays of men's traditional jewellery, including the khanjar, women's jewellery and attire, household items, and swords and firearms. The Omani French Museum celebrates the close ties between these two countries, and is on the site of the first French Embassy. Other highlights include the striking Alam Palace, home of Sultan Qaboos, and Jalali Fort and Mirani Fort overlooking the harbour.

Mutrah

Mutrah rests between the sea and a protective circle of hills, and has grown around its port, which today is far more vibrant than the port of Muscat's old town. Mutrah Corniche is lined with pristine gardens, parks, waterfalls and statues. Further east you'll find Riyam Park, where a huge incense burner sits on a rocky outcrop, while nearby is an ancient watchtower overlooking Mutrah – the view from the top is lovely and well worth the steep climb. One of Muscat's most famous shopping experiences lies in this area: the Mutrah Souk. It is always buzzing with activity and is renowned as one of the best souks in the region.

Other Areas

Although primarily a residential area, Qurum has some great shopping, good quality restaurants and cafes, the

Mutrah Corniche

Weekend Breaks
Oman & UAE

Get the lowdown on the best weekend breaks in Oman and the UAE

city's largest park (Qurum National Park) and arguably the best beach in Muscat. It is also home to some of the top hotels, all of which have superb leisure facilities. The villages of Al Bustan and Sidab provide an interesting diversion from the main Muscat areas. Head south along Al Bustan Street out of Ruwi on the spectacular mountain road to get to the village of Al Bustan and the Al Bustan Palace Hotel, one of the most famous hotels in the region.

Further down the coast, the mountains increase in height and the landscape gets more rugged. However, this undulating rocky coastline hides a number of beautiful secluded coves. These bays, mostly reachable by roads winding over the mountains, are home to the beaches of Qantab and Jassah, the Oman Dive Center (extradivers-worldwide.com) – one of the top dive centres in the world – and the new Shangri-La Barr Al Jissah Resort. Many of the bays in this area have stretches of sandy beach sheltered by the rocky cliffs, and crystal clear waters that are perfect for snorkelling, diving and fishing.

Outside Muscat

Not much further out of Muscat than the Shangri-La Barr Al Jissah Resort, Yiti Beach, while once a popular daytrip from Muscat, is now sadly becoming off limits due to the construction of a huge development called Salam Yiti. As Sifah beach, a little further down the coast, is very popular. The well-travelled path past the last of the houses in As Sifah leads to a beach which slopes gently towards the ocean at low tide. If you're keen to snorkel, head towards the northern edge of the beach. If you enjoy hiking, you can explore the headlands on foot (and maybe even find a secluded beach or two further along).

There are some excellent off-road routes you can take from Muscat within a day, or on an overnight camping trip. For more information on off-roading in Oman, get a copy of the *Oman Off-Road Explorer*.

Novotel Al Dana Resort Bahrain
121 Shk Hamad Causeway, Al Muharraq Manama
+973 1729 8008
novotel.com
Conveniently located on the causeway just minutes from the airport and close to the city, yet with its own beach, this hotel is a great choice for families. There's also a large pool, an indoor and outdoor play area, as well as good watersports facilities.

The Ritz-Carlton, Bahrain Hotel & Spa
Off King Abdulla The Second Ave Manama
+973 1758 0000
ritzcarlton.com
The hotel has one of the best beaches in Bahrain, in a man-made lagoon surrounded by lush gardens. The 600 metre private beach sweeps round the lagoon with its own island and private marina. Along with the nine quality dining venues and comprehensive business facilities, hotel residents have access to all of the club facilities, including the racquet sport courts, the luxurious spa and watersport activities.

Kuwait
Kuwait may be one of the world's smallest countries but its 500 kilometre coastline has endless golden beaches that remain refreshingly tranquil. From the Grand Mosque to the Kuwait Towers, there are many architectural splendours to explore, while Al Qurain House, which still shows the scars of war with its bullet holes, gives you a fascinating insight into the troubled times of the Iraqi invasion. There is also Green Island, an artificial island linked by a short bridge which is home to restaurants, a children's play area and a great view of Kuwait's shoreline. For accommodation, try the Four Points by Sheraton (starwoodhotels.com), Courtyard by Marriott (marriott.com), InterContinental Kuwait, or Radisson Blu (radissonblu.com). There are a few recent additions to Kuwait's hotel scene too, in the shape of Jumeirah Messilah Beach Hotel & Spa (jumeirah.com), Ritz Salmiya Hotel, (ritzkuwait.com) and the glamorous Hotel Missoni (hotelmissoni.com).

Qatar
Qatar once had a sleepy reputation, but things are changing fast. The amount of development and investment in the country means it is becoming increasingly popular with visitors. With an attractive corniche, world-class museums and cultural centres, and plenty of hotels with leisure and entertainment, the capital Doha makes a perfect weekend retreat for UAE residents. Away from the city, the inland sea (Khor Al Udaid) in the south makes a great day trip, usually as part of an organised tour. For further information and full details of the below activities and attractions, grab a copy of Explorer's *Qatar Mini Visitors' Guide*, which also includes a free pull-out map. See askexplorer.com/shop.

Qatar Attractions

Katara Cultural Village
Off Lusail St Doha **+974 4408 0000**
katara.net
This is a unique development, bringing together all the artistic elements in Qatar including music, dance, theatre, photography, painting and sculpture. The site, which looks like a large village, allows artists to meet and collaborate on different projects. It is also open to the public with two concert halls designed for opera, ballet and large theatrical productions, an outdoor amphitheatre which holds 5,000 people, as well as galleries, workshops, cafes, 16 restaurants and souks. There is also a popular public beach.

Doha highrises

Museum Of Islamic Art

The Corniche Doha +974 4422 4444
mia.org.qa
Architect IM Pei has created an elegant home for
this impressive collection. The building is beautifully
subtle, with details drawn from a wide range of Islamic
influences. The collection is showcased as a journey
through time, countries and cultures, and the oldest
pieces date from the ninth century.

Souk Waqif

Off Grand Hamad St Doha
The city's oldest market, Souk Waqif, was renovated
in 2004 using traditional building methods and
materials. The resulting complex is now one of the
most beautiful and authentic modern souks in the
Gulf. The most refreshing aspect of the souk area is
its dual purpose – tourists can easily stroll the narrow
alleys in search of souvenirs while locals can purchase
everything from fishing nets to pots and pans. Aside
from the many shops and restaurants, there is the
Waqif Art Center, which houses several small galleries
and craft shops.

Qatar Hotels

Four Seasons Hotel

Corniche St Doha +974 4494 8888
fourseasons.com
One of the finest hotels in the city, the Four Seasons
has an exclusive beach and marina, first-class service
and excellent restaurants, including the classy Italian
eatery Il Teatro.

La Cigale Hotel

60 Suhaim Bin Hamad St Doha 974 4428 8888
lacigalehotel.com
La Cigale has a reputation for first-class hospitality and
is an exclusive nightlife destination.

Movenpick Hotel Doha

Corniche Rd Doha +974 4429 1111
moevenpick-hotels.com
This modern hotel boasts breathtaking views of the
corniche, where guests can enjoy a morning jog or
afternoon stroll. Popular with business travellers,
this boutique-style hotel also attracts tourists with
its excellent restaurants and leisure facilities which
include a swimming pool, whirlpool and steam bath.

Radisson Blu Hotel, Doha

Salwa Rd Doha +974 4428 1428
radissonblu.com
With a new wing now open and plenty of restaurants,
bars and lounges to enjoy, the Ramada is a staple of
Doha's nightlife.

The Ritz-Carlton, Doha

West Bay Lagoon Doha +974 4484 8000
ritzcarlton.com
The opulent Ritz-Carlton is a perfect stop-off if you're
sailing in the region, with its 235 berth marina and
clubhouse. You can expect 5 star touches as standard
at this resort. All of the 374 rooms and suites have
breathtaking views over the sea or marina. The beach
club has a great selection of watersports and there's
a lavish spa. You'll be spoilt for choice with nine
international and local restaurants, and can finish the
night with either a cigar at Habanos or a cocktail at the
Admiral Club.

Sharq Village & Spa

Ras Abu Abboud St Doha +974 4425 6666
sharqvillage.com
Reminiscent of a traditional Qatari town, Sharq Village
& Spa is another example of Qatar's insistence on
spectacular architecture. The Six Senses Spa was
constructed using traditional building techniques and
the resort's restaurants are some of the finest in Doha.

W Doha Hotel & Residences

Off Diplomatic St, West Bay Doha +974 4453 5000
whoteldoha.com
Adding a touch of fun to Doha's rather conservative
luxury hotel scene, the W Hotel is the only Middle East
offering from the brand that is known for its funky
design. The quality of individualised service here is
just what you'd expect from the renowned W, while
every inch of the hotel is an exercise in architectural
minimalism; you could walk around the hotel and
be every bit as entranced as you would in a modern
art museum. The central location of the W makes
exploring Doha easy.

Saudi Arabia

The largest GCC country, the Kingdom of Saudi Arabia
boasts some incredible scenery, fascinating heritage
and archaeological sites, and diving locations by
the Red Sea that are arguably among the best in the
world. Unfortunately, due to the difficulty in obtaining
tourist visas, most expats and visitors to this part of
the world are unlikely to ever experience the sights
and quirks of this intriguing country. Limited transit
visas are available through agents, allowing visitors
a three day stay in Saudi Arabia en route to another
country, such as the UAE or Bahrain. Recent press
reports suggest that the Kingdom may begin to issue
more tourist visas to boost the country's budding
tourism industry (religious tourism in particular), and
to give better access to business travellers now that
Saudi Arabia is part of the World Trade Organization.
Until then, visit sauditourism.com.sa to see what
you're missing.

HOME TO YOUR FAVOURITE SPORTS BRANDS...

Activities & Hobbies

ACTIVITIES & HOBBIES

With so many different cultures converging in Abu Dhabi, it should come as little surprise that there is such a diverse range of activities to fill your free time with. Everything from simulated jumping out of an airplane to singing is covered in this section, and for every traditional pursuit such as tennis or football, there is the opportunity to try something a little different, such as kitesurfing, martial arts or even a spot of salsa. For the more adventurous at heart, the UAE's diverse topography lends itself perfectly to a wide range of outdoor pursuits, including rock climbing, mountain biking, dune bashing, wadi driving and skydiving. Thanks to the endless kilometres of coastline, watersports are particularly popular as well, with scuba diving, snorkelling, sailing, surfing, jetskiing and water skiing all firm expat favourites. Of course, not all activities require a mammoth dose of adrenaline or even the great outdoors, and there is an increasing number of groups that meet with indoor comforts for everything from art classes to amateur dramatics. Also within easy reach of all parts of the city is the Zayed Sports City. This dedicated sports hub is open seven days a week and provides an ice rink (p.290), bowling alley, tennis courts, gym as well as bumper cars, video games and a cafe. The area is also boasts the UAE's largest stadium (home of the Abu Dhabi Harlequins Rugby Club), as well as a tennis stadium which hosts the annual Mubadala World Tennis Championship (p.177, 179).

American Football

For those who miss their glory days of high school quarterbacking or college wide-receiving, or would just like to give this fun and sociable sport a try, there's 'Monday Night Lights' – Duplays' Abu Dhabi flag football league. Games are played every Monday night between April and June with cross-city games against Dubai's best ball players coming soon too. Cost of joining is Dhs.400 for individuals and Dhs.3,600 for teams. For more information visit duplays.com.

Archery

Following the opening of Al Forsan, there's now a local option for Robin Hood style fun with bows and arrows; more facilities are located a short drive away in Dubai.

Al Forsan International Sports Resort
Nr Abu Dhabi Golf Club & Resort Madinat Khalifa A (Khalifa City A) **02 556 8555**
alforsan.com
Map **1 P8**
The newly opened Al Forsan has 10 archery lanes offering distances of up to 60 metres. Lessons are on offer from Dhs.100 – more for private instruction.

Dubai Archers
Nr Sharjah National Park Sharjah **050 588 0951**
dubaiarchers.com
Meets at Sharjah Wanderers Golf Club on Fridays. Beginners' classes run for two hours and cost Dhs.90 for non-members.

Activity Finder

Hatta Fort Hotel
Dubai – Hatta Rd Hatta 04 809 9333
jaresortshotels.com
The 25 metre range has eight targets and hosts an annual archery competition. Dubai Archers (above) also holds its annual tournament here. Dhs.50 for 30 minutes target practice, with equipment included.

Sharjah Golf & Shooting Club
Nr Tasjeel Auto Village, Emirates Rd Sharjah
06 548 7777
golfandshootingshj.com
The shooting club's indoor range offers target practice at Dhs.60 for 20 arrows. You can also try your hand at pistol and rifle shooting.

Art Classes

Abu Dhabi Music & Arts Foundation
Kanoo Group Bldg, Najda St Markaziya East
02 651 0300
admaf.org
Map **2 P4**
As well as organising and running the annual Abu Dhabi Festival, ADMAF holds year-round educational activities dealing with everything from film and music to poetry. Some of these are open to the public, with others limited to certain professional and academic communities. Often, visiting artists, musicians or writers will lead workshops or give lectures.

Al Qattara Arts Centre
Al Qattara Oasis, Al Qattara Al Ain 03 711 8225
Map **4 D2**
Offers classes in Arabic calligraphy, drawing, oil painting, all aimed at beginners and intermediates.

Art Labs
Dubai 04 374 6208
artlabs.me
Runs training courses in a range of arts and crafts, as well as providing business consultation for arts and crafts based enterprises. Also provides wholesale distribution of hobby materials.

National Theatre
Nr Al Jazira Club, Shk Rashid bin Saeed Al Maktoum St Al Nahyan 02 657 6355
Map **2 L12**
Classes include painting, sculpture, ceramics and silk painting. They run from Sunday to Thursday, and prices start from Dhs.500 for monthly courses.

Aussie Rules
It started with the Dubai Dingoes and then came the Dubai Heat. Now, the Abu Dhabi Falcons have entered the arena. It seems that Aussie Rules is gaining a foothold here in the Emirates, and with the influx of Australian expats it's about time.
The Falcons compete in the Middle East AFL competition that runs from October to March each year with teams based in Dubai, Muscat, Bahrain, Qatar and Abu Dhabi. All are welcome, regardless of skill level or experience. For more information contact Steve Watson on 056 109 2346 or visit abudhabifalcons.com.

Badminton
You wouldn't really think of badminton as a sport with a huge Middle East following, but it seems to be gaining popularity in a big way in Abu Dhabi with a competitive league and a number of die-hard fans of the sport. Members of The Club (p.179) can enjoy weekly matches in the indoor court with occasional leagues introduced, while Duplays (duplays.com) runs a recreational co-ed eight-week season for those who want to meet new people and work up a playful sweat in the process. Games are played on Tuesdays at GEMS World Academy and cost Dhs.350. Alternatively, if you already have the gear and a partner, many sports clubs and hotels have courts that can be hired on an hourly basis.

Basketball
Hoops is certainly alive and well in the capital. In addition to the leagues listed below, there are a number of public ball courts around town. Also, many of Abu Dhabi's hotels have a basketball court (usually outdoor) free for members to use. Duplays runs the Hoosiers League, giving players the chance to run and gun in a competitive set-up for an eight-week season which includes playoffs. Games are usually played on Wednesday nights, and cost Dhs.500 and Dhs.3,200 for a team. New leagues are periodically added, so check the website for more details.

Birdwatching
The increasing lushness of the area attracts ever more birds, many of which are not easily found in Europe or the Middle East. Over 80 species breed locally, while over 400 have been recorded on their migration between Africa and Central Asia. Species spotted include the socotra cormorant, chestnut-bellied sandgrouse, crab plover, and Saunders' little tern. Good areas for birdwatching include the eastern lagoon on the New Corniche, the port area, Mushrif Palace Gardens and around the Abu Dhabi Equestrian Club. Extensive records of sightings and descriptions are kept by Tommy Pedersen who maintains a detailed and constantly updated website (uaebirding.com), and all twitchers are encouraged to participate. Other excellent places for birding around the Emirates include the mangrove swamps in Umm Al Quwain and at Khor Kalba (p.261) – the only place in the world

where you can spot the white-collared kingfisher. During the migrating periods (September/October and March/April), enormous flocks of wading birds can be found. The flamingos that feed here are always a spectacular sight. Access is restricted to permit holders, but birds can be watched from the car if you park along the Ras Al Khor creek and use binoculars. Desert Rangers arrange canoe tours through Kalba's mangroves (04 357 2200).

Bowling

A number of the shopping centres around town have excellent 10 pin bowling facilities which are ideal for an inexpensive family outing. Bowling City has seven locations in the UAE, including three in Abu Dhabi and one in Al Ain. Abu Dhabi Country Club in Al Mushrif (p.190) has a four lane facility which is often booked for birthday parties. The cost for one game is Dhs.20 and to hire the lane for one hour will cost Dhs.100 (adcountry.com). The biggest bowling alley in Abu Dhabi is Khalifa International Bowling Centre, which regularly hosts competitive bowling as well as bowling for the general public.

Bowling City
Al Mariah Mall Markaziya East **02 676 0444**
bowling-city.com
Map **2 P3**
With billiard lounges, karaoke booths, internet cafes and gaming zones, there is so much more to Bowling City than just bowling. If you do feel like hitting the lanes, it costs Dhs.12 per game or Dhs.15 including shoes; socks are an additional Dhs.3. There are seven locations across the country to choose from including Khalidiyah Mall (Sparky's Family Fun Centre, 02 635 4317) and Al Mariah Mall (02 676 0444) in Abu Dhabi, with another at Al Ain Mall (03 751 0006). Parties, corporate events or competitions between groups of friends can all be arranged.

Khalifa International Bowling Centre
Zayed Sports City Al Madina Al Riyadiya **02 403 4648**
zsc.ae
Map **1 J8**
This state-of-the-art bowling centre, located just off Airport Road, boasts 40 lanes and is apparently one of the most modern bowling alleys in the world. Prices start from Dhs.10 per game with shoe hire an additional Dhs.2. Billiards is also on offer, with an hour's play starting at Dhs.30.

Canoeing & Kayaking

Not only are canoeing and kayaking great ways to get out and enjoy the weather when it's not so hot, but both also offer a moment of peace and quiet in a city that can drive one to near craziness with all the horns and jackhammers. Of course, the azure waters of Abu

Dhabi are temptation enough, but with mangrove forests all around the area and a good chance of catching sight of wild flamingos and dolphins, getting out on the water is one of the best ways to get free of the city without actually leaving the city limits. Not only that, but the relatively calm waters can make it easy for beginners to learn, especially in kayaks with their low centre of gravity.

Abu Dhabi Ocean Warriors
Abu Dhabi International Marine Sports Club
Breakwater **050 837 2436**
adowsurfski.wordpress.com
Map **2 E1**
Abu Dhabi Ocean Warriors (ADOW) is a surfski club that operates out of Abu Dhabi International Marine Sports Club near Marina Mall. Surfskis are long kayaks used for ocean racing, and the club caters to paddlers of all abilities, from racing speedsters to those enjoying a leisurely paddle. ADOW meets every Friday morning for a time trial; contact Roland at the above number for more details.

Desert Rangers
Nr American Hospital, Street 18 Dubai **04 357 2200**
desertrangers.com
Metro **Oud Metha**
Desert Rangers offers guided trips through the mangroves of the unique nature reserve at Khor Kalba on the east coast, in two-seater Canadian canoes. Initial instruction is followed by hands on practice to develop skills and confidence. All trips depart from Dubai and cost Dhs.300 per person.

Noukhada Adventure Company
Al Meena St Al Meena **02 650 3600**
noukhada.ae
Map **2 S2**
Noukhada was started over two years ago to promote eco tourism in the area. They offer kayak tours of the mangroves and even offer sunrise/sunset tours for those who want to get out on the water before or after work. However, if you're a keen kayaker, Noukhada also offers an annual membership for Dhs.3,000 to Dhs. 3,500, which gets you free use of kayaks and equipment, a free monthly guided tour and discounts for friends.

Caving

The cave network in the Hajar Mountains is extensive and much of it is yet to be explored. Some of the best caves are located near Al Ain, the Jebel Hafeet area and just past Buraimi near the Oman border. Many of the underground passages and caves have spectacular displays of curtains, stalagmites and stalactites, as well as gypsum flowers. In Oman, the range includes what is believed to be the second largest cave system in the world, as well as the Majlis Al Jinn Cave – the second largest chamber in the world. To arrange caving trips in Oman, contact a local tour operator such as Gulf Leisure (+968 9901 3424, gulfleisure.com) or Muscat Diving & Adventure Centre (+968 2454 3002, holiday-in-oman.com).

Within the region, caving ranges from fairly safe to exceptionally dangerous and, as no mountain rescue services exist, anyone venturing out into the mountains should always be well-equipped and accompanied by an experienced leader. Mountain High (050 659 5536, mountainhighme.com) offers guided tours in and around the caves of Al Ain plus canyoning and other adventures from Dhs.500 per person per day.

Chess

The chess scene revolves around Abu Dhabi Chess & Culture Club, which runs a host of tournaments throughout the year.

Abu Dhabi Chess & Culture Club
Off Baniyas St Madinat Zayed 02 633 1110
abudhabichess.com
Map 2 P5
Abu Dhabi Chess & Culture Club was opened in 1979, and regularly participates in a wealth of local and international chess tournaments, including an annual tournament run by the Abu Dhabi Tourism & Culture Authority. The club has sponsored numerous competitions and enrols members of all ages. All are welcome.

Climbing

For those who feel at home on a vertical plane, excellent climbing can be found in various locations around the UAE, including Ras Al Khaimah, Dibba, Hatta and the Al Ain/Buraimi region; more than 600 routes have been recorded since the 1970s. These vary from short outcrop routes to difficult mountain routes of alpine proportions. Most range from (British) Very Severe, up to extreme grades (E5). However, there are some easier routes for new climbers, especially in Wadi Bih and Wadi Khab Al Shamis.

To meet like-minded people, head to Wadi Bih where you're sure to find climbers nearly every weekend, or go to the climbing walls below, where most of the UAE climbing fraternity hangs around (ahem). One excellent resource is Toby Foord-Kelcey's website redarmadapublishing.com.

Also, uaeclimbing.com features an active forum and a wealth of information for anyone interested in climbing in the UAE. If you're not ready to go it alone, Al Shaheen Adventure Training (alshaheenme.com) offers outdoor lessons for both beginners and more experienced climbers looking to advance their skills and confidence.

Climbing Dubai
Dubai Trade Centre Hotel Apartments Dubai 04 306 5061
dorellsports.com
Map 3 E2 Metro World Trade Centre
Climbing Dubai has daily climbing programmes, outdoor climbing tours and international climbing expeditions. The group seeks to attract new climbers and promotes walk-ins at the evening sessions which cost Dhs.60 and include all necessary equipment.

The Club
Mina Zayed Free Port 02 673 1111
the-club.com
Map 2 V3
The Club has a five metre outdoor climbing wall which overlooks the main swimming pool. Open to members only, adults and children from the age of 4 can try out their climbing skills. Full safety gear is provided.

Desert Rangers
Nr American Hospital, Street 18 Dubai 04 357 2200
desertrangers.com
Map 3 E2 Metro Oud Metha
Desert Rangers offers rock climbing trips to well-established locations, suitable for the absolute beginner or experienced climbers. Trips include instruction, all necessary safety equipment and lunch. All excursions depart from Dubai and a day of scaling the peaks will cost Dhs.400 per person.

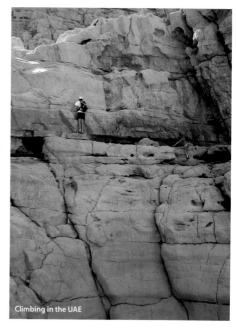
Climbing in the UAE

Pharaohs' Club

Wafi Dubai **04 324 0000**
pyramidsrestaurantsatwafi.com
Map **3 E2** Metro **Dubai Healthcare City**
The indoor climbing wall at Pharaohs' Club lets climbing enthusiasts improve their skills, and offers a range of courses for kids and adults of all abilities, as well as public sessions for experienced climbers. Lessons for non-members cost Dhs.62 per hour, need to be booked in advance and are limited to six people per instructor. The wall consists of varied climbing routes, and crash mats are present for bouldering.

Cookery Classes

Until recently, for a city that is a mixing pot of cultures, backgrounds, sights and sounds, Abu Dhabi was found a little lacking when it came to teaching the tastes. By and large, the responsibility fell to PartiPerfect (02 681 0090, partiperfect@gmail.com) which still offers regular cookery classes: every month (during non-summer months) Chef Lana plans the class schedule and menus range in style from Middle Eastern to Turkish; during holidays, they also bravely run cookery classes for kids. However, the city's hotels are now also shaping up. Royal Orchid on Salam St (02 677 9911) periodically hosts classes for Thai and Indian cooking. The Yacht Club at the InterContinental (800 423 463) runs cookery classes costing Dhs.215 per person, including lunch, with sushi-making lessons held from time to time. Atayeb at Yas Viceroy (02 656 0600) has classes costing Dhs.250 per person, including lunch and soft drinks, while it's also well worth checking the park Hyatt's calendar of events (park.hyatt.com), as the hotel runs special food and drink experiences in both its Abu Dhabi and Dubai properties.

Jones The Grocer (jonesthegrocer.com) also organises popular cookery master classes. These cost Dhs.375 per person and focus on Mediterranean fare, including how to make pastas, breads and pastries.

Cricket

With such a mixture of nationalities and cultures in Abu Dhabi, cricket is a passion shared across many communities. Many organisations have their own cricket teams for inter-company competitions and the sport is becoming more popular in schools. Car parks, rough land and grassy parks all sprout stumps at weekends and evenings, when a mix of ages come out to play. International matches are regularly hosted in the UAE at grounds in Abu Dhabi, Dubai and Sharjah.

Abu Dhabi Cricket Council

Al Salam St Tourist Club Area 02 645 9790
www.uaecricket.com
Map **2 Q4**
The coun7cil was established to promote and run cricket affairs in the emirate. There are currently 65 local clubs registered, with over a thousand players of many nationalities. If you want to play cricket, the council will put you in contact with a suitable club. The council also runs a cricket academy and organises local and international matches at the purpose-built cricket stadium near Khalifa City.

Al Ain Cricket Association

Al Ain **050 515 3537**
alaincricketassociation.org
Map **3 E3**
The association is the oldest cricketing body in the UAE and has been running cricket affairs in Al Ain since April 1989. There are currently 20 teams (seniors and juniors) with over 200 resident players of many nationalities. It has a new location with four new grounds, including a floodlit pitch for play at night. Coaching is available five evenings a week. For more information see the website.

Cycling

Abu Dhabi is not the most bike-friendly of places but if you're willing to brave some crazy drivers, there are plenty of areas where you can ride, including the Corniche (p.194), where there are cycle paths, and it is even possible to hire bikes (q8byky.com).

There is no road cycling group in Abu Dhabi, although Abu Dhabi Tri Club (abudhabitriclub.org) does a good job of organising weekly rides. On Tuesday nights, the Yas Marina Circuit opens up for cyclists, runners and rollerbladers too and this is a great place to ride safely under the floodlights.

Cycling is gaining real traction as a sport in Dubai, with two main cycling groups – Dubai Roadsters (dubairoadsters.ae), and Cycle Safe (cyclechallenge.ae) – both arranging rides throughout the week as well as at the weekend. The Dubai 92 Cycle Challenge – a 92km road race – takes place each December and is the biggest amateur bike race in the Middle East.

Dance Classes

Sociable, great fun and excellent exercise for all ages and levels of ability, dance has a universal appeal that breaks down barriers and inhibitions (sometimes). In addition to the following organisations, some health clubs, bars and restaurants hold weekly sessions in ballroom, flamenco, jazz dance, salsa, samba, and so on. The Club (p.179) offers ballet, hip hop and tap dance classes to children of all ages; the adult lessons include dance fusion and ballet. The Clubhouse at Zayed Sports City hosts regular nights dedicated to salsa lessons and Latin music.

Alternatively, this is definitely the right part of the world to learn belly dancing with all its charms. Surprisingly, there aren't a huge number of studios that advertise it, but health clubs and social clubs will sometimes offer classes, and there are quite a few private teachers. Lessons are also offered at the International Music Institute (02 6211299). Also, don't forget that the true belly dancing capitals of the world, like Cairo and Istanbul, are a short flight away (see Out Of The City, p.264).

Abu Dhabi Salsa
Various locations
abudhabisalsa.com
This organisation's mission is to share the love and passion of Latin dancing and salsa with other people, while promoting the Abu Dhabi salsa scene. Apart from holding classes for different dance styles, it also organises events. Visit the website for more information on the instructors and rates.

Bodytree Studio
Shk Hazaa Bin Zayed St Al Karamah **02 443 4448**
bodytreestudio.com
Map **2 J7**
This studio is rooted in principles of fluidity and grace, with Oriental Dance and Ballet for Girls classes being particularly popular recent additions to the more energetic Xtend Barre, capoeira and Zumba classes.

Dance Abu Dhabi
Various locations **050 410 1535**
danceabudhabi.com
Offering Latin and ballroom dance lessons for everyone from children and beginners to those who already think they can hold their own on the dance floor. With classes taking place at both the Hiltonia Beach and Health Club and the Intercontinental Health Club, there are plenty of opportunities to foxtrot, waltz or cha-cha.

Eden Studio
Le Meridien Abu Dhabi Tourist Club Area
02 697 4354
lemeridienabudhabi.com
Map **2 S4**
One of the newer studios, having opened its doors in 2012, Eden has a vast range of pure dance and dance-fitness classes, which includes the likes of Zumba, belly dancing, Argentine tango, salsa, capoeira and Brazilian dance. The studio also runs yoga (p.306) classes.

Expressions Of Dance & Drama
Al Hilal Bank Bldg, Al Falah St Al Dhafrah **02 448 2778**
expressions-dance.net
Map **2 Q6**
The trainers at Expressions Of Dance & Drama offer children and adults a fun way to exercise or dance their way to fitness. Classes in ballet, tap, jazz, hip hop and even Argentine tango are on offer for the seriously inspired.

International Music Institute
Nr Grand Stores, Shk Zayed The First St Al Manhal
02 621 1299
imi-jmc.net
Map **2 K4**
With classes in ballet, as well as modern dance and even belly dancing, the International Music Institute offers much more than just music. Visit the website for class times and information.

Irish Dancing
Various locations **050 314 1922**
irishsocietyabudhabi.com
Irish dancing lessons for children are available through the hugely active Irish Society Abu Dhabi (p.42). Beginners, intermediate and advanced dancers are taught separately and anyone is welcome to join. For more details, contact Deirdre Mallon.

Salsa With Brando
International Music Institute Al Manhal
050 268 4520
salsawithbrando.com
Map **2 K4**
The founder of the annual Abu Dhabi International Salsa Festival, Orson Brando is passionate about spreading the love of salsa in Abu Dhabi. Not only does he offer classes at the International Music Institute, for both beginners and the more experienced, but he's also a bit of a salsa scholar with plenty of information about the history of salsa in the region. The energetic classes start at Dhs.250 for eight lessons.

Scottish Country Dancing
The Club Mina Zayed Free Port **055 948 4658**
adscots.com
Map **2 V3**
Don your kilt and sporran and join in with this fun class for some traditional highland dancing. People of all levels are welcome – it doesn't matter if you've never danced before. Contact Francine Quastel for more information.

Turning Pointe
V23 Building, Russia Dubai **04 422 1592**
turningpointe.ae
Map **3 E2**
This Dubai-based, RAD-accredited dance school offers lessons at Al Raha International School, Al Yasmeena School, GEMS American Academy, GEMS World Academy and Pearl Primary School in Abu Dhabi. Ballet training, from baby ballet to Grade 1 examinations, is offered, with girls and boys aged 3-10 accepted. Entries are accepted throughout the year, with an admissions and information day held at the beginning of each term; examinations are held in April.

Diving

The warm seas and clear, calm waters of the Arabian Gulf on the UAE west coast and the Gulf of Oman on the east are perfect for exploring the region's varied underwater life. Popular places for snorkelling on the east coast include Snoopy Island, just off the beach of the Sandy Beach Hotel & Resort (p.262).

There are also good spots further north, such as the beach north of Dibba village, where the coast is rocky and there's coral close to the shore. For somewhere closer to home, the seas around Abu Dhabi's numerous islands have a fair amount of marine life. Most hotels or dive centres rent equipment (snorkel, mask and fins); costs vary greatly, so shop around.

If you prefer to go deeper, there are a good number of interesting dive sites, especially wrecks, some of which are within easy reach of Abu Dhabi. There are plenty of dive companies who will get you there and help you improve your diving skills. Courses are offered under the usual international training organisations. If you've already got the know-how and the gear, and want to find out more about diving and snorkelling sites in the UAE, see p.225.

7 Seas Divers

Nr Safeer Centre, Al Mudifi Khor Fakkan **09 238 7400**
7seasdivers.com
This PADI dive centre offers day and night diving trips to sites around Khor Fakkan, Musandam and Lima Rock. Training is provided from beginner to instructor level, in a variety of languages.

Abu Dhabi Sub Aqua Club

The Club Mina Zayed Free Port **02 673 1111**
the-club.com
Map **2 V3**
This club is affiliated to the British Sub Aqua Club (BSAC); safety standards are high, and training courses are regularly held for all levels, including beginners. Dive trips are held at weekends, and include locations around Abu Dhabi, Musandam, Fujairah and five other sites in the region.

Al Mahara Diving Center

Nr Main Taxi/Bus Station Al Nahyan **02 643 7377**
divemahara.com
Map **2 C6**
This centre organises PADI training, ranging from beginner to open water and specialist diving. If you're looking for a career change, the centre also offers instructor training with experienced teachers. special training includes children's programmes, underwater photography and videography. The centre also organises trips to the east coast, Musandam and even overseas; snorkelling sessions near the Breakwater offer a chance to see a number of local species.

Arabian Divers & Sportfishing Charters > p.281

Nr UAE Central Bank, Marina Al Bateen Resort
Al Bateen **050 614 6931**
fishabudhabi.com
Map **2 C6**
With over 20 years of experience in diving, fishing and boat charters, this company has a complete range of on-site facilities based out of the Al Bateen Marina, including a shop, a classroom, a training dive pool and boats for charters. PADI courses from beginner to advanced are available, as well as dives to sites around the UAE coast. The company prioritises individual attention and small diving groups, making sure that safety comes first. In addition to diving and sportfishing, this company also offers dedicated snorkelling charters, with experienced captains who know the best local spots to drop you so that you can spot exotic fish and turtles..

Emirates Diving Association

Heritage & Diving Village Dubai **04 393 9390**
emiratesdiving.com
Map **3 E2** Metro **Al Ghubaiba**
This non-profit group aims to conserve, protect and restore the UAE's marine resources by promoting the importance of the environment. It looks after the well-being of UAE corals as part of its coral monitoring project, and organises annual Clean-Up Arabia campaigns. A quarterly newsletter, Divers for the Environment, details current activities and the website has lots of useful info. Divers are encouraged to join, with membership costing Dhs.100 per year.

Freediving UAE

Various locations
freedivinguae.com
This group of diving enthusiasts promotes and practises the art of freediving – diving without the aid of breathing apparatus. Freediving AIDA accredited courses are also offered to give beginner, intermediate and advanced freedivers the physical skill, mental preparation and theory training required to freedive safely and successfully. Training sessions are held every week on Sundays and Tuesdays, with trips to dive sites in Khor Fakkan organised periodically.

The Oceanic Hotel & Resort

Beach Rd Khor Fakkan **09 238 5111**
oceanichotel.com
Map **3 F1**
The hotel offers boat rides to Shark Island for Dhs.145 per person for a group of four, with every additional person charged at Dhs.30. Snorkelling gear is available for an extra Dhs.30. All prices apply to hotel residents so, if you are just there for the day, entrance to the hotel costs Dhs.45 for adults and Dhs.25 for children.

Sandy Beach Diving Centre

Sandy Beach Hotel & Resort Fujairah **09 244 5555**
sandybm.com
Map **3 F1**
Located in a chalet beach resort, the centre, which
sells and rents dive and snorkelling equipment, is
open year-round. Nearby Snoopy Island, alive with
hard coral and marine life, is an excellent spot for
snorkelling and diving. Beach access for the day is
Dhs.75. Snorkelling equipment is available for hire at
Dhs.60 a day.

Scuba 2000

Al Bidiya Beach, Al Bidiyah Fujairah **09 238 8477**
scuba-2000.com
Map **3 F2**
Located on the east coast between Dibba and
Fujairah, this centre offers boat trips to the east coast's
best diving and snorkelling sites, in addition to diving
courses, night dives, snorkelling trips and equipment
rental. You can also snorkel directly from the beach,
and accommodation is available. A two-dive boat trip
with full equipment costs Dhs.280, while a night dive
with full equipment costs Dhs.230. A Discover Scuba
Diving course is on offer for Dhs.400 and the PADI
Open Water Diving course is available at Dhs.2,000.
Diving packages, with two free dives, are also offered
for certified divers. Snorkelling trips start at Dhs.120,
inclusive of boat ride, fins, mask, snorkel and boots,
plus refreshments.

Dragon Boat Racing

The ancient sport of dragon boat racing involves
long boats, each with 20 members paddling furiously
from the start of the race, like a team paddle boat
sprint, over relatively short distances. The name
comes from the fact that boats are often adorned with
striking dragon heads and tails. Abu Dhabi's pristine
turquoise waters and year-round warm weather
make for a perfect setting for outings of all sorts, and
neighbouring Dubai is home to more dragon boating
activities for dedicated enthusiasts.

The UAE Dragon Boat Association
(dubaidragonboat.com) lists all of the country's
dragon boating crews who meet, along with
international competitors, for the annual Dubai
International Dragon Boating Festival.

Abu Dhabi MAR

Shangri-La Hotel, Qaryat Al Beri Al Maqtaa
Map **1 L8**
This group meets on Monday and Wednesday
evenings at the Shangri-La Hotel, Qaryat Al Beri. The
group is open to absolutely everyone, and there's a
nice balance of competitive spirit with general social
camaraderie between the members.

Capital Dragons

Abu Dhabi Marine Sailing Club Breakwater
050 571 1208
Map **2 E1**
This group is open to paddlers of all ages, and training
sessions run on Monday and Wednesday evenings
at the Marina Yacht Club close to Marina Mall, often
paddling to nearby Lulu Island for a social picnic or
swim. Call the above number for more information.

Drama Groups

The performing arts are growing in popularity both
in terms of performances staged in the capital and
opportunities for residents to get involved themselves.
While major cultural developments are being geared
up by the government, there's already a bunch of
opportunities to give your creative side a go and
release your inner performer. The Abu Dhabi branch
of the New York Film Academy (abudhabifilmschool.
com) opened in 2008 and offers intensive four and
six week film acting courses, as well as one and
two year acting diplomas. Drama Workshops Dubai
(dramaworkshopsdubai.com) sometimes organises
workshops in Abu Dhabi; check the website for
updates. For those who dream of treading the boards
themselves, there are a number of dance schools in
Abu Dhabi (p.278).

Abu Dhabi Dramatic Society

The Club Mina Zayed Free Port **02 673 1111**
the-club.com
Map **2 V3**
As with almost all activities at The Club, the Abu Dhabi
Dramatic Society is open to members only. However,
the productions are open to the public as long as
they're guests of a member. The society puts on four
productions a year and offers children's programmes
and workshops.

Environmental Groups

As it currently stands, there's little chance that Abu
Dhabi would be mistaken for a bastion of greendom,
but the government is committed to ambitious
environmental goals to gradually turn the city into
a model for sustainable development. Masdar City
is at the forefront of the emirate's aim to become a
global leader in environmental development. At the
grass-roots level, there are other developments. For
example, Abu Dhabi's Centre of Waste Management
recently undertook a massive marketing campaign
to encourage adoption of the three 'Rs' – reduce,
reuse, recycle; and private companies like Spinneys
have also implemented recycling efforts. Elsewhere,
a government-led programme to phase out plastic
bags over the next few years is in place. In the
meantime, here are the local standbys when it comes
to the environment.

Activities & Hobbies

Activities & Hobbies *(vertical sidebar)*

Al Ain Zoo

Public Institution Zoo & Aquarium, Nhayyan Al Awwal St Al Ain **03 782 8188**
alainzoo.ae
Map **4 D3**
Al Ain Zoo houses a wide range of animals on its spacious, leafy grounds and one of the park's principal goals is to educate visitors in matters relating to environment, conservation and sustainability. In addition, the park is active through several local schools and communities.

Emirates Environmental Group

Villa JMR 68-117A, Jumeira Rd Dubai **04 344 8622**
eeg-uae.org
Map **3 E2** Metro **Financial Centre**
This voluntary organisation is devoted to protecting the environment through education, action programmes and community involvement across the Emirates. Activities include evening lectures and special events such as recycling collections and clean-up campaigns. Annual membership costs Dhs.200 for adults and Dhs.50 for students.

Emirates Natural History Group

Various locations
enhg.org
The ENHG has groups in both Abu Dhabi and Al Ain, with regular field trips, and lectures on various subjects, ranging from astronomy to zoology. The Abu Dhabi group now meets in the main auditorium at Abu Dhabi Men's College of the Higher Colleges of Technology, at 19:30 on the first and third Tuesdays of each month, with the exception of July and August, when there are no meetings, and during Ramadan when meetings begin no earlier than 20:00. The Al Ain chapter meets on the second and fourth Tuesday of each month (July, August and December excepted) at 19:30 at the Danat Al Ain Resort. Membership costs Dhs.100 per calendar year.

Emirates Wildlife Society

Abu Dhabi Chamber Of Commerce & Industry
Markaziya West **02 634 7117**
uae.panda.org
Map **2 L2**
The Emirates Wildlife Society (EWS) works alongside the World Wildlife Fund (WWF) in the UAE. Together they operate a volunteer programme open to anyone who can spare a few hours a month to assist with valuable conservation work in the Emirates. Volunteer activities include admin, fundraising, assisting with wildlife surveys, clean-up operations and educational presentations, as well as awareness campaigns. To find out more about how to get involved and how to volunteer with the society, log onto uae.panda.org to complete the online application form.

Feline Friends

Various locations **050 582 2916**
felinefriendsuae.com
This non-profit organisation of volunteers aims to care for sick and injured street cats and kittens, as well as controlling the cat population by sterilisation. It rescues abandoned cats and fosters them until permanent homes can be found.

K9 Friends

Dubai **04 885 8031**
k9friends.com
Map **3 E2**
K9 Friends has a re-homing service for stray and abandoned dogs; the group promotes responsible dog ownership and encourages a neutering programme to help control the population of stray dogs. Volunteers and foster homes are always needed.

Fishing

A boat isn't necessarily required to enjoy a great afternoon or evening of fishing. There are plenty of places along the Corniche where fishermen tend to congregate, but be aware that you must first obtain a licence. You can apply and pay online for an annual (Dhs.120) or weekly (Dhs.30) fishing licence (abudhabi. ae). For a chance of hooking bigger bites, or to let someone else handle the licence admin, it's best to get out on the water and hire a fishing guide. From September to April is the peak fishing season, although it's still possible to catch queenfish and sailfish in the summer months. Other commonly caught fish include dorado, jacks, kingfish, shari and tuna. If you're after a really big catch and have some cash to spare, deep-sea fishing and trawling are offered by specialist operators.

Arabian Divers & Sportfishing Charters > p.281

Nr UAE Central Bank, Marina Al Bateen Resort
Al Bateen **050 614 6931**
fishabudhabi.com
Map **2 C6**
This experienced boat charter company offers dolphin watching trips, scuba diving and snorkelling, boat charters and big game sport fishing. An IGFA (International Game Fishing Association) certified captain is on hand to help you reel in your catch.

Beach Rotana Abu Dhabi

Nr Abu Dhabi Mall, Tourist Club St Tourist Club Area
02 697 9000
rotana.com
Map **2 S5**
The hotel's boat is available for hire for fishing or cruising the pristine waters of the Arabian Gulf. The driver will suggest different fishing spots depending on the season, but with hundreds of small islands

Activities & Hobbies

just off the coast, good fishing and scenery are guaranteed. For details, contact the hotel or call Mr Anamul on 050 315 9181.

Hiltonia Health Club & Spa
Hilton Abu Dhabi Al Khubeirah **02 692 4205**
hilton.com
Map **2 C3**
An experienced guide from the Hiltonia Beach Club can organise fishing trips, an island cruise or a combination of both which includes a barbecue for the catch. Though the best fishing is during the cooler months, under expert guidance there are big fish to be caught even in the height of summer.

Noukhada Adventure Company
Al Meena St Al Meena **02 650 3600**
noukhada.ae
Map **2 S2**
For something a little different, Noukhada brings you closer to the action with kayak fishing. Because the company focuses on eco-tourism, catch and release is promoted, but that only means bigger fish in the stories you tell your friends. Fly fishing options are also offered.

The Oceanic Hotel & Resort
Beach Rd Khor Fakkan **09 238 5111**
oceanichotel.com
Map **3 F1**
Fishing trips from the hotel head to a favourite local spot where catches are guaranteed. For hotel guests, the catch of the day can then be cooked according to your taste by the hotel chef. Non-guests can take their catch home with them. Trips leave from 14:00 onwards. The hotel also organises whale and dolphin watching trips, as well as the chance to swim with sharks.

Sheraton Resort Health Club
Sheraton Abu Dhabi Hotel & Resort Markaziya East
02 677 3333
sheratonabudhabihotel.com
Map **2 Q2**
Expeditions are run from the resort for deep sea fishing, with large catches of barracuda, hammour, kingfish and shari (seasonal) virtually guaranteed. Everything is provided, including refreshments, equipment and experienced guides to ensure every trip is a success.

Flying
At present, there are no private flying clubs up and running in the Abu Dhabi or Al Ain areas. However, Dubai-based Micro Aviation Club (see below) occasionally offers lessons in Abu Dhabi too. Otherwise, those keen to learn can travel north to Dubai or Umm Al Quwain, or even east to Fujairah. Those with a private pilot's licence can contact the

Dubai Flying Association; while at Fujairah Aviation Academy' the brave can pick up the high habit and obtain their pilot's licence. If you are after a private flight, but would prefer someone else to handle the controls, you can arrange a charter through Abu Dhabi Aviation (02 575 8000).

Emirates Flying School
Dubai International Airport Dubai **04 299 5155**
emiratesaviationservices.com
Map **3 E2** Metro **Airport Terminal 1**
The only approved flight training institution in Dubai offers private and commercial licences, and will convert international licences to UAE. A Private Pilot Licence course costs upwards of Dhs.51,920.

Fujairah Aviation Academy
Fujairah International Airport Fujairah **09 222 4747**
fujaa.ae
Map **3 F2**
Facilities include single and twin-engine aircraft, an instrument flight simulator and a repair workshop. Training is offered for private and commercial licences, instrument rating and multi-engine rating. Pleasure flights and sightseeing tours are also available, and those with a pilot's licence can enquire about aircraft for hire by calling the above number.

Jazirah Aviation Club
Dubai – Ras Al Khaimah Highway, Jazirat Al Hamra
Ras Al Khaimah **07 244 6416**
jac-uae.net
Map **3 F1**
The club is dedicated solely to microlight/ultralight flying, although it does also offer training and pleasure flights. A Microlight Pilot's Licence course involves around 25 hours flying time at a cost of Dhs.550 per hour.

Micro Aviation Club
Nr Bab Al Shams, 20km from Emirates Rd
Umm Al Quwain **055 843 5254**
microaviation.org
Map **3 E1**
The Dubai-based Micro Aviation Club offers full training courses in microlight flying, paragliding and paramotoring. Its office is located at Dubai Men's College, in Dubai Academic City. Courses start from Dhs.3,500, with an addtional annual registration fee of Dhs.250; Lessons are sometimes held in Abu Dhabi as well as in Dubai.

Football
Football (or soccer for any American expats) is, as in most of the rest of the world, the most popular sport in the United Arab Emirates and it enjoys a large number of spectators as well as plentiful players.

Abu Dhabi Golf Club

Walking along The Corniche

Zayed Sports City

Sea fishing

Activities & Hobbies

During the evenings and at weekends, parks, beaches and any open areas seem to attract a game, generally with a mix of nationalities taking part.

However, you could also leave the street football behind and join The Club's (p.179) Monday Soccer group, which runs, unsurprisingly, on Monday evenings and is open to men and women (members only). Alternatively, you could try one of the clubs listed below. The football field at Abu Dhabi Country Club (p.178) serves as the primary practice facility for football programmes.

If you'd rather watch than play, the UAE's national league has regular fixtures at the Al Jazira and Al Wahda stadiums in town (see Spectator Sports, p.226). For Gaelic football, see Gaelic Games on p.286; for American football, see p.274; for Australian Rules, see p.275.

Abu Dhabi Strollers
Al Ghazal Golf Club Airport Area 050 818 0685
sundaystrollersfc@hotmail.com
Map 1 V8
This club holds weekly kickabouts every Sunday in Abu Dhabi from 19:30-21:00, and has a team in the seven-a-side and eleven-a-side Abu Dhabi leagues. There's also an annual trip to Phuket in Thailand for the sevens tournament which takes place every November. Email Roland at the above address for more information.

Duplays Fifth Element League
The Dome@Rawdat, Shk Rashid Bin Saeed Al Maktoum Rd Al Madina Al Riyadiya 055 224 0186
duplays.com
Map 1 J8
For some regular five-a-side action, the Abu Dhabi branch of sporting community Duplays organises competitive leagues every couple of months. Games are played weekly at the fairly recently-built Dome @ Rawdhat. It costs Dhs.400 to sign up per individual (you'll be placed in a team), or Dhs. 2,600 per team of eight.

Manchester United Soccer Schools
The Dome@Rawdhat, Shk Rashid Bin Saeed Al Maktoum Rd Al Madina Al Riyadiya 02 449 8480
manutdsoccerschools.ae
Map 1 J8
Manchester United Soccer Schools offers a range of football courses for kids, as well as youth football camps aimed at children and young adults aged between 6 and 18 years. The courses run several times a year at the Dome @ Rawdhat, and there are various age groups on offer. All players are given the opportunity to take part in a series of skills challenges, with selected participants being given the chance to represent the soccer school at the World Skills Final event in the UK.

Gaelic Games

Abu Dhabi Na Fianna
Various locations
abudhabinafianna.com
The sister association of Abu Dhabi Irish Society (p.42), Na Fianna offers a sporting programme of Gaelic games, including Gaelic football and hurling. In addition to regular training and competitions, the group runs a busy social calendar which includes golf days, themed social events and fundraisers.

Gardening

Abu Dhabi Flower & Garden Group
Various locations
adfgg.com
This non-profit volunteer organisation aims to create environmental awareness and promote gardening at home and in the Gulf by planting seeds, flowering plants and trees. Meetings are held once a month, and there are various workshops and field trips, as well as exhibits by floral artists.

Golf

The UAE is quite rightly known as the best golf destination in the Gulf, with excellent year-round facilities and many important tournaments being held here. Courses are either fully grassed or brown (sand) courses, or a mixture of the two. Abu Dhabi is home to a variety of local tournaments held on an annual or monthly basis, such as the regular Abu Dhabi Duty Free Medal, while on the international scene, the Abu Dhabi Golf HSBC Championship (p.26) has become an annual stop on the European PGA Tour. A great event to watch, it attracts some of the sport's top names; and in Dubai, the Emirates Golf Club hosts the well-established Omega Dubai Desert Classic (p.27) and the Jumeirah Golf Estates hosts the DP World Tour Championship (p.28) in November, the culmination of the European Tour's Race to Dubai.

Abu Dhabi City Golf Club
Saeed Bin Tahnoon St Al Mushrif 02 445 9600
adcitygolf.ae
Map 1 C4
This unusual course is set within a horseracing track and its par 70 course boasts one of the longest par five holes in the Gulf, at 630 yards. Competitions are held each Friday and the Junior Golf Academy offers an eight-week teaching programme for 8 to 14 year olds. Although there are only nine holes, there are alternative tees for the back nine. All facilities are free to members. Green fees for visitors vary depending on the time of day and year; an off-peak nine holes during the summer starts at Dhs.145 including cart hire. A range of balls are available starting at Dhs.40.

The luxurious clubhouse also features an excellent restaurant, pool and Jacuzzi for use by members.

Abu Dhabi Golf Club

Umm Al Nar St Madinat Khalifa A (Khalifa City A) **02 558 8990**
adgolfclub.com
Map **1 N8**
Located just 30 minutes from the centre of Abu Dhabi, the club's excellent facilities include 27 holes, including a par 72 world-class 18 hole course, a driving range, putting and pitching greens and a golf academy that holds lessons for juniors as well. There is a wide range of membership categories designed to suit every type of golfer. Managed by Troon Golf, the club is the host of the Abu Dhabi Golf HSBC Championship (p.26), a stop on the European PGA Tour. The falcon-shaped clubhouse also features bars, restaurants, pro-shop, gym, pool and spa.

Al Ain Golf Club

Nr Danat Al Ain Resort Al Ain **03 768 6808**
Map **4 E2**
The Al Ain Golf Club, near the Danat Al Ain Resort, boasts an 18 hole sand course, a clubhouse and a floodlit driving range. Handicaps gained here are valid internationally. Visitors are welcome, but should phone ahead.

Al Ghazal Golf Club

Nr Abu Dhabi Int'l Airport Airport Area **02 575 8040**
alghazalgolf.ae
Map **1 V8**
This golf course has 'browns' instead of 'greens' with a purpose-built 18 hole sand golf course, driving range, academy and licensed clubhouse is situated two minutes from the capital's airport, and is home to the World Sand Golf Championship. Anyone can play here, including transit passengers with a few hours to kill – airlines can arrange free 96 hour passenger transit visas for travellers who want to play golf or use the facilities. Lessons are available, and green fees range from Dhs.70 for nine holes for members (weekdays), to Dhs.165 for 18 holes for non-members at weekends. A branch of the Abu Dhabi Duty Free Shop is situated on the premises (see addf.ae).

Emirates Golf Federation

Dubai Creek Golf & Yacht Club Dubai **04 295 2277**
ugagolf.com
Map **3 E2** Metro **Deira City Centre**
This non-profit organisation governs amateur golf in the UAE. It is overseen by the General Authority of Youth & Sports, and actively supports junior players and the development of the national team. The affiliate membership rate is Dhs.200 per quarter, and the UGA Handicap Scheme costs Dhs.795 per year.

Hilton Al Ain Golf Club

Hilton Al Ain Al Ain **03 768 6666**
al-ain.hilton.com
Map **4 E2**
This par three course has an average distance of about 80 yards between each hole and, although short in length, it can play tough. The course has nearly 30 bunkers and very small quick greens. It is open to non-members, and lessons are available. There is an entrance fee of Dhs.76 for non-members and green fees are also Dhs.23; club hire starts from Dhs.35 for a half set and Dhs.8 per golf ball.

Rotana Junior Golf League

Abu Dhabi City Golf Club Al Mushrif **02 445 9600**
adcitygolf.ae
Map **1 C4**
When it comes to learning golf, the younger you start the better. This junior golf league operates from September to May, with tournaments held every month and lessons given weekly. The cost of instruction is Dhs.625 for eight lessons, plus a registration fee of Dhs.150.

Saadiyat Beach Golf Club

Saadiyat Island 02 557 8000
sbgolfclub.ae
Map **1 H1**
The only local course designed specifically for pay and play daily members, Saadiyat Beach is a par 72, 18 hole links-style Championship course designed by golfing legend Gary Player. The spectacular location features three lakes and 60 bunkers. UAE residents can play at a discounted rate of Dhs.425 during the week and Dhs.595 at weekends. The Golf Institute by Troon Golf can help you perfect your swing with an introduction to the course, world-class coaching for all levels, and a junior development programme.

Yas Links Abu Dhabi

Nr Yas Marina Circuit Yas Island West **02 810 7710**
yaslinks.com
Map **1 T4**
Open since 2010 and designed by Kyle Phillips, Yas Links is undeniably one of the region's top golf destinations. It boasts an 18 hole course in a stunningly scenic setting as part of the Yas Island development, with gorgeous seashore views. Yas Links is also home to a nine hole academy course, clubhouse, golf academy and floodlit practice facilities. Individual membership costs Dhs.25,000 per year, while rack rates start at Dhs.550 for non-members.

Hashing

Billed as 'drinking clubs with a running problem', Hash House Harriers is a worldwide network of social running clubs where the emphasis is on taking part, and socialising afterwards, rather than on serious running. Members run or walk around a course laid out by a couple of 'hares'. It's a fun way to get fit and meet new people.

Abu Dhabi Island Hash House Harriers

Various locations **050 669 2667**
auh4.org
If you think you need the drinking capacity of an elephant and the running ability of Sebastian Coe to join a hash, think again. Sprint, run, walk or hobble – it's up to you. The hash meets on Monday nights at various locations around the city. Membership costs Dhs.150 and includes a welcome pack and T-shirt. Under 16s join free with parents. Runs cost Dhs.50 for adults and Dhs.20 for under 16s. Call Derek Griffin for more information.

Abu Dhabi Mainland Hash House Harriers

Various locations
hhhweb.com
The Mainland Hash was started as an alternative to the Island Hash. More convenient to those living off the island, the Harriers meet on Monday evenings year-round. Food and beverages are provided in return for a small contribution. For more information email John Arkley at jrl-a@hotmail.com.

Al Ain Hash House Harriers

Various locations
Al Ain **050 623 0411**
Started in 1984, this hash has run over a thousand times with no break, despite rain, lightning and the occasional near hurricane. The runs vary in difficulty and start at various locations around Al Ain on Mondays, at 17:30 in the winter and 18:00 in the summer. It's a family affair that welcomes people of all ages and holds special events. Contact George on 050 623 0411 or Jude on 050 618 7244 for further details and information.

Horse Riding

Horses are of great significance and importance in this part of the world, both in historical and modern terms. The UAE has a wealth of equine talent. Recreational riding is extremely well supported, and most stables offer quality horses, whether for hacks out in the desert (with gazelles racing alongside) or rides along the beach.

Courses are on offer from the beginner level all the way to advanced. Horse racing and endurance riding are also extremely popular and races are held throughout the year. In March each year, Dubai hosts the world's richest horse race, the $10 million Dubai World Cup (p.28), which is one of the major events on the UAE's social calendar and takes place at the impressive Meydan racetrack.

Abu Dhabi Equestrian Club

Al Saada St Al Mushrif **02 445 5500**
adec-web.com
Map **2 H13**
As well as races and show jumping events during the cooler winter months, the club offers comprehensive instruction at different levels of expertise, starting with riding for beginners right through to show jumping. Private lessons start from Dhs.200 for members and Dhs.350 for non-members. The facilities include modern stables, a polo field and an equine swimming pool.

Al Forsan International Sports Resort

Nr Abu Dhabi Golf Club & Resort Madinat Khalifa A (Khalifa City A) **02 556 8555**
alforsan.com
Map **1 P8**
The newly-opened complex offers fantastic premises and lessons for all levels; indoor and outdoor training areas; show jumping facilities; and a polo field. Lessons start from Dhs.180 and discounted package deals are available.

Sir Bani Yas Stables

Sir Bani Yas Island 02 406 1400
desertislands.com
Map **3 B2**
The latest addition to Desert Islands is a luxury equestrian complex, featuring barns, training arenas, paddocks, lunge rings and training rings. Catering for everyone from beginners to advanced riders, guests can do anything from private lessons to guided rides through the island, getting a unique perspective of the Arabian Wildlife from horseback. More experienced riders can tackle the Royal Bay Ride along a golden beach.

Ice Hockey

Abu Dhabi Falcons Ice Hockey

Zayed Sports City Al Safarat
abudhabifalcons.wetpaint.com
Map **1 J8**
This club is dedicated to the development of youth ice hockey in a fun, safe environment. Practice sessions are held at Sheikh Zayed Sports City and the teams participate in local tournaments against Al Ain, Dubai, Dhahran, Doha and Muscat. The club also holds an annual camp with professional Canadian coaches. Boys and girls aged between 5 and 18 are welcome.

Abu Dhabi Scorpions Ice Hockey

Abu Dhabi Ice Rink Al Safarat **050 621 6464**
Map **1 J8**
You don't have to play like Wayne Gretsky, Bobby Orr or Patrick Roy to join this team – all players over

I ♥ ZSC

LOVE SPORTS?
We have everything you need at Zayed Sports City

With a mission to ensure that every visitor has a great sporting experience, whether they watch or participate, Zayed Sports City is continuing to grow its services and offerings.

With a reputation as the best place for sport in the UAE, over 17 athletic pursuits are on offer between the International Tennis Centre, Khalifa International Bowling Centre, Zayed Sports City Ice Rink and Haddins Gym. In addition to these feature activities, billiards, cycle hire, table tennis, padel tennis, football, rugby, basketball, netball and softball are among the other ways to get active on site. Memberships are available for avid athletes and casual players can take advantage of 'pay as you play' rates at each venue. Throughout the year special ways to participate will appear, such as tournaments, clinics, holiday camps and community nights.

In addition to this wide range of sporting facilities the entire site has become multi-purpose, hosting events from birthday parties to international sporting matches and popular family entertainment shows.

zsc.ae | facebook.com/ZayedSportsCity
02 403 4200

مدينة زايد الرياضية
ZAYED SPORTS CITY

18 are welcome. The Scorpions participated in the inaugural Emirates Hockey League, along with the Abu Dhabi Storms (an Emirati team), two teams from Al Ain and a team from Dubai. The league is impressively organised, and highly competitive. For more information about either the Scorpions or the Storms, contact chairman Ali Kaddas (alikaddas1976@gmail.com).

Ice Skating

Abu Dhabi now has two ice rinks to call its own. The Abu Dhabi Ice Rink is the oldest and largest, and it's where most of the capital's ice sporting events take place. The newest edition, the SnowWorld rink at Marina Mall (02 681 8300), is a smaller rink, but it should prove to be popular with children, and with shoppers who are looking for exercise that's a little more interesting and challenging than mall walking. Similarly, Al Ain has a small rink in Al Ain Mall (03 766 0333) to supplement the more serious, full-size rink at Hili Fun City.

Abu Dhabi Ice Rink
Zayed Sports City Al Safarat **02 403 4333**
Map **1 J8**
This Olympic size rink has great facilities with a separate children's area, a French cafe and arcade entertainment. Lessons for all levels of ability are

Ice skating

available. There is a Dhs.5 entrance fee and a Dhs.15 skating fee but children under 3 get in for free. It's advisable to call ahead as the rink is sometimes closed for ice hockey practice.

Hili Fun City > *p.239*
Off Emirates St Al Ain **03 784 5542**
hilifuncity.ae
Map **4 G7**
Located on the eastern side of the park, this mammoth 60 by 30 metre rink has seating for 3,000 spectators. Besides public skating sessions, there are ice hockey tournaments and ice skating competitions held throughout the year.

Karting

Al Ain Raceway
Off Al Khatam St Al Ain **03 768 6662**
alainraceway.com
Map **4 F3**
Not a place for a leisurely drive, the high-tech karts send drivers roaring around the track at speeds in excess of 60kph. After donning race suits and listening to a safety briefing, drivers are led out to the track – you can choose to ride solo or race as part of a group. Computers record speed and lap times and can be printed out at the end. Open 14:00-22:00, Monday to Friday, and 10:00-18:00 on Saturday; basic practice sessions cost Dhs.100 for 15 minutes on the Indy circuit or Dhs.150 on the International circuit.

Kitesurfing

Kitepro Abu Dhabi
Various locations **050 544 1494**
kitepro.ae
With a couple of good areas for kiteboarding, there's a decent little community in Abu Dhabi. As well as forming something of a hub for kiters, Kitepro Abu Dhabi has a school that covers basic, intermediate and advanced kiteboarding, with all the latest equipment such as radio helmets. Lessons cost Dhs.350 for a 60 minute private tutorial or Dhs.500 for a 90 minute two-person lesson. Packages are also available.

Kitesurfinguae.com
Dubai **050 456 5951**
kitesurfinguae.com
Map **3 E2**
A collection of international IKO-certified instructors who are available for lessons in Abu Dhabi and Dubai. A private one hour lesson starts at Dhs.300 including all gear, going down to Dhs.150 per person for a four person, one hour group lesson. Also organises trips to Oman.

HOW BIG IS
146,000
DAILY READERS?

SPORT 360°

**7HE
SEVENS
STADIUM**

**DUBAI
CRICKET
STADIUM**

**YAS
MARINA
CIRCUIT**

**DUBAI
TENNIS
STADIUM**

Martial Arts

Abu Dhabi Aikido Club
Various locations **050 412 2395**
Aikido literally means harmony and love with the spirit of the universe, and the training is designed to give you the ability to defend yourself while gaining control of your assailant without inflicting injury. Classes take place at the Abu Dhabi Hilton and Asian Karate Center (behind the Russian Embassy). Call Freddie on the number above for more information.

Fighting Fit
Karate, kung fu, kickboxing and self defence classes taught by Sensai Shan, a bronze medal winner in the Karate World Championships, are available for adults and junior members of The Club (p.179). Call 02 673 1111 for enquiries.

Abu Dhabi Combat Club
Abu Dhabi Equestrian Club Al Mushrif **050 561 5176**
adcombat.com
Map **2 H13**
This club focuses on Brazilian jiu-jitsu but cross-trains in boxing, kickboxing, judo, wrestling and various other arts beneficial to no rules fighting. Membership costs Dhs.200 for one month and Dhs.800 for six months for children, and Dhs.200 for one month and Dhs.1,500 for one year for adults. Classes take place every day except Friday and Saturday, from 17:00 to 18:00 for children and 19:00 to 20:00 for adults.

Baroudy's Sports Club
ADCB Building, Corniche St Markaziya East
02 626 8122
Map **2 Q2**
Baroudy's teaches taekwondo, which embraces the traditional beliefs of honour, integrity, loyalty and compassion. Taekwondo teaches self defence and also improves physical fitness and mental discipline. The club runs a children's summer camp. For details, contact Tony Baroudy on the number above.

Cobra Muay Thai Abu Dhabi
Zayed Sports City Al Safarat **055 616 0996**
cobramuaythai.com
Map **1 J8**
Cobra Muay Thai has something to offer everybody, welcoming all skill levels from beginners to advanced

students. Chief instructor Mat Dryden divides his time between hosting classes at Zayed Sports City but is looking for a dedicated facility. Classes include Muay Thai and traditional boxing training as well as a Fitness for Fighters class that promises to push even the most in-shape participants to their limits. For details, call Mat at the above number.

Emirates Sports Centre
Nr Al Salama Hospital Tourist Club Area **050 820 5734**
Map **2 R3**
Sessions in karate and kung fu are conducted by Master Jai. With over 15 years of martial arts experience and a trunkload of awards, expect only the best level of instruction.

The Oriental Karate & Kobudo Club
Tourist Club Area **02 677 1611**
orientalkarate.com
Map **2 R4**
This active Abu Dhabi club offers classes for all skill levels. Lessons are held at various locations; call the number above or get in touch with one of the following centres: Madinat Zayed (02 634 5080), Airport Road (02 445 7375), Khalifa Street (02 622 4182) and Al Khalidiyah (02 621 8773). Classes cost Dhs.250 a month (two sessions per week), excluding a Dhs.100 admission fee and Dhs.100 for the uniform.

Sheraton Resort Health Club
Sheraton Abu Dhabi Hotel & Resort Markaziya East
02 677 3333
sheratonabudhabihotel.com
Map **2 Q2**
Sheraton Resort Health Club offers classes in martial arts ranging from judo and kickboxing to karate at the club facility. The instructor is a highly experienced martial arts black belt who focuses on defence and safety. Lessons are available for different levels of skill, as well as for children. Individual sessions costs Dhs.40 for non-member adults and Dhs.30 for children.

Tai Chi Club
The Club Mina Zayed Free Port **02 673 1111**
the-club.com
Map **2 V3**
The Tai Chi Club has a trained professional leading regular, weekly sessions of the ancient Chinese martial art; you must be a member of The Club (p.179) or be accompanied by a member to take part.

Martial Arts Dan Cady, participant at Cobra Muay Thai

I've been training martial arts for several years now, but Muay Thai is a new discipline for me. I train because it makes me recognise my own limitations physically and mentally and work to surpass them. Martial Arts add balance and discipline to my life and really help me alleviate the stresses of work and everyday life.

Mini Golf

To combine a spot of mini golf with a trip out of town, day visitors can play at the Hatta Fort Hotel (04 809 9333) for Dhs.30 per hour, from 09:00 till 18:00, while at the Mercure Grand Jebel Hafeet (03 783 8888), mini golf is charged at Dhs.24 per hour from 09:00 till 23:00. Guests can play at both hotels for free. The Mercure Grand's course is set against a backdrop of the magnificent mountains. Balls and clubs can be hired from the hotel.

Motorsports

Abu Dhabi MX Club

Various locations **050 818 4668**
Abu Dhabi MX Club is a social group that meets on certain weekends and some week nights (from about 16:00 to 19:00) to ride in the desert. It has several practice tracks that it uses and riders of all standards are welcome.

Al Forsan International Sports Resort

Nr Abu Dhabi Golf Club & Resort Madinat Khalifa A (Khalifa City A) **02 556 8555**
alforsan.com
Map **1 P8**
Abu Dhabi finally has a karting facility: the ultra-modern Motor Sports Centre at Al Forsan boasts a

1.2km track with a Supermoto section built to FIM regulations and three models of karts, the fastest of which reaches impressive speeds of 110kmph. There is also a child-safe track, while adventurous drivers may like to tackle the 2km off-road circuit.

Emirates Motor Sports Federation

Villa 1, Nr Aviation Club, Casablanca Rd Dubai
04 282 7111
emsf.ae
Map **3 E2** Metro **GGICO**
Emirates Motor Sports Federation organises events throughout the year, such as the 4WD 1000 Dunes Rally, the Champions Rally for saloon cars, road safety campaigns and classic car exhibitions. Membership including competition licence is Dhs.500 per year; non-members can race for a fee. Check out the website for a full calendar of events and keep an eye on daily newspapers. A number of international rallies either start or end in Abu Dhabi, or pass through during their stages.

Ferrari World Abu Dhabi > *p.295*

Yas Island West **02 496 8001**
ferrariworldabudhabi.com
Map **1 T4**
The world's largest indoor theme park has enough attractions to keep motorsports enthusiasts of all ages

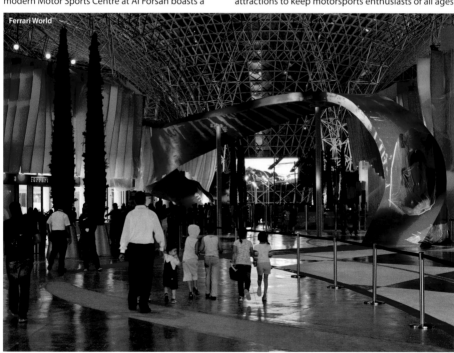
Ferrari World

entertained. Kids can learn to drive in a miniature Ferrari, while grown-up fans get to take a glimpse into the F1 paddock or experience race driving in a simulator. For thrillseekers, there's the world's fastest rollercoaster and the G-Force tower.

Yas Marina Circuit
Yas Island **02 659 9800**
yasmarinacircuit.com
Map **1 T5**
Although most famous for being the home of the annual Formula 1 Etihad Airways Grand Prix, Yas Marina Circuit is actually a year-round venue where petrolheads can put their driving skills to the test, or take high-speed driving lessons. The possibilities include drag racing, as well as a host of other options from supercar and Formula Yas 3000 driving to passenger experiences.

Mountain Biking
Away from the cities, the UAE has a lot to offer outdoor enthusiasts, especially mountain bikers. On a mountain bike it's possible to see the most remote and untouched places that are not even accessible in 4WDs. For hardcore, experienced mountain bikers there is a good range of terrain, from the super-technical rocky trails in areas like Shuwayah and Shawka, to mountain routes like Wadi Bih, which climb to over a thousand metres and can be descended in minutes.

The riding is mainly rocky, technical and challenging. Even if you are an experienced biker, always be sensible and go prepared – it's important to remember that the sun can be very strong, you will need far more water than you think, and it's easy to get lost. You'll find wide, knobbly tyres work much better on the loose, sharp rocks. For further information on mountain biking in the UAE, including details of possible routes, refer to the *UAE Off-Road Explorer*.

Hot-Cog Mountain Bike Club
Dubai **056 170 8087**
hot-cog.com
Map **3 E2**
Hot Cog MTB is an active group of Dubai-based enthusiasts who ride every weekend, all over the country, all year round. They also camp, hike and barbecue, and new riders are always welcome. Visit the website for more information.

Noukhada Adventure Company
Al Meena St Al Meena **02 650 3600**
noukhada.ae
Map **2 S2**
Since there are no mountains in the area, Noukhada will take you on trails out in the deepest desert. Expect

to run into camels, gazelles and people riding horses, and to view the setting sun and stars coming out over the impressive dunes and vast salt flats. Noukhada supplies a helmet, gloves and a bike for Dhs.50 per person per hour. Individuals with their own gear can join for free on Tuesday nights at Yas Island.

Music Lessons
There are a few companies that offer music lessons in Abu Dhabi for both children and adults. As well as the companies included below, Royal Music & Arts (02 622 5442) also offers lessons for a range of common instruments.

Beethoven Institute Of Music
Nr Clock Tower & Fish Market, Al Nasr St
Al Khalidiyah **02 632 7588**
Map **2 K3**
Started in 1984, this was one of the first music institutes to set up in the UAE. On offer are lessons on the drums, guitar, piano and organ. Children can start from as young as 6 years old, and summer 'immersion' courses are also held. For more information about timetables and prices, contact the number listed or Ms Shahnaz on 050 782 7947.

International Music Institute
Nr Grand Stores, Shk Zayed The First St Al Manhal
02 621 1299
imi-jmc.net
Map **2 K4**
Founded in 1994 in order to nurture musical education in the capital, IMI offers lessons taught by professionally trained instructors of piano, string, wind and percussion instruments. The institute offers both individual lessons and group classes based upon the skill levels of its students.

Royal Music Academy
Nr Eldorado Cinema Markaziya East
Map **2 P3**
The instruments taught here include guitar, drums and keyboard and the school serves as preparation for the internationally-renowned Trinity College and Royal School of Music, London.

The Young Musician Music Institute
Al Raha Mall Al Raha **02 556 2080**
theyoungmusician.com
Map **1 R7**
With a highly trained faculty, this institute teaches a variety of instruments and genres including classical, rock, jazz, blues, pop, flamenco and even heavy metal. The organisation offers custom-made and advanced courses which are recognised by the Trinity College of Music, Royal School of Music, Trinity Rock School of Music and London College of Music.

Netball

Abu Dhabi Netball League

Various locations **050 277 5650**
adnetball.com

Netball is the largest organised weekly women's sporting event in Abu Dhabi. This league has been in existence for 10 years and the teams also participate in the Inter-Gulf Netball Championships. The players range from beginners to experts and even men – and it now has 150 girls playing every week. New players are always welcome. A annual membership fee of Dhs.400 is payable by each player to cover administration costs.

Off-Road Driving

With vast areas of rarely visited wilderness to explore, dune and wadi bashing are popular pastimes in the UAE. When heading off-road, it's always advisable to travel with at least two vehicles. If anything goes wrong, you'll be glad of an extra pair of hands, or a tow. If you're desert driving for the first time, go with an experienced person – driving on sand requires very different skills to other surfaces. Tour companies offer a range of desert and mountain safaris (see Tour Operators p.231). 4WDs can be hired from most car hire companies (for Car Hire Companies see p.60). One point about the word 'bashing' – while it is a popular term for this form of entertainment, it can be misleading. Most, if not all, of your journey should be on existing tracks to protect the environment from further damage. For more information of where to head, get a copy of the *UAE Off-Road Explorer*.

Abu Dhabi 4x4 The Capital Off-road Club

Various locations
ad4x4.com

This off-road club welcomes off-roaders based in Abu Dhabi. The club also tries to include family members in its range of activities and events. Members can meet other enthusiasts and share off-road driving tips and experiences. The club's website is also very informative.

Paintballing & Laser Games

Al Forsan International Sports Resort

Nr Abu Dhabi Golf Club & Resort Madinat Khalifa A (Khalifa City A) **02 556 8555**
alforsan.com
Map **1 P8**

Paintballing fans get to choose from three separate, themed indoor spaces: The Wild West, Alien Encounter and Pacific Island Zone. It also contains an international standard tournament field, as well as laser tag modifications for children.

Armed Forces Officers Club & Hotel

Nr Grand Mosque Al Maqtaa Officers Club
02 441 5900
afoc.mil.ae
Map **1 K9**

The club boasts two paintball fields complete with cinder block shelters, wrecked cars and other detritus of urban warfare. The cost is Dhs.150 for an hour, with a minimum of seven players to reserve exclusive use of the field. Advance bookings are essential.

Off-road adventures

The Emirates National Paintball League
Various locations
enpl.ae
Dying to hurl a few paintballs at unsuspecting victims? Get it in contact with ENPL through the website above and get started. The group is run by experienced paintball players who want to share their passion for the game with other enthusiasts. The club also holds four tournaments every year.

Polo

Ghantoot Racing & Polo Club
Ghantoot **02 562 9050**
grpc.ae
Map **3 D3**
Popularity for this sport has increased dramatically over the last few years. Ghantoot Racing & Polo Club boasts modern infrastructure for sports and events, and the centre's calendar features regular chukka tournaments and high profile international games. The club sprawls over 300 hectares close to the Abu Dhabi–Dubai highway. The quality of horses and play is high, and spectators are always welcome. There is also a restaurant and a library on the premises.

Pottery

Abu Dhabi Pottery
Nr Khalidiya Garden, 16th Street, Shk Zayed The First St Al Khalidiyah **02 666 7079**
abudhabipottery.com
Map **3 C3**
Creative-minded adults and children aged 5 and up can try hand building and wheel pottery under the guidance of friendly staff. A chance to explore your creative side costs Dhs.185 per session for adults and Dhs.100 for children.

Rugby
Rugby is played by men, ladies and children throughout the UAE, with the larger teams taking part in Gulf league and cup competitions. The highlight of the year, for players and fans, is the annual Emirates Airlines Dubai Rugby Sevens Tournament (p.29), held at the new ground, The Sevens.

Abu Dhabi Harlequins Rugby Club
Al Ghazal Golf Club Airport Area **050 614 5199**
abudhabiquins.com
Map **1 V8**
Formerly the Abu Dhabi Rugby Football Club, the Abu Dhabi Harlequins is an active club boasting over 400 members, including men, women and children. All are welcome to join in. For further information contact chairman Richard Harris at the above number, or club captain David Stolzenberg at 050 592 0717.

Running along the Corniche

Al Ain Amblers Rugby Club
Al Ain Equestrian, Shooting & Golf Club Al Ain **03 702 6431**
aesgclub.com
Map **4 C3**
Formed back in 1981, the club embraces rugby players of all standards. Future plans include a youth set-up and a mini section for children aged 10 to 16. For more information contact the club chairman.

Ecole Française de Rugby
Sports Stadium, Delma St Al Nahyan
efrabudhabi.com
Map **2 P9**
If your child is a fan of this adrenaline-pumping sport, and they are between the ages of 6 and 19, then look no further. This club has several groups welcoming beginners and players of all nationalities. Visit the website for information on training sessions, coaches and the season schedule.

Running
For more than half the year, the weather is ideal for running, although even in the height of summer, you'll find dedicated types pounding the streets across the country. In the hottest months, the evenings and early mornings are the best times to run. Clubs and informal groups meet regularly, for casual and competitive runs and for training towards running events organised throughout the year. Regular, short distance races are held, as well as a variety of biathlons, triathlons and hashes. A favourite competition is the epic Wadi Bih Run. Teams of five run the 70km from Ras Al Khaimah to Dibba over mountains topping out at more than a thousand metres. Backed by a support vehicle, runners take turns on the different stages. The Dubai Marathon (p.27) is held in January each year.

Abu Dhabi Striders

Various locations
abudhabistriders.com
Formed in 1983 by runners in search of fellow enthusiasts, members come from all walks of life with varying standards of fitness. There are organised runs every Wednesday and interval training on Sundays. Each year the club holds 10km, half marathon, full marathon and cross-country races, and participates in races across the UAE, while organising various social events. Contact them on admin@abudhabistriders.com.

Al Ain Road Runners

Nr Danat Al Ain Resort Al Ain **050 472 1566**
Map **4 E2**
Al Ain Road Runners are generally runners and hashers who want to do a 'bit more'. Each training session encompasses two routes: a 5km jogging route, and a longer one for the more serious runners. The group meets outside the Danat Al Ain Resort on Sundays and Thursdays, and all are welcome. Contact Phil (philip. almond@hct.ac.ae) for more details.

Sailing

While the summer months can be scorching, the winter is perfect for setting sail. From hotels that charter boats for excursions to an offshore island, to friends who moor their catamarans and speedboats at the marina – opportunities to get out on the water are plentiful. Membership at one of the sailing clubs will often mean you can use its leisure facilities, join in with activities, hire sailing and water sports equipment and moor or store your boat. Several clubs offer lessons if you are new to sailing.

A racing dhow

courses or one-to-one private onboard training in boat handling. The courses include handling marina situations, long distance voyages and high speed night navigation, as well as first aid and emergency medical techniques.

Abu Dhabi Sailing Club

The Club Mina Zayed Free Port **02 673 1111**
abudhabisailing.com
Map **2 V3**
Abu Dhabi Sailing Club is a sub-section of The Club (p.179). It has a fleet of Kestrels, Lasers and Optimists, and meets regularly both on the water and socially. Social races are held every week and they participate in a number of national regattas every year in Dubai and Abu Dhabi. Membership is open only to members of The Club but beginner sailing courses are offered for adults and children from the age of 6. Annual membership of the sailing club is Dhs.1,600. For more information contact them on the number above or see the website.

Coastal Safety

Dubai
coastalsafety.com
Map **3 E2**
Based in both Dubai and the UK, Coastal Sea Schools is the place to head for if you're looking for RYA

Noukhada Adventure Company

Al Meena St Al Meena **02 650 3600**
noukhada.ae
Map **2 S2**
For those who want to learn how to sail, Noukhada is a perfect starting point. Its Hobie catamarans are light and easy to manoeuvre and the staff have been sailing for years. For expats who are already accomplished sailors without access to a boat, Noukhada's sailing club (Dhs.5,000 per year) offers the use of its boats for a set number of hours and a discounted rate once those hours have been exceeded. And there's not the headache of storage or upkeep.

Sandboarding & Skiing

The big dunes at Liwa are a wonderful place to try these exciting and unusual sports. It's easy to learn and it doesn't hurt (too much) when you fall. The boards used are usually standard snowboards but, as the sand is quite abrasive for them, they often can't be used for anything else afterwards. Some sports stores sell purpose-built 'sand boards', which are a cheaper and more basic type of snowboard. As an alternative for children, a plastic sledge is more than enough to provide a lot of fun. All the major tour companies (p.231) offer sandboarding or skiing experiences with basic instruction on how to stay up, surf and fall properly and safely. This experience is often available either as part of another tour or as a dedicated sand boarding tour.

Shooting

The shooting ranges and facilities available in Abu Dhabi have increased significantly following the opening of the extensive facilities at Al Forsan. Alternatively, more options are available just a short drive away in neighbouring Dubai, Hatta and Ras Al Khaimah.

Al Forsan International Sports Resort

Nr Abu Dhabi Golf Club & Resort Madinat Khalifa A (Khalifa City A) **02 556 8555**
alforsan.com
Map **1 P8**
The newly-opened shooting ranges at Al Forsan provide what Abu Dhabians were previously lacking: dedicated indoor and outdoor ranges, including the first clay shooting course in the Gulf region. With simulated game flush shooting, Olympic trap and skeet fields, rifle ranges and a laser shooting simulator, the options are plentiful. Lane rentals start from Dhs.100 and training is available.

Caracal Shooting Club

Armed Forces Officers Club & Hotel Officers Club **02 441 6404**
caracalsc.ae
Map **1 K9**
Caracal has a 25 metre shooting range as well as a simulator room, so, if your day at work has been a particularly bad one, you can relieve a little stress the Wild West way. Entry to the club costs Dhs.130 – after that, you will then have to pay for your bullets as you go so accuracy is the name of the game.

Jebel Ali International Shooting Club & Centre Of Excellence

Nr Jebel Ali Golf Resort & Spa Dubai **04 883 6555**
jebelali-international.com
Map **3 E2**
This club has five floodlit clay shooting ranges that consist of skeet, trap and sporting. Professional instructors give comprehensive lessons and experienced shooters are welcome to try their hand at clay shooting or archery. Indoor and outdoor ranges, as well as a specialised pistol range, are available. Non-members are welcome. Refreshments are available and corporate or group activities can be arranged. Prices available on request.

Ras Al Khaimah Shooting Club

Nr RAK Airport Ras Al Khaimah **07 236 3622**
Map **3 F1**
This club welcomes interested parties that want to learn how to shoot, whether it's shotguns or long rifles. The club boasts a 50m indoor and 200m outdoor rifle range, and has a canteen selling snacks and soft drinks. If you ring them you may want to have an Arabic speaker standing by. Otherwise, just drop by the next time you're in RAK.

Singing

Abu Dhabi Choral Group

Al Muna School, Nr Hamdan Centre Al Markaziyah **050 442 0029**
abudhabichoralgroup.com
Map **2 N4**
The largest and longest-running choral group in the capital, ADCG has been active for over three decades. It's open to anyone, and annual membership dues are Dhs.100 with rehearsals normally held on Tuesday evenings at Al Muna School in Khalidiyah. The four part harmony choir stages two major performances a year, selecting pieces from popular musicals for a spring production and festive tunes for a series of December concerts.

Blue Fever

Various locations **050 442 0029**
Passionately belting out love songs and big band hits (in a four to eight part harmony), these jazz and a cappella singers have performed at a range of locations including the Emirates Palace. Contact coordinator and founder Laura Roberts on the number above for more details. Space is limited, so there are friendly auditions.

Men's Barbershop

Various locations **050 442 0029**
This brand new group sings songs from doo-wop style to traditional barbershop blends in a cappella concerts. This is the first group of its kind in Abu Dhabi. A 'friendly' audition is required and there must be a commitment to attend practices regularly. Call or email for more information.

Voices Of Harmony

Abu Dhabi Tourism & Culture Authority Al Matar **050 442 0029**
Map **1 K7**
An all-women's barbershop group in Abu Dhabi that sings a cappella style. The group performs at hotel events, fund raisers and dinner parties, as well as at National Day parties for the United States Embassy, Abu Dhabi Tourism & Culture Authority, the Emirates Palace Hotel and the Crowne Plaza. A casual audition and commitment to attend practices is required.

Skating, Rollerskating & Rollerblading

Good fun and great exercise, rollerblading is a sport for all the family. The best places to skate have few people and enough slopes and turns to make it interesting and to improve your balance and skill. The Corniche (p.194) and Breakwater have long paved areas, best when they're not too crowded – the view is a bonus. Although it gets busy in the evenings, the New Corniche (p.198) is another good spot, with views across the mangroves. Prepare for the inevitable falls by wearing the necessary safety gear: a helmet and elbow, knee and wrist pads. See p.334 for sportswear stockists. For more serious skaters, there is a skate park opposite the Hilton Baynunah. Skate Arabia (skatearabia.com) is an online skating community which posts blogs, information about events being held in the region and photos of enthusiasts. It also occasionally organises competitions and events in Abu Dhabi.

Skiing & Snowboarding

The ski slope at SnowWorld in Marina Mall (p.345) is still under construction and is already years past its opening date so, in the meantime, those wanting to hit the slopes will have to either buy a plane ticket or head to Dubai for their snow fix.

Dubai Ski Club

Ski Dubai Dubai dubaiskiclub.com
Map **3 E2** Metro **Mall of the Emirates**
The club has over 1,400 members and meets at 18:00 on the last Saturday of every month, next to Ski Dubai's ticket counter, for social skiing or snowboarding, race training and races, followed by apres ski. Membership benefits include a reduced fee for the slope pass and use of the 'advance booking' lane when purchasing tickets, plus special offers on equipment, clothing, accessories and holidays. Membership is Dhs.300.

Ski Dubai > p.301

Mall Of The Emirates Dubai 800 386
skidxb.com
Map **3 E2** Metro **Mall of the Emirates**
When temperatures outside are melting your sunglasses, you can go sub-zero with a visit to Ski Dubai. The indoor ski resort is home to five slopes to suit all skill levels. The attractions also include the unique opportunity to get up and close with some irresistibly cute resident penguins. The slope itself has both chair lifts and tow lifts, and there's a well-stocked retail shop selling skis, boards, and clothing. Entrance to the Snow Park is Dhs.130 for adults and Dhs.120 for children. Prices for a two-hour Ski Slope Pass start at Dhs.180 for adults and Dhs.150 for kids; the prices include equipment and clothing (except gloves).

Skydiving

iFLY Dubai

Mirdif City Centre Dubai 04 231 6292
theplaymania.com
Map **3 E2** Metro **Rashidiya**
You can get a taste of the adrenalin-soaked sport at iFly in Dubai. Using super strong fans, the experience is realistic and challenging. First flight packages (instruction, gear and two flights) cost Dhs.195.

SkyDive Dubai

Dubai 050 153 3222
skydivedubai.ae
Map **3 E2**
The only 'true' skydiving provider in the UAE, the company has two drop zones. Easily the most popular for one-and-done and tourist skydivers is the skydive centre located on the beachfront near Dubai Marina, which gives jumpers the incredible experience of jumping above The Palm Jumeirah. But there's also a desert camp near Al Maha which is worth considering and this is where courses to become a qualified skydiver are held. A tandem jump costs Dhs.1,750.

Spacewalk Indoor Skydiving

Abu Dhabi Country Club Al Mushrif 02 657 7777
spacewalk.ae
Map **2 J13**
The perfect way to safely experience the thrill of free falling and skydiving without jumping out of an airplane. It is safe, fun for the whole family and an exhilarating experience for beginners (ages 3 and up) and those with experience. An Intro Flight ticket costs Dhs.180, with a First Class ticket costing Dhs.290. Your introductory flight includes your training session, use of all flight gear, two one-minute flights (two two-minute flights for First Class), and one-on-one personal assistance from your instructor. You will also learn the basic free fall position. A family package (up to five flyers) costs Dhs.720.

Snooker

Snooker here is a largely informal affair. A number of golf clubs have snooker and billiards facilities available for practising and for friendly competitions, but other than at The Club, there are no formal leagues.

The Club

Mina Zayed Free Port 02 673 1111
the-club.com
Map **2 V3**
The Snooker Section at The Club (p.179) has a snooker room with three full size tables available for members only. Weekly league matches and regular tournaments are played. In addition to The Club membership fees,

Do Something Different!

Shake up the routine and discover something new for the whole family at Ski Dubai.
Whether it's twisting and turning down the tube slides,
rolling down in a Giant Snow Ball, experiencing the thrills of a family chairlift ride
or enjoying a mug of the Avalanche Café's famous hot chocolate at minus 4 degrees,
you'll always find **something new at Ski Dubai.**

SKI DUBAI
سكي دبي

For more information please visit www.skidxb.com and 👍 us on facebook.com/skidxb an additional Dhs.125 annual subscription is required for The Snooker Section. For more information call The Club or see abudhabisnooker.com.

Shooters
Danat Al Ain Resort Al Ain **03 768 6686**
danathotels.com
Map **4 E2**
Home to four pool tables and a snooker table, available for use by anyone wanting to brush up their skills. Prices are Dhs.30 per table per hour; free if you order drinks. The club aims to be closely associated with other pool and snooker clubs around the country. Refreshments and snacks are available.

Squash
Courts are available for hire through hotel sports and health clubs and private clubs. The squash league at The Club provides the best opportunities for competitive playing and meeting new players, although Duplays (duplays.com) has recently launched its own league at the Officers' Club. Duplays' online noticeboard is also a good place to get in touch with other players looking for a game.

Abu Dhabi Golf Club
Umm Al Nar St Madinat Khalifa A (Khalifa City A) **02 558 8990**
adgolfclub.com
Map **1 N8**
Squash courts are available here, although they are for members' use only. Guests of members are charged Dhs.100 per hour.

The Club
Mina Zayed Free Port **02 673 1111**
the-club.com
Map **2 V3**
The Club has an active squash section with social evenings, internal box leagues and, for the more competitive player, representation in the Abu Dhabi Squash League. There is also a junior squash section with regularly organised games, practice sessions and tournaments. You must be a member of The Club (p.179) to play in competitions. Call for more details and timings, or see abudhabisquash.com.

Hiltonia Health Club & Spa
Hilton Abu Dhabi Al Khubeirah **02 692 4205**
hilton.com
Map **2 C3**
Squash coaching is available at the Hiltonia Health Club & Spa. Prices for a single lesson start at Dhs.115 for members and Dhs.125 for non-members. A discounted package is available if you book a set of 10 lessons: Dhs.1,035 for members and Dhs.1,150 for non-members.

Le Meridien Abu Dhabi
Nr Old Abu Dhabi Co-Op Society Tourist Club Area **02 644 6666**
lemeridienabudhabi.com
Map **2 S4**
Le Meridien's squash courts are available to outside guests at Dhs.120 per person for 45 minutes. Health club members and hotel guests can use the courts for free. Health club membership starts at Dhs.8,500 per year.

Sheraton Abu Dhabi Hotel & Resort
Corniche Rd Markaziya East **02 677 3333**
sheratonabudhabihotel.com
Map **2 Q2**
Squash court hire is Dhs.50 per hour to non-members and non-guests. Individual membership to the healthclub starts at Dhs.7,700 and includes use of the squash courts.

Swimming
Abu Dhabi's location on the Arabian Gulf means easy access to water that's relatively clean and at a pleasant temperature for most of the year. During the hottest months, the water near the beach is often warmer than a bath. Swimming off the beaches is possible at public beaches (p.215), beach parks (p.214) and private beaches belonging to hotels (p.198). On public beaches, you're advised to be modest in your choice of swimwear and, while bikinis and other swimwear are perfectly acceptable at most hotel pools, beaches and beach parks, be sure to cover up as soon as you leave the beach or pool area. Don't underestimate the strength of the tides and currents when swimming in the sea. Even off the safest-looking beaches rip tides have been known to carry people out to sea. Also, it's advisable to keep an eye out for jellyfish.

There are no public swimming pools but most hotels have swimming pools that are open for use by the public for a day entrance fee; the Abu Dhabi Marina and Yacht Club also has a pool open to day guests, as does the Monte Carlo Beach Club on Saadiyat Island. Entrance charges vary, but range from Dhs.50 to Dhs.400 on weekdays and Dhs.100 to Dhs.600 at weekends, and sometimes include beach access if the hotel has a private beach. Swimming lessons are available. Pools are usually cooled for the summer months. Hiltonia Health Club & Spa offers swimming lessons for kids and adults. Prices start from Dhs.120 (members) or Dhs.150 (non-members) for a private lesson, while group lessons are on offer from Dhs.270 for a set of four sessions.

Table Tennis
Most beach, health and sports clubs offer at least one table tennis table. Contact the hotels (p.198), and gyms and fitness centres (p.177) for more details.

Tennis

Tennis players are well catered for in Abu Dhabi, with courts available for public use in Abu Dhabi hotels (p.198), or for members only in private clubs. Nearly all courts are floodlit to allow play in the evenings – the coolest time of the day, and about the only time you'll want to play outside in the summer. Prices for hiring courts vary between Dhs.25 and Dhs.50 on weekdays, but you may be charged as much as Dhs.100 at the weekends. Group and individual coaching is widely available.

For those interested in professional tennis, the Mubadala World Tennis Championship (p.29) has become an annual fixture which kickstarts the sporting year. Abu Dhabi's first international tennis championship was held in January 2009 and the event has attracted top names in men's tennis each year ever since. The event features family attractions as well as a series of tennis-based activities and tournaments during the run-up to the event, including the Community Cup.

A month later, Dubai's now well-established annual competition, the million dollar Dubai Duty Free Tennis Championships, is held at Dubai Tennis Stadium and attracts big crowds, with most matches selling out. For further information and to buy tickets, see dubaidutyfreetennischampionships.com.

Abu Dhabi International Tennis Complex

Zayed Sport City Al Madina Al Riyadiya
capitala.ae
Map **1 J8**
Part of Zayed Sports City, the Abu Dhabi International Tennis Complex is home to Abu Dhabi's Mubadala World Tennis Championship each January. The state-of-the-art, Association of Tennis Professionals (ATP) standard tennis facility has six training courts and a centre court with a spectator capacity of 5,000. Family membership is available from Dhs.2,500 and individuals from Dhs.1,200, while court hire starts from Dhs.40 per hour. In addition to the court facilities, members have access to a gym, sauna and steam room for the post-play wind-down.

The Club

Mina Zayed Free Port **02 673 1111**
the-club.com
Map **2 V3**
With four floodlit tennis courts and a professional coach available for members at The Club, you're sure to have your backhand perfected in no time. Tennis social evenings and tournaments regularly take place. For those after a more competitive edge, there are annual club championships and teams from The Club are put forward to compete in the Abu Dhabi Tennis League. For more details, call The Club or see abudhabitennis.com.

Hiltonia Health Club & Spa

Hilton Abu Dhabi Al Khubeirah **02 692 4205**
hilton.com
Map **2 C3**
Tennis coaching is available from Dhs.180 (members) and Dhs.200 (non-members). Ten lessons for two people costs Dhs.1,000 per person (members) and Dhs.1,100 (non-members). Group lessons are also available and all groups will be divided by ability and age into Maxi, Midi and Mini tennis groups.

Triathlon

Abu Dhabi Triathlon Club

Various locations **050 610 9506**
abudhabitriclub.org
The Abu Dhabi Triathlon Club is a friendly and active group of swimming, running and cycling enthusiasts who train all year round. In addition to regular training sessions, the members organise and attend competitions and events across the region. There is no formal membership; just show up to the next session.

Emirates Triathlete

Golden Tulip Al Jazira Hotel & Resort Ghantoot
emiratestriathlete.com
Map **3 D3**
Emirates Triathlete organises monthly sprint distance triathlon races at Golden Tulip Al Jazira (p.202) in Ghantoot throughout the year (with the exception of the most sizzling summer months), which are aimed at absolute beginners as well as the more serious athletes.

Walking

The Corniche

The Corniche is a special place. Nearly seven kilometres long, it is a place where everyone can get away from the city without actually leaving it. The turquoise waters soothe and calm the most harassed city dweller and, in the evening, there's usually a breeze blowing in, bringing welcome respite in hot weather. It's easily the most popular gathering place in the city and is great, not only for stretching your legs, but for people-watching. On the city side of the street, there are parks, gardens and play areas, which make for a pleasant walk as well. In the evenings, the parks are busy with families who congregate while the kids let off steam.

Khalifa Park

At the opposite end of the island is the huge Khalifa Park. The expansive area makes the park a favourite among walkers and, with a miniature train that circles the perimeter, it gets the kids excited as well. There is plenty of other play equipment for the young at heart, with a pool for women and children only. The many trees, pergolas and gazebos offer shade from the hot sun, and the fountains add to the park's pleasant feel. If you want a break from walking, duck into the Heritage and Maritime Museums.

Khalidya Park

Another favourite for families with children, this park boasts lots of grass and space, so is perfect for walks. There's a charge of Dhs.1 in the evenings and on Fridays, but it's worth it for all the play equipment geared to younger children, such as swings, slides, climbing frames, monkey bars and the climbing wall, and areas for football and bike riding.

Al Mushrif Central Park

The renamed Al Mushrif Central Park has been completely renovated with new fountains, a shaded promenade and a sculpture garden. It will also be open to men for the first time ever, and there are plans to hold a Friday souk. Three kilometres of jogging and cycling trails, which wind their way through and around the green spaces, are promised for walkers, joggers and cyclists.

Tourist Club Area

No one in their right mind would recommend this as a place for a pleasant stroll, but for sheer activity it can't be beaten. The sights, sounds and smells lurking on every corner promise something new with every visit to the area. And with hole-in-the-wall restaurants dotted around, there are plenty of places to refuel when you become tired from dodging cars, construction and the seemingly endless stream of pedestrians. It's not an easy walk, but it certainly does have its rewards.

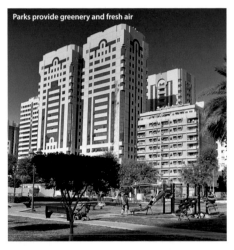

Parks provide greenery and fresh air

Watersports

During cooler months, beaches come alive as people enjoy water-based activities. Most beach hotels offer watersports and there are a handful of special interest groups if you want to take one up on a regular basis. Activities at hotel beach clubs are often discounted to members and guests; day guests will likely have to pay a fee to access the beach, although some hotels offer a special weekend brunch and beach package. Call hotels directly for details, as week and weekend charges vary. For info on canoeing and kayaking, see p.276; for snorkelling and diving, see p.224, 280; for sailing, see p.298; for boating, see p.226.

Jetski Restrictions

Private jetski owners must now license their jetskis but you can jetski almost anywhere. It is prohibited around the public beaches and, in 2010, the Abu Dhabi Coast Guard began to crack down on jetskiers driving recklessly or getting too close to beaches and other boats. There are patrols near Corniche Beach Park that chase away violators getting too close to shore. A good location for launching is Al Bateen Beach (p.215), and jetskiing here is popular. Despite restrictions, there's a lot of water out there to cover, and many hotels, such as the Hilton Abu Dhabi (p.202) rent jetskis for private use.

Abu Dhabi Stand Up Paddle Club

Various locations **050 905 9743**
abudhabisup.com
Stand up paddling, or SUP, is exactly what it sounds like: participants stand on an oversized surfboard and use a paddle to propel the board. Hour-long group lessons are available through the club for Dhs.200 per person, and boards may be rented at Noukhada Adventure Company at the new Eastern Mangroves Hotal & Spa by Anantara. The group is active, with paddle fit lessons on a weekly basis and occasional group paddles through the mangroves. Check the website for details.

Al Forsan International Sports Resort

Nr Abu Dhabi Golf Club & Resort Madinat Khalifa A (Khalifa City A) **02 556 8555**
alforsan.com
Map **1 P8**
If you're tired of rinsing the salt out of your hair, Al Forsan is the place to go. Two purpose-built freshwater lakes, one for beginners and the other for experts, offer the only cable system in the Middle East. Wakeboarders, kneeboarders, and waterskiers are pulled along at speeds of 29-38km/h, the controlled environment allowing for quick progress. When you've fallen one too many times, nurse your wounded pride at the adjacent Beach Bar.

THERE'S MORE TO LIFE THAN BRUNCH

ask**explorer**.com/shop

 ask**explorer**

Beach Rotana Abu Dhabi
Nr Abu Dhabi Mall, Tourist Club St
Tourist Club Area **02 697 9000**
rotana.com
Map **2 S5**
Offers a good range of watersports, including windsurfing, waterskiing, wakeboarding, banana boat rides and laser dinghies. There's a beach access charge but, if you visit on a weekday for watersports without beach access, the fee is waived. Windsurfing is Dhs.90 per hour, waterskiing costs Dhs.75 for two sessions of 10 minutes each, and a wakeboarding taster costs Dhs.75 for two circuits of around 10 minutes each.

Hiltonia Health Club & Spa
Hilton Abu Dhabi Al Khubeirah **02 692 4205**
hilton.com
Map **2 C3**
For non-club members, a day pass will set you back Dhs.150 on a weekday, and Dhs.185 at weekends and holidays. A range of watersports is then available to you; try wakeboarding at Dhs.75 for 20 minutes.

Kite4Fun
Various locations **050 813 3134**
kite4fun.net
Learn kitesurfing with IKO certified instructor Marc Hofrichter, or up to five people can head out on the Kite4Fun Sea Ray for wakeboarding or waterskiing. Prices range from Dhs.300 to Dhs.1,000.

Sheraton Abu Dhabi Hotel & Resort
Corniche Rd Markaziya East **02 677 3333**
sheratonabudhabihotel.com
Map **2 Q2**
Has a range of beach activities and watersports. High-adrenaline wakeboarding is available for Dhs.70 for 10 minutes; waterskiing is charged at the same rate.

Wadi Adventure *> p.307*
Off Al Ain Fayda Rd Jebel Hafeet **03 781 8422**
wadiadventure.ae
Map **3 E3**
Located on the foothills of Al Ain's Jebel Hafeet (p.236), this new resort has three world-class white water rafting and kayaking runs, totalling over one kilometre in length. There's also a huge surf pool that generates a three metre high wave every 90 seconds. Entrance costs Dhs.100, while the activities are charged separately; lessons are also available.

UAE Kitesurfing
Various locations **050 562 6383**
ad-kitesurfing.net
Kitesurfing is a fast-growing sport which has a good UAE following. It's not windsurfing, it's not surfing, it's not wakeboarding, and it's not kite flying, but a fusion of all four. With instructors in both Abu Dhabi and Dubai, UAE Kitesurfing is a group of IKO certified gurus who will get you up and kiteing in no time. Call Jakub at the above number for details.

UAE SUP
Various locations **050 951 7226**
uaesup.com
As well as selling boards and paddles from the likes of EZ Rider, Angler and Malibu, UAESUP rents out gear all over Abu Dhabi and hosts Stand Up Paddle sessions in Yas Marina every Thursday from 17:00-21:00.

Wine Tasting
African & Eastern (02 631 2300) and Gray Mackenzie & Partners (02 676 5954) both arrange occasional tastings on an ad hoc basis at various branches around town. To take part in either, you do, however, need to have a liquor licence. Contact them directly to find out when the next sessions take place. MMI (04 424 5000) also has a Wine Society in Dubai – Grapewine members receive monthly newsletters, discounts and invites to tastings and dinners.

Yoga
Yoga is a low-impact (but challenging) form of holistic exercise that has been practised in the East for centuries. It involves holding sequences of poses, or 'asanas' that, combined with breathing exercises, gently but powerfully help your body to become stronger and more flexible. In addition to the studios below, many health and fitness clubs (p.177) offer yoga as part of their weekly schedule, as do some of Abu Dhabi's alternative therapy centres (p.173).

Bodytree Studio
Shk Hazaa Bin Zayed St Al Karamah **02 443 4448**
bodytreestudio.com
Map **2 J7**
A favourite with local yoga and Pilates enthusiasts. Offers group, individual and partner training sessions, pre-natal and natal partner yoga, Hatha, Kripalu Flow, Ashtanga and Vinyasa practices, children's yoga and belly dancing. Group drop-in classes cost Dhs.60 an hour with a 10 class package priced at Dhs.540. Private classes are available for Dhs.280 per hour. See the website to download the latest schedule.

Eden Studio
Le Meridien Abu Dhabi Tourist Club Area **02 697 4354**
lemeridienabudhabi.com
Map **2 S4**
The recently-opened studio runs regular yoga sessions (usually 09:00, 18:00 and 19:00, Saturday to Wednesday); some are mixed classes while there are also a good number of women-only classes, for those who find that more comfortable.

Wadi Adventure
explore your limits

Wadi Adventure is the Middle East's first man made surfing, whitewater rafting, and kayaking destination and it is located right here in Al Ain! We also have an airpark, climbing wall and zip line just in case your adventure fix needs topping up!

With our world class activities and facilities, excellent service and a backdrop like no other, your day with us can be as exhilarating or relaxed as you want it to be. You will also find a family swimming pool and splash pad for our younger adventurers, as well as a number of food outlets to satisfy a variety of tastes.

If you are thinking of bringing a group of friends or your colleagues from work for some team building fun, then Wadi Adventure can cater for that too. With event space to seat upto 160 indoors (overlooking the surf pool) and a further outside, its the perfect venue for your party, meeting or just about any function.

For further information, get in touch with the team at Wadi Adventure.

explore your limits!

For enquiries please call us on +971 (0)3 781 8422
email: info@wadiadventure.ae
www.wadiadventure.ae

EXPERIENCE NEW LUXURY

A truly spectacular oasis in the heart of the capital yet sheltered from the bustling city, Al Raha Beach Hotel now offers 144 additional reasons to visit! Nestled among blonde sands overlooking the turquoise Gulf, explore our brand new extended bouquet of rooms and suites with uninterrupted views of the shimmering water or sun drenched courtyard.

Book now at Al Raha Beach Hotel and get an exclusive 30% discount* on our best available rate that comes with a delectable breakfast buffet, VIP treatment and free WiFi.

Call on +971 2 508 0555 or 800 ALRAHA for reservations

*Terms & conditions apply

Al Raha Beach Hotel

Managed by Danat Hotels & Resorts, a Division of National Corporation for Tourism and Hotels
PO Box 38616, Abu Dhabi, U.A.E. | T. +971 2 508 0555 | F. +971 2 508 0444 | E. info.alraha@danathotels.com | www.danathotels.com
A Member of Preferred Hotels & Resorts

Shopping

SHOPPING

Shopping plays a big role in everyday life in this part of the world. The malls are gathering places, especially during the hotter summer months when they offer an oasis of cool in the sweltering city – somewhere to walk, shop, eat and be entertained.

One thing that makes shopping here so appealing is the variety – you can offload Dhs.30,000 on a state-of-the-art watch, or pick up one for Dhs.10 in a supermarket or souk (p.339). You can spend thousands on a designer outfit from one of the top names in fashion, or buy a length of fabric and have a tailor make you up your very own creation for next to nothing. You can buy a treasured Arabian antique from days gone by, or a super-modern home entertainment system (p.327).

The variety of goods on sale in the city means there is very little that is not available. For most items there is enough choice to fit any budget, from the fake designer goods in Markaziya East (between Sheikh Khalifa Bin Zayed Street and Sheikh Zayed Second Street), to the shops in the malls that sell the real thing.

You will be amazed at how cosmopolitan the goodies are that are loaded in your shopping trolley. However, like many countries, the cost of living is increasing and while some of what is available is still cheaper than elsewhere, groceries seem to be more expensive every week. You may find that imported items and brands, particularly from the international high-street stores, carry an extra few dirhams to compensate for the cost of importing the goods. If you are an expert bargainer (p.311), you can get better deals at the souks (p.339). And for those items with non-negotiable prices, the trick is to wait for the sales – they happen a few times a year and prices are slashed quite significantly.

Cars are, on the whole, a good buy and petrol, though prices are rising, is still cheap enough to make large 4WDs practical for the school run. Electronics can be cheaper but it depends what you are used to; this region is also a major re-exporter of gold.

One of the few retail sectors where Abu Dhabi is still lacking is second-hand shops (see Second-Hand Items on p.333), although there are a few linked to various charities. With the population still being largely transitory, there is no shortage of second-hand goods, many of which are advertised on notice boards in supermarkets, in the classified section of newspapers, and on websites (such as expatwoman.com).

Shopping hours take some getting used to and a bit of forward planning, especially over Ramadan when almost all shops are closed from noon until about 19:00. However, you can often do your grocery shopping till midnight, and a few of the major supermarkets are even open 24 hours. The malls are particularly busy at the weekends, especially on Friday evenings.

Online Shopping

The online shopping scene in Abu Dhabi is still developing; unlike in some other countries, you won't find a huge catalogue of online fashion stores and you usually can't do your grocery shopping online. There are, however, a few exceptions as more local retailers get on the online bandwagon.

The past few years have seen the birth of online shopping sites such as souq.com and uaemall.com, which sell items from a number of companies. There's a wide range of products available to buy, but navigation can prove a bit time consuming. In addition, a growing number of independent retailers are setting up an online presence with quick and affordable nationwide delivery. For example, Jacky's Electronics (jackys.com) has a fairly comprehensive site with good online deals; Magrudy's website (magrudy.com) allows for both buying and reserving books and kentessa.com offers gifts for delivery.

There are also sites based in the region that will arrange for gifts to be delivered both here and internationally, for example, papagiftexpress.com, which deals with India, Sri Lanka and the UAE.

Hellwafashion (hellwafashion.com) is an online resource providing information on the clothes on offer

Quick Reference

in nearby Dubai's independent stores and designer boutiques, and online shopping is also available at designer wear specialist Boutique 1 (boutique1.com). For books detailing the best off-road routes in the UAE or Oman or a guide to weekend breaks in the region, visit the online store at askexplorer.com.

The web is an increasingly good bet to hunt down second-hand items; try sites such as dubizzle.com and expatwoman.com.

The range of products you can find on international online shopping sites adds to the retail therapy available in Abu Dhabi's many malls and souks. If you shop around, you may be able to find discounted prices, which make online shopping more appealing, particularly for items you can't find locally. More and more international online retailers now deliver to the UAE, so it may make sense to shop around if you are after a special purchase. However, not all companies will ship to the UAE and if they do, the shipping charges can be prohibitive and it may take time for the goods to clear customs.

International credit cards are accepted by most vendors and you should have no problems paying with your UAE card provided international delivery is available. The use of PayPal can often cause problems, but vendors on sites like eBay may be flexible if you explain the situation. Many sites will accept other forms of payment. Sites like Amazon should provide little difficulty, although its branded packaging may be opened at customs. Companies without representation in the region will sometimes agree to sell directly to individual customers, so it is worth sending them an email.

Aramex (see also Shipping p.313) provide a 'Shop & Ship' service which sets up a mailbox in both the UK and US, great for dealing with sites which do not offer international shipping. Borderlinx (borderlinx. com) provides a similar service for stores that will only ship to the USA. Aramex also offers a Web Surfer card, a prepaid MasterCard for use online – this can be set up through the mailboxes and is a solution to PayPal problems.

Refunds, Exchanges & Consumer Rights

The policies on refunds and exchanges vary from shop to shop. There is more chance of success with faulty goods rather than if you have simply changed your mind, and it is more common to be offered an exchange or credit note rather than a refund. Even with tags attached, many stores will not even consider an exchange unless you have the receipt. For some items, such as those in sealed packages, shops insist that the packaging should be intact so that the item can be resold. This is okay if the item was unwanted – however, it has been known for claims for faulty goods to be rejected as the packaging has been damaged;

but how could you know if it was faulty if you hadn't opened it?

If you are having no success with customer services, ask to speak to the manager, as the person on the shop floor is often not authorised to deviate from standard policy whereas managers may be more flexible.

The Consumer Protection Department of the UAE Ministry of Economy has been established to safeguard the interests of shoppers. The department tracks and regulates retail prices and has rejected planned price increases for staple goods. Consumers wishing to complain about a retailer can complete a form on the website adeconomy.ae, send an email to consumer@adeconomy.ae, or call the freephone hotline on 600 522 225. The hotline is manned by non-English speakers so it may be best to stick to other methods. The Abu Dhabi Food Control Authority (02 495 4000, adfca.ae) primarily deals with unfit food. The Dubai Government's consumer rights website (consumerrights.ae) provides tips and further information on consumer rights.

How To Pay

There are facilities for exchanging or withdrawing money pretty much everywhere there is a chance to spend it. If you need to withdraw cash, ATMs are available all over the country, in banks, malls and some petrol stations. They accept most cards – check your bank card for logos of international organisations like CIRRUS or PLUS, and look out for cash machines bearing the same logos. Credit cards are widely accepted in malls and bigger shops but cash still rules in the souks and local convenience stores. Most international credit cards are accepted, including American Express, Visa, MasterCard and sometimes Diners Club. Discounting the high rates of interest you will have to pay, local banks reward their credit card users with a number of promotions, competitions and discounts. If you want to pay in foreign currency, you'll find that dollars, sterling and GCC currencies are accepted in really big stores like Carrefour and IKEA, but in other shops they may only accept dollars, if anything. For the astute shopper though, the best bargains are secured by using local currency; there are numerous money exchange bureaus in all major shopping areas. Having dirhams in your pocket will make shopping quicker and easier, and can potentially translate into some great discounts for you.

Bargaining

Bargaining is still common practise in the souks and shopping areas of the UAE; you'll need to give it a go to get the best prices. Before you take the plunge, try to get an idea of prices from a few shops, as there can often be a significant difference in prices. Once you've decided how much you are willing to spend, offer an initial bid that is roughly around half that price. Stay laidback and vaguely uninterested. When your initial offer is rejected (and it will be), keep going until you reach an agreement or until you have reached your limit. If the price isn't right, say so and walk out – the vendor will often follow and suggest a compromise price. The more you buy, the better the discount. When the price is agreed, it is considered bad form to back out of the sale.

Bargaining isn't commonly accepted in malls and independent shops. However, use your discretion, as some shops such as jewellery stores, smaller electronics stores and eyewear optical centres do operate a set discount system and the price shown may be 'before discount'. Ask whether there is a discount on the marked price and you may bag a bargain.

Buyer Beware

Traps for the unwary shopper do exist in Abu Dhabi. Some of the international stores sell items that are far more expensive than in their country of origin (you can often even still see the original price tags). Prices can be as much as 30% higher, so beware.

Sending Gifts Home

Sending gifts to your friends and family back home shouldn't be too taxing as there are several online stores that offer international delivery services. For cards and flowers, moonpig.com is a great online store where you can customise your own cards by uploading photos and have them sent to a variety of locations. Interflora (interflora.co.uk) also delivers a selection of gifts internationally and can often accommodate same day or next day delivery.

Shoes & Clothing Sizes

Figuring out your size isn't rocket science, just a bit of a pain. Firstly, check the label – international sizes are often printed on them. Secondly, check the store – they will often have a conversion chart on display. Otherwise, a UK size is always two higher than a US size (so a UK 10 is a US 6). To convert European sizes into US sizes, subtract 32 (so a European 38 is actually a US 6). To convert European sizes into UK sizes, a 38 is roughly a 10. As for shoes, a woman's UK 6 is a European 39 or US 8.5 and a men's UK 10 is a European 44 or a US 10.5. If in doubt, ask for help.

Sizing

Clothing sizes in Abu Dhabi's stores usually range from a UK 8 to 16. Petite ranges are available in many stores including Debenhams (p.336) and Marks & Spencer (p.336). For plus-size clothing you can head to H&M, New Look, Wallis, Bhs, Liz Claiborne, Debenhams (p.336), Marks & Spencer and Splash (look out for Evans in Debenhams and Scarlett's in Splash). For more exclusive lines for the fuller figure, head to Dubai for Oui (04 324 2167) or Charisma (04 324 0200) in Wafi City. Men looking for larger sizes should head to Big & Tall (02 681 6703) in Marina Mall which caters for waist sizes from 40 plus and shirts up to 6XL.

Repairs & Cobbling

Abu Dhabi's multitude of tailors will repair or alter garments for a reasonable price, but there are fewer companies who mend shoes. However, there a re a few specialists to rely on to fix a broken heal or to pick up a pair of new laces. Minutes (02 681 6380) in Marina Mall also offer shoe repairs as well as their key cutting service. You can also try Clogs Shoe Repair (02 626 2750) on Hamdan Street or Jeeves (02 667 4299) in Abela Supermarket (p.336).

An abundance of products to choose from

Shipping

Due to the number of international and local shipping and courier agencies, it is possible to transport just about anything. Both air freight and sea freight are available; air freight is faster and you can track the items, but it's more expensive and not really suitable for large or heavy objects. Sea freight takes several weeks to arrive but it is cheaper and you can rent containers for larger items. It is worth getting a few quotes and finding out what will happen when the goods arrive; some offer no services at the destination while others, usually the bigger ones, will clear customs and deliver right to the door. Empost (600 565 555), the Emirates Postal Service, offers both local and international courier and air freight services – its prices are competitive and packages can be tracked.

Several courier companies can arrange for items to be delivered to Abu Dhabi, and Aramex (02 555 1911) offers a great service called 'Shop & Ship', for those wishing to buy online. If a site doesn't offer international delivery or their postage rates are high, for a one-off payment of $45, Aramex will set up a mailbox for you in both the UK and the US. The company will then arrange deliveries up to three times a week and packages can be tracked; the rates are calculated by the total weight of your packages.

WHAT & WHERE TO BUY

With so much choice there should be little problem finding what you need. From antiques to the latest technology, and from tools to toys, the aim of this section is to let you know what is available in Abu Dhabi and the best places to buy it.

Alcohol

It is legal for anyone over the age of 21 to buy alcohol in Abu Dhabi's licensed restaurants and bars, and some clubs, for consumption on the premises. If you wish to drink at home you will need a liquor licence (see p.44 for more information). While it is relatively easy to get your licence, there are certain limits – Muslims, for example, are not permitted to apply, and the amount of alcohol you are allowed to buy is dependent on your monthly salary.

Four companies operate liquor stores in Abu Dhabi. All have several branches in the city, the most handy being the ones near supermarkets. Visit the websites on the right for details of locations. Generally speaking, the selection is decent but certain brands are offered exclusively in certain stores, so it is worth looking around if you are after something specific, or something a little different. Unlike in Abu Dhabi's neighbouring emirate Dubai, where a 30% tax is added at the till, no tax is added in Abu Dhabi – the price you see on the shelf is exactly what you end up forking out at the till. There is also a good selection of alcohol (and several other products including perfume, confectionary and cosmetics) available at the airport Duty Free.

There are a number of 'hole in the wall' stores in the northern Emirates that sell duty-free alcohol to members of the public, even if you don't have a licence. Prices are reasonable and there is no tax. There is a large store within the Barracuda Beach Resort (06 768 1555, barracuda.ae), next to Dreamland Aqua Park in Umm Al Quwain (p.216), and also Al Hamra Cellar in Ras Al Khaimah (mmidubai.com) is another. You don't need to worry about being busted buying booze illegally, but you should be careful when driving home, because it is the transporting of alcohol that could get you into trouble, especially if you are stopped within the borders of Sharjah emirate, which is completely dry. There have been reports of random police checks on vehicles driving from Ajman into Sharjah. Also, if you have an accident and you're found to have a boot full of liquor, your day could take a sudden turn for the worse.

African+Eastern > *p.315* Shk Zayed First St, Al Khalidiyah, 02 667 6041, *africaneastern.com*
Gray Mackenzie Partners Nr Mitsubishi Showroom, Baniyas St, Al Baladia, 02 671 4400, *admmi.com*
High Spirits Nr Carrefour, Off Mussafah Rd, Al Madina Al Riyadiya, 02 444 9821, *highspirits-adnh.com*
Spinneys Liquor Nr Khalidiyah Public Gardens, Al Khubeirah, 02 681 2356, *spinneysonline.com*

Art

Abu Dhabi is not well known historically for its galleries and exhibitions, but the capital's art scene is on the verge of new realms of cultural diversity with branches of the Louvre and Guggenheim due to open by 2015, and the industry is enjoying steady growth in preparation. Most of the galleries in Abu Dhabi display traditional and contemporary art by Arabic and international artists, and many of the works are for sale.

At the higher end of the spectrum is Gallery One (p.212), at Emirates Palace, which hosts art fairs throughout the year showcasing modern and contemporary art from all over the world. Emirates Palace is also home to The Barakat Gallery (p.212) which has branches in London and Los Angeles, and specialises in ancient art. On display are antiquities from China, Egypt, the Near East, Africa and ancient Greece and Rome. Every item on display in the cabinets is also for sale.

The Emirates Palace is something of an arts hub and, in November, it's the venue for Abu Dhabi Art (p.29) – an innovative new platform for modern and contemporary art from the four corners of the globe. It's also a great opportunity to snap up a bargain or something truly original. Acento Gallery (p.212) specialises in Mexican and Spanish art, but also displays works by artists from other parts of the world. Salwa Zeidan Gallery (p.212) showcases a varied range of art by international and Middle Eastern contemporary artists; in addition to paintings, photography and sculpture art, the gallery occasionally houses installations and performance art.

For more traditional, and affordable, art, craft and gift items from the Arab World, check out the Folklore Gallery (p.212) in Khalidiya which sells prints and paintings inspired by the UAE landscape, as well as traditional Bedouin jewellery, ceramics and a picture framing service. If it's framing that you're after, you can also head for Posters in the Tourist Club Area (02 672 4724) or Al Wahda Mall (02 443 7089).

Art & Craft Supplies

A number of shops sell art and craft supplies and you should find there is enough choice, whether you need paints and crayons for children or top quality oils. Particularly good places to find materials are All Prints in Khalidiya (02 633 6999) and United Bookstore in Mina Zayed (02 673 3999), both of which stock an extensive range of stationery, arts and craft supplies for all ages, in addition to related specialist and educational books. The Tourist Club branch of Posters (02 672 4724) also offers a limited range of painting and watercolour supplies, as well as a picture framing service. Magrudy's (p.320) in Al Wahda Mall sells stationery items, as well as knitting needles and wool, and a few haberdashery items. For more specialist artist materials, check out Green Branch on Sheikh Zayed the Second Street (02 621 4507), Folklore Gallery (p.212) and Artists Material Suppliers in the Mohamed Al Makhawi Establishment (02 644 3141).

Baby Items

Basic baby items are all available in Abu Dhabi and, while you may not find the range you would back home, you should find nursery essentials, like bottles, buggies, car seats, changing bags, cots, prams, rocking chairs and travel cots. Supermarkets stock formula, nappies and wipes and many also sell bottles and feeding equipment. If you can't find an item, check with the store because some are kept behind the counter. A good range of jars of baby food are available but prices are slightly higher than you'd pay at home. Pharmacies sell baby essentials and some also have products such as breast pumps.

For bigger baby items, such as pushchairs and car seats, try Mamas & Papas, Mothercare or Toys R Us (p.330). The quality of the items is good and most conform to international safety standards. Various brands of car seats are available and should fit most cars; all shops will offer to help fit car seats but the

staff aren't always knowledgeable about what is most suitable. You can also rent car seats, buggies, strollers and other equipment from Dubai-based Rentacrib (rentacrib.ae) – if you hire a car seat its staff will fit it for you free of charge. Call 050 253 2535 to find out delivery options for Abu Dhabi. The range of slings on sale is pretty limited and backpacks to put your baby in are hard to find, so you may want to order these items from overseas or look online at Bubs Boutique (bubsboutique.com) or BabySouk.com.

When it comes to clothing, there are several stores to choose from. Abu Dhabi Mall (p.341) has the widest range of well-known stores, offering brands such as Mothercare, Adams and Bossini. Online store DubaiBabies (dubaibabies.com) also stocks a fabulous range of products for babies and parents, and delivers to Abu Dhabi for a nominal fee. IKEA (p.324) has nursery furniture such as cots, changing tables and bathtubs. It also makes cot sheets and blankets and some baby-safe toys. Worth waiting for are Babyshop's sales which occur several times a year. For more information on having a baby, see p.129.

Babyshop

Marina Mall Breakwater **02 681 8894**
babyshopstores.com
Map **2 D1**
Babyshop sells low-cost baby clothing and essentials; pick up feeding items, clothing, toys and even baby monitors here. It also stocks feeding pillows, safety rails and sterilisers. Its affordable newborn items come in value packs, perfect for the temporary items you can't live without, but know you won't keep. Other locations are on Sheikh Zayed Bin Saeed Al Maktoum Road (02 634 7012), Tourist Club Area (02 644 7739) and in Madinat Zayed (02 884 0438).

DubaiBabies

Dubai **050 600 3199**
dubaibabies.com
Map **3 E2**
You can shop at your leisure at this online boutique selling blankets, feeding essentials, slings and skincare products, among other items. The store also offers a good selection of gifts that are perfect for baby showers, such as cupcakes, gift baskets, balloons and books for new parents.

Happy Baby

Al Jaber Bldg, Shk Zayed The First St Markaziya West
02 632 3266
happybabyuae.com
Map **2 K4**
Abu Dhabi's answer to the baby boutique. With an extensive range of designer baby gear, including names like Dior, Monalisa Babywear and Lessy, this is the place to go if style is paramount.

NOTHING
stopping you...

from 8 conveniently located stores

in Abu Dhabi and Al Ain
with the widest product
range in the region

Top 10 Things That Are Cheaper In Abu Dhabi

Eating Out

Enjoying a three-course dinner and a few rounds of drinks in a fine-dining restaurant will probably cost more-or-less the same as in other cities, but cheap, street-side dining is one of Abu Dhabi's great bargains. Whether you snack on a Dhs.3 chicken shawarma in the Tourist Club Area, or feast on a Thali lunch (refillable pots of yummy vegetarian curry) from one of Hamdan Street's many great curry houses, it's hard to find such delicious, authentic food at a cheaper price.

Home Help

Having a cleaner come in a few times a week to hoover and dust would be an unaffordable luxury for most people living in the UK, but here in Abu Dhabi it is as normal as eating breakfast in the morning. For as little as Dhs.40 per hour, you can get a maid service in to do all the stuff you're too busy – or too lazy – to do. Frazzled parents can also rejoice at the bargain babysitters' rates available in Abu Dhabi. Call Abu Dhabi Maids for more info (p.96).

Personal Grooming

Having pretty hands and feet comes cheap in Abu Dhabi, where there is seemingly a nail salon on every street corner, and you'll pay as little as Dhs.120 for a manicure and pedicure. Even the boys aren't left out: gents can enjoy a shampoo, a hot oil treatment, a haircut, a shave and a head massage all for around Dhs.40 at your typical city centre men's salon.

Cigarettes

That Dhs.9 pack of Marlboro Lights would set you back the equivalent of over Dhs.30 in the UK, around Dhs.15 in the USA, and Dhs.25 in Australia. It's good news for visiting relatives, who always want to take back a few sneaky cartons, and bad news for smokers, who have little financial incentive to quit here; but at least you don't have to charge your friends every time they pinch a smoke off you.

Taxis

In many of our home countries, a night on the tiles would involve an elaborate plan to recruit a designated driver, or a lengthy wait in a queue for a taxi. Here in Abu Dhabi, walking out of a restaurant or club to find a line of cabs ready and waiting to take you home, at a very reasonable price, never gets old. And just when you thought it couldn't get any better, a whole new fleet of taxis have been put on the roads, to make sure you never have to wait too long.

Soft Drinks

Seemingly, since the beginning of time, a can of Coke or Pepsi cost just one little dirham in a corner shop, a petrol station or a supermarket. The price per can was even cheaper when you bought your favourite fizzy drink by the case. Recently, inflation caught up with the soft drinks industry and a can now costs Dhs.1.50. It's still a bargain by international standards but, unfortunately, the price doesn't always survive the transition to restaurant menus, where that same drink can set you back a shocking Dhs.15 or more. That's quite a mark-up.

Petrol

Although the price of petrol has been increased in the UAE of late, filling up the tank here is cheaper than in many other countries, and often significantly so. For a litre of petrol you'll pay around Dhs.1.70 at an Abu Dhabi pump. As a rule of thumb, to fill a tank it costs roughly one fourth of what you'd pay in parts of Europe; a third of that in Australia or India, and about half of the price in America.

Cinema Tickets

You'll pay between Dhs.30 and Dhs.40 for a cinema ticket in Abu Dhabi (Dhs.40 is becoming standard if you opt for a 3D performance). A ticket will set you back around Dhs.50 in London, Dhs.45 in New York, Dhs.45 in Dublin and Dhs.67 in Tokyo. The downside is that here in Abu Dhabi there are no concessions if you are a child, a student or a pensioner, and the ticket price is the same, no matter what time of day it is (whereas in other cities, morning and matinee shows are cheaper).

Tailoring

Having a tailor whip up a made-to-measure piece of clothing is prohibitively expensive in cities such as London, where a simple shift dress could cost you as much as Dhs.1,000 and you'll need at least Dhs.5,000 for a bespoke suit. In Abu Dhabi, however, there are tailors who can whip up a long dress for around Dhs.100, a blouse for Dhs.50, and a suit starting from as little as Dhs.1,600.

Trips To Oman

It's fast becoming one of the most popular Middle Eastern destinations for tourists from Europe, and it's not hard to understand why. Oman is a breathtaking country combining scenery, culture and luxury hotels. And it's just a one-hour flight or a five-hour drive to Muscat from Abu Dhabi. For more information see Out Of The City, p.263.

Just Kidding

Gold & Diamond Park Dubai **04 341 3922**
justkidding-uae.com
Map **3 E2** Metro **First Gulf Bank**

Not for the budget conscious, but still worth a browse, Just Kidding sells a good range of baby items, furniture and clothes from Europe, including Bugaboo buggies, Little Company bags and Stokke high chairs. You'll find interesting toys for playtime and a catalogue of items that includes maternity wear, gift sets and slings. The store is located in Al Quoz in Dubai, but you can also shop online and have your items delivered. The store also offers an online gift registry service for baby showers.

Mamas & Papas

Marina Mall Breakwater **02 681 6689**
mamasandpapas.com
Map **2 D1**

This store has become a household name for providing well-designed, stylish products for babies and mums-to-be. A good variety of items are on offer including toys, car seats, pushchairs, cribs, nursery items and decorations, maternity clothes and feeding items. Although this is one of the more costly options, it remains a popular spot for gifts and newborn essentials. Another branch is located in Al Wahda Mall (02 443 7273).

Mothercare

Abu Dhabi Mall Tourist Club Area **02 645 4894**
mothercare.com
Map **2 S5**

Mothercare is a long-established store which remains a reliable place to shop for baby essentials. It has a particularly good selection of clothes and many of its larger stores stock cots, prams and car seats. You can order mattresses in specific sizes, and items you've seen online or in a UK catalogue can also be ordered, but the delivery time is a minimum of four weeks and often longer. There are other branches on Hamdan Street (02 621 9700), in Al Muroor (02 449 8115), at Marina Mall (02 681 1781) and at Al Wahda Mall (02 443 7252).

Bicycles

There aren't a lot of bike shops in Abu Dhabi for serious cyclists, but things have got a lot better in the last few years. Studio R (02 681 7676) in Marina Mall has a concession for specialised bikes, clothing and accessories, while Tamreen Sports (02 622 2525) stocks Cannondale, GT, Mongoose and Schwinn. For the BMX biker, there's a branch of Rage in Al Wahda Mall (02 443 7617). Alternatively, head out to Dubai where Wolfi's Bike Shop (04 339 4453) stocks the likes of Kona, Santa Cruz, Scott, Felt, Merida and Storck; there's also a Trek shop (04 323 7966) in the Gold & Diamond Park. Probike (probike.ae) is the official UAE

importer of Planet X, with prices often little more expensive than they are in the UK or USA. Revolution Cycles (04 369 7441) is a recent addition to the scene, with its new store in Motor City, while Ride Bike Shop (ridebikeshop.com) has just opened a large flagship store on Sheikh Zayed Road, stocking mainly Giant.

For the casual cyclist, various sports shops (p.334) sell more basic models at reasonable prices, while fans of something a little different can check out the eccentric vintage bike selection at Middle East Bicycle Trading (050 541 5170) on Post Office Road in Madinat Zayed. Children's bicycles are widely available in bike and sports shops, and shops like Babyshop (p.314) and Toys R Us (p.330) have a range for tiny Bradley Wiggins wannabes, as do some supermarkets, such as Carrefour (p.336). Both adults' and children's helmets are available at the main retailers. Supermarket noticeboards and online classifieds, such as dubizzle.com, are good places to look for second-hand bikes.

Books

You'll find both international bookstores and good local bookstores in Abu Dhabi which stock a decent selection of international books and magazines. Virgin Megastore (02 644 7882) carries an interesting selection of books related to music and popular culture. Magrudys, Jashanmal Bookstore and United Bookstore have a wide selection of English language books, covering everything from popular fiction and self-help to classics, autobiographies, guide books and photography books. United Bookstore also happens to have one of the best arts and crafts selections in town; it stocks stationery and office supplies, computers and accessories, school supplies, magazines, party goods, gifts and a very good selection of greetings cards. You will also find a small selection of books in larger supermarkets like Carrefour (p.336), Abela

Explorer products

RELAY

Relay offers travellers an extensive range of products –
latest newspapers and magazines, bestsellers, souvenirs,
travelling accessories, food products and much more.
Make your travel experience more enjoyable.
Shop at Relay. Over 1300 shops at 100 international airports
around the world.

Abu Dhabi International Airport
Terminal 1 - Airside 02 5758779, Terminal 3 - Landside 02 5759810
Terminal 3 - Airside 02 5759797

Supermarket (p.336) and Abu Dhabi Co-operative Society (p.336).

If you cannot find a publication, the larger stores often have customer service sections where you can search for titles, place an order or enquire whether it is available in another branch. Most shops are happy to order the title for you if you are not in a last minute rush. Otherwise, popular online store Amazon delivers to the UAE – it's usually better to order from the UK site (amazon.co.uk) than the US site (amazon.com), so that you can take advantage of cheaper delivery rates. Unless you choose the super-expensive express delivery, it will take around two weeks to receive your order and your package may be inspected by UAE customs.

Become An Explorer

If you've found this book useful, pick up some of Explorer's other popular titles. Find out more about the region with the *Mini Visitors' Guides* to cities such as Dubai, Muscat and Doha. Get adventurous with off-road guides to the UAE and Oman, *Ultimate UAE & Oman Explorer*, *UAE Boating & Yachting*, or *UAE Underwater*. Or get a souvenir of your time in the UAE with a photography book like *Impressions of Abu Dhabi*.

For second hand books, try St Andrews Thrift Centre (02 446 4193) or look out for car boot and yard sales advertised on supermarket noticeboards and in online classifieds. Alternatively, House of Prose stocks a wide selection of used books at its new store in the Dubai Garden Centre (04 344 9021).

Book Corner Marina Mall, Breakwater, 02 681 7662, *bookcorner.ae*
Booksplus Khalidiyah Mall, Al Khalidiyah, 02 635 4944, *appareluae.com*
Isam Bookshop & Stationery Electra Street, Markaziya East, 02 634 3557
Jashanmal Bookstore Abu Dhabi Mall, Tourist Club Area, 02 645 6454, *jashanmalgroup.com*
Magrudy's Al Wahda Mall, Al Dhafrah, 02 443 7172, *magrudy.com*
United Bookstore Mina Centre, Al Meena, 02 673 3999, *jarirbookstore.com/*

Camera Equipment

Both amateur and serious photographers will be able to find most of what they need on the shelves in Abu Dhabi. Prices from agents are usually fixed but quite reasonable, although it is still a good idea to shop around before you buy, as many of the best-known brands can be found in smaller shops where the price is negotiable. Asking for added extras, such as free memory cards, camera cases or print vouchers, can add extra value to your purchase. However, watch out for parallel (or grey) imports – these products are not counterfeit but they have been imported from another country where they are cheaper, so that dealers can increase profits or undercut the competition. The problem arises if the item is faulty, because you won't have a valid warranty. Similarly, if you are buying the camera to take to another country, ensure that the warranty is an international one: don't just take the retailer's word for it; ask if you can open the box and read the warranty to make sure. Always make sure that the warranty is stamped and dated upon purchase.

Opinion is divided as to whether it's cheaper to buy cameras in the UAE than elsewhere. Due to low import costs, cameras here are less expensive than in the UK, for instance, but that doesn't mean that the UAE is the cheapest place in the world – Hong Kong and Singapore are both cheaper, if you know what you are looking for. It's always worth waiting for the sales to begin before splashing out on big ticket items such as SLR cameras. Don't be afraid to ask the staff — some camera and electronics store sales staff will happily tell you when the next sale is coming up, and a few weeks' wait can save you big bucks on the same item.

For specialist equipment and a good range of film cameras, the main outlets are Grand Stores, Salam and National Store. Grand Stores sells Fuji, Nikon, Canon and Mamiya; Salam Studio carries Bronica, Leica, Minolta and Pentax, and National Store stocks Canon, Lexar, Petra, Karcher, Moser, and Westinghouse products. They all sell a selection of filters, tripods and studio equipment. The alternative to buying locally is to use an online retailer. B&H Photo (bandhphoto. com) and Adorama (adorama.com), in New York, are extremely popular.

For compact, point-and-shoot cameras, basic model SLRs, video cameras and simple home printers, you should find a decent selection of competitively priced items at electrical stores like Plug-Ins (p.327), Jumbo Electronics (p.327), and at major hypermarkets like Carrefour (p.336).

For second-hand photography equipment, gulfphotoplus.com has an active equipment noticeboard, as well as being a great source of information and a good networking site for locally based photography enthusiasts, with information on everything from photography tips to training courses and shooting trips in the vicinity. Keep an eye on dubizzle.com too.

Should your equipment need to be repaired, Grand Stores offers a repair service. Film and disposable cameras are readily available in supermarkets, local shops and hotel foyer shops, and there are plenty of outlets such as United Colour Film (02 677 1967, ucfq.com), in the Tourist Club Area, that can develop films for you.

Grand Stores

Abu Dhabi Mall Tourist Club Area **02 645 1115**
grandstores.com
Map **2 S5**
This is the main retailer for Nikon cameras in Abu Dhabi. The store also stocks Fuji, Canon and Mamiya too and you can also have your camera cleaned and repaired in its stores. Also at Marina Mall (02 681 7817) and in Al Khalidiyah (02 631 2100).

National Store

Omeir Travel Agency Bldg, Skh Khalifa Bin Zayed St
Markaziya East **02 622 2437**
jk.ae
Map **2 N3**
This store is a distributor of Canon, Lexar, Petra, Karcher, Moser, and Westinghouse products and you'll find a good selection of cameras, printers and camera accessories in store.

Salam

Abu Dhabi Mall Tourist Club Area **02 645 6999**
salams.com
Map **2 S5**
Salam stocks a complete range of professional-grade camera and studio equipment, including a good selection of filters and tripods. It carries Bronica, Leica, Minolita and Pentax. Also in Al Ain Mall (03 751 5000).

Car Accessories

Cars and their accessories are big business in Abu Dhabi, so you won't struggle to find the accessories you need. ACE (p.332) and Carrefour (p.336) have large departments selling everything from steering wheel covers to fridges which run off the car battery. Near the intersection of Al Salam and Al Falah streets you'll find a number of small workshops where you can buy accessories such as alloys, window tints and custom seat covers and you can get them all fitted there too. It's worth taking a drive to Yellow Hat (04 341 8592) in Times Square in Dubai for a fantastic range of products from spare parts and in-car technology, to imported, custom-made alloys and under car lighting. GPS systems are available from major stores such as Plug-Ins (p.327), Sharaf DG (p.327) and Jumbo Electronics (p.327), plus other big retailers such as Carrefour (p.336) and ACE (p.332). Car stereos are widely available, and are sold by most electronics shops, with some of the car dealerships stocking alternative models for their cars. To have them fitted, head either to a dealer, service centre or to the workshops around Al Salam and Al Falah – it should cost around Dhs.500 if you are providing all the parts.

Many car owners try to beat the heat by having their car windows tinted. The legal limit is 30% tint; if you get your windows tinted any darker you could be fined, and your car won't pass its annual inspection. The options range from the Dhs.75 plastic film from the workshops around Al Salam and Al Falah, up to Dhs.5,000 at V-Kool (02 443 5333), which is also covered by a warranty, and its clear film is more heat resistant than the tinted one.

If you are just looking for some memorabilia, or if you simply love fast cars, head out to Ferrari World (p.293).

Carpets

Carpets are one of the region's signature items. The ones on sale here tend to be imported from Iran, Turkey, Pakistan and Central Asia. Carpets vary in price depending on a number of factors such as its origin, the material used, the number of knots, and whether or not it is handmade. The most expensive carpets are usually those hand-made with silk, in Iran.

Traditional carpets

Inspect carpets by turning them over – if the pattern is clear on the back and the knots are all neat, the carpet is of higher quality than those that are indistinct. Do some research, so you have a basic idea of what you are looking for before you go, just in case you happen to meet an unscrupulous carpet dealer who could take advantage of your naivety. Fortunately, crooked carpet conmen are rare, and most will happily explain the differences between the rugs and share their extensive knowledge. If you ask the dealer, you can often garner some interesting information about the carpets and where they were made – for example some carpets have family names sewn into the designs.

The Carpet Souk at the Port end of Meena Road is the most obvious place to start; Meena Souk (also known as Afghan Souk) is similarly well stocked. However, if you prefer a more genteel way of purchasing your carpet, a number of the malls have well-stocked carpet shops. For instance, Gulf Antiques & Carpets (02 645 9956) and Handmade Carpet House & Antiques (02 645 7220), both located in the Tourist Club's Khalifa Centre, are a good place to start your carpet hunt. They're less crowded and pushy than the myriad vendors at the Carpet Souk. Most places will not deliver, so it is best to purchase them one at a time.

Ask to see a variety of carpets so that you can get a feel for the differences between hand-made or machine-made, silk, wool or blend carpets. Of course, asking may not be necessary, since vendors will undoubtedly start unrolling carpets before you at a furious pace.

Carpets range in price from a few hundred dirhams to tens of thousands. It is always worth bargaining; make sure the seller knows you are not a tourist, and remain polite at all times to maximise the success of your haggling.

If you happen to venture further out, the road to Hatta (p.246) is lined with stalls selling carpets and the Friday Market in Fujairah is also a good place to pick them up. The Blue Souk in Sharjah has a great range as well.

Mall of the Emirates and The Dubai Mall have a good selection of shops selling traditional carpets; just bear in mind that prices may be steeper here.

For something practical rather than decorative, IKEA (p.324) is always a safe bet, or try Carrefour (p.336) and THE One (02 644 8100).

Computers

You should have few problems submerging yourself in the latest technology here – whether it's hardware or software, numerous outlets sell up-to-the-minute merchandise. The major electronics stores, including Jumbo (p.327), Sharaf DG (p.327) and Plug-Ins (p.327) all sell computer hardware and software, and EMax

(02 674 4937) on Hamdan Street is particularly good for gamers. You will even find a small selection of computers at Carrefour (02 681 7100). The market is dominated by PCs, but Macs are available from iSTYLE (istyle.ae) in Abu Dhabi Mall (02 644 4934) and Marina Mall (02 681 9161). The UAE government, together with the Business Software Alliance is clamping down heavily on the sale of pirated software. As a result, most computer shops are reputable and offer the usual international guarantees.

If you are really serious about computers and the latest technology, it's worth driving to Dubai to check out GITEX (gitex.com). Each year, usually during October, the Dubai World Trade Centre houses this exhibition and a broad range of computer companies participate. There's also a GITEX Shopper held at the Airport Expo in Dubai, so when you've cruised the stands and decided which latest gizmo you can't live without, you can pop along and buy it, with a good discount.

Fashion

From Bhs to Benetton, and Mango to Marchesa, Abu Dhabi has clothes shopping covered. Upmarket designer stores are usually found in shopping malls and hotels. If your budget doesn't stretch to thousand-dollar threads, department stores like Next (02 443 7033), Marks & Spencer (p.336) and Woolworths (p.336) will probably be your hunting ground. In addition, the new branches of H&M (02 671 8799) and Desigual (02 671 9975) in Abu Dhabi Mall certainly caused ripples among the budget-minded fashionistas of late. And if you're on a really tight budget, you can sometimes find some excellent bargains in the souks (p.339). Hypermarkets such as Carrefour (p.336) are another option, or you could try your luck at affordable boutiques like Splash (02 644 5565) and Forever 21 (02 681 8118).

High street fashion

There is a good range of international high street brands including Topshop (02 681 8242), Banana Republic (Al Wahda Mall, 02 443 7006) and Gap (Marina Mall, 02 681 1255).

For something that stands out of the crowd, boutiques (p.338) like S*uce (p.339), Ounass (p.338) and Grafika (02 441 0511, grafikauae.com) step away from the mainstream selections and offer trendy togs from up-and-coming designers. Fancy lingerie is on offer from La Maison De Reve (Al Muhairy Centre, 02 628 2886) and Frederick's Of Hollywood (Mushrif Mall, fredericks.com).

If you love designers but not the price tags, browse the selection online at mapochette.com. The online store stocks designer bags from Miu Miu, Versace and Prada, and offers a rental service which will deliver one of its designer bags straight to your door.

Of course, most of the shops loved by women also have excellent men's sections, such as Debenhams (p.336), Marks & Spencer (p.336), Next (02 443 7033), or Zara in Marina Mall (02 681 8080).

When it comes to shoes, the choice is enormous. Designer labels like Jimmy Choo (sold at Ounass, p.338) and Gucci (Marina Mall, 02 681 6844) mingle with middle-of-the-range creations from the likes of Aldo (02 644 4058), while cheap-as-chips flip-flops and sandals are sold in the big hypermarkets. For stylish shoes on a budget try Shoe Mart (02 644 9543) which carries fashionable and practical shoes.

Most malls have a good selection of quality clothing outlets and there is an increasing trend towards international brands that sell the same items the world over, changing their stock every four to six weeks. Handily, most of these shops also show the retail price in each country on the tag, so it can be quite satisfying to know that you are paying no more than your friends back home (although some stores do charge slightly inflated prices compared to your home country). Mass summer sales generally take place around August or September, and there are more in January when stores get rid of the old and bring in the new. During the January sales in particular, the offers here can be amazing. The Eid sales, around the end of Ramadan, are like the January sales back home – busy and intense, but well worth it if you're an avid bargain hunter unafraid of equally fervent fellow shoppers.

Fashion – Shoes

AK Anne Klein Abu Dhabi Mall, Tourist Club Area, 02 644 4710, *anneklein.com*
ALDO Abu Dhabi Mall, Tourist Club Area, 02 644 4058, *aldoshoes.com*
Bata Marina Mall, Breakwater, 02 681 6834, *bata.com*
Cesare Paciotti Marina Mall, Breakwater, 02 681 3900, *tfgroup.ae*
Charles & Keith Abu Dhabi Mall, Tourist Club Area, 02 645 6240, *charleskeith.com*

Clarks Marina Mall, Breakwater, 02 681 0520, *clarks.com*
Dumond Al Wahda Mall, Al Dhafrah, 02 443 7497, *dumond.com.br*
Dune Abu Dhabi Mall, Tourist Club Area, 02 645 0315, *dune.co.uk/international*
Ecco Marina Mall, Breakwater, 02 681 7120, *ecco.com*
Harrys Of London Marina Mall, Breakwater, 02 665 3299, *harrysoflondon.com*
Hush Puppies Al Wahda Mall, Al Dhafrah, 02 443 7447, *hushpuppies.com*
K Corner Khalidiyah Mall, Al Khalidiyah, 02 635 4418, *kcornershoes.com*
Nine West Abu Dhabi Mall, Tourist Club Area, 02 645 6880, *ninewest.com*
Paris Hilton Marina Mall, Breakwater, 02 681 4993, *http://parishiltonme.com*
Shoe Mart Abu Dhabi Cooperative Society Bldg, Al Baladia, 02 644 9543, *shoemartgulf.com*
Spring Abu Dhabi Mall, Tourist Club Area, 02 645 1297, *myspringshoes.com*
Tod's Marina Mall, Breakwater, 02 681 6562, *tods.com*

Furniture

This is one of Abu Dhabi's most buoyant retail sectors, perhaps because of the wide variety of villas and apartments all in need of furnishing. Most tastes are catered for, from ethnic pieces to the latest designer concepts and specialist children's furniture stores.

Some of the more popular furniture shops sell just about everything you need to furnish your entire home under one roof (the only thing they don't sell is electrical appliances). Fans of IKEA (p.324) will love the giant store on Yas Island. At 33,000 square metres, it's the largest in the Emirates. IKEA is famous around the world for its basic (but attractive) designs, low prices and huge range – the only downside is that you have to assemble it all yourself. However, they do offer a home delivery and assembly service at a nominal rate (and it's free if you spend over Dhs.2,500).

Office Furniture

Whether you're looking to set up shop in Abu Dhabi or need to kit out a home office, there are several general furnishers you can turn to; for example IKEA (p.324) and Home Centre (p.324), while BAFCO (bafco.com) is an office furniture specialist with stores in Abu Dhabi and Dubai.

Other large furniture shops specialise in different styles: 2XL Furniture & Home Décor (02 673 3008, 2xlme.com) is middle-of-the-range as far as prices go, whereas Home Centre (p.324) and Homes r Us (02 631 2020) both stock some lovely furniture at bargain prices. Zara Home's (02 681 5560, zarahome.com) fresh, European designs are available in Marina Mall, or try the stylish range of contemporary furniture at

What & Where To Buy

Natuzzi in Abu Dhabi Mall (02 644 4048, natuzzi.com). Heritage Touch (heritagetouch-me.com) has a number of branches all over Abu Dhabi selling handmade furniture from South Africa, Iran, India and Indonesia.

You can also pick up a good selection of outdoor furniture at ACE on Mina Zayed road (02 673 1665, aceuae.com), while those seeking something for the children's rooms will be happy to know that a Pottery Barn Kids has recently opened in Dalma Mall.

Second-hand bargain hunters can either pay a visit to Nefertiti's warehouse on the Corniche at Khaleej Al Arabi St or peruse the offerings online (useditemsuae. com, 050 641 3677). Then of course, there are plenty of deals to be found in the classified section of newspapers or on supermarket noticeboards. For something completely different, head to the warehouse stores in Sharjah. The hot, dusty warehouses are not the choicest of options, but prices are excellent and after a good polish the furniture looks fabulous. This is a particularly good place to pick up wooden furniture – Pinky Furniture & Novelties in Industrial Area 10 (06 534 1714, pinkyfurnitureuae.com) is a great option; Bayti in Marina Mall (02 681 8107) also stocks a good selection.

Genuine antiques are available but very rare (and therefore very expensive); many antique pieces come from Oman and Yemen. You'll also find plenty of shops selling accessories to add the finishing touches to your home. Souvenir shops (p.333) often sell a good range of regional items including fabric wall-hangings and ornaments. For something unique, MacKenzie Art (04 341 9803, dubaimurals.com, can assist you with some amazing finishing touches to your home, including murals and trompe l'oeils.

Chenone
Marina Mall Breakwater **02 681 8110**
chenonehome.com
Map **2 D1**
An online store stocked with furniture and goodies for the house – so you can beautify your home without leaving it!

Grand Royal
Das Tower Al Khalidiyah **02 639 5565**
grandroyalarabian.com
Map **2 F3**
The Abu Dhabi stockist of a range of top-notch Italian designer brands, such as Versace Home, Blumarine, Ipe Cavalli, Francesco Molon, Jumbo Collection, Rozzoni, Faustig, Mechini and Alexander's Collection.

Home Centre
Liwa Centre Markaziya East **02 639 1918**
homecentre.net
Map **2 M4**
Step into this store and you won't know which way to turn – it is crammed with bath towels, kitchenware

and accessories. You'll also find a conservative selection of wooden tables, sofas and bedroom furniture. Its other branches are located in Centrepoint (02 681 4050) and Dalma Mall (02 550 2415).

IKEA
Nr Ferrari World Abu Dhabi Yas Island West
02 493 5888
ikeauae.com
Map **1 T4**
IKEA's enormous showroom sells a great range of good value furniture. Its selection is suitable for most budgets, and it stocks everything from Dhs.1 tealight holders to Dhs.20,000 kitchens. The store also has a selection of reasonably priced kids' furniture (its range of bunkbeds is consistently popular).

Lucky's
Street No. 2 Sharjah **06 534 1937**
http://luckyfurnitureuae.com
Map **3 E1**
Although this store is in Sharjah, it remains popular with expats looking for well-priced wooden furniture. The range of products is vast, but one of the staff will happily explain the origin and design of the pieces and they can also varnish, paint or make alterations.

Marina Exotic Home Interiors
Abu Dhabi Mall Tourist Club Area **02 645 5488**
marinagulf.com
Map **2 S5**
The items sold here should add an exotic touch to your home – you can pick up key pieces that reflect the region, as well as far-off places from the Orient to New York. The selection includes large wardrobes, tables, ornate chests and various other types of wooden furniture and garden furniture.

THE One
Abu Dhabi Mall Tourist Club Area **02 644 8100**
theoneplanet.com
Map **2 S5**
A favourite among the expat crowd, this store's only downfall is the fact that those divine cushions you bought will most likely pop up in your acquaintances' homes from time to time. But, there is a reason why it's so popular: its funky, modern style (that is highly decorative, but not gaudy) and good selection of home accessories can add a much-needed flourish to impersonal apartments. Another branch is located in Khalidiya (02 681 6500).

ID Design Al Wahda Mall, Al Dhafrah, 02 443 7557, *iddesignuae.com*
Interiors Emirates Tower Bldg, Shk Hamdan Bin Mohammed St, Markaziya East, 02 6797 040, *interiorsfurniture.com*

Shopper's delight

Pan Emirates Shk Rashid Bin Al Maktoum Rd, Madinat Zayed, 02 621 1030, *panemirates.com*
PF Emirates Interiors Al Sahel Tower,Corniche Rd, Al Khalidiyah, 02 667 9588, *pfemirates.ae*
Pier Import Villa 22, Nr Sheraton Khalidiya, Al Nasr St, Markaziya West, 02 665 8395, *pierimport-me.com*

Gold & Diamonds

Whatever your taste in jewellery you'll find an abundant supply here. Gold is available in 18, 21, 22 or 24 carats and is sold according to the international daily gold rate. This means that for an identical piece, whether you buy it in the mall or the Gold Souk, there will be very little difference in the price of the actual gold. Where the price varies is in the workmanship that has gone into a particular piece.

For adventurous jewellery shoppers, there is plenty to choose from, such as silver jewellery from Oman, cultured pearls from Japan, and ethnic creations from India crafted in rich yellow gold. The Gold Souk (p.348) in Madinat Zayed on 4th Street has many jewellers including some of the largest jewellery shops in the Gulf. The outlets in these areas cater for all tastes, so have a browse around to see a full variety of Arabic, Indian and European styles.

Costume jewellery can be found in most department stores; several fashion stores also stock a small range of jewellery. Branches of Accessorize (02 681 3431) and Claire's Accessories (02 645 4861) are great for inexpensive items and hair accessories for children and they can be found in many of the malls.

When it comes to watches, there is also plenty of choice. You'll get plastic cheapies for no more than a few dirhams, or diamond-encrusted designer time pieces coming in at over a hundred thousand dirhams, and everything in between. Check out the souks – not only will you find all the brands you know, plus some you don't, but you'll have fun haggling with the colourful shop owners – The Hamdan Centre (p.347) is a good place to start.

Al Futtaim Jewellery Abu Dhabi Mall, Tourist Club Area, 02 645 2004, *watches.ae*
Al Jazira Jewellery Shk Hamdan Bin Mohammed St, Markaziya East, 02 634 4141
Al Manara Jewellery Marina Mall, Breakwater, 02 627 2222
Al Mandoos Jewellery Marina Mall, Breakwater, 02 681 6555, *mandoosjewel.com*
Carcassone Gold & Diamond Hamdan Centre, Markaziya East, 02 634 7676
Damas Khalidiyah Mall, Al Khalidiyah, 02 635 4420, *mydamas.com*
Le Portique Jewellery Sheikh Khalifa Bin Zayed St, Markaziya East, 02 626 9133
Tiffany & Co. Abu Dhabi Mall, Tourist Club Area, 02 644 1182, *tiffany.com*

Home Appliances

Whether you are setting up home in Abu Dhabi, or you are moving house, you'll have to spend some time looking for white goods. While you may be used to essential items like a cooker, washing machine or fridge, coming as part and parcel of a lease, in Abu Dhabi, unfurnished really means unfurnished and you'll have to fork out for the most standard items like curtain rails for your windows.

Unsurprisingly, there are several places for you to buy goods and several large international brands are sold here like LG, Samsung and Siemens. Marina Mall (p.345) and Abu Dhabi Mall (p.341) have a large selection of shops.

Many of the larger hypermarkets like Carrefour (p.336) and Lulu (p.337) stock a superb range of goods

Abu Dhabi Mall

from well-known brands (and some lesser known ones that also do the job) and they usually offer a delivery and installation service. Sharaf DG (p.327), Jacky's Express (p.327), Jumbo Electronics (p.327), Better Life (02 556 2894), Costless Electronics (02 673 4150), Eros Electricals (02633 6432), Geco (02 443 6866) and Universal Electricals (02 633 6252) all stock a selection of home appliances. Al Ghandi Electronics (alghandielectronics.com) stocks Kitchen Aid products in addition to more mainstream brands such as Philips and Whirlpool.

You can buy coolers and water dispensers in the larger supermarkets or you can buy them directly from the companies that deliver bottled water (see p.92).

Competition is high, so prices are reasonable and most dealers will offer warranties – some will offer a warranty extension for an extra year or two. Check that the warranty is valid internationally if you wish to take items back to your home country. Also check that the item will work in all areas of the world and whether you will have to pay any import duty if you return back home. Also check who will service the items if there are problems. For second-hand items, check the adverts placed on supermarket noticeboards and online classifieds like dubizzle.com.

Mobile Phones

Mobiles are big business and you won't need to go too far to find one. Most of the larger supermarkets have areas dedicated to the bigger brands, while smaller shops around the Madinat Zayed and Al Markaziyah areas may offer some bargains on older models. Handsets can also be bought directly from du (p.93) or Etisalat (p.93); it is often cheaper to buy a phone from them as part of a package.

Home Audio & Visual

When it comes to home entertainment, the stores in Abu Dhabi don't scrimp on size, quality or range. There are several stores dedicated to electronics in each of the larger malls and you'll find large sections in the supermarkets which stock top-of-the-range high-definition televisions, plasma screens, DVD players, games consoles and stereos. Whether or not the items sold here are cheaper than those sold in other countries depends on where you compare it to, but it does pay to wait for the sales as there can be a noticeable difference in prices.

Many stores display operational products so you can check the quality, and staff are happy to explain the differences between models and brands. Bang & Olufsen (Abu Dhabi Mall, 02 644 0587) and Bose (Marina Mall, 800 758 4467) offer a pricey but stylish range of goods for the home, but you'll find a good range of products in all of the electronic stores. Many stores also offer delivery and installation services,

which take the hassle out of mounting a plasma screen or setting up your surround sound system.

Jacky's Express

Bawadi Mall Al Ain **03 784 0747**
jackys.com
Map **4 E3**

A wide range of electronics is stocked here including well-known brands – particularly Sony products. The store offers home delivery and installation for some of its products as well as warranties and protection plans.

Home Audio & Visual

If you are looking for ways to amp up your parties, or you want to set up a home cinema or sound system in your home, AVE (050 676 2864) offer all the advice and assistance you'll need. An independent audiovisual consultant will provide installation services for home audio equipment, projector systems and multi-room audio installation.

Jumbo Electronics

Shk Hamdan Bin Mohammed St Markaziya East
02 632 7001
jumbocorp.com
Map **2 P4**

The selection on offer at this store is vast; head here for its popular brands, good deals and helpful staff. This is also a good place to go to if you are looking for Sony LCD televisions and home theatre systems. Several branches of this store are located in Abu Dhabi in the Marina Mall (02 681 0116) and the Al Nahyan area (02 445 5835) among others.

Plug-Ins

Marina Mall Breakwater **800 758 4467**
pluginselectronix.com
Map **2 D1**

Representing over 300 brands, a full range of electronics is offered at this store. From audio to appliances and from entertainment to office gadgets, you're likely to find what you're looking for here. Some of the brands include Panasonic, Bose, Sony and LG.

Sharaf DG

Times Square Dubai **04 341 8060**
sharafdg.com
Map **3 E2** Metro **First Gulf Bank**

This is many residents' first port of call because of its range of gadgets and good service. Its stores carry everything from plasma televisions and laptop computers to mobile phones and irons. Previously, the only Abu Dhabi store was in the airport, but there are now branches at Abu Dhabi Mall (02 650 3570) and Mushrif Mall (800 344 357).

Places To Shop For Kids

Whether you need to get a gift, re-stock a wardrobe or fulfil a curriculum requirement, shopping for your (or your friends') kids can be an expensive and exhausting task. But with a little bit of planning and a lot of imagination you can have the best-dressed, educated and well-occupied child in Abu Dhabi.

Kids' Fashion

The good news is that Abu Dhabi has a wide variety of international brands (see Kids' Items, p.330) and many adult fashion stores have kids' ranges. Marks & Spencer (p.336) has a great range of on-trend kids' clothes and shoes, while Bhs (02 621 1242) and Next (02 443 7033) have good quality ranges. Check out Women'secret (02 681 8070) for unique items for children, and Beyond the Beach (02 443 7201) for some super cool surf gear. For novelty t-shirts and babygrows with 'My Dad's Cooler Than Yours' across the front, check out concession stalls found in the bigger malls. Katakeet (02 650 3604) stocks brands like Baby Dior, Tartine et Chocolat and Burberry. The latest addition is Gocco (02 586 8120) – a Spanish brand that has opened a kids' fashion store in Abu Dhabi.

Kids' Sportsgear

For swimming suits with built in floats check out Mothercare (p.318), Early Learning Centre (p.330) and most sports shops (p.334). Sun and Sand Sports (02 681 8330) has a great range of sporting items for kids, including roller blades, trampolines (also try Toys R Us, p.330), bikes (see also p.318), miniature pool tables, tennis racquets and golf clubs. For specialist sportswear, like martial arts outfits and ballet outfits you will probably have to buy from one of the academies (see Activities for Kids, p.132), although Marks & Spencer (p.336) and Claire Kids (02 681 7786) sometimes carry ballet outfits.

Musical Instruments

There are a few specialist shops (see p.331) but you can also find basic drum kits and keyboards in Toys R Us, and Virgin Megastore (02 644 7882) have an excellent range of keyboards, as well as digital music games. You might be able to pick up a second-hand guitar or piano from dubizzle.com or put a notice on expatwoman.com. If you're looking for sheet music (often teachers will request parents to buy the required sheet music) Magrudy's has a large range, including exam papers, and can generally order specific books for you.

Bedroom Design

If you want to decorate your kid's room but don't want to paint it you can get family photos printed on canvas, recreate a night time scene (with stars and a moon) or garden setting (with flowers and a ladybird) in wall lighting from IKEA (p.324). Alternatively go for wall stickers – Just Kidding in Dubai stocks wall stickers for children, from funky and friendly animal stickers for nurseries to flowers and rockets for young children's rooms. Order online at justkidding-me.com or pop to Dubai to browse the store (800 5878).

Abu Dhabi is home to all manner of kids' items – from novelty t-shirts to toys galore. So, head out for a shopping trip and get ready to spoil the little ones!

Bags & Stationery

While a lot of schools have book bags as part of their uniform, many kids also take their own school bag in order to fit in their gym kit and packed lunch. Pull along wheeled bags are popular and can be found in Toys R Us in all manner of characters. If you're looking for pencil cases and the like, then Magrudy's, Toys R Us and Early Learning Centre stock good ranges, as do almost all of the city's biggest hypermarkets. While you're there, you can stock up on most types of stationery – if they don't have something, Magrudys, Book Corner (p.320) or Booksplus (p.320) almost certainly will.

Affordable Gifts

Once your kids get to school age you will find that they will be invited to a birthday party nearly every month. So buying birthday gifts can get expensive – if they have a sweet tooth, try Hey Sugar (056 767 9357) or Cupoof Cupcakes (050 660 6964) for the very best cupcakes in town. Rico Gifts (02 681 7622) in Marina Mall has all sorts of fun items like glow sticks, temporary tattoos, wacky T-shirts and wigs, while The Party Centre in Raha Mall is ideal for novelty balloons and costumes (02 556 5563).

Hardware & DIY

While it is usually easier to get someone in to tackle all those niggling domestic jobs, many still prefer to do it themselves. DIY enthusiasts will find the tools they need to get the job done at ACE (p.332). Customised paints, glazes, special paint effect materials, electronic tools and hardware materials can also be found here. A basic range of items can be bought at IKEA (p.324). Carrefour (p.336), in Marina Mall, also has a DIY section where you can pick up the basics.

Health Food & Special Dietary Requirements

The health food trend is growing in Abu Dhabi and there are now quite a few specialist stores. Nutrition Zone (nutritionzoneltd.com), which specialises in vitamins and other health supplements, has branches in both Abu Dhabi Mall and Marina Mall. Longstanding Dubai institution, the Organic Food & Cafe (p.337), opened its first Abu Dhabi branch in Masdar City, bringing a wide selection of organic food and eco-friendly home care products to the doorstep of capital dwellers.

Eat Smart Market (p.337) also offers a range of organic products, while jones the grocer (p.337), the Australian purveyor of gourmet and artisan foods, also carries a range of organic produce at its three Abu Dhabi locations.

Larger supermarkets sell an increasing (but still limited) range of organic and allergy-friendly products and they all carry products for diabetics; Spinneys (p.338), for example, carries a limited selection of organic products. Abu Dhabi Co-operative stores (p.336) have aisles dedicated to organic foods, including muesli, honey, biscuits and teas, while Carrefour's (p.336) range is increasing and, in addition to the basic items that most supermarkets carry, it has a selection of its own brand of organic products; readymade meals are an alternative option for those with special dietary requirements and those counting calories. BiteRite Cafe and Restaurant (p.372) specialises in healthy balanced foods, which are particularly good if you want to lose weight, or if you have a restricted diet due to conditions such as diabetes or high cholesterol levels. For added convenience, you can also try its four week or 14 day meal plans, which are delivered free to home and office (biterite.ae). BiteRite approved products are also available at Zari Zardozi restaurant (p.395) in Al Raha Mall and Foodlands Restaurant (p.376), and you can find its range of guilt-free, meal-on-the-go options in ADNOC garages. The D Club (thedclub.com, 02 644 6461) specialises in balanced, nutritious organic meals, painstakingly planned down to the last calorie. There are packages available for monthly meal deliveries, and options for specific health needs, as well as a catering service for events. Keep an eye out for a D Club restaurant opening in the future.

Kids' Items

There is a high concentration of shops selling toys and clothes for children and you'll find a good selection of well-known stores and smaller outlets. Most electronics stores stock a wide range of games for the various platforms. Carrefour (p.336) also has a good selection, and the hypermarket's toy department is a good address to stock up on inexpensive birthday presents and stocking fillers. Remember that not all toys conform to international safety standards and therefore should only be used under supervision. When it comes to clothing, many of the department stores (p.336) have children's departments or you could splash out on high-end designer gear at Cacharel (02 681 6633).

For babies and younger children, Babyshop (02 681 8894), Mamas and Papas (02 681 6689), Mothercare (02 645 4894), Woolworths (p.336) and Next (02 443 7033) carry the essentials and have some great outfits at reasonable prices. Okaidi (02 681 7740) and Pumpkin Patch (02 635 4527) sell bright, colourful and practical clothes. Monsoon (02 635 4523) has a great range of party clothes, particularly for girls. The majority of children's clothes shops also stock shoes and there are some specialist stores. Shoe Mart (p.323) and Debenhams (p.336) have children's sections. Adams (02 443 7233) and The Athlete's Foot (04 368 5246) also carry a good range. For party costumes check out the Early Learning Centre (p.330) or Toys R Us (p.330), year round. Supermarkets and hypermarkets (p.336) stock some items in the run up to festive events like Halloween and Christmas.

Early Learning Centre

Abu Dhabi Mall Tourist Club Area **02 645 4766**
elc.com
Map **2 S5**
Early Learning Centre stocks a good range of educational products and toys that stimulate play and imagination. There are several outlets in Abu Dhabi stocking a good selection of children's books and some wooden toys.

Toys R Us

Nr Royal Furniture, Mina Zayed Rd Al Meena
02 673 2332
toysrus.com
Map **1 D2**
This well-known emporium offers a good selection of products, whether you are looking for small toys to amuse kids or larger gifts like bikes, electronic games and play sets.

Maternity Items

While maternity fashion is still limited in Abu Dhabi, if you shop around you will find an interesting range to cater to different price brackets. Many of the main retailers have jumped on the maternity fashion bandwagon and now offer fashionable outfits, so that mums-to-be can look as stylish as everyone else. Zara (02 681 8080) stocks a limited range of stylish maternity wear. Similarly, the new H&M (02 671 8799) in Abu Dhabi Mall has a small but trendy selection available at affordable prices. Woolworths at Marina Mall (p.345) also stocks some maternity clothes. Specialist stockists include Mamas & Papas (p.318), Mothercare (p.318), Premaman (02 645 8600) in Abu Dhabi Mall, and Formes in Marina Mall. Next (02 443 7033) and the eclectic Najo Secret (02 673 6622) in Mina Centre also stock some maternity wear. Online shopping is an alternative if you can't find what you're after in store. Just Kidding (justkidding-me.com), which carries Noppies (noppies.com) maternity wear from the Netherlands, and Isabella Oliver (isabellaoliver.com) both deliver to Abu Dhabi, and while they are comparatively expensive, they offer a huge variety of extremely stylish choice. Another option could be to join Abu Dhabi Mums (abudhabimums.ae), where you can hire maternity wear. For other maternity items, such as cool packs, creams and bras, you'll have to shop around in Mothercare (p.318), Babyshop (p.314), and Marks & Spencer (p.336), as available ranges vary and may be limited. Babyshop, Mothercare and Najo Secret all stock a range of breast pumps, or you could try one of the larger pharmacies (p.160) if you want a really heavy duty one. Other essential accessories for pregnancy are available here – one example is a 'Bump Belt', which redirects your car seatbelt under your bump, and can be found in Mothercare. For more information on having a baby see p.129, and for shopping for items for your new arrival, see Baby Items, p.314.

Music & Movies

Although the selection isn't as large or as up to date as in North America, Asia or Europe, you will find a number of audio and video stores selling the latest releases from all over the world. Unless you have particularly eclectic taste, you should find a satisfying collection of music in the city's supermarkets and record stores. The advantage of Abu Dhabi's multicultural society is that you can open yourself up to new genres – Arabic dance music, for example, is very popular. Everything has to go through the censor, so any music or DVDs deemed offensive will not be sold here, unless it can be edited to make it more acceptable. Hollywood blockbusters and mainstream titles can be picked up in many supermarkets. Music and DVDs are generally more expensive than they are in other countries. Virgin Megastore (02 644 7882) at Abu Dhabi Mall has the widest range of new music, as well as classics. It also stocks a great selection of films and TV series box sets on DVD, at competitive prices.

There are numerous rental stores around the city – check one out in your area. Rental prices range from Dhs.4 to Dhs.10 per DVD, or just for membership when you join. Recordable CDs, DVDs, audio and videotapes are sold at major grocery stores.

Carrefour (p.336) and Spinneys (p.338) have good value bargain bins and, although they are usually filled with Hollywood titles, there are occasional gems and the odd BBC children's title. Bollywood films are extremely popular and available in most shops. Retailers will order titles that are on the approved list for the UAE. Online shopping is an alternative if you can't find an item and you'll find more variety on sites like Amazon (amazon.com and amazon.co.uk). Amazon's postal charges are often fairly high and its branded packages are occasionally inspected at the post office (see Online Shopping p.310).

Musical Instruments

Whether you are already an accomplished musician or you have recently decided to explore your hidden talents, you may find the selection of musical instrument stores in Abu Dhabi a little disappointing. Thomsun Electronics (02 672 4703) on Hamdan Street has a decent range of acoustic and electric guitars as well as some keyboard models. Sonia Electronics sells some musical instruments as well as leasing sound equipment. The company has an office in Abu Dhabi, but its main showroom is located in Dubai (04 227 2395, soniaelectronic.com) – you can view its selection of electronics on its website.

Some basic items are sold in Carrefour (p.336) and AKM Music Centre (02 621 9929) which has a decent range of musical instruments including pianos and sheet music. If you can't find what you're looking for, it may be worth a trip to Sadek Music (04 368 6570, sadek-music.com) and Zak Electronics (04 336 8857, zakelectronics.com) in Dubai where you'll find a greater choice. Sadek Music offers a repair service and music lessons and you can also rent a selection of its instruments.

Outdoor Goods

Exploring the great outdoors is a popular pastime in the UAE, especially when the weather cools. While there are no specialist camping shops, the basic gear is readily available in Carrefour (p.336) and ACE (p.337). Items are suitable for weekend campers, but would not withstand extremes, so if you are intending to do anything more strenuous you should consider ordering kit online.

Caveman Make Fire (04 347 6167, cavemanmakefire. com) produces a range of barbecues and heaters which you can have delivered free of charge. GPS equipment can be found in most electronics stores. For outdoor sports enthusiasts there are a number of options (see Sports Goods, p.334).

Serious climbers and hikers should consider getting their boots and equipment from overseas, but a small and decent selection of packs and boots are available at Jack Wolfskin (02 443 7802) in Al Wahda Mall. Alternately, you can order a good range of items from REI (rei.com) and Mountain Equipment Co-op (mec.ca). While hydration packs (backpacks that you can fill with water, complete with a long tube and mouthpiece) are becoming more widely available in sports shops, anything larger than a day pack should be bought overseas.

Similarly, hiking accessories for people with small children, such as backpack carriers, are not widely available here and your best bet would be to buy these goods overseas or order them online.

ACE

Mina Zayed Rd Al Meena 02 673 1665
aceuae.com
Map 1 D2

ACE is the place to go to for hardware, outdoors equipment and camping gear. You can buy all the basic equipment you need for your jaunt in the desert at this store, including tents, sleeping bags and cool boxes. The store stocks a good range of hardware and accessories. It also has a giant superstore near IKEA on Yas Island (02 565 1945).

Party Accessories

Most major supermarkets and stationery stores sell the basic party paraphernalia, and if you go to the more specialised shops, you'll find an even wider range. From cards, balloons, candles, table settings and room decorations to gift wrapping, fancy dress outfits, bouncy castles and entertainers, the choice for both children's and adults' parties is comprehensive. If you're entertaining at home, but don't want the hassle of cooking, there are a number of companies who will be happy to relieve you of the burden (see Parties At Home, p.358).

Carrefour (p.336) and Toys R Us (p.330) stock party essentials such as themed plates, cups and hats. The selection isn't great though, so if your child is attached to a particular character, you may find that online options are more fruitful. UK-based Heroes For Kids (heroesforkids.co.uk) have an endless range of products for kids' birthday parties. US store Oriental Trading Company (+1 800 875 8480, orientaltrading. com) accepts international orders by phone. With any online retailer, be sure to order in plenty of time to allow for delivery hold-ups.

Japanese discount store Daiso (02 631 1514), in Madinat Zayed Shopping Centre, is good for stocking up on knick-knacks for children's party bags. If you're after a fancy dress costume, many of the small tailors in Abu Dhabi are able to copy designs from pictures. Expressions Dancewear & Costumes (expressions-

dancewear.net) has a fancy dress hire department. You can order your costume online and have it delivered, or collect it from the shop. For everything else, try The Party Centre in Al Raha Mall (02 556 5563, mypartycentre.com).

Alcohol retailer Gray Mackenzie, on Najda Street (02 671 4400, admmi.com) offers a free party service. A deposit of Dhs.500 will allow you use of 24 pint beer glasses, 24 wine glasses, two ice buckets, two waiter trays, two bar towels and 24 coasters. Items should be returned within five days of payment of the deposit – a minimum breakage charge of Dhs.6 per glass will be deducted from the deposit and the balance refunded.

Birthday cakes are available in the bakery section of all major supermarkets. You can have custom made cakes created by Tickls Celebration Cakes (055 516 0825, ticklscakes.webs.com). Ice cream cakes are available from Baskin Robbins (baskinrobbins.com).

If you'd rather someone did all the work, leaving you to enjoy the event along with your guests, Events R Us (02 645 6605, events-r-us.net) can provide everything from the catering and balloons, to entertainment. Although they are based in Dubai, the Balloon Lady (04 344 1062, balloonladyme. com), Cheeky Monkey Parties (056 691 3552, cheekymonkeyparties.com) and Flying Elephant (800 72789, flyingelephantuae.com) can provide bouncy castles, fancy-dress costumes, party favours and games. And if you need a marquee (of any size), you should contact Harlequin Marquees and Event Services (04 347 0110, harlequinmarquees.com).

Perfumes & Cosmetics

Perfumes and cosmetics are big business here, from the local scents like frankincense and oudh, to the latest designer offerings. These perfumes and scents tend to be strong and spicy – you can often locate the stores by the smell of the incense they burn in their doorways. The department stores (p.336) and local chains such as Areej (altayer.com) and Paris Gallery (parisgallery.com) are located in most of the larger malls and they stock the most comprehensive ranges of international brand perfumes and cosmetics. The Body Shop, Boots, Red Earth, M.A.C and Make Up Forever are also located in many of the city's malls. M.A.C has a great selection and its staff will also offer tips on application. Larger supermarkets and pharmacies stock skincare products and some make-up. Anti-allergenic ranges are available at some of the larger pharmacies. Most needs are covered but if yours aren't, specialist retailers often have online shopping facilities.

Fragrant outlets of Arabian Oud (arabianoud.com) are found in most malls, but they tend to cater to the Arab population and don't always have English-speaking shop assistants on duty. Prices for perfumes and cosmetics are similar to those in some other countries, although certain nationalities might find perfume is cheaper here than in their home country. There are no sales taxes, so there is rarely a difference between Duty Free and shopping mall prices.

Amouage

Marina Mall Breakwater **02 681 6662**
amouage.com
Map **2 D1**

Made in Oman, Amouage, 'the world's most expensive perfume,' is a high-end brand that can also be found in Paris Gallery. The brand is the epitome of luxury with a range of perfumes that smell fantastic and are totally unique.

L'Occitane

Marina Mall Breakwater **02 681 6691**
loccitane-me.com
Map **2 D1**

Head here for natural skin care products and fragrances; all of its products are certified 100% organic and are made using ingredients like almond, orange, lavender, green tea and shea butter.

Second-Hand Items

The fairly transitory nature of much of the population results in an active second-hand market. If you are looking to buy or sell second-hand goods, the

Arabic perfumes

supermarket noticeboards and the classifieds sections in newspapers are a good place to start. There are also several community websites with classifieds sections – try dubizzle.com, abudhabiwoman.com, expatwoman. com, souq.com and websouq.com.

In most cases you will have to arrange for the items you buy to be transported – head down to the carpark next to the Central Post Office in Madinat Zayed, and negotiate with the drivers there for the use of a small truck. The price should include a driver and a few men to help you carry larger items.

The St Andrew's Thrift Shop (02 446 4193) sells a range of second-hand items. If you are selling second-hand goods, a number of the local second-hand shops will come to your home and give you a quote (usually way below the purchase price, so be prepared to haggle).

Souvenirs

From typical holiday trinkets to tasteful ornaments and keepsakes, there is a wide and often mindboggling range of souvenirs to be found in Abu Dhabi. Many of the items are regional rather than local, and several are actually mass-produced in India, Pakistan and Oman. The generic holiday mementos such as t-shirts, mugs, key rings and, of course, stuffed camels, can be found in the retail outlets in the international airport as well as at Posters (02 672 4724) in the Tourist Club Area and most of the larger hotel gift shops.

The range of ornamental gifts available is endless, with perennial favourites being the Arabic coffee pot and cups (a symbol of Arabic hospitality), metallic decorative plates (traditionally used for serving coffee, and the larger ones for food), framed khanjars (traditional, curved Arabian daggers), wooden trinket boxes and larger handcrafted wooden wedding chests and furniture. For these kind of traditional or regional items, the souks (p.339), particularly the Iranian Souk (p.340), and individual gift shops are the best places to look. Prices and quality can vary enormously, and the souks generally offer the best prices – as long as you haggle.

Within the Tourist Club Area are an array of souk-style shops; inside the Khalifa Centre (p.347), opposite Abu Dhabi Mall, are such stores that sell Persian rugs and other carpets from the Middle East, in addition to trinkets and cultural souvenirs; try Gulf Antiques & Carpets Exhibition (02 645 9956) or Handmade Carpet House & Antiques (02 644 0344). More expensive souk-style shops can be found in The Souk At Qaryat Al Beri (p.348), including Gallery One (g-1.com) which sells a selection of stylish photographs and canvas prints and is particularly good if you want to take home some images of the region. You'll also find some of these items at the Heritage Village (p.208) in the workshops where traditional craftsmen ply their trades and produce souvenir replicas, as well as more contemporary keepsakes such as keyrings, t-shirts and bags. Reshie Handicrafts (reshie.com, 02 681 2747) in Marina Mall, Khalidiyah Mall and Madinat Zayed Shopping Centre sells a variety of embroidered, decorative fabrics including pashminas, wall hangings, rugs and garments, which make beautiful souvenirs but, being imported from Kashmir, aren't indicative of the Middle East.

For ladies, pashminas are in abundant supply and make lightweight, handy gifts for family and friends. The Women's Handicraft Center (p.210) showcases and sells local handicrafts and is ideal for picking up authentic jewellery or pashminas. In some of the souvenir shops, you'll find simple, but extremely heavy, silver wedding jewellery. If the style is not to your liking, these coveted pieces of historical art make excellent displays when mounted in a glass box frame.

Alternatively, if gold is more to your taste, the UAE's legacy as a gold trading post means a vast selection of jewellery and excellent prices for shoppers. The Gold Centre at Madinat Zayed Shopping Centre (p.348) offers the capital's largest collection of gold vendors and jewellers under one roof. The cost of workmanship is also very competitive, so if you have something specific in mind, but don't find the exact piece, you can create your own designs. For more on buying gold, see Gold & Diamonds, p.326.

Once valued more highly than gold, the dried resin from the frankincense tree of southern Oman has been traded for centuries and, nowadays, is often sold in a small wooden chest and with a charcoal burner to give off its evocative scent. You will either love or hate the smell of incense and the heavy local perfumes, but they are great as authentic Middle East gifts, and all available from the souks in Al Meena (p.192). Oud is a popular and expensive oil used in many of the perfumes, while myrrh and other sweet smelling mixtures are also sold. Ask for some to be burned, so you can smell it before deciding on your purchase. Arabian Oud has kiosks and shops in most malls (arabianoud.com). Amouage is an exclusive Omani brand of frankincense based-perfumes, which includes some of the world's most valuable perfumes, made from rare ingredients. Its products can be found in branches of Paris Gallery (02 681 6662) and in Abu Dhabi Duty Free at the airport.

Shisha or hubbly bubbly pipes are fun souvenirs which, along with flavoured tobacco, make a great gift. The more authentic versions can be picked up in the souks or in the Arabic stores on the top level of Marina Mall but, if your friends and family are unlikely to know any better, good but cheaper shisha pipes and tobacco, in flavours such as apple, strawberry and grape, are sold in Carrefour (p.336).

Where edible souvenirs are concerned, look out for delicious Lebanese sweets (usually made from pastry, honey, ground nuts and dates) or local dates. You can find dates, both preserved and (in season) fresh, plus date-based products like date paste and date-flavoured honey, in all supermarkets (p.336). Most are imported from Iran or Saudi Arabia. Iranian caviar is widely available and good value for money, as it is sold without import duty or any added tax.

For a more easily transportable souvenir, pick up a good coffee table book such as *Images of Abu Dhabi and the United Arab Emirates* by Explorer Publishing. This artistic photographic book, available in all good bookshops, offers a refreshing and insightful visual perspective on this part of the world. Explorer's range of photographic calendars also make great gifts and mementos. In addition, most of Abu Dhabi's tourist attractions also offer their own souvenir shops where you can purchase items to remember your visit.

Sports Goods
Abu Dhabi is a great place for a variety of sports, from common activities such as tennis, sailing, golf or football, to more unusual pursuits like sand skiing. General sports shops stock a good variety of items including racquets or sports clothing. You can also find specialist sports shops around the city. For the fishing fanatic, there is a string of bait and tackle shops along Tourist Club St near Hamdan St, while BMX enthusiasts will find a range of bikes at Rage in Al Wahda Mall (02 443 7617). Indeed, unless yours is a very unusual sport, you should have little difficulty finding what you require. The huge Sports Direct store (04 635 9888) in Khalidiyah Mall (p.344) is among the city's best bets for anything from sports gear to clothing and accessories; another branch is set to open in the World Trade Centre Mall in 2013. Studio R (02 681 7676) in Marina Mall sells a selection of active wear lifestyle brands such as Quiksilver, Rockport and Union Bay, and sports brands (Adidas, New Balance, Reebok and Speedo). Many of the major brand names have multiple outlets in Abu Dhabi, including Adidas (02 681 4046), Nike (02 635 4707) and Timberland (02 681 2611). Larger shops dedicated to sportswear such as Sun & Sand Sports (02 681 8330), City Sports (02 681 4922) in Marina Mall and Megasports (02 645 6166) stock a variety of brands. You can also pick up a few basic items at Carrefour (p.336).

Tailoring & Bespoke Services
There are numerous tailors in Abu Dhabi and most operate from small shops tucked away down side streets. The cost of fabric and workmanship is comparatively cheap, and having a shirt, suit, summer dress or even wedding dress custom made can be a surprisingly affordable option. Tailors can copy a pattern, a garment, or even a photograph, and any good service will include at least one fitting before the garment is finished. Standards of workmanship

vary, so ask around to get recommendations of good tailors. In addition, different tailors specialise in different styles of garment, such as saris, abayas, western-style clothes, suits and wedding dresses, so while most tailors will tell you that they can stitch anything you need, you're more likely to be happy with the results if you go to one that can demonstrate their experience in that style.

Agree on the price of the item before the tailor starts work. When the garment is finished, you will be able to try it on and have minor adjustments made if necessary. Personal recommendations are the best way to find a trusted tailor, but Sposa Haute Couture (02 622 1768), The Raymond Shop (02 671 2478) or Joury Tailors (02 631 7323) are good places to start. See Textiles & Haberdashery on p.335 for places to buy fabric.

Textiles & Haberdashery

To buy fabric, head to Madinat Zayed Shopping Centre & Gold Centre, or the streets behind Marks & Spencer in Markaziyah, both of which have a high concentration of textile stores. You'll find all kinds of fabric from the most delicate broderie anglaise to practical cottons. Compare prices between stores and don't forget to haggle. Look out for sales – the prices are too low to resist. Cairo is a fabric emporium located near Al Noor Hospital on Khalifa Street. It has three floors of textiles from elegant silks to plain cotton. Also look out for Green Branch (02 621 4507) on Electra Street, Kashmir Traders (02 621 0347) on Al Nasr St or Rivoli Textiles (02 679 2996) on Hamdan Street. Al Omara Textiles has branches in Madinat Zayed (02 634 5292) and Madinat Zayed Shopping Centre & Gold Centre (02 632 1930), and Paris Textiles has branches on Khalifa Street (02 622 5030), in Al Khalidiyah (02 632 6156) and Al Ain (03 766 7723). If you don't fancy pounding the streets, Al Esayi Textile (02 645 0313), in Abu Dhabi Mall, stocks a range of printed and plain cottons and silks, and IKEA (p.324) has a good range of bright, colourful cottons, plus curtain fabrics.

For embroidery details such as pearls, thread and ribbons, try Malik & Shaheed behind Madinat Zayed Shopping Centre. If it's quality European upholstery fabrics you're after, Areeca Furniture & Curtains in the Tourist Club Area (02 679 0010) and Sedar just opposite have an impressive range, but you'll need to order in advance as they don't keep stock.

Wedding Items

Abu Dhabi is a great place to have your wedding, with sunshine pretty much guaranteed for your big day and a whole host of world-class five-star hotel venues to choose from to make sure you have an unforgettable day. Almost all the large hotels offer wedding planning services if you book your

wedding and/or reception with them, and can guide you through every little detail to ensure it all comes together perfectly on the day.

Bridal gowns are, however, hard to come by in the capital with most options reflecting the flamboyant Arabic style. The best-known bridal shop in Abu Dhabi is Rahmanian (02 676 7079) at the Tourist Club Area end of Hamdan Street. Dubai has a broader range of dresses on offer and has several excellent bridal shops to choose from. Beach Road is home to several bridal stores, including The Bridal Room (04 344 6076) and Frost (04 345 5690, frostdubai.com). Pronovias (04 339 8770, pronovias.com) has a store in The Dubai Mall. For high-end designer gowns head to Saks Fifth Avenue's (04 351 5551, saksfifthavenue.com) bridal department in the BurJuman Centre which stocks the latest off-the-peg designer wedding gowns by Vera Wang and Reem Acra. The store keeps some gowns in stock, but others can be ordered (allow around four months for delivery). The bride will need to attend a number of fittings, but alterations are done in-house and are to couture standards.

There are several specialist bridal designers with workshops in Dubai, but Arushi (04 344 2277, arushifashion.com) is renowned as one of the best. You can select the fabric yourself or it can be selected during the first meeting with the designer. Gowns take around one month to make, but as Arushi is so popular, there is often a waiting list. Some of the tailors in Abu Dhabi are also able to work from pictures to create your ideal dress, but proceed with caution as, while most tailors will tell you they can sew anything you want, standards vary hugely, so it's best to ask to see some samples of similar work before commissioning an expensive garment like a wedding dress. Bridesmaids and other wedding guests, as well as mothers of the bride and groom, are well catered for at stores such as Coast, Debenhams and Monsoon among many others.

Studio Sol (studiosol.me) and Chic Design (chicdesign.org) both make bespoke wedding stationery. For any items you can't find here, confetti.co.uk accepts international orders. Debenhams (p.336) and THE One (p.324) both offer wedding list services and there are also a couple of local online gift list services (whiteme.net).

As well as offering wedding planning services, several of Abu Dhabi's main hotels can be commissioned to make the wedding cake; alternatively, Le Pont Café in Khalidiya (02 666 4022, lepontcafe.com) and Tickls Celebration Cakes (ticklscakes.webs.com) create beautiful wedding cakes. Most of the capital's florists can turn their hands to wedding bouquets and arrangements; discuss your requirements with them to find out what will be available. For more information on tying the knot in Abu Dhabi, see Getting Married on p.128.

PLACES TO SHOP

Department Stores

Department stores anchor some of Abu Dhabi's biggest malls and in addition to British stalwarts like Marks & Spencer and Debenhams, South Africa's trusted Woolworths and regional powerhouse Jashanmal provide the essentials for the whole family.

Debenhams

Khalidiyah Mall Al Khalidiyah **02 635 4994**
debenhams.com
Map 2 H5
A mainstay of the British high street, Debenhams is a go-to for perfumes, cosmetics and clothing for men, women and children. There are also several concessions including Evans, for plus-size clothing, Motivi, Warehouse, Oasis and Dorothy Perkins. There's also a good selection of homeware, including cookware by Jamie Oliver. Debenhams' reputation for selling good quality items at reasonable prices is continued by its Designers at Debenhams ranges by John Rocha, Jasper Conran and Pearce Fionda.

Jashanmal

Abu Dhabi Mall Tourist Club Area **02 645 6454**
jashanmalgroup.com
Map 2 S5
This department store may have escaped your notice but it offers an interesting selection of items. Its homeware section is particularly good for linen and crockery. It also sells a small range of clothing and underwear, perfume and books, and its luggage section is particularly good. It's also located in Marina Mall (02 681 5419) and Khalidiyah Mall (02 635 4545).

Marks & Spencer

Fotouh Al Khair Centre Markaziya East **02 621 3646**
marksandspencerme.com
Map 2 L4
One of the best known brands from the UK, M&S, as it is known, sells men's, women's and children's clothes and shoes, along with a small, but ever popular, selection of food. The clothing lines are not the most exciting from the fashion point of view, but M&S is famous for their underwear and have a reputation for quality. The UAE stores carry selected ranges which include Per Una – high street chic – as well as more classic lines.

Woolworths

Marina Mall Breakwater **02 681 0881**
woolworths.co.za
Map 2 D1
This is home away from home for South Africans – Woolworths in South Africa is similar to Marks &

Spencer in the UK. It is renowned as the place to go for high-quality clothes, shoes and home textiles (towels and bedding). They also do a great range of accessories and underwear. In the UAE, Woolworths may be slightly less impressive than the original stores, but the items are still high quality and the range offers something a little different to standard (UK) goods.

Supermarkets & Hypermarkets

Abela Supermarket

Khalidiya Centre Al Khalidiyah **02 667 4675**
Map 2 H4
Abela is a 'super-store', with a range of shops offering stationery, video rental, books and magazines, dry-cleaning services and jewellery (and much more). In terms of food, Abela has a good selection with a pork section and a good fresh fish counter. Also located at the Shangri-la Hotel (02 558 1468) and Khalifa Street (02 556 7061).

Abu Dhabi Co-Operative Society

Abu Dhabi Mall Tourist Club Area **02 645 9777**
adcoops.com
Map 2 S5
With branches all over the city, Abu Dhabi Co-operative Society is a popular store selling international products. It has a good selection of fresh food and vegetables and it sells its own brand of goods. Other locations include the Mina Centre (02 673 4848), Hamdan Street (02 676 6766) and Madinat Zayed Shopping Centre & Gold Centre (02 632 4500).

Al Maya Supermarket

Nr Hitachi Showroom Tourist Club Area **02 644 4012**
almayagroup.com
Map 2 R6
With enough items to help you keep your pantry well-stocked, Al Maya Supermarkets sell moderately priced goods. Its stores offer a good selection of regional and international items, and often have a small bakery and fresh meat and fish sections. Other branches are located in Al Dhafrah (02 8840 410) and Al Ain City Centre (03 768 8777).

Carrefour

Rashid Bin Al Maktoum Rd Al Madina Al Riyadiya **800 732 32**
carrefouruae.com
Map 1 J8
Branches of this French hypermarket chain can be found throughout the city. As well as a full range of foods, each large store carries fairly comprehensive ranges of electronics, household goods, luggage, mobile phones, and white goods. Camping gear, sporting and car accessories are also on sale, in addition to clothes and shoes for men, women and

children, garden furniture, hardware, music and DVDs, and stationery. The store offers a good range of French products (it's the best place to get crusty, freshly baked French sticks) and it even has a small health food section. Carrefour is renowned for its competitive pricing and special offers. Other branches are located in Dalma Mall (02 652 5999), Marina Mall (02 681 7100), Al Jimi Mall (03 762 0044) and Bawadi Mall (03 703 5101).

Shop & Drop

Carrefour is the latest store in the UAE to launch itself into the digital world. You can buy a range of electrical, household and non-perishable personal items from its online shop, ic4uae.com, and have them delivered directly to your door.

Choithrams

Nr Sheraton Khalidiya Hotel Al Khalidiya
02 666 0610
choithram.com
Map **2 J4**
Choithram has several outlets in the UAE. It is renowned for stocking British, American and Asian products, some of which cannot be found elsewhere, but Choithrams is also known for being fairly expensive. Its stores have excellent frozen sections and a great range of baby products – particularly food and formula. Other branches can be found on Corniche Road (02 681 6930), Al Mada Complex (03 765 6798), Khalifa Street (03 765 6300) and Mega Mart in Al Ain (03 755 8620).

Eat Smart Organic Market & Cafe

Fotouh Al Khair Centre Markaziya East **02 634 6624**
Map **2 L4**
Conveniently located in the city, Eat Smart has a range of organic products, as well as a cafe offering tasty, healthy meals. The products are sourced from around the world and include a range of natural delicacies such as Manuka honey from New Zealand.

Emirates General Market

Shk Zayed The First St Markaziya East **02 631 6262**
luluhypermarket.com
Map **2 N3**
Owned by the same group as the Lulu chain of supermarkets, Emirates General Market is a destination for the cheap and cheerful rather than designer chic. Known locally as EmGen, you'll find clothes, sportswear, watches, electronics, music and more at this lively and affordable mall. The store is also located in Ruwais (02 876 2272), Muroor Road (02 448 0490), Shawamekh (02 584 0850) and Hamdan Street (02 674 7500).

Jones The Grocer

Al Mamoura Bldg B, Muroor Rd Al Dhafrah
02 443 8762
jonesthegrocer.com
Map **2 N10**
A gourmet food store that offers deli items and fresh produce. It stocks international produce (that is largely free from additives and preservatives) and is a particularly good place to fill up your picnic basket. It also has a bakery and cafe and offers a catering service. Also located in Al Raha Gardens (02 557 4882) and Khalidiyah (02 639 5883), in the Pearl Plaza Tower.

KM Trading

Nr Emirates Driving School Mussafah **02 551 2030**
kmt-group.com
Map **1 M10**
Large new hypermarket serving the Mussafah area with a huge range of goods: from fresh fruit and vegetables, bread and hot takeaway food, to fashion, footwear, toys, luggage, electronics, household and more. K.M. Trading also has five more locations throughout Abu Dhabi island and two in Al Ain.

Lulu Hypermarket

Khalidiyah Mall Al Khalidiya **02 635 4100**
luluhypermarket.com
Map **2 H5**
Great for those on a budget; its hot food counters, salad bars and fishmonger are particularly good value. There's not much that isn't sold here – from luggage and electronics to food, clothing and home appliances. The Lulu Center on Salam Street (02 678 0707) is more like a mini mall selling practically everything under the sun. Other branches can be found at Al Wahda Mall (02 443 7500), Al Sanaiya (03 722 0055) and Al Kuwaitat (03 711 8600).

Organic Foods & Cafe

Masdar City
organicfoodsandcafe.com
Map **1 U7**
Long an institution in Dubai, Organic Foods and Cafe now has a branch in Abu Dhabi. The store is an organic supermarket, as well as a cafe, and has a good range of products from fruits and vegetables to skincare and cleaning products. Catering and delivery services are also available. Check the website for details of regular monthly promotions.

Spar

Nr Prestige Cars Al Khalidiya **02 679 6491**
spar-international.com
Map **2 G4**
The Dutch retail giant Spar has opened its first supermarket near the Corniche, and a hypermarket is set to follow.

Places To Shop

Shopping

Spinneys
Nr Adnoc, Corniche St Al Khubeirah **02 681 2897**
spinneys-dubai.com
Map **2 E4**
Spinneys keeps the Brits happy with its Waitrose range among other British products, but the store also stocks a great range of South African, Australian and American products. The bakery is always brimming with freshly baked treats and it is definitely one of the best places to go for fresh fish and pork. It also has its very own car park so parking is never a problem. See the website for a full list of its outlets.

Waitrose
Boutik Sun & Sky Towers Al Reem Island
Map **1 F3**
British expats after a taste of home no longer need to head for Dubai, as the UK supermarket giant has now opened a large store on Reem Island.

Boutiques & Independent Shops
The independent shopping scene is not as prolific in the UAE as it is in other countries. However, there are a few stores, mainly selling fashion, that offer capsule collections of regional and international designers.

Avenue At Etihad Towers
Etihad Towers Al Ras Al Akhdar **800 384 4238**
Map **2 B3**
A sort of boutique mall – a small shopping space containing a handful of small stores from the most luxurious brands on the planet. Spread over two levels you'll find offerings from Cartier, Hermès, Van Cleef & Arpels, Manolo Blahnik, Salvatore Ferragamo, Vertu and a handful of other designers.

Grafika
Nr ADCB Bank, Delma St Al Nahyan **02 441 0511**
grafikauae.com
Map **2 N9**
Grafika is all about stunning Emirati elegance. It offers one-of-a-kind gowns, blouses and dresses from vibrant designers and, although the emphasis is very much on Arabic and Indian inspired shapes and colours, women of all cultures will enjoy checking out the designs, especially those wanting something a little special or different. Prices range from the 'well, I guess I could…' to the 'how much?' category. If you shop here however, you can be more confident that you'll not turn up to a party in the same outfit as someone else.

My Vintage Parlour
050 550 4249
myvintageparlour.com
Offers timeless pieces that date from the 1900s through to 1970s. You can also book private appointments to save having to personally trawl through the collections yourself.

Ounass
Marina Mall Breakwater **02 681 8667**
altayer.com
Map **2 D1**
Ounass (which means 'people' in Arabic) appeals to the ultra-sophisticated party people of the UAE, stocking lines from Marchesa and Alberta Ferretti. As well as fashionable creations and designer treats, the walls are lined with artwork from regional artists, so you can buy beautiful creations for your home as well as your wardrobe.

Regional ceramics

Fruit & Vegetable Souk

Pleats
Nr GEMS Academy, Najda St Al Dhafrah
02 443 3027
pleatscouture.com
Map **2 P6**
Offering ready-to-wear as well as bespoke tailoring, with a team of in-house designers on hand to create lavish designs to suit the occasion.

S*uce
Marina Mall Breakwater **02 681 8650**
shopatsauce.com
Map **2 D1**
Unapologetically girlie, S*uce is a haven for those who like things chic with a feminine touch. All of its stores follow the same theme and funky accessories, quirky fashion and individual pieces are the hallmark of this boutique. Head here for unique items and international designers.

The Vintage Closet
050 988 8542
vintageclosetuae.com
Another vintage offering, this store opened in March 2010, catering to those who love snapping up rare finds and inspirational pieces from years gone by. Extensive international sources means the store can order in specific pieces from established designers too.

Markets & Souks
Souk is the Arabic word for market or a place where any goods are bought or exchanged. Historically, dhows from the Far East, China, Ceylon (Sri Lanka) and India would offload their cargo, and the goods would then be haggled over in the souks adjacent to the docks. Souks have traditionally been the social and commercial centres of life across the wider Arab world, providing a place to meet friends and socialise outside the family. In lots of ways, the souk is the Arabic equivalent of a Western style mall, and, increasingly so, modern souks and malls tend to feature elements of both here. Over the years, the items on sale have diversified dramatically from spices, silks and perfumes, to include electronic goods and the latest kitsch consumer trends. Traditionally, the souks developed organically and were a maze of shady alleyways, with small shops opening on to the paths. Nowadays most have been redesigned and replaced by large, air-conditioned developments. Although Abu Dhabi's souks aren't as fascinating as others in the Arab world, such as Fes in Morocco or Mutrah in Oman, they are worth a visit for their bustling atmosphere, eclectic variety of goods, and the traditional way of doing business. Some have porters who will carry your goods and follow you around, for a few dirhams.

Souk shopping

Al Ain Souk
Zayed Bin Sultan St Al Ain
Map **4 G8**
Also known as the Central or Old Souk, the Al Ain Souk is a great place to explore, savour the local atmosphere, and to practise your bargaining skills. Selling an interesting mix of household goods – including pots and pans, and plastic buckets of every size and colour – and fruit and vegetables, the souk itself is a fittingly diverse affair, but the prices are good and it is different from many of the other modern, rather sterile, air-conditioned markets that are appearing elsewhere.

Carpet Souk
Al Meena Rd Al Meena **02 444 0444**
Map **3 H2**
Also known as the Afghan Souk, Yemeni mattresses and machine-made carpets dominate here, but bargains can be found if you know what you are looking for. Some of the vendors will make Arabic 'majlis' cushions to order for a very reasonable price. Don't forget to haggle.

Fish, Fruit & Vegetable Souk
Nr Iranian Souk Al Meena
Map **2 U1**
Fish doesn't get much fresher than this. The day's catch is loaded onto the quayside and sold wholesale for the first two hours of trading (usually 04:30 to 06:30). They move onto smaller quantities after 06:30 and you have to be there early to get the best fish. While the atmosphere is electric, it is not a place for the faint-hearted, as the smell can be pretty strong. Don't wear your best clothes – you'll be closer to the action than you'd think.

Places To Shop

Across the road from the Fish Market, a visit to Al Meena Fruit and Vegetable Market is a more relaxed affair. Cruise around until you spot a shop stocking most of the items you need – their wares are normally arranged outside the shops. The price and quality of the stock is often better than in the supermarkets and you can buy by the kilo or the box, but do arrive early as the best produce exchanges hand in the first hours of trading. There is another fish and vegetable souk in town between Al Istiqlal Street and Al Nasr Street.

Iranian Souk
Nr Fish, Fruit & Vegetable Souk Al Meena
Map **2 U2**
It may not be air-conditioned, but fresh batches of Iranian goods arrive at this authentic souk every three days by dhow or barge. Everything is on sale, from household goods and terracotta urns, to decorative metal, cane and glass items. It's also a great place for plants – both indoor and outdoor. As it is part of the working port, photography is prohibited.

Muwajei Souk
Nr Jebel R/A, Shk Khalifa Bin Zayed St Al Ain
Map **4 D2**
This modern souk is a long strip of handy shops, including big guns like Choithram, Shoe Mart and The Body Shop. There is also a bakery, a baby shop, a butcher's and a toy shop – and even more outlets can be found across the road.

Ripe
Khalifa Park Garden Centre Al Matar **0551 2517**
ripeme.com
Map **1 K7**
Having enjoyed success and popularity in Dubai, RIPE Farmers Markets brought its organic food boxes to Abu Dhabi. Markets are held on Friday mornings between 09:30 and 13:00 in Khalifa Park's Desert Garden Centre.

Souk Al Bawadi & Al Qaws
Bawadi Mall Al Ain **03 784 0000**
bawadimall.com
Map **4 E3**
Along with Souk Al Qaws, this makes up part of the Bawadi Mall complex. While Souk Al Qaws is more a tourist construct for modern services, Souk Al Bawadi does focus on more traditional and heritage type items. It's well worth visiting if you're in Al Ain and searching for souvenirs.

Souq Al Zaafarana
Nr Emirates International Hospital Al Ain
Map **4 D2**
A few years ago, Al Ain's traditional souk was handed a new home in the shape of Souk Al Zaafarana.

Although it took a while for the old vendors to warm to the idea, there are now plenty of stores in the souk selling lots of traditional items, including a vast variety of dates and spices, although souvenirs and knick-knacks are also plentiful.

Shopping Malls
Shopping malls are not just places to shop; a definite mall culture exists here and people come to the malls to meet, eat, play and mingle. Many malls provide entertainment and people of all ages can easily spend hours in them. Recent changes to the law have resulted in a smoking ban in all of Abu Dhabi's malls (and some of the bars attached to them) which has been welcomed across the city.

With so much choice out there, most malls try to offer something unique to draw the crowds. In terms of architecture, Souk Qaryat Al Beri and the World Trade Center Central Market feature remarkable, modern re-imagining of a traditional Middle Eastern marketplace. Indeed, the line between a mall and a souk is becoming increasingly blurred as developers roll out modern 'souks' which are effectively malls.

Khalidiyah Mall boasts stunning Islamic architecture and is home to over 160 shops, a cinema and the ever-popular Sparky's Family Fun Centre (02 635 4317). The Marina Mall has a couple of top attractions, including an indoor ice skating rink. Abu Dhabi Mall offers all the biggest brands right in the city centre, while Mushrif Mall has generated a buzz with its ambitious architecture and an array of shops and entertainment options – including Abu Dhabi's first indoor waterpark.

Summer in Abu Dhabi (summerinabudhabi.ae) is a festival that runs through the summer months in malls throughout the capital, as well as at Abu Dhabi National Exhibition Centre. In addition to prize giveaways and special offers in almost all stores, there are several other events and attractions aimed at the younger members of the family.

There is another sale period in January and February, when big discounts are offered throughout stores. In addition, the annual Dubai Shopping Festival, which runs for a month around this time of the year and features gradually increasing discounts, is an important attraction (p.27). Although they're often remarkably quiet and pleasant to stroll through during the day, almost all of Abu Dhabi's malls get extremely busy during special events such as Summer in Abu Dhabi.

Regular weekends and evenings, particularly weekend evenings, also attract hoards of shoppers to the malls; if you're not a fan of big crowds, it's probably best to avoid hitting the mall at these times. Most of the malls have plenty of parking and well-served taxi ranks, although both are often stretched to their limits at the weekends when everyone turns up to shop and stroll.

Abu Dhabi Mall

Nr Beach Rotana Abu Dhabi Tourist Club Area
02 645 4858
abudhabi-mall.com
Map **2 S5**

One of the main destinations for shopaholics, Abu Dhabi Mall has more than 200 retail outlets spread over four floors, and attracts 25,000 visitors each day. It has a broad range of shops and is particularly good if you're looking for jewellery or gifts. The stores that really bring in the shoppers are the large Abu Dhabi Co-op (p.336), Paris Gallery (02 645 5004) and Virgin Megastore (02 644 7882) which, as well as music, games and DVDs, also sells tickets to local events. There are some gems in terms of smaller boutiques, such as The White Company (02 645 7002). Visiting Abu Dhabi Mall is about more than just shopping, and there are restaurants on every floor, a nine-screen cineplex, a food court and a children's play area. The 3,000 covered parking spaces and the taxi rank mean you won't struggle to get home. The mall is good at looking after the needs of shoppers; baby trolleys are available for hire, and you can pick them up next to Mugg & Bean (a good place to stop for a pre-shop breakfast) on level one. The mall also provides shop-mobility assistance and rents electric wheelchairs at the customer service desk on level one. There is a

mother and child room and a feeding area. The mall hosts promotional exhibitions throughout the year, including the popular Christmas Market, which takes over the walkways and, if you like to combine window shopping with a workout, the mall is open every day from 07:00 to 10:00 for members of its walking club. Pick up a registration form at customer service.

Abu Dhabi Mall Stores

Books & Stationery
Book Gallery (Jashanmal)
Carlton Cards
Gulf Greetings
Paper Moon

Department Stores
Al Sharief
Bhs
Grand Stores
Salam

Electronics & Computers
Axiom Telecom
Bang & Olufsen
Braun
iStyle
Nokia
Virgin Megastore

Fashion
Aeropostale
Bench
Bershka
Bossini
Bugatti
Cartise
Enrico Marinelli

Evans
Gant
Giordano
Guy Laroche
Hang Ten
Jack & Jones
Jeans West
La Senza
Levi's
Liz Claiborne
Mango
Massimo Dutti
Nautica
Nayomi
Next
Pepe Jeans
Phat Farm & Baby Phat
Pierre Cardin
Pull & Bear
Salsa
Share
Springfield
Stradivarius
Tommy Hilfiger
Triumph
Uterque
Vero Moda
Women'secret

Xanaka
Zara

Furniture & Home Appliances
2XL
Marina Furniture
Museum for Linens & Embroidery
Natuzzi
Sara (Villeroy & Boch)
THE One
The White Company

Kids' Items
Adams
Early Learning Centre
Geekay Games
Krash Toys & Gadgets
La Senza Girl
Mothercare
Pablosky
Premaman

Perfume & Cosmetics
Al Jazira Perfumes
M.A.C
Paris Gallery

Red Earth
The Body Shop
Yas

Services & Utilities
Al Ansari Exchange
Etihad
Al Manara Pharmacy
Al Masood Travel & Services
Dry Cleaning
Fast Rent-A-Car
NBAD
UAE Exchange

Sports & Outdoor Goods
Adidas
Fila
Mega Sport
Puma

Supermarkets, Hypermarkets & Confectionery
Abu Dhabi Co-Operative
Salehia Dates
Bateel
La Casa Del Habano
Patchi

Shopping

Al Ain Mall

Al Qwaitat St Al Ain **03 766 0333**
alainmall.net
Map **4 E2**

When it opened in 2001, Al Ain Mall changed the face of not just shopping in the 'garden city' but of its leisure time and attractions too. Although it has since been eclipsed in size, it's still the city's most popular mall and meeting place. There are more than 100,000 square metres of retail and entertainment space, spread over three floors, in this bright and modern mall, with the 175 stores selling everything from greeting cards to gold jewellery. Large anchor stores include Grand Stores, Home Centre, Splash, Peacocks, Paris Gallery and a MegaMart Hypermarket, but there's plenty of choice and more than enough to satisfy even the most hardcore shopper. There are a number of stores focused on high-end goods and fashion, while The Bride's House is a must-visit for those preparing for their wedding. Electra, Jumbo and i2 should have all the electronics you'll need.

If you're all shopped out, head for the family entertainment area with its 12 lane bowling alley and multi-screen cinema – there's even an indoor ice-skating rink, bumper cars and an action games zone. There are coffee shops throughout, for quick shopping pitstops, and you'll find most of the big fastfood chains present. Covered parking for 1,000 cars is located on the ground floor.

Al Ain Mall Stores

Department Stores	Mexx	Peacocks	Mikyagi
Al Mandoos	Nayomi	Shoe Mart	Nabeel Perfume
LifeStyle	Next	Spring	Nectar
Salam	Parma Moda		Paris Gallery
Sana	Paul Jordan	**Furniture & Home**	Sterling Perfume
	Peacocks	**Appliances**	Tawash
Electronics & Computers	Pierre Cardin	Unique Furniture	Yas
Axiom Telecom	Sahra	Design Furniture	
Cellucom	Splash	Grand Stores	**Services & Utilities**
Grand Stores	Ted Lapidus	Intercoil Therapedic	Al Ansari Exchange
i2	The Bride's House	LifeStyle	Al Manara Pharmacy
Jumbo Electronics	Tina Fashion		Al Masaood Travel
	Velvet	**Kids' Items**	& Services
Fashion		Babyshop	Al Tawash Rent A Car
Balestra Fashion Design	**Eyewear & Opticians**	Bambini	Mall Automatic Laundry
Blue Ocean	Al Ain Optical	Early Learning Centre	Mall Car Wash
Can Can	Badie Optical	Hobby Centre	VIP Rent A Car
Cloud Nine	Grand Sunglasses	Microbio	
Enzo Studio	NYS	MotherCare	**Sports & Outdoor Goods**
Evans	Optifashion		Adidas
Giordano	Yateem Optician	**Perfume & Cosmetics**	Nike
Hang Ten		Arabian Oud	
Heaven	**Footwear**	Grand Stores	**Supermarkets,**
High Fashion	K-Corner	Karji Perfumes	**Hypermarkets &**
Kayra	Milano	M.A.C	**Confectionery**
La Senza	Nicoli	Make Up For Ever	Megamart

Al Wahda Mall

Nr Al Wahda Sports Club, Hazaa Bin Zayed
The First St Al Dhafrah **02 443 7070**
alwahda-mall.com
Map **2 M7**

Located right in the heart of the city, Al Wahda is one of Abu Dhabi's most popular shopping destinations, especially since the recent renovation that saw the number of stores almost double. Its spacious sun-roofed design is fresh and inviting and, although the layout is open and spacious, it also has a myriad of side passages leading shoppers to hidden delights. In one store you can taste-test various Italian and Spanish olive oils and vinegars, or you can eat at a restaurant dedicated to chocoholics. The mall features a wide range of western brand stores including Gap, Banana Republic, Next and Mamas & Papas, while there's a sizeable branch of Magrudy's that doesn't just cater to the needs of reading fans, but also stocks toys and supplies for a whole host of crafts and hobbies. One of the mall's biggest draws is Lulu Hypermarket which has a huge choice of quality products and is particularly popular for its deli counter and pre-prepared meals and salads. As for entertainment, Wanasa Land is the mall's family entertainment centre which has 10 pin bowling, arcades and pool tables. The mall is home to the usual host of cafes and fast

food joints, and there is a sprinkling of higher end restaurants providing more substantial fare too. The hypermarket is open daily from 08:00 to 00:00, while the rest of the mall is open between 10:00 and 22:00.

Al Wahda Mall Stores

Books & Stationery
Gulf Greetings (Hallmark)
Magrudy's
Red Rock

Electronics & Computers
Axiom Telecom
E-City
Jumbo Electronics
Techzone

Eyewear & Opticians
Optifashion
Pearle Opticians
Sunglass Hut
X-Stream Sunglasses
Yateem Optician

Fashion
Armani Exchange
Banana Republic
Cache Cache
Gap
Giordano
Grafika
Intimo Tre
La Senza
Le Chateau

Mango
Marco Firri
Nayomi
Next
Oysho
Pierre Cardin
Pimkie
Riva
Springfield
Ted Lapidus
Tommy Hilfiger
Xanaka

Footwear
Aldo
Bata
Dumond
Hush Puppies
Milano
Moreschi
Tala Shoes

Furniture & Home Appliances
@Home
Better Life
Dwell
Id Design

Stokes
Wall Arts Decor

Jewellery & Accessories
Al Futtaim Jewellery
Aldo Accessories
Claire's
Damas Les Exclusive
Pure Gold
Rivoli
Swatch
The Watch House

Kids' Items
Accessorize Tape A Loeil
Adams Kids
Early Learning Centre
Mamas & Papas
Mothercare
Pumpkin Patch

Perfume & Cosmetics
Areej
Inglot
Mikyajy
Missha
Solace Organics
Swiss Arabian

Tammy Vipera Cosmetics
The Body Shop

Services & Utilities
Abu Dhabi Islamic Bank
Al Ansari Exchange
Al Fardan Exchange
Boots Pharmacy
Etihad Airways
Saber Watch Repairing

Sports & Outdoor Goods
Adidas
Animal
Columbia
Ecko Unltd
Jack Wolfskin
Nike
Oakley, Ripcurl &
  Beyond The Beach
Orlando Sports
Rocawear

Supermarkets, Hypermarkets & Confectionery
Quatro Dates & Nuts
Sweet Factory

Places To Shop

Khalidiyah Mall
King Khalid Bin Abdulaziz Saeed St Al Khalidiyah
02 635 4000
khalidiyahmall.com
Map **2 H5**

Not to be confused with the older, smaller Khalidiyah Centre just up the road, Khalidiyah Mall opened in 2008 and has become one of Abu Dhabi's most popular shopping venues. Located on Al Nahyan Street in the city centre, it is designed in a distinctive Islamic architectural style and is nicely spaced out over three floors.

Home to over 160 stores, the highlights are a large branch of Lulu Hypermarket, which is spread over the first and second floors, and department stores such as Debenhams, Bhs and Paris Gallery. There are plenty of choices for fashionistas with high street labels like Monsoon and Springfield teamed with a couple of higher-end and more traditional outlets. Sports enthusiasts can turn to the excellent, bargain-filled Sports Direct, and other stores sell everything from electronics to accessories and books.

The food and drink outlets go a little further than the bog standard food court offerings, with Bricco Café, Cantina Laredo and Chilis offering more substantial and higher quality fare. Khalidiyah Mall is particularly popular thanks to its entertainment attractions: the large Sparky's Family Fun Centre 02 635 4317) includes rides and a bowling alley, while the CineRoyal cinema shows all the latest Hollywood flicks.

Khalidiyah Mall Stores

Books & Stationery
Booksplus
Bookworm
Gulf Greetings
Photo Magic

Department Stores
Jashanmal
Lulu Deparment Store
Tchibo

Electronics & Computers
Jumbo Electronics
Nokia
Techzone

Eyewear & Opticians
Optifashion
Rivoli Eye Zone
Yateem Optician

Fashion
Alcott
Aldo
Azzaro

Bendon
BHS
Bossini
Brantano
Calonge
Debenhams
Fouad Sarkis
Giordano
K Corner
La Senza
Laura Ashley
Marco Firri
Mario Zognelle
Monsoon
Nayomi
Nine West
Piquadro
Signe
Springfield
Tammy
Via Spiga

Furniture & Home Appliances
Options Furniture

Jewellery & Accessories
Accessorize
Al Zain
Aldo Accessories
Claire's
Damas 22K
Damas Les Exclusive
Hour Choice
Lozan House
Oriental Stores
Paris Gallery
Rivoli
Visconti

Kids' Items
Adams
Bhs Kids
Early Learning Centre
Khabbaz Kids
Pumpkin Patch
Tape A Loeil

Perfume & Cosmetics
Ajmal Perfumes
Faces

Loccitane
Mikyajy
Paris Gallery
The Body Shop
Yas Perfumes

Services & Utilities
ADCB
Al Ansari Exchange
Etihad Holidays
Lulu Khalidiyah Pharmacy
UAE Exchange

Sports & Outdoor Goods
Nike
Sports Direct
Sun & Sands Sports
Timberland

Supermarkets, Hypermarkets & Confectionery
Bateel
Edible Arrangements
Lulu Hypermarket

Marina Mall

Kasser Al Amwaj, Corniche St Breakwater **02 681 2310**
marinamall.ae
Map **2 D1**

Situated in Breakwater, but still within easy reach of the city's main residential areas, this mall offers a breath of fresh (sea) air to its customers, especially those looking for a mix of familiar western brands with a few individual boutiques and a sprinkling of local goods. Popular outlets include global favourites, such as Carrefour, IKEA, Plug-Ins, Sun & Sand Sports and Woolworths. Restaurants, fastfood outlets and coffee shops aplenty offer fuel for weary shoppers, while committed bargain hunters should pencil in a couple of visits during the big sale period that lasts from mid January to the end of February.

If you get bored of shopping, the nine-screen Cinestar complex, Fun City (02 681 5527), and the musical fountains near the main entrance will keep you entertained. There's also one of the city's biggest bowling centres and a small ice rink, while those with a taste for heights and views can have a coffee or a bite to eat in the mall's viewing tower.

On the same plot but with a separate entrance is the large Centrepoint department store, where you'll find everything from shoes, fashion and baby items to a home and garden store.

Marina Mall Stores

Books & Stationery
Book Corner
Gulf Greetings

Department Stores
Jashanmal
Woolworths

Electronics & Computers
Cool Gadgets
I Style
Plug-Ins
Vertu

Fashion
Armani Exchange
Baby Phat
BC Bulgari
Bench
BillaBong
Burberry
Calvin Klein
Chanel
Converse
Diesel
Dior
Ed Hardy
Ermenegildo Zegna

Esprit
Fendi
Gap
Guess
Hugo Boss
Jennyfer
Kookai
La Senza
Lacoste
Levi's
Mango
Monsoon
Nayomi
Next
Oasis
Phat Farm
Pierre Cardin
Quiksilver
S*uce
Springfield
Steve Madden
Stradivarius
Ted Lapidus
Timberland
Top Shop
Valentino
Women'secret
Zara

Furniture & Home
Appliances
Home Sweet Home
Homes Art
IKEA
Silica
Zara Home

Kids' Items
Adams Kids
Bambini
Early Learning Centre
Mamas & Papas
Mothercare
Pumpkin Patch
Sanrio
Tape A L'oeil

Perfume & Cosmetics
Arabian Oud
Areej
Faces
L'Occitane
M.A.C
Natural Looks
Paris Gallery
Swiss Arabian Perfumes
The Body Shop

Services & Utilities
Al Ansari Exchange
Al Manara Pharmacy
Bin Sina Pharmacy
Etihad Airways
Etisalat
Minutes
Moments
Orbit Showtime
Tamweel
UAE Exchange

Sports & Outdoor Goods
Adidas
Studio R
City Sport/Sports Link
Ocean & Woods
Sun & Sand Sports
Timberland

Supermarkets, Hypermarkets & Confectionery
Al Dhafra Dates
Candy Land
Carrefour
Patchi
Sweet Factory

Places To Shop

Al Falah Plaza

Nr Jumbo Electronics, Al Falah St Al Dhafrah
02 642 5800
Map **2 N6**
Situated near Habib Bank, this mall is a cheap and
cheerful place to stock up on household essentials.
Apart from the Lulu Hypermarket on the ground floor,
you'll also find a music shop, a pharmacy, a fastfood
restaurant, a cafe, and much more. Timings for the
supermarket are from 08:00 to 23:30, while stores are
open from 09:00 to 23:30.

Al Foah Mall

Al Ain – Dubai Rd, Al Foah Al Ain 03 704 1010
alfoahmall.com
Map **4 E1**
Al Ain's latest mall opened its doors in December
2010 to bring shopping facilities, including a Lulu
Hypermarket, closer to residents in this part of town.

Al Mariah Mall

Shk Hamdan Bin Mohammed St Markaziya East
02 677 1741
almariah.com
Map **2 P3**
Located in downtown Abu Dhabi, this mall hosts
a range of regional and international shops with a
focus on brands that won't break the bank. The shops
include Milano and Splash, while eating options range
from Chilli's to MacDonald's.

Al Muhairy Centre

Shk Zayed The First St Al Manhal 02 632 2228
Map **2 L4**
This shopping centre occupies the commercial floors
of one of new Abu Dhabi's most recognisable mixed-
use developments. It is yet to fully find its place in the
hearts and minds of Abu Dhabi residents – mainly
as there's nothing here you can't find elsewhere –
although the mall does have a nice collection of
stores, with a focus on high-end shopping. You'll find
a couple of designer labels, as well as some of the
city's top-end tailors and dressmakers here, with a
smattering of coffee shops, cafes, a doctor's surgery
and a couple of beauty salons. Perhaps its greatest
offering is for kids: in addition to children's accessories
and a medical shoe store, there are two play areas for
the younger family members.

Al Raha Mall

Off Abu Dhabi-Dubai Rd Al Raha 02 556 2229
al-rahamall.com
Map **1 R7**
A welcome addition to this rapidly developing area,
Al Raha Mall provides all the daily necessities and
some entertainment options to those living in the
new, off-island, residential communities nearby. Al

Raha Mall is more for local convenience than a tourist
attraction in its own right. This said, the mall succeeds
in offering locals more than the bare essentials. The
Lulu Express supermarket is not huge, but it is well-
stocked and has fresh, appetising produce. The mall
also has a pharmacy, an optician and several of the
biggest banks are represented. Grooming and beauty
care services are also available, including hair saloons,
a Kaya Skincare Clinic and Nails Magic. There are a
few fashion outlets; Betterlife provides homeware
and appliances; Avenue Home Furniture other house
fixtures; while Orlando's Sport is a decent sports
shop with a wide enough stock to suit most needs.
There are a number of restaurants and cafes in the
foodcourt, and a small cinema plays the latest releases.
For parents with younger children, Play & Learn (p.220)
is a supervised children's centre. Parking is plentiful,
and the mall is open from 10:00 to 23:00 during the
week, and from 14:00 to 23:00 on Fridays.

Bawabat Al Sharq Mall

Nr Baniyas Police Station Baniyas East 02 445 2525
bawabatalsharq.ae
Map **3 D3**
The latest addition to Abu Dhabi's retail scene is a
shopper's paradise, consisting of more than 300 stores,
a Carrefour hypermarket, a Grand Cinemas complex,
and a Wanasa family entertainment centre. The mall

is spread out over two floors, and the 2,000+ parking spaces makes it one of the easier of Abu Dhabi's mall to find parking at. As well as fashion staples, such as H&M, Springfield and Centre Point, there's a Victoria's Secret and the city's first branch of Gocco (p.328) – the kids' fashion brand from Spain. You'll also find useful stores like Boots Pharmacy, Ibn Sina Pharmacy and Grand Optics. In total, there are 22 food and drink outlets scattered throughout the food court and the rest of the mall. BAS Mall is open 10:00-22:00 during the week, with opening hours extended to midnight on Thursday and Friday nights.

Bawadi Mall
Zayed Bin Sultan St Al Ain **03 784 0000**
bawadimall.com
Map **4 E3**
The modern, bright and spacious building houses almost 400 stores covering every possible purchasing need, from the giant Carrefour hypermarket and department stores such as Centrepoint and Marks & Spencer, to high street fashion chains (including Zara, Oasis, La Senza and Etam) and shops selling more specialist goods (including sports gear, sunglasses, jewellery, luggage and DIY items). Bawadi Mall is packed with banks, services and eateries (there's a particularly good foodcourt), but it also has a unique offering: there is a separate heritage village and two other souk sections, which resemble traditional Arabic marketplaces, with over 100 stores. There's also a Grand Bawadi Cinema, which has a VIP screen, and a 10,000 square metre family entertainment centre with an arcade, bowling alley and ice rink.

Boutik Sun & Sky Towers
Shams Abu Dhabi Al Reem Island **800 767 684**
sorouh.com
Map **1 F3**
A sort of mini-mall serving residents of Shams Abu Dhabi and Al Reem Island, by far the biggest attraction here is the large Waitrose supermarket. However there are also many other fashion and lifestyle stores spread out over the two levels, and a variety of food and drink outlets to choose from too, such as La Brioche, Yogen Früz and Macondo Colombian Café.

Dalma Mall
Nr Mohammed Bin Zayed City, Abu Dhabi – Tarif – Al Ain Highway Mussafah **02 550 6111**
dalmamall.ae
Map **1 N13**
Located in Mussafah, this fairly new mall caters mainly to residents of Mohammed Bin Zayed City but is a favourite destination for off-island dwellers who don't want to battle the traffic of the island. The mall is anchored by Carrefour, Home Centre, Matalan and one of the country's biggest Marks & Spencer stores. It is

also home to the usual array of international brands, like H&M, American Eagle, Debenhams and Topshop. One recent addition is Pottery Barn Kids – a great place to head to if you're decorating your children's rooms. As for entertainment, there is a food court that has branches of Soy Express, Koala, Special Juice Bar and Yogen Früz, with seating for 500 visitors. In addition, mall-goers can enjoy a giant 14 screen CineStar Cineplex, while kids will love the FunCity play zone.

Dana Plaza
Nr Khalidiya Garden, Khalidiya St Al Khalidiyah **02 665 1333**
Map **2 H4**
Packed with outlets selling everything from cosmetics and stationery, to household goods, linen and fashions for the whole family; most of the stores cater largely to local tastes. The ground floor houses a branch of the Abu Dhabi Co-op (open 24 hours a day) and bargain hunters should head for the third floor to find a selection of purse-friendly outlets.

Fotouh Al Khair Centre
Shk Rashid Bin Saeed Al Maktoum St Markaziya East **02 681 1130**
fotouhalkhair.com
Map **2 L4**
Several of the world's favourite brands are jammed into this spacious mall – Marks & Spencer, Adams, Monsoon, Nine West, and more. Other shops include Al Rani Bridal Wear, Bendon Lingerie, Dune, Nail Fashion, Pumpkin Patch, Watch House, and Falcon Gallery – great for Christmas decorations.

Hamdan Centre
Shk Hamdan Bin Mohd St Markaziya East **02 632 8555**
Map **2 N4**
Something of a local shopping institution and located in the heart of the city, this vibrant centre is a good place to buy clothing, leather, shoes, bags, perfumes, sports equipment and touristy knick-knacks, all at reasonable prices. Look carefully, and you'll also find a few designer outlets.

Khalifa Centre
Nr Abu Dhabi Co-Operative Society
Tourist Club Area
Map **2 R4**
Located behind the Abu Dhabi Co-op building and opposite Abu Dhabi Mall (look for Al Mandoos), this mall is teeming with craft and souvenir shops, as well as shops selling Persian and Baluchi carpets. It's a great place to look for such mementos in air-conditioned comfort. Be aware that you may find a few controversial items, such as African ivory. If you have strong feelings about this, check before you buy.

Places To Shop

Liwa Centre
Shk Hamdan Bin Mohd St Markaziya East 02 6320 344
Map 2 M4
This is where to head on Hamdan Street for designer jewellery, clothes, makeup, perfume and more. Be sure to visit the vibrant food court on the second level or relax in the coffee shop, which is open until midnight.

Madinat Zayed Shopping Centre & Gold Centre
Nr Post Office, East Rd Madinat Zayed 02 633 3311
madinatzayed-mall.com
Map 2 M5
Shopaholics will love this mall – it has over 400 outlets selling just about everything from home accessories to clothing. The Madinat Zayed Gold Centre, adjacent to the main mall, glitters with the finest gold, diamond and pearl jewellery. The supervised toddlers' area and the games arcade will keep the kids entertained.

Mazyad Mall
79th Street Mohammed Bin Zayed City 02 553 2200
mazyadmall.com
Map 1 P10
This light, airy mall is not what you'd call a shopping hotspot, but there's a well stocked Lulu Express supermarket, as well as fashion outlets, cafes and a small foodcourt. Great for general mall outings, and with sporting goods, jewellery stores and electronics all covered, Mazyad Mall leans more towards family outings than fashionista shopping sprees.

Mina Centre
Nr Toys R Us Al Meena 02 673 4848
Map 1 D2
This small and quiet commercial centre in the port area of the city is mainly visited for three reasons: the excellent branch of the Abu Dhabi Co-op, the Costless Electronics that it houses, and the great art and craft section in the United Bookstore. The Co-op has arguably the city's largest assortment of fruit, vegetables, fresh bread, meat and fish, while the Costless has the capital's biggest collection of electronic goods under one roof. United Bookstore has a vast array of art and craft supplies, and a good range of educational books. There's the usual collection of coffee shops, fastfood joints and a kids' play centre, plus a carpet store and an interiors store.

MultiBrand
Nr Shk Hamdan Bin Mohd St & Baniyas St Markaziya East 02 621 9700
alshaya.com
Map 2 P4
This large, open plan store houses well known shops such as Mothercare, Claire's, Next and Oasis. If your taste in fashion is more USA than UK, you'll find the Liz Claiborne outlet a welcome addition. Alternatively, indulge your shoe fetish at Milano.

Mushrif Mall
Shk Rashid Bin Saeed Al Maktoum St Al Mushrif
02 690 4422
mushrifmall.com
Map 1 G7
The newest of the capital's mall options has generated a buzz among Mushrif residents with its ambitious architecture and an array of shops and entertainment options. Anchored by Lulu Hypermarket, there's also the Indoor Market, which is the largest of its kind in Abu Dhabi and a destination in itself. What's more, many of the branded retail outlets are the first of their kind in Abu Dhabi, and some stores indeed in the whole country. Finally, there's an enormous dining court and a small indoor water park – another first for the UAE.

Rotana Mall
Al Khaleej Al Arabi St Al Khalidiyah 02 681 4433
Map 2 G4
Located between Khaleej Al Arabi Street and Sheikh Zayed The First Street, this mall is best known for a couple of shops selling antiques, carpets, handicrafts, Arabic pottery and wall hangings.

The Souk At Qaryat Al Beri
Qaryat Al Beri Complex Al Maqtaa 02 558 1670
soukqaryatalberi.com
Map 1 L8
A contemporary adaptation of a typical souk, Qaryat Al Beri forms part of a larger creekside complex with the Shangri-la and Traders hotels. This area is a rabbit's warren of outlets, bound together by romantic water canals on which abras transport visitors. The outlets are predominantly aimed at tourists and, as such, are a little over priced, although residents looking for certain niche items, such as antiques, heritage items, souvenirs or even gifts of flowers, dates and chocolates will find what they're looking for here. The real reason for Souk Qaryat Al Beri's increasing popularity, however, is its extensive and diverse collection of cafes, bars and restaurants. Almost all offer alfresco dining with views over the creek.

World Trade Center Central Market
Nr Hamdan St Markaziya East 02 810 7810
wtcad.com
Map 2 M3
Opened in 2011 after extensive redevelopment, this beautifully themed setting has already attracted faithful regulars, particularly at its many cafes and restaurants. With a growing number of shops and boutiques now opening their doors, the development looks set to transform the shopping scene in this part of town.

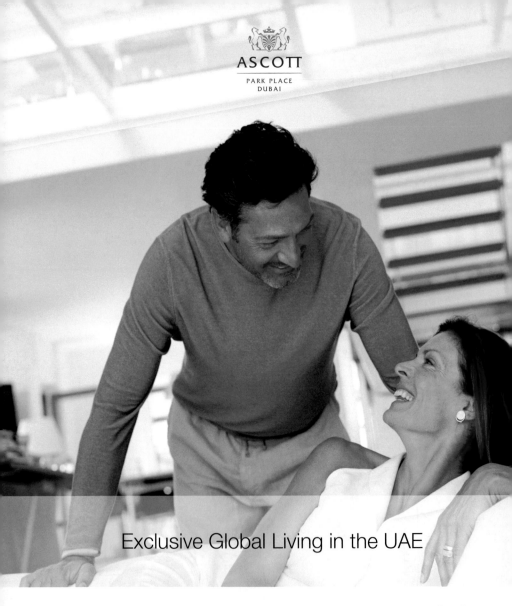

ASCOTT
PARK PLACE
DUBAI

Exclusive Global Living in the UAE

Stay along the exclusive Sheikh Zayed Road. Ascott Park Place Dubai provides luxury residences overlooking magnificent views of the city, with comprehensive services and modern facilities in the iconic Park Place Tower. Indulge in our 40-metre temperature controlled swimming pool, work out in our state-of-the-art gymnasium or unwind in our steam & sauna rooms. Relax, recharge and stay at your peak with us. **Because life is about living.**

Managed by

THE
ASCOTT
LIMITED

A Member of CapitaLand

For further information and global reservations, please visit
www.the-ascott.com, call (971) 4310 8555 or email enquiry.dubai@the-ascott.com

Ascott Park Place Dubai is managed by The Ascott Limited, a member of CapitaLand. It is the largest global serviced residence owner-operator in Asia Pacific, Europe and the Gulf region, managing the *Ascott*, *Citadines* and *Somerset* brands in over 70 cities across more than 20 countries.

Going Out

GOING OUT

Abu Dhabi's gastronomic landscape is fairly impressive, and continues to grow at an ever-increasing rate. At one end of the spectrum, celebrity chefs, picturesque cocktail lounges and well-appointed clubs compete for your hard-earned dirhams. At the other end, bargain eateries, drink-deal bars and bang-for-your-buck brunches are there to help at the end of the month. Abu Dhabi's social scene revolves around club nights, raucous brunches and laid-back shisha cafes, so expect to go out more than you ever did back home.

Thursday and Friday nights are the big ones, with reservations required in restaurants. During the week you'll find drinks deals across the city and all manner of dining promotions, so the town is still buzzing. Since alcohol can only be served in hotels and sports clubs, chances are you won't have a 'local' at the end of your street; instead, you might have a 10 minute taxi drive. Most of the city's popular restaurants are located in hotels for the same reason – but don't let the absence of a wine list deter you from exploring the many outstanding independent restaurants that Abu Dhabi has to offer. You can always eat first and drink later.

The live entertainment scene lags behind other cities, but with ADNEC focusing increasingly on live events, Emirates Palace and Yas Island opening their doors to concerts, and some of the city's festivals incorporating a healthy dose of music, more and more big names are being lured over to perform and the scene is improving all the time (see Concerts & Live Music, p.357).

┌ Ramadan Rules ─────────────

During Ramadan, opening and closing times of restaurants change considerably. Because eating and drinking in public is forbidden during daylight hours, many places only open after sunset and then keep going well into the early hours. Restaurants in some hotels remain open, but will be screened off from public view. Alcohol will also only be sold after sunset. Live entertainment is not allowed, so while some nightclubs remain open, all dancefloors are closed.

Opening Hours

In general, cafes and restaurants close between 23:00 and 01:00, with bars and nightclubs split between those that close 'early' at 01:00 and those that go on until 03:00. The legal drinking age is 21, and it's best to avoid getting staggeringly drunk as it may land you behind bars. Most importantly, don't even think about getting behind the wheel of a car after drinking – Abu Dhabi maintains a strict zero tolerance stance on drunk driving. Respect the laws and you'll have nothing to worry about – apart from your dwindling finances.

┌ Dressing Up ─────────────

Generally speaking, shorts and T-shirts are a no-no for Abu Dhabi's bars and restaurants, and even some pubs will frown at your beach-bum attire, especially at the weekend. While trainers aren't strictly outlawed it will depend on the whole ensemble, and many places don't let you in wearing flip-flops – even if they're nice ones. Abu Dhabi's dress code is on the smarter side – more beautiful than bohemian – so shine your shoes when you're stepping out.

EATING OUT

The majority of Abu Dhabi's most popular restaurants are located within hotels and leisure clubs, and their popularity is partly down to the fact that these are virtually the only outlets where you can drink alcohol with your meal. Almost all other restaurants are unlicensed. If you're the type who requires a glass of vino to make a meal complete, it's best to phone ahead to check whether the establishment serves alcohol. There's quite a hefty mark-up on drinks, with a decent bottle of wine often costing as much as your meal.

Bottled water also seems to rocket in price in the five-star venues, and if you ask for water you'll often be given an imported brand, costing up to Dhs.40 a bottle. You should specify 'local' water when ordering, but even then you can expect to pay Dhs.10 or Dhs.20 for a bottle of still water that costs less than Dhs.2 in the supermarket.

However, the city has some superb independent restaurants and cafes that shouldn't be ignored just because they don't serve booze. Most of these serve up Arabic or Asian cuisines and, along with a more traditional dining experience, you'll often be faced with a bill that, for two people, comes to less than that bottle of imported water.

Hygiene

Food and drink outlets are subject to regular checks by the Abu Dhabi Food Control Authority (adfca. ae), and unclean outlets are warned to either scrub up or shut down. ADFCA also regulates food stores and wholesalers. You can be fairly confident that restaurants within hotels and most independent restaurants meet basic health and hygiene requirements. The city isn't immune to the odd food poisoning incident, however, so if a place looks like it might have some hygiene issues, it's best to avoid it. If you feel a restaurant you have visited could use an inspection, you can call ADFCA (800 555).

Arabic coffee

especially in the small restaurants centred around the Tourist Club and Al Markaziyah areas. Try Evergreen Vegetarian Restaurant (p.376) or opt for super budget Ruchi (02 679 5679). In other restaurants (even in steakhouses), you'll often find at least one or two vegetarian options. Arabic cuisine, although heavy on meat-based mains, offers a great range of mezze that are mostly vegetarian.

Abu Dhabi's cafes also represent decent sources for vegetarian food. Of particular note is BiteRite (p.372). The D Club, (thedclub.com) offers an organic food delivery service in the capital, and has plans to open a restaurant in the near future.

A word of warning: if you are a strict veggie, confirm that your meal is completely meat free. Some smaller restaurants cook their 'vegetarian' selection with animal fat or on the same grill as the meat dishes. Also, in some places you may need to check the ingredients of the vegetarian items before ordering.

Food Allergies

If you suffer from food allergies, take extra care when eating out in Abu Dhabi's restaurants. Many restaurants in the larger chain hotels now adhere to western practices in catering to and warning those with allergies about the contents of dishes, and menus are generally well-labelled for nuts and shellfish. In smaller and independent eateries, however, a lack of clearly-marked menus and a serving culture that is trained to tell customers what they think they want to hear can combine to form a dangerous situation. Don't hesitate to inform servers about the seriousness of your allergies if you don't think they are catching the drift of your questioning.

Taxes & Service Charges

Look out for the small print at the bottom of your menu and you may spot the dreaded 'prices are subject to 10% service charge and 6% tourism fee'. In some hotel restaurants and bars, these extras are already included, but they appear as extras on bills in a large number of outlets, particularly independent eateries. The 10% service charge is perhaps incorrectly named as often it isn't passed on to the staff, and you have no option of withholding it if you receive poor service. If you want to reward the waiting staff directly then the standard rule of a 10 – 12.5% tip will be appreciated, but give them cash if you can, or your tip may go straight in the till.

Vegetarian Food

Vegetarians should be pleasantly surprised by the variety available to them in Abu Dhabi's restaurants. For starters, Abu Dhabi is home to a large population from the subcontinent who are vegetarian by religion, and numerous Indian restaurants offer a range of cooking styles and tasty vegetarian dishes,

Cultural Meals

Al Markaziyah is the best place in the city to eat while soaking up some of the local atmosphere. This traditional city centre may be non-stop hustle and bustle, but strolling through the streets and dining at one of the many small, independent restaurants and cafes is an enjoyable experience. Both the Heritage Village (p.208) and Women's Handicraft Center (p.210) have small eateries where you can try traditional Emirati flavours, while an Emirati buffet is there to be dived into at Al Arish (02 673 2266) – a real local, cultural gem in the Al Meena port area. To enjoy Abu Dhabi – and the Corniche in particular – in the

Street Food

Throughout the city, you will find counter windows selling 'shawarma' (rolled pita bread filled with lamb or chicken as well as chips and a yogurt sauce). Costing about Dhs.5 each, this is not only an inexpensive option but also well worth trying as an excellent alternative fast food to the usual hamburger. These places usually sell other dishes too, such as 'foul' (a paste made from fava beans) and 'falafel' (or ta'amiya), small savoury balls of deep fried chickpeas. And if it's value for money you're after, for just Dhs.15, you can buy a whole grilled chicken, salad and hummus. While most counter window restaurants offer virtually the same thing, slight differences make some stand out from the rest. People are often adamant that their particular favourite serves, for example, the best falafel in town. Every restaurant has its own way of doing things and you might find that the best place is, surprisingly, the smallest, most low key restaurant you happened upon by chance.

way that Abu Dhabians themselves enjoy it, head for Mirage Marine Café (p.384) or Café Layali Zaman (02 626 4555), which both serve up local cuisine and shisha in waterfront locations. Top-end Emirati cuisine is on offer at Mezlai (p.384), located in the sumptuous Emirates Palace (p.201).

Independent Restaurants

While hotel restaurants tend to draw in the crowds, especially at the weekend, Abu Dhabi's independent choices are not to be missed. Areas like Al Markaziyah, Tourist Club Area and Al Khalidiyah are home to restaurants serving everything from authentic Arabic kebabs (Lebanese Flower, p.382) and tempting teppanyaki (Samurai, p.388) to Indonesian dishes (Bandung, p.369) and fiery Pakistani curry (Karachi City, 02 677 6055). Whether you pop in for a hearty lunch or have a teetotal evening you shouldn't ignore the culinary, and affordable, delights of these independent restaurants.

NIGHTLIFE
Bars, Pubs & Clubs

You can't expect authenticity from Abu Dhabi's pubs, but then when they're mostly in hotels, in the desert, in the Middle East, that won't come as a surprise. What you can look forward to is some inviting, friendly spots with a decent selection of draught and bottled beers and reliably good grub. Many of these mostly English and Irish places are popular when there's a big game on. And they're all comfortable, raucous and smoky enough to feel like the real thing.

Local Liquids

Fresh juices are widely available, either from small restaurants or juice shops. They are delicious, healthy and cheap, and made on the spot from fresh fruits such as orange, mango, banana, kiwi, strawberry, avocado, cantaloupe melon, watermelon, grapefruit and pineapple. If you can't decide, go for the mixed fruit cocktail or the refreshing lemon mint. Yoghurt is also a popular drink, often served with nuts, and the local milk is called 'laban' (a heavy, salty buttermilk that doesn't go well in tea or coffee). Arabic mint tea is available but probably not drunk as widely here as it is in other parts of the Arab world. However, Arabic coffee (thick, heavy and strong) is extremely popular and will have you buzzing on a caffeine high for days.

Door Policy

Certain bars and nightclubs have a 'selective' entry policy, and sometimes the 'members only' sign on the entrance needs a bit of explaining. Membership is usually introduced to control the clientele frequenting the establishment, but is often only enforced during busy periods. At quieter times, non-members may have no problems getting in, even if not accompanied by a member. Some places seem to use the rule to disallow entry if they don't like the look of you or your group.

Large groups (especially all males), single men and, sometimes, certain nationalities may be turned away without explanation. You can avoid the inconvenience, and the embarrassment, by breaking the group up

The Gateway to Abu Dhabi.
Discover the Fairmont experience.

Set on the creek side beach-front at the entrance to Abu Dhabi, Fairmont Bab Al Bahr offers the highest level of elegance and comfort throughout its luxuriously appointed guestrooms and suites and a variety of award winning dining venues - including Frankie's Italian Restaurant & Bar and Marco Pierre White Steakhouse & Grill.

This iconic landmark hotel stages the perfect setting for the modern traveller, while its contemporary designed ballroom with a capacity of up to 1,100 guests is the perfect venue for corporate or social events.

Introduce yourself to a century of service excellence as you check into Fairmont Bab Al Bahr.

For reservations or more information, please call **+971 2 654 3000** or toll free (UAE) **800 848 000**, email **babalbahr.reservations@fairmont.com** or visit **fairmont.com/babalbahr**

Nightlife

or by going in a mixed-gender group. If you do find yourself being discriminated against it's not worth arguing with the doorman – it won't work. Most companies do everything to avoid bad publicity, so try taking the issue up with the local media instead.

Pre-booking a table is a good option for ensuring that you gain entrance into a popular club. But keep in mind that table reservations usually come with a required minimum spend.

Dress Code
While many bars have a reasonably relaxed attitude towards dress code, some places will not allow you in if you are wearing shorts and sandals, while others require a collared shirt and have a 'no jeans or trainers' policy. You'll find that dress codes get stricter at the weekend too, when relaxed sports bars you've watched matches in wearing shorts and flip-flops during the week will turn you away for the same attire. In general, nightclubs are stricter, so dress to impress.

Under Age
The law in Abu Dhabi states that drinkers must be 21 or over. If you're lucky enough to look like you were born after the 1980s, make sure you carry some form of ID that shows your age – a passport or driving licence is best. Even if you think you're flattering your slightly wrinkled self, it's better to be safe than sorry. Otherwise you'll be on lemonade all night, or, worse still, left outside alone.

Driving Under The Influence
Drinking and driving is illegal in Abu Dhabi. There is zero tolerance; if you are caught with even a hint of alcohol in your system you will be sent to prison. Be responsible and always take a taxi – they're cheap, reliable and plentiful. For more information on drink driving and the law, see p.59, 123.

Cinemas
There are a number of cinemas around Abu Dhabi – the majority of them situated in shopping malls. Grand Cinemas operates a couple of cinemas, while Vox Cinemas runs the Marina Mall cinema. Abu Dhabi's movie offerings are largely mainstream Hollywood and Bollywood films with multiple screenings. There are also a couple of smaller independent cinemas in Abu Dhabi, which focus mainly on Hindi films. Unfortunately, there are no IMAX screens in Abu Dhabi, so those wanting the full 3D experience will have to head for Ibn Battuta Mall in Dubai where the Grand Megaplex has an IMAX screen, the IMAX at Meydan, or to Screen 22 at Dubai Mall's Reel Cinema which offers an IMAX-like experience.

There are local cinema idiosyncrasies – freezing air conditioning, people chatting to each other or talking on their mobile phones, and the heavy hand of the

censor can all affect your experience. Also, the sound quality can be a little off and Arabic (and often French) subtitles cover the bottom of the screen.

An annual cinematic highlight is the Abu Dhabi Film Festival (p.29). The event runs for a week in October, taking place mainly at the Emirates Palace and showcasing an impressive mix of mainstream, world and local cinema, from short films and documentaries to full-length features.

Alternative Screenings
Several of Abu Dhabi's big hotels hold occasional movie nights featuring giant or even poolside screens but, unfortunately, none of these as yet make regular appearances on the cultural calendar. The Alliance Française's Cine Club (af-aboudabi.net) has regular screenings of French language films while some of the more progressive art spaces occasionally arrange film nights. ADACH (the cultural foundation, see p.207) teams up with consulates and embassies to put on film nights from time to time, although these have become less frequent since the foundation moved from its Al Hosn home. Check adach.ae for details of upcoming screenings and events. New York University Abu Dhabi (nyuad.nyu.edu), in collaboration with the Abu Dhabi Film Festival, runs a series of Cinema Chats during the academic year. The series generally features movies by Arab filmmakers, who take questions from the audience following the film. Check the website for scheduled viewings.

Cine Royal Khalidiyah Mall, Al Khalidiyah, 02 681 9444, *cineroyal.ae*
Grand Abu Dhabi Mall Abu Dhabi Mall, Tourist Club Area, 02 645 8988, *grandcinemas.com*
Grand Cineplex Cinema Al Ain Mall, Al Ain, 03 751 1228, *grandcinemas.com*
Grand Rotana Al Ain Rotana, Al Ain, 03 754 4447, *grandcinemas.com*
Vox Cinemas Marina Mall, Breakwater, 02 681 8484, *voxcinemas.com*

Comedy Nights
The regular comedy scene in Abu Dhabi is, unfortunately, quite limited. However, there are regular visits from The Laughter Factory as well as the occasional comical theatre production or one-off event. Comedy shows tend to be aimed at the British population, so other nationalities may not always get the joke. Events are often promoted only a short time before they actually take place, so keep your ears to the ground for what's coming up.

Based on a concept that has been tremendously successful in the UK, America and Hong Kong, The Laughter Factory (thelaughterfactory.com) provides acts by both established and up and coming comedians. The artists, imported straight from the UK comedy circuit, are carefully selected to entertain the mainly expat audiences in this region. The winning formula of three distinct comedy styles performed in one evening caters to a wide range of comic tastes. Shows are usually held monthly at the Crowne Plaza Yas Island (p.201). If you can't make the Abu Dhabi date, see the website for the busier Dubai schedule.

Concerts & Live Music

In Abu Dhabi, there is no regular calendar of events for music lovers, although recent years have seen a decided increase in happenings in the music scene. At different times of the year (mainly in winter), international sporting events, concerts and festivals feature international artists, bands and classical musicians (see Abu Dhabi Calendar, p.26). Ticket prices may be higher than you would expect to pay elsewhere.

Emirates Palace has established itself as a venue for large scale concerts in the capital and, in the couple of years since opening, a number of international artists have played in the palace gardens including Andrea Boccelli, Bon Jovi, The Killers and Coldplay; Emirates Palace's concert hall has also played host to a number of renowned international orchestras. More recently, however, the biggest concerts have taken place on Yas Island in Flash Forum, a large concert pavilion adjacent to Ferrari World. Linkin Park, Kings of Leon, Beyonce,

Kanye West, and Prince have played the Formula One Weekend, while Stevie Wonder, Snoop Dogg, Eric Clapton, Madonna and Shakira have also performed at other times.

⌐ Stretch In Style

If you're feeling a bit flash (or are on a stag or hen party), you can rent a stretch Lincoln, SUV or even Hummer limo from Dubai-based company Connection Chauffeur (uae-limousine.com) so that you can arrive at your destination in style. Al Ghazal (adnh.com) also has a fleet of Mercedes, Audi and Chevrolet limos ready to dispatch.

Club events, such as Ministry of Sound nights, have also taken place in Abu Dhabi, and the Abu Dhabi Music & Arts Foundation (admaf.org) has hosted several cultural events. The Abu Dhabi Classics programme, which runs throughout the winter months, is well attended (abudhabiclassics.com). Dubai's popular Jazz Festival (p.27) and Gulf Bike Week (big name rock bands play at the weekend) are two annual musical events that are not to be missed.

Also worth noting is that WOMAD (p.28), Peter Gabriel's 'World of Music and Dance' festival, appears to have become a regular fixture.

WOMAD

Nightlife

Promoters usually have no long term programmes and details are only available about a month in advance, so for details of events, visit Explorer's website at askexplorer.com, check the daily press or monthly magazines, and listen out for announcements and advertisements on Emirates 1 and 2 FM as well as the northern radio stations Channel 4 FM and Dubai 92 FM.

Ticket Tips

Tickets for concerts and events go on sale at the venues and often through other diverse outlets, such as Virgin Megastore, Centrepoint and Starbucks too. Of course, tickets for the majority of events can be purchased online at sites such as boxofficeme.com, thinkflash.ae or itptickets.com.

Parties At Home

There are several companies in Abu Dhabi that can do all the cooking, decorating and cleaning up for you, leaving you with more time to concentrate on your witty after-dinner anecdotes. All of the companies listed offer a complete service from event organisation to the hiring of performers and equipment rental. For a novel outdoor party idea, you can get your own shawarma stand set up in the garden, complete with shawarma maker. Several Arabic restaurants provide this service, which works out as a very reasonable and easy way to sustain hordes of party guests. Also, many popular Indian restaurants offer catering services at great prices. You can order off the menu and specify the number of guests (although the general rule is reduce it by a few unless you want to be eating curry for a week). In addition to specialist companies, many restaurants, hotels, and clubs, including the Beach Rotana (p.200), Hilton Abu Dhabi (p.202) and The Club (p.179), have catering departments, so pick your favourite and ask if they can help out. Depending on what you require, caterers can provide just the food or everything from crockery, napkins, tables, chairs, waiters and doormen to a clearing up service for afterwards.

The D Club

The first totally organic catering company in the UAE, The D Club can arrange healthy food for your get-togethers at home.
Nr Baynuna Flowershop Tourist Club Area
02 644 6461
thedclub.com
Map **2 N4**

Events R' Us

This events company can take care of all your party requirements from delivering quality catering for an intimate dinner to providing party food, themed decor and serving staff for big bashes.
Sultan Al Qubeisy Bldg Tourist Club Area
02 645 6605
events-r-us.net
Map **2 R4**

Flying Elephant

This Dubai-based events company offers everything from entertainment and themed decorations to catering and waiting staff for all kinds of events. Whether it's for weddings, kids' birthday parties, office parties or corporate team-building events, Flying Elephant can look after the whole process.
Shk Zayed Rd Dubai **04 347 9170**
flyingelephantuae.com
Map **3 E2** Metro **Noor Islamic Bank**

Parti Perfect

This company offers a variety of food-themed parties where you or, better still, your kids get to create your own party food as part of the celebrations. For those who don't like getting their hands dirty, standard party catering is also available.
Al Khaleej Al Arabi St Al Manhal **050 126 4819**
Map **2 G5**

Theatre

The theatre scene in Abu Dhabi remains rather limited, with fans relying chiefly on touring companies and the occasional amateur dramatics performance. However, there are some developments. Amateur theatre, in the form of Abu Dhabi Dramatic Society (p.282), always welcomes new members, and there are occasional drama workshops to get involved with, most of which hold a performance at the end of the workshop (see Drama Groups, p.282).

As for bigger shows, the usual suspects – ADNEC (adnec.ae) and Emirates Palace (p.201) – are usually the venues. However, the National Theatre (p.275) does see some performances. Much like musical concerts, shows tend to come in fits and starts rather than on any consistent basis. The exception is the Abu Dhabi Festival (p.27), during which there should be plenty to keep theatre fans happy.

The recently opened Manarat Al Saadiyat (p.212) has a large auditorium which may well attract performances – especially as the venue is a precursor to Saadiyat's Performing Arts Centre, due for completion in the next couple of years, and will then surely make theatre a staple part of the Abu Dhabi events calendar.

In the meantime, you could head to Dubai, where the First Group Theatre at Madinat Jumeirah (madinattheatre.com), the Palladium and the Centrepoint Theatre at DUCTAC (ductac.org) have regular shows.

Savour The Souk Flavour

Got the munchies? Head to Souk Qaryat Al Beri, arguably Abu Dhabi's top foodie destination that's packed with a multitude of restaurants and cafes.

Although it's located away from the traditional city centre and the tourist magnet that is the Corniche, the southeast end of the island and just across the bridge on the mainland are arguably Abu Dhabi's most up-and-coming areas. And in the middle of it all is Souk Qaryat Al Beri.

There are some lovely, unique stores and boutiques in this traditional style marketplace, but this is one souk where shopping doesn't take centre stage. Here, you'll find everything from simple bites to some seriously high-end fine dining restaurants, but the main draw is the relaxed atmosphere, alfresco eating and drinking. The maze of walkways is interlinked by canals on which small abras motor, delivering visitors from one end to the other of the complex.

There are piles of dining options in Souk Qaryat Al Beri, serving up just about every popular cuisine available. If you can't decide what you're in the mood for, just go for a wander and you'll soon stumble upon something that takes your fancy. For lunch, there's little to rival the healthy skewers, salads, pita sandwiches and smoothies from Le Paradis du Fruit (02 558 1212), although coffee and carrot cake from Starbucks is always a decent back-up option.

Come dinnertime, steak and burger lovers will likely head straight for The Meat Co (p.384). The Lebanese restaurant Abdel Wahab (p.367) offers more than just meat, but its kebabs are really something special.

Luxurious European option, Eight Restaurant & Bar (p.375), is fairly new on the scene but has already won rave reviews and is among your top choices when it comes to top-quality continental cuisine.

As you look east on your global Souk Qaryat Al Beri gastronomy tour, you arrive at the award-winning Indian fare of Ushna (p.394); this classy restaurant proves that there's more to curries than you might expect. Elsewhere, the simple servings from The Noodle House (p.385) are always an unfussy delight, while the super chic Sho Cho restaurant serves up cool Japanese cuisine.

Although it may be best to enjoy dining at Souk Qaryat Al Beri's restaurants at night, when they spill out on to the creekside and offer up amazing views across the water to an illuminated Sheikh Zayed Mosque and Abu Dhabi island, bear in mind that many of the flashier restaurants also have some jaw-droppingly good lunch deals.

Finally, if you feel like continuing your evening, head to the excellent Left Bank (p.400) which serves up all manner of beers, wines and cocktails, while also having a pretty decent bar food menu. And, if all that's not enough, all the goodies in the Shangri-La, Traders and the Fairmont, including Hoi An (p.378), Pearls and Caviar (p.401) and Frankie's (p.376) and Chameleon (02 654 3238) are a short stroll away.

Souk Qaryat Al Beri

RESTAURANTS BY CUISINE

Afternoon Tea

American

Asian

Asian Subcontinent

Brazilian

Buffet

Cafes & Coffee Shops

Chinese

Contemporary Asian

Dinner Cruises

Emirati

Far Eastern

French

Fusion

Health Food

Indian

Indonesian

International

Going Out

Going Out (side tab)

Saadiyat Island

Park Hyatt Abu Dhabi Hotel & Villas
Beach House, Mediterranean — p.372

Saadiyat Beach Golf Club
Hawksbill Restaurant, International — p.378
The Park Bar & Grill, Steakhouse — p.386

The St Regis Saadiyat Island Resort
55&5th, The Grill, Steakhouses — p.366

Sas Al Nakhl Island

The Westin Abu Dhabi Golf Resort & Spa
Lemon & Lime, Bars, Pubs & Clubs — p.401

Tourist Club Area

Abu Dhabi Marina & Yacht Club
Bam Bu!, Chinese — p.369
Colosseum, Nightclubs — p.398
Portofino, Italian — p.387
The Alamo, Tex Mex — p.367

Al Diar Capital Hotel
Ciro's Pomodoro, Italian — p.375
Rock Bottom Cafe, American Bars — p.402
The Palm, International — p.386

Al Diar Dana Hotel
49er's The Gold Rush, American — p.366

Beach Rotana Abu Dhabi
Bay View, International — p.369
Benihana, Japanese — p.372
Brauhaus, German — p.396
Essence, Buffet — p.375
Finz, Seafood — p.376
Indigo, Indian — p.379
Prego's, Italian — p.387
Rodeo Grill, Steakhouses — p.388
Trader Vic's, Polynesian — p.394

Le Meridien Abu Dhabi
Al Birkeh, Middle Eastern — p.367
Captain's Arms, Bars — p.397
G Club, Nightclubs — p.398
La Brasserie, Buffet — p.380
Le Bistrot, French — p.382
NRG Sports Cafe, International — p.401
Opus Bar, Bars — p.401
Pappagallo, Italian — p.386
Talay, Seafood — p.394
Wakataua Terrace, Beach/Waterfront Bars — p.403

Nr ADNOC, Al Salam St
India Palace, Indian — p.379

Nr Al Diar Capital Hotel, Al Meena St
Samurai Restaurant, Japanese — p.388

Nr Al Madina Supermarket, Nadi Shahid St
Bandung, Indonesian — p.369

Nr Kia Showroom, Al Salam St
Le Shaderwan, Middle Eastern — p.382

Nr Lebanese Flower Restaurant, Al Salam St
Al Aqsa Sweets, Middle Eastern — p.367

Obaid Al Romaisi Bldg, Nr Emirates Islamic Bank
Al Qasr Restaurant & Grill, Middle Eastern — p.367

Yas Island West

Crowne Plaza Abu Dhabi Yas Island
Barouk, Middle Eastern — p.369
Jing Asia, Asian Subcontinent — p.379
Stills Bar & Brasserie, Bars, Pubs & Clubs — p.403

Park Inn By Radisson Abu Dhabi, Yas Island Hotel
Amerigos, Mexican — p.368

Radisson Blu Hotel, Abu Dhabi Yas Island
Assymetri, International — p.368
Filini, Italian — p.376

Yas Island Rotana
Blue Grill, Steakhouses — p.372
Rangoli, Indian — p.388
Y Bar, Bars, Pubs & Clubs — p.403

Yas Links Abu Dhabi
Hickory's Sports Bar, Sports Bars — p.400

Yas Viceroy Abu Dhabi
Amici, Italian — p.368
Angar, Indian — p.368
Atayeb, Middle Eastern — p.368
Kazu, Japanese — p.379
Nautilus, Seafood — p.385
Noodle Box, Contemporary Asian — p.385
Origins, International — p.385
Rush, Bars, Pubs & Clubs — p.402
Skylite, Bars, Pubs & Clubs — p.403

Yas Yacht Club
Allure By Capriani, Nightclubs — p.396
Cipriani, Italian — p.375
Stars 'n' Bars, American — p.403
Yotto, Japanese — p.395

RESTAURANTS & CAFES

┌─ **The Yellow Star** ─────────────
│ This yellow star highlights places that merit extra
│ praise. It might be the atmosphere, the food, the
│ cocktails, the music or the crowd, but any review
│ that you see with the star attached is sure to be
│ somewhere that's a bit special.
└──────────────────────────────────

18°   Mediterranean

Although officially Hyatt Capital Gate's all-day dining
restaurant, it does 18° something of a disservice to
describe it as such. Located right on the most leaning
section of the world's most leaning tower (hence the
name), 18° is an evening venue worthy of visiting for
more than just the awe-inspiring floor to ceiling views.
Focused on Eastern Mediterranean cuisine, you can
opt for an Italian, Greek, Turkish, Syrian or Lebanese
dishes. Try the melt-in-the-mouth burrata cheese,
crispy calamari or pickled halwayo to start; the Syrian
beef tenderloin is hard to beat for meat-lovers. Service
is exceptional and the range of wines on offer is as
good as you'll find anywhere. For a special occasion,
try either the chef's table, right next to the open
kitchen, or the private hidden table.
Hyatt Capital Gate Abu Dhabi Al Safarat
02 596 1440
abudhabi.capitalgate.hyatt.com
Map **1 H8**

18Oz   Steakhouses

This elegant restaurant is an ever-popular part of Abu
Dhabi's dining scene. 18Oz specialises in mouth-
watering steaks and chops, serving choice cuts of
Angus beef drenched in a selection of no fewer than
eight sauces. Non-carnivorous diners are catered to as
well, however; seafood appetisers and lamb, chicken
and vegetarian main dishes can also be found on the
menu. The modern decor and attentive service feels
just right, and even the desserts are delicious – if you
have any space left after the meaty feast. They're open
for lunch (12:30 to 15:30) and dinner.
One To One Hotel – The Village Al Dhafrah
02 495 2000
onetoonehotels.com
Map **2 Q8**

49er's The Gold Rush   American

Centrally situated, this popular venue is usually
packed, so get there early to enjoy an entire evening
of entertainment American-style. The rich timber
finishes reflect the ranch style atmosphere, and the
food is delicious, with steaks that melt in your mouth.
Service is excellent, and with live music and quite

reasonable prices, you can't go too wrong – this is a
great venue. Check out the various theme nights for
added spice.
Al Diar Dana Hotel Tourist Club Area **02 645 6000**
aldiarhotels.com
Map **2 R4**

55&5th, The Grill   Steakhouses

Out on this wind-swept stretch of Saadiyat is an East
Coast-style high-end steakhouse. From the brick
and leather decor, which makes it look like a modern
gents' club, to the predominantly surf and turf
inspired menu, this is upper-crust Big Apple through
and through. In fact, the jazz, cocktails and cigar
atmosphere is a nod to the original St Regis New York.
Starters of foie gras, scallops or beef crudo are delicate
but flavourful, while main courses are dominated
by the excellent 'vintage beef from the aging room',
although Scottish salmon, veal and lobster casserole
also feature. The wine list is impressive and there's an
exceptional private chef's table perched in a 'wine
library' high above the rest of the restaurant – perfect
for parties. None of this, of course, comes particularly
cheaply, but it's very nice.
The St Regis Saadiyat Island Resort Sadiyat Island
02 498 8888
stregissaadiyatisland.com
Map **1 G1**

55&5th, The Grill

Abdel Wahab
Middle Eastern

The Abu Dhabi branch of this legendary Beirut establishment does, by and large, live up to the hype, with authentic but refined Lebanese cuisine in nice, if not stunning, surroundings. The Levantine-inspired menu won't shock anyone with novelty – think flatbread, hummus, mezzes and lamb dishes – but it's all prepared as well as you'll find anywhere else, and with reasonable prices to boot.

The Souk At Qaryat Al Beri Al Maqtaa **02 558 1616**
Map **1 L8**

Al Aqsa Sweets
Middle Eastern

Al Aqsa does only one thing and it does it extremely well: kanafeh. Made of very fine shredded pastry dough on top of a soft cheese, drizzled with sugary syrup and crushed pistachios, and served hot, the sweet is beloved throughout the Arab world. This tiny shop, near Gad Restaurant, sells two kinds of kanafeh by weight; there are small tables to sit at but you'd be just as well to take it wrapped to go.

Nr Lebanese Flower Restaurant, Al Salam St
Tourist Club Area **02 644 2159**
Map **2 Q5**

Al Birkeh
Middle Eastern

Widely touted as one of the best pan-Arabic restaurants in town, this established venue serves traditional Middle Eastern fare in an atmospheric setting, complete with live music and a belly dancer to set the mood. Start your culinary journey with a selection of hot and cold mezze before moving on to a main course of grilled meat or fish (and lots of it, too). The portions are generous and, for the adventurous or gastronomically brave, the menu also includes some rather exotic Lebanese dishes such as raw liver, washed down with the strong aniseed drink, arak, that perfectly cleans the plate.

Le Meridien Abu Dhabi Tourist Club Area **02 644 6666**
lemeridienabudhabi.com
Map **2 S4**

Al Dhafra
Dinner Cruises

This traditional dhow offers daily dinner cruises in a tranquil setting as the atmospheric vessel floats along the picturesque Corniche. The upper deck boasts a majlis while the lower deck is air-conditioned and can seat approximately 50 people. A sumptuous menu includes lavish international fare which can be tailored to individual preferences. As you dine, the ethnic charm of the dhow, and the serenity of the calm Arabian waters, ensures an unforgettable evening. The dhow can also be hired for private functions.

Nr Meena Fish Market Al Meena **02 673 2266**
aldhafra.net
Map **2 S1**

Al Fanar
International

The revolving Al Fanar restaurant on the very top of the Le Royal Meridien hotel in Abu Dhabi is the perfect venue for a first date: the constantly changing vista of the capital's skyline offers welcome opportunities to fill any awkward conversation lulls while the extensive menu provides a good selection of inventive dishes including seafood, meat and vegetarian options. Al Fanar takes 1 hour and 45 minutes to do a full rotation – during which the polite waiters cater to your every whim, enhancing the feeling of other-worldliness. If you are all romanced out, Al Fanar also hosts lively Friday brunches and has set course business lunches.

Le Royal Meridien Abu Dhabi Markaziya East
02 674 2020
alfanarabudhabi.com
Map **2 P3**

Al Qasr Restaurant & Grill
Middle Eastern

Tender appetisers of stuffed vine leaves and well balanced moutabal pave the way for Middle Eastern main courses that include some tasty hammour creations (fish) and a fabulous selection of mixed grill specialities. Lunch offers an astounding selection of no fewer than 99 dishes, including Middle Eastern rice, curries and other regional delicacies. No matter when you go, you can expect to be served by staff that are capable and eager to please.

Obaid Al Romaisi Bldg, Nr Emirates Islamic Bank
Tourist Club Area **02 644 9933**
Map **2 R5**

The Alamo
Tex Mex

The Alamo, with its cantina-style atmosphere and Mexican-inspired memorabilia, is renowned for its frozen margaritas, succulent spare ribs, sizzling fajitas and Friday brunch. Friendly and polite service staff complete the ingredients for a perfect 'casual night out' venue.

Abu Dhabi Marina & Yacht Club Tourist Club Area
02 644 0300
Map **2 P3**

Amalfi
Italian

The chef is Italian and so are many of the guests – the fact that Amalfi is favoured by Italian expats speaks volumes of the restaurant's commitment to produce all-Italian classics using top-notch ingredients. From antipasti to pesce, insalate and carni, you'll find all the usual suspects on the menu; the home-made pasta dishes are a particular standout. The grandiose setting, an extensive wine list and live music top the experience.

Le Royal Meridien Abu Dhabi Markaziya East
02 674 2020
amalfiabudhabi.com
Map **2 P3**

Restaurants & Cafes

Amerigos
Mexican

Suitable for casual or formal occasions, this spacious Mexican restaurant has modern colourful decor with a large TV at one end, dedicated mainly to sports. If you prefer, you can enjoy the views from the poolside restaurant area. Choose from traditional fajitas and quesadillas with fresh guacamole, or try tender meats and fish dishes, all prepared to a high standard and served by friendly staff. Alternatively, just sip a long cocktail at the large bar. A bustling restaurant that almost always results in a lively, social evening.

Park Inn By Radisson Abu Dhabi, Yas Island Hotel
Yas Island West **02 656 2222**
parkinn.com
Map **1 T5**

Amici
Italian

Amici is an Italian restaurant with an almost futuristic vibe thanks to a large outside dining terrace, calming water feature, moulded white structures and furniture and green glass hanging sculptures. Fresh bread and a trio of flavoured olive oils start your meal, delivered by staff who are attentive and helpful. While the menu is small (you choose from an antipasti buffet for your appetiser), there is quite obviously an Italian chef passionate about food in the kitchen, as every morsel is authentic and delicious.

Yas Viceroy Abu Dhabi Yas Island West **02 656 0600**
viceroyhotelsandresorts.com
Map **1 T5**

Angar
Indian

Follow your nose through The Yas Viceroy, and you'll be lead straight to Angar, the hotel's delightful Indian eatery. Authentic tastes of India mix with contemporary luxury, served in one of the most exciting recent additions to Abu Dhabi's five-star dining scene. The beautiful terrace has views of the brightly coloured hotel dome and a small water feature; inside, you can watch chefs prepare your curries from scratch to whet your appetite. Each course is carefully constructed, balancing flavours and textures. The extensive menu features authentic dishes in numbers that prove that variety really is the spice of life.

Yas Viceroy Abu Dhabi Yas Island West **02 656 0600**
viceroyhotelsandresorts.com
Map **1 T5**

Arabic Cafe
Middle Eastern

The waft of fruity shisha and dulcet notes of Arabic music welcome you to this relaxed little cafe set in the heart of the Hiltonia Beach Club overlooking the shimmery, turquoise waters of the Arabian Gulf. The concise menu offers Arabic staples from mezze to Shawarma and grilled chicken with sumac alongside international bar food classics from burgers to croque

monsieurs. Similarly, the desserts menu features regional treats like Umm Ali and halawat al geban as well as ice cream and eclairs.

Hilton Abu Dhabi Al Khubeirah **02 681 4344**
hilton.com
Map **2 C3**

Independent Reviews

All of the outlets in this book have been independently reviewed by writers based in Abu Dhabi. Their aim is to give clear, realistic and unbiased views of each venue. If you feel you have been unwittingly led astray, or your much-loved local or hidden gastronomic gem has not been included, let us know by emailing info@askexplorer.com. Alternatively, if you think you know better and have sufficiently discerning taste buds, log on to askexplorer.com and submit your own reviews.

Asian Garden
Asian

Don't let the rather plain look of this restaurant fool you – what's on offer is a culinary tour of East Asia at bargain prices. From Thai curries to Filipino noodles and Chinese fried rice, the food is faultless and the prices cheaper than what you'd pay at a mall food court. Watch out if you order something spicy, though: perhaps true to authentic Southeast Asian cooking styles, the chef can have a heavy hand with the chilli peppers.

Nr El Dorado Cinema, Shk Zayed The Second St
Markaziya East **02 676 3350**
asiangarden-restaurant.com
Map **2 Q4**

Assymetri
International

Perfect for families with children, this restaurant has its own clown, an assortment of toys and a swimming pool right on the doorstep. The international cuisine, by its very nature, caters for all and the live cooking stations make for dynamic entertainment as fresh dishes are concocted before your very eyes. The restaurant itself is large, with an abundance of natural light and views over the Arabian Gulf, allowing you to admire the beauty of Abu Dhabi's islands.

Radisson Blu Hotel, Abu Dhabi Yas Island
Yas Island West **02 656 2000**
radissonblu.com
Map **1 S5**

Atayeb
Middle Eastern

There are a few things that you can take for granted when walking into a Yas Viceroy restaurant: thoroughly modern but extremely considered design; a dramatic open kitchen; pitch perfect service; large outdoor areas with race track views. But the clutch of awards that adorn the entry to Atayeb also mean that

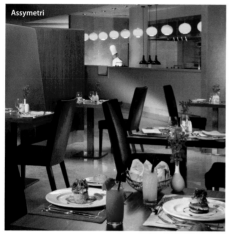

Assymetri

you can take the quality of the food for granted – Chef Wafaei, by many experts' reckoning, serves up the best Middle Eastern cuisine in Abu Dhabi. There are no real surprises – it's hot and cold mezze, grilled meat platters and fresh, grilled fish, and the dishes aren't too fussy, but sheer quality makes this restaurant stand out. Atayeb has a large terrace – ideal for a relaxing post-meal shisha.
Yas Viceroy Abu Dhabi Yas Island West **02 656 0600**
viceroyhotelsandresorts.com
Map **1 T5**

Azur > p.308   Mediterranean
At a first glance, the rather clinical modern decor could be off-putting, which is a pity since 'Azur' hides a cornucopia of wholesome high-end dishes predominantly made with organic ingredients. The menu features hearty meat dishes, seafood and super fresh vegetables; there's even organic wine on menu. The food arrives piping hot and service is surprisingly knowledgeable and friendly, albeit a little slow.
Al Raha Beach Hotel Al Raha **02 5080 555**
danathotels.com
Map **1 R7**

Bam Bu!   Chinese
Whether out for a romantic dinner or a celebration with all your friends, you can't go wrong with Bam Bu! – a little slice of the Orient with an enchanting view of the yachts in the marina. The brunch option is a good choice for the uninitiated – just sit back and relax while a constant stream of freshly prepared delicacies are brought to your table. Speciality dishes such as lobster or peking duck are charged for accordingly.
Abu Dhabi Marina & Yacht Club Tourist Club Area **02 645 6373**
Map **2 S4**

Bandung   Indonesian
Another of the Tourist Club's hidden gems, this Indonesian restaurant might not be a delight for the eyes but its food is a feast for the taste buds. The meat and fried fish dishes are all tasty and the food always arrives piled high.
Nr Al Madina Supermarket, Nadi Shahid St Tourist Club Area **02 645 2008**
Map **2 R5**

Barouk   Middle Eastern
This Lebanese joint offers an authentic taste of the Middle East – with a Turkish twist. With a wide selection of hot and cold mezze, sharing is advisable in order to sample a range of the delights. Main course options are predominately a choice of juicy lamb or chicken kebabs. To sweeten things up, try the exquisite Turkish delight to accompany the restaurant's own belly dancer who makes an appearance between 21:00 and 22:00, transforming the atmosphere from quiet and refined to lively and vibrant.
Crowne Plaza Abu Dhabi Yas Island Yas Island West **02 656 3000**
ichotelsgroup.com
Map **1 S5**

Bay View   International
If alfresco dining beneath beach brollies, sipping cocktails and watching sunsets sounds appealing, then head to Bay View in the Beach Rotana's rather plush sports complex (you need to be a club member or pay the 'day guest' entry fee to eat here). An abundance of freshly prepared salads, mains and desserts awaits, and there's also a fine choice of drinks. The food, although pricey, is tasty, healthy and well presented, but the service could use a bit of fine tuning.
Beach Rotana Abu Dhabi Tourist Club Area **02 697 9011**
rotana.com
Map **2 S5**

BBQ Al Qasr   Middle Eastern
With high-quality chargrilled food, served on purpose-built pagoda platforms right on Emirates Palace's very own private stretch of beach, this is barbecuing VIP style. The setting is perfect for a romantic evening out; musicians play chilled out tunes until late into the night as you sample the Arabic-inspired barbecue menu. Although there are non-meat options – such as tasty grilled seafood dishes – ultimately this is carnivore territory. A shisha is the perfect way to end the meal.
Emirates Palace Al Ras Al Akhdar **02 690 7999**
kempinski.com
Map **2 B2**

Where To Go For What

Abu Dhabi is a pick 'n' mix of eateries, drinking spots and entertainment options vying to please a highly diverse audience. Whether you want a daytime binge of five-star cuisine, a raucous night out dancing to live music, an evening of brain teasers or an early morning rendition of I Will Survive, you will find it all within Abu Dhabi's restaurants, cafes, pubs, bars and nightclubs.

Alfresco

Between late October and early May, the weather in Abu Dhabi is perfect for alfresco dining. Popular spots for dinner with a waterfront view are The Fishmarket (p.376) and The Yacht Club (p.403) at the InterContinental Abu Dhabi, while Finz (p.376) at the Beach Rotana is on a pontoon-like wooden structure that stretches out over the water and BBQ Al Qasr (p.369) at Emirates Palace is right there on the sand. Boccaccio (p.373) and Riviera (p.388) both have lovely outdoor areas. Several venues, including Pearls and Caviar (p.401), Left Bank (p.400) and Ushna (p.394), at Souk Qaryat Al Beri are great alfresco watering holes that also serve up tasty treats under the stars. The recently opened Central Market development is home to several increasingly popular options too; try Tarbouche (p.394) for shisha and fruit mocktails unders the stars.

Celebrity Chefs

Does food prepared by famous hands really taste better? Check out Marco Pierre White's eponymous grill restaurant (p.378) or Frankie's (p.372), both found at the Fairmont Bab Al Bahr, to see for yourself. At Emirates Palace, the delectable Emirati dishes on offer at Mezlai (p.379) are created by the country's first Emirati chef, Chef Ali Salem Musbeh Al Badawi. Alternatively, hop over to Dubai to check out what's cooking by chefs including Gordon Ramsay, Pierre Gagnaire, Gary Rhodes, Nobu Matsuhisa, Santi Santamari and Michel Rostang.

Fish & Chips

You may not find a British-style 'chippy' in Abu Dhabi, but if you're really hankering for some good old fish and chips there are a few choices at your disposal. To keep the takeaway feel, head for Al Wahda Mall where there's a London Fish & Chips (02 443 7701) in the foodcourt, although these are a far cry from the real deal. For something more authentic, Ally Pally Corner (p.396) and Rock Bottom Café (p.402) get the big British pub portions and low prices spot on while, if you take your fish and chips seriously, try Hemingway's (p.400) or Stills (p.403), for some of the best fish and chips in the city.

Dancing

There are a few clubs to boogie the night away in, as well as a handful of places for impromptu dance routines. Should you fancy wiggling to something slightly more alternative while out on the town, then you're likely to be disappointed. Rock Bottom Café (p.402) is about the only place in town where rock or indie are played, although the cover band at The Tavern (p.403) on Thursday nights is worth checking out. Cinnabar's (p.397) dance floors are often full, especially for Saturday's salsa night. By and large,

Skylite at Yas Viceroy

dancing in the capital is a fairly glitzy affair, with Etoiles (p.398), Pearls and Caviar (p.401) and Sho Cho (p.402) popular options.

Late & Lively

In addition to the dedicated clubs listed in this chapter, Abu Dhabi's nightlife also includes several bars and restaurants which transform late evening into lively joints with hopping dancefloors. These include Beachcomber (p.396), Colosseum (p.398), Aloft's Relax@12 (p.402) and Skylite (p.403) at The Yas Viceroy.

Karaoke Bars

There are a few places in Abu Dhabi where you can show off your vocal abilities, or even just belt out a comedy version of Ice Ice Baby. Wasabi (02 678 1000) in the Al Diar Mina Hotel is a popular haunt, with its authentic Japanese style private booths, while the karaoke cabins at Bowling City (p.276) even allow you to record your vocal gymnastics on to CD for future playback. Tambayan (02 679 4777) at Al Ain Palace Hotel is a popular choice, as is the karaoke room at PJ O'Reilly's (p.402).

Ladies' Nights

Lucky ladies in this fair city can go out almost any night of the week and enjoy free drinks. Of course, this isn't a charitable venture for Abu Dhabi's bar scene; where ladies are drinking, the men and their wallets inevitably follow. Wednesday is the biggest ladies' night with many bars and pubs offering at least two free drinks, and some of the most popular venues include PJ O'Reilly's (p.402), Cooper's (p.398), Zenith (p.403), Left Bank (p.400), 49er's (p.366) and Etoiles (p.398).

Quiz Nights

If you want to test your brain power and knowledge of useless trivia then head to one of Abu Dhabi's many quiz nights. Try Hemingway's (p.400) on a Sunday, Heroes (p.400) on a Monday or Ally Pally Corner (p.396) every Tuesday. If you're lucky enough to be a member of The Club (p.179), then the bar there runs a popular quiz on Wednesdays which always attracts a decent crowd.

And The Rest…

Abu Dhabi also has a few fun alternatives for when you need a break from the bar and restaurant scene. Aloft's Mai Café (p.401) takes the party to the pool with its Full Moon Splash parties, which include a shisha lounge. On the water, several large dhows, including Al Dhafra (p.367), offer dinner cruises for the best Corniche view in town, while numerous charter companies (p.230) will provide boats for hire – you can then bring your own food and drinks on board. For something really different, why not head for one of the quiet islands off the coast and set up camp with a barbecue?

Restaurants & Cafes

Beach House — Mediterranean

The setting is beautiful, with palm trees and idyllic pools leading the way to the extremely sophisticated and picturesque restaurant on the beachfront. Once there, the attentive staff will see to your every need – and ordering is a breeze thanks to the large menu full of delectable Mediterranean titbits. Much like a Spanish tapas bar, the idea here is to share dishes, and the fantastic array of little plates of deliciousness will make sure there's a taste for every palate. A serviceable wine list – not to mention sangrias and cocktails – cheese platters and innovative desserts round off a meal that will have you returning time and again to relax by the shore. And since the restaurant is away from the bustle of the city, overlooking the waters of Saadiyat Beach, the Beach House makes for a great romantic spot. Open for lunch between 12:30 and 16:00, and for dinner between 18:30 and midnight.
Park Hyatt Abu Dhabi Hotel & Villas Saadiyat Island **02 407 1138**
abudhabi.park.hyatt.com
Map **1 H1**

The Beach Restaurant — Seafood

Located next to the beach and pool, this aptly named restaurant offers a reasonably priced range of internationally-inspired seafood. You'll have the choice to dine alfresco by the pool or indoors within the cosy terracotta walls and murals. The Atlantis, an iced seafood platter, is worth a special mention – not only does it come overflowing with aquatic treats of all manner, but it also features rare-to-find Ceviche. Otherwise, the menu features dishes ranging from Mexican lobster quesadillas to Mediterranean coconut crusted yellow fin tuna.
Khalidiya Palace Rayhaan By Rotana
Al Ras Al Akhdar **02 657 0000**
rotana.com
Map **2 A3**

Beijing Restaurant — Chinese

The large restaurant, tucked away behind Madinat Zayed mall, gets packed at the weekend and doesn't win many points for ambience, but with food this authentic, it doesn't need to. Classics like scallion pancakes, fried green beans and Kung Pao chicken are perfect for sharing and the rotating tabletops mean that everyone gets a chance to dig in.
Nr Shoe Mart, Al Falah St Madinat Zayed **02 621 0708**
Map **2 M5**

Benihana — Japanese

Contemporary Asian cuisine, minimalist decor and crowd-pleasing chefs make this a 'must do' on the Abu Dhabi restaurant circuit. The menu includes soups, salads and desserts, but don't miss out on the sushi teppanyaki, prepared at live stations by entertaining chefs. Prices seem high, but for a feast of treats, it's good value, especially on the teppanyaki theme nights. Fans of Japanese food looking for a lively night out will not be disappointed.
Beach Rotana Abu Dhabi Tourist Club Area
02 697 9011
rotana.com
Map **2 S5**

Biancorosso Pizza — Italian

Biancorosso is not a restaurant, it is a pizzeria. Accordingly, the Italian owners have put a lot of effort into developing their signature dish, and the attention to detail pays off. It is quite possibly the best pizza in the capital, with crisp, light dough, a subtle hint of tomato sauce, and the perfect amount of fresh toppings. Though the menu also features traditional antipasti, salads, and pastas (which are well worth a sample), the pizza is the focus of biancorosso, and even the pasta bowls come covered with pizza dough that you can use to soak up the sauce. While you might be tempted to devour the entire dish, you'd be remiss not to save room for an Italian espresso and the creamy tiramisu. Biancorosso is one of many new eateries in the quickly developing Al Dhafrah neighbourhood, but the delicious food and reasonable prices make it one that should not be missed.
Y Tower, Nr Al Mamoura Bldg Al Dhafrah
02 658 4244
biancorossoitaly.com
Map **2 N10**

BiteRite — Health Food

A healthy eating cafe-cum-restaurant where nutritional, well-balanced lunches and dinners are the name of the game. The menu offers a jigsaw of flavours, with sandwiches, wraps and stir-fries rubbing shoulders with health-conscious curries, pizzas and pastas. The decor is reflective of the menu – clean, bright and original. BiteRite also does a range of healthy-eating programmes and can deliver nutritionally-controlled meals direct to your doorstep whether at home or in the office.
Nr Red Crescent Bldg, East Rd Al Dhafrah **02 641 1660**
biterite.ae
Map **2 N8**

Blue Grill — Steakhouses

Elegant in shades of blue with touches of dark wood, this light and airy restaurant displays an extensive wine cellar and an impressively large show kitchen. An innovative a la carte menu focuses on prime beef and seafood, and is replaced on Fridays with a truly fine dining brunch experience. With freshly squeezed juices and the option of free flowing Laurent Perrier champagne served by attentive staff, your gastronomic journey starts with an exquisite array of appetisers including oysters, foie gras and lobster. Follow with your choice of freshly prepared main, including fillet steak with truffle mash, eggs Benedict with smoked haddock and perfectly cooked duck breast, but save room to sample the enticing handmade desserts on display.

Yas Island Rotana Yas Island West **02 656 4000**
rotana.com
Map **1 T4**

Bocca
Italian

For modern Italian cooking with a touch of romance, Bocca is a good choice. Low lighting and flickering candles create an intimate atmosphere, and the crisp white tablecloths offset by dark wood fittings provide a feeling of relaxed elegance. The hand-made pasta, and good range of seafood dishes, are all prepared with care and presented with a flourish. It's Italian but with a twist on the traditional recipes; expect to spot specialities such as spaghetti with lobster bolognaise. The service is professional and prompt, and the staff are friendly. Live piano music provides a nice touch, though the acoustics are not great and it's a little too easy to overhear the conversations at neighbouring tables.

Hilton Abu Dhabi Al Khubeirah **02 681 1900**
hilton.com
Map **2 C3**

Boccaccio
Mediterranean

Boccaccio offers some of the best Italian food in town, at surprisingly reasonable prices. Choose between dining outside on the deck overlooking the charming marina or eating in the elegant, warmly lit interior, decorated by the illuminated bar and wine rack, where the mood is added to by the talented, resident acoustic trio. The newly expanded menu contains a large number of pastas, pizzas, starters and mains, all extremely well prepared. The quality of the food makes dining here a real pleasure, and it is equally suitable for a romantic tete a tete as for a group gathering, as it's fairly buzzing when it's busy. To round off a superb meal, ask for the chef's recommendations for his truly wicked, adult desserts.

InterContinental Abu Dhabi Al Bateen **02 666 6888**
ichotelsgroup.com
Map **2 C4**

Bord Eau
French

Bord Eau has quickly established itself as one of the very best restaurants in the city, but good food doesn't come cheap here and, while the chef produces some undeniable gastronomic masterpieces, dinner for two will do some considerable damage to your wallet. The menu takes established luxuries – delicacies such as foie gras, scallops, lobster thermidor and Wagyu beef – and adds a subtle but distinctive twist. There

Chamas Brazilian Churrascaria Restaurant & Bar

is the hushed and refined air of fine dining, and people come here for business (when someone else is picking up the cheque) or for special occasions. The views of the creek through the large picture windows are interesting, and the service faultless. One of Abu Dhabi's finest.

Shangri-La Hotel, Qaryat Al Beri Al Maqtaa
02 509 8888
shangri-la.com
Map **1 L8**

Cafe Arabia
Cafes & Coffee Shops

Located in a nondescript villa out of the heart of the city, Cafe Arabia is worlds apart from the typical cafe in the capital. Each of the three floors, as well as the rooftop terrace, is tastefully decorated with plush sofas, elegant tables, and bookcases inviting you to stay and read over coffee. The menu offers light fare based on recipes the owner has collected from family and friends, as well as some inventive hot and cold beverages. Thanks to art shows and coffee mornings, this new spot has quickly established a well-deserved following among local expats.

Nr Mushrif Park, Mohammed Bin Khalifa St Al Mushrif **02 643 9699**
Map **2 K10**

Caravan Restaurant
Indian

If you're looking for a cheap, 'no frills' Asian meal, Caravan delivers the goods. The menu offers a tasty selection of Chinese, Indian and Thai cuisine, and the evening buffet (incredible value for money) includes soups, salads, a selection of main courses and desserts. The service is remarkably friendly and helpful given that this is a low cost venue. A home delivery service is available.

Al Hamed Centre Madinat Zayed **02 639 3370**
sterlingcaravan.com
Map **2 M4**

Chamas Churrascaria & Bar
Brazilian

Eat as much red meat as you like for a fixed price; Chamas' concept is great but the road to red-meat heaven is a long one. First navigate salad bar purgatory, before steering through steaming bowls of polenta, hash browns, black beans, vegetable rice and fried bananas; then negotiate various barbecued meats. Resist all of these wayside temptations and you'll finally arrive at steak heaven, serving sirloin, flank, rib eye and tenderloin. This noisy, frantic place with its enthusiastic band is great for large groups and is packed every night, proving that Chamas has got the formula for Brazilian churrascaria (that's barbecue for the uninitiated) just right.

InterContinental Abu Dhabi Al Bateen **02 666 6888**
ichotelsgroup.com
Map **2 C4**

Chequers
Mediterranean

This modern, intimate venue is a pleasing choice if you fancy a cosy meal accompanied by good wine and a spot of live music. The service is attentive and the meals beautifully presented, but if you are a particularly picky diner, you may find the food a little bland. However, thanks to the excellent wine list, the singer and her sidekick on the baby grand piano, your evening at Chequers will be a largely enjoyable one.

Sands Hotel Madinat Zayed **02 615 6666**
danathotels.com
Map **2 N4**

China Restaurant
Chinese

This restaurant has been dishing up yummy Chinese cuisine for 24 years and it is still going strong. The food and service are both of consistently high standards, with the peking duck and kung pao prawns worthy of a special mention. The authentic decor and lighting enhance the warm, welcoming ambience – all in all this is a highly recommended venue.

Mercure Abu Dhabi Centre Hotel Markaziya East
02 633 3555
mercure.com
Map **2 M4**

Cho Gao
Asian

The menu reads like an eclectic collection from a food travelogue – an ingredient from China, a recipe from Thailand, a technique from Vietnam; salad, soup, dim sum. Recommended are the steak, duck and seafood options, but you'll also find some of the most creative vegetarian options in town. The ambience is calm and the decor authentic, while the service is attentive without being intrusive. It's the perfect place for a low-key but special night out with friends or loved ones.

Cho Gao

The bar, with its two-for-one happy hour, is great for a quick drink and a snack after work.
Crowne Plaza Abu Dhabi Markaziya East
02 616 6166
ichotelsgroup.com
Map **2 N4**

The Chocolate
Gallery > *p.355*   Cafes & Coffee Shops
This restaurant-cafe-heaven is a chocoholic's paradise. Choose between chocolate delights from crepes to muffins, and chocolate martinis to a mouth watering, not to be missed, chocolate fondue with all the trimmings. Special sculptured chocolate models and cakes can be ordered in advance and can be seen on display around the cafe; you can watch the talented chocolatiers work their Willy Wonka magic through glass windows too. Don't fret if you don't have a sweet tooth – an array of savoury paninis, crepes and salads are also available.
Fairmont Bab Al Bahr Al Maqtaa **02 654 3333**
fairmont.com
Map **1 L8**

Cipriani   Italian
This nautically-themed joint's sleek cream and navy interiors make it feel like a superyacht – complete with an attentive crew and top-notch chef. The menu offers signature Italian fare from light bites to soups, pasta and risotto, as well as tasty grilled mains. Culinary treats aside, the adjacent bar is an atmospheric hangout; with its eclectic collection of coffee table books to flick through, it's an easy place to while away the hours over a drink.
Yas Yacht Club Yas Island **02 657 5400**
cipriani.com
Map **1 T5**

Ciro's Pomodoro   Italian
If you just can't resist a charming Italian, then this unique, trendy venue is perfect for you. The menu covers all the classics like pastas, salads, pizzas and grilled dishes, and the numerous pictures of celebrities visiting Ciro's around the world will keep you entertained while you wait for your meal to arrive. The food is delectable, the service friendly and attentive, and a live band is there most days to serenade you through your meal.
Al Diar Capital Hotel Tourist Club Area **02 678 7700**
aldiarhotels.com
Map **2 R3**

Curry House   Nepalese
Take your tastebuds on a culinary journey to Nepal at this unpretentious restaurant. The traditional Nepalese fare includes vegetable dishes, soups and curries, as well as a variety of momos (Nepalese dumplings)

accompanied by a spicy sauce. The naan bread, served fresh and hot, is particularly memorable. Indian and Chinese specialities are also available. This venue is a bit more upmarket than your local thali joint, and is recommended for a tasty, inexpensive meal.
Nr Janata Bank, Shk Zayed First St Markaziya East
02 632 8860
Map **2 N4**

Eight Restaurant & Bar   International
Another big name establishment with a track record elsewhere – this time in Lebanon – that has transferred its success to Abu Dhabi. Style and class are two words that spring immediately to mind as you enter, and the food has all the idiosyncratic delights of the decor. From spinach-fringed gnocchi and grilled fish, to beef fillet and ribs, each dish feels like a luxurious treat, as do the wines and cocktails.
The Souk At Qaryat Al Beri Al Maqtaa **02 558 1988**
Map **1 L8**

El Sombrero   Mexican
Peachy terracotta walls, signature sombreros and live Mexican music set the scene at this lively restaurant, which comes recommended, whether you're out for a relaxed dinner for two or a raucous night with your amigos. The impeccably dressed maitre d plays an active role in servicing the tables as guests wade through the menu which offers Mexican staples. The Fiesta Platter is perfect for sharing and the house specialty, homemade guacamole, is prepared fresh at the table. Mains are a feast of Mexican-style meat and fish dishes, burritos, tacos and enchiladas.
Sheraton Abu Dhabi Hotel & Resort Markaziya East
02 6970 224
elsombreroabudhabi.com
Map **2 Q2**

Escape   International
Swimmers and beach-goers alike can find welcome refuge from the sun in this casual poolside restaurant with its full canvas canopies and multiple electric fans; the setting is ideal for a casual family dinner or a few lazy sundowners. The hearty sandwiches and healthy, original salads make Escape a great place to recharge after a hard day relaxing on the beach. Kids are welcome and there's a special menu for hungry little tummies.
Hilton Abu Dhabi Al Khubeirah **02 681 1900**
hilton.com
Map **2 C3**

Essence   Buffet
A hotel buffet can fall victim to trying to cater to everybody, but Essence manages to do a decent job of the tricky task. The food is of solid quality, the setting classy and even though it's a family-friendly

Restaurants & Cafes

restaurant, there's an unusual aura of serenity. The international buffet has something for just about anyone and some of it you get to witness being prepared at the live cooking stations.

Beach Rotana Abu Dhabi Tourist Club Area
02 697 9011
rotana.com
Map **2 S5**

Evergreen Vegetarian Restaurant
This is a traditional vegetarian Indian restaurant where the emphasis is very much on fresh, healthy ingredients. The restaurant is clean but reassuringly basic in the way that only the very best independent restaurants get away with and, true to form, the food is authenticity itself. To delight local residents, the restaurant also does takeaways.

Nr Al Safa Supermarket, Shk Zayed The Second St
Madinat Zayed **02 676 7361**
Map **2 M4**

Yas Marina Yacht Club
One of Abu Dhabi's most popular dining destinations is also one of the city's swankiest – which is saying something in this five-star city. You can sample exquisite sushi at Yotto, taste Italian treats at fine-dining Cipriani (p.375), enjoy bar food and big screen sports at Stars 'n' Bars (p.403) or sashay the night away to DJ tunes at Allure by Cipriani (p.396).

Figaro's Pizza   Italian
More a family or fast food style Italian restaurant than a venue for a romantic evening, Figaro's serves up pizza and pasta which are both fairly tasty and decent value. It's a good place to stop and carb-up before taking on a second round of shopping.

Marina Mall Breakwater **02 681 3300**
figaros.com
Map **2 D1**

Filini   Italian
This is a spacious, modern restaurant where warm beiges, creams and dark woods calm the senses; if the weather allows, the terrace is equally as peaceful a dining space. Filini is unashamedly Italian, and classic, simple and seasonal fare is served up from a menu that holds no surprises. Pizza, fish, meat or pasta are the main choices, but they're done very well, and the wine list, like the service and presentation, is excellent. The bar is also very good for a quiet chat over a deep claret tinto.

Radisson Blu Hotel, Abu Dhabi Yas Island Yas Island West **02 656 2000**
radissonblu.com
Map **1 S5**

Finz   Seafood
Sitting apart from the other Beach Rotana restaurants, Finz feels like something of a seafood pilgrimage. Finz is serious about seafood and, with several pages detailing different preparations and offerings, the place doesn't disappoint. From lobster to sea bass to huge prawns, Finz keeps you salivating. It's not cheap, but it's almost worth it for the half shell oysters alone. Attentive service and a gorgeous terrace setting (currently suffering from construction noise) can turn a Monday night into an evening fit for a holiday.

Beach Rotana Abu Dhabi Tourist Club Area
02 697 9011
rotana.com
Map **2 S5**

Fishmarket   Seafood
With the tropical island decor and the always smiley service, the Fishmarket feels a very long way from Abu Dhabi, and the food furthers that illusion. From the extensive array of fresh seafood and the cartload of fresh vegetables, noodles and rice, customers choose the style of cooking (grilled, sautéed or fried), the kind of sauce (green curry, red curry or oyster sauce), and the accompaniments. Not a place for committed meat lovers, this place concentrates on seafood and raises the bar to another level by doing so.

InterContinental Abu Dhabi Al Bateen **02 666 6888**
ichotelsgroup.com
Map **2 C4**

Foodlands Restaurant   Indian
Foodlands is a good place to go for a reasonably priced family meal. There are two separate areas, depending on whether you are dining or just fancy a quick snack, and both offer tasty Indian, Chinese, Arabic and continental cuisine, all served with a smile. Parking can be a problem, so prevent road rage on busy nights by taking a taxi. Foodlands is also open for breakfast.

Al Hamily Bldg, Shk Rashid Bin Al Maktoum St
Al Manhal **02 633 0099**
foodlands.com
Map **2 K5**

Frankie's Italian Restaurant
& Bar > p.355   Italian
Frankie Dettori's collaboration with Marco Pierre White offers world-class dining in a chic setting. Diners can feast on the freshest Italian fare, ranging from homemade pastas and wood-fired pizzas to grilled lobster. The gelatos and tiramisu are a must for dessert. Keep an eye out for midweek early bird offers on main courses and cocktails..

Fairmont Bab Al Bahr Al Maqtaa **02 654 3238**
fairmont.com
Map **1 L8**

Filini

The Garden Restaurant

Jing Asia

El Sombrero

Frankie's Italian Restaurant & Bar

The Garden Restaurant International

This lovely eatery offers an assortment of themed brunches through the week. Stylish decor, an easy atmosphere and homely charm make it a thriving favourite. The Mojito Bubbly Brunch (Dhs.160) on Fridays offers unlimited mojitos, bubbly and live music. A divine buffet, live cooking stations and an exceptional wine list accompany every meal. So whether you're into Mexican, Far Eastern, seafood, Italian, or all of these (international night), book a table and enjoy, but remember to dress on the smart side.
Crowne Plaza Abu Dhabi Markaziya East **02 616 6166**
ichotelsgroup.com
Map **2 N4**

Hakkasan Far Eastern

Since opening its doors in June 2010, this famous establishment has been a popular choice for lovers of Cantonese cooking. The restaurant's layout offers each party of diners a secluded area where they can enjoy privacy, but still observe their surroundings and the stunning interiors. The menu offers a mouthwatering choice of southern Chinese specialities and innovative creations. For those who may fear a dent to your wallet due to Hakkasan's location in Emirates Palace, fear not; whilst it is possible to spend a fortune on the a la carte menu, there are very reasonable options too – particularly the highly recommended dim sum brunch.
Emirates Palace Al Ras Al Akhdar **02 690 7999**
hakkasan.com
Map **2 B2**

Haveli Indian

This pleasantly unfussy restaurant delivers hearty Indian fare – with warm service and rock bottom prices to boot. What's on offer is a range of chicken and lamb kebabs prepared in a tandoor oven, as well as tasty curries, ranging from mild to fiery. Traditional north Indian thalis offer the chance to sample a number of curries and desserts in small portions.
Nr New Etisalat Bldg Al Dhafrah **02 632 1448**
Map **2 M6**

Hawksbill Restaurant International

It may be a golf course restaurant but Hawksbill offers much more than your average clubhouse. Named after Saadiyat's local turtle species, it welcomes non-member diners in search of a modern setting, great views, a range of reasonably priced drinks and a varied menu. It serves up everything from designer burgers to Thai dishes, but the common theme is huge portion sizes. The large terrace is great for a long weekend lunch.
Saadiyat Beach Golf Club 02 557 8000
sbgolfclub.ae
Map **1 H1**

Hoi An Vietnamese

An upmarket taste of Vietnam overlooking the shores of Al Maqta Channel. The comprehensive menu comprises traditional Vietnamese favourites and delicious originals, such as kobe steak in a rich foie gras sauce. The staff are friendly and accommodating, tailoring dishes to suit the palates of chilli lovers and loathers alike. Subtly decorated in a far eastern style indoors, the outdoor tables offer a more secluded dining experience.
Shangri-La Hotel, Qaryat Al Beri Al Maqtaa
02 509 8888
shangri-la.com
Map **1 L8**

Il Porto Italian

Il Porto is located in the Mirage Marine complex. The restaurant's stylish interior is eclipsed by its outdoor terrace with views over blue waters. On offer is an intriguing mix of contemporary Italian fare and sushi (which feels a bit odd, but just about works). Food is simple, service is fine, and dishes are mouth-watering, but this good restaurant is elevated by its location. Within the complex, a Lebanese restaurant, shisha garden and cafe also serve up treats, and Mirage Marine is fast becoming an essential (though unlicensed) hangout.
Mirage Marine Complex, Nr Marina Mall Breakwater
02 635 9957
Map **2 D2**

Hakkasan

India Palace
Indian

This unassuming restaurant features an extensive menu and is busy at lunchtimes and evenings with a mix of diners. The flavoursome, authentic dishes are generously portioned and offer good value for money. As certain dishes are pretty fiery, those with delicate palates can request milder versions. Quick, courteous waiters will patiently guide you through the menu if you are not an expert on north Indian cuisine.
Nr ADNOC, Al Salam St Tourist Club Area
02 644 8777
sfcgroup.com
Map **2 Q5**

Indigo
Indian

Offering a lighter take on Indian cuisine, with distinct Thai and Malaysian twists to some of the dishes, Indigo is popular with Indian families as well as expats. Although one of the more expensive Indian restaurants in the capital, Indigo serves high quality fare in stylish surroundings with a good atmosphere. Wooden screens separate the restaurant into private areas making it suitable for groups of all sizes as well as intimate couples. Opt for terrace dining to make the most of the view of the beach and harbour, with the lights of the ever-growing Reem Island twinkling in the distance.
Beach Rotana Abu Dhabi Tourist Club Area
02 697 9011
rotana.com
Map **2 S5**

Jing Asia
Asian Subcontinent

Contemporary and colourful on the inside, with a rejuvenating sea view from the outside, the ambience at Jing Asia is impressive either way. Attentive, friendly staff prepare fresh ingredients in the open kitchen which hosts traditional Asian cuisine, from sushi to stir fries; Friday brunch casts the net wider, even boasting a traditional roast with Yorkshire puddings. Ideal for large groups or parties, there are a variety of themed nights throughout the week.
Crowne Plaza Abu Dhabi Yas Island Yas Island West
02 656 3000
ichotelsgroup.com
Map **1 S5**

Jones The Grocer
Cafes & Coffee Shops

The Australian-based chain is a firm favourite among Abu Dhabi expats with a taste for high quality food, organic produce and rustic style ingredients. The cafe, nestled within a larger food emporium that includes a fromagerie and bakery, offers natural gourmet food sourced from around the world. It has a decidedly countryside, rural feel, with simple decor and food often served on cutting boards. Sit outside on wooden benches to soak up some sun as you enjoy a mouth-watering brunch or light lunch, and you'll soon understand the hype; the breakfast here comes particularly highly recommended and is definitely among the best in town. Jones The Grocer has four other locations throughout the city – see the website for details.
Al Mamoura Bldg B, Muroor Rd Al Dhafrah
02 443 8762
jonesthegrocer.com
Map **2 N10**

Kababs & Kurries
Indian

Located in the brand-new World Trade Center Central Market, this upscale restaurant offers, as the name suggests, both Indian and Arabic food. The selection of kababs, ranging from chicken tikka to a more adventurous shikampuri lamb, should please any meat lover while the curry selection showcases the best of the subcontinent.
World Trade Center Central Market Markaziya East
02 628 2522
Map **2 M3**

Kazu
Japanese

There are some very good restaurants in Abu Dhabi but Kazu makes the difficult leap to exceptional. The interior is nothing too spectacular – it's simple, modern and nicely lit; however the terrace, overlooking Yas Marina and the race circuit, makes for a unique backdrop to a social restaurant where sharing is the best way to sample as much of the menu as possible. Head chef Yu Cao trained under Nobu Matsuhisa but, in Kazu, it's possible that the apprentice has eclipsed his master's Dubai offering. The exceptional lightness and clarity of flavours almost defies belief; wash them down with a Japanese beer or some sake. Presentation is excellent, as is service.
Yas Viceroy Abu Dhabi Yas Island West **02 656 0600**
viceroyhotelsandresorts.com
Map **1 T5**

Kwality
Indian

If you like authentic Indian food at almost unbelievably reasonable prices, then Kwality is one of the best options in town. From north Indian tandoori dishes to Goan curries, Kwality offers the diner a wonderful culinary tour through India. Watch the chefs in the open kitchen as they prepare succulent kebabs and hot, fluffy naans, while you whet your appetite with peppery poppadoms and spicy chutneys. The food, service and welcoming atmosphere make this one of the 'must do' Indian restaurants in the capital.
Nr National Bank of Fujairah, Al Salam St Markaziya East **02 672 7337**
Map **2 Q3**

Restaurants & Cafes

L'Auberge
Middle Eastern

Although L'Auberge may have slipped down somewhat on the list of top Arabic restaurants in the city, its prime location in the heart of the business district ensures a bustling lunchtime trade. The menu covers a wide range of Lebanese specialities and European fare, and the Friday brunch is very popular. The venue is modern and spacious, albeit fairly plain, but the waiters are all friendly and very helpful. Prices veer a little towards the high side.
Shk Khalifa Bin Zayed St Markaziya East **02 627 3070**
Map **2 N3**

Central Market

Located on the site of the city's old souk, the newest destination for shopping and dining in Abu Dhabi is exquisite, with intricate wood architecture and a rooftop terrace perfect for enjoying a (non-alcoholic) drink with friends. Although the Market is still in its infancy, there are already many shops and restaurants open. Stop by Kababs & Kurries (p.379) for upscale Indian, feel Parisian at the Crepe Café, sample some of the Southern hemisphere's finest ice cream at New Zealand Natural, or get a taste of the Middle East at Tarbouche (p.394). The Central Market often holds cultural events and book fairs on weekends, so stay tuned as Abu Dhabi's newest souk finds its niche.

L'Opera Brasserie
International

At first glimpse, this restaurant may appear small, but once you're seated, it doesn't feel crowded and the small size makes for an intimate ambience. Alfresco dining next to the hotel pool is an option in cooler weather. The Friday brunch offers a good quality buffet with a wide selection of well presented international dishes. It also caters for children, with a separate mini-buffet and TV to keep the kids entertained and allowing parents the freedom to eat in peace. It has a calm, relaxed atmosphere with prompt, responsive staff. During the rest of the week, the restaurant offers an a la carte menu, and caters for breakfast, lunch and light dinners.
Le Royal Meridien Abu Dhabi Markaziya East **02 674 2020**
leroyalmeridienabudhabi.com
Map **2 P3**

La Brasserie
Buffet

This little oasis in the heart of the bustling Tourist Club area serves a good selection of buffet fare. Each night is different as the themes differ from evening to evening: Monday's Seafood affair is particularly popular due to the wide range of treats on offer – crab,

lobster and crayfish sit alongside sushi and all manner of fish dishes from near and far. Thursday nights are Meat Nights, featuring a carnivorous buffet, while Flavours of the World are on offer come Saturday. Live music completes the ambiance and when the weather is cooler, the terrace is a wonderful place for an evening of laidback alfresco dining.
Le Meridien Abu Dhabi Tourist Club Area **02 6446 666**
labrasserie-abudhabi.com
Map **2 S4**

La Mamma
Italian

This spacious, well-appointed restaurant has a homely atmosphere, which makes you immediately feel welcome. With the exception of the antipasti buffet which has a number of exotic dishes, the food is fairly standard but is well prepared and of good quality. Presentation is unfussy and leaves the food to speak for itself. The restaurant caters to a wide range of appetites, from quick and filling pizza to delicious and generous helpings of pasta and seafood. The staff are unobtrusive but attentive and quick to offer extras such as perfumed towels and freshly grated parmesan cheese. An excellent choice for an intimate romantic evening or a fun family feast.
Sheraton Abu Dhabi Hotel & Resort Markaziya East **02 6970 224**
lamammaabudhabi.com
Map **2 Q2**

La Piazza
Italian

Refreshingly free from cliched 'traditional' decor, La Piazza offers quiet respite. The menu, on the other hand, stays true to its Italian theme with a good selection of authentic starters, main dishes and desserts that are all enjoyable, good value and well presented. A popular buffet is also available.
Sands Hotel Madinat Zayed **02 615 6666**
danathotels.com
Map **2 N4**

La Terrazza
Mediterranean

The decor of this bustling, open-plan restaurant is stylish and modern, and the dazzling buffet display doubles up as decoration. There are a number of stations, each with a culinary theme, and it is easy to miss one out in your enthusiasm to pile your plate with delectable titbits. For all the quantity of food, the quality is not compromised. Resist the temptation to fill up before reaching the exquisitely presented dessert table. Busy, without being crowded, Wednesdays and Thursdays are theme nights, and on all other nights the buffet serves international cuisine.
Hilton Abu Dhabi Al Khubeirah **02 681 1900**
hilton.com
Map **2 C3**

Amici

Noodle Box

Barouk

Angar

Pachaylen

La Veranda   International

This intimate, formal dining establishment has four different reasonably priced dinner menus, plus a brunch buffet, and the excellent quality of food makes up for the somewhat limited choice. There is a tempting selection of international dishes and, if you fancy lobster, steak or prawns, each food type has its own menu, detailing the varying sauces, cooking methods and accompaniments. Reserve a table by the windows for a view of Al Khalidiya Street.
Sheraton Khalidiya Hotel Abu Dhabi Markaziya West
02 666 6220
Map **2 J4**

Le Beaujolais   French

With its red checked tablecloths and French speaking, glass clinking clientele, Le Beaujolais transports you to a charming little bistro in Paris. The menu offers a choice of traditionally prepared seafood and meat dishes, rounded off perfectly by a dessert selection which includes favourites such as creme brulee and cheese plates. A daily set menu is also available. This is one of the few places in Abu Dhabi where you can treat yourself to a cheese or meat fondue. The service, headed by a friendly maitre d', is welcoming and attentive, but never obtrusive.
Mercure Abu Dhabi Centre Hotel Markaziya East
02 633 3555
mercure.com
Map **2 M4**

Le Bistrot   French

Fans of locally-produced ingredients and elegant food with a French twist will enjoy a superb dining experience at surprisingly affordable prices in Le Meridien's central garden. Le Bistrot's decor is in keeping with the restaurant's all-natural, eco-driven theme and the tree-shaded terrace offers a great opportunity to watch the world go by. The menu is not long, but all the essentials are covered and the dishes delight with classy simplicity that lets the quality of the ingredients shine through. The only downside is the loud music played at Le Meridien's Village at the weekends.
Le Meridien Abu Dhabi Tourist Club Area
02 644 6666
lebistroabudhabi.com
Map **2 S4**

Le Shaderwan   Middle Eastern

Le Shaderwan is one of the few Arabic restaurants that are neither high-end hotel nor chaotic cafe. The atmosphere is almost cave-like and the menu, which features informative images of the dishes, has all the traditional Arabic staples covered. Prices are reasonable, portions generous, and the food served promptly. The restaurant is also a popular indoor

La Mamma

shisha spot for those seeking tranquillity amid the hustle and bustle of Tourist Club.
Nr Kia Showroom, Al Salam St Tourist Club Area
02 645 5400
Map **2 Q4**

Le Vendôme Brasserie   International

If you are a fan of luxurious opulence and sampling cuisines from all around the world in one sitting, then Le Vendôme is your kind of place. This all-day restaurant offers a wonderful buffet and, if weather permits, you can choose to sit outside on the beautiful terrace. Alternatively, you can enjoy the stunning decor inside the restaurant, where tables are laid out under gothic-inspired archways. In a happy departure from the norm at buffet restaurants, the tables at Le Vendôme are set well apart from each other, so you won't be knocking elbows with the strangers at the next table.
Emirates Palace Al Ras Al Akhdar **02 690 7999**
kempinski.com
Map **2 B2**

Lebanese Flower   Middle Eastern

The pavement location of this popular joint results in a few parking difficulties, with cars lining up outside to collect takeaway orders. Once inside the brightly lit, comfortable interior, you'll find a range of high quality grilled meats and fish accompanied by fresh Arabic bread from the nearby bakery. A selection of Middle Eastern curries and meat dishes are available at lunchtime. The service is super efficient.
Nr Shk Zayed The First & Al Nahyan Sts Al Khalidiyah
02 665 8700
Map **2 H4**

Li Beirut
Lebanese

A fine-looking, modern and elegant restaurant, bright white table clothes team with deep red chairs and dark wooden finishes. On the terrace, views over the pool provide a wow factor you may not expect – but then Li Beirut is an unexpected delight. Officially classed as a Lebanese restaurant, it'd be more accurate to describe it as a European restaurant that uses Lebanese flavours. The traditional breads and mezze and creatively reinvented as yummy starters, while the main courses are much more focused on great cuts of meat and fish prepared beautifully, with pomegranates, pistachios, aubergine and splashes of kebbeh and zaatar providing added panache. The honey fudge dessert has a reputation for being one of the city's tastiest indulgences.
Jumeirah At Etihad Towers Al Ras Al Akhdar
02 811 5666
jumeirah.com
Map **2 B3**

Marakesh
Moroccan

Despite the elaborate decor, Marakesh has a fairly casual ambience which suits business and leisure diners alike. Exotic and delectable Moroccan food (with more than a hint of Lebanese influence) is served in generous portions and delivered to your table by a team of highly efficient waiters. A live band adds atmosphere and, later in the evening, an eye-poppingly beautiful belly dancer makes a dramatic appearance. The air conditioning is rather frosty, so go prepared. Marakesh is open seven days a week for dinner only.
Millennium Hotel Abu Dhabi Markaziya East
02 614 6020
milleniumhotels.com
Map **2 P3**

Marco Pierre White Steakhouse & Grill > *p.355*
Steakhouse

If a beautifully appointed restaurant with exact yet friendly service delivering classic, hearty British comfort food, elevated to superbly delicious standards, sounds like your idea of heaven, then get yourself to Marco's Abu Dhabi restaurant. He may be a celeb chef but one bite into the foie gras or pepper sauce topped fillet and you'll know this is anything but style over substance. It's a dinner only restaurant but you'll want to spend the whole night wallowing in the wine-fuelled experience.
Fairmont Bab Al Bahr Al Maqtaa **02 654 3238**
fairmont.com
Map **1 L8**

Marroush
Middle Eastern

The multitude of cars lined up outside this Lebanese street cafe is the first thing to catch your attention – and given the somewhat grimy decor, it is not surprising that the bevy of drive-by customers choose to take their food away. However, the standard Lebanese dishes on the menu are delicious and freshly grilled, and there is the usual range of decadent fruit cocktails piled high with syrup, nuts and cream. Marroush is recommended as a cost effective venue for light meals and takeaways.
Nr Abu Dhabi Chamber of Commerce & Industry Markaziya West **02 621 4434**
Map **2 L2**

Mawal
Middle Eastern

An Arabian belly dancer and singer top the bill at Mawal, but the excellent food, colourful service and lively atmosphere are enough draw in themselves. In addition to an exhaustive range of hot and cold Lebanese mezze, there's a selection of superb kebabs

Marco Pierre White Steakhouse & Grill

grilled to perfection. If you plan to stay for the show, reservations are essential as the place really comes alive later on. The show starts at 22:30 Saturday to Wednesday and at 23:00 at weekends, and there is a minimum spend on food of Dhs. 275 (weekdays) or Dhs. 325 (weekends) per person for the show.
Hilton Abu Dhabi Al Khubeirah **02 681 1900**
hilton.com
Map **2 C3**

The Meat Co   Steakhouses
The Meat Co is a deceptively large restaurant, covering two floors plus a big outdoor deck. It's open plan to the extreme with an open kitchen, and even an open pantry and store cupboard. The energy of the kitchen spills out to the restaurant giving the place a frenetic atmosphere, which is augmented by the loud music, making it popular with large groups. When not rushed, the service has a casualness that isn't reflected in the steep prices. The meat, the best reason for coming here, is good with Wagyu sirloin, Australian and South African Grade A, and US Black Angus beef on offer.
The Souk At Qaryat Al Beri Al Maqtaa **02 558 1713**
themeatco.com
Map **1 L8**

Mezlai   Emirati
Appropriate for a restaurant which prides itself on being the UAE's first Emirati restaurant, Mezlai's Arabic-themed decor features majlis corners and memorabilia from the country's early days while stained glass lanterns cast an atmospheric spell. The food relies on traditional staples – rice, meat and fish – with a sprinkling of regional influences from across the Middle East. True to the UAE's culinary traditions, there's a definite emphasis on seafood and you'll get to sample specialities like Weld-Al Walad – a shark soup – and grilled Gulf hammour, while carnivores are treated to camel meat and Lamb Medfoun. The restaurant's Emirati chef (see p.364) is also touted as a regional first.
Emirates Palace Al Ras Al Akhdar **02 6907 999**
kempinski.com
Map **2 B2**

Mezzaluna   Italian
From the moment the complimentary breads and olives are placed in front of you, until the time you devour the last crumb of your wicked (but wonderful) dessert, your experience at Mezzaluna will be heavenly. The Italian head chef uses divine inspiration to create a host of beautifully presented dishes that include fresh pasta concoctions, seafood creations and meat dishes, many of which are surprisingly easy on the pocket. Whether seated out on the covered terrace or indoors, the stunning decor set beneath church-like arches creates an opulent atmosphere that you'll want

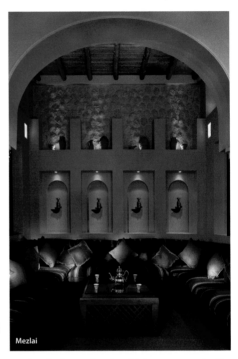

Mezlai

to return to time and again – this is a rare opportunity to experience food and service of regal standards, without having to pay a king's ransom.
Emirates Palace Al Ras Al Akhdar **02 690 7999**
kempinski.com
Map **2 B2**

Mirabel   International
Located in the Marks & Spencer building, Mirabel stands out from the standard shopping mall cafes; the menu encompasses delicious breakfast, lunch and dinner options made of fresh ingredients by the European-led kitchen crew – and if you can't leave the office for lunch, the online automated ordering system will see a warm delicious meal delivered without the usual hassle of location explanation.
Fotouh Al Khair Centre Markaziya East **02 631 5111**
mirabel.ae
Map **2 L4**

Mirage Marine Cafe   Middle Eastern
A favourite among locals, this large Lebanese restaurant-cafe features a main restaurant, a covered shisha bar and an outdoor garden. Very popular for shisha and coffees, the mezze and mixed grills are also all well above par.
Mirage Marine Complex Breakwater **02 635 9957**
Map **2 D2**

Nautilus — Seafood

Nautilus may lack the trademark futuristic styling of the rest of Yas Viceroy Abu Dhabi, but its theme is strong nonetheless, with waiters in blue neckerchiefs, a white and blue nautical interior and, of course, a seafood menu. It isn't cheap (especially with the 16% tax on top) but the food is excellent, and the terrace view of Yas Marina is magical. The set menu (Dhs.1,000 for two with a bottle of wine) is a good choice, offering high-end fish and seafood dishes, and desserts to die for. Everything comes in perfect proportions, and the splendid amuse-bouches set the scene for the extravaganza that follows.
Yas Viceroy Abu Dhabi Yas Island West **02 656 0600**
viceroyhotelsandresorts.com
Map **1 T5**

Nihal Restaurant — Indian

This well-established restaurant offers great curries at very reasonable prices, and the menu is extensive enough to tickle just about anyone's fancy. The fragrant spices of the subcontinent are expertly blended into tasty traditional dishes, served up with the usual relishes, yoghurts and chutneys. If Indian food is not your favourite, there are also various Chinese dishes on offer. Nihal does a bustling takeaway trade, and has a well reputed outside catering service. This is cheap chow at its best.
Nr Sands Hotel, Shk Zayed The Second St Madinat Zayed **02 631 8088**
Map **2 N4**

Noodle Box — Contemporary Asian

The Noodle Box boasts a chic but calm romantic setting with an outdoor terrace overlooking Yas Marina and the F1 track. The menu is simple, but expertly designed. From signature dim sum and prawn cakes with fresh chillies and lime leaves, to wok specialties that include Singaporean black pepper crab and a tantalising Thai green chicken curry, each dish holds a myriad of flavours to tempt even the most discerning of taste buds. The well selected wine list and, particularly, the house speciality beer, Tsingtao, complement the cuisine perfectly. To top it up, the service is impeccable.
Yas Viceroy Abu Dhabi Yas Island West **02 656 0600**
viceroyhotelsandresorts.com
Map **1 T5**

The Noodle House — Chinese

Views of the Souk Qaryat Al Beri, coupled with delicately prepared oriental dishes, mean that The Noodle House is a popular choice at any time of the day. With a wide selection for vegetarians, spice lovers and healthy eaters, everyone leaves satisfied. The zen ambience and oriental music make this modern slice of Asia ideal for any type of social gathering, although it's best suited to lunch with friends and family, or dinner before a night out. The service is fast but this doesn't hinder the excellent quality of the food. Another branch in Al Wahda mall is also popular for those seeking a quick, quality meal between shops.
The Souk At Qaryat Al Beri Al Maqtaa **02 558 1699**
thenoodlehouse.com
Map **1 L8**

Ocean's Seafood Kitchen & Lounge — Seafood

African masks and heavy wicker furniture decorate this excellent restaurant. Offering a range of Indian, Thai and Malay dishes, the menu is dominated by seafood, though it does have a good selection of meat dishes, and there are a few salads. Low lighting and widely spaced tables offer a feeling of intimacy, although the tables are a little large for two people. There are special promotions and occasional live music. The venue also offers terrace dining in the cooler weather, as well as a private function room.
Le Royal Meridien Abu Dhabi Markaziya East **02 674 2020**
leroyalmeridienabudhabi.com
Map **2 P3**

THE One — Cafes & Coffee Shops

Located inside the eponymous furniture store in Khalidiya, THE One cafe is a great place to relax in the middle of a shopping adventure. Not surprisingly, given the location, the cafe is strikingly decorated, and the menu, though not extensive, offers both traditional and more inventive cuisine, as well as delicious desserts.
Khalidiya Theatre & Restaurant, Shk Zayed The First St Al Khalidiyah **02 681 6500**
theoneme.com
Map **2 G4**

Gourmet Abu Dhabi

Abu Dhabi gastrophiles should look forward to the month of February as that's when Gourmet Abu Dhabi hits the kitchens of the capital. Organised by Abu Dhabi Tourism Authority, Gourmet Abu Dhabi is a 10 day culinary tour-de-force that sees Michelin-starred and celebrity chefs from all over the world showcase their skills, and discuss their art, at several of Abu Dhabi's biggest hotels. See gourmetabudhabi.ae for more info.

Origins — International

The most striking feature of Origins is the amazing view of the Yas Marina Circuit (and some pretty swanky boats). The international buffet is well spread out and presented, with loads of time honoured favourites from around the world. The salad and dessert bars stand out, offering an excellent selection

of fresh, quality produce, and tempting sweet treats. Come the weekend, brunch deals are offered.
Yas Viceroy Abu Dhabi Yas Island West **02 656 0600**
viceroyhotelsandresorts.com
Map **1 T5**

Oro
Italian

Billed as 'signature Italian', Oro is all about the meats, fish and fresh ingredients that Italy is famous for rather than the chequered red and white tablecloth style eatery that serves up pizzas and pastas – although prices do, of course, reflect this. The restaurant is large and nicely decked out, although it does feel a little cold rather than cozy, but the staff are excellent. Recommendations for both food and wine flow readily, with a number of specialties highlighted. Steaks and well-prepared seafood are tempting, but the highlights are Oro's high-end interpretations of classic Italian fare, such as carpaccio, risotto and lasagne. There's a good tasting menu if you're not sure what to opt for, while the range of wines is impressive.
Rocco Forte Hotel Abu Dhabi Al Madina Al Riyadiya **02 617 0000**
roccofortehotelabudhabi.com
Map **1 J7**

Pachaylen
Thai

If the rest of Eastern Mangroves Hotel & Spa is a delicate balance between the Arabian and the Far Eastern, Pachaylen is a full embrace of Anantara's Thai heritage, from the all-Thai kitchen and waiting staff to the menu. You'll be hard-pressed to find a more beautifully decked-out restaurant in Abu Dhabi, or a tastier, lovelier welcome than the authentic miang kham street snack. After that, it's traditional Thai done in the tastiest way you'll find anywhere outside of Bangkok. The soft shell crab salad is the standout starter, while you should look no further than the slow-cooked Thai curries for main course. This is a long way from traditional street food and the spice isn't overdone either. The banana pancake spring rolls or sticky rice and fruit are the perfect ways to finish.
Eastern Mangroves Hotel & Spa By Anantara Al Matar **02 656 1000**
anantara.com
Map **1 H6**

The Palm
International

Ideal for families, The Palm offers a reasonably priced buffet packed with fresh, tasty salads, hot meals and desserts, with various theme nights during the week. The simple decor is clean and inviting, and large glass windows allow an abundance of light into the cheerful dining area.
Al Diar Capital Hotel Tourist Club Area **02 678 7700**
aldiarhotels.com
Map **2 R3**

Pappagallo
Italian

Pappagallo is like a little slice of Tuscan dolce vita right in the heart of Le Meridien's Culinary Village. The menu offers few culinary novelties, focusing instead on time-tested classics from the Italian kitchen. Indeed, with over a page each dedicated to pasta and pizza in the menu, it can take a while to make a decision – but if non-fussy all-Italian food in an informal trattoria-style setting is what you're after, Pappagallo fits the bill.
Le Meridien Abu Dhabi Tourist Club Area **02 644 6666**
pappagallo-abudhabi.com
Map **2 S4**

The Park Bar & Grill
Steakhouse

Spread over two levels, with an effortlessly chic speak-easy serving up cocktails, scotches, cognacs and cigars on the upper level, and a modern, classy restaurant with poolside terrace on the lower level, The Park Bar & Grill may lie 20 minutes' drive from town but is well worth the drive for an exuberant night out – this is a venue that would grace anywhere from New York to Nice. The restaurant is spacious but well laid-out and creatively-lit to create a feeling of intimacy, while there are enough design points to keep conversation flowing over dinner. Food is generally high-end bistro fare, with charcoal-grilled meats and fish at the top of the menu, although Asian flavours add a nice twist. The Wagyu tenderloin is hard to beat. Desserts too tick all the right boxes – if you're unable to decide, there's a special taster menu that delivers small tastes of the best sweet bites. Weather permitting, dining out by the pool with the sound of waves crashing in the background just about trumps the lovely interiors.
Park Hyatt Abu Dhabi Hotel & Villas Saadiyat Island **02 407 1138**
abudhabi.park.hyatt.com
Map **1 H1**

Peppino
Italian

Peppino has been around for a long time and, although this shows in the decor, the food is still good. While it offers a decent spread of standard Italian fare, Peppino is most famous for its pizza with interesting toppings; note that the wine list is no longer on offer, though. The service here is good, but takeaways and home delivery options are available, if you prefer.
Grand Continental Flamingo Hotel Markaziya East **02 690 4000**
gcfh.ae
Map **2 P3**

Poolside
> p.355 · International

Set alongside the beach and overlooking the creek, Poolside serves great food with signature cocktails and juices. Healthy dishes, such as tuna tartare with avocado, cucumber and arugula and an interesting array of salads feature alongside more calorific mains.

The gourmet burgers are delicious – choose from Atlantic lobster, chargrilled lamb loin, or The Full Monty: Australian Wagyu beef, black truffle, foie gras, caramelised onions and parmesan in a onion bun.
Fairmont Bab Al Bahr Al Maqtaa 02 654 3238
fairmont.com
Map **1 L8**

Porto Bello   Italian
Porto Bello stands out among Abu Dhabi's many Italian restaurants thanks to its first-class food, discreet service and classy setting. Whether you dine indoors or on the atmospheric terrace, you'll get to sample a good but not confusingly large choice of dishes, each of which is a lesson is flavoursome simplicity. The lasagna – overpowering bechamel is shunned in favour of layers of ricotta and mozzarella cheese – is a fine example of its attributes, as are the smoked duck risotto and osso buco Milanese.
Grand Millennium Al Wahda Al Dhafrah 02 443 9999
millenniumhotels.com
Map **2 M7**

Portofino   Italian
Although it probably won't win any awards for food quality, the menu offers nicely prepared Italian classics like pizza, pasta and tiramisu. On the plus side, portions are generous and prices are reasonable. The main draw is the pleasant location overlooking the pool, which lends itself to relaxed outdoor dining in the winter months. Shisha pipes are available, if desired.
Abu Dhabi Marina & Yacht Club Tourist Club Area
02 644 0300
Map **2 S4**

Prego's   Italian
Prego's boasts an enchanting setting with its large, airy interior and superb terrace overlooking the beach. The food is wonderful – in addition to a varied pizza bar, the menu has a selection of both classic and innovative pasta dishes, main courses and desserts, and an impressive wine selection. Pizzas are prepared in an authentic wood-fired oven. Prego's is family friendly, but it's good for an intimate dinner too.
Beach Rotana Abu Dhabi Tourist Club Area
02 697 9011
rotana.com
Map **2 S5**

Quest   Asian
Abu Dhabi is jam-packed with very good restaurants but, until recently, it has lacked something really world-class. That's a gap that Quest fills with ease and a good splash of panache. The restaurant is beautiful and elegant – all tables offer incredible views from the 63rd floor as well as being spread around the

open kitchen. But, as Abu Dhabi sparkles below, it's the service – just about perfect – and the food that captures the attention. Officially, it's Pan-Asian fare, but this is the kind of Cantonese or Malaysian food that Heston Blumenthal or Ferran Adria might serve up – deconstructed and reinterpreted, never pretentious but intriguing, fun and downright tasty. Salads appear in plant pots, foie gras comes served on spoons, soup is created at the table, popping candy 'pops up' in the desserts. For the full experience, try the tasting menu along with an accompanying selection of wines chosen by the sommelier (although it's fun to play with the iPad wine menu too). An exciting and innovative culinary experience.
Jumeirah At Etihad Towers Al Ras Al Akhdar
02 811 5666
jumeirah.com
Map **2 B3**

Rainbow Steak House   Restaurants & Cafes
This refurbished venue is definitely worth a visit. Contrary to its name, steaks are not its forte so stick to the seafood, Chinese, Indian and continental cuisine. Lunch and dinner buffets are available daily at unbelievably low prices, with friendly, efficient service.
Rainbow Hotel Apartments Markaziya East
02 632 6333
Map **2 N3**

Porto Bello

Rangoli
Indian

With a la carte options available and friendly staff, Rangoli offers a good value curry fix. The buffet, with a focus on North and South Indian cuisine, is fresh and attractive. Starters and mains include vegetable samosas and meat, fish and vegetable curries. Sweet lovers can choose from traditional desserts. Cushioned booths and a formal dining area enveloped in dark wood with flashes of bright colour, and a glass-fronted show kitchen, create a laid back atmosphere.
Yas Island Rotana Yas Island West **02 656 4000**
rotana.com
Map **1 T4**

The Restaurant
Buffet

This members-only dinner venue features an impressive entrance area, complete with a fireplace constructed of stone and wine bottles, which leads to a softly lit, Roman-style interior – the perfect setting for a romantic evening out. With theme nights every night except Saturdays and brunches on Friday and Saturday, The Restaurant offers a superb choice of tasty cuisines and culinary experiences. The prices are reasonable and there is live music on most nights.
The Club Mina Zayed Free Port **02 673 1111**
the-club.com
Map **2 V3**

Resto!
International

Warm, modern decor, the quiet hum of easy listening tunes, and friendly staff set the tone at Resto! and the international menu is equally crowd-pleasing: the buffet includes curries, sushi, grilled meats and vegetarian dishes, with the pasta bar a definite highlight – closely followed by the colourful desserts.
One To One Hotel – The Village Al Dhafrah
02 495 2000
onetoonehotels.com
Map **2 Q8**

Riviera
Italian

Riviera is a guilty pleasure courtesy of executive chef Salvatore Cozzi, who came from Naples to bring authentic Italian cooking to the heart of Abu Dhabi. From hearty homemade pasta, pizza and irresistible breads that will satisfy your carb cravings to the terraced seating that overlooks the tranquil marina, dining at Riviera is a relaxed affair that deserves ample time to savour.
Marina Al Bateen Resort Al Bateen **02 665 0144**
marinaalbateen.com
Map **2 C6**

Rodeo Grill
Steakhouse

Part old English drawing room, part old American shooting lodge, Rodeo Grill is reminiscent of a high-end Argentinean ranch. Resplendent in green leathers and deeply hued wood, it's an unashamedly masculine restaurant geared to carnivores who enjoy full-bodied reds. That said, salads, seafood and even a few veggie options make it on to the menu, but the spotlight shines firmly on the fantastic range of steak cuts, with the grade nine marble Wagyu and the bison rib eye stealing the show. Wash it all down with a pinot noir and you're in meat-lovers' heaven. Prices are certainly not cheap, but this is a truly excellent restaurant.
Beach Rotana Abu Dhabi Tourist Club Area
02 697 9011
rotana.com
Map **2 S5**

Royal Orchid
Thai

The extensive menu at this small tucked away joint allows you to break convention. It alternates between light, fragrant Thai and succulent Chinese spices – the deep fried black bean chilli chicken wings are as deliciously indulgent as they sound. Like the cooking, the decor effuses elegant Thai style with more than a hint of Chinese flair. Families are welcome, but the intimate seating is best suited to couples, small groups and business occasions. Ample portions and reasonable prices make for a satisfying experience.
Hilton Abu Dhabi Al Khubeirah **02 681 1900**
hilton.com
Map **2 C3**

Samak
Seafood

It may take an hour by seaplane to get here, but the long trek to the Desert Islands feels truly worthwhile as you dine on the pristine beach, sampling Samak restaurant's extensive seafood menu in flickering candle light. Opt for the dine-by-design concept and you'll be whisked away to a private table set out on the sand – as far as settings go, it doesn't get much more romantic. The Asian-inspired cuisine can't be faulted either: the Thai-style starters are of top calibre and when it comes to the mains, you have the option to create your very own combination of a dish.
Desert Islands Resort & Spa By Anantara Ruwais
02 801 5400
desertislands.anantara.com
Map **3 B3**

Samurai Restaurant
Japanese

There aren't too many Japanese restaurants in Abu Dhabi, and those that there are tend to veer towards the pricier end of the spectrum. If you're a devotee of sushi, maki and yakiniku, then Samurai is a special little find. The food is top draw, while the atmosphere, like the decor, is a lot of fun.
Nr Al Diar Capital Hotel, Al Meena St
Tourist Club Area **02 676 6612**
samurai.ae
Map **2 R3**

Let's Do Brunch

Brunch may have been invented in the States, given kudos in New York, and be setting itself a place mat in the hipper centres of western Europe, but in this particular Middle Eastern city, it's a hobby, a social skill, a weekend institution. It's the calorific glue that holds the weekend together.

Far from the genteel image of croissants, scrambled eggs and good coffee over the day's newspapers, brunch in Abu Dhabi is synonymous with triumphantly eating your own body weight in food and washing it down with free-flowing champagne. And all for a set price.

Having eaten and quaffed the entire day away, brunchers are renowned for then throwing themselves into misguided rampages around the city's nightspots, and suffering spirit-crushing hangovers the following morning. New arrivals are quickly asked whether they've been to a brunch yet, typically by an expat with more Abu Dhabi-years under their (loosened) belt, and a knowing glint in their eye.

So why is this gluttonous sport so popular in Abu Dhabi? This city's predominantly expat community probably has a lot to do with it. There are plenty of work-hard, play-even-harder type young revellers looking to blow off steam and mingle, so Abu Dhabi has a sociable culture to match. The fact that you boil alive if you venture outside for more than 10 minutes during at least three months of the year also helps keep people inside and ingesting at the weekends.

Whatever the reason, brunch has become quite the art form; one which diners master by flexing their (softening) stomach muscles at the masses of competitive, creative and uniquely reasonable deals available from the city's fleet of five-star hotels. Formerly purely a Friday fun-for-all, the pursuit is now spreading through the week, almost to the point where brunch becomes a round-the-clock way of living, rather than just a way of eating.

The Yacht Club

Brunch. You might think that the word is self-explanatory: a portmanteau of 'breakfast' and 'lunch' – a meal you have between the two more widely accepted dining anchors. If so, you clearly haven't lived in Abu Dhabi for very long.

If you want to throw yourself in at the deep end, head out to Viceroy Brunch at Origins. Held every Friday, Dhs.295 will buy you an extensive array of dishes to choose from and you'll get to wash it all down with unlimited house beverages – before heading to the Skylite bar for an after party; and you even have the option to stay overnight at The Yas Viceroy for a discount, should the party carry on to the point of no return.

Once you've flaunted your daytime partying prowess, you might want to prove you can keep the same pace going. In that case, head for the InterContinental's Yacht Club (p.463) where the Friday lunch runs from 12:00 to 16:00 and offers unlimited food from the menu along with more mojitos than are served during the average Havana public holiday.

Le Vendome Brasserie (p.382) offers a brunch experience with finesse. The deal at this Emirates Palace favourite epitomises Abu Dhabi's posh and pricey all-inclusive. For a princely sum, you can feed on the entire world (from Japan to Europe via India), and swig from a champagne flute all afternoon. And while at Emirates Palace, there's no better address in town for local flavour than Mezlai (p.384). A booze-fuelled fiesta it may not be, but for Dhs.280, you can tuck into Emirati delicacies from camel shawarma to grilled Gulf hammour every Friday. Prepared under the guidance of the UAE's first Emirati chef, it's a local feast, in a spectacular Emirates Palace setting to boot.

Across town, you could do worse than head out to Fairmont Bab Al Bahr's CuiScene, where Dhs.469 buys you a brunch with unlimited Moet & Chandon. Bubble lovers would be equally pleased at Left Bank (p.400), where you get to select whatever you fancy from an a la carte menu and the bubbly is free-flowing too.

Thankfully, tucking into the stuff of brunch-time legends need not mean breaking the bank. Priced at Dhs.149, C.Taste's budget option is hard to beat. In addition to the offerings of an irresistible waffle station, you'll be treated to unlimited house beverages and complimentary pool access.

Somewhere in the middle of the brunch-ometer lies a trove of average-priced bargains that take the feasting mission slightly less seriously, and are therefore ideal for a laidback meal with chums or a family outing. Assymetri's Friday Family Brunch is priced at Dhs.195 and the deal runs till 15:30 every Friday.

Talking of families, both Sevilla (p.392) and Assymetri (p.368) have fun-filled Friday family brunches with both food and entertainment aimed at kids as well as parents. Both also represent fantastic value. Sevilla costs Dhs.174, while Assymetri sneaks in at Dhs.245. Both include certain house beverages, while children are half price. Just as fun is the Friday Family Brunch at Jing Asia (p.379), where you can enjoy an extensive selection of eastern and international delicacies. And so there it is. Brunching in Abu Dhabi is as big as football in the UK, sumo wrestling in Japan and basketball in the US. So raise your fork and join in.

Restaurants & Cafes

Eat In Al Ain

It may not be a global culinary capital but find yourself in Al Ain and there are a few decent options to help ward off hunger. Danat Al Ain's (p238) Luce, The Wok and Tanjore are all excellent eateries, while Casa Romana at the Hilton Al Ain (p.238) is an Italian restaurant worth checking out. The Al Ain Rotana (p.238) also has some good restaurants, with Gardenia and Trader Vic's arguably the top picks.

Sardinia
Mediterranean

Hidden away in an area not known for its fine dining, every course at Sardinia is both an event and a work of art, served by a white-gloved, highly professional waiting team. Only the finest ingredients are used and while some of the amuse-bouches are off-the-wall, such as foie gras with chocolate and passion fruit, most are sublime mouthfuls. Opt for the 12 course 'regular' dinner accompanied by four types of wine (Dhs.750) for a sensational culinary journey. Certainly one of the best restaurants in Abu Dhabi.
Abu Dhabi Country Club Al Mushrif **02 657 7777**
adcountryclub.com
Map **2 J13**

Sayad
Seafood

As one of the key restaurants at the luxurious Emirates Palace, you can expect the ultimate high-end dining experience. This superb eatery offers a seasonal menu of fresh seafood, sourced from across the globe. The modern glass interior could look stark, but the blue-green lighting adds a touch of class and quiet charm. The wine list is extensive, offering the top eight wines from every wine-producing region in the world. You can select your own fish or lobster

from the tanks along the wall to be prepared to your taste. If the choice of so many well-designed dishes is overwhelming, simply opt for the five-course set menu for a taste of everything from sushi to the catch of the day. A sublime dining option.
Emirates Palace Al Ras Al Akhdar **02 690 7999**
kempinski.com
Map **2 B2**

Sevilla > *p.308*
International

Situated in the grand lobby of Al Raha Beach Hotel, Sevilla offers a daily dining buffet with a different theme depending on the night of the week. There is an extensive wine list and the buffet which is supplemented with a salad bar, a large selection of breads, as well as a small but tempting dessert trolley. Inside you can relax to the tinkling sounds of the harpist and outside on the terrace overlooking the pool and the gardens of the hotel, enjoy your evening under the stars.
Al Raha Beach Hotel Al Raha **02 508 0555**
danathotels.com
Map **1 R7**

Sevilo's
Italian

In the more temperate months, make use of Sevilo's poolside terrace which offers stunning views of the city and gardens. The varied yet uncomplicated menu delivers classic Italian cuisine, which is freshly prepared and generally of a high standard. Sevilo's is a pleasant, intimate and trustworthy eatery which delivers a trio of high points: good food, pleasant setting and great service, which should provide an enjoyable evening.
Millennium Hotel Abu Dhabi Markaziya East
02 614 6020
milleniumhotels.com
Map **2 P3**

Sayad

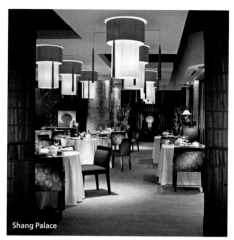

Shang Palace

the signature sushi rolls are perfectly formed and delicious, but if raw fish isn't your thing there are plenty of cooked alternatives to tempt the taste buds. The dessert menu is limited, but a great end to the meal – the green tea icecream is particularly good. Open for lunch and dinner, Soba is perfect for groups and singles, but may not be the best place for children due to the muted ambience. The open kitchen gives a view of the quiet skill of the chefs, and if the menu inspires you, Soba offers sushi-making classes on Saturdays, morning and afternoon.
Le Royal Meridien Abu Dhabi Markaziya East
02 674 2020
leroyalmeridienabudhabi.com
Map **2 P3**

Shakespeare & Co   International
Stepping into Shakespeare & Co. is a little like stepping into the book Alice In Wonderland; the shabby chic Victorian decor, with pastel colours and mismatched chairs, is delightful and instantly inspires an urge for a cup of tea and some sweets. The menu has an eclectic mix of English, American, Italian, and Arab cuisine at moderate prices. The desserts, neatly showcased in a pastry case, are decadent and – almost – too beautiful to eat.
World Trade Center Central Market Markaziya East
02 639 9626
shakespeareandco.ae
Map **2 M3**

Shang Palace   Chinese
There are so many reasons to visit Shang Palace. The extensive menu covers Cantonese and Szechuan cuisine in addition to many non-Chinese items, and seafood features prominently. The atmosphere is great, the service faultless, the staff impeccably dressed, the food superb, and the large portions offer excellent value for money. The breathtaking views from the romantic terrace are more than enough reason to come and linger for the evening in the large, solid chairs. Highly recommended, and deservedly popular, reservations for terrace dining are advised.
Shangri-La Hotel, Qaryat Al Beri Al Maqtaa
02 509 8503
shangri-la.com
Map **1 L8**

Soba   Japanese
Soba is a tranquil, comfortable, minimalist haven, where you'll find a taste of the far east and a chance to unwind. The emphasis is on fresh, good quality:

Sofra Bld   International
Any restaurant that can boast three chocolate fountains is worth a visit, and while an a la carte menu is available, it is Sofra's luxury buffet, surrounding its centrepiece of fountains, that is the restaurant's main attraction. A breathtaking selection of cuisine is offered which covers all four corners of the globe – from fresh sushi to shawarmas, kebabs and parrot fish. The light and airy interior is less suited to intimate occasions, while the outside terrace provides a perfect vantage point for viewing the neighbouring Sheikh Zayed Grand Mosque.
Shangri-La Hotel, Qaryat Al Beri Al Maqtaa
02 509 8555
shangri-la.com
Map **1 L8**

Spaccanapoli Ristorante   Italian
This Italian haunt is squarely Neapolitan and, although thoroughly modern, it has plenty of rustic features which nod to a menu that embraces the traditional quality of simple Italian fare, rather than the modern trend for fusion offerings. Treats such as baked aubergine with mozzarella, parmesan, tomato and basil get the meal off to an excellent start, and all the traditional main courses are represented. Try the veal escalope, the fresh fish or, if you're hungry, the metre-long pizza. The food is excellent, the prices reasonable and, best of all, the atmosphere is traditionally Italian.
Crowne Plaza Abu Dhabi Markaziya East
02 616 6166
ichotelsgroup.com
Map **2 N4**

T-Garden   Afternoon Tea
Tea aficionados in the capital are treated to a wide range of brews from ginger to Darjeeling and the comfortable sofas make a good spot for relaxing with a book. Should you get peckish sipping your third cup, there's a selection of finger food – choose from

a range of panini, sandwiches and Asian small eats, or satiate your sweet tooth by opting for one of the luxurious cakes on display.
One To One Hotel – The Village Al Dhafrah
02 495 2000
onetoonehotels.com
Map **2 Q8**

Taiki
Japanese

While the minimalist decor is a touch on the drab side, and the high-pitched, xylophonic zinging of the background music is clanging at times, Zen has a string of satisfied customers, including many from the Japanese expat community of Abu Dhabi. The secret of this success is simple: the food is authentic, delicious and fresh. Whether you choose the sophisticated sushi or the dishes served at the teppanyaki bar, you'll quickly forgive the shortcomings of the decor thanks to the simplicity and subtlety of the flavours on offer.
Al Ain Palace Hotel Markaziya East **02 679 4777**
alainpalacehotel.com
Map **2 P3**

Talay
Seafood

This Thai restaurant's strongest point is the freshness of the food on offer: choose from a wide display of seafood (with live lobsters), and have it prepared to your personal tastes – the Chu Chee prawns are a particular treat. Alternatively, the a la carte menu offers a good range of starters, seafood, meat, rice and noodle dishes – all flavoured to suit individual palates. The typically Thai service is attentive but not intrusive and, despite the range of wine and drinks on offer, this restaurant is more on the quiet side, making it a good choice for an intimate occasion – sip cocktails as you watch the daylight fade away over a quiet beach, then tuck into tasty aquatic treats.
Le Meridien Abu Dhabi Tourist Club Area
02 644 6666
talayabudhabi.com
Map **2 S4**

Tarbouche
Middle Eastern

The ground floor location offers views of the new souk, but it's the roof terrace where Tarbouche excels: alive and buzzing with people drinking fruit cocktails and enjoying shishas, it's fast becoming one of the most popular lounges in the city. Comfortable sofas and chairs are arranged in groups to allow you and your friends to socialise while taking in the downtown view. Both food and drinks are available and service is efficient, though expect to pay slightly higher prices than average.
World Trade Center Central Market Markaziya East
02 626 0700
Map **2 M3**

Teatro
Fusion

An eclectic mix of Venetian masks, crystal beads, thick white candles and modern furniture creates a dramatic, but informal, atmosphere at Teatro, which is echoed by a huge show kitchen that hides nothing. Choose from an impressive and extensive a la carte menu, which covers a spectrum of east to west fine dining cuisine with many favourites available. For special occasions, you can book the exclusive chef's table which can seat up to eight people. Service is impeccable, with nothing too much trouble. Teatro is fast becoming a firm favourite.
Park Rotana Abu Dhabi Al Matar **02 657 3333**
rotana.com
Map **1 K7**

Toshi
Asian

'Fusion' is sometimes shorthand for a restaurant with an identity crisis but when it's done well – as it is here at Toshi – it gives you access to a wide-ranging and delicious menu. The restaurant delivers a good range of Japanese, Chinese and Thai dishes, but it's the teppanyaki that steals the show – try black tiger prawns, Canadian lobster or jumbo scallop: light, healthy and delicious.
Grand Millennium Al Wahda Al Dhafrah **02 443 9999**
millenniumhotels.com
Map **2 M7**

Trader Vic's
Polynesian

A tropical retreat serving fusion cuisine from Polynesia alongside the chain's legendary cocktail menu, of course. Live Cuban and Latin music complete the picture and the lively atmosphere draws in the crowds most days of the week. The menu ranges from finger food to tasty treats from the Wood Fire Oven selection.
Beach Rotana Abu Dhabi Tourist Club Area
02 697 9011
tradervics.com
Map **2 S5**

Ushna
Indian

Ushna's sophisticated surroundings perfectly complement the beautifully prepared food. The service mirrors the superb setting and there's a good selection of traditional North Indian dishes to choose from, as well as a large range of premium wines and cocktails. During the cooler months, bag a table by the water overlooking the Grand Mosque.
The Souk At Qaryat Al Beri Al Maqtaa **02 558 1769**
Map **1 L8**

Vasco's
Portuguese

A contemporary, fine-dining venue that serves up a fusion of European, Arabic and Asian cuisines. Food is prepared to a very high standard, imaginatively presented, and delivered to your table by friendly,

knowledgeable waiters. As one of the more popular restaurants in the capital, reservations are essential for lunch and dinner. The patio offers a pleasant setting.
Hilton Abu Dhabi Al Khubeirah **02 681 1900**
hilton.com
Map **2 C3**

The Village Club
International
Situated in a garden with huge, shady trees, this is a great place to linger over a leisurely lunch or a relaxed supper. Buffet starters include soup, mezze and salads; the BBQ offers a variety of meat, fish and side dishes. Weekends are good for families.
One To One Hotel – The Village Al Dhafrah
02 495 2000
onetoonehotels.com
Map **2 Q8**

The Vista
International
A great outdoor venue with one of the best views in Abu Dhabi. Steaks, tapas, grills and seafood dominate the menu; best of all may be the Wagyu tenderloin and Omani lobster. The reasonable prices make it a regular hangout for club members and their families.
The Club Mina Zayed Free Port **02 673 1111**
the-club.com
Map **2 V3**

Waves
Far Eastern
This relaxed beachfront joint caters to fans of pan-Asian cuisine. The menu offers a fusion of Far Eastern flavours from Peking Duck to tempura and kim-chi. Open for members and their guests, the alfresco setting makes for a tranquil evening out.
The Club Mina Zayed Free Port **02 673 1111**
the-club.com
Map **2 V3**

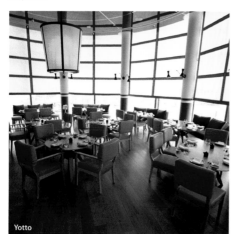

Yotto

Wokcano
Far Eastern
This friendly joint with creative flair offers a taste of Asia: the glossary at the back of the extensive Pan-Asian menu guides your decision between a range of sushi, dim sum and a host of innovative specialities as you dine in the beautifully presented setting.
One To One Hotel – The Village Al Dhafrah
02 495 2000
onetoonehotels.com
Map **2 Q8**

Yotto
Japanese
This bright and minimalist restaurant, located in Yas Yacht Club, features a pleasing fusion of nautical and Japanese design. Japanese classics from sushi to noodles and tempura grace the menu; the signature Alaskan black cod with sweet miso glaze merits a return visit – and is often sold out at the weekends. End your meal with the pastel mocha: sweet and chewy bites of pounded rice moulded around ice cream. Though dinner for two, at upwards of Dhs.700, does not come cheaply, it is difficult to find a more memorable Japanese meal in the capital.
Yas Yacht Club Yas Island **02 657 5400**
cipriani.com
Map **1 T5**

Zari Zardozi
Indian
The theme of Indian opulence, silk and spice is clearly reflected in Zari Zardozi with its rich red walls, copper ceiling and fragrant incense. Intimate seating arrangements add to the exotic mood and accompany the north and south Indian menu – which is extensive to say the least. The chef and staff will happily come to your table and discuss your preferences for spicy culinary treats. Other options include fusion food, a diet menu and 'tandushi' – which combines tandoori cooking with sushi.
Al Raha Mall Al Raha **02 556 5188**
zarizardozi.com
Map **1 R7**

Zest
Cafes & Coffee Shops
With a light, zesty twist throughout the menu, this bistro style eatery offers an array of light, healthy snacks and fillers. Delectable soups, salads and sandwiches appeal, with the roasted corn and pumpkin soup and the chicken and mango Thai style salad recommended. Situated in the fitness centre of The Club, Zest also provides pump for the pros with a range of Myoplex infused smoothies, and low carb and high protein alternatives. For the not so health conscious, there is a selection of well earned afters to indulge in.
The Club Mina Zayed Free Port **02 673 1111**
the-club.com
Map **2 V3**

BARS, PUBS & CLUBS

Allure By Capriani · Nightclubs

High-end nightclubs can be synonymous with a pretentious crowd too beautiful to dance, but Allure, even while offering Dhs.68,000 bottles of champagne, strikes a fine balance and does a decent job in its attempt to create a club scene reminiscent of Ibiza. Stunning all-white decor, top DJs and monthly theme nights attract a crowd looking to genuinely have a good time while moving to pulsating beats.
Yas Yacht Club Yas Island **050 596 9543**
nightcluballure.com
Map **1 T5**

Ally Pally Corner · Sports Bars

A bit of an expat institution, the goal is a British style boozer and the execution is almost perfect. Beers, wines and spirits run freely, while the food is hearty and, in most cases, served with chips. Sport is shown on large screens, and there's a pool table and darts.
Al Ain Palace Hotel Markaziya East **02 679 4777**
alainpalacehotel.com
Map **2 P3**

The Beachcomber · Bars

This chilled-out beach bar feels more Caribbean than UAE. Popular with after-work and weekend crowds, it serves up a tapas menu that, while not truly Spanish, ideally accompanies the cocktails and shisha that are both also must-tries. Beachcombers is closed during the warmest summer months.
Sheraton Abu Dhabi Hotel & Resort Markaziya East **02 677 3333**
sheraton.com
Map **2 Q2**

Belgian Beer Cafe · Belgian

A lively, European-style café setting with lots of noise and hearty laughter coming from the bar. The specialty is steamed mussels – what else, this being a Belgian joint – and you'll get to sample the Belgian classic dish cooked with broths ranging from curry to white wine and tarragon. The restaurant boasts some of the best fries in the city, as well as pork cooked in a number of ways. Other alternatives include steaks, chicken and vegetarian selections, all of which makes for an escape into Belgian vibes, if only for a few hours. The extensive choice of beers makes this a favourite hangout among expats.
InterContinental Abu Dhabi Al Bateen **02 666 6888**
ichotelsgroup.com
Map **2 C4**

Black Pearl > p.308 · Bars

An excellent choice for a super sophisticated evening out. The bar has a small but varied menu of mostly

Allure By Cipriani

light meals and, while the food served up here is delicious, it is definitely more a bar than a restaurant. Black Pearl is a great choice for pre-dinner drinks or as a stop-off during an evening out. The comfortable leather couches provide intimacy, while stools grouped around the bar are ripe for those who want to mix and mingle. Black Pearl also has a small selection of cigars on offer.
Al Raha Beach Hotel Al Raha **02 508 0555**
danathotels.com
Map **1 R7**

Brauhaus · German

This cosy pub features all things German in a setting almost authentic enough to make you forget you are in Abu Dhabi. Dark wood panelling and hunting gear mounted on the walls give this establishment a feel of a remote lodge and European sports is shown on the many TV screens. The menu offers hearty German fare including pretzel dumplings with a ragout of forest mushrooms; pork knuckle with sauerkraut and mashed potato; as well as five types of German sausages – with all the trimmings. The signature apple strudel with vanilla sauce and cinnamon ice cream is the perfect finish if you can fit it in.
Beach Rotana Abu Dhabi Tourist Club Area **02 6979 011**
rotana.com
Map **2 S5**

Bravo – Spanish Tapas Bar & Restaurant · Bars

An intimate setting with lovely decor, Bravo makes for a great place for a date or simply catching up with a friend. While chatting away and sipping on a fruity glass of Iberian tinto or refreshingly cold Estrella beer, you'd do well to dive into the exceptional tapas menu,

whioch features the usual Spanish treats.
Sheraton Abu Dhabi Hotel & Resort Markaziya East
02 6770 224
bravoabudhabi.com
Map **2 Q2**

Captain's Arms
Bars

Located in the Village Courtyard and overlooking the gardens, this tavern has a cosy interior and upbeat, outdoor terrace. It offers a traditional British pub ambience and, by and large, Abu Dhabi's expat scene soaks it up. The daily happy hour (17:00 to 19:00), nightly entertainment and food and drink specials bring in those crowds and, although you won't find many culinary surprises, food portions are generous and satisfying. The service could be better, but it is the value for money on drink specials that appeals.
Le Meridien Abu Dhabi Tourist Club Area **02 644 6666**
captainsarms-abudhabi.com
Map **2 S4**

Sporting Life

The glitz and glamour of the A-lister bars is all very well, but sometimes you just want a joint where you can catch the big match and enjoy a pint with your mates. Unfortunately, Abu Dhabi is a little lacking when it comes to out-and-out sports bars (try Heroes p.400, or NRG p.401) but there are plenty of other bars where the screens are big and the beers are cold. Harvester's (02 615 6666) and The Captain's Arms (above) are popular options, while Cooper's (p.398) is a good venue for those living at the other end or off the island.

Chill Out Lounge
Bars

The unrivalled views from the top floor location make Chill Out Lounge a perfect spot to while away the hours over drinks and shisha. The in-house band provides cool tunes to relax to while the attentive staff make sure you won't run out of anything while watching the sun go down. Whether you turn up solo to wind down, or with friends to chill out, you'll be soaking up some of the best vistas in town.
Grand Millennium Al Wahda Al Dhafrah **02 443 9999**
millenniumhotels.com
Map **2 M7**

Cinnabar
Nightclubs

With an eclectic mix of RnB and popular funk, Cinnabar offers a stylish way to round off your night. From the rich ruby drapes to the minimalist sofas and candlelit tables, it is more sophisticated than most Abu Dhabi nightspots. Guests can either strut their stuff on the dancefloor or simply sit back, relax and let one of the waitresses guide them through the cocktail menu. The champagne and fresh strawberry cocktails

slip down very easily but, don't fear, the Dhs.100 price tag will keep your excesses in check and sore heads at bay. Quiet on weeknights, the club comes alive after midnight at weekends when the party set let their hair down. It is also the venue for weekly salsa nights.
Hilton Abu Dhabi Al Khubeirah **02 681 1900**
hilton.com
Map **2 C3**

Cloud Nine – Cigar & Champagne Bar
Cigar Bars

If a refined evening of cognac, caviar and the finest cigars appeals to you, Cloud Nine is a place you'll want to call home. From the first puff on your hand-picked Cohiba, Monte Cristo or Bolivar (delivered to you on a silver platter, of course), to the last taste of Beluga, this venue exudes a pleasing mix of old boys' club charm and trendy sophistication. Service is pleasant and discreet, and a pianist adds further elegance to a classy (if a bit smoky) evening out. Try the 'Sheraton Social Hour' between 19:00 and 20:00 on Monday, Wednesday and Saturday, when the hotel wine expert serves up special, assorted wines that cost just Dhs.25 a glass.
Sheraton Abu Dhabi Hotel & Resort Markaziya East
02 677 3333
sheratonabudhabihotel.com
Map **2 Q2**

The Club Bar
Bars, Pubs & Clubs

A lively members' bar, with an extensive drinks menu and a great range of pub food at attractive prices. It shows major sporting events and there's a weekly quiz night on Wednesdays. The Club's Sports Bar is similar and is also an excellent, laidback venue.
The Club Mina Zayed Free Port **02 673 1111**
the-club.com
Map **2 V3**

Cinnabar

Going Out

Colosseum — Nightclubs

Visit this Roman-style nightclub any night of the week to rub shoulders with the young and hip on the snug, yet pumping, dancefloor. Tuesday is Arabic night, while the rest of the week sees a live band and decent DJs belting out the latest RnB and pop beats, making this multi-cultural venue one of the city's favourite hotspots. Entrance is Dhs.100 (which includes three free drinks). As an added bonus, drinks are reasonably priced and ladies get in free.

Abu Dhabi Marina & Yacht Club Tourist Club Area
02 644 0300
Map **2 S4**

Cooper's Bar & Restaurant — Pubs

Coopers draws in the football fans: not only can you find a friendly pint and some superb pub grub, the pub also shows all major football matches (call ahead for details), is convenient for both on-island and off-island clientele and boasts competitive prices with 50% off selected beverages during its extended 'happy hour'. It can entertain a large number of drinkers and diners with its spacious interior and additional seating outside, making it a handy location for informal social gatherings.

Park Rotana Abu Dhabi Al Matar **02 657 3333**
rotana.com
Map **1 K7**

Cristal — Cigar Bars

Experience the tranquil but trendy ambience of this bar, where elegantly understated decor is set off perfectly by an excellent range of champagne, sparkling wine and other tipples. The bar manager will help you select the perfect drink while you sit back and relax in surroundings of polished wood, leather and subdued lighting – the tinkling tunes played by the in-house classical jazz pianist are the perfect accompaniment. 17:00 to 19:00 is happy hour.

Millennium Hotel Abu Dhabi Markaziya East
02 6146 020
millenniumhotels.ae
Map **2 P3**

Dock Side Pool Bar — Bars

After a hectic week, relaxing by the water with a drink in hand is just what the doctor ordered. Dock Side Pool Bar, at Marina Al Bateen Resort, is the ideal place to kick back with friends or get the family together for a casual meal overlooking the marina. Dine alfresco on home-made baguettes, hearty kebabs and steaks, or just watch the sun go down with a drink from the licensed bar with a shisha pipe at your side. Open from 11:00 until late.

Marina Al Bateen Resort Al Bateen **055 871 8644**
marinaalbateen.com
Map **2 C6**

Etoiles — International

It's hard to decide whether this is a lounge bar, restaurant or nightclub, such is the venue's success at walking a delicate line between all three. The food is tasty European haute cuisine, while the decor is Paris, New York or Milan chic turned all the way up to 11. A backdrop of loud house music may be a little bizarre as you finish your meal, but as the evening gets later and the venue hits full on club mode, Etoiles stands out as one of the UAE's very best. It's where the A-listers party when they're in town, which pretty much says it all.

Emirates Palace Al Ras Al Akhdar **02 690 8960**
etoilesuae.com
Map **2 B2**

G Club — Nightclubs

G Club, previously known as Gauloises, may be a nightclub that is a little past its peak, but its drink promotions and prime location seem to keep it hopping along. The dancefloor is vastly under-used, thanks in part to the rather lacklustre DJ.

Le Meridien Abu Dhabi Tourist Club Area
02 644 6666
lemeridienabudhabi.com
Map **2 S4**

— Al Ain Watering Holes —

Wetting your whistle in the oasis city of Al Ain is a generally quiet but enjoyable affair, with the Horse & Jockey (03 704 6000) offering the most authentic pub ambiance in town – come the weekend, the atmosphere can get pretty lively too. Across town is Paco's (03 768 6666), part bar part Mexican cantina and an equally popular haunt among local expats. And that's not even mentioning the ever reliable Trader Vic's (03 754 5111) where the cocktails are so strong they should come with health warnings, and the live entertainment is just as addictive.

Havana Club — Bars

In keeping with the grandeur and opulence of the hotel, the Havana Club exudes sumptuousness and luxury. The delicious lingering scent of fine cigars and cigarillos entices from the moment you set foot in this old boys' bar. The club itself has a split personality, with the rowdy bar area having a younger, more outgoing spirit, while the leather armchairs in the back recess are the epitome of refinement. Relax and enjoy the imaginatively mixed and decorated exotic cocktails or sample one of the many vintage brandies and other spirits – or even test-smoke the cigars and cigarillos.

Emirates Palace Al Ras Al Akhdar **02 690 7999**
kempinski.com
Map **2 B2**

NRG Sports Café

Cloud Nine – Cigar & Champagne Bar

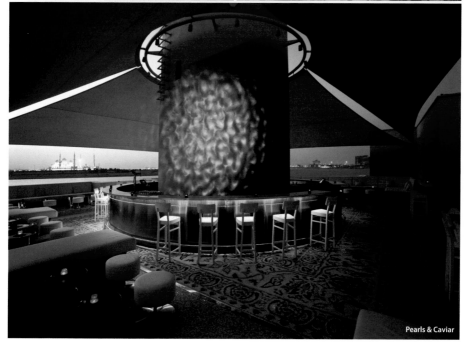

Pearls & Caviar

Bars, Pubs & Clubs

Hemingway's
Pubs

Tucked away at the back of the Hilton hotel, this lively bar-restaurant offers an unpretentious all-in-one experience. The restaurant area serves the standard Mexican fare and it opens out onto a bar (which can get quite raucous at the weekends) with TV screens and live music, making Hemingway's more of a fun venue than one for an intimate rendezvous. There are regular ladies' nights and quiz nights.
Hilton Abu Dhabi Al Khubeirah **02 681 1900**
hilton.com
Map **2 C3**

Heroes
American

Heroes is your typical sports bar early in the evening and during weekend afternoons. However, once the DJ begins at 21:00, followed by the band at 22:00, don't bother trying to watch TV – the lively, good-natured crowd will be more interested in throwing shapes on the dancefloor. The pub grub is plentiful and well-priced, with mains around Dhs.60. Arrive early if you plan to eat – seats are hard to come by once things kick off. Monday is quiz night and Tuesday is ladies' night. Parking around the hotel is nightmarish so use the underground carpark next to the Crowne Plaza or take a cab.
Crowne Plaza Abu Dhabi Markaziya East
02 616 6166
ichotelsgroup.com
Map **2 N4**

Hickory's Sports Bar
Sports Bars

A cosy club restaurant with sensational views over the lake and golf course, Hickory's is a sports bar, but that title doesn't really do it justice. Sure, major sporting events and news adorn the large plasma screens, but the feel is of a private members' club; the robust menu

of wood-fired pizzas, huge pies and steaks is also a cut above. For something different, try the tasty tapas-style snacks on the terrace.
Yas Links Abu Dhabi Yas Island West **02 810 7710**
yaslinks.com
Map **1 T4**

Illusions
Bars

One of Abu Dhabi's best known nightspots, Illusions plays loud, banging dance music in a futuristic venue. The crowd tends to be fairly male dominated and it's not the place to go if you're after a cosy chat with friends. Saturday and Monday are ladies' nights.
Le Royal Meridien Abu Dhabi Markaziya East
02 674 2020
leroyalmeridienabudhabi.com
Map **2 P3**

The Jazz Bar & Dining
Jazz Bars

Small tables and hug-around chairs allow you to rub elbows with neighbours also enjoying the music at this stylish but laidback nightspot. The select menu offers elite bites, including oysters and foie gras, and is priced to match, while dishes in the dining area are more conducive to larger and less exclusive appetites. The floor staff keep the unique, jazz-themed cocktails flowing and the live band entertains with cover versions; although there's no official dance floor, at weekends, wherever there's floor there's dancing.
Hilton Abu Dhabi Al Khubeirah **02 681 1900**
hilton.com
Map **2 C3**

Left Bank
Bars

With views of Sheikh Zayed Grand Mosque, and chic contemporary European cuisine, Left Bank has a lot to offer. The terrace bears Arabic influences, while the

Left Bank

interior echoes any exclusive London venue, complete with VIP section and inexhaustible cocktail menu. The combination of excellent food, friendly staff and stylish surroundings has earned Left Bank a good reputation among the expat community, so visitors are advised to book ahead.
The Souk At Qaryat Al Beri Al Maqtaa **02 558 1680**
emiratesleisureretail.com
Map **1 L8**

Lemon & Lime
Bars, Pubs & Clubs

An extremely elegant wine and cigar bar, Lemon & Lime is the kind of lace you can pop to after work, start your night at, or just spend the whole evening soaking up the chic atmosphere. The decor is contemporary luxury, although the amazing golf course views dominate. There are some delicious snacks available, and the variety of wines on offer is exceptional. Fans of fine vintages should keep their eye out for both the weekly offers and the one-off special nights, which provide real value for money.
The Westin Abu Dhabi Golf Resort & Spa
Sas Al Nakhl Island **02 616 9999**
westinabudhabigolfresort.com
Map **1 N8**

Level Lounge
Bars

High above Hamdan Street, Level Lounge serves up mellow tunes and tasty tapas in a cosy, chilled-out rooftop setting. Wild risotto balls and braised calamari will take the edge off your appetite and, without a roof to obstruct the view, you can hunt for stars or just enjoy the twinkling city lights. Cooling off in the swimming pool next to the bar is an option on Friday afternoons, otherwise, Level Lounge is open nightly from 19:00. Check it out on Thursday and Friday nights when a DJ drops by to spin some tunes.
Crowne Plaza Abu Dhabi Markaziya East **02 616 6166**
ichotelsgroup.com
Map **2 N4**

Mai Cafe > *p.iv*
Bars, Pubs & Clubs

A poolside restaurant-cum-lounge bar, ideal for spending hours draped over retro lounge chairs with drinks and shisha for company. Alternatively, move to the poolside tables and choose from the many Arabic and international dishes that adorn the menu. On Thursday evenings, get down early to make the most of the all-you-can-eat BBQ which includes unlimited house drinks.
Aloft Abu Dhabi Al Safarat **02 654 5111**
aloftabudhabi.com
Map **1 H8**

Mood Indigo
Pubs

With its colonial furnishings and live music, which is courtesy of the resident pianist and band, this is a

sophisticated hangout. A snack menu of sandwiches, burgers and light bites is available as you prop up the very long, custom-made bar. This all-day bar stays open later than most other outlets at the hotel, closing at 02:00.
Mercure Abu Dhabi Centre Hotel Markaziya East **02 633 3555**
mercure.com
Map **2 M4**

NRG Sports Cafe
International

Armchair athletes of all sporting preferences flock to this sports cafe, with its multitude of TV screens, reasonably priced snacks and happy hour that lasts from 19:00 to 21:00. Decorated in sporting colours and paraphernalia, it combines an arena ambience with an open kitchen that pumps out fast and furious fusion food; NRG is a great spot to catch your favourite game live on TV. You can try out your best moves on the dancefloor or, better still, keep your eyes glued to the score line.
Le Meridien Abu Dhabi Tourist Club Area **02 644 6666**
nrg-sportscafe.com
Map **2 S4**

Opus Bar
Bars

This elegant bar is the kind of place you might take your boss for an after-work drink – with its comfy chairs and civilised noise levels, you'll be able to discreetly demand that promotion without having to shout over the music. The food is the usual pub fare (think Arabic mezze, chicken fingers, burgers and sandwiches), and it is served up in a more refined setting than your usual local.
Le Meridien Abu Dhabi Tourist Club Area **02 644 6666**
lemeridienabudhabi.com
Map **2 S4**

Pearls & Caviar
Mediterranean

Inside, this popular venue is a sleek world of black, white and chrome. Downstairs, you can enjoy Mediterranean-Levantine culinary treats in a soothingly dark decor (Caviar), while the airy rooftop lounge (Pearls) serves cocktails and tapas to the backdrop of the white marble of Sheikh Zayed Mosque. As you might expect, three types of caviar are on offer: Beluga, Sevruga and Oscietra. Prices and service reflect the luxury and, while dinner for two will set you back around Dhs.1,200, this has not dimmed the restaurant's popularity. Expect a lively Lebanese and Emirati contingent on Fridays.
Shangri-La Hotel, Qaryat Al Beri Al Maqtaa **02 509 8777**
pearlsandcaviar.com
Map **1 L8**

Bars, Pubs & Clubs

PJ O'Reilly's · Pubs

One of Abu Dhabi's most popular pubs, with a friendly atmosphere. The menu is bar grub with flair – large portions prove good value for money. There's a lively bar downstairs, but you can escape to the quieter upstairs or outdoor areas. Bright and comfortable, it seldom feels crowded, despite its popularity. Large screen TVs show sport, though the sound is generally only on during live matches. Happy hour runs from 12:00 to 19:00 every day.
Le Royal Meridien Abu Dhabi Markaziya East
02 674 2020
leroyalmeridienabudhabi.com
Map **2 P3**

Relax@12 > p.iv · Bars, Pubs & Clubs

The name says it all – chill out in the sleek lounge, nibble on some Asian bites and down a cocktail or two as you sink into one of the inviting sofas on the terrace overlooking Abu Dhabi's gorgeous skyline. The decor is modern with glowing bars, dim lighting and angular furniture, and both the terrace and huge-windowed bar attract a refreshingly broad mix of clientele. The view alone is worth a visit, but the extensive menu of beer, wine and cocktails, along with sushi and Japanese snacks, makes this a perfect spot for a night out.
Aloft Abu Dhabi Al Safarat **02 6545 183**
relaxat12.com
Map **1 H8**

Rock Bottom Cafe · American Bars

This vibrant American diner has a split personality – go early in the evening to enjoy a quiet dinner, or hang around until later when the live music starts and the pace becomes frenetic. The menu features succulent steaks, sizzling seafood and innovative salads, as well as a range of lighter snacks. Quality food and value for money are distinct characteristics. The daily happy hour extends until 21:00.
Al Diar Capital Hotel Tourist Club Area **02 678 7700**
aldiarhotels.com
Map **2 R3**

Rush · Bars, Pubs & Clubs

The sort of swanky and effortlessly elegant lounge bar you'd expect from the people behind the global Buddha Bar chain. It still hasn't quite hit its stride and is not always as busy as the bar and setting merit, but Rush is still a great place for afterwork cocktails, an early stop or a chilled-out but classy night out. The cocktails are excellent, and there's some top quality finger food on the menu too.
Yas Viceroy Abu Dhabi Yas Island West **02 656 0600**
viceroyhotelsandresorts.com
Map **1 T5**

Rush

SAX · Jazz Bars

Loved by the chic set for its vibrant and trendy NYC style. Staff are welcoming and remain so throughout the evening. A live jazz band and a well-stocked bar contribute to the vibey atmosphere as you unwind on comfortable sofas in the sunken lounge area, with one of the many exotic cocktails on offer. The decor is clean-cut with avant-garde lighting, which suits the sophisticated young clientele looking for a stylish venue to meet and mingle.
Le Royal Meridien Abu Dhabi Markaziya East
02 674 2020
leroyalmeridienabudhabi.com
Map **2 P3**

Sho Cho · Bars

One of Dubai's most achingly hip restaurants and nightspots has successfully made the leap to Abu Dhabi. The interiors are a delight, while the decking area boasts enviably incredible creekside views. The cuisine is perhaps best described as oriental fusion, with plenty of fish and sushi dishes on the menu. This is fast becoming a weekend favourite among Abu Dhabi's elite socialites.
The Souk At Qaryat Al Beri Al Maqtaa **02 558 1117**
sho-cho.com
Map **1 L8**

The Shore · Bars, Pubs & Clubs

The Club's members all tend to talk highly of The Shore which brings to mind the easy glamour of old St Tropez. Located on the beachside, during the day members can dip in the sea and then head straight for a light bite and cocktail at The Shore.
The Club Mina Zayed Free Port **02 673 1111**
the-club.com
Map **2 V3**

Skylite
Bars, Pubs & Clubs

You can't help but be blown away by the stunning views from this rooftop lounge bar, and even the most style conscious will appreciate the modern, imaginative decor. There are light bites and long wine, champagne and cocktail lists to choose from, while the dress code errs on the smart. The best time to enjoy Skylite is as the sun goes down, but it's easy enough to spend all night here too.

Yas Viceroy Abu Dhabi Yas Island West **02 656 0600**
viceroyhotelsandresorts.com
Map **1 T5**

Stars 'n' Bars
American

Located on the water's edge of the Yas Marina, this hive of fun with an unmistakable all-American facade gives out its welcome message loud and clear: Stars n Bars prides itself on being far more than a restaurant – it offers 'eatertainment'. In addition to serving unashamedly American food from Tex Mex favourites to the ultimate 'Burgernator,' there's a pool table, live music, DJ and dancing – not to mention the countless screens showing sports of all kind.

Yas Yacht Club Yas Island **02 565 0101**
starsnbars.ae
Map **1 T5**

Stills Bar & Brasserie
Bars, Pubs & Clubs

This lively bar serves the cool youth as well as the gracefully aged. There's a nice list of speciality cocktails and whiskys, as well as several beers on tap and a cigar humidor. The gastro-pub menu serves light bites. There's also a DJ Pool Party night once a month, and Stills serves as a sometime-stopover for touring bands.

Crowne Plaza Abu Dhabi Yas Island Yas Island West
02 656 3000
ichotelsgroup.com
Map **1 S5**

The Tavern
Pubs

The Tavern may not epitomise sophisticated dining, but it does cracking roast dinners which will please those in need of some 'morning after' carb-loading. The no frills approach, comfortable dining area and the limited yet familiar menu create a relaxed, functional atmosphere with no pretension. Early birds get the armchairs.

Sheraton Abu Dhabi Hotel & Resort Markaziya East
02 677 3333
sheraton.com
Map **2 Q2**

Wakataua Terrace
Beach/Waterfront Bars

With an idyllic setting on the water's edge, Wakataua is popular with those seeking a sundowner spot. A limited range of light snacks (chicken satay, buffalo wings and nachos) is available to help you curb the munchies.

Le Meridien Abu Dhabi Tourist Club Area **02 644 6666**
lemeridienabudhabi.com
Map **2 S4**

Y Bar
Bars, Pubs & Clubs

Hit the bar area, with its long wooden tables and sport on TV, or try the outside terrace with its views of the other Yas hotels. The drinks menu focuses on cocktails and spirits while the food menu provides tasty basics, such as shepherd's pie, steak and chips and bar snacks.

Yas Island Rotana Yas Island West **02 656 4000**
rotana.com
Map **1 T4**

The Yacht Club
Fusion

If you're a vodka martinis fan then, with 52 different kinds of vodka, The Yacht Club should definitely be on your hit list. An excellent fusion menu is jam-packed with tasty Asian and western dishes. The terrace benefits from harbour vistas, while, inside, the sparkly decor is one part disco and one part ship's galley. There's a DJ on hand at the weekend.

InterContinental Abu Dhabi Al Bateen **02 666 6888**
ichotelsgroup.com
Map **2 C4**

Zenith
Nightclubs

One of the city's most popular clubs, tunes are of the house and RnB varieties and the crowd is diverse and intent on partying. Saturday is Arabic night, and ladies drink for free on Mondays, Tuesdays and Wednesdays.

Sheraton Abu Dhabi Hotel & Resort Markaziya East
02 6970 224
zenithabudhabi.com
Map **2 Q2**

Zenith

Explorer Products

Residents' Guides

Mini Visitors' Guides

Photography Books & Calendars

Maps

Adventure & Lifestyle Guides

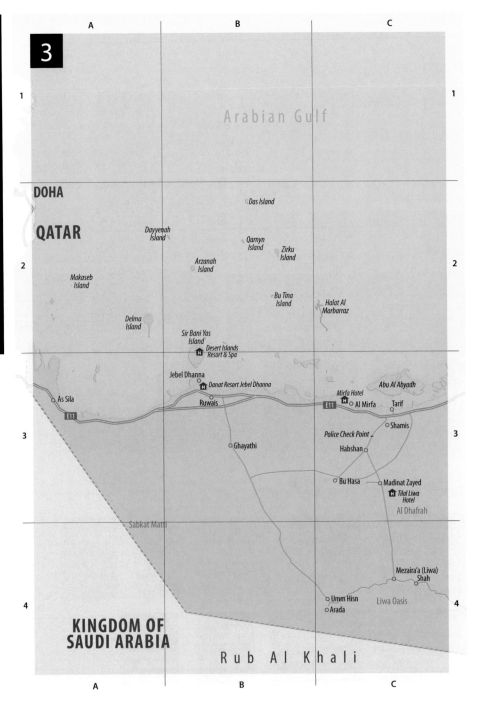

3

A **B** **C**

1 1

Arabian Gulf

DOHA

Das Island

QATAR

Dayyenah
Island

Qarnyn
Island

Zirku
Island

Arzanah
Island

2 2

Makaseb
Island

Bu Tina
Island

Halat Al
Marbarraz

Delma
Island

Sir Bani Yas
Island

Desert Islands
Resort & Spa

Jebel Dhanna

Danat Resort Jebel Dhanna

Abu Al Abyadh

Mirfa Hotel

As Sila

Al Mirfa

Tarif

E11

Ruwais

E11

3 3

Shamis

Police Check Point

Ghayathi

Habshan

Bu Hasa

Madinat Zayed

Tilal Liwa
Hotel

Al Dhafrah

Sabkat Matti

Mezaira'a (Liwa)
Shah

4 4

Umm Hisn

Liwa Oasis

Arada

**KINGDOM OF
SAUDI ARABIA**

Rub Al Khali

A **B** **C**

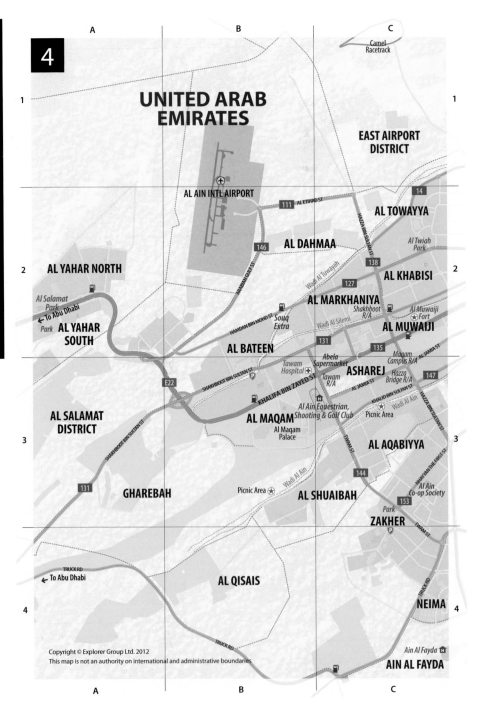

4

UNITED ARAB EMIRATES

EAST AIRPORT DISTRICT

AL AIN INTL AIRPORT

AL ETIHAD ST

111

14

AL TOWAYYA

146

AL DAHMAA

Al Twiah Park

138

AL YAHAR NORTH

Wadi Al Towayah

AL KHABISI

127

Al Salamat Park

To Abu Dhabi

Park AL YAHAR SOUTH

AL MARKHANIYA

Shakhboot R/A

Al Muwaiji Fort

AL MUWAIJI

Souq Extra

Wadi Al Silemi

HAMDAN BIN MOHD ST

AL BATEEN

131

135

Tawam Hospital

Abela Supermarket

ASHAREJ

Maqam Campus R/A

147

Tawam R/A

Hazza Bridge R/A

E22

SHAKHBOOT BIN SULTAN ST

KHALIFA BIN ZAYED ST

AL JAMIA ST

AL SALAMAT DISTRICT

Al Ain Equestrian, Shooting & Golf Club

AL MAQAM

Picnic Area

Wadi Al Ain

KHALID BIN SULTAN ST

Al Maqam Palace

AL AQABIYYA

131

GHAREBAH

Picnic Area

Wadi Al Ain

AL SHUAIBAH

144

AL AIN Co-op Society

153

Park

ZAKHER

TRUCK RD

To Abu Dhabi

AL QISAIS

NEIMA

TRUCK RD

Copyright © Explorer Group Ltd. 2012
This map is not an authority on international and administrative boundaries

Ain Al Fayda

AIN AL FAYDA

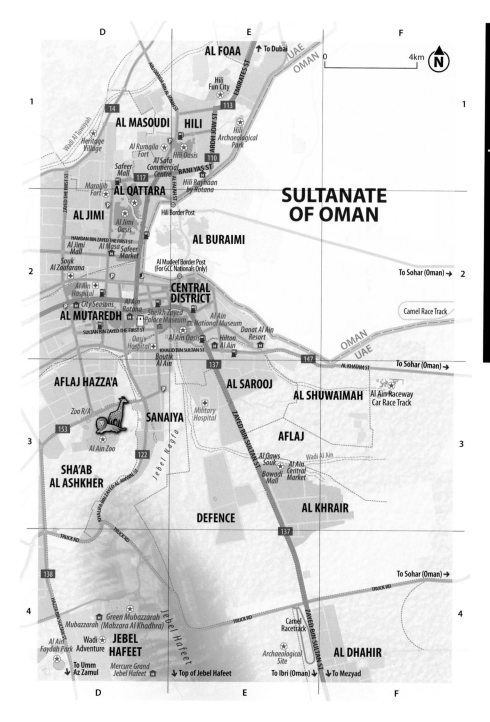

AL FOAA

↑ To Dubai

0   4km   **N**

Hili
Fun City

D

14

113

AL MASOUDI   **HILI**

Heritage
Village

Hili
Archaeological
Park

Al Rumaila
Fort

Hili Oasis

110

Safeer
Mall

Al Safa
Commercial
Centre

BANI YAS ST

117

Hili Rayhaan
by Rotana

Maraijib
Fort

AL QATTARA

**SULTANATE
OF OMAN**

Hili Border Post

AL JIMI

Al Jimi
Oasis

HAMDAN BIN ZAYED THE FIRST ST

Al Jimi
Mall

Al Masa
Safeer
Market

AL BURAIMI

Souk
Al Zaafarana

Al Mudeef Border Post
(For GCC Nationals Only)

To Sohar (Oman) →

Al Ain
Hospital

City Seasons

Al Ain
Rotana

**CENTRAL
DISTRICT**

Camel Race Track

AL MUTAREDH

Sheikh Zayed
Palace Museum

SULTAN BIN ZAYED THE FIRST ST

Al Ain
National Museum

Al Ain Oasis

Oasis
Hospital

Hilton
Al Ain

Danat Al Ain
Resort

KHALID BIN SULTAN ST

OMAN

UAE

Boutik
Al Ain

137

147

AL KHATAM ST

To Sohar (Oman) →

AFLAJ HAZZA'A

AL SAROOJ

AL SHUWAIMAH

Al Ain Raceway
Car Race Track

Zoo R/A

153

SANAIYA

Military
Hospital

AFLAJ

Al Ain Zoo

122

Jebel Nagfa

**SHA'AB
AL ASHKHER**

KHALIFA BIN ZAYED AL AWWAL ST

ZAYED BIN SULTAN ST

Al Qaws
Souk

Al Ain
Central
Market

Bawadi
Mall

Wadi Al Ain

AL KHRAIR

DEFENCE

137

TRUCK RD

TRUCK RD

138

Jebel Hafeet

To Sohar (Oman) →

TRUCK RD

ZAYED BIN SULTAN ST

HAZZA BIN SULTAN ST

Green Mubazzarah
Mubazzarah (Mabzara Al Khadhra)

TRUCK RD

Camel
Racetrack

Al Ain
Faydah Park

Wadi
Adventure

**JEBEL
HAFEET**

↓ To Umm
Az Zamul

Mercure Grand
Jebel Hafeet

↓ Top of Jebel Hafeet

Archaeological
Site

To Ibri (Oman) ↓

AL DHAHIR

↓ To Mezyad

D   **E**   **F**

there's more to life...
just ask us.

Is there more to Dubai than brunches and ladies' nights?

Where are the best off-roading spots in Oman?

Do you need your PADI to dive off Fujairah's coast?

What concerts are on in Abu Dhabi?

explorer

askexplorer.com

   askexplorer